Georgina Weldon

Georgina Weldon

The Fearless Life of a Victorian Celebrity

Joanna Martin

THE BOYDELL PRESS

First published 2021
The Boydell Press, Woodbridge

ISBN 978 1 78327 582 3

The Boydell Press is an imprint of Boydell & Brewer Ltd
PO Box 9, Woodbridge, Suffolk IP12 3DF, UK
and of Boydell & Brewer Inc.

668 Mt Hope Avenue, Rochester, NY 14620–2731, USA
website: www.boydellandbrewer.com

A CIP catalogue record for this book is available from the British Library

This publication is printed on acid-free paper

Printed in the UK by TJ Books Limited, Padstow, Cornwall

For my goddaughter
Georgina Treherne

Contents

Illustrations

All illustrations belong to the Treherne family, unless otherwise stated

Acknowledgements

The completion of this book is the fulfilment of a promise made many years ago to my mother, Oona Methuen-Campbell (née Treherne) and her first cousin Geoffrey Treherne. Unfortunately, neither of them lived long enough to see it published. Other members of the family have also helped and encouraged me over the years, most notably the late Robert Treherne, my sister Catherine Benjamin, Franco da Conturbia, and my goddaughter Georgina Treherne.

I would also like to acknowledge, with gratitude, the help and interest of the following: Charles Brett, Niccolò Capponi, Charles Frankiss, Veronica Franklin Gould, Mike Hickox, Tim Lindholm, Fernando Mascarenhas (Palacio Fronteira, Lisbon), Camelia Miller (great-granddaughter of Charles Rawlings), Anne Monroe, Helen Nicholson, Marcus Risdell, Martin Sheppard, Patrick Treherne, Philip Ward-Jackson, Peter Watson, Christopher Whittick, Thomas Woodcock (Garter King of Arms), and Robert Yorke; also Cristina Fantacci and Francesca Baldry, who showed me the Villa La Pietra, Florence.

I am particularly grateful to Martin Sheppard, the publisher of my last two books, who showed great patience in reading, and commenting on, the first (much longer) draft of this one. And finally, I could not have finished the book without the help and forbearance of my husband (and photographer) Edward Martin, who has lived with Georgina Weldon as well as me for so many years.

Acknowledgements

Abbreviations

AM	Angèle Ménier
BL	British Library
DT	Dal[rymple] Treherne
ESRO	East Sussex Record Office, Brighton
GFW	George Frederick Watts
GW	Georgina Treherne (to 1860), then Weldon
JPR	Jules Prudence Rivière
LFT	Louisa Frances Treherne
PA	Percy Anderson
PCY	Probate Court, York
PMG	*Pall Mall Gazette*
POB	Proceedings of the Old Bailey
PPR	Principal Probate Registry
SC	Statement of Claim
TNA	The National Archives
WHW	William Henry Weldon

Newspapers and magazines

Daily News	*London Daily News*
Entr'acte	*Entr'acte and Limelight*
Standard	*London Evening Standard*
Times	*The [London] Times*, law reports

Published works by Georgina Weldon (see bibliography for further details)

GWL	'French and British Law and Justice: England As It is: Is the Law An Honourable Profession?' (1906)
GWM	*Mémoires Weldon* (1902)[1]
GWO	*My Orphanage and Gounod in England* (1882)
SS	*Social Salvation* (1883–4)

1 Quotations from this book have been translated from the original French.

Manuscript sources

GWJ	Georgina Weldon's journals
GWMSM	Georgina Weldon's manuscript memoirs
GWT	MS book beginning 'today is the 7th January 1870'

Georgina Weldon's Archive and her Biographers

When Georgina Weldon died in 1914, she bequeathed all her papers to her friend Lise Gray, fearing that they would be burnt if she left them to her relations. There were hundreds of letters, together with manuscript memoirs, records of her innumerable lawsuits, and twenty-four journals, covering the years from 1852 to 1854, and from 1860 to 1913. Georgina had also published numerous articles, pamphlets and books, together with six volumes of '*Mémoires Weldon*' – in reality a chaotic compilation of transcripts of letters and legal papers, interspersed with autobiography, all translated into French. In fact all her published works were largely autobiograpical.

The first book about Georgina was *A Plaintiff in Person*, which was written by her nephew Philip Treherne and published posthumously in 1923. Treherne, who was born in 1872, first visited Georgina in 1893, and he saw her often after that. His biography is uncritical, and he is at his best when recounting his personal reminiscences of his notorious aunt, especially during her latter years.

Lise Gray died in 1923 and her niece, Marjory Pegram, inherited sixty-five packing cases full of Georgina's books and papers, which had remained in a furniture repository in Brighton since Georgina's death. It was, as she wrote, 'an awe-inspiring sight.' Miss Pegram then spent many years sorting and arranging the archive. She must have thrown a large proportion of the contents of the packing cases away, but much still remained. In the 1950s, she commissioned Edward Grierson to write a new biography. Grierson, a barrister and prolific writer of both fiction and non-fiction, was born a few weeks after Georgina's death. His book, *Storm Bird*, was published in 1959. It is a masterpiece of compression and remarkably fair, if one considers that he was a barrister working at a time when there were still lawyers around who remembered Georgina, by repute if not in person. Grierson is particularly good on her court cases, but seems rather to have lost interest towards the end of her life.

In the mid 1970s Marjory Pegram went into a care home and her family decided to dispose of Georgina's papers. Some, mainly those written by well-known people such as Gounod and the artist G.F. Watts, were sold to collectors, but the diaries and a number of letters and photographs were sold to my mother and her first cousin, Georgina's great-niece and great-nephew. At that time I was a history research student at Cambridge and the intention always was that I would eventually write a new biography. More recently, and thanks to a fellow researcher, I have been able to acquire a number of papers that had remained with Edward Grierson's family after his book was completed. I have thus been able to reassemble the major part of the surviving Weldon archive for the first time since the 1950s.

In 2000 another biography of Georgina was published. This book, *A Monkey among Crocodiles*, was written by Brian Thompson, who had bought *Mémoires Weldon* from a French bookseller five years earlier. Thompson neither had – nor sought – access to the main Weldon archive, and his book is based on the *Mémoires*, with extensive borrowing from *Storm Bird*. The book is poorly researched and carelessly written, and should be regarded as a work of fiction loosely based on the events of Georgina's life, rather than a biography. Even the title is based on a mistranscription (by Grierson) of something that Georgina herself wrote.[1]

Thompson's book did, however, help to reawaken interest in Georgina – much of it, unfortunately, somewhat misdirected. She is included in several recent books, including *Inconvenient People: Lunacy, Liberty and the Mad Doctors in Victorian England* by Sarah Wise (2012); and *Changing the Rules: Women and Victorian Marriage* by Jennifer C. Kelsey (2016). She also has her own entry in the *Oxford Dictionary of National Biography* (2004), a recognition of her importance that would have pleased her greatly. She was highly indignant that her name was omitted from editions of *Who's Who* published in her lifetime.

Useful though *Storm Bird* is, there have been significant changes in historical interests in the sixty years since the book was published. In particular, the whole field of women's history and gender studies has been opened up. Much more material is available too: online resources, including genealogical sites and newspaper archives, have made it possible to fill in the background to Georgina's own writings in a way that would have been impossible even ten years ago.

1 See below, p. 159 n. 7.

Prologue

> What I find people in general the most interested in concerning my career is the transformation of myself from a lady in the best society, a vocalist, an educationalist, a philanthropist, into a quarrelsome, litigious female, wasting the time of the Court [and] irritating the 'poor Judges' almost to the verge of insanity. How could Mrs Weldon, so charming, so gifted, so beautiful, so amiable, become a kind of Megæra – a being to avoid, to run away from, a social pariah?
>
> (Georgina Weldon, 1906)[1]

A little while before ten o'clock on the evening of Sunday 14 April 1878, a closed carriage drew up outside Tavistock House, an imposing, if somewhat run-down, Georgian mansion in Tavistock Square, Bloomsbury. Shortly afterwards the doorbell rang and a man's voice was heard, demanding admission. He wanted, he said, to see Mrs Weldon, the mistress of the house. Anticipating trouble, the manservant kept the chain on when he opened the door. There stood a man and two women: a madhouse keeper and two nurses. They had been sent, under an order signed by Mrs Weldon's estranged husband, to carry her off to a private lunatic asylum. The three visitors tried first to force, and then to bribe, their way into the house, but the servant managed to close the door and they went away empty-handed. The events that led to this dramatic scene, and its far-reaching consequences, form the framework of this book.

Georgina Weldon was born a month before Queen Victoria came to the throne; she died when Victoria's grandson, George V, was king. These years, from 1837 to 1914, were a time of unprecedented change. When Georgina and her family travelled from Florence to Lake Constance in 1854, the railway only took them as far as Pisa; the rest of the journey was accomplished by means of horse-drawn carriages and a steamboat. In the early twentieth century Georgina used motor buses, cars and taxis, and marvelled at the exploits of the early aviators. She was born three years before the introduction of Rowland Hill's Uniform Penny Post; in old age she

1 GWL, p. 1. Megæra was one of the Furies in Greek mythology.

occasionally used the telephone. As a child, she was entertained by magic lantern slides; in 1902 she saw 'cinematograph living pictures' showing the Boer leaders laying down their arms at the end of the Second Boer War. Georgina lived through the Crimean War, the American Civil War (which she witnessed at first hand), the Franco-Prussian War, the Boer War and the Russo-Japanese War, writing at the end of the last, 'I hope I shall not live to hear of any more Wars.'

As a young woman, Georgina sang before the cream of Society in some of the grandest houses in London. She knew many of the most famous artists and musicians of her day. In middle age she served two prison sentences, and even in old age her activities were still of considerable public interest. She was born a year before the publication of *Women of England*, the first book by Sarah Stickney Ellis, who believed that wives should respect, and defer to, their husbands, and lead by example; in the years immediately before Georgina's death the suffragettes were busy chaining themselves to railings, setting fire to post boxes and smashing windows. Georgina, who had previously derided the suffragists, supported their more radical sisters at the end of her life. She was a pioneer in many spheres of female activity. She pursued a relentless campaign against the male establishment, especially the members of the medical and legal professions, making speeches and giving lectures, writing books and pamphlets, and taking every opportunity to publicise her own causes. She was almost certainly the first married female litigant in person to appear in the English courts, and she acted as a legal adviser to fellow litigants at a time when women were not allowed to practise law on a professional basis. A friend of the most famous French composer of the day, Charles Gounod, she gave singing lessons, organised concerts and conducted choirs and orchestras. Later, she also sang in music halls, at a time when no respectable lady would even enter such establishments. She co-wrote, and acted in, a semi-autobiographical play. For a decade her name was hardly out of the newspapers; after her death most of the major newspapers (including *The Times*) carried her obituary.

Georgina Weldon died on the eve of the First World War, which would radically alter the world that she had known. And she recorded her thoughts and feelings, together with the events of her long life, in her journals over a period of almost sixty years.

1

Georgina

Georgina Thomas was born on 24 May 1837, a day of general rejoicing throughout Great Britain.[1] Church bells rang; schools and shops were closed; and there were firework displays, tea parties and public dinners with speeches and toasts. It was 'a day that the old would talk about for a long time, and the young would never forget'.[2] This had, however, nothing whatsoever to do with Georgina, who happened to share her birthday with the young heir to the throne, Princess Victoria. In May 1837 Victoria turned eighteen and, under the provisions of the Regency Bill of 1831, attained her 'royal majority'. This meant that she was able to rule alone, in her own right, when her uncle William IV died, less than a month after her birthday. The knowledge that she had been born on such an important day gave Georgina a 'vague idea of superiority and of relationship to the Royal Family' from an early age. This feeling was reinforced by the erroneous belief that the Thomases were descended from Edward III and would be entitled to claim the throne of England 'if anything should happen to the reigning family'.

Georgina was the second daughter of Morgan Thomas of Gate House in the parish of Mayfield in Sussex and his wife, Louisa Frances Dalrymple. An elder sister, Cordelia, died of whooping cough when she was just seventeen months old, a few weeks after Georgina's birth. Morgan and Louisa had convinced themselves that their second child would be the longed-for son who was to continue the family line, and they made no attempt to hide their disappointment when the new baby turned out to be a girl. Georgina always felt that her parents had been dissatisfied with her since the day of her birth, somehow blaming her for her sister's early death. As Louisa wept beside Cordelia's empty cot, Georgina (with, as she later wrote, her habitual lack of tact) 'kicked and screamed with life and joy'.[3]

1 The family name was changed to Treherne in 1856.

2 *Ipswich Journal*, 27/5/1837, p. 2.

3 GWMSM, p. 13.

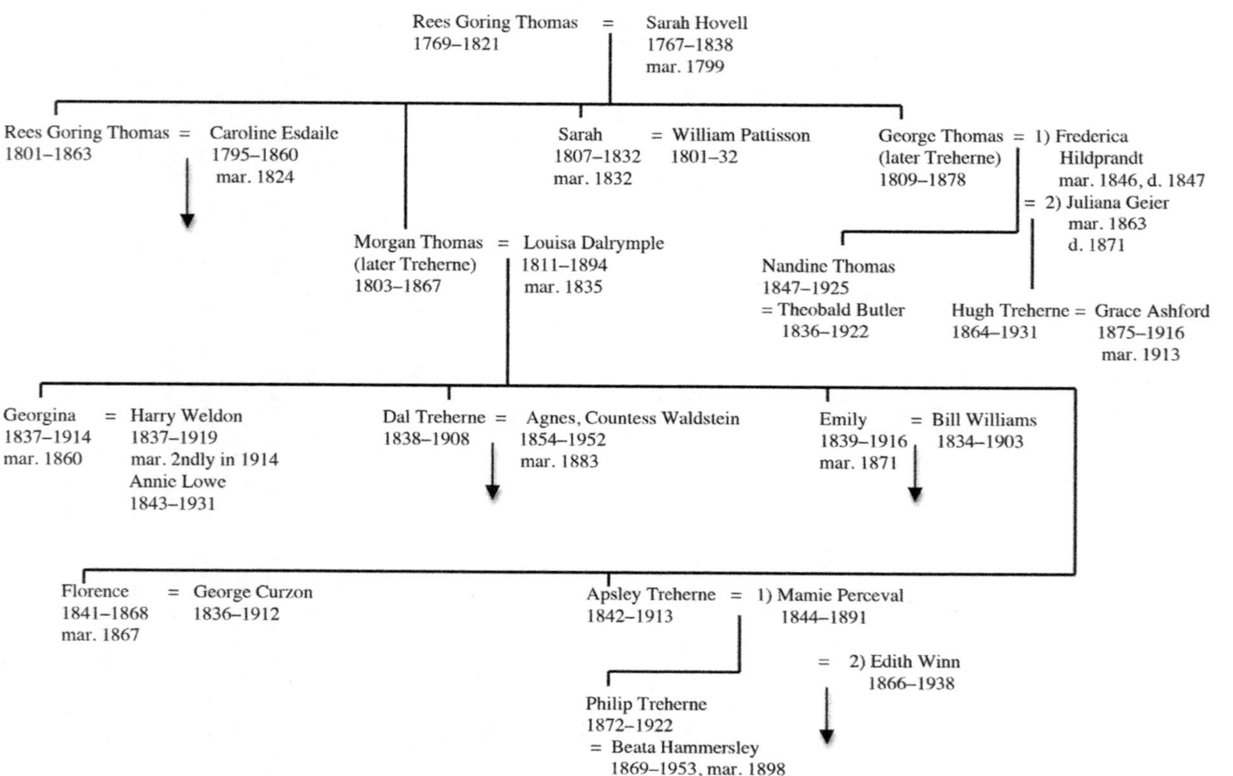

Fig. 1. The Thomas/Treherne family.

The Thomas family was of Welsh origin. There is no evidence for their supposed royal descent, but they could trace their ancestry back in the male line to one Traherne ap Thomas, who was living at Lletty Mawr in Llannon, Carmarthenshire, in 1597. Georgina's great-grandfather Morgan Thomas, a lawyer and estate agent, settled in London in the mid eighteenth century. His son, Rees Goring Thomas, married Sarah Hovell in Fulham in 1799. Rees was thirty years old at the time; Sarah was almost two years his senior. It may have been a love match: the attraction for the upwardly-mobile lawyer was certainly not Sarah's social position, for her father, Richard Hovell, had been in trade as a corn chandler. One of Sarah's brothers was a saddler; another was a haberdasher. The haberdasher, Thomas Hovell of Cambridge, prospered, however, and when he died, unmarried, in 1837 he left most of his money and property to his sister and her sons.[4]

In 1807 Rees Goring Thomas bought a large villa in Surrey, on the outskirts of London. This was Tooting Lodge, built four years earlier, which stood in twenty-four acres overlooking Tooting Common.[5] Rees and Sarah lived there with their four children: Rees (born 1801), Morgan (1803), Sarah Frances (1807) and George (1809). Morgan was his mother's favourite: a spoiled child who was to become an overbearing bully in later life. After several years at Cheam School in Surrey, he went up to Trinity College, Cambridge, in 1820. He stayed there until 1824 and then trained as a barrister at the Inner Temple in London. He was called to the Bar in 1827, but never practised: his father, who had died in 1821, had left him enough to live on, for the time being at least. Instead, he set his sights on the House of Commons, standing three times as a Tory candidate for Coventry. In this he showed characteristic perversity, for the borough was a Whig stronghold with which his family had no obvious connection. Morgan came bottom of the poll each time. Shortly after his third attempt, in January 1835, he left England. Four months later, he married Louisa Frances Dalrymple, at the house of the British minister (ambassador) in Naples. Georgina's claim that her father had 'sighed for' her mother for ten years before she accepted him is probably an exaggeration, but she does appear to have turned him down more than once. They had known each other for some time, as Louisa's father, John Apsley Dalrymple, had been a friend of Morgan's father.

4 TNA, PCC, PROB11/1880/459.

5 *Morning Chronicle*, 28/6/1806, p. 1. The house eventually became part of Tooting Bec Asylum.

Louisa was pretty enough, though her face was rather too red, and her nose a little too much like a bird's beak. The celebrated dandy and wit Count D'Orsay, who met her when she was young, thought that she looked like 'the offspring of Punch and Venus'.[6] She was fond of bright colours – so much so that her appearance was often somewhat peculiar in middle age, as she liked to wear a sky-blue bonnet with a red China shawl, which clashed with her 'startling complexion'. She looked (in her daughter's words) rather like a macaw.[7] But, if she was not a beauty, Louisa had the great advantage of being an heiress, wealthy enough to allow her husband to overlook the disadvantages of her background. For she was illegitimate – a fact that her descendants, not surprisingly, tried to forget, preferring to believe that she was the daughter of a Spanish princess. The identity of Louisa's mother is unknown, but there were rumours that she was the daughter of a coachman. Census returns suggest that she was born in London, probably in 1811. By 1832, when John Apsley Dalrymple wrote his will, Louisa was living with him, and he made her his sole heir.[8]

With his new bride Morgan Thomas gained an estate of approximately 1500 acres in East Sussex, and a mansion dating from the mid eighteenth century, Gate House in Mayfield. This was the birthplace of Morgan and Louisa's first child, Cordelia, but Georgina was born at Tooting Lodge, the home of her widowed grandmother Sarah Thomas. A month later, the king died and a general election was called. Morgan, whose funds had recently been replenished by an inheritance from his uncle Thomas Hovell, made yet another attempt to become an MP. Once again, he was unsuccessful. This election was to see the end of his parliamentary ambitions for the time being: he did not stand again for another twenty years.

Exactly a year after Georgina's birth, Louisa dutifully produced the much-wanted son and heir. He was named Morgan Dalrymple, though he was always known as Dal. Another eighteen months passed, and another girl, Emily Louisa, was born, in November 1839. By this time, having given birth to four children in less than four years, Louisa's health was beginning to fail. Her doctors recommended that she should go abroad for a while, to escape the cold and damp of the English climate, and the whole family set off for Italy in the following year. Although she was only three at the time, Georgina always remembered travelling through the Black Forest in a diligence or *vettura* (a large, four-wheeled carriage) in a 'tremendous' storm. Her feeling of being the least-favoured child was reinforced by

6 Philip Treherne, *A Plaintiff in Person* (London, 1923), p. 4.

7 GWMSM, p. 34.

8 TNA, PCC, PROB11/1841/133.

Fig. 2. The Thomas family at the Villa Capponi, *c.*1847–8. Left to right: Apsley, Louisa, Emily (above), Florence (below), Morgan, Georgina, Dal.

the fact that her younger brother and sister each had 'a clean little white pillow' to lean on, whilst she had to make do with the dirty blue cloth sides of the coach, which she hated.[9]

The Thomas family's destination was Florence, where there was a large British community at this time. The climate was agreeable and the cost of living low, an added attraction to a man such as Morgan Thomas, whose social aspirations tended to outrun his financial resources. He may, moreover, have been in somewhat straitened circumstances in 1840. Sixteen years earlier his elder brother, Rees Goring Thomas, had married Caroline Esdaile, the daughter of a wealthy London banker. The failure of the Esdaile bank in 1837 seems to have brought financial problems for Rees. According to Georgina, her father helped his brother and then took his family abroad 'to retrench.'[10] They settled first at the Casa Rendlesham near Florence, where Morgan and Louisa's youngest daughter, Mary Florence (Florence), was born in March 1841. But for most of their stay in

9 GWMSM, p. 14.
10 GW, *Louis XVII*, pp. 10–11.

Fig. 3. Villa Capponi (now Villa La Pietra), near Florence, c.1850.

Italy, which was to last on and off for the next ten years, the family's home was a villa rented from the blind Marchese Gino Capponi, an Anglophile historian and reformer who was briefly Prime Minister of Tuscany in 1848. Two more sons were born there: Goring Apsley (known as Apsley) in August 1842 and Gilbert Offley in 1845. Gilbert lived for less than a year, dying while teething in June 1846.

The Villa Capponi, one of the most magnificent country houses in the Florence region, stands in its own grounds to the north of the city, a mile beyond the Porta San Gallo and not far from the village of La Pietra.[11] In the mid nineteenth century this was an area of streams, and low wooded hills dotted with cypress trees. Amongst the vineyards and olive groves stood the 'ornamental and picturesque' villas of the Tuscan nobility, many of which were leased out to foreigners.[12] Georgina describes the Villa Capponi as 'a splendid residence ... a beautiful and spacious palace'. In later years, like Goethe's Mignon, she was to dream of 'The orange flowers and marble statues, the palaces of marble, the grand staircases, the spacious courtyards, the lovely gardens filled with myrtle, jessamine, geraniums and varied perfumes, and also with muscatel vines

[11] Later called Villa La Pietra, it now belongs to New York University.

[12] BL Holland House, Add. MS 51352, pp. 136–7, William Fox Strangways–Lady Susan O'Brien, 12/6/1825.

with sunburnt clusters of grapes, which we were forbidden to touch'.[13] The Thomases lived in the villa in considerable comfort, looked after by a large household of servants, including a butler, footmen, cook, kitchen-boys and several maids. Clearly their 'retrenchment' was only relative, for the Villa Capponi was much larger and grander than their own home in Sussex.

~

The expatriate inhabitants of Florence and the surrounding area enjoyed a lively social life, with a succession of balls, dinners, picnics, concerts and theatrical performances. Society in the city, described by Shelley twenty years before the Thomas family's arrival as 'the paradise of exiles and the retreat of pariahs', was less exclusive than in London.[14] Bohemian artists and writers mingled with aristocrats and wealthy members of the middle class, and there were many who were reluctant to give too detailed an account of their own background and financial situation. New arrivals would hope to gain an *entrée* to the fashionable world by being presented to the Grand Duke of Tuscany by the British Minister (ambassador). Lord Holland, the Minister from 1839 to 1846, adopted a policy of presenting everyone who desired it. In this he was encouraged by Leopold II, the Grand Duke of the time, who hoped to gain the support of the Florentine tradesmen and letters of apartments by attracting wealthy foreigners to the city.

Proud, rigorously conventional and obsessed with genealogy, Morgan Thomas was out of place in Florence, where, as Georgina put it, 'Individuals with more-or-less shady reputations flourished'. Georgina's portrait of her father suggests that his undoubted virtues were balanced – if not outweighed – by a much darker side to his personality. Morgan was a talented man, with 'a great turn for mathematics, poetry, foreign languages and music'. He was musical, and had an exceptionally fine voice. In a good mood, he could be charming, but he also had a foul temper, which could erupt into violence at the least provocation, and he 'swore constantly'.[15] He was unsociable and preferred to stay at home, whilst his wife loved to go out to parties. The couple's social life was further restricted by the fact that Morgan declined to meet anyone whose name brought with it the faintest hint of scandal. As this included the coquettish wife of the British Minister, Augusta, Lady Holland, he refused to set foot inside the British Legation, the Casa Feroni.

13 GWO, i, p. 2.
14 Quoted in Pamela Neville-Sington, *Fanny Trollope* (London, 1997), p. 315.
15 GWO, i, pp. 4, 20; GWMSM, p. 56.

In Florence his fellow-countrymen mocked Morgan with the nicknames 'the policeman of society', and 'the *carbonaio*' [coal-man], and he lost many opportunities to make useful contacts amongst them.[16] Perhaps surprisingly, in view of her father's determination to associate only with those who, in his opinion, had attained 'the Parnassus of Virtue', Georgina remembered many visitors to the Villa Capponi, including Peter Scarlett, the secretary to the British Legation, and Lord Vernon who shared Morgan's interest in the poet Dante.[17] Nor was Morgan entirely consistent: one of his 'favourites' was the *grande dame* of Florence, the talented and independent-minded Princess Mathilde Demidoff, wife of a Russian diplomat and art-collector. Princess Mathilde was godmother to Morgan and Louisa's son Gilbert, but in 1846, shortly after the child's christening, she left Florence in secret and fled alone to Paris. Morgan never forgave her for this 'cowardly' act, believing that it was a wife's duty to stay with her husband, no matter how badly he behaved. He forbade his wife and children ever to speak of the princess again, though the fact that Prince Demidoff was subsequently shunned by polite society in Tuscany suggests that rumours that he had beaten his wife were probably well founded.[18]

~

As small children, Georgina and her brothers and sisters spent most of their time with their nanny, Eleanor Leath. Georgina hated Mrs Leath, 'a horrid woman', who made little attempt to hide her dislike of her two elder charges, Georgina (known as Missy) and Dal (Bobby). She much preferred Emily, who was 'her' baby. Not surprisingly, Georgina and Emily (Zizi) did not get on. The jealousy and resentment that the two sisters felt towards each other in their early childhood was to permeate their relationship for the rest of their lives. Georgina liked her younger sister Florence (Ninny) better, though she was jealous of her too. She always remembered how, as small children, Emily and Florence had been dressed alike in brightly-coloured silks, whilst she had been forced to wear 'dingy' colours. Georgina also looked different from the other two. She was a slim, wiry child, with long thin legs: Florence and Emily were shorter, and they were both 'as dark as gypsies', with black hair and eyes 'as black as berries', whilst Georgina had grey eyes and reddish-brown hair. The others teased Georgina, telling her that she had green eyes, which, according to Mrs Leath, were 'a sign of every bad quality under the sun'. More sympathetic was the family's Italian butler, Antonio Castellani, but his apparent devotion to the *Moschina* [little

16 The second nickname was presumably a reference to his Welsh ancestry.
17 GW, *Louis XVII*, p. 13.
18 GWO, i, pp. 4–5.

fly], as he called Georgina, hid a dark secret: when she was about four or five years old she had 'witnessed something which, had I repeated it to a living soul, would have consigned him for life to the galleys'. She did not say anything until many years later, when she told her mother. Louisa merely replied that she was not surprised, and that Georgina's story explained why the nanny had disliked Antonio so much. After this incident Georgina had a hold over Antonio that was to prove very useful in later years when she wanted to send or receive letters without her parents' knowledge.

The children all quarrelled continually, and Dal and Emily bullied their younger siblings and 'teased them to distraction'. Mrs Leath spoiled Emily, but treated the others with 'great severity': they were 'slapped constantly and otherwise harshly handled'. 'Spare the rod and spoil the child' was one of Morgan's favourite maxims. He was 'a terror' who said 'No' to everything and was always threatening to send his children to bed for a fortnight. 'Papa used to perform the rod part of our education; Mrs Leath did the slapping, and Mama had a very long knitting needle, with which she rapped me on the knuckles when I played a wrong note on the piano'. Nevertheless, Georgina later claimed that, as a child, she had been 'no more unhappy than I have been through life'.[19]

They were educated by a series of governesses – a grand total of seven of them whilst the family was at the Villa Capponi. Georgina seems to have been a diligent pupil, anxious to please her tutors. By her own account, she was their favourite: Emily was 'a very dull, stupid child' and the others were all 'extraordinarily lazy'. Georgina's claim that none of the rest of her family 'are, or were, capable of any intellectual pursuit' is no doubt an exaggeration, but she was certainly the brightest of Morgan and Louisa's children.[20] Intelligent as she was, it was not difficult to excel, for the education given to girls such as Georgina and her sisters at this time was not particularly demanding.

Above all, girls were brought up to be good wives and mothers. They learned to be modest, virtuous and self-effacing, obedient first to their parents and later to their husbands. They were taught that they should not argue with men, but should give them emotional support and lead by example. Since their brains were smaller than those of men, their understanding was thought to be shallower. As a result, they were deemed to be incapable of prolonged intellectual effort. Their bodies were weaker, so it was believed that they lacked the physical resources necessary to support academic study as well as reproduction. For females the latter was, of

19 GWMSM, pp. 15–16, 31–2; GW–LFT, 10/11/1880.

20 GWMSM, p. 59.

course, much more important than the former. Any skills that would raise their profile in the marriage market were desirable, but too much learning was likely to put prospective husbands off.

Georgina could read when she was four; her spelling and punctuation were excellent; and she learned to write English fluently and grammatically in the beautifully clear hand that she kept to the end of her life. She knew some German, and could read, write and speak French and Italian well. She claimed many years later that she had learned 'botany, mineralogy, conchology, chemistry, history, geology, meteorology, and all sorts of sciences, comparatively useless to common every-day life.'[21] She certainly read any books she could get her hands on. Like many of her female contemporaries, she was self-educated to a significant extent.

Morgan would have liked the girls to learn 'farming and dairy work,' and it was at his insistence that they were taught to sew and knit. His wife thought such mundane occupations *infra dig.* Like most women in wealthy families, Louisa attached great importance to ornamental accomplishments such as drawing, dancing and playing the piano.[22] Georgina could never draw well, though she became a competent pianist. She had a naturally beautiful soprano voice, but this received little training when she was young, apart from a few singing lessons with her mother. It is difficult to know how seriously to take her claims that she was made nervous as a child by constant exhortations to behave like a young lady, not to be vulgar, and to maintain the good name of her family. As she wrote many years later, Georgina 'bristled with virtue.' 'I had,' she wrote 'inherited to the full my father's mania to keep my reputation inviolate.'[23]

In 1852 Morgan gave up his lease of the Villa Capponi. By this time he had fallen out with almost everyone in Florence and had decided that the city was a den of iniquity – a modern Sodom and Gomorrah. The children were, moreover, beginning to grow up, and the boys were destined for schools in England. Georgina's first journal starts just over a fortnight before she and the rest of the family left Florence. The last days at the Villa Capponi were spent packing, saying goodbye to friends and visiting favourite haunts for the last time. The children were forced to give all their toys away to save the expense of sending them to England. On 18 May Morgan and Dal (who were to stay in Florence for a few days longer) waved goodbye to the three

21 SS, 7–10/1884, p. 6.
22 GWMSM, p. 136.
23 GWO, i, p. 4.

girls, their mother and their brother Apsley at the railway station. The rail network in Tuscany had been expanding rapidly since 1844, when work on the first line, from Livorno to Pisa, had been started. But in 1852 the train took them only as far as Pisa, a journey that lasted about two hours. After this they used carriages, drawn by hired post-horses. From Pisa they made their way northwards along the coast road to La Spezia, where they stayed for almost a fortnight, waiting for the rest of the family to catch them up.

Fig. 4. Schloss Hard, Ermatingen, Lake Constance, 1853.

On 9 June the travellers finally arrived at their destination, Schloss Hard at Ermatingen, on the Swiss shore of Lake Constance, a few miles beyond the town of Konstanz. Schloss Hard, the former home of the courtesan Anna Lindsay, now belonged to Georgina's uncle, George Treherne Thomas, a widower who lived there with his five-year-old daughter Fernandina (Nandine) and his mother-in-law Caroline, Baroness Hildprandt. To Georgina, the house, which stood in a large garden surrounded by an ornamental park, was a paradise: the interior was like fairyland and there were two conservatories, both full of flowers, creepers and hanging plants.

Schloss Hard was to be the Thomas family's home for a little over a year, though only Louisa and her daughters stayed there for the whole of this time. The boys were sent to school in England, where their father also spent some time attending to his business affairs. Governesses were brought in to teach the girls; Mme Hildprandt gave Georgina German lessons, and her mother taught her to sing. She also had music lessons with Father Fischer, 'an old German canon', who could 'play Mozart all through'. When they were not occupied in the school-room, the three girls explored the countryside, sketched, shopped with their mother and paid visits. Hildprandt relations and friends of the family came and went. Georgina disapproved of many of them, commenting in her diary: 'The company at Hard is very odd and not in the highest degree *comme il le faut*'.[24] On rainy days (of which there seem to have been a great many), there were games of billiards, amateur dramatics and informal concerts. Georgina overcame her nerves and sang to her family and friends in the evenings. She also read her way through every book she could find, including the works of Sir Walter Scott. Conscious that many adults believed that reading fiction had a bad effect on young ladies, she claimed in her diary that her head was 'not turned' by novels. When she could, she slipped into Anna Lindsay's apartments, which had been 'preserved (as it were) sacred' by Uncle George and were only used on special occasions. There, Georgina 'devoured' the contents of Anna Lindsay's 'prettily-bound' books, which for the most part consisted of works on the French Revolution of 1793.[25]

At fifteen Georgina was, by her own account, innocent and childish. She had been very reluctant to give her favourite doll Eglantine (with which she still played) to the Italian master's daughter before leaving Florence; she enjoyed skipping, playing at horses and climbing. She had little interest in boys. But she was growing into a beauty – a fact of which she had until recently been quite unaware. Indeed, she had been astonished and displeased on hearing a friend of her parents, the Queen's Messenger Robert Haviland, describe her as 'a lovely child', and thought that he was teasing her. She asked her mother, 'Is it true I am lovely?' Louisa replied that Georgina was pretty, but that she was 'not to think about it'. But, with long, glossy brown hair and a good figure, it was not long before she discovered that boys – and men – were beginning to take an interest in her. Quite why they were so interested was still something of a mystery to Georgina, not least because the prudery of the time meant that her knowledge of the facts of life was distinctly limited.

Less than a fortnight after their arrival in Switzerland, the Thomases were surprised by the arrival of an Irish acquaintance from Florence, 'the O'Donoghoe', together with two friends, Peter Wills and Frederick

24 GWJ, 9/6/1852, 6/9/1852.

25 GW, *Louis XVII*, pp. 10–11.

Weatherly.[26] At first Georgina disliked the O'Donoghoe and thought him 'very rough and rude'. But in the evening they all danced until nearly eleven. After polkas, waltzes, quadrilles and polka-mazurkas Georgina decided that Mr Wills was 'a delightful partner', though Mr Weatherly danced 'as if he were mad, with *such* pulling'. She even warmed to the O'Donoghoe, and concluded 'I got on very well. I enjoyed myself that evening very much'.[27] On the next day the O'Donoghoe and his friends gave Georgina a lift in their drag and 'I first experienced what Mama told me some time ago about young men making themselves agreeable to me'. Edouard Rausch, who lived nearby, was also attentive. He presented Georgina with 'a beautifully done drawing', but she dismissed him with the comment 'A very amusing, nice boy. Puppy love', though he was two years older than her.[28] Nor were these young men her only admirers, for Father Fischer (whom the Thomases called *Canonicus*) had taken a great fancy to his pretty pupil. As Georgina wrote in her diary, 'Canonicus is a very nice old man. He squeezes me a little *too* much and kisses my hand in raptures. *Rather* suspicious'. Canonicus presented Georgina with 'a quantity of roses' and 'told *me* I was a rose!' A fortnight later he gave her 'a *love* letter!!' Georgina thought him 'an old fool' and very wisely showed the letter to her mother, who returned it to the writer.[29] Canonicus left Schloss Hard three weeks after this episode.

~

By the middle of April 1853 Louisa had persuaded her husband that the family's next destination should be Brussels, a cosmopolitan city with a lively social life. They all started packing on 24 August, with Morgan in 'a towering passion' and his wife and children in a state of nervous collapse. 'Papa is very fiery, and my idea of a smothered violence', wrote Georgina. After everything had been packed and unpacked several times, they set off on 27 August, travelling by steamboat across the lake to Friedrichshafen, where they caught a train to Heilbronn. They arrived in Brussels three days later.

Georgina was overjoyed to be back in a large city again. 'Such lovely shops! Lace! Watches! Porcelain! It is really delightful to behold'.[30] They all stayed at the Hôtel d'Europe while Mama and Papa began to look for a house to rent. But on 4 September, Morgan left for England. He had been in a furious temper throughout the journey from Switzerland, worried by

26 The title *The* was used in Ireland for the chief of a clan or sept. He was probably Daniel O'Donoghoe of the Glens, Co. Kerry (1833–89).

27 GWJ, 21/6/1852.

28 GWJ, 19/10/1852.

29 GWJ, 2–19/7/1852.

30 GWJ, 31/8/1853.

problems with the management of the estate in Sussex; threatening to sell everything in England; and telling his wife and children that they were all beggars. Everyone heaved a sign of relief after his departure and Georgina and her mother got down to the serious business of shopping and house hunting. At thirteen and twelve, Emily and Florence were too young to help their mother and, in her husband's absence, Louisa – never the most energetic or assertive of women – came to rely heavily on the company and practical assistance of her eldest daughter.

After several disappointments, Louisa decided on a suitable house: 1 Rue de Luxembourg. Servants were engaged; cases of the family's belongings began to arrive from Switzerland and Italy; and a piano was bought for 680 francs. They were beginning to make some friends too. Amongst their first callers were Sir Thomas Waller, the secretary to the British Legation, and his wife, to whom Louisa had been given a letter of introduction. Having walked or taken a hackney carriage during their first weeks in Brussels, Louisa hired a four-wheeled carriage with black horses and a coachman. Georgina noted in some excitement in her diary: 'We went about in our carriage, and all our ancient admirers on foot stare at us as if we were risen from the grave. It is very amusing!'[31]

Morgan returned from England at the end of October, bearing a letter of introduction to Lord Howard de Walden, written by his friend Peter Scarlett. This was a great prize, for Lord Howard was the British Minister at Brussels, and he and his formidable wife, a daughter of the fourth Duke of Portland, belonged to the highest level of Brussels society. On the day after his arrival, therefore, Morgan called on Lord Howard and 'sat a whole hour', and he also 'left cards at nearly all our acquaintance'. During the next few days, he and Louisa were invited to dine with Sir Thomas and Lady Waller, and Lord Howard paid them 'a very long visit'.[32] Other new friends included Mr and Mrs Stanley Curwen, who had several daughters. The girls had fine voices, but they were 'not considered proper'. They had, Georgina noted with some satisfaction 'the worst characters in all Brussels, and to be seen with them might lose one's reputation'. They even went 'roaming about in the woods with men who are not gentlemen'.[33] More satisfactory from the social point of view were the Bonnor Maurices, whose elder daughter Judith could sing well. On Twelfth Night 1854 Georgina and her mother went to a ball at the Bonnor Maurices, leaving Morgan at home. Georgina had a wonderful time: 'I was engaged every dance. I like going

31 GWJ, 29/10/1853.

32 GWJ, 9/11/1853.

33 GWJ, 31/12/1853, 4/1/1854, 22/4/1854.

Fig. 5. Georgina Thomas in Brussels, 1856. 'This is the way I used to be drest in my best! Had I been a man I would not have danced with such a caricature.'

to the ball. I looked so pretty, and my hair was very nicely dressed. I think Mama and I were the prettiest there.' On the following Sunday the whole family attended the chapel at the Royal Observatory, where they met an interesting young man, Montague Peacock, 'a gent worth £10,000 a year, and £16,000 in store. Cousin to an old lover of Mama's, Sir Francis Peacock.' 'I should not,' wrote Georgina, 'mind catching Mr Peacock. Good-looking, too – Oh Lud!'[34]

[34] GWJ, 6,8/1/1854.

Fig. 6. Some of Georgina Thomas's admirers in Brussels, 1856. Left to right: standing: Marquis Silva da Peñeranda, Baron de Moncorvo, Baron de Pfüel; seated: Henry Winston Barron, Chevalier de Heydebrand.

Despite their best efforts, it was some time before Lady Howard de Walden took much notice of the Thomases. The British Minister's wife was said to be 'very uncertain in her favors, and often most shockingly rude'.[35] But she was fond of music, and singing classes were held in her house (or at least under her sponsorship). One of the pupils was Judith Bonnor Maurice, and it was on a visit to her that Georgina first encountered the singing teacher Jules de Glimes. He was 'charmed' when she sang Rossini's 'Assisa a piè d'un salice' to him, and she longed to join the class.[36] Two weeks later, after singing for him

35 GWJ, 2/11/1854.

36 Desdemona's 'Willow Song' from Rossini's *Otello*.

again, she noted with great satisfaction 'He was much gratified. My voice is getting beautiful and divinely sweet.' Lady Howard began to thaw and invited Louisa to a ball. 'Fashionable are we going to be', wrote Georgina. It was agreed that 'old ferocious de Glimes' should come to the Thomases' house to teach Georgina once a week. The first class went well: de Glimes taught 'beautifully' and was 'in ecstasies' after hearing his new pupil sing.[37] Two days later he brought a message from Lady Howard, asking Georgina to sing at her next concert. For some reason she does not appear to have done so, but Lady Howard then graciously accepted an invitation to attend an evening concert and ball at the Thomases' house in the Rue de Luxembourg.

It was probably fortunate that Morgan was out of the way in England again. By this time Georgina had collected a number of admirers, several of whom came to the party. They included Baron Ferdinand de Marches, 'a great *vaurien* [good-for-nothing], for he makes regular love to me'; the Baron de Pfüel 'a jolly little dog' who, at an earlier party, had 'helped himself' to Georgina 'most liberally'; Victor Limnander de Nieuwenhove, 'rather a nice man, and very funny'; Captain Aitkens, who danced well; Eugène O'Sullivan, a 'hideous little monster'; Edward Hyde Hewett; and Skelton, one of Apsley's school friends.[38] Georgina sang 'Robert, toi que j'aime' by Meyerbeer and 'Tranquillo ei posa', which was one of her favourite party pieces. In her own opinion she sang 'like an angel', and Lady Howard was said to be delighted. After this success the invitations for Louisa and her daughter came in thick and fast. Eighty-five people attended a party they gave on Easter Monday (Morgan was in England again). In spite of a sore throat that prevented Georgina from singing, she and the others danced until three in the morning. It was 'a beautiful night'.[39] She sang, danced and flirted at another party on 25 April at which Limnander was 'desperate' and Hewett ('poor little beast') was 'bordering on distraction'. Three weeks later, a fall prevented Louisa from accompanying her eldest daughter to a party held by Madame de Gériche, but Georgina succeeded in persuading another friend, Madame Huüghe de Penterine, to accompany her instead:

> So at a quarter past nine, I presented myself there, and were not they all charmed to see me!!! I wore a white muslin dress, with three flounces bordered with pink and black, and pink spots, and my stomacher was very prettily arranged with black and pink ribbons, and my

37 GWJ, 24/1/1854, 10,22/2/1854.

38 The prep school in England had evidently not been a success; Apsley attended a school in Brussels from January 1854.

39 GWJ, 17/4/1854.

> coiffure pink silk ribbands with three ends behind and narrow velvet black ribbons. I was irresistible!! They encored me in 'Senti, senti'. I was obliged to sing it over again, and such a stamping, banging, and clapping of hands, and shouts and screams, I never heard, except at the opera. I sang the *Puritani* affair pretty well, and the slow part beautifully. Madame Montalto was very civil, and in fact I had a most brilliant *succès*.[40]

Georgina, now nearly seventeen, had clearly changed a great deal in the previous two years. In 1882 she claimed that she had been 'shy, painfully shy and sensitive' when she was young. Even at seventeen, she tells us, she remained 'so innocent, so well trained': 'I was, and have ever remained, so ingenuous and so credulous!'[41] Naive she may have been, but she certainly revelled in the attention. She enjoyed playing her followers off against each other, though there is little sign that she was really interested in any of them – except, perhaps, for 'the precious wicked Limnander' – who, however, was engaged to someone else by the end of the summer.

~

Georgina's reign over the young (and not so young) men of Brussels came to an abrupt end on 23 May, when her father returned. On the following day, Georgina's seventeenth birthday, Morgan intercepted a love letter to his daughter, written by 'an *étudiant des sciences* at Brussels', who wrote that he had fallen for her beautiful eyes, was miserable and unable to sleep, and wished to make her acquaintance. 'Poor stupid ass!' commented Georgina, as Papa sent Antonio to the police with the letter. Then, on 25 May, Morgan 'made a row' and forbade his wife and daughter to go to a concert, declaring that they were 'not proper'. He was, Georgina decided, 'a horrid old tyrant'.[42]

Until this time, Georgina's relationship with her father seems to have been amicable, if not particularly close. She claimed in her memoirs that Morgan had never shown the slightest affection for any of his children and had never spoken to them, other than to rebuke them or call them 'damned fools'. His temper was volatile and his mood swings were terrifying: genial at one moment, he could rapidly work himself up into a fury which inspired 'hatred and terror' in anyone who was unfortunate enough to cross his path.[43] He and Georgina had a good deal in common,

40 GWJ, 11/5/1854.
41 GWO, i, p. 6.
42 GWJ, 24–5/5/1854.
43 GWM, i, p. 45.

for both were tidy, orderly and methodical, and they shared an interest in genealogy and a pride in their family history (whether true or imagined). Both were also equally intractable, and clashes between them were inevitable sooner or later.

~

Georgina and her mother and sisters spent the last week of May saying goodbye to all their friends and acquaintances in Brussels. On 31 May 1854 the whole family left the city by train at seven in the morning. They reached their home in Sussex at a quarter to eleven in the evening of the same day.

2

Mayfield

For the next eight years the home of Morgan and Louisa Thomas and their children was to be Gate House in the south-western corner of the parish of Mayfield in East Sussex. The Georgian mansion of the same name that Louisa had inherited from her father had been demolished after her marriage, and had been replaced with a modern house half a mile away, on the site of a farm called Merriams, which belonged to the estate. The name Gate House was transferred to the new building, though the local people continued to refer to the place as Merriams.

Whilst the old Gate House had stood close to the turnpike road leading from Mayfield to Heathfield, its replacement, 'a stone cottage or shooting box', lay 'low, and hidden from the road'. It was, Georgina thought when she first saw it, 'a horrid little place'.[1] No doubt it suited Morgan's increasingly unsociable disposition, but for his wife and children it brought loneliness and isolation. Sale particulars of 1862 describe Gate House as 'a commodious residence in the Elizabethan style of architecture ... surrounded by park-like paddocks and ornamental woods', with twenty-three bedrooms in addition to large drawing and dining rooms, a library, a billiard room, and the usual domestic offices, stables and outbuildings.[2] Drawings and photographs show a somewhat curious jumble of buildings resembling two or three houses joined together, and it is possible that the new Gate House incorporated at least part of the old Merriams farmhouse. The house was added to, in a somewhat haphazard manner, during the 1850s.

Three weeks after their arrival in Sussex, Georgina and her mother escaped from their rural confinement and went up to London for a few days. The ostensible reason for their visit was the need to engage a governess for

1 ESRO, XA38/2, microfilm copy of College of Arms, antiquarian notebooks of William Courthope, xxiii, p. 209; GWJ, 31/12/1899.
2 *Sussex Express*, 3/5/1862, p. 8.

Fig. 7. Gate House, Mayfield, 1861.

Emily and Florence, but they also found time to enjoy themselves. They drove in Hyde Park and visited the Botanical Gardens. Dressed in her 'silk *écossais,* white bonnet and new *mantille*', Georgina found that she attracted a certain amount of attention, though this was not entirely welcome, for the English men looked 'such fools' and stared at her in 'such a disagreeable, impudent way'. They were, however, 'very tall'.[3] Georgina and her mother spent an evening at Covent Garden and visited the Crystal Palace with Uncle George, who was paying one of his occasional visits to England. Joseph Paxton's vast exhibition hall of glass and iron, which had originally been erected in Hyde Park for the Great Exhibition in 1851, had recently been moved to Sydenham, six miles south of the Thames. Newly enlarged, it had been opened by Queen Victoria on 10 June 1854, just a fortnight before the Thomas family visited. Georgina thought that it was wonderful: 'A more beautiful, fairy-like place I never saw nor could imagine. Stupendous, yet lovely! Massive, but aerial! Magnificent and simple! It is not to be described.' They stayed there for three hours and had 'a very good dinner', which cost two shillings a head.[4]

3 GWJ, 20–1/6/1854.

4 GWJ, 23/6/1854.

Six weeks later, Louisa and Georgina accepted a pressing invitation to visit Aldermaston Court in Berkshire, a large new Elizabethan-style house which belonged to a wealthy couple, Daniel Higford Burr and his wife Anne Margaretta, who were old friends of the family. Morgan, who had also been invited, refused to go. At Aldermaston they found a large, mainly youthful, house party. Georgina danced, played the piano, sang and flirted. She enjoyed herself 'exceedingly' and decided that the English men were 'not so bad after all', though Mr Fellowes, who had £40,000 a year, and Mr Griffiths, who had £20,000, were both 'very ugly'. She was, however, disappointed by Lady Annabella Lovelace, granddaughter of 'the adorable, *elegantissimo* first Lord Byron'. Though clever and 'pleasant enough', Annabella was 'an ugly, cooksmaid-looking person with small bright black eyes'.[5]

In November, Morgan and his family returned to Brussels for the winter. It was there, at the beginning of 1855, that Georgina fell in love for the first time. The object of her affection was the brother of one her friends, Maria de Moncorvo. Pedro, Baron da Torre de Moncorvo had witnessed Georgina's 'brilliant *succès*' at Madame de Gériche's party nine months earlier but he had not been introduced to her then. They met for the first time on 8 January. Georgina called him 'Crow' – *corvus* being the Latin name for the crow family. Crow was twenty-five years old and 'almost English', as his father had been the Portuguese ambassador in London for a quarter of a century. He was also, in Georgina's parents' eyes, totally unsuitable, being poor – and a Catholic. But Crow pursued Georgina with determination, declaring that he loved her to distraction: 'He treated me in a manner by turns dictatorial, submissive, savage, tender, ferocious and caressing, brusque and gentle, at the same time.' He was a gifted musician who played the piano well and criticised her singing, teasing her about her faults. He was also as jealous as a tiger and Georgina was terrified of displeasing him.

This was carnival time in Brussels, and on 17 February the Baronne de Goethals invited Georgina and her mother to a costume ball. Alluringly dressed as a *grisette* [a young working-class Frenchwoman] of the time of Louis XV, Georgina was constantly surrounded by a swarm of young men. She danced the cotillion with a rich admirer of whom her mother approved – but the only partner she really wanted was Crow, who stood and watched her, refusing to dance with anyone else. He told Georgina that she was so beautiful that he would like to live with her in a thatched cottage for the rest of his life. Georgina was entranced. Returning to the family's lodgings after

5 GWJ, 17–18/8/1854.

the party at five o'clock in the morning, she burst into tears: taking off the costume that Crow had admired so much would bring the wonderful evening to an end. Recognising the strength of her feelings for the young nobleman, she was also afraid, for her mother had convinced her that no young lady who was *comme il faut* ever fell in love before she was married. According to her memoirs, Georgina then fell into a 'mechanical and mournful stupor', which lasted for several weeks – though her diaries record that Crow and his sister were 'constantly with us' during the month of April.

On 28 May, a few days after Georgina's eighteenth birthday, she left Brussels 'in bitter tears'. She and the rest of the family were to spend a month in Boulogne before returning to England. Feeling that she would die of misery, Georgina was certain that the reason for the journey was her mother's desire to get her away from Crow (Morgan appears to have known nothing about this love affair). She began to practise the piano in a frenzy, recalling 'with love and sorrow' all that her beloved had said about her faults. 'Thus it was', she wrote many years later 'that I became a great musician'.

To everyone's astonishment, Crow followed the Thomases to Boulogne after a fortnight, and they found him waiting for them in their lodgings one Sunday on their return from church. Snatching a few minutes alone with Georgina, sitting on the chalk cliffs overlooking the Channel, Crow asked her about a letter that she had written to his sister, in which she had hinted at her feelings. 'If you did love me', he said, 'we could be married in that little church.' He gazed at Georgina, whilst she gazed at the sea: 'I made no reply, he bent towards me, his lips almost touched my cheek. I drew back gently. He did not kiss me, but left the same afternoon – and I have never seen him since.'[6]

Georgina would remember this moment for the rest of her life. A year later, however, Crow married a Portuguese noblewoman and heiress, Maria, Marquesa da Fronteira, who was seven years older than he was. Nevertheless, he and Georgina remained in contact on and off for several years, and he even sent her his photograph in 1869. On the back of it she wrote 'He whom I should have married'. But she was deluding herself: if she had been able to marry Pedro de Moncorvo the outcome would surely have been disastrous. It seems most unlikely that Moncorvo's family in Portugal would have welcomed a new baroness who was neither a Catholic nor an aristocrat. Even if Georgina's parents had agreed to the wedding, her dowry would not have been large enough to outweigh her other disadvantages. Nevertheless, Georgina continued to think of Crow, on his birthday and on the anniversaries of their meeting and final

6 GWJ index, 28/5/1855; GWO, i, pp. 6–7.

parting. And after his death in 1903, when she herself was sixty-six and no longer in the best of health, Georgina travelled to Portugal to visit Crow's grave and see the palace in Bemfica (now on the outskirts of Lisbon) where he and his wife had lived.

Georgina's heart may have been broken, but life continued much as it had done before. She and her mother returned to Brussels early in 1856, and there were balls and parties almost every night. At the beginning of May Georgina was confirmed by the Bishop of Jamaica: 'All the other girls were decently dressed in white muslin. I wore a black silk skirt of Mama's, a corsage of my own which fit [*sic*] very badly, and, as a veil, a Brussels lace shawl belonging to Mama. Horrible caricature! I shall never forget my feelings.' In spite of her somewhat eccentric clothing, however, Georgina claimed, 'I not only never missed a dance, but was engaged balls ahead for the whole winter. Had I been a man, I would not have danced with such a caricature.'[7] Edward Hyde Hewett was still desperately in love: he wrote poems for Georgina and begged her to marry him. She refused, offering him friendship, but not love: 'So many people love me, Ted – there is nobody I have so much friendship for as you. Papa would not give his consent to my marriage with anybody less than £5000 a year, and poor Mama has set her mind upon my being a great lady.'[8] She was, moreover, still in love with Crow.

~

In November 1856 Morgan Thomas, with his wife and children assumed – or, as the family claimed, reassumed – the surname of Treherne. There was some justification for doing this: hereditary surnames came relatively late in Wales and Morgan's ancestors had settled on the name Thomas only in the latter part of the seventeenth century. According to family tradition, Morgan changed his name because he had fallen out with his elder brother, Rees, and no longer wished to bear the same name as his hated sibling. Treherne is a more distinctive name than Thomas, and Morgan may also have hoped that a new name would help him to achieve the ambition of becoming a member of parliament, which had never quite left him. Whatever the reason may have been, Georgina Thomas now became Georgina Treherne.

By this time Morgan and Louisa were becoming increasingly preoccupied with the need to get their attractive, but wilful, eldest daughter safely married off. If Georgina is to be believed, it was her 'matchmaking mother' who took the lead in this, doing everything she could to indoctrinate her

7 GW, scrapbook.

8 GW–Edward Hyde Hewett, *c.*1856.

daughter with the belief that it was her duty to marry well for the sake of her younger sisters. This was 'agony' to Georgina, as it made her feel 'as tho' I were cattle, ready for market'. Additional pressure came from Emily. She and Florence had both been sent to a boarding school in Brighton in the autumn of 1855 – due, according to Georgina, to their 'insubordination, bad tempers and impudence', which made it 'impossible to keep them at home', as no governess could stand them. This made Emily ('lazy, stupid and quarrelsome') even more jealous of her elder sister than she had been before, and she 'martyred' Georgina by mocking her 'sadness and distress' and ridiculing her admirers. As a result of all this teasing, according to Georgina, she became *maigre comme un clou* [as thin as a nail] and the doctors began to suspect that she might be consumptive. But Georgina's account of these years was written many years later, when her attitude to marriage had changed. As a girl of nineteen or twenty, she seems to have entered into the search for an eligible partner with considerable enthusiasm.[9]

~

The vast majority of girls of the upper-middle or upper class in Victorian Britain expected (or, at least, hoped) to marry. The education that they received – such as it was – trained them for lives as wives and mothers but for little else. Women lower down the social scale might become governesses, teachers or housekeepers, or they might earn a living as dressmakers or milliners; if a family belonged to the gentry or aristocracy it was felt to be demeaning if the women undertook paid work. Most girls dreamt of becoming mistress of their own house and hoped that this would give them a degree of independence. Spinsters were seen as failures, condemned to spend their lives caring for others and dependent on their parents or brothers for financial support.

Unfortunately for the Treherne girls, their father had very definite ideas about the qualifications needed by a prospective son-in-law. Morgan was 'a monomaniac' on the subject of marriage. He 'tabooed Irish and Yankees and Papists' and insisted that his children should only marry into families of high social status, preferably with titles.[10] For a son-in-law, an annual income of at least £10,000 was an absolute necessity. This was distinctly optimistic: Morgan's own income was much less than this, and he was only prepared to give dowries of £7000 to his daughters. Nevertheless, his goal may have seemed attainable for a while, as Georgina's social circle widened. Between November 1856 and May 1857, she and her mother

9 GWL, p. 14; GWJ, 31/12/1899.

10 GWMSM, p. 28.

spent most of their time in Brighton, and it was during these months that Georgina formed a number of friendships that were to have a decisive impact on the next phase of her life.

Only twenty miles from Mayfield, Brighton was a lively, fashionable social centre in the mid nineteenth century, with a winter season that attracted some of the richest and most influential people in the land. At the end of 1856 these included Lady Charlotte Schreiber, daughter of the ninth Earl of Lindsey, who was a contemporary of Georgina's mother. A forceful and highly intelligent woman, she had married the wealthy Welsh ironmaster John Guest in 1833 when she was twenty-one. Guest had died twenty years later, leaving his widow with ten children. In 1855 Lady Charlotte had married her son's tutor Charles Schreiber, a man fourteen years her junior. Homesickness for Wales, where she had spent most of the previous twenty years, probably encouraged Lady Charlotte to make the acquaintance of a family of Welsh origin, and her children were the same age as the young Trehernes. In Georgina she may have recognised a kindred spirit: both women were the oldest (and brightest) children in families which prized sons more than daughters; both had suffered from the embarrassment caused by the behaviour of an unpredictable and ill-tempered parent (Lady Charlotte had loathed her stepfather the Reverend Peter Pegus); and both had used a journal as an outlet for their innermost thoughts from an early age. Both women, too, had a strong sense of the importance of their own lineage (better founded in Lady Charlotte's case than Georgina's) and of the superiority of their own talents to those of ordinary people. And both were, at the time, somewhat on the margins of society: Georgina because of her background and the fact that she had spent so much time abroad, and Lady Charlotte because of the widespread disapproval of her second marriage.[11]

Several friends visited Lady Charlotte and her children whilst they were in Brighton, and Georgina met many of them – including Mr and Mrs John Warrender Dalrymple. John Dalrymple was a distant relative of Georgina's mother. There is no indication that Louisa Treherne had ever had any contact with her father's relatives before this time, but, given Morgan's obsession with ancestry, it seems likely that they soon worked out the connection between the two families. Mrs Dalrymple (born Sophia Pattle) was of Anglo-Indian descent, one of seven beautiful and talented sisters, several of whom Georgina was soon to meet. In April, however, Lady Charlotte left Brighton for Roehampton, where she was to rent Exeter House (next door to the home of Sophia Dalrymple's sister, Julia Margaret Cameron) for

[11] Revel Guest and Angela V. John, *Lady Charlotte* (London, 1989), pp. 1–12.

three years.[12] The other winter visitors drifted away too, and Georgina and her mother returned to Gate House at the beginning of May. Three weeks later there was 'an awful row' after Morgan discovered that Georgina had been corresponding with one of her Belgian admirers, Guillaume van der Burch, in secret. He seized his daughter's journal 'which called him names and compromised the rest of the family'. Then, 'in a fright', Louisa burnt all the journals that Georgina had written since September 1854. When, in the 1880s, Georgina wrote her account of these events, she added: 'Papa, in reality, had led us all a most wretched life. We all deceived him as much as we possibly could – servants and all.'[13]

After Morgan's violent reaction to the discovery of his eldest daughter's latest love affair, it is somewhat surprising that he allowed her, a month after the 'awful row', to accept an invitation to visit some of her new acquaintances. She was asked to stay at Little Holland House, the home of Sophia Dalrymple's sister Sara and her husband Henry Thoby Prinsep. Sara and another sister, Virginia (later Lady Somers), both beautiful and 'passionately unconventional', had met the artist George Frederick Watts in 1849, and Sara had looked after Watts at her house in Chesterfield Street when he fell seriously ill in 1850.[14] Later that year Watts had taken Sara and her husband to look at Little Holland House, a rambling farmhouse in Kensington which belonged to his patrons Lord and Lady Holland. The Prinseps were enchanted with Little Holland House, which was surrounded by gardens and open countryside. It would be an ideal setting for gatherings of the artists and writers that Sara wished to cultivate. They invited Watts to join them when they moved into the house early in the following year. The arrangement was mutually beneficial: Watts found a comfortable home, where his eccentricities would be tolerated and he would be nursed, cherished and revered, and Thoby and Sara gained an eminent artist who would attract other well-known people to their salon.

Georgina arrived at Little Holland House for the first time on 22 June 1857. She stayed there for six weeks, until 5 August. It was like a new world – an exotic one of colour, mystery and excitement, full of 'pictures and music and gentle, artistic people with quiet voices and elegant manners'.[15] Sara Prinsep and her sisters did not dress like other women of the period: their hair was simply styled and they favoured flowing robes and Indian jewellery. On Sunday afternoons, when the house and gardens were thrown

[12] Julia would later become a well-known portrait photographer.

[13] GWJ index, later addition to entry of 27/5/1857.

[14] Veronica Franklin Gould, *G.F. Watts* (New Haven and London, 2004), p. 27.

[15] Ellen Terry, *The Story of My Life* (London, 1908), pp. 47–8.

Fig. 8. Georgina in 1857, from the watercolour by J.R. Parsons after the oil portrait by G.F. Watts.

open, the visitors included many of the best-known men and women of the day. All kinds of people – politicians, painters, writers and musicians – were welcome, so long as they were interesting. Julia Margaret Cameron and Lady Charlotte Schreiber were both there when Georgina arrived, as were the Dalrymples and the Prinseps: Thoby and Sara, their second son Val, and their daughter Alice, a girl of ten or eleven. Also present was 'Mr George F. Watts', who, with Val Prinsep, had just returned from an expedition to Turkey.

During this stay at Little Holland House, Georgina met the writers Lady Theresa Lewis and Caroline Norton; the composers Julius Benedict and Fabio Campana; and the artist and illustrator Richard (Dickie) Doyle. One day, three of the most famous artists of the day turned up: Dante Gabriel

Rosetti, William Holman Hunt and Edward Burne-Jones. The Prinseps took Georgina to balls and operas, and on 3 August there was a party at Lincoln's Inn Fields to inspect the frescoes that Watts had been working on for several years. Georgina had struck up a somewhat unlikely friendship with the artist, who was to paint two portraits of her. Watts was twice her age and, in the words of his biographer, 'relished the idea of taming excitable young women.'[16]

These, as Georgina later wrote, were 'happy days.' On 5 August she returned to Mayfield, to 'isolation and constant warfare,' but not for long.[17] In October she, with her mother and sister Florence, went to stay at Beechwood Park in Hertfordshire, the home of Sir Thomas Sebright, an old friend of the Treherne family, who was Florence's godfather. Georgina had been invited to take part in a private production of a musical comedy, *Hearts and Tarts, or The Knave Turned Honest* by Augustus Stafford, which was to be performed on 16 October at Ashridge House, a few miles from Beechwood. Ashridge was the home of a wealthy and artistic widow, Lady Marian Alford, and Georgina's fellow actors included the Duke of Manchester, who played the King of Hearts, and Princess Mary of Cambridge (later Duchess of Teck) who was the Queen. Georgina (the Eight of Hearts) was one of only two adults on the main cast list without a title. The prompter was the Hon. Frederick ('Poodle') Byng, 'the last of the Regency bucks,' who was soon Georgina's devoted admirer, though he was well over seventy years old and married.[18] Augustus Stafford praised Georgina's performance, telling her that she was 'not like other people.' She was, he told her, 'simple, unaffected and without pretensions.' She gave herself no airs and followed his instructions. Enjoying all the attention, Georgina decided that she could (if she chose) have a future as an actress.[19]

Watts paid a brief visit to Beechwood whilst the Trehernes were there, and Louisa was warned about him and the rest of the Little Holland House set by her host. Georgina and Watts were already exchanging letters by this time, and Georgina was making use of the older man as a confidant – somewhat to his dismay, it would appear, especially after he discovered that her mother knew nothing of their correspondence. Like everyone else at Little Holland House, Georgina called Watts 'Signor'; he called her 'Bambina' (soon shortened to 'Bam') and wrote of his 'true, brotherly

16 Gould, *Watts*, p. 50. Veronica Franklin Gould believes (pers. comm.) that Georgina is also the central figure in Watts's Lincoln's Inn mural, *A Hemicycle of Lawgivers*.

17 Lindholm Collection, GFW–GW, 25/8/1857. I am grateful to Tim Lindholm for permission to quote from this letter, and from other letters in his collection.

18 Edward Grierson, *Storm Bird* (London, 1959), p. 18.

19 GWO, i, p. 11.

affection' for her. In one of his first letters he told her that he missed 'the effervescing stimulant that was sparkling and overflowing' about the house, though he had always been 'in a fidget about the wild little girl' (Georgina). She should, he warned her, be 'very wise' in her choice of a husband,

> for everything will depend upon the person or persons with whom you may live. If you are fortunate in this respect you will be, as you ought to be, an ornament and a delight to society. If the contrary, I dread more than I can say for the little Bambina. I do not think you would be happy as the wife of a poor man.[20]

In another letter Watts chided Georgina for being 'frank and thoughtless' and told her that she never 'said a word, or did a thing' that did not tend towards her own advantage. He advised her to do everything that she could to avoid scandal, and to 'bear your troubles and annoyances nobly and give up your time to improvement in every way'. Georgina promised him that she would be 'prudent and wise'.[21]

It is clear from this correspondence that Georgina had embarked on another romance, this time with Lady Charlotte Schreiber's second son Merthyr Guest, an undergraduate at Trinity College, Cambridge. Merthyr, who was eight months younger than Georgina, was clearly smitten, and he had already proposed. Watts advised caution: they were both very young and need not be in a hurry to commit themselves:

> Marriage is a serious thing, and when a mistake has been made by two poor creatures, God help them! Be not rash, Bambina. If Merthyr Guest cares for you, and is worthy of you, he will not forget you or change for a year or more. If he should, then you will have had an escape ... Be sure of your own feelings, don't let opposition, or love for Kate [Merthyr's sister], cause you to nourish a romance into a fictitious passion. Be well sure of yourself.[22]

At the end of this eventful year, Georgina summed up her feelings in her diary:

[20] Lindholm Collection, GFW–GW, 5,25/8/1857.

[21] GFW–GW, n.d., quoted in Grierson, *Storm Bird*, p. 19; Watts Gallery, transcripts of letter GFW–GW, 20/9/1857 and n.d./10/1857. I am grateful to Veronica Franklin Gould for copies of these transcripts, and for copies of other material at the Watts Gallery.

[22] Watts Gallery, Compton, transcript of letter GFW–GW, 28/10/1857.

> How all the scenes of my life are changed! New and different friends since last year ... TMG [Merthyr Guest] and all belonging to Little Holland House uppermost in my heart and mind. My mind also is more changed than I could have imagined. I see things, I hope, in a better and more reasonable light. At any rate, Signor is a good and kind friend I can depend on. If I could cure myself of my heedlessness I should hope and feel sure for a happy future, but I am so excitable. Poor old TMG, I am afraid I shall never marry him.[23]

She was right, though the story of Georgina's relationship with Merthyr Guest had not ended yet.

[23] GWJ index, 1857. TMG is [Thomas] Merthyr Guest.

3
Harry

Georgina saw out the year 1857 at Gate House feeling 'unwell, cold and wretched', surrounded by her unsympathetic family and wondering how she would get through the rest of the winter. The bleakness of her mood was enhanced when Florence and Emily, home from school for the Christmas holidays, told her a terrible secret. They had discovered, from reading the diary of a fellow pupil, that their 'aristocratic, noble mother' was illegitimate – a fact which had been concealed from them up to this time. Emily and Florence thought that this was 'rather fun', but Georgina was horrified. She rushed to her mother 'with red and flaming eyes', sobbing 'It can't be true! It can't be true!' When Louisa 'flushed scarlet all over her face', and admitted that it was indeed true, Georgina felt 'turned to stone'.

She was particularly worried about the effect that this revelation might have on her marriage prospects:

> I dreaded any man of family wanting to marry me, as I looked on ourselves, henceforth, as imposters, and all our airs as imposture. Either the engagement would be broken off – on the wedding day, perhaps! – or it would be found out afterwards. The thought was to me a perpetual nightmare.[1]

Relief was, however, at hand. Early in the New Year Louisa received a letter from Tizey Smith, an old school-friend, informing her that she had just met a junior officer in the 6th (Inniskilling) Regiment of Dragoons, who was 'The most charming, most adorable boy who could be imagined'. He was 'handsome, tall and rich'; he already had an income of £10,000 a year, and he was heir to his mother and grandmother. Louisa was urged to make sure that this paragon met Georgina as soon as possible. And, in Georgina's own words, Louisa and her three daughters 'went running'.[2] The officer was William Henry (Harry) Weldon, and he and Georgina met for the first

1 GWJ index, 1857; GWMSM, pp. 32–3.
2 GWM, i, pp. 30–1. In the original French, Georgina wrote '*Nous accourûmes*'.

time at a party in Brighton at the end of January. Harry was twenty, a few weeks older than Georgina, and he had joined the dragoons as a cornet eight months earlier.

Harry was just as keen to meet Georgina as she was to meet him, though for rather different reasons. She had clearly acquired a somewhat dubious reputation in the drawing rooms of the leaders of Brighton society. This might well have tarnished her marriage prospects, but it only made her more attractive in the eyes of the young cavalry officer. Everyone had told him that Georgina was 'a great flirt' and would only amuse herself with him. But Harry was, as he himself boasted, 'a most *dreadful* flirt'. He later informed Georgina that 'I thought it would be the greatest fun in the world to flirt with you – it would be "diamond cut diamond", and we would see who would be the strongest.' But, if their subsequent letters are to be believed, it was love at first sight for both of them. Georgina later told Harry that she had fallen for 'the tone of your voice, the glance of your dark eye, and the radiant smile of your countenance'.[3] He had no aristocratic connections, but to Georgina, still shaken by the discovery of her mother's illegitimacy, this was an advantage, as his family 'could never make any objection to pedigree'. She hailed Harry as a deliverer.[4] Harry appeared to be equally entranced by Georgina and the two danced together all evening. They saw each other again several times during the days that followed, before the Trehernes returned home on 6 February. A week later Georgina received, by the same post, her first letter from Harry – and a valentine from Merthyr Guest.

On 13 February Cornet Weldon was promoted to the rank of lieutenant. A week later he rode over to Gate House from Brighton on his charger Multum and was kindly received by Georgina's parents. Morgan thought him charming, especially after his wife had told him that the young man had £10,000 a year and high expectations. Admittedly, his family was in trade – a disadvantage that would have disqualified him in the eyes of many élite parents – but in Morgan's eyes this was outweighed by his apparent wealth. He was quite respectable – and he was already in love with Georgina. During his next visit, a week later, Harry told Morgan that he would ask his lawyer exactly how much money he could expect to have when he came of age in April. He also promised that Georgina would have an income of £4000 if he should die before her. It all sounded too good to be true – as, indeed, it was. Georgina's suitor soon admitted to her that his income was nowhere near £10,000 a year and his mother was 'quite poor'. He claimed, nevertheless, that she had £2000 a year; he thought that he had

[3] WHW–GW, 7/7/1859; GW–WHW, 16–19/6/1859.

[4] GWMSM, p. 33.

about £6000, but would eventually have £10,000. Georgina reassured him: her parents liked him, and all would be well. Unfortunately, Harry was still being less than totally honest.

~

William Henry Weldon was born at Wath-upon-Dearne in Yorkshire on 8 April 1837, the son of William and Hannah Weldon. William's father was Thomas Weldon, a coal merchant who had made enough money to buy up a number of properties around Sheffield, including a mansion, Bramley Hall in Handsworth, where he and his family lived. Thomas was also wealthy enough to enable William, his only son, to call himself a gentleman, with no obvious occupation. William had married Hannah Wright in Liverpool ten months before Harry's birth. Hannah, the daughter of a ship-builder, was a plain girl, but she had money – perhaps as much as £20,000.[5] Unfortunately for her, William died of smallpox in March 1838, when his son was less than a year old. Little love seems to have been lost between Hannah and her in-laws, and it was not long before she took her young son to live in Wales. They went to Beaumaris on the island of Anglesey, closer to members of her own family. What Hannah lived on at this time is unclear, but her income is likely to have been much less than a thousand pounds a year.

Thomas Weldon died in 1846. He left most of his estates to his widow for life, after which they would be divided between the family of his daughter, Mary Dymond, and his grandson Harry. The depth of his antipathy towards Harry's mother is indicated by his revocation of a bequest of £500 to her. Harry had been made a ward in Chancery shortly before his grandfather's death, and his grandmother and uncle Robert Dymond had been appointed guardians.[6] They sent Harry to Harrow School when he was thirteen years old and he stayed there until midsummer 1853. Around this time, as Georgina was to discover many years later, Harry seduced his mother's parlour maid, then 'stoutly denied it, spoke to the poor girl like a dog, and got her sent away in disgrace'.[7] Harry tried to get into the army after leaving school, but failed his exams at least once. He eventually succeeded in 1857, when he was able to purchase his cornetcy for £840. In the intervening period he had been made a lieutenant in a volunteer regiment, the Royal Lancashire Militia Artillery, which was commanded by his great-uncle, Sir Duncan MacDougall.

5 GWMSM, p. 35.

6 Borthwick Institute, York, PCY wills, Thomas Weldon of Bramley Hall, Handsworth, Yorkshire, 1847.

7 GWMSM, p. 42.

The truth about Harry's financial position began to come out a week after his second visit to Gate House. Early one morning Louisa Treherne rushed into her daughter's room when Georgina was still in bed, declaring that Harry was 'a blackguard' and 'a vile crook'. She showed Georgina a letter from her beloved, who admitted that his means were 'far inferior to what he had been brought up to expect'. He would have £1000 a year in April when he came of age, and another £1000 when his grandmother died. He would also inherit £2000 a year from his mother – but she was only forty-five and could live for many more years. Louisa told Georgina that she would be mad to marry Harry – the whole idea was 'ridiculous, infamous'. Two thousand a year was 'beggary', but one thousand meant starvation – 'it means dying of hunger'.[8]

Harry was immediately informed that he would not be welcome at Gate House again, and would not, under any circumstances, be permitted to marry into the Treherne family. But he was not prepared to give up so easily. Having been refused admittance on his next visit, he wrote to Georgina, threatening to take his revenge on her father and trying to persuade her to elope with him. The letter arrived during the morning of 10 March. When Harry rode over to Mayfield several hours later, on a 'dark, cold, snowy winter's night', Georgina, frightened by the tone of the letter and unwilling to embark on a course of action that would alienate her from her parents and siblings, refused to see him and told the butler to send him away.[9] In his final letter, Harry accused Georgina of selfish pride and ambition, and of writing to him with 'a cold heart and an iron pen'.[10] Soon afterwards, he left Brighton for Leeds, having been transferred from the Inniskilling Dragoons to the recently re-raised 18th Hussars.

At the beginning of May Georgina went to stay with Lady Charlotte Schreiber and her family at Exeter House, and on 5 May Lady Charlotte presented her young friend at Court.[11] Most girls were presented when they were seventeen or eighteen: Georgina was almost twenty-one, but the delay could be explained by the fact that she had been living on the Continent – and she had already been presented to King Leopold in Brussels in 1855. Three days later, Merthyr Guest proposed to her. He was still infatuated, though he must have known something of her recent love affair, as his sisters Kate and Maria had stayed at Gate House for a fortnight in March and his brother Augustus had also been a regular visitor there. Merthyr

8 GWM, i, pp. 33–4; GWL, p. 14.

9 WHW–GW, 23/6/1859.

10 GW–WHW, 16–19/6/1859 (referring to letter of 23/3/1858).

11 Earl of Bessborough (ed.), *Lady Charlotte Schreiber* (London, 1952), pp. 82–7.

had told his mother of his intentions before asking Georgina to marry him. Lady Charlotte was less than enthusiastic about the match, but she did not absolutely forbid him to propose.

This time, Georgina accepted Merthyr's proposal, having already decided that if she could not have Harry she would marry someone 'of high rank and enormously rich.' Merthyr went to visit Georgina's parents, and Morgan then wrote to the boy's mother, asking how much money would be settled on his daughter, and how much she and Merthyr would have to live on. It turned out that Merthyr could expect to have £2000 a year in two years' time, rising to £40,000 a year 'some day.'[12] This reply was not good enough for Morgan, whose subsequent letters to Lady Charlotte were described by the recipient as 'violent.' As she noted in her journal 'He evidently expected to make great terms as to settlement, believing that we were all anxious for the match.' Georgina, for her part, decided that her prospective mother-in-law was 'a humbug.' In June there was a showdown at Little Holland House, where Georgina was staying. With Sara Prinsep acting as an intermediary, it was agreed that there should be a 'tacit engagement' between Georgina and Merthyr, but that the two should not meet, write or marry until Merthyr came of age in the following January. The lovers took leave of each other in Julia Margaret Cameron's house four days later, and Merthyr left for a fishing trip to Scotland soon afterwards.[13]

Georgina was, however, having second thoughts about Merthyr by this time. During the next few weeks she seems to have done her best to convince Lady Charlotte that she would be totally unsuitable as a daughter-in-law by flirting with William, Lord Ward, a wealthy widower with a scandalous past, who was twenty years her senior. Ward was said to admire Georgina very much, and the two were soon 'inseparable.' On 14 June Lady Charlotte drove over to Little Holland House, where she spent several hours with Mrs Prinsep. 'And all that while,' as she later wrote in her journal, 'Miss Treherne was closeted with Lord Ward alone in Watts' studio.' Watts himself was away, at Bowood. Both women were disgusted by Georgina's behaviour, for a young unmarried girl was not supposed to spend time alone with any man – let alone one like Lord Ward. It is difficult to believe that Georgina was naive enough to believe that she could get away with this – unless she saw a flirtation with the widower as the best way of ending an engagement that she now deeply regretted. Predictably enough, Lady Charlotte soon decided that it was her duty to tell her son what his beloved was up to. At the end of June, after Georgina sent Merthyr a 'pert and dictatorial letter,'

12 GW–WHW, 17/6/1859, 11/7/1859.
13 GWJ index, 31/5/1858.

he asked her to return all the letters that he had sent her.[14] By the beginning of July it was 'all over' between them. Georgina went home to Gate House and then, with her brother Dal and sister Emily, set off for Switzerland to stay with Uncle George at Schloss Hard.

The young Trehernes were in Switzerland for the next five months, returning home to Gate House just before Christmas. It was not a particularly happy time: when Georgina arrived she found that George (whose favourite she had been) was 'completely changed towards me in consequence of my love affairs', and she felt anxious and unwell. A tour of Switzerland with George and Nandine was not a success, and Georgina and Emily were both 'bored to extinction'.[15] There were, nevertheless, some compensations: on 23 September the eminent conductor and composer Julius Benedict, whom Georgina had first met at Little Holland House a year earlier, arrived at Schloss Hard with his daughters Georgy and Alice. They were there on and off for the next month, forming the basis of a friendship with Georgina that was to last for many years.

~

Back at Gate House at the end of another year, Georgina wrote of her unhappiness. Merthyr was lost to her for ever and 'all hopes of Little Holland House' were gone:

> I have no hope and no future before me. It is to be resigned here at Gate House, where everything is uncongenial to my feelings, but it is my home and I must bear it. Crow I love as much, and more, than ever. Guillaume van der Burch I have heard from and written to. He is the same, and I love him as much as ever. This year I have lost the only object of my wild fancy and fervent dreams, Harry Weldon. Never can I admire anyone so much as I did him.[16]

She had not, however, entirely given up all hopes of seeing Harry again, having realised during the negotiations with the Guest family that an income of £1000 a year was not, as she had been led to believe, too little for a married couple to live on.

Whilst she was still in Switzerland, Georgina had received a letter from one of her friends, Frances Beckett, the wife of a wealthy banker and former MP. The Becketts, who spent every winter in Brighton, knew Harry and thought him 'very agreeable and gentlemanlike'. He had told Mrs Beckett

14 Bessborough, *Lady Charlotte Schreiber*, p. 84.
15 GWJ index, 6/9/1858.
16 GWJ index, end 1858.

that he was still in love with Georgina, and she had decided to try to bring the two together again. When Georgina saw the Becketts in Brighton in January 1859, they told her what Harry had said and described his 'mad, restless look'. They teased Georgina, telling her that Harry was being pursued by several rich, beautiful girls, and that Mrs Beckett would find an heiress for him if Georgina did not want him. They also told her that Harry had been seriously ill and close to death for some time, and had been sent home to his mother in Wales. All this made him quite irresistible in Georgina's eyes. She sent him two valentines in February, but he does not appear to have realised that they came from her.

Harry rejoined his regiment in March, at a time when war in Europe was imminent. Three months later, fearing (as she claimed) that her beloved might be sent abroad to fight, Georgina finally took the plunge and wrote to him, asking if he still loved her. That she did so is a sign of her growing desperation: men were supposed to take the initiative in love affairs, and many would have been surprised and shocked to receive a letter of this kind from a girl with whom they had had no contact for over a year. Receiving no reply to her first short note, she wrote a much longer letter a week later, telling Harry that she loved him and had pined to be with him for eighteen 'long, sad months':

> Have not I prayed to God to let me forget you and drive away the maddening thoughts that would throng my brain to bursting? Have not I laughed at the love I have for you, talked of it jestingly, forced myself to hear your name, to become familiar with the agony of hopelessness that name involved?[17]

The longed-for reply arrived at Gate House on 25 June. In it Harry asked Georgina how she could doubt for a single moment that he loved her 'truly, dearly, fondly as ever', and told her that he had imagined that she was with him when he was delirious with fever during his long sickness.

For reasons that eventually became clear, Harry was reluctant to tell Georgina exactly what he had been doing since his last visit to Gate House on 10 March 1858, but the story gradually came out. On reaching the age of 21 on 8 April of that year he had received the money left to him by his father, a total of £7000. Much of this had already been spent by the time Georgina wrote to him. He claimed that he had tried to write to her to tell her 'how truly wretched, miserable and wicked' she had made him, but had fallen ill before he could do so.[18]

17 GW–WHW, 10,16,25/6/1859, 4,10/7/1859; WHW–GW, 20/7/1859.

18 WHW–GW, 23,30/6/1859.

Harry thus made Georgina (already stricken with guilt for having rejected him in the first place) feel that his troubles had been all her fault. She believed his claim that he had been 'a better boy' since his illness, and ignored rumours that he had changed regiments only because his colonel had ordered him to leave the Inniskillings.[19] Magnanimously (and naively, since she clearly had little real idea of what he had been up to) she forgave Harry, and the resolution of saving him from himself began to form in her mind. She was, as she wrote many years later, led astray by 'reading the lying pernicious, mischievous tales of Charlotte Yonge'.[20] C.M. Yonge, an enormously popular and influential novelist in the mid nineteenth century, believed that it was the duty of women to support men, and that they could redeem them through their example of virtue and ultimate sacrifice.

Georgina was to play many different parts in her life: having hitherto acted the dutiful daughter at home, and the fascinating siren in society, she now began to represent herself to Harry as an obedient and dutiful little wife. She had, she told him, been 'brought up to pride, and worse, ambition', but now wanted nothing more than 'to be a good wife and possess a happy husband'. Only when she was singing, she claimed, did she feel that she was great and powerful. Georgina was not, however, entirely convincing in this new role, even at this stage. She poured out torrents of words, telling Harry how much she loved him, suggesting that they marry in secret and making plans for their future together. But she also complained about the brevity and irregularity of Harry's replies to her letters. She demanded a photograph of her beloved, then criticised the one that he sent her:

> Your little photo made me very happy, although you hold your little chin too high and your trousers fit you very badly, at any rate your right leg looks very crooked, little sunburnt boy that you are ... but your dear eyes and nose are beautiful, and your little moustache is a wee bit more evident.

Further requests followed: in one letter Georgina asked Harry to buy a horse cheaply and break it in for her; two weeks later he was to send her a ten-pound note, so that she could buy a pair of earrings and a brooch.

It is obvious from their correspondence that it was Georgina, not Harry, who made most of the running – though he provoked her by telling her of the other girls he had been flirting with. Georgina described herself as 'a weak, yielding little girl', but it was she who kept coming up with (often hare-brained)

[19] GW–WHW, 9/7/1859.

[20] GWJ, 25/2/1904.

schemes for them to meet.[21] They would go riding together in London, and she would wear a false nose 'so as not to be found out'; she would go and stay with the Becketts in Brighton and Harry would stay in an hotel there, calling himself 'Mr Smith'; or Harry would introduce himself to the people at Little Holland House by asking Watts to draw him. It was Georgina, too, who devised a way of continuing their correspondence in secret when Antonio, the butler, fell ill. It was he who usually sorted the mail and made it possible for Georgina to send and receive letters without her parents' knowledge. Georgina instructed Harry to buy a piece of music (an aria from Verdi's *Sicilian Vespers*) and send it, rolled, with his letter between the pages.[22]

Harry meekly did his best to obey most of Georgina's instructions, though he was dismayed when it became obvious that his inamorata planned to change him so that he would fit in with her own social circle. She wanted him to meet the people at Little Holland House, she wrote:

> You will, then, my darling, know what kind of society I like, and make acquaintance with me by my own friends. In the Season (in the course of time) you shall go to every fine party, and then you will know what good society is. You will then more understand what my tastes are, for tho' I greatly prefer the literary and artistic society at Little Holland House, yet as when I am in the world I must necessarily go to a few parties, I wish you to go where I shall meet you if I go out. I do not care for Society, but the little I must meet, I like to be good. I should like to send you to live with the Becketts, to teach you to be exclusive. Then you should be presented next year by the colonel of your regiment. I make one hundred thousand little plans for you, darling, and for your advantage and your amusement. I want you, in the Season, always to go to Covent Garden, hear good music, and feel there is no voice there like your own Gem's! I want you to feel with me, to think with me, before I can be with you, and then when you have had your full swing of pleasure, that you know how the world goes, we will quietly pair off together and go and talk alone of our love and all we have seen and heard: we shall remember the same things and talk of the same pleasures.[23]

When Harry protested that Georgina's friends would surely see through this plan, 'and I should get a snubbing,' she replied dismissively, 'I do not know what you mean by saying you might get a snubbing at Little Holland House, but I suppose it is an excuse, as you do not want to go.' She ordered Harry to stop gambling, but told him that she approved of him taking part

21 GW–WHW, 4,10,31/7/1859, 13,16/8/1859, 17,30/9/1859.

22 GW–WHW, 24,31/7/1859, 14/8/1859, n.d./8/1859.

23 GW–WHW, 13/8/1859. 'Gem' was Harry's pet name for Georgina.

in amateur theatricals 'because I believe that among the people belonging to the stage there is more real heart and feeling than is to be found in the higher classes of society'.[24]

Dreaming about a happy future with Harry made it possible for Georgina to endure the quarrels and tension at home. Morgan was becoming increasingly difficult, even forbidding his daughters to give singing lessons to the choir in Mayfield parish church. Fortunately, he was 'a most unsuspicious individual', and his wife and children had all become very good at deceiving him. Georgina went ahead and taught the choir, in spite of the veto.[25] But she received no support from Emily, who teased her by telling her that she had read in the paper that Harry had been seriously wounded. There followed a 'stand-up fight' between all three sisters, which had to be broken up by their mother.

There was, however, little prospect that Georgina and Harry would be able to marry in the foreseeable future, since she had 'not the half shadow of a farthing' and he had little more. As a junior officer he would be expected to remain single until he was thirty, so he would almost certainly have to leave the army if he married Georgina. Sometimes Georgina, who was enjoying the sensation of being in love, was quite happy with this situation, but even she realised that Harry would not wait for ever.[26]

After they had been exchanging letters for several months, Georgina and Harry arranged to meet again at the Brighton Hospital Ball on 28 November. It was almost two years since they had seen each other, and they had never spent more than a few minutes alone together – indeed, up to this time, they had met no more than ten times in all. All did not go according to plan. Georgina had assured Harry that her mother would not go to the ball, 'So there will be no one to prevent us talking the whole night together', but Louisa was there, and it was not long before she put two and two together and asked her daughter point blank if she was engaged to the young hussar. Stunned, Georgina replied 'Yes'. When the other guests realised what had happened, they all ignored Harry and he was forced to leave.

The repercussions continued during the days that followed, as rumours of Harry's past misdeeds flew from one house to another. The story about him having been ordered to quit the Inniskillings or face a court martial resurfaced, and he was also said to be rather too friendly with a number of actresses. Louisa wrote to Harry, ordering him to stay away from her daughter. He agreed to do so. Having been told that marriage to Harry

[24] WHW–GW, 15/9/1859; GW–WHW, 17,30/9/1859.

[25] GWO, i, pp. 10, 22; GWMSM, p. 33.

[26] GW–WHW, 24,30/7/1859.

would 'bring disgrace' upon her name, Georgina obeyed her mother's orders – outwardly, at least.[27] But she continued to write to him, and she also wrote to Colonel Shute to ask about Harry's army record. At the end of 1859 Georgina wrote bitterly of her mother's 'cold, unjust, ambitious and total disregard of her daughter's earthly happiness'. She was, she continued, resigned to her fate and no longer had any desire to marry. That she was not being entirely truthful to herself is indicated by subsequent speculations on the suitability of a new acquaintance, Martin Smith of the Royal Irish Dragoons, as a potential husband. He seemed to her to be 'peculiar, passionate, of stronger intellect and firmer purpose than I am composed of, and I have thought how he might love me and how I might love him, very dearly, heart and mind'. Significantly, Georgina dreamt one night that she was married to Harry, who had gone mad and tried to kill her – and that it was Martin Smith who had saved her.[28]

Georgina was back in Brighton in the first weeks of 1860, singing in All Saints church and enjoying dinners and dancing parties. She soon discovered that Harry was still thought to be 'the greatest blackguard unhanged', and Lady Abinger had been told that he had a mistress living in the barracks with him.[29] When she heard this, Georgina felt 'as if all my clothes had fallen off in a room full of people'. She claimed much later that she had, at this time, completely lost her 'idiotic, unreasoning feeling' for Harry. She stopped writing to him for a while, though he sent her a pair of earrings (but no letter) early in February. But she soon started to write again, having decided to ignore the rumours about his mistress. On 1 March Georgina took the train to London. She did not know it at the time, but she was never to see her home – or speak to her father – again. Shortly after her arrival she asked Harry to come and see her.

Georgina's accounts of the life-changing meeting with Harry that followed are inconsistent. According to memoirs written in 1903, she began by telling him that she 'cared no longer one button for him'. Harry then burst into tears, vowed that Georgina was his only love, and told her that he had become desperate for love of her, had spent all his money (£25,000, he said) and had not one penny left. All that remained for him was to go out to India and get himself killed. He 'begged and prayed' Georgina to marry him. She told him that she would never do so, but would not marry anyone else either; she was terribly delicate and the doctors believed that she was

[27] GW–WHW, 2/12/1859.
[28] GWJ index, end 1859.
[29] GW–WHW, 14/3/1860.

in a decline. She hoped that she was dying, so that she could go to 'a world where there would be no more question of marriage, or giving in marriage'.

Her journal tells a rather different story. The entry for 11 March runs as follows:

> My very darling and best love Harry Weldon came to see me at half past eleven a.m. Oh! It seems to me there was never love so pure, passionate, young or fresh as he is. He was so gentle, so good. He is an angel, I believe. How I pray to God he may remain good and pure, as he is now. He looked so bright and beautiful now.[30]

Whatever actually happened, Georgina decided that she was still in love with Harry. He was certainly not perfect, but her mission in life would be to save him from himself. She told him off for not praying and reading his Bible every night, as she did, and urged him to be 'a good boy'. 'Of course', she told him, 'you will do a naughty little thing now and then, but you will not gamble or do anything horrid.' She still felt that she could not look forward to anything but 'a very dim and distant day' for their marriage, but expressed the hope that 'I may remain your friend through life, and die your wife'.

For the next few weeks Georgina felt that she was 'three parts crazed'. She admitted that she hardly knew Harry, but she had decided that she loved him 'more than any one I had ever or have ever seen, and more than I can ever love again'. She tried to set up an assignation, for which she planned to disguise herself with 'a double Shetland vail and a respirator', and told Harry that her health was 'vile', and her spirits 'all broken and gone'. In Harry's reply to this letter he repeated his threat to go to India. He ended with the words 'God forgive me for all I have done to you, for I now see you never will'.[31] If Harry intended to make Georgina feel guilty again, he was successful, especially after she received a 'very satisfactory' letter from Colonel Shute, telling her that the rumours about her beloved's less-than-creditable army career were untrue. Suddenly, everything became clear and she knew what she should do. Several friends, including Julius Benedict, had told her that she could make a fortune on the stage. So, as she wrote in her journal, 'I have formed the resolution of marrying Harry and going on the stage, for I cannot bear this any longer. I am quite ill with fever, anxiety and love. With God's help, and my own earnest desire to do right and good, it may yet be.'[32]

30 GWMSM, pp. 35–6; GWJ, 11/3/1860.

31 GW–WHW, 19,24,28/3/1860; WHW–GW, 30/3/1860.

32 GWJ, 3/4/1860.

A week later Georgina saw Harry again. They met at 15 Westbourne Place, the home of Fabio Campana and his wife Nina, with whom Georgina was staying, and spent most of the day alone together. Harry assured Georgina that he did, indeed, love her, and they agreed to marry soon. Their wedding would, however, be kept a secret until October, by which time Harry would have sold out of the army. He promised to think about her hopes of a career in the theatre. Four days after this meeting Harry wrote to Georgina: 'Yes, my own pet, you shall in this instance have all your own way. We will be married as soon as possible, and in October you will come to me and we will at once go to Florence, and you may go on the stage.' There was no going back now, though Harry may well have had second thoughts when he read Georgina's next letter:

> I keep on thinking how very, very happy we shall be when October comes, and we shall be together to love each other all the day round. I think, darling, we have both very soft, gentle minds; we remind me of two good little cats who sit and purr together all day and never get tired of each other. I hope, my dear love, I shall be a good little wife. Harry will never do anything his little wife does not like, and Gem will never do anything her own husband does not approve of. I know, darling, you hate and abominate my going on the stage, but I will do it. I will be married on Wednesday or Thursday, it's me who will do everything this time, and you must now do as I bid you.[33]

At midday on Saturday 21 April William Henry Weldon and Georgina Treherne were married in the parish church in Aldershot, near the cavalry barracks where Harry was stationed. Their witnesses were Tommy Howe, a barrister friend of Georgina, and two of Harry's army colleagues. Georgina, 'nervous and happy' at the same time, almost disgraced herself by giggling when the clergyman called her 'Georgi-Anna.' Harry was shocked, and gave her a 'reproving look.' Two hours after the ceremony the newly-weds said goodbye to each other at Farnborough station and Georgina returned to London, to the home of her godmother Ellen Hills.

Why did this singularly ill-assorted couple marry? Georgina found Harry physically attractive, but she was by no means sure that she was in love with him. She had vowed not to marry a man who was 'inferior in intellect,' but it is clear that she did not believe that Harry was her social or intellectual equal. He had almost no money, and had admitted that the sale of his commission would do little more than clear his outstanding debts.[34]

33 WHW–GW, 13/4/1860; GW–WHW, 14/4/1860.

34 GWJ index, 1859; GWMSM, p. 37.

Marriage to him would inevitably cut Georgina off from the rest of her family. She was only twenty-two and had already received numerous proposals, including two – from older men – in the months leading up to her elopement with Harry.

Much later, Georgina wrote: 'The crusader in me urged me to save the poor youth who, out of love, had ruined himself, and I very foolishly married this penniless adventurer, who had insinuated himself into my society by his Hussar uniform and his charming manners.' The truth is probably that she saw marriage to Harry as her best way of escaping from 'the eternal calculations of a match-making mother' whom she had come to despise, and from a father whom she both feared and hated. She was sick of being 'bartered for as if I was cattle'.[35] And, though many men had fallen in love with her and wanted to marry her, none had come up to her father's exacting – and unrealistic – standards. By the beginning of 1860 she had begun to believe that none ever would. She was, by her own admission, impulsive, and she was also extremely stubborn. She was, moreover, in many respects still surprisingly naive, and – encouraged by the praise of Julius Benedict and other musical friends – genuinely believed that she would be able to make a living as an actress or singer.

Harry's real motives are equally hard to fathom. No doubt he desired Georgina who was, by all accounts, extremely attractive. But he was young and good-looking, and he had had plenty of female friends – and at least one mistress. Georgina had no money of her own, and there was a distinct possibility that her father would refuse to give her a dowry if she married against his wishes. If he married Georgina, Harry would almost certainly have to leave the army. This may, however, have been one of the reasons why he agreed to her proposals: his army career up to this time had been less than glorious; and he may not have welcomed the prospect of being sent to India, only two or three years after the Mutiny in which so many British subjects had been killed. Was Harry really desperately in love with Georgina – or was he simply carried along by the force of her personality, until they both reached the point of no return?

What is certain is that these two young people, who barely knew each other, had no idea what they were letting themselves in for.

[35] GWL, p. 14; GWM proof, vii, p. 8.

4

Beaumaris

Georgina and Harry's plan of concealing their marriage until the autumn proved to be hopelessly naive. Four days after the event they went to Phillips, a jeweller in Cockspur Street, and ordered a 'sham ring' to conceal Georgina's wedding ring. Whilst they were in the shop, the author William Makepeace Thackeray came in. Georgina rushed into a back room to hide, but Thackeray, whom she had met at Little Holland House, spotted her. He immediately put two and two together. When he met Poodle Byng in the street a short while later he stopped him with the words 'Poodle, you've lost your singing-bird! Miss Treherne has married some fellow!'[1] Poodle was an inveterate gossip, and the news was soon all over London.

A more judicious couple might have decided to lie low until the initial storm had subsided, but Georgina and Harry had no intention of doing so. Instead they came out fighting: on the following evening Harry got Lord Palmerston's box for the first night of Fabio Campana's opera *Almina* at Her Majesty's Theatre. He and Georgina bought 'all the bouquets with the tricolor Italian colors, red, green and white' and they and their friends 'made a great row'. Four days later they took another box at the same theatre for a benefit performance for the soprano Marietta Piccolomini.

Though she had as yet received no word from her family, it was now obvious that Georgina could not simply return home to Gate House as she had intended. She therefore decided that she had better go and live with her husband. The marriage was consummated on 28 April at Long's Hotel in Bond Street. Georgina's accounts of her first night with Harry vary. In her diary she wrote: 'Nothing can be more kind or more gentle than my own darling husband – so kind to his poor weak little wife. God bless us both – it surely can't be wrong to love as we do.' But, as Georgina noted many years later, this diary was originally written in shorthand, and Harry subsequently made her rewrite it all in longhand as he was unable to read

1 GWMSM, p. 38.

it. She may well have edited some of the original entries. The description of the same event in her unpublished memoirs is rather different:

> Needless to say, I was absolutely ignorant. I therefore made up my mind that my parents, somehow, knew Weldon was a horrible monster, an unnatural creature. That was the real reason why they had so strongly objected to my marrying. I was horrified, but I did not dare say a word.

Georgina concluded that Harry's mistress must have 'taught him these dreadful ways.' It would, she thought, be up to her to 'cure' him. She was highly relieved on the following evening, when Harry was a 'dear good darling.' He simply undressed her, put her to bed, and 'left me quiet all night.' During the next few weeks, however, Georgina was to learn a good deal about her husband's former mistress, who was known as 'Mufti.' She was, Harry said, 'a very nice little body, who he had taught to write.' Harry claimed that he had 'done all he could to instruct her and make her lead a better life.' It soon became clear that Mufti had suited Harry a great deal better than Georgina ever could.[2]

A few days after his first night with Georgina, Harry received a letter from his mother who was in London. She forgave him for his secret marriage and he took Georgina to see her. Her new daughter-in-law thought that Hannah Weldon was 'a dear old thing' (she was forty-seven), 'and very kind.' Before long, however, Hannah made it quite clear that she did not approve of Georgina's plan to earn her living on the stage. But Georgina refused to give way. Harry's income was only £300 a year, and she had decided that 'we *cannot* and I *will not*' live on so little. 'But for silly pride and scruples,' she wrote, 'we may make a good fortune. If the husband *cannot* keep the wife, surely the wife, if she can, may keep her husband.'[3]

Somehow, Harry negotiated his way out of the army, enabling him and Georgina to make hasty plans for their honeymoon. On 3 May Hannah Weldon waved goodbye to them at the station as they set off for Folkestone. On the following day they crossed the Channel to Boulogne, accompanied by Georgina's new maid, Anna Price, and Harry's poodles, Topsy and Mose. Harry, who spoke no foreign languages, left most of the arrangements to his energetic wife, who 'was courier, ticket taker, looked after the luggage, spoke all the languages, bargained with *vetturini* [coachmen], argued with *facchini* [porters], wrangled with *cochers* [coachmen], and paid all the bills.'[4]

2 GWJ, 24–29/4/1860; GWMSM, pp. 16, 47.
3 GW–Apsley Treherne, 9/5/1860.
4 *London Figaro*, 25/12/1878, p. 4.

Their first destination was Paris. It was not long before Georgina discovered that Harry had visited the French capital with Mufti two or three months earlier. He had taken her to dine with an old military friend, Colonel Johnston of Balcarry, telling him that Mufti was his wife. When Harry turned up with Georgina, the colonel's Italian housekeeper took her aside and asked her if she was sure she was married to him. The housekeeper made it only too clear that she did not like Harry. Georgina complained to her husband, but he merely sulked and informed her that he was 'very much injured' by her sentiments. He soon found out that Georgina's tastes were rather different from Mufti's. His mistress, who had been dressed as a boy for part of their stay in Paris, had particularly enjoyed visiting 'horrid places', such as the city morgue. Georgina refused to go there; she much preferred the Louvre and the Bois de Boulogne. Both enjoyed the circus, and Georgina persuaded Harry to take her to the opera to see *Pierre de Médicis* by Prince Poniatowski. They went shopping too: Harry spent 800 francs (£32) on a pair of gold bracelets for Georgina, and 195 francs (£7 15s) on a Turkish dressing gown and slippers for himself.

Georgina and Harry left Paris on 9 May. They headed for Lake Constance, spending a night in Schaffhausen on the way. From there, Georgina sent a letter to Uncle George, who had recently moved from Schloss Hard to a chalet at Müllberg near Raperswilen, on high ground a few miles further from the lake. Unfortunately for his niece, George had already received a letter from her parents, informing him that she had married without their consent. As Georgina was later to discover, her father, 'the dirty old Guv', had disinherited her within twenty-four hours of finding out about her marriage. He and Louisa had also written to Harry's mother and to several of their daughter's friends, including the Becketts, Lord Essex and the Prinseps, telling them that Georgina was 'a cruel, unnatural creature'.[5] Georgina and Harry got as far as Konstanz, where they received 'an impudent letter' from George, who absolutely refused to receive them.[6] There was nothing for it but to pack up and set off again, this time for Italy. On the evening of Sunday 20 May they reached Florence, where they found lodgings on the second floor of a house in the Piazza della Independenza.

The honeymooners were in Florence for nearly two months. One of their first visitors was the Treherne family's old Italian tutor, Pietro Arettini, and Georgina made arrangements for him to give Harry some lessons. She also hired a piano and music, and contacted a singing teacher, 'old Maestro Pietro Romani', who agreed to take her on as a pupil. He would, Georgina

5 GWJ, 19/4/1861; GWM, iii, pp. 9–10.

6 GWJ, 11/5/1860.

hoped, prepare her for her 'public career'.[7] She and Harry also received calls from some of the most prominent members of the city's expatriate community, including the scholar and art collector Francis Sloane and his wife, and William Blundell Spence, the English art dealer, painter and writer. They soon fell into a routine of walking or driving to the Cascine almost every day, taking the two dogs with them. In the evenings they ate ices and drank *spuma bianca* [white fizz] at Castelmuro, went to the opera, or visited the Sloanes. Harry did not, however, seem to be enjoying himself much. The Italian lessons were not a success: he hardly learned a word and sat 'as glum as Pluto and as silent as a bat' whilst his wife chattered away in Italian, French or German. He also claimed that he felt unwell, though Georgina thought that many of his ailments were imaginary: 'He was always complaining, either of toothache, sore throat, stiff neck, pain in the stomach, wretched spirits, morose, hypochondriacal.'[8]

Georgina had her first singing lesson with Romani, 'a nice old man', on 28 May. Later that day, however, she wrote in her diary, 'I feel privately I am giving way about the stage'. She does not make it clear if this was due to Romani's comments on her voice, or the result of continuing pressure from Harry's mother, who wrote regularly to her son. Respectable people such as Hannah Weldon believed that the centre of a woman's world must be her home. She should not flaunt herself on a public stage in front of an audience; anyone who did so was little better than a prostitute. It was generally understood that real ladies did not sing, dance or act before strangers except at private parties.

Georgina's brother Apsley was horrified by her plans, telling her in a letter that was waiting for her when she reached Florence:

> You were never born to be on the stage, where women are anything but delicately talked about, and just fancy if I happened to hear you discussed by a party of men, it would nearly drive me mad, or some foolish thing, so don't go, dearest G., without *actual necessity*, on the stage.

Apsley also passed on a message from sister Florence, complaining about the consequences for herself and Emily of Georgina's elopement: 'You may tell [Georgina] that she has been thoroughly selfish for, knowing the Governor's disposition, she has made matters a thousand times worse here for me and Emily, for he is nothing but cross now – doesn't let us stir anywhere.'[9] Before long, Georgina also received a letter from her mother,

7 GWT, p. 24.
8 GWMSM, p. 45.
9 Apsley Treherne–GW, n.d./5/1860.

telling her that she was 'quite quite mad.' Letters from Harry's mother were much more friendly. By this time Hannah Weldon was refusing to communicate with Georgina's parents other than through her lawyer, having taken offence at the 'heartlessness and want of proper feeling' displayed in their letters to her. She had taken particular umbrage at their description of her son as 'mean,' and their implication that he was their daughter's social inferior. Harry was, Hannah asserted, Morgan and Louisa's 'equal by birth, education and position.'[10] Few of her contemporaries would have agreed.

By the end of May, Georgina had other things on her mind. 'Dirty old Joe' (her period) was a week overdue, and she was starting to think that she might be pregnant. A month later her suspicions were confirmed when she began to throw up at regular intervals. She told Romani that she had given up all thoughts of going on the stage for the time being. He was, she wrote, 'very much disappointed.'[11]

Harry and Georgina left Florence on 13 July after spending a few days with the Spences at the Villa Mozzi in Fiesole, where they were plagued by fleas and mosquitoes and slept badly. William Spence, 'a generous host and passable painter' attempted a portrait of Georgina, but she and Harry both thought that the picture was a failure.[12] From Florence they travelled to Livorno, where they left the dogs with the Sloanes, who were staying in the town. They were to be shipped from Livorno directly to Liverpool. Taking the dogs to Italy had been, as Georgina admitted later, a great mistake: their foreign holiday had cost over £60 – money that their owners could ill afford.

After a night in Pisa, Harry and Georgina travelled to La Spezia, then took a boat to the Isola di Palmaria, which Georgina had visited eight years earlier. Her delight in being there was, however, tempered by worries about Harry, who was ill again. He had been grumpy whilst they were in Pisa and had provoked an argument about religion. Georgina, who had absorbed some of her uncle George's atheistical beliefs, had long since decided that she did not believe in Hell. Harry's own beliefs were much more conventional, and he told his wife that her ideas made him unhappy. The two had 'a long religious conversation, in which we both nearly cried our eyes out, and both nearly died of grief.' Georgina vowed that she would 'change and try to be truly good.' She even gave in when Harry, 'to revenge himself on me for my unbelief,' ordered her to stop writing to, or receiving letters from, her sisters, claiming that he did not want her to deceive her father. They left Palmaria on 23 July and journeyed gradually back to England by

10 GWJ, copy letter, 1860.

11 GWJ, 29/6/1860.

12 Katie Campbell, *Paradise of Exiles* (London, 2009), p. 141; GWJ, 11/7/1860.

steamer, horse-drawn coach and train. The journey was difficult and tiring. Georgina was so uncomfortable during the night that they spent in the mail coach 'bolting, jolting and bumping' over Mont Cenis that she thought she would have a miscarriage.

When, on 30 July, they finally arrived in London, Georgina was feeling sick and 'quite knocked up'. But a few days' rest at Long's Hotel restored her, and she soon felt strong enough to go shopping and pay some visits. She took Harry to Little Holland House, where she introduced him to Watts and the Prinseps, who all appeared to be delighted to see her again and eager to meet her new husband. After this, there was nothing for it but to head for Beaumaris. Harry had no job, he and Georgina had no home of their own, and they had only £118 12s 11d in the bank. Their honeymoon, which had cost £200, had been heavily subsidised by gifts of money from two of Georgina's friends.[13]

~

Georgina and Harry reached Beaumaris late on the evening of 3 August, having travelled all day by train and ferry from London. Hannah Weldon lived in a terraced house, no. 3 in a row of four called Tros-yr-afon which stood – and still stands – on the outskirts of the town, beside the road from Llansadwrn. Though it was much smaller than she had expected, Georgina was determined to like her new home, writing on her first evening there:

> This is a most dear, pretty little place and house, and I think Mother will be very dear and kind to us. I should like to stay here a long time. We had evening prayers. My room is so prettily arranged with pink. The bells rang and the boys hurrahed to welcome us when we arrived.[14]

Beaumaris, a town with approximately 2500 inhabitants in the 1860s, stands overlooking the Menai Strait. The old part of the town, with its ancient buildings and narrow streets, runs westwards from the stone castle built for Edward I in the 1290s. For many centuries Beaumaris had been the administrative and social centre of Anglesey, but the opening of the Menai Bridge in the 1826 and the Britannia railway bridge in 1850 had taken away much of its importance, as traffic bound for Ireland bypassed the town and headed, instead, for Holyhead. But Beaumaris retained a county hall and courthouse, as well as the county gaol, and by mid century it was becoming well known as a bathing resort. A pier, built in 1846, was long enough to take the steam packets which brought tourists from Liverpool.

13 GWJ, 10–30/7/1860; GWMSM, p. 45.
14 GWJ, 3/8/1860.

There were several hotels and lodging houses for visitors, who could enjoy the 'charming walks and pleasant recreations' offered by the town and its surrounding countryside.[15]

Georgina spent her first few days in Beaumaris writing letters and getting to know the town and its inhabitants. But she felt tired and listless, and after ten days she began to feel ill, suffering from 'great pain in my lower stomach or womb'. Early in the morning of 19 August, after 'agonizing pains', her baby was born dead. It was a boy, and Georgina persuaded her maid, Anna, to let her see the lifeless little body before it was taken to Llanfaes churchyard to be buried. She was devastated, writing in her diary, 'My darling baby, my first little one. I am sure I shall never again love any other so well as this my poor first dead little one'. She concluded that God had taken her baby from her 'because I should have loved him too much'.[16] But she was young and healthy and there was no reason to think that she would not become pregnant again quite soon.

Georgina was very much on her best behaviour at this stage, though the novelty of life with her mother-in-law at Tros-yr-afon soon began to wear off. Many of Hannah Weldon's friends were condemned as 'bores', 'snobs' or 'fossils', and it soon became clear that she and Georgina had little in common apart from their connection with Harry. Sundays were particularly difficult: Hannah would go to church in the morning and then spend the rest of the day 'gossipping with a Bible on the table'. She protested if Georgina tried to do anything else. Harry sided with his Mama, so his wife had to sit doing nothing. To Georgina this was 'torture'. The sooner she and Harry moved out into a place of their own, the better.[17] Fortunately, the cottage next door (no. 2) was empty, and the owner, Sir Richard Bulkeley of Baron Hill, appeared to be willing to let it to them.

Towards the end of October, Georgina and Harry escaped from Anglesey and headed for Manchester, where they bought furnishings for their new home. They then travelled to Sheffield and paid a visit to Harry's grandmother at Bramley Hall. Old Mrs Weldon was now eighty-six: no doubt she thought (with some justification) that her grandson and his new wife wanted to find out for themselves how much longer she was likely to last. Grandmother Weldon seems to have taken an instant dislike to Georgina, while Georgina decided that the old lady was 'a nasty old cat'. Nor did she take to Harry's aunt, Mary Dymond.[18] But, with her usual talent for charming elderly gen-

15 John Marius Wilson, *Imperial Gazetteer of England and Wales* (London, 1870–2), p. 136.

16 GWJ, 19–21/8/1860.

17 GWMSM, p. 46; GWJ, 16/9/1860.

18 GWJ, 25/10/1860.

tlemen, she got on well with Harry's great-uncle, William Stacey, a Sheffield ironmonger who had managed Harry's estates for him during his minority. Stacey told Georgina all about her mother-in-law's financial situation. After a fortnight the Weldons headed home again. By the time they reached Beaumaris, Georgina had a streaming cold, but she was determined nevertheless go to a ball in the town on the following evening. It was Hunt Week, the height of the town's social season, and she wanted to impress the cream of county society, which included Lady Willoughby de Broke of Plas Newydd with nineteen guests, and Georgina's old friend Higford Burr. She dressed carefully in a white silk dress and wore her coral and diamond necklace and earrings. At the Hunt Dinner on the next evening she sat next to Sir Richard Bulkeley. They met again at the Hunt Ball, where they had 'a little confab' about the house that Georgina and Harry wished to rent.[19]

A few days later, Harry and Georgina received an invitation to dine at Baron Hill with Sir Richard and his wife. This was a great honour, for the Bulkeleys were the most important family in Beaumaris. Sir Richard, who was MP for Anglesey, owned 30,000 acres including a large part of the town and the countryside around it. Baron Hill, a large neo-classical mansion that had been rebuilt after a fire in the 1830s, was the grandest house in the area. If the Bulkeleys approved of the young Weldons, other invitations were certain to follow. The summons to Baron Hill did nothing to improve Georgina's relationship with her mother-in-law, who had never been asked to go there. This reinforced Georgina's feeling of superiority, and she wrote (with some glee) that 'Mammy' was 'in an awful rage'. For several hours she was 'as silent as a door nail', after which she made 'a terrible scene'. Harry and Georgina ignored her and enjoyed a most satisfactory evening. Georgina persuaded Sir Richard to let them have their 'little house' rent-free for three years, thus saving them £111. She sang in the evening, as did a Miss Massey. Georgina was very nervous, but pleased with herself, having, in her words, 'considerably smashed' her fellow singer.[20]

Georgina and Harry's new home, no. 2 Tros-yr-afon, was in poor condition when they agreed to lease it. It was probably for this reason that Sir Richard Bulkeley was prepared to forego three years' rent. The roof was under repair in December, and by mid January the walls were being papered. The work was expensive: in December alone they paid £55 to the builder, in addition to £55 16s 7d for furniture and fittings. If Hannah Weldon had not given them £82 they would have ended the year with just £12 9s 7d in the bank. The goods that had been ordered in Manchester and

19 GWJ, 6–8/11/1860.

20 GWJ, 12–16/11/1860.

Sheffield arrived over the next few weeks: stoves, a washing machine and a sewing machine. The carpets were put down and the beds were unpacked. Both worked on the sewing machine, making sheets, curtains and dusters, and they began to move their furniture and other possessions from next door. In mid May they were finally able to sleep in their 'own little nest'. Compared with the houses in which Georgina had grown up it was tiny, the main structure consisting of a drawing room and dining room downstairs and two bedrooms upstairs, with the usual offices (including a kitchen and wash-house and an outdoor privy) and a servant's room at the back. There was also a garden, with an area for growing vegetables. Georgina grew very fond of the 'dear little house opposite the sea, and the mountains of Carnarvonshire [*sic*]', and in later years she looked back with nostalgia to the ten years during which it had been her home.

Before her marriage Georgina had always had a personal maid to look after her clothes, do her hair and run errands. Now she had to do all this for herself, in addition to looking after Harry's clothes since he was (as she said) too lazy to do anything for himself. She had to learn quickly how to cook and keep house. These were not accomplishments that were usually needed by girls such as Georgina and her sisters, who expected to have

Fig. 9. 2 Tros-yr-afon, Beaumaris. Georgina Weldon's home from 1860 to 1869.

plenty of servants, but she found that she rather enjoyed her everyday chores. 'I am fond of all that is domesticated', she wrote, 'mending clothes, making my own wardrobe, cooking, washing up, tidying.' She later advised all women to 'Study earnestly, be good housewives above all, and then even if everything has failed, you will have the satisfaction left you of keeping your four walls neat and clean, of keeping your clothes well mended, and of preparing your simple meals with taste and cleanliness.'[21]

Georgina and Harry generally had at least one maid, but most of these were young girls who had received very little, if any, training. Many stayed for only a few weeks – or days. One became pregnant; one was dismissed after 'sending in the dinner disgustingly'; and another was 'packed off for dirt and lies'. A few of the girls could cook, but Georgina had to buy and prepare much of the food herself. Some of their fruit and vegetables came from the kitchen garden behind the cottage, and friends were generous with seasonal gifts of game, fish and fruit. Georgina acquired a copy of Alexis Soyer's best-selling book, *Shilling Cookery* and tried out the recipes that she found in it. Her first efforts were surprisingly successful. Four months after moving into the cottage she was confident enough to give a dinner party, though it took her two days to prepare and cook the food.[22] She later claimed that she and Harry had been so poor in the early years of their marriage that they could not afford to buy wine, beer or sugar.[23] Georgina gave up butter too, but Harry decided that he could not do without it.

Apart from her domestic duties, which included gardening as well as cooking and housework, Georgina found time for a multitude of other occupations. She cleaned and mended her own clothes and those of her husband, knitted socks for Harry, and made many of her own dresses. It was fortunate that Morgan Treherne had insisted on his daughters learning to sew, for Georgina could not afford to pay a professional dressmaker. Her own efforts were supplemented by gifts of bonnets, dresses and other garments from her friends. She wrote and received letters almost every day and made daily entries in her journal. She also began to collect coins, stamps, monograms, seals and autographs, and badgered her friends and acquaintances for contributions. Apart from their intrinsic interest, the collections were useful for impressing her new neighbours with the breadth of Georgina's connections with high society.

[21] GWO, i, pp. 10, 16.
[22] GWJ, 7/9/1861.
[23] GWO, i, p. 12.

Fig. 10. Georgina and Harry Weldon, 1861.

Georgina and Harry's social circle widened quickly. Georgina was bored by most of her mother-in-law's friends and complained that going out in Anglesey society was 'quite a penance,' as 'one is always having one's fur rubbed the wrong way up.'[24] But she liked the Beaumaris doctor, Robert Wynne Jones, and his wife Catherine, who was Harry's godmother. Harry spent much of his time with Sir Richard and Lady Bulkeley's youngest son, Charlie, and he and Georgina often

[24] GWJ, 7/2/1861.

dined at Baron Hill, which was within walking distance of their own home. Lady Bulkeley, who had four sons but no daughters, took a motherly interest in Georgina and was very kind to her. She even called on the Weldons at their cottage from time to time, though Georgina was somewhat dismayed when her ladyship turned up one morning whilst she and Harry were still having breakfast and before she had done her hair.[25]

At the end of November 1860 Harry was elected captain and commanding officer of the newly formed Beaumaris Artillery Volunteer Corps, one of a number of such forces raised at this time in response to instability in Europe and fears of war with France. Georgina was delighted, having already decided that her husband was lazy and needed something to occupy him other than sailing or playing rackets and billiards with his friends. After this, Harry devoted much of his time to the Volunteers – with some success, as Georgina was able to write on 15 December that the Beaumaris corps was the only one that had so far been embodied, as the others could not enlist enough men.[26]

Georgina's diaries describe a number of events connected with the Artillery Volunteers. The government was prepared to supply guns and ammunition, but each Volunteer corps had to raise the money needed to pay for uniforms and other expenses. Harry's responsibilities as commanding officer included fundraising and he enlisted Georgina's help to put on a series of concerts. She sang in them, of course. She also trained a choir of thirty men and boys and did her best to persuade her friends and acquaintances to take part. The first 'Grand Amateur Concert' was held in August 1861, with Georgina as the star of the show. She was 'very much terrified' at the beginning, but sang (she thought) 'lovelily'. Everyone was enthusiastic, and Lady Bulkeley sent her a bouquet of flowers and a basket of grapes. The concert was such a success that it was repeated in the evening. The reporter for the *North Wales Chronicle* was particularly enthusiastic:

> Mrs Weldon is a musician of the first order, gifted by nature with such a voice as falls to the lot of very few; and endowed with all delicacy of musical sensibility. It was to Mrs Weldon's singing the concert owed its charm; and we believe that the steady and efficient chorus of members of the battery was by her trained for the occasion – a work of no small enterprise.

The audience was 'fairly carried away' by Georgina's rendition of 'Jeanie with the light brown hair', which was 'uproariously redemanded'.[27] Further, equally successful, concerts would be given in subsequent years.

[25] GWJ, 21/8/1861.
[26] GWJ, 26/11/1860–21/12/1860.
[27] *North Wales Chronicle and Advertiser*, 24/8/1861, p. 6.

5

Friends and Relations

There were few years during the 1860s in which Georgina and Harry did not spend several months away from Beaumaris. To begin with they were heavily dependent on their friends, without whose generosity they could not have afforded to stay in London or travel abroad. The sale of Harry's commissions raised almost £2000, but most of this was swallowed up by his outstanding debts, so they often had to borrow money from Hannah Weldon to enable them to pay their day-to-day living expenses.

Somehow they scraped together enough money to take them up to London early in April 1861. They were away from home for nearly two months, staying mainly with friends. For a few nights, however, there was nothing for it but to stay in a hotel. Georgina hated it, writing in her diary one evening when Harry was out gambling with his old army colleagues:

> I feel dreadfully sad. The thought that we are so very poor troubles me sadly – not that I should mind it a bit if Harry would have a higher feeling about him and not think this and that below his dignity. He insists on going to this Westminster Palace Hotel. For one night it has cost 18 shillings! He is above carrying a brown paper parcel in the streets of London at a fashionable hour. I cannot tell how miserable from my heart it makes me to find how mistaken I am, and what hard work lies before me. It is so, so disheartening, I could cry all day and all night.

Harry returned at one in the morning, smelling 'most odiously' of smoke and stale wine, and very pleased with himself as he had won £21 14s playing at loo.[1] Complaints about his extravagance were to be a recurrent theme in the diaries during the next few years. Saving him from himself was going to be a much harder task than Georgina had at first imagined.

In spite of Georgina's parents' best efforts to turn her friends against her, most people seemed to be pleased to see her and her new husband. Several acquaintances invited them to tea or dinner, and some asked Georgina to

[1] GWJ, 12–13/4/1861.

sing. She was happy to oblige, though she was 'dreadfully out of practice'. One Sunday a hansom cab took them to 'dear Little Holland House'. The Prinseps greeted them warmly and were 'so kind, *as ever*'. Watts, 'poor dear little Signor' was laid up with a boil on his leg, but they visited him in his room. The artist promised to do a pencil drawing of Harry and said that he would never let anyone else have his portrait of Georgina. Thackeray came, and Dickie Doyle and Merthyr Guest were there for dinner. Georgina thought that her erstwhile suitor looked 'very stoical', but decided that, although he was 'rather improved', she was glad that she had not married Merthyr, as she would have become 'awfully tired and disgusted with him'.[2]

Georgina's next visit to Little Holland House a week later was less successful. Signor was 'out of sorts' and Sara Prinsep was distant. It was, Georgina decided, all 'very different'. Her feelings were soon confirmed, for she received 'a most extraordinary note' telling her that Sara and her husband did not intend to have any more dinner parties at Little Holland House. It was clear that Georgina would not be welcome there any more. 'I wonder', she reflected, 'if, after all, Aunt Sara only liked me out of worldliness, that's all.' She 'howled' out her woes to Mrs Burr – but then went off to a party, where she sang to the assembled company. Georgina was rarely downhearted for long.[3]

~

Later in the same year, Georgina and Harry made a much longer trip, to visit Hannah Weldon's sister Ellen, who had emigrated to Canada with her husband and children in 1859. They had settled in Lennoxville, a small town in the province of Quebec, eighty miles east of Montreal. On 26 October Harry and Georgina boarded the SS *Persia*, which was to carry them from Liverpool to New York. The *Persia*, the largest steamship afloat in the world when she was launched in 1855, was vast, with accommodation for 260 passengers and a crew of 150. She was the fastest ship crossing the Atlantic at the time, able to complete the voyage in just eight days. Harry and Georgina's passage, which took ten days, cost them £26 each, excluding wine and beer.[4] After suffering from seasickness for the first couple of days, Georgina spent the rest of the trip walking on deck, playing whist, and flirting with the captain, Charles Judkins, and some of her fellow passengers.

They arrived in New York on 5 November and spent a few days sight-seeing. Georgina was much struck by 'the gaudy manner American ladies dress', but worried that they would themselves be stared at as Harry insisted on

2 GWJ, 14/4/1861.
3 GWJ, 21,28/4/1861.
4 GWJ, 11/10/1861.

wearing knickerbockers. Ever-present in the background was the American Civil War. In the months before the Weldons' visit a total of eleven slave-owning states had seceded from the Union and formed the Confederate States of America under the leadership of Jefferson Davis. In May Abraham Lincoln (who had been sworn in as President a few weeks earlier) had proclaimed a blockade of all southern ports. In New York the newspapers were full of the latest events, and Harry Weldon watched the presentation of military colours to a volunteer regiment 'en route for the seat of war'.[5]

From New York the Weldons travelled by train to Washington, where they were met by Georgina's old friend Percy Anderson, a clerk at the British embassy. He told them of other acquaintances who were in the town, and introduced them to his former lodger, 'Russell of *The Times*', the journalist William Howard Russell, who was already a household name in Britain as a result of his reports from the Crimea in 1854 and 1855. Georgina thought him 'very jolly and very clever', though he was also 'very fat'. It was, no doubt, through Percy Anderson that Georgina and Harry received an invitation to dine with the British ambassador, Lord Lyons, 'a very agreeable man'.[6] They were to dine at the embassy several times more during their stay in Washington, which lasted for a fortnight. Apart from Russell and Anderson, the company there included Freddy Warre, Ernest Clay and George Sheffield, most of whom Georgina had met before.

On 20 November, armed with a pass and invitation from the United States Secretary of State, William H. Seward, Georgina and Madame de Hurtado, the wife of the Spanish ambassador, 'bumped, scrambled and waded' their way in a carriage to see a review of the Union troops. Harry accompanied them on a horse lent to him by William Russell. They arrived just after Mrs Lincoln and Mrs Seward, and watched as 30,000 men marched past. It was, Georgina wrote, all 'beautifully organized'.[7] After another week she and Harry said goodbye to Lord Lyons and their other friends and set off on their travels again. On 4 December they finally reached Lennoxville, where 'Aunt Ellen' and her husband, Christopher Rawson, met them at the station in a sledge. Exhausted, they fell into bed at two in the morning.

In Canada, as in the United States, it was impossible to ignore the effects of the Civil War. It was feared that the Northern states would try to divert attention from their domestic problems by attacking foreign powers, especially Britain. Canada was likely to be their first target – and Lennoxville was only twenty-five miles from the border with the Union state of Vermont.

5 GWJ, 7/11/1861.

6 GWJ, 15–16/11/1861.

7 GWJ, 20/11/1861.

By the time Georgina and Harry arrived, men were flocking to join the local militia regiments and Georgina had already been asked to help with a concert to raise money for them. The first rehearsal, which was held two days after her arrival, was 'grand, but most ill-organized'. The ladies' voices were 'squealy and out of tune', and it was 'altogether a sadly slow affair'.[8] When Georgina went down with a cold, which prevented her from singing in the first concert, she was not too upset, having decided that the people were 'horrid'. But she was well enough to sing at the second one, held in Lennoxville on Shrove Tuesday. The room was 'very full' and she thought it all went off very well. The audience was 'stupid', but she was asked to sing several encores and the Rawsons were delighted.

The fourth, and last, concert was the most successful. Georgina, who was later to claim that she could never appear on a platform or stage without first drinking 'as much as would suffice to render me intoxicated for hours at any other time', fortified herself with two and a half glasses of beer, and sang several of her favourite songs, including 'Jeanie' and 'When the elves at dawn do pass' out of *The Amber Witch*, a new opera by William Vincent Wallace. The local newspapers were full of praise, hailing Georgina as 'the very Napoleon of Music', and the militia officers presented her and Harry with three complimentary addresses of white satin lettered in gold, with 'splendid margins and very pretty designs'.[9]

After a stay of four months, Georgina and Harry left Lennoxville on 5 April, 'in tears', taking Frances Rawson, the eldest daughter, with them. All the schoolboys came to see them off at the station when they set off by train to Montreal. After ten days there they travelled to Boston, where they boarded the steam packet *Niagara*, which was to take them back to England. The return crossing was a rough one, but on 28 April, twelve days after leaving Boston, they passed Holyhead and the Anglesey coast before the ship anchored in the River Mersey. On 30 April they returned to Beaumaris, having been away for six months.

~

Georgina did not see any members of her family for three years after her marriage, though she received occasional letters from her mother and sisters. Gate House was sold in 1862 and 'the family Treherne' spent much of that year abroad. But by November they were back in London, where they rented a house in Eaton Square. Morgan Treherne still refused to have

8 GWJ, 6/12/1861.

9 GWJ, 3/4/1862; GWO, i, p. 22.

anything to do with his errant daughter, though it was thanks to Georgina that he was presented at Court by Poodle Byng early in the following year.

In the spring of 1863, Georgina and Harry learned that Georgina's mother wanted to see them. She came to their lodgings, 17 Mount Street, near Grosvenor Square, looking 'just the same as ever'. After this, the younger of Georgina's two brothers paid her a visit, as did her two sisters, Emily and Florence. Georgina noted with some satisfaction that Emily looked 'very brown'. She was, however, happy to see the girls again. Apart from her father, the only member of her immediate family who did not come to see her was brother Dal, whose 'pecuniary interests guided his honourable feelings'.[10] He kept his distance for fear that fraternisation with the enemy would bring down Morgan's wrath upon him. Georgina did, however, run into Dal with a friend at the Lyceum a few days later.

In the meantime, Georgina was back in the social and musical whirl of fashionable London. On 28 May she sang in a concert in the Hanover Square Rooms put on by the composer Frederic Clay, who was an old friend. She started nervously, but then got on 'famously' and was 'much applauded'.[11] Three weeks later, she was asked to sing at a party given by a Mrs Stephenson. Fred Clay accompanied her 'vilely', and she met Arthur Sullivan, 'such a dear little man', who was beginning to make a name for himself at this time. She introduced Harry to the Duchess of Cambridge, who remembered her from the amateur theatricals at Ashridge six years earlier. On the following day she was presented at Court. Though she had been presented before, in 1858, it was the custom for a woman to be re-presented after her marriage. On this occasion Georgina's sponsor was Henrietta, Countess de Grey and Ripon, the wife of the Secretary of State for War, whom she had known for several years. With no maid to assist her, Georgina dressed herself and did her own hair ('very well'). She wore 'a white brocaded moiré antique dress trimmed with tulle rosettes, and a petticoat, white tulle bouillonné', with pearls and diamonds borrowed from friends. That evening she and Harry were in the Marquess of Sligo's box in Her Majesty's theatre in the Haymarket for one of the first London performances of Charles Gounod's opera, *Faust*. They left after the fourth act to go to a party given by Lady Palmerston.[12]

Georgina seems to have made a good impression on Lady Palmerston, who asked her to sing for her a few days later. Catherine Gladstone, the wife of the future Prime Minister, was friendly, and so was Lady Zetland, who gave Georgina two Shetland shawls. After a visit to Little Holland

10 GWMSM, p. 72.

11 GWJ, 28/5/1863–1/6/1863.

12 GWJ, 19–20/6/1863.

Fig. 11. The Treherne family at Gate House, Mayfield 1861. Left to right: Emily, Dal, Florence, Charles Oakes (friend), Apsley, Louisa, Morgan.

House (where they missed seeing the Poet Laureate Alfred Tennyson, who was ill with varicose veins and nettle rash), she and Harry spent several weeks moving from one acquaintance's country house to another, unable to return home as their cottage had been rented out, and too poor to pay for lodgings.[13]

On 7 September, when they were staying with Lord and Lady Zetland at Upleatham near Redcar, the news came that Harry's grandmother had died. The old lady's death would eventually mean an improvement in the Weldons' finances – though she had done her best to ensure that they would receive as little as possible, leaving everything that she could to her daughter's family. In her will, which was made a few months after Harry and Georgina's marriage, Grandmother Weldon made no reference at all to her grandson or his new wife.[14] The most immediate consequence of her death was the arrival two months later at Tros-yr-Afon of five cases of stuffed birds and beasts; a portrait of Harry as a child; and 'a lot of stones

[13] GWJ, 8/7/1863.

[14] PPR, will of Elizabeth Weldon of Bramley Hall, Handsworth, Yorkshire, 1864.

and rubbish which belonged to his father.'[15] A rather more welcome acquisition at this time was Watts's portrait of Georgina when she was nineteen, which the artist sold to her for the bargain price of fifty guineas. His usual price for a portrait, Watts told Harry, was a hundred guineas – more for a 'fancy head' such as Georgina's picture, for which Lord Lansdowne had already offered him £200.[16]

During the months that followed, letters from her sisters told Georgina about their father's increasing mental instability. When she heard that Morgan had dismissed the faithful Antonio and quarrelled with Dal, Georgina concluded that he had 'evidently lost all his tiles' and was now 'as mad as a hatter.'[17] She felt sorry for Emily and Florence, who were being 'led such a life.' Florence, now aged twenty-three, had an admirer, 'little George' Curzon, 'a small man with a red nose, blue eyes and blonde sideboards.'[18] Georgina was not impressed when she met him. A great-grandson of the first Viscount Curzon, George was well connected, but his income as a junior army officer fell far short of Morgan's exacting standards. The bar may even have risen since Georgina's elopement, for Morgan had at last achieved his long-held ambition of becoming MP for Coventry following the death of the sitting member, Edward Ellice. Morgan's victory in October 1863, with a majority of just 134, came thirty-two years after his first attempt to take the seat. It was probably not entirely coincidental that the sale of the Gate House estate in the previous year had raised £50,000.[19]

In June 1864 Mrs Gladstone asked Georgina to sing at a charity concert. Her fellow performer was Jenny Lind, one of the most famous singers of the day, who had settled in England with her husband six years earlier. By this time Lind had long since ceased singing professionally, though she continued to give performances for charity. Georgina, who was determined to dislike her, decided that Lind was 'a horrid old scarecrow and humbug' when she discovered that the Swedish soprano proposed to sing five solos, whilst Georgina was down for only one. She did concede that Lind's style was good, and that her singing 'would be nice if she herself were not so unpleasant.' Jenny Lind's reaction to Georgina's performance was not complimentary: 'she looked as if a toad had croaked, and took not the slightest notice.' Undaunted, Georgina sang at another party later that evening.[20]

15 GWJ, 9–10/11/1863.
16 GWJ, 10,15/9/1863, 1/10/1863, 31/12/1863; Lindholm Collection, G.F. Watts–WHW, 5/9/1863.
17 GWJ, 22/1/1864, 13/2/1864.
18 GWM, ii, pp. 45–6.
19 *Mid Sussex Times*, 16/5/1893, p. 1.
20 GWJ, 23/6/1864.

During this stay in London, too, Georgina consulted a gynaecological specialist for the first time. Though her periods were regular and there had been a number of false alarms, she had failed to become pregnant during the four years since her miscarriage. Dr de Mussy examined her and told her that she should visit Spa to seek a cure.[21] Delighted with this proposal, she set off a month later with two old friends, Arthur and Sophie Chapman, but without Harry, who had made plans to go on a sailing expedition to the Isle of Wight. In Spa, Georgina consulted Dr Jules Lezaack, who told her that she should bathe twenty-four times and drink water from the Pouhon spring. Dutifully, she rose at half-past six the following morning and went to the baths, and then drank three glasses of water. The next few days were spent bathing, taking the waters and playing whist. The town was 'crammed full' and there were concerts, balls, illuminations and cricket matches. Georgina was hardly missing Harry at all. She had a new admirer, Robert Tennent, the son of an Irish landowner, with whom she had long theological discussions. Her Belgian friend Guillaume van der Burch also turned up for a few days, 'much changed' and wearing 'a horrible beard and whiskers'.[22] He and Georgina spent several happy hours together, comparing stamp collections and reminiscing about old times.

After a month Georgina and the Chapmans left Spa and headed for Brussels, where they were to meet Harry. The joy of Georgina and Harry's reunion was tempered – from Harry's point of view, at least – by the fact he had 'given himself some kind of strain', which put him *hors de combat* for a month. Georgina was not too upset. The injury was, she thought, very sad for Harry, but 'I shall be in peace till after my next Joe [period]. A good thing for me!!'[23] Nor was Harry pleased when Robert Tennent sent Georgina his photograph and then turned up in person. Harry sulked, refused to eat, and forbade his wife to write to her new friend. Relations between husband and wife improved only when they left Brussels for Lake Constance, which they reached on 24 September.

Georgina had had no direct contact with her uncle George Thomas for almost three years, after his refusal to receive her and Harry during their honeymoon. Early in 1863, however, she had heard that George was now somewhat more kindly disposed towards them. An exchange of letters followed, and the older man wrote to Harry, apologising for doing him a 'great injustice'. The apology was graciously received. George's attitude towards his niece mellowed even further when, a few months later, he married his

21 GWJ, 2/7/1864.
22 GWJ, 22/8/1864.
23 GWJ, 8/9/1864.

daughter's governess, Juliana Geier, and Georgina's father (certain that his brother had married beneath him) sent him a number of 'rude and insulting letters'. There would be no contact between the two brothers after this.[24]

George and Juliana received their visitors kindly at Müllberg. After a month Georgina and Harry continued their journey to Florence, where they were to stay with the Spences at the Villa Mozzi. Their hosts knew everyone who was anyone in the city and there was a dinner party almost every evening. Visitors included the composer and pianist Jacques Blumenthal, whom Georgina had met in London a year earlier, and the 'great Italian historian' Thomas Adolphus Trollope (elder brother of Anthony).[25] Harry and Georgina went 'curiosity hunting' and visited the studio of an old acquaintance, the English sculptor Charles Francis Fuller, where they commissioned a terracotta bust of Georgina. Early in December the party at the Villa Mozzi was joined by Higford Burr, the eldest son of Georgina's old friends at Aldermaston Court, and it was agreed that he and the Weldons should go to Sicily together. They changed their minds after talking to Blumenthal, who gave a 'most dreadful account' of Palermo, which was, he said, both unpleasant and very expensive. He advised them to go to Capri instead, as it was both warm and cheap. Higford and the Weldons set off on 29 December, travelling by train to Livorno and then by steamer to Naples, where bad weather kept them for several days. At last, on 5 January, they were able to board a boat for the short trip to Capri. Their arrival was chaotic, but Georgina climbed onto a white pony that carried her up to the Hotel de Tiberio, where they were all to stay. Blumenthal was already on Capri, staying with his cousin Madame Loeser at the Quisisana.

Higford left at the end of January, but Georgina and Harry were to stay on Capri until mid March. There was not a great deal to do on the island, but they kept themselves occupied walking, bathing and picking watercress. Finding her dresses too constricting, Georgina ordered an outfit like those worn by the local women so that she could scramble up and down the hills. Her new clothes (which consisted of 'a cloth pair of trowsers and ditto petticoat') were very convenient, though the local boys all ran after her the first time she wore them. She and Harry spent most evenings playing whist or writing letters. Sometimes Harry read aloud (Dickens's *Dombey and Son*) to Georgina whilst she mended her stockings or tried to teach herself to play the guitar. Blumenthal was friendly and they enjoyed musical evenings together. The Weldons also made a new friend, the young English artist John Brett, who was romantically

[24] GWM, iii, pp. 3–5.
[25] GWJ, 23/11/1864.

involved with Madame Loeser. Brett joined them on their walks and began to sketch Georgina in her Capri dress. The result was a tremendous row between him and Madame Loeser, who saw Georgina as a rival. She warned Georgina that Brett was 'a most dangerous *seducteur*.' 'There is some method in her madness,' commented Georgina, 'but not much.'[26] There were other English visitors too, including some 'affable' cousins of Freddy Warre who joined their evening card parties.

Harry and Georgina arrived back in England at the end of May after ten months on the Continent. For the next few weeks they stayed with the solicitor-general Sir Robert Collier and his wife Isabella at 2 Eaton Place West, near Sloane Square. Four days after their arrival the Colliers' daughter Margaret (Madge) took them to Lavender Sweep near Clapham Common to visit the playwright and *Punch* columnist Tom Taylor and his family. The Taylors' house was a gathering place for a wide variety of politicians and artists, and Georgina found several old friends there, including the actress Kate Terry and her sister Ellen (Nelly), who had married G.F. Watts at the beginning of 1864 and was living with him at Little Holland House. At Lavender Sweep Georgina, Kate and Nelly were 'quite inseparable, talking over Little Holland House iniquities.' 'I am determined' wrote Georgina 'the world shall know about that and me too!' That evening Georgina and Harry dined with the Benedicts, where their fellow guests included two of the most famous musicians of the day, the violinist Joseph Joachim and the pianist and composer Clara Schumann. Madame Schumann played to the assembled company 'most deliciously,' whilst Benedict 'purred.'[27]

Early in the following January Fred Clay stayed with the Weldons in Beaumaris for several days. He wanted to Georgina to sing one of the leading roles in his operetta *Out of Sight*, which was to be performed in London. They practised hard, and Georgina and Harry travelled to London a few days later. Georgina met her fellow performers (all men) who were to include Quintin Twiss, one of Clay's fellow clerks at the Treasury, and Colonel Henry de Bathe, a man with whom the Weldons would subsequently become much better acquainted. By the time of the first performance, on 21 February, Georgina had a bad cough and cold, but she was determined to take part, though her voice was weak and she was 'quite speechless' afterwards. She sang again at the next performance, two days later, when her voice was 'worse than ever.' The invited audience included 'loads of jolly people,' such as Tom Taylor and his wife, Kate Terry, the artist John Everett Millais, Dickie Doyle and Val Prinsep. Then, on

26 GWJ, 8/2/1865.

27 GWJ, 4/6/1865.

24 March, *Out of Sight* was put on again, this time at the Gallery of Illustration in Regent Street, in the presence of the Duke and Duchess of Cambridge. The room was 'crammed full' for this performance, which was given in aid of the charities of the Brigade of Guards. The show was a great success, and Georgina 'acted and sang better than ever' – in her own opinion, at least.[28]

It was at this time, too, that Georgina and Harry made friends with the Scott Russell family, who lived at Westwood Lodge in Sydenham, not far from the Crystal Palace. As joint secretary of the Royal Society of Arts, the engineer John Scott Russell had been involved with the organisation of the Great Exhibition in 1851. There was a son, Norman, the same age as Harry and Georgina, and three daughters, Louise, Rachel and Alice (known as 'Fluffy May'), a few years younger. The Scott Russells knew many of the same people as the Weldons, and regular visitors to their hospitable home included John Millais, Val Prinsep, Freddy Warre, Fred Clay and George Grove with his friend Arthur Sullivan.

Arthur Sullivan was a few years younger than Georgina. She liked him, but she and her friends did not take him very seriously:

> He was a small, dark young man with enormous hands on very long arms. In our circle he was known as 'Jackie,' but he was a small, comic person who made everyone laugh. As a musician he was a very adept plagiarist, a veritable parakeet. When he imitated Handel, Fred Clay, Mendelssohn or Gounod he was very good, but when he tried to be original his music was nothing.[29]

On 9 March Georgina and Harry went to a rehearsal of Sullivan's new symphony at the Crystal Palace. The music was, Georgina thought, 'very lovely.'[30] A few weeks later Harry went with John Scott Russell to Moray Lodge on Campden Hill, the home of the silk mercer and part-time artist Arthur Lewis, to see the first performance of Sullivan's new operetta, *Cox and Box*, which was put on by the Moray Minstrels, a group of amateur singers. Harry saw 'loads' of acquaintances at this all-male gathering, including G.F. Watts. Neither man acknowledged the other. Sullivan brought Georgina a copy of his new song, 'Little birdie,' and accompanied her when she sang it at a party given by Julius Benedict. One of the guests at this party was Rachel Scott Russell.[31]

Few, if any, people appear to have suspected that Rachel and Sullivan were embarking on a love affair at this time, least of all Harry, who spent much of

[28] GWJ, 21–4/2/1866, 24/3/1866.
[29] GWM, i, pp. 37–8.
[30] GWJ, 9/3/1866.
[31] GWJ, 24–9/5/1866.

his time at Sydenham without Georgina – so much time, indeed, that Freddy Warre became suspicious and asked in one letter if Harry and Rachel had 'exchanged hair' yet.[32] On 1 August Georgina was given a ticket for a soirée at the Royal Academy by her old friend Frances Beckett, now a widow and living in London. She went with two new friends, the wealthy surgeon and amateur artist Henry Thompson and his wife Kate, a pianist and composer. To her surprise, Harry was there with the Scott Russell girls. He returned to Sydenham with them, whilst the Thompsons took his wife home.

In mid September the Weldons visited Uncle George at Müllberg again, taking Rachel Scott Russell with them. There were parties as usual, and paper-chases and games of billiards and croquet. Georgina hunted for curios in the old shops in Konstanz and learned to play the zither. The only problem was Rachel – who was, by this time, corresponding regularly with Sullivan. Nobody liked her and Georgina decided that the girl was 'the most self-assuming, shallow person' she had ever met.[33] Not surprisingly, Georgina saw rather less of Rachel after their return to England. Arthur Sullivan, too, was less attentive than he had been – influenced, Georgina believed, by Rachel's jealousy of her. But she had plenty of other friends in London. When Harry went off to Wales without her, she hardly noticed his absence.

[32] Frederick Warre–GW, 27/5/1866. Locks of hair were often given as love tokens.

[33] GWJ, 9/10/1866.

6
Discontent

By the mid 1860s the relationship between Georgina and her husband was beginning to change. In the early days of their marriage Harry had been ill at ease with his wife's old friends, some of whom made it clear that they thought him their social inferior. He had been reluctant to go anywhere without Georgina. Now he was more self-confident: he had friends of his own and was elected to the Garrick Club in 1867. Harry had previously been inclined to jealousy, tearing the photographs of Georgina's former admirers out of her album, but in the summer of 1866 he did not complain when she spent hours alone with John Brett whilst the artist sketched her. Nor did he object to Georgina staying with Freddy Warre in his new house at 44 Great Ormond Street. It is probably significant that Freddy never married – or came anywhere near doing so. Harry never seems to have seen him as a threat. Freddy was a good friend to Georgina, running errands and buying presents for her. Both were fond of knick-knacks, which they called 'grabs', and they wrote silly, teasing letters to each other. Freddy called Georgina 'Grabkins' or 'Georgina Graspall' and frequently referred to her strong acquisitive streak. He was only too well aware of Georgina's somewhat imperious nature, telling her 'Sometimes I wish I was your pardner [*sic*], and then I should be fed and led about like a slave.'[1] Georgina took all this in good part, and she continued to confide in Freddy and enjoy his visits.

Fred Clay was another close friend. Like Freddy Warre, he teased Georgina and did not take her too seriously, addressing her in one letter as 'Wondrous Madarme! Ray of Light from Realms above! You 'eavenborn Female.'[2] Harry showed no signs of jealousy of Fred Clay either. Much more dangerous was Henry Thompson, who paid Georgina more attention than was entirely proper. He took her to the theatre in London without Harry and brought her chocolate truffles and champagne. Thompson and Georgina began a regular correspondence after she returned to Wales in

1 Frederick Warre–GW, 28/7/1864.
2 Frederic Clay–GW, 25/11/1867.

October, and his gift of a box of marrons glacés on New Year's Day was received with rather more enthusiasm than Harry's aluminium saucepan.

In March 1867 Georgina sang Julius Benedict's new cantata *The Legend of St Cecilia* at a party given by her sisters' friend Lady Downshire. She was very nervous, as she was out of practice and had never sung with an orchestra before. As a result, she wrote, 'I sang flat the whole way through and did not know what I was doing.'[3] But she was well received and saw lots of friends, including Henry Thompson and his wife, and Gertrude Jekyll, 'a very jolly, clever, good-natured girl', whom Georgina had met at Aldermaston the previous summer.[4] Henry Thompson was still attentive: he took Georgina out in a hansom cab to buy shoes before a second performance of *St Cecilia*. With the help of four glasses of wine, Georgina sang much more confidently this time, though the audience included the Duke and Duchess of Cambridge and the Prince and Princess of Teck. Everyone was 'affable and complimentary' and the guests of honour asked for Georgina's photograph and promised to give her theirs.

Henry Thompson was, Georgina decided, 'a delightful man'. They saw each other almost every day during the weeks that followed. Sometimes he was with his wife and family, but they were often alone together. He began to paint a portrait of her; took her around in his carriage; and gave her presents, including a gold pen, a veil and a parasol. Such behaviour by a married woman – with a man who was not her husband – cannot have done Georgina's reputation any good. Was she being naive – or simply reckless? She wrote many years later that she had been 'too young and innocent' to understand the likely consequences.[5] It seems, however, that Harry was encouraging his wife to play up to Thompson, as he was hoping that her new admirer would invest £500 in the North Wales Granite Company, an enterprise in which he had an interest. Quite what Henry Thompson's intentions were, one can only speculate; that they were not honourable is suggested by a reference to a morning when he 'forgot himself and attempted to take liberties' when attending Georgina after an 'accident' with a bottle of chloroform, which she had been using to relieve a headache. When Harry found out about this a few months later, all relations between the Weldons and the Thompsons were broken off.[6]

In July Georgina and Harry travelled to Switzerland once again, to attend the wedding of Nandine Thomas, who was to marry a Bavarian count, Theobald Butler. Six days after their arrival, they received a telegram from

3 GWT, p. 1.

4 GWJ, 15/7/1866.

5 GWJ, 20,24/3/1867, 9/5/1867; GWM, iii, p. 219.

6 GW–T. Disney Leaver, 9/4/1881; GWM, iii, pp. 219–20.

London informing them of the death of Georgina's father. The madness that had been stalking Morgan Treherne for so long had finally caught up with him. For several years he had dragged his reluctant family around Europe for months at a time, never staying in one place for very long. In the summer of 1864 they had all taken up residence at 10 Stratford Place in central London, and Georgina had visited her mother and sisters there quite often – always making sure that Morgan was safely out of the way. He had been re-elected to Parliament in 1865, but in May of the following year Georgina was informed that her father was full of 'violent, terrible and mad ideas'. He was in such a 'terrible state' that the 'mad-doctor Blandford' had been called in to see him.[7] This was the eminent physician and psychiatrist George Fielding Blandford, who combined his post as lecturer in psychological medicine at St George's Hospital with an extensive private practice.

Shortly afterwards, Georgina 'took the bull by the horns' and wrote to her father, telling him that she hoped that the forthcoming marriage of her brother Apsley would be a good opportunity for the whole family to be reunited and let bygones be bygones. She continued:

> My unhappy girlhood is by me quite forgotten and forgiven, and I am quite prepared to be a kind and affectionate child to you. If you *will* but forgive my one act of insubordination we could all be so happy together. It is pure affection for you and the desire to see dear Mama, brothers and sisters again which makes me write to you.[8]

She received no reply, though she heard that 'the Guv'nor' had informed Dal 'a person' had written to him. By the end of the year Georgina's mother and sisters had moved out of Stratford Place, leaving Morgan in sole possession. 'Oh that Mama had done this years ago!' wrote Georgina in her diary on 31 December. In reflective mood, she continued:

> Even though one has no reason to love one's father, one cannot help feeling grieved to think he is in an irretrievably mad state, and so miserable. What we have all suffered through him, and what those poor children have suffered for the last 5 or 6 years with him, is dreadful. It was bad enough in my time. Ever since I can remember him, he has not been fit to be the father of a family.

Though she longed for a child of her own, she was worried that it might inherit 'this horrid curse'.[9] The idea that insanity might be hereditary in

7 GWJ, 10/5/1866; GWM, v, pp. 72–3; GW–DT, 5/5/1884.

8 GW–Morgan Treherne, 25/6/1866.

9 GWJ, 26–7/6/1866, 31/12/1866.

the Treherne family was to reappear several years later – with disastrous consequences for Georgina.

In March 1867 Georgina heard that her father had been confined in a private lunatic asylum. This was probably The Dell in Long Ditton, where he died after a succession of epileptic fits brought on, it was believed, by his 'addiction to onanism.' 'He was always so malicious – like a spirit of evil,' his daughter wrote.[10] If she mourned his death, she gave little sign of it. The event was, she thought 'a blessing for everybody.' She wondered if her mother would cry at all, and if she would feel at all sorry. Nobody else at Müllberg seems to have regretted Morgan's passing either. When Uncle George was asked if Nandine's wedding should be postponed, his reply was 'Certainly not.' The wedding duly took place on 23 July. Georgina commented cattily that the bride 'did not look at all pretty,' though she was 'a Venus' compared with her Butler sisters-in-law.[11]

Back in London at the end of October, Georgina went for the first time to see Joseph Kidd, a well-known homeopathic doctor. She and other members of her family had been using homeopathic remedies for many years, and she had great faith in Kidd to begin with, deciding that he was 'a nice, gentle man.' He gave her some medicine and told her that she would be 'quite cured' if she followed his advice. 'I do hope and pray he is right,' she wrote 'if I had only one child I should be perfectly happy.'[12] When, early in the following year, sister Flo announced that she was 'on the high road to a babbie,' but did not like 'the prospect of being a beast and a load for the next nine months,' Georgina commented 'Quite different to me!!! Ha!' She was still seeing Dr Kidd regularly, though he hurt her so much during one examination that she had to lie on the bed for an hour and a half after he had finished.[13]

In mid July Georgina and her sisters went to a party at the Gladstones'. Afterwards Florence, whose pregnancy had gone well up to this time, complained that she was very tired. Within three days she was dangerously ill and the doctors told her that the baby had died. Delirium and convulsions followed, and Flo sank into unconsciousness. She recovered a little, and the baby, a girl, was born on 19 July, having apparently been dead for two or three weeks. Two days later 'poor little Flo' died 'quite quietly, without pain.'[14] Georgina was devastated. Flo had always been her favourite sister, 'the loveliest, winsomest, merriest, cleverest child,' and the only one who had ever given her 'the merest shadow of sympathy.' Georgina was reluctant

10 GWJ, 16/3/1867, 31/12/1899; GWM, ii, p. 45.
11 GWJ, 11,23/7/1867.
12 GWJ, 30/10/1867.
13 GWJ, 14/2/1868, 23/6/1868.
14 GWJ, 14–21/7/1868.

to look at the body, but was eventually persuaded to do so by Dal and Emily. She kissed her dead sister over and over again until the others took her away. Afterwards she much regretted seeing Flo's corpse, and wrote that she would have given ten years of her life 'not to have seen her dead before me, and a smile which was not hers on her stiff little face'.

The reaction of her mother, sisters and brothers to their bereavement soon reawakened Georgina's old feelings of resentment at being undervalued by the other members of her family. On the day after Flo's death she wrote:

> It is so sad for me to see they don't care a scrap for me, when I cling to them so and might be such a resource to them, but I will not leave them, as I know – if they only try – they will find great consolation in our being all together.

Flo was buried on 25 July in the Curzon family plot in the churchyard at Parham in Sussex. Harry, Dal and George Curzon all went there by train, leaving the female members of the family at 10 Stratford Place. After their return Georgina was 'most astounded and deeply hurt' at being asked to go away and leave the house to her mother, sister, brother and brother-in-law, 'quite putting me and my feelings about Flo out of the question'. Not only was she excluded from the close family circle, she and Harry were forced to go and dine that evening at the Solferino, a 'public café'.[15] A fortnight after Flo's funeral, Georgina and Harry set off for the Continent once again. This time, however, Harry only went as far as Paris, whilst his wife travelled on by *coupé lit* [sleeper] to Basle and then Lucerne. Her final destination was the Rigi Kaltbad, a popular watering place on Lake Lucerne, where she met up with Uncle George and his wife and their three-year-old son Hugh. Georgina's mood lifted when she was persuaded to sing to 'a dreadful big audience' who applauded her enthusiastically. When they all left she had 'pretty verses' written for her, 'and such music and cheers when we departed, and bouquets of flowers'.[16] A day's journey took the family party to Müllberg, where Harry joined them a fortnight later.

By the beginning of September Georgina's period was ten days overdue. 'I can think of nothing but myself and my hopes all day, and almost when I am sleeping', she wrote. 'How cruel it will be to be disappointed!' But 'that cruel friend Joe' arrived three days later. She was dreadfully upset, but decided that 'certainty of disappointment is much easier to bear than fear of disappointment'.[17] She had still not entirely given up hope of bearing a

15 GWJ, 21–5/7/1868.
16 GWJ, 16/8/1868.
17 GWJ, 2,5/9/1868.

child, but she never did become pregnant again after the miscarriage in 1860. The most likely explanation is she had caught a sexually-transmitted disease from Harry, who been 'a most dissolute fellow' from his early youth and admitted that he had suffered badly from gonorrhoea and syphilis whilst a bachelor. Within a year or two after their marriage, Georgina had begun to experience the symptoms of 'a disease' of which, she was informed by the doctors and midwives she consulted, her husband was the cause. Harry, too, admitted that he was suffering from a 'mysterious disease'. This was the subject of some gossip among the servants: the laundress informed Louisa Treherne's butler, Antonio, that Harry had 'a dreadful disease' and said that she hoped to God that Georgina did not sleep with him'.[18] Harry's attempts to convince Georgina that his illness was a consequence of her lack of enthusiasm for sex were unsuccessful, and marital relations appear to have ceased by the end of the 1860s.[19]

~

For nearly a decade Georgina had 'enchanted' the best society in London with her singing:

> No one was so good-natured (the general term applied to an amateur fond of, or coerced into, showing off), no one was so clever, no one was so gifted as Miss Treherne. '*She was coming*!' Parties were made up, dinners given to the highest, the best, the most fashionable in the land. Their Ladyships, their Lordships – nay, their Royal Highnesses themselves – were safe to be amused! 'Miss Treherne would be there!'[20]

By the mid 1860s, however, she was becoming increasingly dissatisfied with her role as an amateur musician. The 'Tea-Urn' (Treherne), as she had sometimes been jokingly called before her marriage, was now less keen to pour out her melodies and felt that she was being exploited. When, in June 1865, she received 'an impudent invite' from Mrs Gladstone, she replied that she would come 'if I had nothing better'.[21] Catherine Gladstone does not seem to have been offended by this, for she continued to invite Georgina in subsequent years. Across the page of her diary covering September 1868 Georgina scrawled: 'Oh what a despicable creature an amateur is! In such a

18 GWMSM, p. 133. Morgan Treherne had dismissed Antonio in 1864, but the butler returned to the family after his death.

19 GWMSM, p. 52.

20 *Illustrated Sporting and Dramatic News*, 2/11/1878, p. 7.

21 GWJ, 10/6/1865.

false position. How I regret my lost life – which now is gone past recovery!' Two years later she wrote in more detail of her feelings at this time:

> An amateur is an unfortunate creature; he is without a standard. An amateur, however good, however excellent he may be, is 'Only an amateur'. The worst professional artist that ever ventured to sing in public is worth in the market more than he is. The public – always ignorant – would have more respect for the worst professional artist than for the best amateur artist. The professional's lessons would be paid for; the amateur's (however stupendous his genius might be) gentlest hints would not be listened to. An amateur, if he is at all good-natured, is a slave to the public, from whom he gets nothing but criticism – ignorant, of course, whether complimentary or the reverse. He would be mercilessly expected out to luncheon every day; to five o'clock tea and to 'At Homes' in the evening. A dinner is generally grudged an amateur. This is the life an amateur who is at all in Society or good-natured must lead. He has never time to speak to a friend or cultivate an acquaintance; people talk when he sings; he must listen, smirking with a polite face the while, to people giving him their opinion about his voice. Whatever a professional artist may suffer, he or she has the consolation of knowing the sufferings are *paid for*, and that if he or she is worried by criticism or rudeness or ignorance, he or she is at any rate a gainer in point of profit.[22]

Another problem, in Georgina's eyes, was the fact that Harry still had no real occupation – and no obvious desire to find one. Visits to his mother in Chester, and to Liverpool for meetings connected with the North Wales Granite Company, now kept him away from her for days, or even weeks, at a time. Nevertheless, and spite of all the evidence to the contrary, Georgina continued to see herself as 'a quiet, gentle wife, endowed with the most placid temperament in the world'. Saving Harry from himself had, however, turned out to be much more difficult than she had anticipated, as he stubbornly resisted all her attempts to improve him:

> My husband said he adored me. His way of adoring me showed itself in never being at home, in doing nothing, and in interesting himself in nothing. I would have wished to keep him at home, to teach him something – French, Italian or music – or get him to cultivate our garden, in which I used to go and dig myself, in the hope that he would be induced to acquire some love for the flowers, fruit or vegetables. I had hoped he would have amused himself doing a little carpenter's work. No, in vain! I have never succeeded in interesting him in any way whatever.[23]

22 GWT, pp. 1–3.
23 GWO, i, pp. 10–11.

These and other grievances had built up over the years:

> I've introduced him into the best, the highest society; I gave up my own chance of going on the stage and making a large fortune; I gave way to his mopes and his growls. I've made my own dresses, my own cloaks, my own bonnets; knitted my own stockings; valeted him; cleaned his clothes, mended them; paid all his debts; have been disinherited for marrying him; have humoured this diseased, degenerate creature in every sort of way. No one could have been a better or more devoted wife than me.[24]

Georgina's enthusiasm for sex – never very great – had soon decreased, and she had concluded that she was not an 'animal woman', though Harry was an 'animal man' with 'a very low and bestial nature'. 'A ram would not suit a marmoset, and a marmoset would not suit a ram. So we were unsuited to each other'. Her conviction that she and her husband were incompatible was reinforced when Harry tried to persuade Georgina to let him whip her 'as they do the Guards or naughty gentlemen at Eton'. Harry's former mistress, Mufti, had 'positively liked to be whipped'. His wife, however, was less co-operative:

> I, playfully at first, then indignantly, refused. One night he came to the bedroom as naked as the worm and as nude as Adam before the Fall, with a beautiful little rod tied up with pretty blue ribbon (in a true lover's knot, I suppose); wanted to strip me and administer personal chastisement. I sprang out of bed on the opposite side. 'If you touch me, you beast' (said I in a very quiet tone of voice, but with a very ugly look in my eyes) 'I'll kill you'.[25]

Harry never attempted to whip his wife again. Georgina also claimed some years later that his hands had been 'up every woman's petticoats'; and that, whilst they were living in Beaumaris, her husband had made a habit of asking 'old flirts' of his to come and stay in the spare bedroom at Tros-yr-afon. He would then send Georgina to get into bed with the girls so that he might 'follow me, get into bed with them and take liberties with them' – leaving Georgina to return to her own bed alone.[26]

The main objects of Georgina's affection by the late 1860s were her dogs, on which she lavished the love that she would otherwise have given to a child. As she herself wrote, she had decided that her husband was 'not

24 GWMSM, p. 53.
25 GWMSM, pp. 41–3, 133.
26 GWMSM, p. 49; GW–WHW, 15/7/1882.

interesting,' so 'after having loved him very much, I took to loving my dogs frantically!'[27] Georgina was fond of all kinds of animals: there was a pet hedgehog at Tros-yr-afon, also a tortoise, a goldfinch and several cats. But dogs were her favourites, and she and Harry always had at least one during their time in Beaumaris. In 1862 they were given a pug called Dan Tucker. This was the beginning of a love affair with pugs that was to last for the rest of Georgina's life. Dan went everywhere with her, to London and even to Switzerland. Harry was almost as besotted, taking Dan to have a Turkish bath on one occasion and insisting that 'dearest Minkin' should accompany him on visits away from home, in spite of Georgina's protestations. When Dan ran off during one visit to London, they were both distraught. The dog was found after a few days, but they had to pay five guineas to get him back. In the years that followed Dan was joined by a Willoughby pug bitch named Titania and then another pug, Jarba, 'a nice funny little thing' though very 'piddly-widdly'.[28]

Had Georgina borne a child, the rest of her life would no doubt have turned out very differently. But she showed early signs of the lack of regard for contemporary conventions that was ultimately to prove her downfall. At the age of sixteen she – like all fashionable young ladies of the day – was expected to wear stays or corsets. She endured these 'horrid inventions' for two years and then refused to wear them ever again, claiming that they made her back ache. She refused to believe that a woman had to suffer to be beautiful. Proud of her own good looks though she was, she eventually came to the conclusion that 'The only good of being beautiful is that it helps men, who are no good, to fall in love with you and create enemies.' In 1866 she also had her hair cut short – a step that was almost unheard of at the time. This was not quite as drastic as it appears, however, as the hair that had been cut off was made into a hairpiece or 'tail' that she could wear when she went out.[29]

To a certain extent, Georgina's unconventionality was forced on her by poverty. Unable to afford to dress like most of her friends, and largely dependent on garments that she made for herself or was given by friends, she adopted a certain eccentricity of clothing. How much she told her London friends about her home in Beaumaris is unclear, but few, if any, of them can have lived as frugally as she was forced to do. Even in Beaumaris there were not many ladies who lived in quite such reduced circumstances. Many years later Georgina summed up her family's attitude towards her life there:

27 GWO, i, p. 13.
28 GWJ, 21–4/6/1864, 17,28/2/1868.
29 GWO, i, p. 16; GWJ, 10/9/1866.

She must be mad!
She manages to do without a man servant!
She has only two little Welsh girls at £7 and £8 a year!
She cooks!
She skins rabbits!
She plucks fowls and game!
She opens oysters!
She has no carriage of any sort!
She wears an apron!
When the county people call on her she does not take off her apron!
She does not return their visits!
I wonder they take any notice of her!
She must be mad.[30]

The 1860s also saw the first stirrings of the campaigning spirit that was to sustain Georgina in later decades. Firstly, there was the Post Office affair. Harry's mother left Beaumaris for Chester in 1863, tired of competing for the attention of her son and of the local gentry. Hannah Weldon's insistence that all letters addressed to 'Mrs Weldon' should be sent directly to her in Chester meant that a large number of her daughter-in-law's letters went astray. At Georgina's instigation a letter was sent to the Postmaster General, threatening legal action if the order concerning the redirection of letters was not revoked. Mother Weldon proved to be uncooperative and wrote a disagreeable letter to her son. The dispute dragged on for two years, until Hannah Weldon finally gave in and told the Post Office authorities that she no longer wanted Georgina's letters to be forwarded to her.

In the meantime, Georgina had taken up another cause. One day in 1865 she was at Bangor station when the Irish express train arrived. She watched as a small, plump woman descended from a second-class carriage 'with the greatest care.' The train jerked and the woman, Mrs Fanny Duval Clarke, missed her step and fell onto the platform, breaking – as it turned out – her nose and two front teeth. She then passed out. Georgina had Mrs Clarke carried to the ladies' waiting room, sent for the doctor, washed the blood off her face, and telegraphed for her husband. She then took the injured woman to a hotel, made her lie down, and returned home thinking no more of the incident.

Mrs Clarke then attempted to claim damages from the railway company. The case came up the following year at the Spring Assizes, which were held in Beaumaris's small, ancient courthouse. The lawyer for the railway company suggested that Mrs Clarke might have had too much to drink, and claimed that her own negligence had caused the accident. Georgina was

[30] GWMSM, p. 138.

called to the witness stand and told the court that she was positive that Mrs Clarke had not been drunk and that the steps of the railway carriage were dangerously far apart. The accident had not been Mrs Clarke's fault in any way. Georgina thoroughly enjoyed her day in court. In her eyes she was the star of the show:

> The judge and lawyers all tried to make us, Mrs Clarke and me, appear to be imbeciles. But I found, myself, that I was well able to pay them back. The defence, using their sacred rights, could not shake my testimony at all! I felt myself to be in my element, neither nervous nor alarmed, nor timid. I found with joy that I enraged and irritated the opposing party.

Enraging and irritating the opposing party was to be one of Georgina's principal tactics during her subsequent legal career. In this instance, however, her evidence failed to persuade the court, and Mrs Clarke lost her case, having 'capsized' in the face of the lawyer representing the railway company, who shouted at her, threatened her with everlasting damnation if she was lying, and made her admit that she could, perhaps, have paid a little more attention to the place where she put her foot. Georgina's day in court had given her a taste for litigation, but the outcome was a disaster for Mrs Clarke, the wife of a 'poor little shopkeeper'. Costs of over £200 were awarded against her, and she and her husband were ruined.[31]

It was not long before Georgina found yet another campaign to occupy her attention. Early in 1866 news came that Robert Tennent, whom she had met at Spa two years earlier, had been fined £100 and sentenced to a year's imprisonment for attacking his 'wicked' brother-in-law, whom he accused of beating his wife, who was Tennent's favourite sister.[32] Always an indefatigable letter-writer, Georgina lobbied several friends and acquaintances, including Poodle Byng, Lord Abercorn and W.E. Lendrick, secretary to Lord Naas (an MP and Chief Secretary for Ireland), asking them to help Tennent, whose health had deteriorated during his stay in gaol. After Tennent's release, two months early, Byng forwarded a letter from Lord Abercorn, who wrote:

> I have done the bidding of your lovely client (I wish she were mine) and have today signed the discharge of Mr Tennent. It was not altogether

31 *North Wales Chronicle and Advertiser*, 31/3/1866, p. 6; GWM, ii, pp. 1–5; GWM proof, vii, pp. 11–12; GWL, pp. 2–3. Mr Clarke was the plaintiff on behalf of his wife, since married women could not sue for damages until 1883.

32 GWJ, 22/3/1866.

> easy to do, as the judicial opinion was rather the other way, but there were very strong representations from influential people in his favor, which enabled me to feel that I was not giving way only to the smiles of beauty, and not of justice.

A few days later Georgina received a letter from Arthur Sullivan, congratulating her on obtaining Tennent's release and expressing the opinion that the young man owed 'every bit of it to your untiring efforts.' 'We will all throw our hats in the air,' he wrote, 'and shout bravo! and hurrah! and above all "long live Mrs Weldon."'[33] Later in the same year Georgina did her best to obtain promotion for her brother-in-law, 'little George' Curzon, suggesting to Colonel James MacDonald that the young man should be made ADC to Lord George Paget. In this she was eventually successful. She also tried to obtain positions in the library of the House of Commons for W.E. Lendrick and George Grove and attempted to obtain leave of absence for one of John Brett's brothers.

Perceived injustice towards others of her sex also attracted Georgina's attention. During the winter of 1868–9, with other ladies of Beaumaris, she helped to run a soup kitchen for the poor of the town. In January a kitchen maid committed suicide. The girl was pregnant and her employers had turned her out 'neck and crop.' A few days later, whilst they were giving out soup, Georgina gave the other women a 'jobation' [lecture] 'as they were *at first* rather inclined to be hard on her [the girl who had killed herself] expecting, I suppose, I was one of the harshly virtuous ones':

> I said to them: 'You are women yourselves, and you never know when you may be led astray, and if you yourselves escape free, you do not know what may happen to your daughters, so never say an unkind word of any poor girl who gets into that state, but help her. If one could punish the man I'd do it, and flog him at the cart's wheel, but the girl is quite punished enough without your abusing her, and women's abuse of women does not make the world either better, happier, or more virtuous.'[34]

The reaction of the Welshwomen to this sermon is not recorded.

At home in Beaumaris at the end of 1868, a 'cruel' year which had seen the death of her younger sister and the end of her hopes of bearing a child, Georgina reflected on the events of the previous twelve months. She wanted a change from the 'hugger mugger' way in which she and Harry lived. Their financial situation had improved considerably since the death

[33] GWJ, 5/1/1867; Arthur Sullivan–GW, 9/1/1867.

[34] GWJ, 23,27/1/1869.

of old Mrs Weldon: Harry's inherited property was now bringing in about £800 a year, and this was likely to increase as coal had been found beneath his land. Although Georgina's father had left her nothing, her mother had been giving her £100 a year since the end of 1867. She wanted to be nearer to the rest of her family, and believed that a more settled life would be 'so much better for me morally'.[35]

The speech that she later claimed to have made to Harry at this time summed up all her pent-up grievances and resentment:

> Do you think I am going to remain here where I am losing my nerves, my habit of mixing with the world; where my natural terrible shyness paralyses me; where you leave me alone to saunter all day in the lanes with some man; where the gentry are afraid of asking you to their shooting parties because you so cruelly maim the poor birds? You know you never had the chance of shooting with the gentry until you married me. Am I to lose my voice, my beautiful voice, because I have got so cowed, so timid as to dread the very sound of it? You are enough to depress the liveliest, merriest nature in the world! Can I go on loving my home, where you flop in bed till mid-day; a home in which you can never stay; in which I can hardly get you to read the newspapers; a home you have defiled in every way, where you grudge me being happy, occupied, interested in my cottage and my garden; where you never miss a chance of snubbing me because I will not dress for dinner and allow you to wear an evening dress and white tie. I do not snub you back, though you know I might, by telling you no member of your family has ever worn an evening coat, nor ever dreamed of such a thing – they are honest, active tradespeople; I am not ashamed of them, and I learn more from them than I do from my own set.[36]

It was time, Georgina told Harry, to leave Anglesey and set up home in London.

[35] GWM, i, p. 36; GWO, i, p. 10; GWJ, 31/12/1868.
[36] Draft letter in GW's hand, n.d.

7
Gwen

Harry agreed, albeit reluctantly, to try living in London for a year. In May 1869 he and Georgina, accompanied by a servant maid and three pugs, left Beaumaris and took the train to the capital. Georgina was to stay with her mother in Stratford Place, and Harry with Freddy Warre, whilst they looked for lodgings.

By this time a great plan was beginning to evolve in Georgina's mind. Since her theatrical ambitions had been thwarted, she would become a music teacher instead. She had already achieved some success with her first pupil, a sickly, nervous girl called Gwendoline Jones, the daughter of a clergyman and goddaughter to Georgina's friend Catherine Wynne Jones. In 1866 Catherine had brought Gwen to see Georgina. The girl, who was said to have 'a great taste for music', had already had some lessons with Manuel García at the Royal Academy of Music in London and wished to become a professional singer. Her neighbours all thought that she had 'such a sweet voice' and sang 'so charmingly'. Georgina, as 'the great musical oracle of the county' was asked to hear her sing. She agreed to do so, and gave her opinion that Gwen's talent was 'very mediocre' and 'needed cultivation'. The girl was, moreover, 'very unattractive in appearance' and had 'no more manner than might be expected of a Welsh goat'. Nevertheless, Catherine begged her friend to take the girl under her wing, to help her with her singing and to sing with her. Flattered by this request, and wishing to please the older woman who had been kind to her, Georgina agreed.[1]

During the first few months of 1867 Gwen came for a lesson every few days – rather more often than she was really wanted. But she soon fell ill and returned to her parents, suffering (it was said) from 'hysteria'.[2] Two years later, just before the Weldons left Beaumaris, Gwen turned up again, apparently recovered, and told Georgina that she wished to settle in London, to study singing seriously, and to become a professional singer.

1 GWT is the main source for this chapter, unless otherwise stated.

2 GWO, pp. 21–3.

She begged Georgina to recommend a suitable master. Georgina suggested that they should try Alberto Randegger, a well-known music teacher and composer, who had recently been appointed professor of singing at the Royal Academy. Georgina, who had met Randegger the year before, had been informed that he took pupils as apprentices, charging them nothing until they had begun to earn money from their singing. She wrote to him, but he replied that he no longer took apprentices free of charge, 'as they always turned out ungrateful and invariably cheated him.' Nevertheless, he agreed to hear Gwen sing.

Randegger's verdict was bitterly disappointing: he told Georgina that the 'poor child' had 'neither voice nor ear.' She was mad to wish to make her protégée sing. Undaunted, however, Georgina decided that she would teach the girl herself. For a month Gwen spent two or three hours every day going through the singing exercises that Georgina had devised for her own use. Gwen's voice improved so much that Georgina told her that nothing stood between her and 'perfect success' but 'life and health.' Gwen returned home to Wales with orders to practise regularly, and Georgina did not see her again for several months. But she was now convinced that she had something unique to offer. As she wrote later 'the teaching mania was beginning to invade me.' She began to dream of establishing a music school, in which she would teach fifteen 'young ladies of good family' to sing. She would train them for two years, after which they would 'make a triumphant entry in the professional world.' She could, Georgina thought, earn some money by doing this. Gwen's mother was unstinting in her praise, telling Georgina that God had given her great talents, which she should not allow to be buried. It was encouragement such as this, Georgina wrote some years later, that 'helped to turn my head.'[3]

~

Another, quite different, preoccupation at this time was the need to find something for Harry to do. In this, the impetus came entirely from Georgina, for Harry was perfectly happy visiting friends, learning to ride a bicycle, spending long evenings at the Garrick Club, and visiting his mother in Chester. Georgina decided that he should become a herald at the College of Arms. 'The great inducement,' she later wrote 'was to get him a nice occupation and me an apartment – free of rent – in London.' The heralds had their own quarters in the College and Harry could hope to earn at least £200 a year. He might even enjoy the work.[4]

3 GWO, i, pp. 24–28; Mrs J.O. Jones–GW, 16/6/1869.

4 GWMSM, p. 52.

Georgina began to bombard with letters any acquaintance who might have some influence with the Duke of Norfolk, who, as Earl Marshal and hereditary judge in the Court of Chivalry, had jurisdiction over the officers of arms. These included the Gladstones, the Earl of Denbigh, and the Countess of Suffolk. They were unable to help, apparently because the Duke of Norfolk refused to consider anyone who was not a Roman Catholic. Then, in May, Georgina met Sir William Alexander, an old acquaintance of her family, who had been on holiday in the Pyrenees in 1832 when her uncle and aunt, William and Sarah Pattisson, had been drowned in the Lac de Guave during their honeymoon. Alexander had been present when the bodies were dragged from the lake and had stayed with them until Georgina's father and his brother had arrived to take the corpses back to England for burial. A barrister, Alexander had subsequently become Solicitor General to the Prince of Wales, and a baronet on the death of his father in 1859. Georgina must have pricked up her ears when she was told that the Duke of Norfolk had recently asked Alexander to preside over a commission of enquiry into the state of the College of Arms.

With her usual talent for charming elderly men, Georgina soon had the seventy-two-year-old bachelor eating out of her hand. He promised that he would do all he could to help and would ask for a position for Harry in lieu of the fee (at least £500) for his work on the commission.[5] Georgina was delighted, but Harry was much less enthusiastic, telling his wife:

> My sides with lafter [*sic*] fairly ache at your sudden idea of getting me made a herald. No, no Mrs Weldon, I am not going to have one little thread wound round me that will help to keep me in the great metrolepus [*sic*] until I have fully satisfied myself whether I can be content to live there. Besides, heraldry, tho' charming as an amusement, is not a profession I have the slightest desire to follow. You believe every word of nonsense people tell you if it only happens to agree with some plan you, at the time, may have in your head.

He was prepared to give London a fair trial, but would not commit himself to staying there for more than a year. A few weeks later, however, Georgina wrote in her diary, 'Harry and I do our heraldry lesson every night'.[6] Why Harry had changed his mind is unclear, but he seems to have succeeded in convincing Alexander of his new-found interest in heraldry. At the end of the year the news came through that he had secured the appointment of

5 Sir William Alexander–GW, quoted in Philip Treherne, *A Plaintiff in Person: Life of Mrs Weldon* (London, 1923), p. 23.

6 WHW–GW, 1/6/1869; GWJ, 13/7/1869.

Rouge Dragon Pursuivant, a junior officer at the College. Georgina congratulated herself on 'extreme luck' in obtaining this vacancy for her husband.[7]

~

In the autumn of 1869, Georgina travelled to North Wales to check on Gwen Jones's progress and give her further lessons. The girl's voice had improved 'miraculously' and she had also been trying to teach her sisters to sing. After a fortnight Georgina decided that she and Gwen should spend the winter with Uncle George in Switzerland, where she would be able to give her pupil her undivided attention. Within two years, she believed, she would be able to present Gwen to the musical world as a great singer.[8] In London, on their way to the Continent, Gwen sang to Julius Benedict, who appeared to be impressed and assured Georgina that nobody was being better trained than her pupil. He had not the slightest doubt that Georgina would be able to bring the girl out as a public concert singer at the beginning of the next London season.

Georgina and Gwen reached Müllberg two days before Christmas. Georgina had a piano sent from Zurich and the singing lessons began at once. But Gwen's sight was so poor that she found reading difficult and Georgina discovered that her voice was 'very much out of tune and very bleaty'. Georgina refused to give up, writing at the end of the year:

> Unpromising as people about me think [Gwen], I am sure I must make something of her, and I should like to have several pupils. I think of my singing plans day and night, and have no more wish for a baby, and I am glad (almost) I did not go on the stage, as perhaps if I had the idea of teaching others would not have come into my head. Now I feel certain all has happened for the best, and that this was my fate, and I like the idea of it very much. I never get impatient or tired in teaching, and appear to be very successful.[9]

Gwen's voice improved gradually, though her pronunciation was poor. Unfortunately, however, the girl's general health seemed to be deteriorating and she was often too unwell to practise. Georgina was only moderately sympathetic, suspecting that many of Gwen's 'everlasting ailments' were psychosomatic. But Gwen's condition worsened and her mother insisted on taking her back to Wales in spite of Georgina's protestations. Georgina stayed on at Müllberg, practising her singing and cursing Harry, who had stayed

7 GWJ, 10/12/1869.
8 GWJ, 24/9/1869–1/10/1869; GWO, i, p. 24.
9 GWJ, 31/12/1869.

behind in London and seemed unaccountably reluctant to leave, claiming that his duties at the College of Arms prevented him from travelling. He finally turned up on 8 May and they returned to England two weeks later.

Back in London, Georgina and Harry went into lodgings at 24 Welbeck Street. Georgina had given up all hope of putting Gwen on the stage, but she had great hopes of her younger sisters. She and Harry were soon joined by three of them, who were to form the nucleus of Georgina's music school. But she found to her dismay that they were all 'raw Welsh.' None of the girls could hold a tune and one lisped badly, but Georgina believed that she could train them all in spite of all their defects. Harry was distinctly unenthusiastic about his wife's new project, though he knew better than to oppose her openly. As she herself wrote, 'My character is in all things never to let go of anything I have once taken in hand.' The music school was beginning to assume the dimensions of 'a gigantic and superb fairy castle.'[10] Now, Georgina also took on two adult pupils. At a party given by her mother she met a young Polish baritone, Jean de Reszke, who had 'a lovely voice' and sang 'remarkably well.' They sang duets together, after which he visited Georgina every day for a fortnight 'to practise and study.' She tried to improve his pronunciation and believed that she could 'cure him of a great many tricks.'[11] She also did her best to help a thirty-year-old actress, Nelly Craven, who was one of Harry's old girlfriends. According to Georgina, Nelly had been 'inveigled' to go to Randegger's class at the Royal Academy. This was no great recommendation as far as Georgina was concerned, as she had decided that the Academy was 'nothing but a den of thieves and robbers.' Nor was she impressed by Nelly herself: teaching her a song was impossible, and her voice sounded 'hollow, like a soda water siphon.' The only thing in her favour was 'her evident anxiety to study properly.'

Occasional lessons did not bring in much – if any – money, and Georgina's most pressing need at this time was to raise enough to 'dress, doctor and feed' the Jones girls, since it was clear that Harry was unlikely to give her much financial assistance. She decided, therefore, to give a concert to raise money for her music school, confident that her friends and acquaintances would fall over themselves to support her:

> I have already given an idea of the select society in which I moved and reigned, which was only too happy to associate with me, and of which I was the 'Peri'; the 'Queen of Song'; the 'Semiramis'; the 'Corinna'; the 'Nightingale'; the 'Muse,' etc., and all those other pretty

10 GWO, i, pp. 27–8.

11 Jean de Reszke (1850–1925) became one of the greatest operatic tenors of his generation.

> flattering names which are accorded to the worst amateur, as well as to the greatest artist. I was acquainted with all the richest and noblest among those who were in the habit of throwing their money out of the window, and as my runaway marriage, beneath me and *sans façon*, had not been the signal for a shower of wedding presents (such as I should have received under other circumstances), I thought that my friends would have seized this opportunity of repairing their want of generosity ten years after my very happy marriage in order to give me proofs of their regard, their appreciation, their admiration and their gratitude. How often, with eyes suffused with tears, with smothered sighs, had I not been accosted with 'Ah, Mrs Weldon, what ought we not to do for you who lavish so bountifully your divine gifts on your fellow-creatures! What have you not a right to demand of us?' I graciously supplied them with the opportunity demanded.[12]

She wrote to Fred Clay to enlist his help, telling him, 'Nothing on this earth will keep me from doing as I say, and I know I shall be truly happy in my work, and work I must have, else I shall grow crazy!' She also managed to persuade her old admirer Lord Ward, now the Earl of Lord Dudley, to let her use his house in Park Lane.

The 'Grand Morning Concert' did not, however, go entirely according to plan.[13] The three daughters of the famous soprano Giulia Grisi, whom Georgina had met at Wiesbaden a year earlier, were unable to sing for her as they were in mourning for their recently-deceased mother, whilst Frederick Gye, the manager of Covent Garden, refused to allow their father, the tenor Giovanni Matteo de Candia (Mario) to take part in the concert. Several of Georgina's friends advised her not to let the Jones girls sing either, as they were 'so very plain and awkward-looking.' Others, who were against the whole idea of a benefit concert, 'sermonised me or wrote me letters full of reproaches,' telling her that her plans 'could not be pleasing to my husband.' Georgina commented scathingly that 'The affection and esteem for my husband (who had been considered up to that time more as a fifth wheel to a coach than anything else) was remarkable.'

~

These objections only served to spur Georgina on, and the date of the concert was set for 5 July. Georgina sent notes to everyone she could think of, explaining her reason for putting on the concert and asking them to 'help me to do good.' She began to worry that the room might be too full.

12 GWO, i, pp. 29–30.
13 Advertised in *Bell's Weekly Messenger*, 2/7/1870, p. 4.

Finally, the great day came. More than 250 people had taken tickets and many of the Weldons' friends were there. The actor Arthur Blunt, an old friend, was steward, and the audience included Henry de Bathe (now a general), James Robinson Planché (Somerset Herald), Sir William Alexander and Ferdinand de Lesseps, the man responsible for the construction of the Suez Canal. The composer Ciro Pinsuti accompanied Georgina as she performed one of her favourite party pieces, the 'Jewel Song' from Gounod's *Faust*. She was not frightened at all; she sang well and was 'so much applauded'. She was, however, disappointed that none of her family had turned up, apart from her mother, who had come in at the end, having been too nervous to sit through the whole event.[14] It was not until a few days later that Georgina began to realise that the concert had not been quite as successful as she thought. Instead of the £3000 that she had expected to raise, she collected £199 from the 'vast' audience, which had appeared to be 'so appreciative, so admiring, so enthusiastic'. She was so 'astonished and indignant' that she vowed never again to sing a single note for 'My Society, so false and so ungrateful!' unless they paid her. Instead, she would appeal to 'the public, to the real public'.[15]

It is not difficult to work out the reasons why the receipts from this concert were so disappointing. Georgina's expectation of raising £3000 was wildly over-optimistic: this would have meant each member of the audience of 250 paying an average of £12 – a large sum to contribute towards what many people must have felt to be a hare-brained, ill-thought-out scheme that might well benefit nobody but Georgina. In putting this concert on at all, Georgina was coming dangerously close to overstepping the critical boundary between amateur and professional – one that no lady could afford to cross without severe damage to her social status. Moreover, Georgina had evidently overestimated the regard that many of her acquaintances had for her, and had ignored the fact that her entrée to fashionable society owed a good deal to her readiness to sing for her supper. With little money and no house of their own, either in London or the country, the Weldons did not have much else to offer in return for the hospitality of their 'friends'.

Georgina's reaction to this setback was one of defiance, rather than discouragement. As she wrote many years later, 'I never say die until I am dead, and then whistle, as the saying goes.'[16] Her next step was to set up a series of smaller concerts in North Wales, hoping that they would attract members of the general public as well as her own friends and acquaintances.

14 GWJ, 5/7/1870.

15 GWO, i, pp. 29–30.

16 GWMSM, p. 52.

A local agent was engaged as impresario and Georgina set off on her tour in August, taking Gwen Jones with her. They gave a total of sixteen recitals, most of which were poorly attended. Gwen did her best, but she had not sung at all for seven months and was poorly for much of the time. After the concerts were over, Georgina reflected that her decision to allow Gwen to sing with her had been an unwise one. 'I think,' she admitted, 'people who were of opinion I had better have waited to produce her till she sang in tune were quite right.' The local newspapers were complimentary, but the audiences had been disappointing. Georgina blamed her agent, Mr Ellis for this: he had turned out to be 'a real donkey' and 'an awful bungler.'[17] Letters from Harry, who had refused to travel to North Wales with her, were less than encouraging:

> I don't care whose fault it may be, or might be – the fact of having to sing to a handfull [*sic*] of people in a huge room indicates a want of success somewhere which, if I were, like you, the person principally interested, would give me a shamefaced feeling, and the mismanagement, although done by my agent, would really be mine.[18]

Georgina's profit from this tour was just £17, but she was relieved that she had not actually lost money by it. Much more upsetting was the behaviour of Gwen's mother. Even before the concerts began, Mrs Jones had suggested that her daughter was ready to perform on her own and no longer needed a teacher. Georgina had hoped that, by letting the girl sing with her, she would prove that she was not ready for a public career, but once the recitals were over, Mrs Jones informed her that she 'no longer had any necessity to have recourse to my charity.' Georgina decided that Gwen's mother was 'a most unreasonable, impatient, faith-breaking woman.' In desperation, she offered the Joneses £50 a year if they would leave their daughter alone and 'give her the necessary time to perfect herself with me.' The offer was rejected and Georgina soon came to the conclusion that she should in future avoid outside interference by taking only 'orphans of both sexes from the lower classes.'[19] None of the Jones girls returned to London after this and Gwen, whose health had never really recovered, was to die less than a year later. Now Georgina's only pupil was Nelly Craven, who did at least seem to be making some progress.

At the end of August, Georgina met Harry in Chester and they travelled on to Birmingham, where the Music Festival was in full swing. There they met up with Benedict, Randegger and the conductor Michael Costa. They

17 GWJ, 26/8/1870.
18 WHW–GW, 22/8/1870.
19 GWO, i, p. 30.

attended the first performance of Benedict's new oratorio, *St Peter*, which was 'an enormous success'.[20] Benedict came to see them with Randegger afterwards and repeated his advice – first given ten years earlier – that Georgina should seriously consider a professional singing career, telling Harry, 'She is so gifted – she is a star which the world has lost. It is a real misfortune you did not make me your impresario – we should have both made our fortunes long ago'. To Georgina's astonishment, Harry replied that 'all was perhaps not lost', and he promised that his wife would sing at one of Benedict's concerts in the following year. This was, Georgina claimed, 'the first word that was spoken about engaging me to sing seriously in public'.[21]

Two weeks later, Harry's willingness to let Georgina take part in a public concert was tested when Benedict asked her to sing a solo contralto part in Handel's *Messiah*, which was to be performed in Liverpool on 27 December. She accepted immediately and begin to dream of the fame and adulation that were to come. 'How I should like to go as *prima donna* to Lisbon', she wrote in her diary. 'I should get, I think, about £240 a week and I should not let Crow inside my house!'[22] As it turned out, her first professional performance came before this, when Benedict engaged her to sing at a concert that was to be given by the Liverpool Philharmonic Society to celebrate the centenary of Beethoven's birth. Georgina agreed to take part, though she hated Beethoven's vocal music. 'I must have a beginning, and I shall get thirty guineas for doing so', she wrote.

Georgina's attitude to her début was somewhat ambivalent. She claimed a fortnight before it took place that she felt no interest in the occasion, perhaps because she could not admit, even to herself, how much it meant to her:

> I only look forward to how the public will like me in two or three years. I expect all the press to be against me for a long time, I am too entirely different to anybody or anything they have ever heard or seen before. They are sure to think absence of affectation, smirking and *minanderies* [simpering] want of artistic finish! I shall not dress myself up for the occasion or do a single thing to draw attention. But I shall like to see how the public will receive an utter stranger to them as I shall be.

Her attitude was certainly unusual. Henry Ludlow of the Philharmonic Society must have been surprised to receive a letter a few days later, in which Georgina asked him to alter the programme to suit her preferences, informing him:

20 GWJ, 2/9/1870.
21 GWO, i, 30–1.
22 GWJ, 30/9/1870.

> I don't know if Mr Benedict has told you that, having had the fortune or misfortune of being born what is called 'a lady', I have been only an amateur up to the present moment, and that I shall make my début as a paid artist at Liverpool. My reason for doing so is that my system and method of training the human voice is utterly different, in fact diametrically opposite, to any other musician's, but that I have found them so infallible as regards the production of the voice and consequent enunciation of the words that I have determined to lose no time in proving my system publicly, and what I earn I mean to devote to keeping six young girls (orphans) in my own house from the age of thirteen and educating them for the musical profession. I am no longer young, so I cannot have much of a career myself, but what I shall have, I look forward to as a means of helping my pupils on in the musical world.
>
> I have never had a master myself, but I believe I have worked harder than any artist ever worked. I have told you all this as I suppose there may be some mention of me as a new singer, and I should like what I have said to be reported.[23]

Ten days after writing this, on 21 November, Georgina travelled with Benedict to Liverpool for her first rehearsal. At the concert on the following day she sang three songs by Beethoven: 'In questa tomba', 'Oh beauteous daughter' and 'Ah perfido!' Immediately after the performance, she wrote that Benedict was 'in the highest possible spirits' and 'delighted with the praise bestowed on me'. 'I think I was immensely applauded', she added, 'considering I was an utter stranger. I did not give the public credit for so much discernment'. The critics were less complimentary – indeed, most of them were 'more or less abusive'. The man from the *Liverpool Courier* referred to Georgina's 'peculiar style of vocalisation', though he did think that her singing displayed 'much ability ... fine dramatic expression and fervent vocalisation'.[24]

Back in London again after the concert, Georgina had a terrible quarrel with Harry, who had changed his mind about the whole idea of her singing in public. He was also being difficult about money, claiming that she wanted to save money to please herself, rather than for their mutual benefit. That evening, Georgina cried until she was 'quite ill and exhausted'. Her mother, too, made it quite clear that she disapproved of Georgina's actions, telling her: 'I think, unless the necessity was paramount (nothing less than starvation) it is dreadful (respecting your beautiful talent) to make a business of

23 GW–Henry Ludlow, 12 November 1870.

24 GWJ, 22/11/1870; *The Liverpool Courier and Commercial Advertiser*, 23/11/1870, p. 6.

a pleasure. You cannot think how painful it is to see one's child have such opposite ideas in life to oneself.'[25] Georgina would not, however, give way, and she continued to practise the *Messiah* with Benedict. Harry did go with her to Liverpool on Boxing Day, but he was 'odious and tiresome'.

On the following day Georgina felt unwell, and 'nearly froze to death' at the rehearsal. But she put on her 'geranium dress' in the evening and got through the performance, in spite of nerves which meant that she sang 'without any genius'. The critic for the *Courier* thought that she was mistaken in singing the alto part 'for which the timber [*sic*] of her voice, which is really a very agreeable *mezzo soprano*, is by no means suited'. Some of her solos were coldly received, though '"He shall feed his flock", which was in her natural register, was sung in a manner we have seldom, if ever, heard surpassed for sweetness and religious feeling'. The same critic commented on Georgina's 'peculiar style', which was, in his opinion, 'disfigured by an exaggerated pronunciation, in which euphony is sacrificed to distinctness'. But Benedict seemed to be 'very much pleased' with her performance – and she earned £20.[26]

'The sun has (quite) gone down on my beautiful past', and I could never care or believe in any one single thing again', Georgina wrote in her diary at the end of a year in which she had decisively crossed the line between amateur and professional. Harry, who was suffering from 'depression of spirits', was still being disagreeable, but she was determined to persevere in her pursuit of a career. She had no intention of giving up her dream of setting up a school where her own idiosyncratic theories on the teaching of singing could be put into practice. There was to be no going back – especially after her first meeting with the composer Charles Gounod early in the following year.

25 GWMSM, p. 54; GWJ, 24/11/1870; LFT–GW, 13/10/1870.

26 *The Liverpool Courier and Commercial Advertiser*, 28/12/1870, p. 6; GWJ, 26–7/12/1870.

~8~
Gounod

The year 1871 did not start well. Georgina was left in no doubt that her friends and family disapproved of her recent activities when she received a letter from her sister Emily:

> I have had several letters from people, Alice Bective amongst the number, asking me if you had become professional, and so I say 'I am sure I don't know what new freak you may be up to', but I am sorry since I said that to see your name in the *Times* advertisement among second-rate artistes. Why don't you take another name? I heard at Liverpool you were placarded about the town in red and green letters (alternately) on large boards – with Arabella Goddard, and some others. I know with you it is no good saying anything, but poor Mama is awfully worried about all this, tho' I have told her, what is the good, and the best is to try and not care and not think about it.[1]

A few days later Georgina wrote to Alice, Countess of Bective, justifying her course of action. Her family had all known about her decision to turn professional 'for months' and she had already given her mother a full explanation of her motives. She had devoted herself to teaching, but could not afford to continue without the financial support of her friends. This had not been forthcoming, so

> I made up my mind to do what I have been told all my life I ought to do, and determined to earn the money myself with which, without being indebted to anyone but my own exertions, I hope to carry out my plan for the complete education of a certain number of young girls. Entering the profession is the most disagreeable and humiliating thing you can possibly imagine, but it is not more humiliating, in my opinion, than the way people fight to get to one party and the other in Society, and the way dukes and duchesses are run after for no reason

1 Emily Treherne–GW, 21/1/1871. Arabella Goddard was a well-known concert pianist.

> or object in life that *I* can see. I *always* hated Society and its mean ways, and never have I asked to go to a party in my life. Whatever I go through now is for a purpose, and in my opinion, as well as that of many persons, a good one.

She asked Lady Alice to tell everyone the truth.[2] Whatever anyone said, she was determined to pursue what her family described as her 'childish wild schemes'. Harry told his mother-in-law that nothing would stop Georgina but experience. 'All the talking in the world will do no good', he wrote, 'and driving would only make her worse and more determined.'[3] At this stage, however, it seemed possible that Georgina's public career would stall as soon as it had started. She had 'looked forward to a Barnum of some kind picking me up and making for me the reputation I knew I deserved', but soon found that the music publishers who promoted many of the most prestigious concerts seemed curiously reluctant to take her on.

Some years later, Georgina wrote of the disappointment she had felt at this time:

> I had been cradled with the choicest flattery since my entrance into Society, and I was convinced that I had but to show myself in public to turn the world upside down! I imagined that I was going to make the fortune of concert managers. That they would tear Mrs Weldon to pieces amongst them!!! A misgiving never entered my mind. I saw London – all my London – all the 'upper ten thousand' thronging in mass to hear their idol sing in public. However, not a soul troubled their heads about me. Not a soul spent a shilling to hear Mrs Weldon sing in public, although she had deprived the world of the ineffable happiness of hearing her in private!!![4]

The faithful Benedict did, however, secure a request for her to sing at a London Ballad Concert at St James's Hall in Piccadilly on 18 January. She wore her geranium dress again, and sang Benedict's 'The rose of Erin', and 'She wandered down the mountainside' by Fred Clay. Though in 'a fearful fright', she was 'very much applauded'. She met three of the most famous singers of the day, Sims Reeves, Charles Santley and Helen Lemmens-Sherrington whom she had known in Brussels sixteen years earlier. Three days later she sang at a concert put on by Signor Urio, to whom she had been introduced by a new admirer, the wealthy merchant Alexander Ionides. She also joined the well-regarded choir led by the composer and conductor

2 GW–Alice, Countess of Bective, 23/1/1871.
3 WHW–LFT, –/–/1871.
4 GW, 'Quarrel', p. 7; GWO, i, p. 34.

Henry Leslie, who was, she thought, 'a good, kind, businesslike man'.[5] In mid February Georgina set off for the south coast, having been engaged by an old acquaintance, the pianist and composer Wilhelm Kuhe, to sing a solo at the Brighton Festival. The critic from the *Musical Times,* which was published by the all-powerful firm Novello's, made no comment on her performance at the Dome.

It was later in the same month that Georgina met Charles Gounod for the first time. This encounter with the leading French composer of the day – her saviour and, ultimately, her nemesis – was to change Georgina's life for ever. Gounod, who was best known for his enormously successful opera *Faust,* had left Paris and fled to London with his family in the previous September, following the outbreak of the Franco-Prussian War. At first, they had sought sanctuary in Blackheath with Louisa Brown, a friend of Gounod's mother-in-law, Hortense Zimmermann, who had come to London with them. By the time Georgina met the Gounods they were living at 9 Park Place, near Regent's Park.

Georgina had first heard of Charles Gounod in 1862 and had at once been 'charmed and interested' by his music. Before that, she had cut her musical teeth on the works of the 'old Italian masters', such as Bellini, Donizetti, Verdi and Rossini. In 1858 Benedict had persuaded her to study the music of Richard Wagner, but she had not taken to it, finding that 'One had to pay, by hours of spiral and labyrinthian [*sic*] passages of almost unbearable weariness, for a quarter of an hour of dazzling music'. Georgina had attended one of the first London performances of *Faust* in 1863 and had been completely bowled over. The opera was 'a revelation'. From then on, she later wrote, 'I no longer dreamt of anything but *Faust.* I played nothing, I sang nothing but *Faust*.'

Some years later, Georgina wrote ecstatically of the impression that Gounod's music had made on her, contrasting it with that of Wagner:

> I compare Wagner to a brilliant sunny garden plot, where tulips and gaudy flowers, with long branches and curious leaves, bloom, before which one stands and gazes, bewildered by their beauty; but Gounod appeared to me as a mossy dell in some wood, lit up by great rays of sunlight athwart the foliage – a dell where, in dreaming repose, hours might be spent. What did not the beautiful new music speak of, say to me? Of cathedrals, of incense, of anthems, of plain-chant, of processions! It was a world in itself! *My world.* It spoke to me of simple farm-yards, of courtly castle-yards, of hell, of heaven.

5 GWJ, 18–21,31/1/1871.

The French composer seemed to have invented a new and simple style of singing, which Georgina tried to imitate, comparing it favourably with the affected manner adopted by many contemporary performers. She was convinced that she alone knew how to interpret Gounod's music correctly: 'I felt that a peculiar delicacy was needed to avoid depriving it of its effect or of rendering it coarse, or absolutely devoid of attraction.'[6]

On Sunday 26 February the Weldons dined with Fred Clay and his parents at their house in Montagu Square, and then walked a few hundred yards to 2 Manchester Square, the home of Julius Benedict. Georgina wanted to say goodbye to Benedict's married daughter, Alice Boulan, who was to leave England for France on the following day. To her surprise, Benedict seized her by the arm as soon as she entered the house and introduced her to 'a gentleman dressed in a brown suit.' This was Charles Gounod. Her favourite composer was not at all what Georgina had expected. She had visualised him as 'a Trappist; a silent young man, pious and holy' – though she must have known that he was in fact fifty-two. Her first impression of him was profoundly disappointing:

> Gounod's appearance did not charm me, because he had a muddy complexion; his hands seemed dirty; his clothes scrubby and too short. Gounod seemed to me *round*; his closely shaped beard *round*, not a hair longer than the other (bristles like box-hedge trimming); his short neck, his *round* stomach, his *round* shoulders, his *round* eyes with which he had glared at me.

Georgina's hero was, in short, 'fat and old.'

Gounod gazed at Georgina, 'very searching and interrogative.' He seemed, she thought, to recognise her. Benedict asked him to sing to the assembled company and he seated himself at the piano. Georgina went and sat next to Alice Boulan in her usual place, on a sofa from which she could see the pianist's hands. The two friends were joined by 'an ugly little brown woman,' whose dress and way of dressing her hair were 'vulgar.' Georgina took an immediate dislike to her, though she had no idea who she was. The woman, 'with broad nostrils turned up all round like those of a Japanese crockery dog, with a mocking smile on her lips,' seemed, Georgina thought, to sneer at Gounod. But she forgot her unappealing companion when Gounod began to sing his song 'À une jeune fille.' He kept looking at Georgina and seemed to be specially addressing himself to her. This was flattering since, at thirty-three, she was no longer a young girl. But it was the words of the song that 'went straight to my heart [and] stirred every fibre of my being':

6 GWT; GWO, i, pp. 36–7, 51.

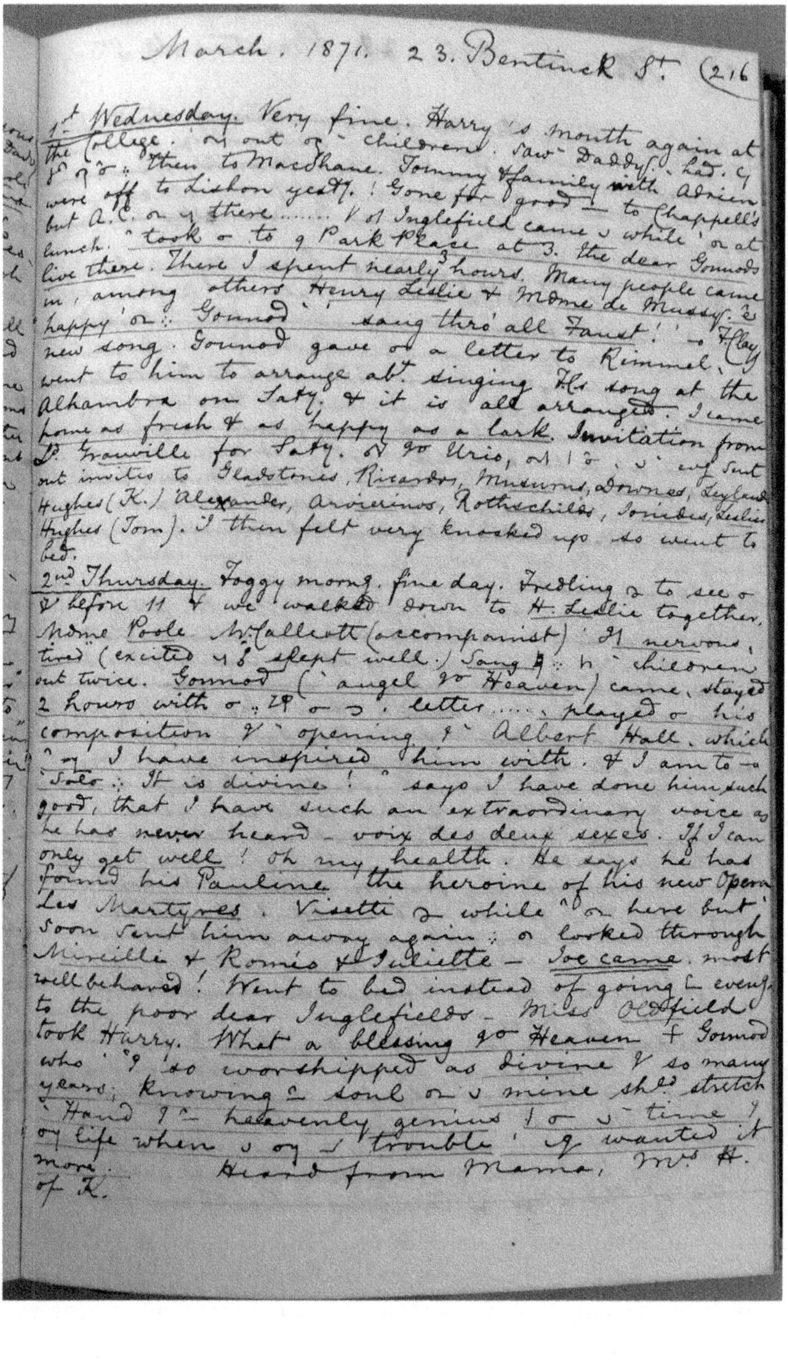

Fig. 12. A page from Georgina Weldon's diary, March 1871. Note use of shorthand symbols.

Poor child, who would'st struggle against nature,
Who doubtest of Love and would'st ignore its laws.
What hast thou then suffered? And from what wound
Has this heart of eighteen lost its faith?

Georgina, who was already feeling miserable, began to cry: 'My tears, which had begun to flow at the first line, had become a rivulet, the rivulet had become a stream, the stream a torrent, the torrent sobs, the sobs almost a fit!' Gounod sang several other songs, but Georgina did not hear them, having hidden herself behind some curtains to drink a glass of water and try to calm herself. Harry was furious and wanted to take her home at once, but she did not emerge from her retreat until most of the other guests had left. She asked Benedict who the 'ugly little old brown woman' was, and was stunned when her host told her that this was Madame Gounod. 'Good Heavens! What did he marry her for?' Georgina asked. 'Because she had a fortune and a position which he had not' was the reply. She went home feeling dissatisfied with the evening. Not only had she, as Harry put it, 'behaved like an idiot', but her favourite composer 'had not a good natural look' and had married for money 'the ugliest, the most common, sneering, disagreeable little woman in the world!!!'[7]

Two days after the party at Benedict's, Georgina went to Store Street Hall in Bedford Square for a rehearsal, having been asked to sing a solo at one of Henry Leslie's concerts. Gounod came in while she was practising, accompanied by his wife and mother-in-law and a friend, the Abbé Boudier, vicar of St-Cloud near Paris. Once she had finished, Georgina was applauded by the choir, and Gounod, 'in ecstasies', left his seat 'precipitately' to congratulate her. He wrote later that he had been struck by 'the sureness of her technique and the noble simplicity of her voice', and had proved to himself that Benedict's assessment of her 'remarkable talent' as a singer was fully justified.[8] Gounod introduced Georgina to his companions, who were all 'very amiable'. She could not talk to them for long, as she had to leave for the Hanover Square Rooms, where she was to perform at a concert in aid of the French soldiers who had been wounded in the conflict with the Prussians. She sang 'Albion, O soeur généreuse', a song specially written for the occasion, accompanied by Fred Clay, who had composed the music. Afterwards, Georgina told everyone that Gounod had heard her sing and had paid her a number of compliments. She was advised to go to see the composer and to ask him to allow her to sing the same song at a charity concert that he was putting on at the Alhambra in Leicester Square on 4 March.

7 GWO, i, pp. 38–40.
8 James Harding, *Gounod* (London, 1973), p. 166.

So, on 1 March, Georgina went to call on the Gounods at 9 Park Place, taking her music with her. Gounod asked her to sing 'Albion, O soeur généreuse' and the effect on her audience was most gratifying: they all burst into tears. Even Madame Gounod wept and 'forgot to sneer.' Gounod pressed both her hands with his eyes full of tears and exclaimed, 'What a singular voice! It is the voice of both sexes.' It was, as Georgina put it, 'a perfect shower of tears and compliments.' And it got better: Gounod sat down at the piano and he and Georgina sang *Faust* right through from beginning to end. Afterwards there were 'bravos and sighs without end.' Even Anna Gounod was enthusiastic: she told Georgina that she was 'born for Gounod.' Madame Zimmermann agreed, and Gounod himself was 'jubilant.' Georgina was with the Gounods for three hours and it was arranged that she should sing at the Alhambra. She came home 'as fresh and as happy as a lark,' having decided that Madame Gounod was not so bad after all. 'I argued with myself that if she were ugly it was not her fault, and that if Gounod had married her it must have been for some great qualities which she possessed which were not apparent at first sight, and not for her fortune.'[9]

On the following afternoon Gounod, 'the angel from heaven,' turned up at the Weldons' lodgings and stayed for two hours. He played *Gallia*, his new cantata for the opening of the Albert Hall, to them, telling Georgina that she had inspired him, and that she should sing a solo at the first performance. Georgina was almost overcome with joy: 'What a blessing from heaven that Gounod, who I have worshipped as divine for so many years, knowing his soul was in mine, should stretch a hand of his heavenly genius to me in a time of my life when, in my sore trouble, I never wanted it more.'[10] Gounod might be the means of reviving her flagging singing career. He might also help her to launch her music school. At this time she still had just one pupil: Harry's former girlfriend Nelly Craven.

Two days later Harry and Georgina went to the Alhambra in the afternoon. Gounod was there, of course, and so were Fred Clay, Arthur Sullivan and 'lots more artists.' Georgina sang her song 'very well.' She was not at all nervous. 'I do not think I should ever feel nervous if Gounod was there,' she wrote. She then hurried off to St James's Hall for another concert, in which the performers included a 'stringed quartett,' and Clara Schumann, who played a solo. Georgina sang 'My mother bids me bind my hair,' accompanied by Julius Benedict. After this she returned to the Alhambra, to join Enrico Delle Sedie, Madame Lablache and Urio in a quartet from

9 GWJ, 1/3/1871; GWO, i, p. 40.
10 GWJ, 2/3/1871; GWO, i, p. 41.

Rigoletto. It was, Georgina thought, 'the most marvellous feat; Arditi [the conductor], orchestra and selves arriving at the end together!'[11]

On the next day Georgina was unable to walk, having sprained her ankle badly as she returned to the platform at the Alhambra to take her bow. But she was absolutely determined to accept an invitation to spend the evening with the Gounods. With her foot heavily bandaged, she was carried downstairs by Harry, who took her to Park Place in a carriage. She spent the evening very happily, sitting in a corner of the drawing room with her leg on a stool near the piano. Gounod's seven-year-old daughter, Jeanne, played duets with her father, and her brother Jean (aged fourteen) and Gounod sang a duet. The children were badly behaved, but Madame Zimmermann was friendly, and she asked Gounod and Harry to return on the following evening to make up a party for whist. They went, and enjoyed themselves, though Georgina was dismayed when Gounod told her that she would not, after all, be required to sing a solo at the Albert Hall. He claimed to have forgotten that he had promised long ago to ask Madame Conneau, a well-known semi-professional singer, to perform for him on that important occasion.[12]

Henry Leslie's concert was held on 9 March at St James's Hall. Georgina sang her solo, 'Hear my prayer', and did better than she expected. The critic from the *Musical Times* thought that her performance was 'highly successful'. He also commended her rendition of Leslie's own song, 'The Rainbow', which Georgina thought ugly.[13] Sims Reeves was 'uncommonly civil' and, to Georgina's delight, said that he would like to sing a duet with her. The other members of the choir were complimentary too and Georgina went home happy. A few days later, she went to a rehearsal for another of Leslie's concerts. Gounod was there too, to conduct his 'Ave verum' and 'O salutaris'. Georgina 'nearly burst with pride' when he singled her out for special attention.[14] She saw and corresponded with Gounod and his family almost every day during the weeks that followed.

On 23 March Julius Benedict rushed to the Weldons' lodgings 'in the state of the greatest excitement' to tell them that he was to be knighted by the Queen at Windsor on the following day. Georgina's claim that she secured the honour for her friend seems to have been justified, for she received a letter from Gladstone on the same day, in which the Prime Minister told her that he was 'able to pay the regard which I so much wished to

11 'Arditi' was the conductor Luigi Arditi.

12 GWJ, 6/3/1871; GWO, i, p. 41.

13 GWJ, 9/3/1871; *Musical Times*, 1/4/1871, p. 45.

14 GWJ, 14/3/1871.

your recommendation of Mr Benedict.'[15] Things were looking up, not least because Georgina and Harry had at last found a permanent residence in London. During the second half of 1870 they had been busy searching for a house, having discovered that they could not live together at the College of Arms, as junior heralds such as Harry were only entitled to have one room each. They looked at dozens of houses, but nothing was suitable. Then, in September, Harry came home and said that he had seen somewhere that might do, 'a nice large house surrounded by gardens and large trees, as pleasant for the pupils as for the pugs.'[16]

This was Tavistock House, just off Tavistock Square, not far from Euston station. Part of an imposing late-Georgian mansion belonging to the Bedford Estate, it stood behind iron railings alongside Bedford and Russell Houses. The building was spacious enough, in Georgina's words, 'to quarter a regiment' – the drawing room alone could take three hundred guests. There was also a large garden, which gave the house 'a countryfied look.'[17] It was well known, having been the home from 1851 to 1860 of Charles Dickens and his family, who had often used the schoolroom on the first floor as a theatre. Since 1860, the house had been leased to a Mr and Mrs Davis. Harry and Georgina saw Tavistock House for the first time on 9 September 1870. They immediately 'took a great fancy' to it, though Georgina's mother told her that it was 'very indecent' of her to want to live in the WC district of London.[18] Nevertheless, Harry offered the Davises £2500 for the lease a few days later. The contract was signed on 3 December, but it was agreed that the Davises should stay in the house until the following May.

In the middle of April Harry and Georgina travelled to Beaumaris to pack up all their possessions at Tros-yr-afon, returning to London just in time for Gounod's concert at the recently-opened Royal Albert Hall on 1 May. Harry had been to the opening of the Hall at the end of March, but Georgina had missed the great event as she was ill. The concert on 1 May was, therefore, her first visit. All ten thousand seats were occupied, and Gounod was enthusiastically applauded when he walked onto the platform. Georgina thought the Hall 'the most magnificent thing I ever saw, and splendid for sound.' She was equally impressed by Gounod's *Gallia*, a lament for the fate

15 W.E. Gladstone–GW, 23/3/1871.

16 GWO, i, p. 31.

17 Claire Tomalin, *The Invisible Woman: The Story of Nelly Ternan and Charles Dickens* (London, 1991), p. 80; Edward Grierson, *Storm Bird: The Strange Life of Georgina Weldon* (London, 1959), p. 77; Hans Christian Andersen, quoted in Lucinda Hawkesley, *Katey: The Life and Loves of Dickens's Artist Daughter* (London, 2006), p. 71.

18 GWMSM, p. 53.

Fig. 13. Tavistock House (on the right), c.1900, from F.G. Kitton, *The Dickens Country* (1905).

of his native land based on the *Lamentations of Jeremiah*. The music was 'too heavenly' and made Georgina cry. 'It is all so divine, the finest thing he has written, though *all* he has done is *so* wonderfully beautiful!' For her, it totally overshadowed the other works on the programme, a triumphal march by Ferdinand Hiller and Arthur Sullivan's cantata *On Shore and Sea*. Of the latter she wrote that it was 'like all his music: two lovely bars and then eight ugly ones.'[19]

They spent the next two weeks preparing to move into Tavistock House. Georgina saw Gounod almost every day, and was persuaded to give him a gold pen of which she was very fond. She comforted herself for her loss by thinking of the 'beautiful things' that the composer would write with it. Gounod was full of plans for the formation of 'a great choral union,' which would give concerts at the Albert Hall, with him as conductor. He also told Georgina about a new oratorio, *The Redemption*, that he was composing for

[19] GWJ, 1/5/1871.

her.[20] At last, on 13 May, Georgina was able to sleep in her new home for the first time – without Harry, who stayed with Freddy Warre in Great Ormond Street for some unspecified reason. Three days later she was startled when Gounod burst into the house 'like a thunderbolt, beside himself, foaming at the mouth.' The Abbé Boudier, who came with his friend, tried to calm him. Georgina discovered that Gounod had had a terrible row with his wife. He swore that he would separate from her and claimed that he had led a life of 'hell upon earth' for the last twenty years. This was the end. He would never be dragged into such a life again – death itself would be preferable. Georgina was stunned. This was not the Gounod she thought she knew, a man who was 'calm, dignified and serenely angelic': 'I had imagined him just, without earthly desires, wrapt up in God, and his heart full of love for his fellow-creatures. He kissed all those who came near him, men, women, children and animals. The little he said was full of goodness, and of goodness for all.' The abbé was philosophical, telling Georgina that it was 'the same story every three months' and that Gounod and his wife would make it up again, as they had always done in the past.

When Georgina asked her new friend what he had done to provoke such a quarrel, he explained furiously that his wife was jealous of her. Georgina burst out laughing:

> 'Jealous of me? Can she be capable of imagining by any chance that I could be in love with you?' I asked, still laughing. It would never have occurred to me that *Gounod*, a married man, such a saint, too! could seriously be suspected of being in love. Equally monstrous and impossible did it seem to me that I, a married woman, could fall in love. The idea that Gounod, who was fifty-three, could be loved by me at thirty-four, that Madame Gounod, at forty-six years of age, could be jealous of me and of her husband at such venerable ages filled me with disgust, with horror, and with incredulity.[21]

She loved Gounod, it was true, but 'as an inferior loves a superior': 'I felt myself raised by being at his side, exalted by his grandeur, and blessed in having brought him recreation and consolation during the very painfull [*sic*] period through which he and his country were passing.'[22] As Georgina was subsequently to learn, Anna Gounod had good reason to be suspicious of her husband's intentions, for he had been involved with a succession of

20 GWJ, 9–13/5/1871. Gounod had in fact started work on *Rédemption* two years earlier.

21 GWO, i, pp. 43–6.

22 GWO, i, pp. 52–3.

women over the years. It was not until much later that Georgina admitted to herself that her 'saint' had been 'much more fond of me in a certain way than he ought to have been.' For the time being, however, she still 'set him on a pedestal and worshipped him.'[23]

The immediate result of the row of 16 May was that Anna Gounod returned to France with her daughter, leaving her mother, son and husband behind. Georgina decided that the older woman was 'odious' and that the quarrel must have been entirely her fault. With his wife out of the way, Gounod's visits to Tavistock House became even more frequent. By this time Georgina had discovered that her 'saint,' though keen on earning money, possessed little business sense. He had come to rely on her judgment, telling his wife that Georgina was 'a dear little woman' who would help them 'wonderfully.'[24] Unfortunately the 'dear little woman' was almost as naïve in business matters as she was in affairs of the heart. This did not, however, stop her giving Gounod advice. He already had a grudge against his French publisher, Antoine Choudens, who, he thought, had grown rich whilst he, Gounod, remained poor. Choudens had taken a gamble with *Faust* at a time when no other publisher was interested in the work and had been amply repaid, for the opera had brought him a small fortune. In England every composition had to be entered at Stationers' Hall within three months: Choudens had sent the score of *Faust* to the English publisher, Chappell, but they had failed to register it in time and Gounod had lost all his rights to the opera.[25] There had been similar problems with other compositions: his *Messe Solennelle Sainte-Cécile* had become 'common property through mere ignorance of the law.' Not only had it been published in its original form, it had also been 'attired' as a Protestant service. This adaptation, from which Gounod received no income, was, he claimed, 'a travesty sanctioned by the law.'[26]

When he came to London in 1870, Gounod had anticipated that all the city's music publishers would be eager to compete for the privilege of bringing out his music. But he was disappointed: the only one that showed any interest was Henry Littleton of Novello's. Littleton offered Gounod £40 for the right to publish each song in all countries. At first Gounod was delighted: Choudens had never paid him more than £20. He also sold the rights to *Gallia* to Novello's for £200. But the composer soon became dissatisfied with the English publishers, claiming that they were not paying him as much as they had promised. He had also discovered that many English composers received royalties on

23 *The New York World*, 21/1/1894.

24 GWO, i, p. 44.

25 GWO, ii, pp. 47–8; Philip Treherne, *A Plaintiff in Person: Life of Mrs Weldon* (London, 1923), p. 25.

26 GW, 'Quarrel,' p. 5.

the sale of their sheet music in England, whilst he had previously sold his compositions in return for a lump sum. Julius Benedict and Fred Clay urged him to insist on the royalty system, enthusiastically supported by Georgina. When, early in 1871, Gounod wrote two songs, 'The sea hath its pearls' and 'Oh, that we two were Maying,' they were offered to Duff and Stewart of Oxford Street, a rival publishing firm supported by Benedict. Gounod's command of the English language was poor, so Georgina undertook the negotiations for him. On 16 May, the day of the row that sent Anna Gounod back to France, Georgina settled 'very satisfactorily' with Duff and Stewart for the publication of 'The sea hath its pearls.' Gounod, however, subsequently changed his mind about ending his relationship with Novello's and reopened negotiations with Littleton. The publisher offered him £20 per song plus a royalty of 4d on each copy sold 'for the sake of remaining, as before, his principal publisher.' Gounod accepted this, and it was agreed that Novello's should publish two new songs, 'Queen of love' and 'Sweet baby sleep.'[27]

Once Anna Gounod was safely out of the way, Georgina and Gounod were out and about together almost every day. At Julius Benedict's concert at the Floral Hall on 31 May, Georgina sang 'Oh, that we two were Maying,' accompanied by Gounod on the piano. Her performance was generally well received, though one critic thought that she had not done the song justice. A week later the composer insisted on taking her to a concert, which she did not enjoy at all: 'Classical music? Ugh! Give me one bar of Gounod's for the whole boiling lot of them,' she wrote in her diary.[28] But people were beginning to talk, and one of Benedict's daughters told Georgina that 'everyone' believed that Gounod was in love with her. She denied the allegation vehemently, telling her friend 'Don't say that. He would become a fallen angel in my eyes.'[29] This was only a foretaste of the troubles that were to come but, wrapped up as she was in her adoration of Gounod, Georgina ignored all warnings of this kind.

On 10 June Gounod received a letter offering him the post of director of the Conservatoire in Paris. At first the composer wanted to accept, telling Georgina that he would then be able to offer her a class at the Conservatoire and get plenty of professional engagements for her. Like, as she later admitted, 'a great and never-to-be-forgotten simpleton,' Georgina urged him to turn the offer down, reminding him that he would not be able to show any favouritism to her and telling him that the job would not leave him enough time for composition.[30] He listened to her advice and refused to take up the post.

27 GWJ, 16/5/1871; GWO, ii, pp. 49–54.
28 *Lloyd's Weekly Newspaper*, 4/6/1871, p. 7; GWJ, 6/6/1871.
29 GWO, i, p. 50.
30 GWO, i, p. 54.

Madame Zimmermann followed her daughter back to France in the middle of June, and Harry and Georgina invited Gounod and the Abbé Boudier to lodge with them during the remainder of their stay in London. The abbé refused, afraid of Anna Gounod's reaction, but Gounod moved into Tavistock House on 19 June. He was to stay there for six productive weeks, during which time he worked on his opera *Polyeucte* and *The Redemption* and composed several songs. On 21 July Georgina sang *Gallia* for the first time, at the Albert Hall, dressed in a specially-made 'Gallia deep mourning dress.' With Gounod there she was 'hardly at all frightened' and her voice was 'as firm as a rock.' Gounod, the 'dear old man,' the 'divine being' as Georgina and Harry called him, was delighted and the performers (who included Arthur Sullivan) were 'tremendously applauded.' Afterwards, Gounod presented Georgina with a gold ring with his monogram in memory of her great success.

Gounod left Tavistock House on the last day of July and returned to Paris. 'And so,' wrote Georgina in her diary 'ended the happiest period of the whole of my life': 'He is all I could wish: careful, thoughtful, kind as an angel, good like a saint, economical and without a grain of vanity, tenderer than the tenderest woman and firm in his honor. No words could ever make anyone feel enough how good and how great he is.'[31] Her account of Gounod's visits to England, written ten years later, suggests that he was not, in reality, the ideal house-guest. He had many objectionable habits, including spitting (indoors as well as outdoors) and paring his nails at table. He smoked incessantly and took snuff. Though Georgina claimed that she thought it her duty to put up with anything for the sake of the 'divine being,' it was not long before she tried to tame him. Gounod did his best to comply with her wishes. He was 'a martyr to dyspepsia' and complained that the 'continual worryings' of his wife had 'turned his blood to vinegar and destroyed his digestive organs.' Georgina ordered an india-rubber bath and cold ablutions. Georgina's Protestant inclinations were aroused when, on unpacking his portmanteau, Gounod showed her a long cord and told her that it was the discipline or scourge with which he flagellated himself. She made him promise not to use it. He gave her a copy of the *Imitation of Christ* and a rosary, and they were both soon 'up to our necks in religion.'[32]

With Gounod back in France, Georgina was able to devote more time to her pupils. The numbers grew slowly: by the summer of 1871 these included, in addition to Nelly Craven, the three sons of a blind musician, Arthur Rawlings, whom Georgina had first heard singing in the street. The

[31] GWJ, 21,31/7/1871.

[32] GWO, i, p. 55.

boys, Charlie (fourteen), Alfred (ten) and Walter (five), had 'lovely voices', though they were 'awfully ugly' and had a dreadful 'cockney twang'. They came to Tavistock House two or three times a week. Harry soon began to complain that the boys were driving him mad with their 'hideous discord', but Georgina ignored him.[33]

~

In the summer of 1871 Georgina began work on a pamphlet with the title *Hints for Pronunciation in Singing with Proposals for a Self-Supporting Academy.* Her intention, she wrote, was to found 'an academy wherein the poorest may obtain free instruction in music and singing, and all the educational advantages ordinarily enjoyed only by the rich, including modern languages, general culture, and foreign travel.' In her opinion it was through a lack of such a liberal education for singers and actors that the stage had become 'so vulgarised that a person of refined taste can rarely visit a theatre without being shocked by the ignorance or ill-breeding of at least some of the performers.'[34] This all-too-obvious disdain did not endear Georgina to the members of the music trade. She was later to claim that a singer who wanted to 'get on' had to be

> 'hail fellow, well met' with all the mud and slum, and I, a lady! I was a lady of good birth and breeding, I shrank from it. I was to this band of brigands a stumbling-block, a *bête noire,* a scare-crow! A lady who had enjoyed a good reputation for so many years, there was no chance of pinning a lover on her, there was no way of seducing her – therefore no way of trading on her.[35]

Georgina was sure that the music critics had decided to disparage her talent as much as possible so that Benedict, her protector, would give her up. But her pamphlet on singing would be advertised 'properly', and would make her better known 'in defiance of those horrid critics'. The pamphlet was less well received than its author had hoped. A reviewer commented on her 'eccentric pronunciation' and described her 'so-called method' as 'false and artificial'. 'If', he added, 'an essay written in such a rambling and disconnected manner can rightly be termed a method.'[36]

Georgina also came to regard Arthur Sullivan as an enemy at this time, claiming that he had a grudge against her because she had rejected his advances some years before. When, in 1868, Sullivan had 'pestered' Georgina, 'as indeed he pestered all women, with his disgusting familiarities' she had told Harry,

33 GWJ, 31/7/1871; WHW–GW, 21/10/1871.
34 GW, 'Hints', p. 3.
35 GWO, i, p. 32.
36 GWJ, 11/8/1871; *Morning Post*, 12/12/1871, p. 3.

who had threatened to horsewhip him. After this, Sullivan had taken to leaving the room every time Georgina sang, telling everyone that her voice grated on his ears.[37] He may also have blamed her for his failure to marry Rachel Scott Russell. But Georgina always took criticism or opposition of any kind as a personal affront. In 1870 Louisa Treherne, who knew her daughter only too well, told her 'The only comparison I drew of you and your father was this, that he thought everybody a donkey, or wrong, and his enemy, that differed with him. I certainly think that you are like him in that respect.'[38]

After Gounod's departure, Georgina practised her singing and taught herself to spin to prepare herself for the role of Marguerite in *Faust.* She wrote to Gounod every day, and he wrote to her almost as often. In August he returned to London for ten days, having again fallen out with Henry Littleton, who had published his song 'La Siesta' with words that Georgina thought 'absurd.' As soon as he arrived at Tavistock House, Gounod announced that he wanted to go off and 'kick Littleton.'[39] Over the next few days he and Georgina visited a number of European legations and embassies together, trying to register Gounod's copyright of some of his songs.

Gounod returned to Paris on 3 September and Georgina followed him six weeks later. The first performance of *Gallia* in France was to take place on the occasion of the reopening of the Conservatoire after a closure of eighteen months, and Gounod was insisting that she should sing the solos. This did not go down well with the French, who thought that such an intensely patriotic role should be taken by one of their own countrywomen, but Gounod was obdurate. He took lodgings at 21 Place de la Madeleine for Georgina, and met her at the station when she arrived early in the morning on 14 October. The composer did not look well: he was suffering from a streaming cold and, thought Georgina, 'had the appearance of a poor, driven, hunted wild beast.' He told Georgina that his wife had been driving him 'mad – raving mad!' and that he could stand her no longer.[40] Things could only get worse when Anna Gounod discovered that Georgina had come to Paris without Harry. He had been left behind to look after Freddy Warre, who was seriously ill at Tavistock House.

In Paris Georgina was able to witness at first hand the destruction wrought during the Franco-Prussian War and the weeks of street-to-street fighting that had followed the declaration of autonomy by the Paris government or Commune. She saw that part of the Louvre had been burnt

[37] GWM, i, p. 38; GWT.
[38] LFT–GW, 13/10/1870.
[39] GWO, ii, p. 55; GWJ, 24/8/1871.
[40] GWO, i, p. 58.

down and that the Palais Royal was in ruins. On 17 October she went with Gounod to the Conservatoire for a rehearsal, and met the composer Ambroise Thomas, 'a dear old man', who had recently been appointed to the post that Gounod had turned down. Georgina was disappointed by the Conservatoire: there was 'no WC fit for a pig' and no waiting room for the soloists. The place was 'a real hole altogether', and the people there, apart from the director, were 'a lot of muffs [duffers]'. On 23 October she and Gounod dined together, and then went to see the ninety-eighth performance of *Faust* at the Grand Opéra. Georgina was more impressed by the building than by the singers: 'Never saw such a lovely opera house. So well arranged and good for sound. The singers all more or less poor. The *mise en scène* lovely; "Danse Nubienne" too lovely. The *entreacte* had something civil about me in it!'[41]

On the following day they went together to a party at which Georgina met several members of the Committee of the Conservatoire. Dressed in her 'geranium dress, gold myrtle crown and cameos', Georgina sang 'so exquisitely' and amused herself 'extremely'. She was introduced to Jules Franceschi, a sculptor who had his studio on the courtyard of the house occupied by the Gounods. Franceschi, who was terrified of Anna Gounod, admired Georgina 'tremendously' and began work on a bust of her wearing her special *Gallia* head-dress. He also asked her to model for him, as the Muse of Music, for a monument to the composer Gottschalk that was to be put up in Green-Wood cemetery in New York.[42]

The dress rehearsal at the Conservatoire on 28 October did not go well. The room was so cold that Georgina almost lost her voice during her first solo, and the presence of Anna Gounod (now usually referred to as the *chien de faïence*, or 'c. de f.') made her 'dreadfully nervous'.[43] Nevertheless, she made a favourable impression on the playwright Ernest Legouvé, who wrote immediately to Julius Benedict to tell him of his protégée's success:

> You know that the audience at the Conservatoire are very hard to please, deeming it due to themselves to be very severe, by according their plaudits as though they were awarding diplomas. The success of Mrs Weldon is so much the more honourable. The instant she appeared she pleased, her reserved attitude and well-bred looks and manner seemed to please; she had no appearance of a professional singer. As soon as she opened her mouth her voice struck one as *bien timbrée*, her manner of singing natural, simple and in good style. She

41 GWJ, 17–27/10/1871.

42 GWJ, 24/10/1871; GWO, i, p. 62.

43 Georgina translates this as 'crockery dog'.

> had a great deal of success in her first solo, and was applauded at the end of it. In the second a little more power would have been desirable, and the voice was unavoidably overpowered by the choir; added to which she was frightened out of her wits.[44]

Georgina vowed afterwards that she would drink a tumbler of wine before the performance on the following day. She does not tell us if she did so, though she was certainly still nervous. She wrote that she was well received and loudly applauded, but this does not entirely agree with P.L. Hillemacher's, account, published in 1906: 'Her reception was courteous rather than warm. The vocalist was found, not without reason, to communicate without charm. In fact, with her, the voice is the least of her seductions.'[45] Georgina was delighted when Choudens told her that he wished to engage her as the soloist for some further performances of *Gallia* to be given at the Opéra-Comique.

The *chien de faïence* had good reason to be frosty, for Gounod and Georgina spent much of their time together. When they were not rehearsing they went to mass; she visited his apartments and gave him beef tea. He poured out his troubles to her, confessing that he had in the past suffered from periods of insanity and that it had been necessary to lock him away in Dr Antoine Blanche's clinic at Passy on the outskirts of Paris. He had tried to commit suicide on one occasion and had been confined in a straitjacket for two months. Everything was, of course, Anna Gounod's fault. These confidences thrilled Georgina. It was not until many years later that she asked herself if they had all been true. 'Sometimes,' she wrote, 'I think he trumped up all these stories to get me to take pity on him.'[46] In this he was certainly successful. Though there is no indication that anything improper happened, the hours that Georgina and Gounod spent together, both in private and in public, cannot have done her already-damaged reputation any good.

At twenty past eight on the evening of 8 November Gounod came to the apartment to fetch Georgina for her first performance at the Opéra-Comique. It was to be semi-staged, and she had spent hours practising walking up and down in her *Gallia* dress, which had a long train. Georgina had never appeared publicly on a stage before and there had been only one 'wretched little rehearsal.' She had to stand alone for seventeen minutes, then walk

[44] GWO, i, p. 59.

[45] P.L. Hillemacher, *Charles Gounod* (Paris, 1906), p. 84.

[46] GWO, i, p. 58. Gounod was at the clinic in Passy in 1856: Harding, *Gounod*, pp. 96–7. One of Gounod's most recent biographers, Gérard Condé, comments that the accuracy of Georgina's account of Gounod's time in London can be confirmed from other sources: Gérard Condé, *Charles Gounod* (Paris, 2009): www.books.google.co.uk (no page nos given).

backwards without tripping over her train and seat herself on a stone and 'look round and gaze sadly at the Gallic-Israelites as they passed at the back of the stage.' When she and Gounod reached the theatre Georgina felt 'more dead than alive with fright.' In her costume, with her face rouged and painted, she finally went on stage at 11.15. It all went better than she expected:

> I dragged myself onto the stage amidst a hushed silence! My voice went all right, and I did my *mise en scène* all right, and the whole house applauded me many times quite loudly. I really don't mind it so much nearly as that horrid little Conservatoire. I am sure I should like acting in downright earnest very much, and I shall not feel at all nervous after a bit.

Hillemacher describes how Georgina made her appearance in a plantation of palm trees, with chorists in biblical costumes. She was draped in long veils 'which admirably suited her elegant figure.'[47] Several acquaintances came to see her after the performance: all complimented her, and the manager of the theatre, Camille du Locle, told her that she had 'the genius of gesture.'[48] The French critic M. Reyer wrote, 'It is long since, whether within or without a theatre, I have listened to singing so true, so elegant, and I might say so captivating.' Mrs Weldon's début in Paris had been very successful, he added, in spite of the fact that she was an Englishwoman.[49] There were seven more performances of *Gallia* at the Opéra-Comique, and Georgina was paid 250 francs (£10) for each of them. There was talk of an oratorio, *Ruth and Boaz*, which Gounod would write for her, and she began to dream of her debut as Pauline in *Polyeucte* at the Grand Opéra.

Harry arrived in Paris on 15 November. A week later he went with Georgina to the church of Saint-Eustache, where she was to sing in a concert in aid of the Association of Musical Artistes. This seems to have been a spectacular success. *Gallia* was on the programme again, together with Gounod's *St Cecilia Mass*:

> It was heavenly and such a beautiful church, which held today over 6000 persons. I sang *Gallia* in Latin and it went so grandly! I felt so proud and happy and the old man was so pleased with me and Harry thought my voice sounded grand. No end of people came to congratulate me.

The church was icy cold and Georgina was so 'muffled up' in veils and furs that the audience could hardly see her face. As a result, she felt less nervous

47 Hillemacher, *Gounod*, pp. 84–5.
48 GWJ, 8/11/1871, GWO, i, pp. 63–4.
49 PMG, 17/11/1871, p. 3.

than usual and her voice showed its 'natural brilliancy.' Everyone congratulated her on her performance, and the sculptor Franceschi, 'a most amusing little man,' was 'out of his senses with delight.'[50]

The rows between Gounod and his wife continued. The composer told Georgina that although they both lived in the same house, they had separate apartments and had lived apart for many years. This did not stop them having violent arguments. Every day, Gounod would 'burst like a typhoon' into her apartment, full of his wife's latest iniquities. One day he had been so furious that he had hit her and torn her dressing gown, shouting that she was a 'vile wretch.' Anna Gounod had been telling everybody she knew that her husband was having an affair with Georgina, and that the younger woman was 'a woman on the town who slept with the first comer for £5 a night.' She was, Anna claimed, penniless and avaricious; she did not know how to sing, and she was hideous into the bargain. After several weeks of this Georgina was, she claimed, 'almost out of my mind with nervousness.' It is therefore somewhat surprising that Harry should have initiated a move that would only reinforce the rumours about his wife and Gounod: he suggested to Georgina that they should take the composer back to London with them once the concerts in Paris were over.[51]

Before the final performance of *Gallia* at the Opéra-Comique, Georgina and Victoire, the cook at her lodgings, hatched a plan that was to backfire in a spectacular manner. Victoire suggested that Georgina should arrange for bouquets of flowers to be thrown to her at the end of her performance, as other artists did. Though disapproving at first, Georgina decided that this was not such a bad idea. But instead of fresh flowers, which would fade, she would pay for a garland of *immortelles* [everlasting flowers], which Victoire should bring anonymously to the theatre, with the inscription 'Gallia to G. Weldon' on it. Gounod's reaction to the wreath was not what Georgina had expected. After a 'mournful silence' he told her that it must have been sent by an enemy, perhaps his wife, and that it was 'a piece of foolery.' The meaning of it was clearly that '*Gallia* is a fiasco, Charles Gounod a fiasco, and G. Weldon, ditto' adding 'My poor child! What persecutions! Good God, what persecutions!' Georgina admitted that the wreath had come from her and asked him to forgive her for her 'naughty trick.' He agreed to do so, but begged her never to do anything like it again.[52] She cheered up, however, when she heard that the Conservatoire had awarded her a silver medal.

50 GWJ, 22/11/1871; GWO, i, p. 62.
51 GWO, i, pp. 57–9; WHW–GW, 31/10/1871.
52 GWO, i. pp. 60–1.

By this time Gounod was in a state of nervous collapse. He agreed to return to London with Harry and Georgina, partly to get away from his wife, but also because he had decided to sue Novello's. At the station a pickpocket stole 275 francs (£11) from Georgina. Harry caught the thief, but had to let him go as their train was about to depart and Gounod was 'frantic' to leave, telling his friends that he would die if he had to stay in Paris a day longer. 'Devil take the money,' he declared, promising that he would give them all that they had lost.[53]

[53] GWO, ii, p. 4; GWO, i, p. 65; GWJ, 30/11/1871.

9
Tavistock House

The Weldons and Gounod arrived back at Tavistock House at 7 o'clock in the evening on Friday 1 December 1871 after a terrible crossing of the Channel during which they had all been seasick. It had been arranged that Gounod would stay with his friends for three weeks and then return to Paris for Christmas. In the event, he was to be with them for three years.

The composer appeared to be seriously ill. 'He fluttered into our nest like a wounded bird,' wrote Georgina, 'he crouched down in his bed like a poor hunted animal, and there he lay for several days without moving.' She summoned her own homeopathic physician, Dr Thomas McKern, who examined the patient. A member of the Plymouth Brethren, 'who shun music as the work of Satan,' McKern had never heard of Gounod. He told Georgina and Harry that their friend's condition was much worse than they had supposed. He was 'poisoned with eczema' and might suffer a cerebral attack at any moment. Both lungs were 'highly congested' and his bronchial tubes were 'in a state of chronic irritation.' McKern prescribed some of his own homeopathic medicines and ordered a course of hydropathy. He also recommended rest and quiet.

Every morning after this, Gounod stayed in his bedroom on the third floor of Tavistock House, wrapped up in wet sheets and blankets and smothered in rugs, furs and waterproofs for up to six hours, watched over by Georgina's old pug, Dan Tucker. The aim of this treatment was to make the patient sweat. Whilst Gounod was thus incarcerated, Georgina would climb the stairs from the ground floor room where she gave her music lessons every half hour or so to check on his progress; and Harry would return from the College of Arms two or three times in a morning to ask 'Has the old man perspired? How long will he be today before he perspires?' If the answer was satisfactory, the 'old man' would be released from his bonds, though he was strictly forbidden to smoke or take snuff, and Georgina insisted on cooking all his food on a gas stove close to him. She fed him herself, 'through the spout of a little porcelain jug.'[1]

1 GWO, i, pp. 64–7; GWO, ii, p. 4.

After a few days of rest, Gounod began to rebel against this enforced inactivity. As his boredom increased, he became less and less cooperative. 'I fear', wrote Georgina, 'that he got to look upon his goddess as his nurse and his slave. At first he gently tyrannised over me; little by little he became more exacting.' She was reluctant to let anyone else help, believing that she alone could 'cheer and console' her patient, and that only she knew what was best for him. He required constant attention: nursing and coaxing when he was feeling ill and had no appetite; endless games of cribbage, whist and backgammon when he was feeling better. Harry, who rather enjoyed the role of sick nurse, appeared to give his wife his full support. When the doctor told Gounod that he was too ill to return to Paris, Georgina was certain that the Parisians would say that the composer was pretending to be unwell so that he could stay with his mistress. 'I used then to value above all things my reputation, and I was really frightened', she wrote. But Harry insisted that 'the poor old man' should stay in London, telling his wife and the doctor that he did not care what the 'blackguards' in Paris might say.[2] 'Mercy on us!' was Georgina's comment.

Georgina's duties in the sick room absorbed most of her time and attention. She even burnt Crow's letters, which she had kept for nearly seventeen years, deciding that she wished 'it had never been'.[3] She engaged a cook on a month's trial and took the eldest Rawlings boy, Charlie, into the house to run errands and go out with the carriage. At the end of 1871 she summed up her feelings as usual. The year had been 'brightened by the Messenger of God, my dear blessed poor sick old man'. She hoped that Gounod would 'live to see the triumph and the good of the great work he is helping me to carry out'. She had tried to like Gounod's wife, and could not understand why the *chien de faïence* had taken against her 'in this awful way'. Anna Gounod was evidently a terrible woman: 'She drives him frantic and prevents him being as dignified and holy as I would like to see him at times. I hope I may help to make his name deservedly glorious, and that we may establish together a splendid school of music.' The 'great work' of creating a music academy had, however, a long way to go. Singers who were prepared to pay for lessons were still thin on the ground, and Georgina did not want any pupils who were encumbered with parents. Some, like Mrs Jones, were over-ambitious, whilst others, like Father Rawlings, demanded monetary compensation for their children's lost earnings.[4] Georgina decided instead to take only orphans or beggar children.

2 GWO, i, pp. 66–7.
3 GWJ, 15/12/1871.
4 GWJ, 31/12/1871, 30/1/1872; GW, *Musical Reform*, p. 15.

Visits to the Turkish baths seemed to do Gounod more good than wet sheets, and his health improved gradually. But he was still poorly at the beginning of January, suffering from colic, rheumatism and haemorrhoids in addition to his other woes. The Abbé Boudier and Louisa Brown visited him, but he was convinced that his wife had sent them all to spy on him, to make sure that he really was as ill as he claimed. When Georgina refused to discuss his suspicions, they had a frightful row. It would not be the last. They bickered constantly and their relationship veered continually from one of mutual affection to hostility. Gounod called Georgina 'Mimi', 'my good little mother', 'my dear little girl', and she addressed him as 'tu' rather than the more formal, and proper, 'vous'. He warned her not to use 'tu' when they were in company, as everyone would suspect that he was her lover, but she declared that it had become such a habit that she 'could not have said *vous* to him for the world'.[5] She was almost wilfully naive: it was widely believed, especially in France, that she was Gounod's mistress, and his feelings towards her were certainly not entirely platonic. Nevertheless, she wrote many years later that 'we were so wrapt up in our music, our ideals, I cannot imagine any sexual bearing interfering with those kind of relations'.[6]

At the beginning of February, Gounod was well enough to fulfil an engagement with Wilhelm Kuhe to perform at the Brighton Festival with Georgina. They set off together, with Nelly Craven as a chaperone for Georgina, accompanied by a pet thrush and a canary. Harry joined them a few days later with the pugs. The fresh air and sea bathing seemed to do the composer good and he appeared to be stronger. This was fortunate, because the first rehearsal, of *Gallia* and the *Messe Solennelle* at the Royal Pavilion, was a disaster: the choir 'did not know a single word of their parts', and there were only twenty-nine musicians in the band instead of the expected seventy-six. Gounod was 'beside himself ... a raging lion'. Georgina and Nelly had to take him for a walk afterwards, to calm him down. Julius Benedict, who arrived a few days later for a rehearsal of his oratorio, *St Peter*, did not fare any better. He had just one hour to practise a piece that lasted for four hours. He threatened to throw himself into the sea after the rehearsal.

The first concert went surprisingly well. Georgina, who had drunk several glasses of port wine to calm her nerves, sang Gounod's 'Oh, happy home!' and the *Messe Solennelle*. Charlie and Alfred Rawlings, who sang in the chorus, made their first public appearance. There was plenty of applause for Gounod, though the music publishers had sent two groups of people to

5 GWO, i, p. 67.

6 GWJ, 20/4/1906.

hiss everything of his. Benedict's oratorio, on the following day, was less successful. Georgina thought that he looked 'a hundred years old' after it.

On 13 February Gounod conducted the ballet music from *Faust* at a concert. Two days later he suffered a relapse. Georgina was awoken at half past one in the morning by 'fearful groans, like the cry of a wounded and hunted beast'. She and Nelly ran downstairs to the composer's room and found him sitting up in his bed: 'He did not recognise us. He was shaking his head to and fro, he was looking with a fixed gaze in front of him, and muttered "that for a long time past they had wished to put him in the churchyard"'. Harry telegraphed for Dr McKern, who arrived within a few hours, gave the patient a dose of medicine, ordered a hot bath for his feet, and told Georgina to rub his legs well. Gounod eventually came round, but he felt very sorry for himself, telling Georgina 'I have but a little time to live. I should die happy were you to promise me to become a Catholic'. She duly promised. Gounod then became calmer, though he started howling again during the following night. McKern was sanguine, declaring that Gounod was not insane and that his attacks would be called hysteria if he were a woman. It was only necessary to watch him, make sure that he did not hurt himself, and keep him quiet. The doctor had, he said, been expecting this cerebral attack since the first day he saw his patient.[7]

The show had to go on in spite of Gounod's indisposition. Georgina sang 'The sea hath its pearls' at a concert on the afternoon of 15 February, accompanied by Kuhe. The reception was lukewarm. Gounod was still too ill to take part in the next day's concert, but Georgina went and sang *Gallia*. This time the audience was much more appreciative and called for encores. On the following day, the invalid seemed to be much improved, so they all returned to London, apart from Nelly who stayed behind with some cousins. A few days later, Gounod's 'mad-doctor', Antoine Blanche paid his former patient a flying visit, and he and Georgina had a 'tremendous conversation'.[8] Though Gounod was convinced that Blanche was yet another 'spy from the *chien de faïence*', the doctor seemed to sympathise with him and returned home with a letter from the composer to his wife, declaring that he would never set foot in France again unless she came to fetch him and agreed to stay with him in London for two months.[9]

In mid March Gounod received letters from his librettist and friend Jules Barbier, warning him about the consequences of his relationship with Georgina and making insulting references to her. Gounod was furious and

7 GWO, pp. 71–3; GWJ, 10/2/1872.

8 GWJ, 16,22/2/1872.

9 GWO, i, p. 74.

threatened to challenge Barbier to a duel. Georgina said that she did not blame Barbier, whom she described as 'Madame Gounod's parrot'. The Frenchman clearly believed Anna Gounod's claim that she had been forced to leave England on Georgina's account. This was the cause of yet another furious dispute with Gounod, whose next letter to his wife can only have widened the breach between them. He informed her that 'the state of moral and physical health' into which he had fallen prevented him from returning to Paris: 'The too familiar atmosphere that awaits me there, an atmosphere poisoned by the most odious wickedness, has become too noxious, too deadly, for me to expose to it the little strength remaining to me and the peace of mind which Providence has spared me.'[10] Over the weeks that followed the composer became more and more dependent on his hosts, but also increasingly resentful. Georgina told Harry

> I am sure [he] dreads the very sight of me, the sound of my steps, and cannot help shuddering when he feels that I move my chair, for fear that it should be for the purpose of coming to interrupt him in the middle of a sentence or phrase, by what he calls 'obedience to health'.[11]

'Obedience to health' meant a strictly controlled diet, imposed by Dr McKern and his colleague Wilberforce Smith. Gounod was not allowed to eat pastry, and at every meal Georgina would cut the fat and gristle from his meat and cut up his bread, giving him only the crusts. Gounod was, in short, treated like a child – and not just in matters of health. Georgina 'constituted herself his nurse and impresario, agent, secretary, paymaster, press representative, and even translator'.[12] Convinced that he needed her help in business matters, she got into the habit of opening all his English letters (and some from abroad as well) and replying to them without telling him. Inevitably, this led to further trouble. Gounod accused Georgina of trying to keep him prisoner and making him work 'like a galley-slave'. After one particularly violent row he stormed out of the house on an icy-cold, snowy day clad in a greatcoat and Georgina's sealskin cap. When Harry brought him back and accused him of childish behaviour, the composer responded with 'black fury', telling his host that he was 'a stuck-up jackass who is not fit to black my shoes'. Georgina tried to embrace Gounod, but he shrieked 'Don't touch me! It is *you* who have incited your husband to insult me, to outrage me, to defy me! I will die! and all shall perish with me!' Georgina was terrified, believing that the composer might set the house on fire. He

10 Charles Gounod–Anna Gounod, 18/3/1872.

11 GWO, i, p. 76.

12 George Werrenrath, article in the *New York Sun*, n.d. (1893+).

then rushed 'like a madman' to the cupboard where the orchestral score of *Polyeucte* was kept and seized hold of it, shouting '*Polyeucte* first; *Polyeucte* shall burn!' It was, wrote Georgina 'his custom, at the last contrariety, to burn the manuscript he was composing.' She was determined to preserve the music:

> With strength lent me by the horror of despair, I threw myself on Gounod with all my weight; I knocked him down; I rolled on him; we tussled violently for the possession of the treasure. I tore it from him; I flung it on the sofa; I suddenly picked myself off the floor; I sat upon it and I screamed: 'You shall kill me first, but you shall not burn *Polyeucte*!'

She then burst into tears and cried out 'My old man! My old treasure! Why are you so wicked to me? Don't you see you are killing me? I suffer too much, I can bear it no longer. I do all that is possible to save you useless trouble, useless work. It is all in vain.'[13]

Georgina's account of this episode tells us as much about her own possessiveness and tendency to self-pity as it does about Gounod. She made the composer appear much more of an invalid than he really was in order to control him, treating him as a naughty child. She also intercepted his post and tried to dictate whom he could or could not see. It is hardly surprising that he felt like a prisoner. She did not understand this, still preferring to think of herself as 'a quiet, contented, placid home-bird, happy in being a little mother to everybody: human beings and dear animals.'[14]

Gounod's health improved again and he was able to receive a constant stream of visitors. Many of them were from continental Europe, and the majority were of French origin. By the middle of the nineteenth century the French community in London numbered several thousand, mainly concentrated in Soho and the area north of Oxford Street, between Great Portland Street and Gower Street. Some of these were economic migrants; others were political exiles. From 1870 onwards they were joined by refugees from the Franco-Prussian war and its aftermath. It has been estimated that approximately 3300 Communards fled to Britain with their families after the fall of the Paris Commune in 1871.[15] Most of them settled in London. In the 'French ghetto' there they found French food shops and wine merchants, bars, cafés and restaurants, nightclubs and gambling dens. There were also French barbers and laundries, banks, schools and churches. French newspapers could be bought on the day after publication; a French-language

[13] GWO, i, pp. 76–84.

[14] GWM proof, vii, p. 37.

[15] Caroline Corbeau-Parsons (ed.), *Impressionists in London* (London, 2017), p. 13.

journal was produced locally; and books were available in French libraries. French voices were heard in the streets and a contemporary commentator described the 'social atmosphere' as 'Gallic'.[16]

Most of the people who came to Tavistock House at this time were connected with the music business in some way. Some had taken up permanent residence in London, whilst others, like Gounod, would eventually go back home. Others again were in London on a short-term basis for business or professional reasons, specifically to see Gounod or because the city was a stopping-point on a musical tour. Visitors included the composers, conductors and instrumentalists Charles Abdank, Julius Benedict, Gaston Berardi, Hamilton Clarke, Fred Clay, W.G. (later Sir William) Cusins, Anton de Kontski, Jules de Soria, Auguste Durand, Seymour (Sim) Egerton, Gabriel Fauré, Wilhelm Kuhe, Édouard Lalo, Jules Rivière, Pablo de Sarasate, Auguste van Biene and Louis van Waefelgham; the singers Madame (Juliette) Conneau, Manuel Garcia, Claude Jaquinot, Emilio Naudin, Federico Monari Rocca, Ostava Torriani and Léonce Valdec; the violinist Alfred Viguier; the librettist Jules Barbier; the poet and translator Giuseppe Zaffira; the managers Olivier Halanzier and Maurice Strakosch; and the music publishers Achille Lemoine and Joseph Goddard.

In 1872 Georgina began to organise a series of 'At Homes' on Sunday afternoons. These get-togethers, which included informal concerts, were neither as grand nor as well attended as the parties in the far off days at Little Holland House, but Gounod was nevertheless a significant attraction, and plenty of people wanted to hear him sing and play. The musicians (professional and amateur) were joined by painters and sculptors such as Jean-Baptiste Carpeaux, Alphonse Monchablon, Félix Moscheles, Carlo Pellegrini, Louis-Émile Pinel de Grandchamps, the brothers Félix and Frédéric Régamey, E.M. Ward and Leopold Wiener. There were a few writers and politicians too, most notably the journalist Thomas Gibson Bowles, and the Communard and future diplomat Camille Barrère with his friend, the left-wing journalist Jules Vallès. Other Communards included Gaston da Costa, recently escaped from prison in New Caledonia, and Stefan Polès, a Polish Jew who had bribed his way out of a gaol in Paris and was now looking for work as a theatrical and literary agent. Georgina's old friend Freddy Warre came regularly, but most of her aristocratic acquaintances were conspicuous by their absence, put off by rumours about the scandalous behaviour of the Weldons and their lodger.

~

[16] Anon., *Wonderful London* (London, 1878), p. 149; Jerry White, *London in the Nineteenth Century* (London, 2007), pp. 139–45.

Georgina was at last beginning to attract more singing pupils, but they were a mixed bag. At the end of April 1872 the Rawlings boys, three children of George Tolhurst (a musical acquaintance of Gounod), and Nelly Craven were joined by a young mulatto girl called Nita Gaëtano, who had been recommended by one of Gounod's friends. Nita seemed to be good-natured, and was 'very pretty and ladylike'.[17] She sang beautifully, though 'her voice trembled like a jelly and her pronunciation was absurd'.[18] Georgina took a great fancy to the girl. She agreed to take her on as a pupil and promised to try to get her admitted to the choir that Gounod was trying to form. Nita must, however, have wondered what she was letting herself in for when she received a letter from Georgina, telling her:

> You must know Gounod cares for nothing but my singing (from the first moment he heard me) because it is utterly void of anything like false sentiment and, as regards elocution, everything he wishes.
>
> I would be too delighted to find a young girl to sing to please him, as I am too old to be of any use to him as a prima donna and have not the slightest wish for personal triumph.
>
> I hope you are docile and do not mind being told you must improve and I am sure you may have a splendid career before you!

Nita agreed not to accept any engagements without Georgina's permission, and promised to hand over a third of her earnings above £500 for the support and maintenance of Georgina's other pupils.[19] She moved into Tavistock House, and Harry and Georgina took her to the theatre and to evening parties. At this time, too, Maurice Strakosch brought a young Danish tenor, George Werrenrath, to see Georgina. She agreed to keep him for a month, to see what she could do with him, though 'He sings in his throat, fetches up his voice, and bellows out of tune'. But he seemed to be 'a good beast', and he might do for the role of *Polyeucte* in Gounod's new opera.[20]

It was arranged that Georgina and Gounod should give a number of concerts in Spa. They set off at the end of July, accompanied by Werrenrath, Nita Gaëtano, Georgina's German friend Ottilie Schmidt and the pugs. Harry, who was on duty at the College of Arms, was left behind in London. When they reached Brussels the basket containing the dogs was nowhere to be found. Georgina was distraught, especially as Titania was pregnant. Gounod, who had always been jealous of the dogs, was furious, declaring

17 GWJ, 29/4/1872, 28/8/1872.
18 GWO, ii, p. 38.
19 GW–Nita Gaëtano, 28/4/1872.
20 GWJ, 16,18/5/1872.

that he hoped they were lost for ever. There was, he added, 'nothing more insupportable than a woman who cannot move without dragging after her animals of all kinds.' If the pugs were to darken their doors again, he would take the first train back to London and Georgina and the others would have to fulfil their engagements in Spa without him. It was, perhaps, fortunate that Georgina was not forced to choose between Gounod and her pugs, which eventually turned up safe and sound.

When they arrived in Spa, Georgina, Nita and Werrenrath went to a hotel, whilst Gounod stayed at the Chateau d'Alsa with its owner, Ernest Gambart, a wealthy Belgian-born art dealer who had been based in London since 1840. Georgina quickly decided that Nita was much less amiable than she had thought. The girl grumbled when Georgina insisted on taking the dogs out with her, and 'in fact at *everything* which does not exactly suit her or flatter her ladyship.' The first concert, on 7 August, went 'nicely' and Georgina and Nita were both asked to sing encores. A few days later, Georgina had a long conversation with Gambart who advised her to be on her guard with Gounod. He warned her that it would be impossible for her – or even for 'an angel from heaven' – to satisfy the composer; that he was 'a man of sand'; and that the Weldons would end up losing both time and money. Georgina ignored most of this, dismissing Gambart as 'an excessively crabbed man, autocratic and jealous of the rather tiresome affection Gounod appeared to have for us.' By this time Georgina's own feelings for her 'old man' veered from uncritical adoration to claims that he nearly worried her to death. 'I was convinced,' she later wrote, 'that had I been *his wife* Gounod would not have tormented me as he did.' She still blamed the *chien de faïence* for her husband's ill temper.[21]

In spite of the supposed health-giving properties of the waters at Spa, they were all unwell. Harry, who arrived on 11 August, was plagued by *tic douloureux* or facial neuralgia and Nita was 'weakly.' Gounod came to the hotel every day, but he was 'stormily inclined' and 'practised and snarled by turns.' Nita loathed him, declaring one day that she 'would rather die of starvation than be obliged to live with him and have to listen to the incessant rehearsal of his imaginary poverty.'[22] He flew into a furious temper after the second concert, which was very poorly attended, so Georgina retired to bed and stayed there for two days, during which she 'did nothing but cry.' She recovered in time for the third concert, which was more successful. After a nervous start, she drank a glass of wine and then sang 'Oh, happy home!' and Gounod's new song cycle, *Biondina*. This time the audience was

21 GWO, i, pp. 93–5.

22 GWO, ii, p. 39.

Fig. 14. Georgina Weldon and Charles Gounod in Brussels, 1872. Cabinet card by Eugène Guérin.

much better and the orchestra was 'capital.' There were no more concerts after this and Nita went off by herself to stay with some friends, while the Weldons and Gounod stayed on in Spa with Werrenrath. All was quiet until 13 September, when Gounod announced that he was moving from the Chateau d'Alsa to the Weldons' hotel after 'an awful row.' He was feeling ill again and wanted someone to nurse him. The doctor thought that his brain was 'attacked' and he spent five days in bed.[23]

By the end of the month they were all in Brussels, still without Nita, who seemed to be strangely reluctant to join them. Georgina eventually intercepted one of the girl's letters and discovered that she had made an agreement with the theatre manager George Dolby and was too frightened of Georgina to tell her about it. Nita was, Georgina decided, 'a very bad sly girl.'[24] They left Brussels on 15 October after giving three concerts, and arrived back at Tavistock House two days later. After a week Georgina, who still had a bad cough, took herself off to Brighton alone. She was surprised to find that Nita Gaëtano was due to sing at a recital at the Pavilion given by the pianist and composer Frederic Cowen, a former pupil of Julius Benedict. It is not difficult to discern a certain note of *Schadenfreude* in Georgina's description of the concert:

> [Nita] sang a filthy silly hideous ballad by Cowen, which she was forced to repeat by Cowen himself, who was applauded by five people behind

[23] GWO, i, pp. 96–7; GWJ, 21/8/1872.

[24] GWJ, 28–9/9/1872.

> us. I could not help crying to see her in such a low situation. She sang the air from *Queen of Saba*, without recitatif, infamously: all her high notes were flat and plenty of mistakes. In fact, a hash. She seemed to have no voice.[25]

Back at Tavistock House, Georgina resumed her teaching duties. Alfred and Walter Rawlings reappeared and she decided that their voices had improved, though they had 'lice running about in their heads'. There were others, too, who wanted help of one kind or another. These included Naudin, 'a poor architect from Paris' whose story made Gounod and Georgina cry. He seemed, Georgina thought, 'a nice young man', though he eventually stole her jewellery.[26] Then there was Richard Freemantle, 'a very honest young fellow', whose head had been 'turned with a passion for the stage'.[27] Freemantle, who told Georgina that he wanted to learn to sing properly, seemed to be promising, having a good bass voice, with 'facility'. He appeared to be industrious and devoted to music, and he was anxious to learn. He had, however, only £12. Georgina, who calculated that 'Free', as she called him, could live on £1 a week, agreed to take him on for three months and he moved into the house. 'Now', she reflected, 'I have a poor tenor, a poor bass, and a poor soprano. Never shall get anyone decently off and able to do something for themselves!' Another new pupil was Marion Westmacott, a girl with 'a decided talent'.[28]

Rehearsals for Gounod's choir began again, with Georgina taking the female singers. Only thirty-eight people came to the first session but the numbers gradually picked up. All did not go smoothly, however. At one session Gounod had a tantrum because Werrenrath and the other singers could not read their music well enough, but Georgina ignored him. She was more concerned a few days later when he got angry whilst they were in the carriage, announced that he was going to die, and fainted clean away. On this occasion, he recovered quickly and went off to a fencing lesson later in the same day. But Gounod was soon feeling sorry for himself and 'tantrummy' again. On 5 December he got up with 'the black dog' on his shoulder, ready to pick a fight. When he tried to interfere with Georgina's singing class, she left him to it, confident that he would not be able to manage without her:

25 GWJ, 30/10/1872.
26 GWJ, 8–10/11/1872.
27 GWO, ii, pp. 46–7.
28 GWJ, 9/11/1872, 13/7/1872.

> He had not in reality the least idea of drilling a choir. He is a very excellent conductor of an orchestra and choirs, but to teach them their parts, he had not the least capacity. This he discovered very soon when he found himself at the head of about two dozen ignoramuses without me.

In revenge, Gounod then left the house without saying a word. Convinced that he had gone to drown himself, as he had often threatened to do in the past, Georgina rushed out to two police stations to raise the alarm. Having stayed out long enough to frighten her, the composer eventually came back of his own accord and began 'tormenting' her again. Both stayed in bed, with Gounod sulking and Georgina vomiting and suffering from a headache. And so it went on, with rows and hysterics interspersed with days of apparent peace and harmony. Harry wisely spent much of his time at the College of Arms or his club. When he was at home, however, he was surprisingly supportive. Apart from helping with Gounod when the composer was feeling ill and sorry for himself, he seemed – probably for the first time – to be genuinely enthusiastic about Georgina's plans for a singing school. She thanked God for husband's apparent 'conversion' and looked forward to 'The Peace of God which passeth all understanding'.[29]

Stung by Nita's defection, Georgina now issued a circular setting out her conditions for taking singing pupils:

> 1. To those wishing to know if M. Gounod gives lessons in singing or harmony.
> No, never, upon any condition.
>
> 2. To those wishing to know Mrs Weldon's terms for teaching grown-up pupils or amateurs:
> £600 lodged in the London and Westminster Bank to Mrs Weldon's credit. In the case of a professional, the conditions are that he (or she) must remain for two years regularly training his (or her) voice under Mrs Weldon's superintendence, the £600 being sufficient to keep any young man or woman respectably for two years in London; the balance of that sum to be forfeited by the pupil should the engagement be broken by him (or her). An amateur would not be accepted on any terms except £600 down, and Mrs Weldon hopes she may never have those terms accepted.
>
> 3. To those wishing to ask Mr Gounod's opinion as to their own, or any other person's musical capacity, voice etc.
> Mr Gounod can see no one on this subject.

[29] GWJ, 20/11/1872, 16/12/1872; GWO, pp. 98–9.

> 4. To those wishing to know what Mrs Weldon thinks on the same subject.
> Mrs Weldon knows if anyone chooses to practise conscientiously for two years under her supervision, anyone can make a good deal of his (or her) voice and style. But Mrs Weldon, from experience, is of opinion that it is impossible for a grown-up person to practise patiently for the time specified, and recommends everybody not to try.[30]

To Georgina's surprise, pupils, current and prospective, seemed reluctant to submit to these terms. Even the usually obedient Werrenrath argued with her and refused to sign a contract. 'Stupid old donkey!' was Georgina's comment. 'However, he is quite honest and will write me a letter saying he promises to give the third over £500 a year to my academy.'

Georgina's summary of the year's events at the end of 1872 was surprisingly upbeat in view of the ups and downs of the previous months:

> Heard Big Ben plainly strike the hour, and the most satisfactory year of my life was ended, in spite of the disappointment about Nita. I suppose she hated me because I am good, and because the old man has such a trick of extravagantly praising me to everybody he can get hold [of]. Of course she found him tiresome, and his queer way of everlasting grumbling also. But what was it for her in comparison to what it is for me, poor dear old man. His *chien de faïence*'s evil spirit pervades him and he cannot help himself, but we'll get him all right and happy in time. Everybody is trying to upset our coach at every turn; it requires very steady driving, especially having such a leader as the old man himself, who can't help helping to upset it if he tries to drive it!!! As long as in the end I get my fifty orphans I'll go through anything.[31]

The attempts to upset Gounod and Georgina's coach would continue in the following year.

30 Quoted in Edward Grierson, *Storm Bird* (London, 1959), pp. 94–5.

31 GWJ, 21,31/12/1872.

10
Maestro or Marionette

Georgina was now convinced that the members of the musical establishment were determined to belittle and ignore her because she was 'a lady' and refused to bribe the critics.[1] She was especially vitriolic towards the *Times* critic James Davison, who had been 'particularly prominent' in his 'persecution' of her, refusing to mention her by name in his reviews of concerts in which she had performed.[2] Davison was also against Gounod, she believed, because of a thirty-year feud with Henry Chorley, the music critic of *The Athenaeum*, who had praised Gounod's music when it was first performed in England. By the 1870s, however, Gounod had 'a strong antipathy' to Chorley who, he claimed, had been abusing him and Georgina 'in a shameful manner'. When, in mid September 1871, Gounod finished his *Funeral March of a Marionette*, he and Georgina decided to dedicate it to Chorley, because the critic walked like 'a stuffed red-haired monkey'.[3]

It did not help that Gounod had also fallen out with most of the music publishers in London. He had tried to take legal action against a number of them, accusing them of selling about a hundred compositions to which his name had been falsely affixed. In each instance an out-of-court settlement had been agreed – always, Georgina believed, at the last possible moment 'so as to give the opportunity to solicitors on both sides to run up costs'.[4] Visitors to Tavistock House were left in no doubt as to the composer's opinions. He told them that vampires were not only to be found in 'certain villages in Illyria':

> They come across us in all parts of civilized Europe under the form of music publishers and theatrical managers. They suck the life-blood from the veins of poor inexperienced musicians, swindle them of their finest productions, fill their money bags with the proceeds of the ill-paid manuscripts, and strut about insolently in the plumes of their

1 GW, *History*, p. 14.
2 GWM proof, misc., p. 139.
3 GWO, ii, p. 104; GWJ, 18/12/ 1871.
4 GWM proof, vii, p. 17.

> victims while they throw the poor artist little more than the crumbs from their banquetting table.[5]

The *Funeral March* and two songs, 'Oh, happy home!' and 'Ivy', were offered to the publisher Arthur Chappell, but he refused to buy them. Gounod did, however, receive £50 from Duff and Stewart for the two songs that he had sold to them in 1871. He was also busy writing music for a new choir of 1600 voices, having agreed to conduct a series of choral concerts at the Royal Albert Hall in the spring. On Fred Clay's advice, he decided to have the music printed at his own expense, thus bypassing the professional publishers. He and Georgina both hoped that this would make him 'tremendously rich'.[6] Gounod promised that, once he had made £4000 for his daughter's dowry, he would give Georgina all the royalties on the songs dedicated to her to finance her music school, now given the imposing title of the 'National Training School of Music'. In return, Georgina promised to devote herself to 'singing and pushing Gounod's compositions exclusively'. As it turned out, her estimate of the likely profits from this venture was wildly over-optimistic, for Gounod never appears to have made much more than £600 a year.[7] Only two songs were printed: 'Oh, happy home!' and 'April song', and none of the publishing firms would take them. Nor did they show any interest in the *Funeral March*. Gounod's compositions were, the publishers claimed, 'Not suited to the English taste'.

The printing of the choruses was set in hand, but the work went on very slowly. Georgina was convinced that the Commissioners of the Albert Hall (the promoters of Gounod's concerts) were in league with Novello's and plotted to pay Gounod 'some insignificant sum' for music that they would then sell themselves at a considerable profit.[8] It soon became clear that a professional publisher was an absolute necessity, so Gounod entered into another agreement, this time with Joseph Goddard of St Pancras, to whom he sold the copyright of a number of songs, together with the piano music for the *Funeral March*. Goddard was also to have the copyright of the books of music and choruses for the new Royal Albert Hall Choral Society, for which he was to pay Gounod two-fifths of the marked price.

On 8 April Gounod's choir met at the Royal Albert Hall for their first rehearsal. There were 1200 singers and all seemed to be going well to begin with.[9] Then the arguments began. The composer had firm ideas about the

5 John Urich, 'Gounod's Life and Works in England', *Frankfurter Zeitung* [1876].

6 GWJ, 18/1/1872.

7 GWM proof, vii, p. 32.

8 GWO, ii, pp. 62–3.

9 GWJ, 8/4/1872.

programmes for his concerts and was dismayed to discover that the Commissioners believed that they had some say in the choice of performers. They refused to allow Georgina to sing the National Anthem at the first concert and told Gounod that they wished to introduce other solo singers. Even worse, they omitted Georgina's name from the advertisements for the concert. With Georgina's help, Gounod wrote an abusive letter to the Commissioners, in which he complained about the infringement of his rights as conductor and sole manager of the music to be performed at the concert, and threatened to resign from his position as director of the choir unless he received an apology. 'At the same time', he warned, 'I shall bring an action against you for breach of contract, and claim damages.' Gounod sent a copy of this letter to his friend Mlle Norèle, a member of the Queen's household. He also began to read intemperate letters (composed by Georgina) to the choir during their rehearsals.[10]

The first Albert Hall concert took place on 8 May in the presence of the Queen and other members of the Royal Family. The choir sang well, but the audience showed a distinct lack of enthusiasm – owing, Georgina believed, to the presence of royalty.[11] There were complaints that all the items on the programme, apart from the 'Hallelujah Chorus', had been composed or arranged by Gounod. The composer appears to have decided on this course of action in order to establish his copyright over the pieces played. He also wished to pay back the music publishers, who, he claimed, 'had piratically seized and murderously dealt with' so many of his compositions.[12] The critics were not sympathetic: the *Musical Times* protested that an English choir, in a building under royal patronage, should have been conducted by a 'native professor', of whom there were plenty who were 'qualified by talent and experience for the task'. Gounod had even dared to add some harmonies to the National Anthem 'which by our conservative English ears could scarcely be tolerated'. Another critic found the whole concert 'depressing'.[13] The Albert Hall was half-empty for the second concert and relations between Gounod and the Commissioners continued to deteriorate. At the beginning of June the amateur musician Sim Egerton (whom Georgina thought 'horrid') came to Tavistock House to negotiate with the composer on behalf of the Commissioners. The meeting did not go well and ended with a blazing row, after which Gounod had his visitor thrown out.

10 Charles Gounod–'Her Majesty's Commissioners', 20/4/1872; GWJ, 22/4/1872.
11 GWJ, 8/5/1872.
12 PMG, 13/2/1873, p. 12.
13 *Musical Times*, 1/6/1872, p. 498; *Morning Advertiser*, 9/5/1872, p. 5.

Although the choir continued to support Gounod, the third concert was also poorly attended. By this time it was clear that the series had lost a substantial amount of money for the sponsors, the Royal Choral Society, which had agreed to pay Gounod £400 for four concerts, besides £100 for the rehearsals.[14] After receiving an unpleasant letter from the Commissioners, Gounod and Georgina decided to form their own choir, and a committee was set up with Harry as Honorary Secretary. In the meantime, the disputes continued in the correspondence pages of the *Musical World*, with Georgina taking every opportunity to put forward her side of the argument. At the end of June she and Harry took Gounod to a party at the Gladstones', where the composer had a long talk with the Prince and Princess of Wales. Georgina and Gounod sang together, but the composer was in a furious temper by the end of the evening because the audience had chatted during their performance – a common problem at private parties. He cheered up a few days later, however, when he received the news that Their Royal Highnesses had agreed to give their patronage to his next concert.

In July Gounod resigned from the directorship of the Royal Albert Hall Choral Society. By this time rehearsals of his 'special choir' were being held at Tavistock House. Builders began to knock down the wall between the two drawing rooms on the first floor to create a music room large enough to hold all the singers. Georgina received a letter from a friend who told her that 'all the English music writers' expected Gounod's concerts to be a failure, firstly because he was a foreigner and secondly because he had 'brought a hornet's nest about his ears' by quarrelling with the Albert Hall set.[15] She ignored him.

Gounod's choir gave their first performance at St James's Hall on 15 July: 'The hall looked tidily filled and I was delighted with everything. The choir looked very nice. I was not a bit nervous. The poor old man was very hoarse in "Maid of Athens", but sang without any accent and I was much pleased. He was tremendously applauded.' There was another concert at the Crystal Palace on 27 July, at which the organising committee presented Gounod with a 'beautifully illuminated' testimonial, together with a baton and a sum of money to cover the expenses of the concert at St James's Hall. Georgina sang 'To God, ye choir above' and the 'old man' was, for once, 'happy and well'. Altogether, Georgina thought, it was a most successful day.[16]

14 GWO, ii, p. 19; GWJ, 24/6/1872; GWM proof, vii, p. 27.
15 GW, 'Quarrel', p. 18.
16 GWJ, 15,27/7/1872.

Georgina and Gounod were on the Continent from the end of July to mid October, but the choir rehearsals began again shortly after their return. They were not as well attended as Georgina had hoped. Some singers had, no doubt, been put off by the scandalous stories about the inhabitants of Tavistock House that were circulating by this time. For others, however, such stories were an undoubted attraction: one new choir member, John Urich, had heard 'fabulous rumours' concerning the life of Gounod in England: 'A songstress of dazzling beauty (so it was said) kept him prisoner, and secluded, like a second Tannhäuser, from the world and mankind. She held converse by night with spirits, and kept three dogs, into which animals the spirits of her ancestors had passed.'[17] Georgina thought that the numbers had declined because the subscription was too high: each member of the choir had to pay £2 10s a year, whereas no other musical society asked for more than a guinea – and some charged nothing at all, 'But Gounod (being the *great Gounod*!) considered that one should pay him for the honour of belonging to the "Gounod Choir". He expected to succeed in England in artistic and commercial enterprises of which, I learnt later, in France there could not even have been a question.'[18]

Seventy-five choristers turned up at St James's Hall for the Gounod Choir's first performance of 1873. The women were all dressed alike in a costume specially designed by Georgina, consisting of grey dresses with lace capes, and pink sashes worn 'military fashion'. Georgina thought that Joseph Goddard, who had taken responsibility for the practical arrangements, had 'spread the choir in a most silly manner', trying to make it appear larger than it was. But the hall was well filled and the performers, who included some of Georgina's pupils, were enthusiastically applauded.[19] Some of the reviews were good – the critic for the *Evening Standard* wrote that 'The public was enthusiastic to the highest degree, and evidently enjoyed the evening's entertainment immensely'. *The Era* was, however, dismissive: 'It may be interesting and laudable for a band of enthusiastic amateurs to club together and support a Society with purse as well as voice, but the power to pay for music does not of itself give the necessary qualifications for its artistic rendering.' Another critic found the proceedings 'curious', mainly because most of the music had been composed by Gounod himself. The choir had sung so loudly that the quality of the tone had suffered: the women's voices had been 'especially strained and harsh'. The critic had heard a rumour that a large number of tickets had been given away free, and wrote:

17 Urich, 'Gounod'.
18 GWO, p. 100.
19 GWJ, 8/2/1873.

Fig. 15. The advertisement cart, 1872.

> I grieve to see such a musician as M. Gounod brought to the pass of advertising his own music, by means of a little choir, half trained, to a public who do not care to pay for the privilege of hearing it. Surely so distinguished a man might easily command a nobler fate than this.[20]

Plans for a concert at the newly-built Alexandra Palace came to nothing when the whole building was burnt to the ground a fortnight after its official opening on 24 May. But the concerts at St James's Hall continued. The hall was 'crammed' for one on 8 March and everyone agreed that the choir had improved greatly, but the attendance at most of these concerts fell far short of Georgina's expectations. Certain that this was the result of a conspiracy by the music press, she decided that an extra effort was needed, telling Gounod with what she felt was brutal honesty:

> It is not because you are Gounod that people will come to your concerts, your name is hardly known. A striking colour must be found for the placards; we must have some curiously devised bills with your name carried about the streets. It is not because you have heavenly genius that people will take tickets for the concerts, they buy them of me because I torment them.

20 *Standard*, 10/2/1873, p. 3; *Era*, 16/2/1873, p. 4; *Glasgow Herald*, 15/2/1873, p. 3.

She hit on the idea of sending a cart covered with advertisements round the streets. Such a vehicle was bought for £25 and the words 'Gounod's New Concerts' were painted in large letters on each side. This was described as 'a square wooden affair on wheels, covered with bills in the name of M. Gounod and of his compositions and the dates of his concerts.' The coachman promptly gave notice, but Georgina was able to note in her diary on 26 May that the cart had been out all day.[21]

It is not clear if this made any difference to the size of the audience at the next concert, on 31 May. By this time Georgina was ill again, suffering from 'a fearful influenza.' She was nevertheless determined to sing, and dressed herself in her special choir costume. The choir sang surprisingly well and it all went 'very slick and nice.'[22] The choristers were, however, still complaining about the high subscription rate, and they became increasingly uncooperative. Some refused to sit where they were put for the concerts, and several of the ladies were reluctant to wear their uniform. 'Some wear scarlet ribbons,' Georgina complained, 'some are colour blind and get a blue, instead of a grey dress. Then some are tall and *will* indulge in towers of chignons, false hair and curls.'[23] And there were still too few of them. A notice issued by Gounod (but no doubt composed by Georgina) at this time has a certain air of desperation: 'Those ladies and gentlemen desirous of joining' the choir were asked to contact the Hon. Secretary, and informed that 'there will be no examination as to voice or facility of reading, as Monsieur Gounod considers willingness to learn of more avail than the amount of knowledge choristers generally bring.'[24] If membership of the choir was, as this suggests, open to anyone who applied, it is surprising that they sang as well as they did.

~

On 21 June the long-anticipated court case between Gounod and Henry Littleton of Novello's began. Relations between Gounod and the music publisher had become even more acrimonious during the previous year, with the former claiming that the latter had infringed his copyright. Gounod also took exception to Littleton's attempts to advise him on the suitability of English translations of his songs.[25] At the same time a series of articles and letters written by Gounod and Georgina had appeared in *The Choir*, a weekly journal published by Metzler and Co. It had been agreed that

21 GWO, ii, pp. 12, 48; GWJ, 25/5/1873.
22 GWJ, 31/5/1873.
23 Quoted in Edward Grierson, *Storm Bird* (London, 1959), p. 93.
24 GW, 'Quarrel,' p. 21.
25 Lindholm Collection: draft (by GW) of response to Novello, 21/4/1872.

Gounod should take 250 copies a week, to be distributed amongst his choristers. Inevitably the agreement broke down, but not before the publication of a letter from Gounod in which he claimed that Littleton had 'mulcted me twice of £400'. The problem was the use of the word 'mulcted', which was Georgina's translation of Gounod's original word, *refait* (literally 'done again'). Littleton sued Gounod and asked for damages. The composer's lawyers advised him to retract and apologise, but he (egged on by Georgina, who claimed that Novello's were merely seeking cheap publicity) doggedly refused, insisting that he wanted to go into the witness box to 'tell of the way he was being hounded down, outraged, robbed, libelled and persecuted by all the British trade and press'. He and Georgina were both looking forward to their day in court: 'We glowed with indignation and satisfaction – yes, satisfaction! At last justice would overtake this cowardly crew of miscreants, thanks to the great composer, and punish what Choudens (a great Parisian firm of publishers) called "those English pickpockets."'

On the first day, however, Harry came into Georgina's room early in the morning, 'pale and trembling', with the news that Novello's had retained the fearsome serjeant-at-law William Ballantine as their counsel. 'I'd sooner pay any amount of money than allow you to be cross-examined and insulted by that blackguard', he announced. Georgina, who was looking forward to a good fight, replied, 'radiant as a star, perfectly calm', 'Don't be anxious darling. Neither Ballantine nor any other lawyer would frighten me. Fear nothing.' Harry begged her to think of the scandal that could follow if she and Gounod were to be questioned by Ballantine. When she refused to listen to him, he told her 'I'm off. I'll take the train and go twenty miles out of London. I shall not dare to look at the evening papers. Oh, that Ballantine!' So Harry left London, with 'death in his soul', whilst his wife and Gounod set off in the victoria for the Westminster Sessions House in Broad Sanctuary. Gounod's counsel, Digby Seymour, strongly advised him to apologise and tried to persuade him not to go into the witness box. Gounod refused.

The hearing started badly. Seymour 'did not know one word of the case' and Georgina, who already had a poor opinion of lawyers, observed that this was 'only the usual thing'. Gounod did not make a good impression: he could not understand Ballantine's English, seemed 'deaf and imbecile', and was eventually asked to stand down. Then it was Georgina's turn. Seymour tried to stop her going into the witness box, and again beseeched her to persuade Gounod to apologise. 'He also was terrorised by the terrible Ballantine', wrote Georgina, contemptuously. She was 'burning to avenge Gounod' and insisted on going on. Her own account of what followed cannot be improved on:

Ballantine wriggled like an eel, sniggered, pulled his gown over one shoulder, put his leg on the bench, and said 'Now we are going to hear what this young lady has to say.'

I looked at him, the picture of serenity, and gently murmured: 'I am not a young lady, Serjeant Ballantine.'

Ballantine looked at me – full stop. I do not think he had ever been so surprised in his life. Imagine a wild bull looking at a red rag for the first time!

He then stooped over the desk and whispered something to the solicitor sitting beneath him. The solicitor looked up. He nodded 'Yes.'

I fancy Ballantine's question was, 'Is that impudent hussy Mrs Weldon?'

He gave a sharp little cough.

'You are Mrs *Georgiana* Weldon?

I murmured 'No.'

'You are *not* Mrs *Georgiana* Weldon?'

'No.'

Ballantine again stooped down and inquired of solicitor, who again nodded 'Yes.'

'What do you mean? Your name is not *Georgiana* Weldon?'

'No, I have already told you twice; my name is not *Georgiana* Weldon.'

With a shrug of his shoulders, as if to say, 'I can't help it, they told me her name was Georgiana Weldon,' he stooped again. Solicitor again nodded 'Yes.'

I began to feel a certain pity for their discomfiture, and said: 'Serjeant Ballantine, would you like to know my name?' I said so in the same tone I would have used to a child crying for a toy – 'Do you really want this toy?'

Ballantine, the terrific, naturally found himself obliged to grunt 'Yes.'

'My name is Georg*ina*, not Georg*iana*.'

The judge was beginning to smile, the jury to titter. I was so candid, so calm, so innocent.

Ballantine's chaffy manner had already toned down. He no longer tugged at his gown; his 'side' had collapsed to o [zero]. He turned to his brief, and said respectfully: 'You are the wife of Major Weldon.'

'No!' (very faintly).

'No!!!' thundered Ballantine.

Ballantine, furious, stooped down to his solicitor, who turned round to him insisting that he was right.

'You are not the wife of Major Weldon?'

'No.'

> And again he stooped down for renewed instructions. The solicitor looked puzzled, shrugged his shoulders, as if to say, 'What is to be done?'
>
> Again a feeling of the same kind of pity inspired me, and I amiably asked – oh! so amiably – 'Serjeant Ballantine, would you like to know who I am the wife of?'
>
> What could he reply but 'Yes, madam?'
>
> 'I am the wife of William Henry Weldon, neither Major, Captain, or Lieutenant.'
>
> All in Court were bursting with laughter, except plaintiff's counsel and solicitor. Ballantine was nearly out of his mind with fury.

After this exchange, Ballantine asked Georgina if she knew who had written the 'article' in *The Choir* which contained 'the famous libel.' Georgina replied that she did not.

> He interrupted me rudely, ferociously: '*Letter* or *article*, it's the same thing! Who wrote the letter?'
>
> '*Letters* and *articles* are two distinct things, and you lawyers ought to know how to ask proper and precise questions. *I* wrote the letter!'
>
> 'Thought she did!!!'
>
> 'Never said she didn't!' I retorted.
>
> Everyone was laughing, judge and jury, at seeing the terrible Ballantine meet his match.
>
> At last Ballantine said: 'We do want to hear what Mrs Weldon has to say.'
>
> I turned to the jury: 'Gentlemen, no, they do not want to hear what I have to say. Have you ever heard anything more ridiculous? Neither party knows what they are talking about. Mr Gounod has been most shamefully robbed by these publishers, by all the publishers.'

The jury, Georgina thought, were listening to her 'with delight': 'I was as pleased as Punch. My skirts were being tugged at by counsel and solicitor for the defence; the barristers opposite were shaking their hands or fists at me, either in reprobation or approbation; tears of laughter were running down the judge's face.' The judge, George Denman, told Georgina that it was for him, not her, to make a speech. She was obliged to leave the witness box 'amid a universal din.' Everyone seemed to be shouting at her.[26]

The jury awarded Littleton forty shillings – the lowest damages possible. Afterwards, Georgina was later informed, Ballantine told his cronies at his club that he would have won £500 'had it not been for that d–d woman.'

26 GWL, pp. 5–7; *Morning Post*, 23/6/1873, p. 3.

Her delight was, however, tempered two days later when she discovered that Gounod had to pay Littleton's costs, which came to more than £118. The composer was beside himself with rage. When he and Georgina went to see a friend, Eliza Patterson, to discuss the latest developments, he made a terrible scene, working himself up 'something frightful' and saying 'dreadful things' to Mrs Patterson when she tried to calm him down. He wrote a letter to *The Times*, declaring that he would pay neither damages nor costs, and told everyone that he would rather go to prison.[27] Georgina encouraged him, believing that Littleton would do anything to avoid having Gounod imprisoned because the publicity would draw attention to the 'infamous intrigues of great publishers.' Two weeks later the bailiffs came to Tavistock House to seize goods to the value of the debt, but they had to go away empty-handed, as Gounod claimed that there was nothing in the house that belonged to him. He had already signed a schedule admitting that he owed Georgina £350. Then, on 22 July, 'a little man from Littleton' left an order for Gounod to go to prison.

Gounod was still quite ready to be martyred, but his friend Louisa Brown was horrified at the turn of events. She came to Tavistock House with Mrs Patterson 'in an awful state of mind' and there was a violent scene, during which Mrs Patterson was extremely rude to Georgina. Fortunately for all concerned, the Lord Chief Justice intervened and deferred the committal order, announcing that he did not believe that it would be in Littleton's interest to send Gounod to prison.[28] A month later Georgina was informed that the proceedings had been dropped and Littleton had been paid. She assumed at first that this was simply a ruse to avoid bad publicity, and was furious when she discovered that the money really had been paid – by Gounod's mother-in-law, Hortense Zimmerman. The composer, who had forbidden his wife to pay the publisher, took this surprisingly well at the time, though he was later to accuse Georgina of conspiring with Littleton. He did not, however, give up his campaign against the music publishers.

~

Gounod continued to compose in spite of all these distractions. His years at Tavistock House were a productive period in his life, though few of these compositions have stood the test of time. According to Georgina, he produced sixty-three 'melodies, piano pieces and duets' and twelve choruses; arranged forty-five choruses, psalms and anthems; and also composed a requiem, a mass and an oratorio.[29] In the summer

27 GW, 'Quarrel,' p. 3.
28 GWJ, 14,25/7/1873; Grierson, *Storm Bird*, pp. 103–4.
29 GWO, ii, p. 78.

of 1873 he was, amongst other things, working on the incidental music for Jules Barbier's new drama, *Jeanne d'Arc.* He finished the score on 12 July, and dedicated the work to 'My two dear and courageous friends Henry and Georgina Weldon, in memory of the stake at which public ill-will has condemned them to burn with me, ever since I had the good fortune to have them for friends'.[30] By the end of August Georgina was busy translating the libretto into English. She was also occupied with the composition of a pamphlet entitled 'The Quarrel of the Royal Albert Hall Company with M. Charles Gounod', in which she claimed that she had the spirit of Joan of Arc and would be prepared to go to prison, or die, for her faith. In spite of its title, the pamphlet was mainly concerned with a recital of Georgina and Gounod's grievances against Littleton and the other music publishers, and with Georgina's hopes for her music school. At the same time she wrote a number of letters and articles on the same subjects, which were published in the *Times* and *Cosmopolitan* newspapers.[31]

Gounod was ill again in September after yet another row with Georgina, this time about the dogs, which, he claimed, she loved more than him. For a few hours he was 'completely off his head', not recognising anyone or knowing where he was. After further 'frightful fits' the doctor advised the Weldons to take their friend to the seaside. They all stayed in Margate for three weeks in October, 'dawdling about out of doors', bathing, and playing cards and backgammon. Gounod took time off from his musical compositions to do some painting. This was 'another subject rife with wrangling' between him and Georgina. She complained that 'he had no idea of painting anything but sands'. 'Gifted as he was, with so rich an imagination for music, he seemed destitute of any when he painted'. He did not appreciate Georgina's habit of standing over him while he worked at a picture, suggesting 'improvements'.[32]

They all returned to London at the end of the month. Four days later Georgina set off for Paris, to attend the first performance of *Jeanne d'Arc.* For reasons that are not clear, the composer refused to go to France, but he wanted 'a faithful report of the manner in which the affair went off'. Harry had to stay in London as he was on duty at the College of Arms again, so Georgina travelled alone.[33] She went to the dress rehearsal at the Théatre

30 GWJ, 31/10/1873.

31 GW, 'Quarrel'; GW, *Musical Reform.*

32 GWO, i, pp. 102–3, 119–20. John Urich commented that 'if Gounod had not been a good composer, he would certainly have been a bad painter': Urich, 'Gounod'.

33 GWO, i, p. 121.

de la Gaieté on 6 November, sitting in box 27 with an old friend, Captain Bingham, whom she had met on the boulevards. The *chien de faiënce* and Madame Zimmerman were close by, in box 30, but there is no indication that Georgina spoke to them. The rehearsal lasted from half past seven until after one in the morning. The music, Georgina thought, was 'lovely, quite', and the orchestration was wonderful, but the drama was slow, the brass too loud, and the violins and chorus weak. Harry arrived on the following day and they both went to the first performance, on 8 November. Georgina thought that it all went very well, but not everybody was appreciative. Gounod's old publisher, Choudens, sent a claque to hiss the *Funeral March of a Marionette* and the critics were unenthusiastic, describing Gounod's music as 'a collection of reminiscences'.[34]

The original plan was for Harry to return to London on the following day leaving Georgina in Paris, as Gounod had asked her to see a number of people, including his lawyer. But, as she later wrote, she 'felt an internal presentiment that the old man wanted to see me' and decided that she had better return with her husband. They were met at Charing Cross by Richard Freemantle, who told them that Gounod appeared very strange, that he had not spoken a word to anyone all day long, that he had eaten nothing, and that there seemed to be something 'funny' about him. Georgina jumped into a cab and drove home immediately, leaving Harry to deal with the luggage. As soon as she got home she asked where Gounod was. She found him lying in an armchair in the drawing room:

> He did not look round to see who came in. I went and knelt by him, and kissed his hand. He opened his eyes wide as though he were awaking from a dream, looked at me with an inexpressible look of joy, took my face in his hands, stroked it as if he wanted to feel if it was really me, and said 'Is it really you, Mimi?' Two tears rolled down his cheeks. How happy he was to see me again. Without us he seemed to fade like a flower which thirsts for rain and sunshine. This, at least, was not acting! He loved us, he longed for us, he clung to us.

Gounod seemed to be 'completely restored' by the end of the day, and his health and temper were both 'charming' for several weeks.[35] He 'dragged' Georgina to a concert given by the well-known pianist Hans von Bülow at St James's Hall, but she did not enjoy the outing. Von Bülow played pieces by Hummel, Bach, Sterndale Bennett, Liszt and Beethoven. This was, Georgina thought, 'more stupid music than I ever had to listen before'.

34 GWJ, 6,8/11/1873; James Harding, *Gounod* (London, 1973), p. 179.

35 GWO, i, p. 122.

'He plays magnificently', she conceded, 'but I don't care for anything that has so many notes in it. Such rattling and pretension! *Le joueur*, not *la musique, en avant*.'[36]

~

For some time Georgina and Gounod had been trying to interest Queen Victoria in Gounod's music, hoping that royal patronage would help them to vanquish the music press and hostile critics. At the end of October Gounod had received an encouraging letter from Mlle Norèle, to which he had replied immediately with a mixture of bravado and flattery that must have owed much to Georgina's assistance. He had, he wrote, 'composed, and written myself, the poem of a great sacred trilogy entitled *The Redemption*'. He asked for the Queen's 'gracious patronage' and informed her 'I confidently await Her Majesty's commands for the first execution of *The Redemption* in the Royal Albert Hall.' He had, he wrote, been 'shamefully expulsed, iniquitously turned out of the position of a *Founder Director*' as a result of an 'ill-natured plot', and wished to re-enter the Hall 'with a work worthy of the place and of the name it bears' under the patronage of the Queen herself. Gounod went on to ask Mlle Norèle to let him know unofficially whether the Queen consented to 'second and assure the favourable reception' of his work. He hoped that, by persuading Her Majesty to announce that she wished to hear *The Redemption* in the Albert Hall, he would be able to circumvent the Commissioners, who were refusing to have anything to do with him by this time.[37]

The Queen, who seems to have felt that Gounod had been badly treated in England, appeared to be favourably disposed and the composer was asked to continue negotiations with the royal household. There followed 'a little haggling' about *The Redemption*, perhaps because the words were thought to be too Catholic.[38] It was then suggested that *The Annunciation* would be more suitable, since it was 'much shorter and easier for performance at Windsor'. Subsequently, however, the Queen chose Gounod's songs, 'The worker' and 'Thy will be done'. By 21 November it was, according to Georgina, 'quite settled' that the choir would perform at Windsor and would be conducted by Gounod himself. But then disaster struck. Georgina received a letter from Mlle Norèle telling her that the royal household was 'in a fit', having seen her articles in the *Cosmopolitan*. In a damage limitation exercise Gounod wrote immediately to the

36 GWJ, 19/11/1873.
37 Charles Gounod–Mlle Norèle, 31/11/1873.
38 GWJ, 4/7/1873.

Frenchwoman, denying all responsibility for the articles. They had, he told her, all been written by his friend Mrs Weldon.[39]

Unfortunately for Gounod, 'Mrs Weldon' also decided to write to Mlle Norèle herself, having realised that the publication of her pamphlet on the dispute between Gounod and the Albert Hall was likely to make matters even worse. To begin with she struck a conciliatory note: it would, she wrote, 'be an immense disappointment to me – in fact it would quite break my heart' if the forthcoming pamphlet were to 'deprive our dearly beloved friend of the Queen's gracious patronage'. The pamphlet would be published within the next two or three weeks – but, she added, there was plenty of time for it to be withdrawn.

Edward Grierson describes this letter as 'the only recorded attempt to blackmail Queen Victoria – in the nicest possible way and in terms that command admiration'.[40] By writing it, Georgina hoped that she would be able to persuade the Queen to give her patronage both to Gounod and to the proposed music school. In her usual discursive style, she began by summarising the various grievances and obsessions that were occupying her mind at the time. She had not, she assured the recipient, written the pamphlet for the purpose of doing anyone any injury, but

> for the sole purpose of exposing the intrigues connected with the musical *trade*, and to prove that a distinguished artist like Mr Gounod can be *ruined* through it, and how hard it is for ME, A LADY, born in a brilliant position, with a good and excellent husband like mine who spends all his time and his fortune in doing good, to find it impossible to succeed because English musical *commerce* opposes us.

She and her husband wanted nothing for themselves – he was a member of the Queen's household and had an income of about £2000 a year, and they could no doubt 'live a life of perfect peace and selfishness'. But this was not God's will:

> It is HE who has inspired me to work for the good of my fellow creatures. I never thought of seeking a vocation; I lived, for eight years, very quietly in the country with my husband. It never struck me to try to find something to do. I had no hobby. This turbulent existence is most distasteful to me, and Her Majesty could put an end to it one day.

[39] Charles Gounod–Mlle Norèle, 24/11/1873.

[40] Grierson, *Storm Bird*, p. 114.

Georgina hoped to send 'a little pamphlet' with her letter, explaining her plan of education, and also a letter on the 'National Training School of Music at South Kensington,' which would enable Mlle Norèle and the Queen to understand her aims. She wished, she wrote, to found 'a school of high morality,' and to 'render musical art what it ought to be – an honourable trade.' Although she would be 'deeply grieved to disoblige Her Majesty' – she was, 'by birth and inclination a loyal royalist' – she was determined to publish this pamphlet which would, she thought, 'attract much notice, much interest, towards my system of education.' The pamphlet would be sold for the benefit of her academy. She needed £20,000 to set up her school in a satisfactory manner and she could not hope to get this without publicity.

Having set out her objectives, Georgina went on to tell Mlle Norèle how 'everything may be put straight.' The Queen must get Gounod reinstated in the position at the Albert Hall from which he had been 'so ignominiously expelled.' If Her Majesty would allow Georgina to tell people that her school was 'Under the patronage of Her Gracious Majesty the Queen,' she would be able to get up a subscription, 'and should collect the £20,000 in a very little while.' Whether she went ahead and published her pamphlet depended entirely on the Queen's response to her requests.[41] There is no record of any such response and it seems highly unlikely that Queen Victoria ever saw the letter. Gounod was not restored to his position at the Albert Hall and the Queen showed no interest in the National Training School of Music. Georgina's pamphlet was duly published.[42] She also published her correspondence with Mlle Norèle as part of a special preface to her volumes of recollections, *My Orphanage and Gounod in England.*

The year 1873 ended as it had begun, with squabbles and tantrums. With hindsight it is surprising that Gounod had put up with Georgina's tyrannical ways for so long, but even he was beginning to realise that the 'dear little woman's' advice was often misguided at best, and quite frequently disastrous. Unable, for the time being, to break away, he became even more difficult to live with, and the slightest disagreement could bring on a major row. This time it started with an argument about money. The subject of Gounod's reluctance to contribute more than the bare minimum to the costs of his accommodation at Tavistock House was already a long-standing grievance. He paid Harry £5 a week, but Georgina felt that this was not nearly as much as they spent on him. The composer was, moreover, very generous with the Weldons' hospitality, professing 'the greatest sympathy and pity' for a number of poor people whom his friends had to feed 'day

41 GW–Mlle Norèle, 24/11/1873.

42 GW, 'Quarrel.'

after day and week after week.' He was also 'most curiously avaricious.' 'To hear him speak,' Georgina wrote, 'you would have thought he hadn't a farthing of his own. To get him to buy anything or take money out of his pocket was like swallowing the sea.' He was particularly reluctant to spend money on new clothes, preferring to borrow items from Harry's wardrobe. But Harry's trousers did not fit him, and those that Gounod had brought from France were now worn out and 'disgusting.'

On 19 December the composer finally agreed to go to the tailor, having been given £100 by Baron Alfred de Rothschild. He and Georgina set off in the carriage, but Gounod changed his mind before they reached their destination, repeating excuses that Georgina had heard many times before about his mother's poverty and his reluctance to get into debt. He owed Harry money for his board and lodging, he said, and this meant that he could not afford to buy any new clothes. Georgina exploded. She later claimed that this was 'the first day in my life that I got into a passion.' This is hard to believe, but she was evidently beside herself with rage. She ordered the coachman to return home. Once they were there, she dragged Gounod to the drawing room 'as a mother drags a naughty child,' and told Harry that she would have nothing more to do with the composer unless he wrote and asked for money to be sent to him. If he refused, he must return to France. 'He may do whatever he likes,' she declared. 'I am out of my mind. I shall go mad! I can no longer put up with him!' She then struck the table with her fist and stormed out, slamming the door behind her. After this she shut herself in her room 'rocking myself, screaming in such a state as I had never experienced in my life before!'

Georgina's outburst had the desired effect: Harry soon came to her and reported that she had 'half killed the old man with fright.' Gounod was now crying in despair, making excuses, and prepared to do whatever she required of him. Georgina graciously agreed to see him and he threw his arms around her waist, wept 'as if his heart was breaking' and asked her to forgive him. No money ever came from France, but the new trousers were ordered and Gounod gave Harry £188 to cover his board and some of the other payments that the Weldons had made on his behalf.[43]

43 GWO, ii, pp. 9–14.

11
Loss

In spite of all the evidence to the contrary, Georgina was still convinced at the end of 1873 that everything was working out for the best. She and Harry had tamed the 'old man': he no longer spat all over the place, he took baths, and he changed his clothes regularly. Instead of his brown suit, he had acquired a taste for exotic garments, wearing 'a red flannel blouse and a loose jacket with flowing necktie', which made him look like Garibaldi. Georgina had even made Gounod grow his hair and 'cultivate a saint-like appearance'. He was 'very much changed for the better' and she hoped that he would become 'calmer, happier and gooder, year by year'.[1]

All was quiet until the third week in January, when the composer had another of his 'cerebral attacks' and was 'off his head all day'. In his delirium he recognised nobody and believed that he was in Antoine Blanche's clinic at Passy. He claimed that 'they' wanted to take him and put him in a hole' and only 'Mimi' (Georgina) could save him. The only way that Georgina could persuade him to stay in bed was by lying down on the bedclothes by his side. After her furious outburst a few weeks earlier, Gounod was still somewhat in awe of Georgina and inclined – for the time being – to do as he was told. He seemed to be entirely dependent on her, telling her several times that he saw her 'covered in white light'. He was better in the evening, after Georgina and Harry had given him an 'injection' of warm water and turpentine. On the following day he was weak, but his head was 'right'.[2]

The first concert of the year took place at St James's Hall on 7 February. It did not go entirely according to plan: Gounod made 'an awful mistake' in *Jeanne d'Arc* and the whole performance lasted much too long, not ending until almost eleven. The critic from the *Examiner* wrote that it was 'a fortunate thing' for Gounod that his European reputation did not depend on this concert. It was always 'a dangerous experiment' to fill up the whole evening with the works of one composer and he could not

1 GWJ, 31/12/1873.

2 An 'injection' was an enema; GWJ, 19–20/1/1874.

Fig. 16. Georgina Weldon, Charles Gounod and pupils in the garden at Tavistock House, early 1874. Left to right: Hetty James, Georgina Weldon, Alfred Rawlings, Charles Gounod, Charles Rawlings, Marion Westmacott, Bella Tolhurst, Walter Rawlings.

deny that he had 'experienced the depressing feeling of monotony usual in such cases'.[3] The members of the choir were unhappy too: the singers still complained continually and Georgina was convinced that the music publishers had put in 'grumblers' to spread bad feeling and discontent. To make matters worse, the members of the committee seemed to have an alarming disinclination to do as they were told, and their attempts to raise enough money to put on concerts were largely unsuccessful. Altogether, Gounod was 'bored to death by it all'. He began to make plans for getting rid of the choir.

In mid April Gounod, Harry and Georgina travelled with two pugs to St Leonards, where they were to spend a fortnight. The weather was beautiful; Gounod was still behaving remarkably well and his health was good. During this stay, Gounod worked hard at an instrumental mass that could be

[3] GWJ, 7/2/1874; *Examiner*, 14/2/1874, p. 19.

performed without a choir, and he also composed a shorter work, 'Ilala,' 'an exquisite song,' which was a setting of a poem by Lord Houghton dedicated to David Livingstone. To Georgina's delight he dedicated his new work to:

> Mrs Weldon, whose daily inexhaustible charity I grow to revere more and more, [and who] has consecrated her life to the material guardianship and to the musical instruction of poor children, whom her maternal care seeks to protect by education, trade, and the resources of talent against the trials and the dangers of an artist's life.

To Georgina this was proof that Gounod was genuinely interested in her plans for the future.

When he was not composing, Gounod spent much of his time sketching on the pier. Georgina watched him from the window of the house where they were staying. She saw him 'bathed in light, luminous himself from the brightness of the April sun and the sheen of the illumined sea.' Even Harry seemed to be in good spirits, forgetting the hypochondria and depression that had been plaguing him in recent months. From time to time he would 'stretch himself out on the beach' with the pugs, 'like a big old lizard in the sun,' and Georgina was able to 'contemplate in one glance all the creatures I loved, and of whom I believed myself the darling.' She was convinced – no doubt correctly – that Harry's problems were due in large part to the strain of living with Gounod. The composer was, she thought, usually 'enough to kill a whole colony with despair.' His attempts to cheer Harry up only made him 'ten times worse.' 'When the old man takes me in his arms to comfort me,' he confessed, 'I don't know what I would not do to him; I'd as soon by kissed by a viper as by one of my own sex!'

Three weeks after their return to London at the beginning of May, there was a concert at the Crystal Palace. Though 'weak from cough and asthma,' Georgina sang 'Ilala' twice and it was very well received. The following day was her thirty-seventh birthday.[4] Gounod lavished on her 'all his protestations of affection and gratitude' and gave her two of his father's drawings. A few days after this, Georgina and Gounod with two pugs, Dan and Whiddles, drove out in the Weldons' victoria to Blackheath, where they were to visit Louisa Brown and her husband. It was a glorious day and they were both in good spirits: 'Our hearts beamed full of sun, and the fields beamed full of sun,' wrote Georgina. Just before they reached their destination, however, Whiddles suddenly began to 'scream fearfully.' Georgina was not greatly alarmed – Whiddles had suffered from a similar fit a few months earlier – but Gounod was terrified. He tried to persuade Georgina to put the dog down but she clung to him desperately whilst his cries continued.

4 GWO, i, pp. 133–6; GWJ, 20/4/1874; GWJ, 23–4/5/1874.

A crowd began to gather. The newspapers had recently been full of reports of hydrophobia, and some 'horrid boys' called out 'Mad-dog!' Georgina ignored them: she went to a nearby house to get some water for her pet and then told the coachman 'to drive for his life'. By the time they reached Mr and Mrs Brown's house, Gounod was 'more dead than alive'.[5]

Whiddles was a little better by the evening, but Georgina was afraid that he would have another fit on the way back to Tavistock House. She was even more afraid of Gounod's reaction if this were to happen, so she asked if the composer could stay in Blackheath for few days. At first, Gounod was reluctant to let Georgina go home without him, but he eventually agreed and she promised to send him a portmanteau with some clothes on the following day. When she returned to Blackheath to collect Gounod three days later, he told her that he was 'very much inclined to stay', so she left him there, confident that Mrs Brown would look after him. She was also grateful for the chance to get on with her own work without constant interruptions. During the days that followed Gounod sent Georgina a postcard every day. He complained that she had not been to see him and seemed to be looking forward to coming home.

On the morning of Friday 5 June, after Gounod had been at Blackheath for more than a week, Georgina received a postcard from him, telling her that he was expecting her to collect him on the following day. Just as she was reading this, however, a telegram from Mrs Brown arrived, informing her that the composer was very ill and begging her to come at once. Georgina rushed off to Blackheath immediately and found the Browns 'alarmed, agitated and frightened out of their wits'. One of Gounod's 'cerebral attacks' had come on during the previous day. He had begun by repeating the same words over and over again, and had then begun to 'howl and be violent'. The doctor had been sent for and the patient had improved a little by the time Georgina arrived. But Gounod refused to stay in bed, and the Browns had spent a sleepless night, fearing that he would throw himself out of the window. Mrs Brown had sent a telegram to Gounod's family in France to tell them that the composer was dying. Georgina ran upstairs to Gounod's room: he smiled at her 'vacantly' and rambled on incoherently about papers, money, and his son Jean. He was convinced that he could hear people whispering 'and saying in a low voice that they were going to take him and put him down the black hole'. Georgina lay down on the bed beside him and he became quieter.

Georgina was sure that the attack had been brought on by the Browns, who had 'tormented' Gounod by trying to discuss his business affairs – affairs which, Georgina thought, only she could really understand. She

5 GWO, i, pp. 140–2.

resolved that she would never be separated from the composer again. As she lay there, a vision suddenly appeared before her:

> At that instant I felt an immense net, with great meshes of rays of dazzling light, cover my eyes and my whole body. I felt myself shine in a splendid white light. The rays which proceeded from my body streamed outwards, and went to mix themselves with those of a WHOLE UNIVERSE of light! This light had neither end nor beginning. I seemed to know that what I looked on was IMMORTAL LIGHT. I seemed to understand the INFINITE; my intelligence seemed able to reach it; it seemed as though a thousand years had passed away in the twinkling of an eye.

She saw 'luminous signs which seemed to proceed from JESUS HIMSELF'. They included the injunctions 'Woman, Behold Thy Son', and 'Behold Thy Mother', and told her, amongst other things, that she was destined to have fifty children and nurse the 'old man'. 'It is all I look for', she wrote later, 'I do not look for triumph, or joy, or satisfaction. All I do is for HIM. Perhaps, after me, I shall have pupils who will be remarkable. I shall be dead. It does not signify!' The 'holy vision' faded and Georgina felt 'bowed down under the cold load of a heavy grief, an immense, eternal sorrow which had lasted a thousand years'. In the evening Harry arrived to take over the duty of watching the invalid, and Georgina went home, sad that Gounod still did not appear to recognise her.

On the following day Gaston de Beaucourt, a friend of the Gounod family, arrived from Paris. He announced that he had come to 'take possession' of Gounod, and would allow nobody to enter the composer's room. Georgina could not believe that this included her and set off for Blackheath again in the afternoon. She was informed that Gounod had regained consciousness, but she was not permitted to see him. 'M. Gounod is still very weak', de Beaucourt told her, 'I am afraid the least emotion might bring on the fit again, and as he loves you very much, the sight of you could not fail to cause him strong emotions. I fear the consequences.' Gounod had, he continued, asked de Beaucourt to come and fetch him. Indignant and furious, Georgina refused to believe this and said that she would not leave the house without talking to Gounod. She insisted on waiting to see the doctor, and sat and 'cried silently' whilst de Beaucourt went to sit with the invalid. 'Then', wrote Georgina, 'I got tired of crying silently, I went upstairs into a room next to Gounod's, crying louder'. She hoped that Gounod would hear and ask for her. She sat there for an hour 'crying my eyes out'. Unfortunately for her, however, Gounod had been moved to a different room and he did not know that she was there.

Eventually de Beaucourt relented and allowed Georgina to enter Gounod's room for five minutes. The 'old man' seemed to be 'happy and consoled to see her', but she was dismayed by his appearance: 'Instead of the somewhat stout and robust man I had taken to Mrs Brown's eleven days before, I found a little old man, thin, shrunk; his trousers hung on his shrivelled legs, he was pale, and had a grey and faded look.' Gounod took Georgina in his arms and kissed her 'over and over again', asking her why she had deserted him. She promised that she and Harry would both visit him on the following day. At last, with de Beaucourt 'making grimaces and threatening signs' and pointing at his watch, Georgina was dragged away by Louisa Brown and her daughter. She returned to Tavistock House, 'weeping bitter tears of doubt and anxiety'.

Early on the next day, she had another 'vision'. She saw a group of people, all dressed in the deepest mourning, and herself, wearing a long black dress, a very long cloak, and a veil. She did not seem to walk: 'I appeared rather to glide mechanically'. Behind her was an immense hearse, covered with a funeral pall. 'Something then seemed to draw my eyes to the hearse and signified to me, "*He is there. You will be alone all your life*".' This vision distressed her greatly: 'I no longer had but one idea: "They will take my old man from me, he will die without me! I shall never see him again except in a great hearse!"'[6] At this point she woke up and rushed to Harry, 'sobbing with despair', but he told her that she was 'silly and superstitious'. She was so upset that she did not go to visit Gounod, fearing that she would be unable to control herself. But Harry went to Blackheath and found that Dr Blanche had arrived, having been sent by Gounod's family. Gounod asked after Georgina continually. He told Harry that his friends had suggested that he should set off for Normandy at once, and begged him to join him in France, with Georgina, as soon as possible. Later in the same day, Dr Blanche came to Tavistock House and told the Weldons that he, M. de Beaucourt and Gounod would be going to France on the following day if the latter were well enough. He promised to write or telegraph to let Harry and Georgina know when they would all be leaving, and returned to Blackheath, taking some of Gounod's clothes with him.

After a sleepless night, Georgina got up at three in the morning to write a 'heartrending' letter to Gounod, in which 'I confessed all my wretched, dark suspicions'. She implored Gounod to insist that she should be sent for next time he fell ill. She was not greatly surprised when the hoped-for communication from Dr Blanche failed to arrive. This alarmed even Harry, who had at first been inclined to disregard his wife's fears, and he suggested

6 GWO, i, pp. 144–56.

that they should go at once to Blackheath. They jumped into a hansom cab and set off for Charing Cross station. There, to their (and his) surprise they found Blanche walking up and down the platform. With unusual tact Georgina did not remind him of his promise to contact her. Blanche told Georgina and Harry that he and his fellow travellers were going to start by the 1.25 train, and the three went together to the Browns' house, where they found Gounod lying on the sofa in the drawing room.

The composer appeared to be overjoyed to see Georgina and told her that he would not say good-bye, as they would see each other again soon: 'I cannot bear the idea of being separated from you, my good little father, my good little mother, if you do not swear to me that you will be after me in no time.' Georgina managed to snatch a few minutes alone with the composer, telling the others that he had written a new song for her and she wanted to try it out. Georgina gave Gounod her letter 'bleared and stained with my tears' and made him promise that he would send for her if he became seriously ill, and would die in her arms. Gounod gave her his new song and she sang it, sight-reading, whilst he played the accompaniment. To Georgina the words recalled her vision foreseeing Gounod's death, and she could barely restrain her tears:

> Watchman, what of the night?
> Do the dews of the morning fall?
> Have the Orient skies a border of light
> Like the fringe of a funeral pall?[7]

Her audience, which consisted of Harry, the Browns and the two Frenchmen, were 'transported as usual.' They insisted on her singing another song, and she gave them 'The better land.' After this Gounod said *au revoir* to the Browns, crying and kissing them all over and over again. The Weldons, Gounod, Blanche and de Beaucourt then set off on the journey back to London.

As they waited for the Paris train at Charing Cross, Gounod (who was wearing Harry's best Panama hat) 'cried as if his heart would break.' He held tightly onto Harry and Georgina's hands until the last moment, as Harry promised that Georgina would join him in ten days' time. After the train had left the station, with Gounod gazing through the window as the tears poured down his cheeks, Georgina returned home and, worn out with all the excitement, retired to bed for four hours.[8] Afterwards, when she knew that Gounod was not going to return to her, she

7 The words are from a poem by the Revd Thomas Page, MA.

8 GWJ, 8/6/1874.

wondered if it had all been 'a clever farce, acted to perfection by all the personages of the drama.' 'Or,' she asked herself, 'can it be that it was not until after his return to France that they were able to persuade him?' As she saw it much later, 'It was thus a beautiful drama transformed itself into a frightful nightmare.'[9]

At first, however, Georgina was certain that Gounod would come back very soon. He sent her a telegram as soon as he reached Paris, and it was followed by two 'nice' letters. Then, on 12 June, there came a letter from Paris that, Georgina wrote, 'greatly increased my uneasiness.' 'What shall I do,' she added, 'if, after having sacrificed everything in the world to him, he should fail me?' Georgina sent Dr Blanche a long account of Gounod's 'tempers and *crises cérébrales*' and took to her bed again. After three days with no further letters from Gounod she was 'half dead with anxiety and disappointment,' unable to eat or sleep. She could not believe that the composer did not wish to write to her and convinced herself that he was seriously ill. A 'sweet old letter' was followed by a 'cold' one a few days later. That night, Georgina 'sobbed and howled' herself to sleep. 'I am so miserable!' she wrote, 'If all that has been told me about the old man should come true! Death!' She was also afraid that Gounod was about to make a new agreement with Joseph Goddard, to which she would not be a party.[10]

It was decided that one of Georgina's protégés, the young writer Edmund de la Pole, should be sent to Paris to talk to Gounod. Two days after his departure, Georgina received a 'dreadful' letter from the composer. Other similar letters followed. A translation by Georgina of one of these has survived among her papers. 'My Dear Mimi, My Dear Old Man,' it began, 'I can no longer hide from you the profound and bitter grief which your letters since I have been here have caused me. They have upset all my heart and brought the height to the trouble of my existence.' Gounod assured the Weldons that he believed they meant well, but told them he thought that their efforts on his behalf were devoted to 'an absolutely chimerical end.' Hating rows, he been unable to resist them, but now he felt that:

> To re-enter into this life of anxiety, of submission to the terror of saying the least word, of the sacrifice of my own thoughts so as to feel myself paralysed, is beyond my experience. Since you have desired my peace and my tranquillity, do not dream of re-opening for me an existence which can bring neither you or [*sic*] us peace. All that which

9 GWO, i, pp. 157–64.
10 GWJ, 16–25/6/1874.

> is *admirable* will never destroy your instinct for command, nor my repugnance to this entire annihilation of myself and of my child, the thought of which terrifies me.[11]

Though desperately upset when she read this, Georgina could still not believe that it had all come to an end. 'When all else has failed him,' she wrote, 'he will return to his haven of rest and love.' She sat down and wrote a sixteen-page reply to Gounod's letters, in which she raised no fewer than seventy-two separate points. The letter was sent to de la Pole, who was instructed to read it to Gounod 'word for word, line for line.'

At the end of the letter Georgina wrote that she would be prepared to take the composer back, 'a dissatisfied, miserable, yet more broken-down man than when I first took him in.' But if he did not return, Harry would take her to a place where she would not hear his name, and where she could 'try and live down the infernal scandal this fearful wreck of the three years he has lived with us will cause.' She and Harry had 'wasted three years love, three years anxiety, three years care and watching on what we were told he was – a broken reed.' Whether Gounod actually saw this epistle is unknown, though he did send Georgina a nineteen-page letter of his own.[12] But nothing that he wrote gave her any grounds for optimism and Georgina was left to contemplate the after-effects of his defection. 'Disgrace, ridicule, moral, irretrievable ruin had fallen on me; humiliation, the bitterest disappointment; all my hopes of my musical academy vanished. I did nothing but cry. I cried day and night; always in my sleep the tears silently rolled down my parched cheeks.' 'How it is I keep going, I know not,' she wrote in her diary, 'I can't sleep more than three or four hours. I awake at 3 a.m. and feel quite mad.'

When de la Pole returned from Paris empty-handed, Georgina broke down. That evening, Harry had to carry her upstairs and send for the doctor:[13]

> I was seized for a long time with the idea of burning everything, the house itself – EVERYTHING – sooner than let any one take away from me all that remained to me of what I loved so much. I saw that I was ruined, the scandal Gounod had brought to the affair was moral and pecuniary ruin to me!
>
> I knew I had lost all the friends who might have helped my pupils and me. I had sacrificed them all to Gounod's jealousy and susceptibility, all my old helpers, my old friend, not one remained, not a single

11 Charles Gounod–GW and WHW [July 1874].

12 GWJ, 22/6/1874; GW–Edmund de la Pole, 22/6/1874; GWJ, 2/7/1874.

13 *London Figaro*, 8/1/1879, p. 4; GWJ, 25,29/6/1874.

> one; that, as for HIM, he would die – and to make matters worse, I was firmly convinced that he would die, away from me.
>
> I was done for! cheated! sacrificed! I saw neither compensation nor consolation. No dawn of hope! No love! No friendship! NOTHING LEFT![14]

There was still worse to come. A few days after Georgina wrote her letter, Gounod sent a list of his belongings at Tavistock House to the French ambassador in London, with a request that someone from the embassy should have them packed up and sent to him. In addition to his clothes, books and photographs of his mother and other members of his family, and a collection of drawings done by his father, he asked for all his music manuscripts, apart from a few compositions that he had dedicated to Georgina. In particular, he needed the score of his new opera, *Polyeucte*. In spite of everything, Georgina had been hoping that Gounod would want her and Harry to continue to act as his agents in London, but he would not consider entering into any kind of agreement with them unless they gave him everything that he wanted. When Gounod's London solicitor sent Georgina an 'insulting' letter, demanding that she should hand over all the composer's effects and threatening legal action if she failed to do so, she was furious. She replied that 'rather than give up by force what I never thought of refusing, I would burn the manuscripts.' 'He will not have them, that's all I can say!' she wrote in her journal. Indeed, she rather hoped that Gounod would try to prosecute her and Harry, believing that they would be certain to win. Nothing happened, but the composer had to wait for more than a year before Georgina sent his manuscripts to him.[15]

On 9 July Georgina and Harry set off for the Continent, leaving Marion Westmacott and her mother to look after Tavistock House. A 'very darling' letter from Gounod, which arrived just before their departure, gave Georgina hopes that the composer would agree to see her. 'I hope, I pray', she wrote. 'It cannot have been true. It's like a bad dream.' But Gounod did not come to see them when they reached Paris. Instead, he sent his French lawyer, Albert Delacourtie, with a note claiming that he was ill. Georgina did not believe a word of this and asked her old cook, Victoire, 'to find out how the land lay.' Victoire reported back on the following day: she had not seen Gounod, but his servants confirmed that he was well. 'I had a faint hope till the last, I might see him, that he would come and see poor Mimi – but no! Silence of death', was Georgina's reaction. She suggested a settlement, under which she and Harry would pay Gounod £300 a year in return

14 GWO, i, p. 166.

15 GWJ, 6/7/1874; GWO, ii, p. 97; GWJ, 4/9/1875.

for his English copyrights and the right to publish all his future works in England. But it soon became clear that Gounod and his advisers would not agree to anything until she gave them the score of *Polyeucte* – the opera that Georgina had saved from the fire two years earlier and which had, she claimed, been suggested by, and written for, her.[16]

Declaring that '*Polyeucte* shall be thrown into the sea before it is given up', Georgina left Paris with Harry, 'feeling broken-hearted'. Their destination was the Rigi Kaltbad, where Georgina had stayed with her uncle and his family in 1868. The change of scene had the desired effect: there were new people to talk to and Georgina enjoyed the fresh air and exercise. Arthur Blunt, turned up, and Georgina made friends with 'a queer little man', Dagobert Oppenheim, who presented her with a basket of flowers and two harmonicas, and then 'a lovely plate with a donkey on it'. She began to play the piano and practise her singing again. One evening she sang to the other visitors for several hours and then danced a quadrille with Harry after supper; on another she sang again, to a 'large audience', and Arthur Blunt and Harry 'played all kinds of charades'. It was, she wrote, all 'great fun' – even though there was always 'a stone on my heart'. But she began to plan for the future again, and several of her new friends gave her money for her orphanage. She gave a fund-raising concert with Blunt, which was 'a great success' and made over £30.[17]

Harry returned to England after the concert as September was his month 'in waiting' (on duty) at the College of Arms. Georgina stayed on for another fortnight and then headed for Brussels, where she spent a month seeing old friends, shopping and visiting the zoo with the children of her old drawing master, Charles Ligny. These were all welcome distractions, but the shock waves from Gounod's defection continued to reach her. It had been agreed earlier in the year that his compositions *Jeanne D'Arc* and the *Funeral March of a Marionette*, together with 'Ilala' and one of his masses, should be performed at the Liverpool Music Festival in the autumn, and that Georgina and Gounod should both be there. In spite of everything, Georgina had held on to the hope that they would both be able to fulfil this engagement. At the beginning of August she had written to A.F. Eggers, the chairman of the Festival Committee, and he had replied, confirming that they wanted her to sing 'Ilala' – but also asking if she had heard from Gounod. Clearly, Eggers was beginning to worry. He became even more concerned when Georgina sent him a letter for Gounod, which she asked him to forward. Realising that the composer had no intention of travelling to England, Eggers begged

16 GWJ, 8/7/1874; GWO, ii, p. 97; *The New York World*, 21/1/1894.

17 GWJ, 11/7/1874–14/8/1874.

Georgina to send him the orchestral parts for the music to be played at the Festival, telling her that they wanted her to sing even if Gounod stayed away, and that her name was already on the posters.[18]

Gounod still refused to leave France, claiming that he was seriously ill. Georgina wrote another letter to 'the poor old silly' and blamed his refusal to come to England on his 'demoniacal entourage'. But she did not contact Eggers for more than three weeks. In desperation he wrote to Harry at Tavistock House and then, on 17 September, sent him a 'frantic' telegram, asking him to tell Georgina that the Committee relied on her coming to Liverpool next week. Another desperate telegram from Eggers followed, together with one from Sir Julius Benedict, who had been engaged to conduct Gounod's music at the Festival. Eggers begged Harry to 'insist upon Mrs Weldon returning home, or anyhow upon her assuring us that she will be with us on Tuesday, and with the band parts'. Harry forwarded everything to Georgina in Brussels, and informed Eggers: 'I have done my very best to persuade Mrs Weldon from taking the course she has, for I have opposed it from the commencement. Had I the slightest influence with her in the matter you would long ago have received the scores.'[19]

After another week, Harry could stand it no longer. On 26 September Georgina noted that 'the louse' had sent the scores to Liverpool. She stayed on in Brussels for another ten days, writing in her diary with some satisfaction, 'I am sure the Festival in Liverpool in every way has been a lamentable failure. I'm so glad I did not go.' She was, of course, not prepared to accept any responsibility for the Festival Committee's problems, and even tried to claim that they owed her £84, the fee originally agreed on. Eggers refused to pay on the basis that it was now clear that she was not Gounod's agent, as she had claimed, and warning her that 'as you have completely left us in the lurch and put us to a great deal of expense, you might be made personally liable for it all and have actually to pay us (for damages)!'[20]

Georgina left Brussels for Paris on 8 October. A few days earlier she had bought a pair of slippers and a pipe for Gounod and sent them off to Paris in a parcel. Perhaps she hoped that Gounod would, after all, agree to see her when she followed the parcel to the French capital. If so, she was to be sadly disappointed. Her old friend merely sent her 'a short, cruel little note' shortly after her arrival, and she returned home to London after a week.

18 A.F. Eggers–GW, 20/8/1874.

19 GWJ, 1/9/1874; A.F. Eggers–WHW, 17/9/1874; WHW–A.F. Eggers, 19/9/1874.

20 A.F. Eggers–GW, 17/10/1874.

12
Separation

Gounod had been welcomed back to France in the summer of 1874 as a prodigal son who had at last escaped from the chains of an English enchantress. It had not been long before the tales about him and Georgina, which had been circulating in the French press for several years, had reappeared, newly expanded and embellished. A particularly offensive article by the journalist Albert Wolff had appeared in the Parisian newspaper, *Le Gaulois*, on 24 August. Wolff asked 'Was there ever a more singular history than that of Gounod and the Englishwoman? Since the woman Dalilah, who cut off Gaffer Samson's hair, never was seen anything so curious.' The composer had, he wrote, sacrificed 'first his family; then, step by step, his dignity' to 'the fair-haired one'. He believed he had loved an angel, 'and, in reality, he had sacrificed his best years to a *propriétaire* [lodging-house keeper]'.[1]

Gounod did nothing to contradict these stories, claiming that Georgina was 'violent, passionate and mercenary', and that she had beaten him. He told everyone who would listen that he had been 'the victim of this infamous couple' who had 'fleeced him of everything he possessed'. He had not really been ill whilst he was at Tavistock House, but the Weldons had made him believe that he was in poor health in order to keep him a prisoner and prevent him from returning to his wife and children. Georgina had 'drawn him into her nets by putting on Charity's mask'; her pupils were myths and her school a swindle. The 'children' of the household 'consisted of three little pug dogs who dirtied all over the house'. The Weldons had even plotted to involve him as a co-respondent in their impending divorce proceedings, 'so as to extort an enormous sum as damages out of him'.[2] When news of her daughter's treatment by the foreign press reached Louisa Treherne, she wrote to Harry in a vain attempt to persuade him to restrain his wife, asking

1 *Le Gaulois*, 24/8/1874.
2 GWO, ii, pp. 2, 16, 115, 121; GW, *History*, p. 22.

'Will G. ever stop making herself public?'[3] Making a public spectacle of herself was most definitely not the behaviour of a lady. To the dismay of Harry and the Treherne family, this was only the beginning.

Harry met Georgina at the station when she returned to London in mid October, and for a while life seemed to be returning to normal. Freddy Warre came to dinner looking 'nice and well' and Georgina and Harry went to the theatre together. On 24 October they saw *School for Scandal* at the Prince of Wales Theatre and Georgina had a long talk with her old friend Nelly Watts (Ellen Terry), who now called herself Mrs Godwin.[4] But Harry seemed distant and he was out a great deal. He and Georgina 'wrangled' and she cried. By the end of the month she was exhausted and depressed: she was sleeping very badly and believed that 'the old man' would be the death of her. She could not bear 'the sight of the old trees, the stairs, the empty room, all the same but so different'. She missed having someone to take care of, as Harry 'could never bear to be cuddled or kissed'. The pug Dan Tucker was her only consolation: 'I can't bear to go abroad, and yet I can't stop crying here. Why, oh why, have I been sent such a bitter trial? All by trying to do good.'[5] Georgina did not, however, suspect the real reason for Harry's frequent absences: he now had a mistress. This was Annie Lowe, who had visited Tavistock House at least twice earlier in the year. Harry would maintain a relationship with Annie for forty-five years and she would eventually become his second wife after Georgina's death. The daughter of a barrister, Annie was six years younger than Harry. She had married an army officer, Stanley John Lowe in 1862, and their son, Francis Stanley Lowe (known as Frank), had been born five years later at Kandy in Ceylon, where Captain Lowe had been posted with his regiment.[6] The Lowes had returned to England shortly afterwards. In 1871 Stanley Lowe had sailed for the diamond fields in the Cape of Good Hope, leaving his wife and son behind. They had never heard from him again.

At the end of October, too, Georgina was alarmed by a visit from the Rawlings boys' father. He had, he told her, been 'accosted' by three men who offered to pay him for information about Georgina and Gounod. They wanted proof that Georgina was Gounod's mistress and that she had frightened the composer by her violence. Fortunately for Georgina, Rawlings had refused to co-operate. And there were other worries as well.

3 LFT–WHW, 8/9/1874.

4 Ellen Terry and G.F. Watts had separated within a year of their marriage in 1864, though they did not divorce until 1877. From 1868 to 1875 she lived with the architect, interior designer and essayist Edward William Godwin.

5 GWJ, 30/10/1874.

6 Ceylon is now Sri Lanka.

When Gounod's solicitor asked Georgina for details of all the money that she claimed to have spent on the composer's behalf, her indignation knew no bounds:

> So I was to send in my bill:
> I had been his sick-nurse.
> I had been his secretary.
> I had sold his music.
> I had been the round of the publishers for him.
> I had written all sorts of puffs and advertisements for him.
> I had become his poet.
> I had spent my money.
> I had been agent general for all M. Gounod's affairs.
> I had acted for him in America, in Italy, in Germany, and in France.
> I had sung at all his concerts.
> I had always sung his compositions.
> I had played the devil so that he might appear an angel.
> I had been the rat of the lion.
> I had been the ichneumon among the crocodiles.
> I had been the cat of the monkey.
> I had picked the chestnuts out of the fire; he eat them [*sic*], and threw back the shells into the fire to prevent me profiting by a single crumb that he might accidentally have left.[7]

Nevertheless, she set to work and composed a bill. The final product, which covers sixteen pages of her published memoirs, was no doubt rather more than Gounod and his advisors had bargained for.

Georgina began, innocuously enough, with a few miscellaneous payments:

> Sums spent on engraving several of Gounod's works, £282.
> M. Gounod's Pension for seven months, washing, carriage, wine etc. included, £140.
> Mr Bowen May's (solicitor) account – Metzler, Novello, etc., £110.
> Subscription and entrance fee, Royal Thames Yacht Club, £8.
> English translation (Joan of Arc), Miss Horace Smith, £16.
> Doctors' bills, medicines for two years, £45.

Then she moved on to more important matters: 'The first thing which I consider undoubtedly due *to me* by M. Gounod, is £3000, as compensation

7 GWO, ii, p. 27. An ichneumon is an Egyptian mongoose, well known as a destroyer of crocodiles' eggs. Edward Grierson (p. 140) misquotes this as 'the monkey among the crocodiles'. Unfortunately Brian Thompson took this misquotation as the title of his book about Georgina.

for having prevented me from carrying on a profession by which I was earning money for my Orphanage.' Gounod should, she thought, pay for Nita Gaëtano and Werrenrath's singing lessons, since they had both been introduced to her by the composer's friends. Further expenses, including Gounod's share of the cost of a writing table for Harry; payments made during the visits to Margate and St Leonards; and the cost of a bed for Jean Gounod, took the total to £4181 10s 5d. In addition, the construction of the music room at Tavistock House had cost £400; the expenses of the choir rehearsals came to £84; and the Weldons' bills during their visit to Paris to see *Jeanne D'Arc* had come to £20. With a few other minor payments the grand total amounted to £4891 13s 9d, on top of which Georgina claimed £5000 in damages 'As, to some extent, compensation for the injury done me by the infamous calumnies, lies, and libels, spread about concerning me and M. Gounod and his French friends, and which are FROM BEGINNING TO END unmerited.'[8] The bill was completed on 16 November and sent off to Paris.

~

In the meantime, Georgina pursued her long-held dream of founding an orphanage with her usual determination. London was already Europe's greatest city in extent and population in 1800, with more than 1.1 million people living in the area that would become Greater London. In the century that followed, the population doubled, and then doubled again, as people flooded in looking for work. Many of the city's inhabitants were young and remained very poor. By the 1860s social reformers had begun to recognise that better provision was needed for the tens of thousands of 'neglected and abandoned children' that were, in the words of a modern historian, 'nineteenth-century London's greatest shame.'[9] Some babies were taken in by the Foundling Hospital in Bloomsbury and a few orphanages were established by religious institutions or by individuals, but most children ended up in the workhouse or on the street. Of those who attempted to remedy this desperate situation, many were influenced by their deep Christian faith, most notably Thomas Barnardo, who started his work among destitute children in London's East End in the late 1860s and opened his first home, for boys, in 1870.

Georgina was unusual in that she was motivated neither by religious faith nor, to any great extent, by philanthropic feelings. Her orphanage was to be a social experiment, where she would prove that her own idiosyncratic training programme could produce first-class musicians.[10] At the beginning of November she went to the Foundling Hospital 'to see what I

8 GWO, ii, pp. 2–18.

9 Jerry White, *London in the Nineteenth Century* (London, 2007), pp. 17, 206.

10 GWM, ii, p. 191; GW–AM, 24/7/1889.

could do about getting children.' She was told to go and see a Mrs Main at 35 Great Coram Street, a home for previously respectable women and their illegitimate children. Three days later she 'settled to take three children: a girl eleven, a little boy three and a half, and another three.' Mrs Main gave Georgina £5 for boots and shoes. On the following day the three children were delivered to Tavistock House: a girl called Rosina Strube, and boys called Johnnie and Tommy.[11]

Less than a fortnight after the orphans' arrival, Georgina set off for Paris on the first leg of what she intended to be a 'a three years *tournée* [tour] for the purposes of getting £20,000 wherewith to keep fifty orphans.' The children were left to the care of Marion Westmacott and her mother, who moved into Tavistock House as housekeeper. Georgina left home 'most dreadfully miserable at going away, feeling myself hopeless, thoroughly old and broken-down in spirit.' Her depression was deepened by the news that Gounod had returned to his wife, whom he now described as 'an angel.' Harry, who was on duty at the College of Arms again in December, took her to the station. He was grumpy and told her that her bonnet was crooked. She had offered to delay the start of her journey until January when he would be able to accompany her, but he had seemed 'most anxious to hurry me away from home – *for my good*.'[12]

After a few unsatisfactory days in Paris, Georgina continued her journey, arriving in Florence on the last day of November. She was joined two days later by one of her old governesses, Fräulein Gutmann (Gutie), who was to act as her chaperone and companion. The two women travelled on to Rome, where they were to stay for two months. Georgina renewed her acquaintance with Tom Trollope, whom she and Harry had met in Florence ten years earlier, and was introduced to his 'very nice' second wife, Fanny, the sister of Charles Dickens's mistress Ellen Ternan. Trollope had found an apartment for Georgina and Gutie at 11 Via delle Quattro Fontane, which they decided to take, though it was expensive at 500 francs (£20) a month. Rome was, Georgina thought, 'three times as dear as Florence and not half so nice.' She hired a piano, bought some music, and began to practise her singing again. When Gutie fell ill, Georgina was not at all sympathetic, complaining 'It is a most horrid bore, anybody I have to deal with always is in bad health.'[13]

On New Year's Eve, as usual, Georgina looked back over the year that had begun so happily, but had turned into one of 'perfect wretchedness, the utter demolition of all my hopes, my labor [*sic*], my incessant watching and anxiety

11 GWJ, 2–6/11/1884.

12 GWJ, 1/1/1875, 19/11/1874; GWMSM, p. 65.

13 GW–Marion Westmacott, 27/11/1874; GWJ, 9–14/12/1874.

all thrown away upon a poor old madman.' 'I wish,' she added, I could soon get my £20,000 and go home and be happy and quiet. I do so loathe this life of going about.' So far, however, she had raised only a few pounds. Early in January she moved to a 'charming' apartment at 58 Via Sistina. A few days later she was invited to a party at the Palazzo Buonaparte, where she danced a cotillion with an elderly nobleman, the Marchese di Castel Maurigi. The marchese was attentive and seemed to be enthusiastic about her plans. 'It seems too good to hope for,' she wrote, 'but he seems to think I might get my fifty orphans if I would live in Palermo for three years.' He visited 58 Via Sistina several times after that and encouraged Georgina to believe that she would be able to establish her orphanage in a Sicilian convent. She fell ill with 'nervous rheumatic fever' towards the end of the month, but was well enough to go to the Camera dei Deputati on 25 January to see Garibaldi, one of her heroes, who had entered Rome on the previous day. The whole city was, she wrote, 'wild with excitement.' A fortnight later she met the 'poor dear man' himself at the Villa Severini. Garibaldi was, she declared, 'a wreck, a shade ... such a poor old cripple!' But he was 'a nice old thing, *simpatico*,' and he promised to put in a good word for her convent.

Harry had promised to join Georgina in Rome early in the New Year. Whether he ever intended to do so is unknown, for his mother died suddenly on 17 January. He telegraphed to his wife to tell her that he would have to stay in England. She asked him if he wanted her to return home, but he encouraged her to persevere with her projects. She was tired of Rome by this time and left the city on 9 February, feeling as if she was escaping from prison.[14] She was, however, not yet ready to go back to England. Instead, she travelled to Livorno, where she found lodgings and set to work on the first volume of her book *My Orphanage and Gounod in England*, a justification of her actions during the previous four years.[15] She wrote fast, completing twenty-four pages on the first day. Within a fortnight the book – a total of 350 pages in manuscript – was finished, and she began work on another volume.

Writing left little time for other activities, though she continued to plan her orphanage. The Sicilian project had fallen through when Georgina discovered that she would have to pay for the old marchese's help by spending a fortnight with him at Gaeta on the way to Palermo. She spent some time looking for a suitable building with the encouragement of the city authorities, who appeared to be anxious to help her. Early in March she wrote to tell Marion Westmacott to prepare to travel to Italy with the orphans. Marion's mother soon put a stop to this plan, telling Georgina firmly that

14 GWJ, 31/12/1874–9/2/1875.

15 This volume was published in 1882 as part ii of GWO.

she could not allow her only child to set off for the Continent in sole charge of seven children. Mrs Westmacott's letter ended with the suggestion that Georgina should, in future, select 'children of a higher class only'. '*These* children', she added, 'will never gain you the praise that your great exertions and self sacrifice demand.'[16]

Georgina realised that she would have to think again. She returned to Florence for a week and then set off for Paris, where she went with a friend to a concert of Gounod's music at the Châtelet. She saw the composer there with his wife, son and daughter; if he noticed her he gave no sign of having done so. The main purpose of this visit to Paris seems, however, to have been to consult a number of acquaintances about her book. Georgina had instructed a Parisian attorney, M. Pilastre, to inform Gounod's lawyer that she felt she had been patient for long enough. If her proposals concerning royalties and copyrights were not accepted, she would have no course open to her but to tell the world about the conduct of M. Gounod and his friends. Once her book was published she could not consent to its suppression for less than seventy-five francs (£3) a page – a small recompense, in her eyes, for 'the trouble, the time, and the sorrow which the composition, compilation and printing of the said book have cost me.'[17] She showed her manuscript to several people, including Gounod's friend the composer and critic Oscar Comettant, whom she told in a letter that she would publish the book if Gounod did not apologise to her. She wanted £10,000 in compensation, she added, together with an acknowledgement that Harry was the composer's representative in London. Georgina ended the letter with a threat: 'I know my strength and what is within my power'.

Comettant strongly advised Georgina not to publish the book. So did her mother, who wrote:

> I *suppose* Gounod has compromised himself in his letters to you, and now you threaten to publish! But remember, *whatever* thing he may have said, *You* will be *equally injured* in the world's estimation, as, in publishing, if you were right in your way of acting according to the world's code, the world will say 'She cannot be what she (Mrs Weldon) should be or Gounod would never have dared to write to *her* what was compromising to himself'. Besides, the vengeance would shock people and set them strongly against you, particularly as he is not thought sane. Who will take the trouble – except your enemies, just to pick holes – of wading through 1000 pages? So your truths will be understood in a one-sided manner.

16 S[arah] Westmacott–GW, 15/3/1875.
17 GWO, ii, pp. 106–7.

Julius Benedict joined the chorus of disapproval, telling Georgina that the publication of her book would 'materially increase the number of your enemies and detractors'. He begged her to return to 'old England' and to forget 'Utopias which, though very promising and enticing on paper, are not practicable in this material and matter of fact world'. 'You have now an independent position in life', he continued, and she could make Tavistock House 'a real temple of art for poets, painters and musicians', of which she would be 'the presiding genius'. Life was 'too short to be frittered away in hopeless battles against prejudices and conventional laws'. Georgina was too sensible to sacrifice her present and future happiness 'to an abstract idea of duty, *self-imposed*, and therefore *not* binding'.[18]

But Georgina had no intention of settling down quietly at Tavistock House. She wrote of 'The hell upon earth I consider the life of a lady in society', declaring 'My banner is the white banner of truth and charity, and my shield the light of God'.[19] She proceeded to compose 'a little pamphlet' entitled 'La Destruction de *Polyeucte* de Gounod par Madame Georgina Weldon'. Pilastre told her that she should publish nothing until she had brought an action for libel against Gounod, and advised her to come to an amicable agreement with the composer. For the time being she decided to take no further action.[20] Still half-convinced that everything would be all right if she could only speak to Gounod, Georgina stayed on in Paris, hoping all the while that Harry would join her and take legal action against the composer. He had, after all, threatened several times to horsewhip Gounod 'within an inch of his life'.[21] But Harry refused to leave England, though he did send Georgina a legacy of £100 from his mother. He was, Georgina wrote later, 'sick of all the trouble our philanthropic schemes had brought us, and he wished to dissuade me from working myself to death in a cause which had no chance of success'.[22]

Georgina seemed to be getting nowhere until, in mid May, she received a communication from Gounod's mother or, rather, from her spirit. Spiritualism had been introduced to Europe from America in the early 1850s and had rapidly gained a hold over the public imagination. In London in 1871 Georgina had met the singing teacher and composer Antoinette de Sievers who had told her 'wonderfully' about Spiritualism, but her initial reaction had been sceptical. A séance with Madame de Sievers later in the same year

18 GW–Oscar Commettant, 1/4/1875; LFT–GW, 1/4/1875; Julius Benedict–GW, 25/4/1875.

19 GW, *Musical Reform*, pp. 86–7.

20 GWJ, 10/5/1875; GWO, ii, p. 1.

21 GWMSM, p. 68.

22 GW, *History*, p. 20.

was a little more successful: Georgina thought that the medium, 'an old maid' called Mademoiselle Huet, was 'probably a humbug,' but she wondered how she had made the table 'lift itself right off the ground.'[23] At the Rigi Kaltbad in the summer of 1874 she had attended several séances organised by 'an old Russian gentleman,' Gustave de Veh, and his wife. These were not very successful: nothing happened apart from 'a little table swaying.' But Georgina was sufficiently intrigued to accept an invitation from the de Vehs to a séance at their home in Paris in May 1875. She described the evening's events in some detail in her diary. They started with 'a dark séance,' which Georgina found unconvincing. She was sure that Mlle Rodière (one of the mediums) had cheated. After tea, there was a 'rapping séance' which was 'most remarkable,' and made Georgina cry. Gounod's mother came:

> I asked her if she loved me, if she knew I loved him. The table was lifted right off the ground, came to me and pressed against me. A very heavy table. In fact it was most extraordinary. I asked her if she would send him a message and the table rapped out the following message: 'I desire that Charles should bear witness to your friendship and acknowledge all the proofs of devotion that you have given him. May my memory preserve him from ingratitude. My heart watches over you with happiness.'

Georgina had no doubt that this was all genuine.[24] Five days later, on 24 May, she received a letter from Harry, who had completely forgotten that it was her thirty-eighth birthday. She thought back to the previous year, when Gounod had given her two of his father's drawings. That night she sobbed herself to sleep again. Further séances gave her some comfort, especially when Gounod's mother arrived on cue at a 'curious rapping séance' at the de Vehs and told her that she was 'une pauvre victime de l'amour matrimoniale' [a poor victim of married love]. It was all 'most miraculous' and she hoped desperately that it was not all a trick. At another séance, Victoire Gounod told Georgina that she was very distressed by the behaviour of her son, who was running towards his downfall. 'Our advice will not be listened to,' the spirit continued, 'your great friendship does not touch him.' When Georgina asked if she should send Gounod his mother's message, the answer came back, 'He will not listen to you. Be his friend to the end. My heart blesses you.' At this point in the proceedings the table 'came off the carpet.' Four days later, Georgina paid a visit to the Montparnasse cemetery, where Gounod's parents were buried. She left a wreath of *immortelles* on

[23] GWJ, 13,17/3/1871, 12/8/1871; GWO, ii, p. 132.

[24] GWJ, 9/8/1874, 19/5/1875.

his mother's grave, with the inscription 'Lamentation' on it. That evening Madame Gounod's spirit appeared at another séance and the table 'rose higher than ever, four times.'

On the day after her visit to Montparnasse Georgina left Paris, feeling ill and miserable.[25] She crossed the Channel that night and arrived back in London on the first day of July. She did not, however, go directly to Tavistock House. At long last she had begun to suspect that Harry had not been entirely honest about his reasons for remaining in England. The few letters that she had received from him during her stay on the Continent had been unusually carefully written, and she had concluded that he must have 'found some one whose tender heart he was laying siege to by making the fair one believe he was an ill-treated, much injured husband.' She had been particularly alarmed by one letter, a 'bewildering concoction,' in which Harry complained that he saw his wife only at breakfast, and then against her will. Georgina later claimed that she had contemplated committing suicide when she read this letter, which had 'made me cry bitterly the whole day, so bitterly that I could not write for the constant flow of tears.'[26] So, on reaching London she went first to a private hotel owned by Alfred Nodskou, a Dane who had been a member of the Gounod choir.

All her worst suspicions were confirmed when she was informed that her husband had 'a mistress (very fine)' living in Chelsea. Two days later, Georgina arrived at Tavistock House a little after nine in the morning. When 'My Lord Harry' finally came downstairs, at midday, he did not seem particularly pleased to see 'his dear Wifey':

> As I wished to please him and be pleasant, I had had a complete costume made in Paris in the last fashion, tied back tight as possible. I had done my hair very prettily up in curls all over my head, with a jaunty little bonnet, and thought to myself 'at all events, he shall see he has got a smart wife!' Vain endeavours! Mr Weldon put on a wry face at seeing me in his domain; I do not believe he would have kissed me at all if I had not kissed him; as he did not go into ecstasies at my fashionable appearance, I had to fish for compliments, and asked him if I did not look splendid! 'See,' said I, how tight my dress fits!' 'You must have got on a petticoat,' replied he; 'women who know how to dress wear nothing underneath their dress but tight-fitting wash-leather breeches!' I felt sadly crestfallen, and made up my mind for ever after, it was indeed useless my trying to look fashionable.[27]

25 GWJ, 4,25,29–30/6/1875.
26 GWMSM, pp. 67, 69a.
27 GW, *London Figaro*, 8/1/1879, p. 4.

After this less-than-enthusiastic reception, Georgina retired to bed with a headache and stayed there for the rest of the day. That night she dreamt that Gounod's mother had come to her and told her that she should return Gounod's papers to him. Georgina's insistence on retaining the papers had, said Victoire Gounod, given her son an excuse for refusing to pay the money he owed. Georgina's immediate response was to write to the composer, offering to return his manuscripts to him on condition he gave her the power to manage his affairs in England. Receiving no response, she finally sent the scores of Gounod's operas *Polyeucte* and *Georges Dandin* to him at the beginning of September.[28]

Harry had taken himself off 'bag and baggage' to stay with Freddy Warre on the day after Georgina's unexpected return to Tavistock House.[29] Never again would he and his wife spend a night under the same roof. In later years Georgina was to give several different reasons for this separation, though none of these included any reference to Harry's mistress. She wrote in 1878 that she and Harry loved each other and had never quarrelled, but she felt that she would be 'deservedly calumniated and dishonoured if I lived with a man who had not cared to protect either himself or his wife from the most atrocious slander'. Why, she asked, had Harry not horsewhipped Gounod? A few years later she was to add the claim that Harry had agreed to execute a deed of separation that would enable her to take legal proceedings against the composer for libel and breach of contract.

In her memoirs, published nearly thirty years after these events, Georgina was to write that she had told Harry to leave Tavistock House after discovering that her mother-in-law had possessed an estate worth only £800 a year instead of the £2000 that Harry had talked of when he was courting her. His inheritance was, moreover, burdened with so many legacies that it would take him three or four years to pay them all off. Georgina could, she claimed, not bear to hear the curses that her mother, sister and brothers would pour down on the head of her blackguard of a husband, whom they had named 'Ananias' after a biblical character who had been struck dead for lying. Nor could she bear to send the children 'back to the streets or to the workhouse'. She wished, she told Harry, to 'carry on the work alone, for that I should die were I forced to give in'. So she devised a 'Machiavellian' plan, and told Harry that, in order to prevent her family from finding out

28 GWO, ii, p. 121; GWJ, 2–4/7/1875, 4/9/1875. French sources state that Georgina had used a blue crayon to write her name in large letters on each page of the manuscripts: Yves Bruley, *Charles Gounod* (Paris, 2015), p. 121.

29 GWJ, 5/7/1875.

the truth, he should give her Tavistock House so that she could use it as an orphanage for three years. Then her family would believe that she had been spending her husband's newly-acquired wealth on the children. She also wanted an allowance of £1000 a year. If, after three years, Georgina had not succeeded in getting fifty orphans, she would abandon her enterprise and Harry could come back. By this time the worst of the storm would have passed, and Harry would have paid off all his mother's legacies. They would then, she hoped, be able to 'jog along together as we had for many years – in peace, if not in happiness.'[30]

30 GWM, i, p. 58; GWO, ii, pp. 20–2; SC, *Weldon v. Weldon*, 1884; GW, *Doctors*, p. 6.

13
Orphans

With Harry out of the way, at least for the time being, Georgina could now devote herself to the expansion of her orphanage. There was still a long way to go before she had the fifty children she wanted, but in July 1875 Sarah Palmer, one of the superintendents at 35 Great Coram Street, brought little Katie, 'such a curious quiet little girl', to join Rosie, Tommy and Johnnie. The orphanage continued to grow in the months that followed, though many of the children were less promising than Georgina might have hoped: 'They are all forsaken children without a friend or a relation in the world. Most of them I have taken in undersized, wretched, without a change of rags, with loathsome diseases, with underbred, vicious natures, and often repulsive.'[1] An 'enormous' baby with a bad cold and cough arrived in November. Georgina named him Freddie after her two old friends Fred Clay and Freddy Warre. Three weeks later, he was joined by Janie, a 'pretty fair little spoilt, half-starved wretch. Vulgar in the extreme.' After a few months Janie was given the new name of Beryl.

At the end of 1875 Georgina looked back on the previous twelve months as usual. She had been laid up for several weeks with a sprained ankle, barely able to hobble from one room to another. Harry had come to the house on a few occasions to collect his belongings, but he had never stayed for long. Georgina wondered what he was doing on New Year's Eve, still confidently expecting that he would eventually come back to her:

> I dare say he is with some beastly woman who I suppose he will get heartily sick of and be very glad to come back to his Poomps. What has made him turn so sour? Mrs Weldon number two, no doubt, who I can never help to rivalise [*sic*], with her buckskin or wash-leather breeches. Very unkind of him not to have come to see me since I can't move.[2]

1 GWJ, 22–4/7/1875; GW, *History*, p. 35.

2 GWJ, 25/11/1875, 6,17,31/12/1875.

In the middle of the following April, the Rawlings boys showed Georgina a newspaper article that they thought would interest her. It told the story of one Anacharsis Ménier, who had been imprisoned at the instigation of his brother-in-law, Henri Duprat, having been accused of stealing the latter's two children. The magistrate at Bow Street had ordered that the children should be returned to their father. At this, the children had cried and howled, whilst Madame Ménier had been taken ill, 'mad with despair'. The children's grandmother, who was also in court, had shouted out that Duprat was a 'filthy Communard who killed his wife'. Georgina's eyes filled with 'tears of sympathy and compassion' as she read this sensational account. She recognised the name Anacharsis Ménier – as, indeed, the Rawlingses had done. Introducing himself as 'a journalist of importance', 'founder and former editor-in-chief' of a short-lived journal called *La Liberté Coloniale,* Ménier had written to Gounod in December 1873 in the hope of interesting the composer in a three-act comedy that he had written, and had visited Tavistock House a few times in the early months of the following year. Georgina had not taken to him. He was

> coarse, and dirty, with filthy black fingernails. He had three hairs on either side of his upper lip, a turned-up nose with dirty nostrils which looked like two tunnels at the end of which one expected to see his brain, and two large, colourless eyes which were perpetually hidden behind spectacles. Those teeth that he still had looked like medieval turrets soaked in ink. He had long black hair stiff with dirt, and he was very tall.

Ménier had told Georgina that his wife, like her, adored children, and that they had adopted a little boy. He had left a volume of *La Liberté Coloniale* with Gounod. During Georgina's absence on the Continent in the winter of 1874–5 he had come several times to Tavistock House to ask for the return of the book, but it could not be found. Then, after Georgina's return home in July 1875, the book had been discovered. She had written to Ménier to tell him that he could come and fetch it, but the letter had been returned marked 'gone away without leaving an address'.

After reading the newspaper article, Georgina sent the Rawlings boys to Bow Street to ask for Ménier's address so that she could return his book to him. They came back with the news that the Frenchman and his wife were staying in lodgings very close to the police court. The Méniers came to collect the book later that day and told Georgina what had happened. Ménier's sister, Elma, had married Henri Duprat in 1870 and the couple had had two children, both girls. Elma Duprat had died a fortnight after the birth of her second daughter. Henri Duprat had, for some unspecified reason, been condemned to deportation for life, after which the older girl had lived with her maternal grandmother, and the younger with her uncle, Anacharsis Ménier, and his wife. Quite how or why they had all come to London is unclear, but Duprat had evidently reappeared in France and demanded that his children should be returned to him. After obtaining the court order at Bow Street, he had taken the two little girls to Brussels.

As they told Georgina this sad story, the tears 'poured down Ménier's dirty cheeks', whilst his wife, Angèle, sobbed. They both looked 'very, very poor' and appeared to be deeply upset: Ancharsis had lost a great deal of weight and Angèle looked like a skeleton. She was, Georgina thought, 'nearly out of her mind with despair', though not quite so 'desperate or mad' as she, Georgina, had been when she lost her 'darling old child' [Gounod]. The Méniers assured Georgina that the two little girls would be returned to them immediately in any country apart from Great Britain, after which Georgina asked them why they did not go to Belgium to retrieve the girls. At this, Angèle burst into tears. Convulsed by sobs, she told Georgina that she and her husband had no money left. She had even sold her own wedding ring. Determined to right what she perceived to be a great wrong, Georgina gave Angèle £12 – all the money that she had on her at the time. The three Méniers – Anacharsis, Angèle and the grandmother – left for Brussels almost immediately.

A few days afterwards, Georgina received a letter from Angèle, who told her that there were certain legal formalities that had to be gone through and that she needed more money. Unable to decide what she should do, Georgina resorted to bibliomancy – a practice that she had adopted on previous occasions. She opened her Bible and demanded a sign from Providence. Providence – or rather, as Georgina believed, the spirit of Gounod's mother – directed her finger to a verse in Corinthians: 'Every man according as he purposeth in his heart, so let him give; not grudgingly, or of necessity: for God loveth a cheerful giver'. She sent Angèle £50 at once. Much later, Georgina came to believe that she had been the victim of professional crooks who, she had been told, often used children to entrap 'simpletons, geese, milch-cows'. But at the time she was entirely convinced that the Méniers' plight was genuine and wanted to do everything that she could to help them. She began to think that they might, in return, be able to help her. The domestic arrangements at Tavistock House had always been somewhat haphazard, with maids and housekeepers coming and going with monotonous regularity. Georgina made up her mind to sack all her servants and invite the Méniers to live with her.[3]

3 GWM, i, pp. 39–54; GWJ, 12–14,22/4/1876; GW, *London Figaro*, 29/1/1879, p. 3.

Earlier that year, the composer and former choir member John Urich had come to Georgina with the suggestion that the 'Gounod concerts' should be revived, in spite of the absence of the composer after whom they were named. Now, Georgina sent out circulars inviting the former choristers to a meeting at Tavistock House on 3 April. Very few appeared on that day, but the numbers increased during the next few weeks. In mid May the choir consisted of three men and about twenty women; by the end of the month there were approximately a hundred choristers and they were all busy with rehearsals for their first concert, with Urich as accompanist. He conducted too, though Georgina was not impressed by his efforts. She led the next rehearsal herself, 'got on splendidly' and was 'much applauded'.[4]

The 'Grand Orchestral Concert in Aid of Mrs Weldon's Orphanage' duly took place at St James's Hall on the afternoon of 17 June 1876. In the 'Book of Words', which was sold to members of the audience for one shilling, Georgina proudly announced that she had obtained the 'Royal and Distinguished Patronage' of the Duke and Duchess of Cambridge, the Duke of Teck, and Princess Mary, Duchess of Teck. It was, she claimed, 'perhaps the most important concert of the season', for it brought out new works by 'M. Gounod, the composer of *Faust*', in addition to 'his incidental music to the drama of *Jeanne d'Arc* which had never before been played during the season in London'. There were also new compositions by the conductor and composer Hamilton Clarke, by Georgina's 'youthful pupil' Alfred Rawlings, and by John Urich, whose music, Georgina thought, 'combined the power of Wagner's with the purity of Gounod's music'. Clarke and Urich were the conductors, together with Alfred Cellier.[5]

The performers were a somewhat odd mixture – as, indeed, to modern eyes, was the programme. A chorus of more than three hundred amateur singers, made up of the choir of the Alexandra Palace combined with Georgina's 'Gounod Choir', was joined by a number of professional or semi-professional singers. The orchestra, with more than sixty players, was 'Her Majesty's Band', led by Adolf Pollitzer. The first half opened with an orchestral piece, Gounod's march *Fête de Jupiter* 'arranged expressly for the Gounod Concerts'. This was followed by the first performances of Alfred Rawlings's song 'To the Cuckoo', and 'Fragments from *Nourmahal*' by John Urich, a piece for solo, chorus and orchestra. After this, 'Miss Bertini' sang Rossini's 'Una voce poco fà'. Next came the young Belgian pianist Edgar Tinel who played John Urich's setting of Frederic Clay's dramatic song, 'The sands of Dee'. The baritone Frederick Federici then sang Gounod's 'Oh, that

4 GWJ, 19/2/1876, 22,29/5/1876.

5 GW, *London Figaro*, 15/1/1879, p. 3.

we two were Maying'. Finally the audience heard a Serenade for orchestra by Hamilton Clarke 'composed expressly in aid of Mrs Weldon's Orphanage', and *Amarilla*, a work for solo, chorus and orchestra, with 'an African melody' by John Urich and words by E.J. Maddox.

After this there was an interlude of fifteen minutes, which was taken up by performances by some of Georgina's pupils. Then it was back to the serious music: the last part of the concert began with a performance of Gounod's setting of *On the Sea of Galilee*, 'a Biblical symphony' with a recitative sung by Georgina. It was followed by the *pièce de résistance*, the incidental music from *Jeanne d'Arc*, which involved orchestra and chorus, with Georgina as soloist. In the final scene she was tied to the stake and died as a martyr, accompanied by 'the song of the saints and the chiming of the supernatural bells'.[6] Georgina thought that the afternoon had been 'a very great success', though the hall had been 'disgustingly empty' and the money from ticket sales and donations (a little over £200) did not cover the cost of putting on the concert. She blamed this on a conspiracy between the newspapers, which had failed to display the advertisements prominently enough, and the 'gentlemen of the press', whose aim was 'to prevent me getting on'. The music critics, especially James Davison of *The Times* and Joseph Bennett of the *Daily Telegraph*, were, in Georgina's eyes, responsible for the lack of reviews in the daily newspapers published during the days that followed. A brief notice in the *Musical Times* was, predictably, dismissive. 'We can scarcely imagine', the critic wrote, 'in spite of the attraction of Gounod's *Jeanne d'Arc*, that the appeal [of the programme] to musical people could be largely responded to'.

The longest, and most complimentary, review appeared in the *Spiritualist* newspaper. The editor, who had interviewed Georgina on the day after the concert, wrote that the Hall had been 'well filled by an appreciative audience including several well-known Spiritualists'. The concert had consisted of 'a high-class and appropriate selection, unexceptionably performed'. *Jeanne d'Arc* had 'a decidedly spiritualistic nature', featuring as it did a heroine who was a 'clairaudient medium'. 'It is to be hoped', the reviewer added, 'this unique concert was as useful to the excellent charity of Mrs Weldon as it was interesting to the audience'.[7]

Though this concert had lost money, Georgina was determined to go ahead with another one a month later. The hall was full, largely because she had hit upon the novel tactic of giving the tickets away free and relying

6 Book of Words for Grand Orchestral Concert, 17/6/1876.

7 GW, 'Appeal', pp. 5–6; *Musical Times*, 1/7/1876, pp. 523–4; *Spiritualist*, 23/6/1876, pp. 289–90.

on voluntary donations. A printed address appealing for funds, written by Georgina, was handed out to the members of the audience as they arrived. If there were two and a half thousand people there, she calculated, she should receive at least £150, assuming that everyone gave at least a shilling. Once again, she had badly misjudged her public: the takings came to the 'shabby' sum of £32 3s 9d, an average of little more than threepence a head. With £11 6s 8d from the sale of Books of Words, the total receipts were £43 10s 5d. This sum fell far short of the expenses of putting on the concert, which came to £131 6s 6d. Undaunted, Georgina began to plan further musical events. She was also cheered by the reappearance of Angèle Ménier with the younger of the two Duprat children, a little girl known as Bichette, who was twenty months old. For the next few weeks Angèle and Bichette came to see her almost every day. Angèle was devoted to the child, but Georgina took against her from the start, declaring that she was 'a perfectly spoilt worry', 'a most odious child' and a 'fiendish little beast'. Nevertheless, she asked Angèle and Bichette to come and stay with her at Tavistock House. They moved in on 11 August.

~

Angèle Ménier, who was about eight years younger than Georgina, was a short, plain peroxide blonde. Of peasant stock (Georgina was later to describe her as being 'common and coarse' in appearance), she had left her parents' home in Clermont-Ferrand in the Auvergne for Paris at the age of sixteen. She had been seduced by a married man and had given birth to a stillborn child. Her seducer's mother had subsequently given her a small income and some furniture and she had been able to live fairly comfortably, supplementing her pension by dancing at the Folies Marigny, where she was known as Mademoiselle Lucienne, and by prostitution. She had met 'the great Anacharsis' on a street corner and he had lived off her earnings for six or seven years before marrying her. Georgina did not find most of this out until much later. When they first met, she was impressed by the fact that the Frenchwoman was clean and neat. Angèle had, moreover, endeared herself to Georgina during her absence by writing to tell her how much she admired her 'beautiful and generous enterprise'.[8]

Angèle soon made herself indispensable. She was a skilled needlewoman and a good cook, and she took over much of the day-to-day running of the household, going to market and giving orders to the servants. She kept Georgina company and gave her the emotional support that she so desperately needed. Before long, the two women were sharing a room (and perhaps

[8] GWM, iii, pp. 12–14; GW–AM, 8/3/1878.

Fig. 17. Children in the garden at Tavistock House, 1876, by Lennox Browne. Left to right: Johnnie, Sapho, Beryl, Tommy, Bichette.

a bed). By the end of September they were calling each other 'Minette'. Did Georgina realise that *faire Minette* was a slang term for performing oral sex? As a former Parisian prostitute, Angèle certainly did. Angèle began to wear Georgina's clothes; she accompanied Georgina on excursions to the theatre and social visits and appeared to share her interest in Spiritualism. When, in October, both women went to a 'spiritualist soirée', Angèle dressed herself up in Georgina's black velvet and jet and 'looked very nice and chic'.[9] Angèle even allowed Georgina to cut her hair short. The relationship between Georgina and Angèle Ménier, which to last on and off for thirteen years, was, however, a stormy one from the beginning. Angèle was moody and capricious and a hypochondriac, inclined – as was Georgina herself – to take to her bed and sulk if something displeased her. She was greedy, and it was not long before she began to take advantage of Georgina's reliance on her.

[9] GWJ, 4/10/1876.

Anacharsis Ménier returned from the Continent in February 1877. He stayed at Tavistock House for a month, during which he was mainly preoccupied with an unsuccessful attempt to take out a patent for 'self-steering and self-navigating' hot-air balloons, which were to be used for military purposes. Angèle fell ill after he left and Georgina, who had been unsympathetic at first, felt sorry for her. At the beginning of April the two women signed an agreement, under which Angèle was to live at Tavistock House permanently 'for the purpose of assisting me [Georgina] in clothing, dressing, nursing, and generally looking after the orphans I have adopted.' In return, Georgina promised to 'bring up Bichette and give her the same advantages as to my other children.' If Mr Weldon returned to Tavistock House, Georgina would give Angèle six months' notice; £1000 'as compensation for salary due'; and an annuity of £50 for a period of fifteen years.[10]

With Angèle to help her, Georgina felt able to take on five more orphans. All of them were given the names of her old admirers, or characters in Gounod's operas. First there was 'poor little' Dagobert, two years old, who arrived in August 1876. Georgina was horrified when she saw him. 'He is hideous,' she wrote, 'and his legs are curly.' Dagobert's legs were so bad that she had to take him to be fitted for special boots and irons. Also 'hideous' was Merthyr who was ten months old when he was brought to Tavistock House in mid October. He 'bellowed and roared,' but he had 'a splendid body' and was 'very tall.' Then, just before Christmas, a 'wee little baby girl' arrived. Georgina decided to call her Mireille. The last two orphans, both of whom came in May 1877, were Sapho (later known as Baucis), aged two, and Pauline, who was said to be six, though Georgina thought she must be older.

Problems with the servants continued. 'It is very evident that it is impossible to get good servants,' Georgina wrote, 'All they think of is eating and getting dressed by four o'clock in the afternoon, going out as often and staying out as late as possible.'[11] She later claimed that she had always tried to employ 'middle-aged, respectable, experienced women,' but many of them appear to have been young and most were unsatisfactory. A few, Georgina later admitted, were 'extraordinarily cruel.'[12] Some fell ill and others fell out with Georgina. She boxed one girl's ears and sacked her, declaring that she was 'a slut.' Then there was Mrs Shee, who could not cook, and Ellen White, a poor woman who came to the door one day with a recommendation from

10 *Times*, 1/6/1888.

11 GW–W.H. Harrison, editor of *Spiritualist* [summer, 1876].

12 GWM proof, vii, p. 35; GW–AM, 3/3/1878.

a local clergyman, the Reverend John Hunt, setting forth 'her qualities of honesty, sobriety, industry and cleverness'. Georgina engaged her as a nurse in spite of her 'wretched appearance', but the other servants told her that Mrs White was 'a female of the lowest and loosest description', and also 'a drunkard and a brawler well known in my neighbourhood'. Her husband was in gaol and she was probably Hunt's mistress. Georgina tried to prosecute the clergyman for giving a false reference, but eventually had to give up, defeated by the convolutions of the legal system. 'What a beast nearly all servants are!' she declared at the end of 1876.'[13]

Most of the people who knew Georgina were impressed by her devotion to the children. In an article published in the *Frankfurter Zeitung*, John Urich wrote:

> Whoever should enter Tavistock House will find a merry troop of children thronging round a lady simply dressed in black, with whom they sing songs. The little ones flock shyly to their protectress when any stranger enters, so afraid are they lest any harm should happen to 'Grannie'. They are orphans who have been abandoned in the open streets to the pity of the passers-by. A noble, benevolent heart has taken them to herself and cares for them; may she find consolation in these little ones for all the insults which have been heaped on her![14]

But one observer later recalled the building's 'weird and dreary aspect'. Broken windows remained unmended, and it was rumoured that the children slept in unfurnished rooms, on mattresses on the bare floor. Georgina prided herself on her economical housekeeping 'to which the poor little wizened faces of the orphans bore ample testimony' – though she herself lived comfortably and had plenty to eat.[15] Visitors to Tavistock House at this time certainly found a somewhat ramshackle household. The orphans all ran around barefoot after one evening when Tommy was allowed to take his shoes and socks off 'as a great treat' and the others followed suit. 'We find it an immense economy, a wonderful saving of time, and very conducive to health' wrote Georgina, who recommended that 'children in all classes should not, as a rule, wear any kind of shoe or boot till they are ten years old'. The orphans could be noisy too: 'I often allow all the children to amuse themselves by out-screaming each other', wrote Georgina. 'No cage of macaws ever was so noisy! They seem to find some ecstatic sensation of pleasure in their screeches and shrieks.'

[13] GWJ, 5–11/9/1876; GW, 'Death-Blow', pp. 2–8; GWJ, 23/12/1876.

[14] John Urich, 'Gounod's Life and Works in England', *Frankfurter Zeitung* [1876].

[15] *Birmingham Daily Post*, 9/7/1880, p. 7.

They were left to their own devices for much of the time, with the older children helping to supervise and teach the younger ones.[16]

Georgina was later to claim that her happiest hours had been spent with the orphans, but she could be a strict disciplinarian. The children were tied to their chairs if they misbehaved during their lessons, and whipped if they were naughty. Georgina tried to love all of them equally, declaring that 'children, however stupid they are, are preferable to grown-up persons', but she certainly had favourites. She never liked Rosie, the oldest girl, believing her to be 'sly and clever' and 'an aggravating, vulgar chatterbox, but so sharp.' Rosie was, she thought, a bad influence on the other children and a thief. Johnnie, who wet the bed, had 'every moral defect under the sun.' Little Katie was 'wonderfully clever' – an infant prodigy who could sing and recite beautifully – though she could also be greedy and obstinate. Babies, being more adaptable, were easier to deal with than the older children: Georgina took to Mireille at once, declaring that she was 'a dear little midge.'

The health of the children was a constant worry. Most of them were small and malnourished when they arrived, and they all caught the usual coughs and colds. The medicines that they were given sometimes did more harm than good. 'Beryl very sick all day', Georgina wrote, 'Katie sick, Johnnie sick, Merthyr sick, all from taking the new cough mixture. I got frightened about Beryl. I put them all on wet bandages, gave her ice-cold milk, and the sickness stopped. She brought up blood.' Beryl recovered, but Georgina could do little to help the baby, Freddie, who never thrived. Six months after his arrival he seemed 'very queer'; he had a fit and his hands and feet swelled up. By the beginning of the following year he was seriously ill; a lump appeared on his head and it was obvious that he was dying. The end came in January 1877, after 'a wretched struggle for two days and nights.' The doctor decided that the baby had died of 'an abscess on the brain.' On 1 February Georgina, Angèle, one of the maids and all the children took Freddie in his coffin to Highgate Cemetery where he was buried. To Georgina this was 'a disgusting performance' and the clergyman and clerk who conducted the burial service were 'hateful.'

Georgina freely admitted that her motives in founding her orphanage were not entirely altruistic, telling one interviewer '"Instincts of maternity" had nothing to do with my school. It was the pursuit of Art.'[17] She wanted to put her educational theories to the test and saw the children as raw material, which could be moulded to produce polished performers who could compete with anyone who had received a more orthodox training.

16 GWO, p. 29; GW–W.H. Harrison [summer 1876].

17 MS comments by GW on article in *Truth*, 17/2/1881.

Determined to give the children a sound musical education, she took them to musical performances on a regular basis, and they all turned out for concerts of Gounod's music. At the 'first Gounod night', a promenade concert in August 1876, the orphans, all with bare feet and dressed in the colours of the Gounod choir, 'made quite a sensation'.[18]

A vital component of Georgina's system was performance, as she believed that musicians would be less nervous if they became used to appearing in public from an early age. Thus it was that she began a series of concerts, held at eight o'clock on Monday evenings in the Langham Hall. There were forty-four of these 'Sociable Evenings' altogether, the first being in November 1876 and the last in September 1877. The performers always included Georgina and her choir, with the orphans and the Rawlings boys, together with an ever-changing cast of adult soloists. Sometimes Georgina made a speech and there were usually prose pieces as well as musical items. A regular star was little Katie reciting all forty-four lines of Georgina's allegorical poem 'The Spider of the Period', which tells how 'a poor little credulous fly' is deceived (and eaten) by a spider, who 'talks like a saint, though he sins on the sly'.[19] On one evening Georgina persuaded George Grossmith to take part. He was 'too amusing' and she 'nearly died of laughter'. Less successful were 'Poor Mrs Vere', who was 'a perfect fiasco'; and Madame Augusta Roche, whose singing was 'very vulgar'. Sometimes it was the orphans who let Georgina down: on one memorable occasion poor Beryl 'piddled on the platform before everybody'. Beryl and most of the other children were whipped 'for misbehaviour' on the following day. The choir, too, was a disappointment: some of the former members refused to come after hearing the rumours about Georgina and Gounod, and fewer and fewer came to the regular Saturday rehearsals. 'Not one chorist of any shape or kind' came to the final rehearsal, at the end of August 1877.[20]

The concerts may have given the children useful experience, but they were a disaster from the financial point of view. On most evenings the hall was almost empty: in spite of the best efforts of Angèle and the orphans with their collecting boxes, the takings were rarely more than £2 or £3 – barely enough to cover the two guineas that Georgina paid to hire the hall. As usual, she blamed the newspapers and the music critics. She attempted to circumvent them by buying 'an advert carriage': an old dark brown omnibus to which were attached blackboards giving details of the orphanage and the Langham Hall concerts. In addition to conveying the performers to and from the concerts,

18 GWJ, 1875–7, *passim*.

19 Published in W.H. Harrison, *Rifts in the Veil* (London, 1878).

20 GWJ, 1876–7, *passim*.

this vehicle often carried the children and maids when they were sent out to distribute tickets and programmes in the streets of central London. Such public advertisements were too much for Georgina's family, especially as she also used the bus when she paid visits. One day in January 1877 she took the children to call on her mother at 10 Stratford Place, but found the house empty. Shortly afterwards she received a letter from her brother Dal, whom she had rarely seen since her marriage. 'Dear Georgina,' he wrote, 'The Mother is out of Town. I am not. I shall be obliged by your keeping your insane-looking van away from here.' Georgina's reaction was characteristically defiant. 'Dal frantic about my bus,' she noted in her diary, adding 'What fun!' On her return to London, Louisa Treherne begged Georgina to take a cab (for which Louisa offered to pay) if she came to Stratford Place again – or, if she must use the bus, to make sure she called at the back door. The advertisements did not, however, increase the size of the audience at Georgina's concerts.[21]

The Rawlings boys, who had spent much of their time at Tavistock House for the past six years, still took part in Georgina's concerts. They were usually 'hard working and industrious,' but she was at a loss to know what to do with them. She liked Alfred best, believing him to be 'of very superior stuff' to his elder brother, Charles. Alfred 'sang remarkably, composed wonderfully, and was an excellent deputy teacher.' Georgina could trust him to conduct her classes 'as well as I could myself.' Early in 1876, at the age of sixteen, he fell ill. The doctors told her that he was tuberculous and should be out of doors as much as possible, rest, get up late and go to bed early. He should also 'be fed up, drink good stout and be kept warm.' Alfred recovered, but the attention and cosseting seem to have gone to his head and he became increasingly uncooperative. It is clear that he and his brothers were jealous of the orphans. One of them even went so far as to tell Georgina that 'the best thing to do with me and my beastly orphanage would be to drop a lighted match into the paper-box and burn down the whole house' with Georgina and all the children in it.[22] She decided that Alfred had 'a low, vulgar disposition with nasty mistaken feelings' and wished she had 'never had to do with anything but orphans.' A month later she was angry with Alfred for smoking, commenting 'What dreadful things these common boys are.'[23] Alfred was eventually thrown out: having refused to go out and buy potatoes for the cook, he was insolent to Georgina when she reprimanded him.[24]

21 GWJ, 29/1/1877, 16/3/1877, 9/4/1877; DT–GW, 29/1/1877; GWMSM, p. 86.
22 GW–Anacharsis Ménier, 14/10/1877.
23 GWJ, 9/4/1876, 12/5/1876.
24 GWMSM, pp. 87–8.

Georgina declared that the Rawlings family were all 'stuck up, insolent thieves.' But she still continued to help them. She paid for the boys to learn to play the hand bells, and gave them her old piano. With Angèle she went to see the 'Silver Chime Carilloneurs' in action at the Langham Hall. 'Rather "dog in front" at present,' was her comment. Nevertheless, she went to the Crescent Foundry in Cripplegate a few weeks later and ordered a peal of bells for them.[25] Early in the following year Georgina and the Rawlings family signed an agreement, under which the boys were to call themselves 'Mrs Weldon's Orphanage Hand Bell Ringers.' They rang their bells at her concerts and were, according to Georgina, a great success. She tried to get engagements for them, but it was an uphill task to begin with. In the end, the boys were taken on by the Adelphi Theatre and then by the Aquarium. Before long, they changed their name to 'The Orphanage Hand Bell Ringers,' then to 'The Rawlings Family.'

~

Though most of Georgina's time was occupied with fundraising and teaching the children, she also renewed her interest in Spiritualism and wrote a series of letters on 'The Education of the Children of Spiritualists,' which were published in *The Spiritualist* during the summer of 1876. In these she included some surprisingly radical ideas:

> I consider that the education of the higher classes has to be reformed before any efficient good can be wrought among the lower classes, because till the lower classes can conscientiously look up to the higher ones as their superiors in intellect and righteous behaviour, it cannot be expected that they should respect, obey or devote themselves to them.

She also proposed that the children of rich and poor should be 'brought up together in class and on the same principles' until they were ten years old. Having informed her readers that she had 'by nature a remarkably independent character, one singularly indifferent to praise or blame,' she then went on to criticise contemporary ideas on the relationship between husband and wife, expressing her growing disdain for the male of the species:

> All married women, or housewives, have their time fully taken up by their daily duties. How a married woman finds time to 'go out' and 'amuse' herself is more than I can understand, if only to 'please her husband' (and duty to a husband – a nasty man, most likely – is the first duty of a married woman). So all people say, and there are

[25] GWJ, 7/9/1876–31/12/1876.

> undeniable texts in the Bible which foster this idea of a woman's duty. If the husbands were followers of the Gospel, if men nowadays lived as Christ commanded, I should not speak of them as 'nasty men', nor would I exhibit evident annoyance at the notion that a wife's first duty is to her husband. It cannot be expected that a superior woman, fond of her home, should, for the sake of amusing her husband, leave it.[26]

It was probably curiosity about the writer of these letters that brought a significant number of Spiritualists to Georgina's 'Sociable Evenings'.

In the autumn of 1876 Georgina became involved in the campaign to support the controversial American slate-writing medium 'Dr' Henry Slade, who had come to London a few months earlier. Slade was prosecuted for obtaining money under false pretences, having been exposed as a 'gross scoundrel and imposter' by the eminent zoologist Professor Ray Lankester. The case came up for trial at the Bow Street Police Court on 1 October and lasted until the end of the month. Georgina, who had visited Slade before the trial began, was quite convinced that he really was psychic and that the 'spirit messages' he produced were genuine. She wrote to *The Times* supporting Slade, and then attended the court on at least six occasions 'to show by my presence that I stuck to my colours and that I protected an innocent man'. She was not impressed by Lankester, who was much younger than she had expected, describing him as 'a lout, a real lout' with 'a heavy-jawed, pig-like face'. She was quite sure that Slade would be vindicated and was horrified when, on 31 October, the police magistrate, Frederick Flowers, sentenced the medium under the Vagrancy Act to three months' imprisonment with hard labour. Georgina was in court when the verdict was announced and went afterwards to Slade's lodgings at 8 Upper Bedford Place, where she burst into tears 'after haranguing the crowd to be silent'.[27]

Henry Slade was not sent to gaol immediately. He continued to hold séances, several of which Georgina attended. She wrote to W.H. Harrison, the editor of the *Spiritualist*, proposing the establishment of a fund, to be called the 'Great General and International Medium Defence Fund'. Dr Slade's currently high profile should be used to promote and advertise the fund. Getting somewhat carried away, Georgina promised to protect Slade if, as some feared, he were to be physically attacked by the public: 'I fear no mob, and I will back myself to put the mob in its place. My father, who was Member for Coventry, had that power, and I have it. I would undertake to take Dr Slade safe and bring him back unscathed from any meeting or any performance.' 'I *must* be trusted, and I *must* be obeyed', she added, and

[26] GW–W.H. Harrison, 29/7/1876 and n.d. [summer 1876].

[27] *Times*, 21/10/1876; GWJ, 31/10/1876.

vowed 'to help to rescue the world by the knowledge of Spiritualism from the all-spreading curse of Infidelity and Atheism'. Slade's conviction was quashed on technical grounds at the end of January, and he left almost immediately for the Continent. Whilst he was still in England, Georgina began work on a new pamphlet entitled 'Death-Blow to Spiritualism – Is It?' in which she challenged her fellow spiritualists to 'stand by our acknowledged Mediums'.[28]

Numerous visitors still came to the door of Tavistock House in 1877: some to offer help or – more often – to ask for money. Others were interested in the house because of its connection with Charles Dickens. One such was a young Irishman called Cadwalladwr Waddy, who turned up one afternoon in August with his pregnant wife and two young children. They chatted with Georgina, who was sitting at a downstairs window with the Méniers and some of the orphans. Cadwalladwr was evidently fascinated by Georgina, who told him that her own family was Welsh and that the Treharnes were descended from Edward IV. 'I am Cadwalladwr Waddy, descended in direct line from the first Prince of Wales, Edward II, barrister-at-law', the young man declared, 'and you are the handsomest woman I ever saw!' Georgina replied that she was old enough to be his mother and her hair was going grey, 'so it is no use talking nonsense to me!' After some further conversation Georgina decided that Waddy was 'rather silly and tiresome', and excused herself. On the following day Waddy came again, this time alone, and asked to see Georgina. She told the servant to inform him that she was not at home. He returned a few hours later: again he was told that the mistress of the house would not receive him. This time he gave the servant a white rose and red rose entwined for Georgina, together with a piece of paper on which was written the words 'From HRH the Prince of Wales to HRH the Princess of Wales'. After this he came to Tavistock House or wrote to Georgina every day, sending 'the most ridiculous letters', which Georgina ignored, having decided that the Irishman was 'a stark staring lunatic'.[29]

[28] GWJ, 4,19,31/10/1876, 10/1/1877; GW, 'Death-Blow', pp. 13–14.

[29] GW, *Consequences*, pp. 1–4.

14
Argueil

Money – or rather the lack of it – was now a pressing problem. Georgina had opened a music shop in Great Marlborough Street in 1876, but this lost money and she closed it after a year. Then the hotel-keeper Alfred Nodskou went bankrupt owing her £1000, and Harry threatened to halve her allowance of £1000 a year, claiming that his financial circumstances had changed. It was now obvious that the Rawlings boys had no intention of giving her a share of their earnings from playing the hand bells that she had bought for them. Georgina suspended all payments to them and ordered them to return the bells and her piano. The Gounod choir had now almost ceased to exist and it was clear that the 'Sociable Evenings' were never going to produce enough money to support the orphanage. Everything seemed to be going wrong.

Anacharsis Ménier reappeared at Tavistock House at the end of March 1877, 'as greasy and dirty as ever', claiming that he was about to make his fortune out of his interest in 'millions' of acres of land in New Caledonia.[1] He was full of plans for the revival of *La Liberté Coloniale* and persuaded Georgina that it might be a useful means of conveying her ideas to a wider public. Ever hopeful, she sent £50 to the newspaper's office. Ménier also enlisted her help with his attempts to recover a prototype of his military balloons which had been sent to Woolwich to be assessed by the War Office, offering to give Georgina a third of the profits from the balloon if she could get it back for him.[2]

In April, Angèle left for France without her husband, having agreed to take Bichette to her sister in Normandy. Georgina refused to allow Ménier to sleep at Tavistock House whilst his wife was away because he was 'so dirty, spitting about the house, untidy and disorderly', so he took up residence at the *Liberté Coloniale's* London office. Though she disliked Ménier,

[1] A French penal colony in the South Pacific.

[2] GWJ, 30/3/1877; POB, 9/10/1878.

Georgina trusted him, and he came to dinner almost every day and made himself useful by going to market and running errands. In return, Georgina took him to see her old friend General James Macdonald, who agreed to do what he could to get the balloon back. On 16 May Ménier and his friend André Sauvadet brought 'the Hot Air Military Balloon' from Woolwich, accompanied by a 'grand procession'. Ménier was one of the star turns at Georgina's 'Sociable Evening' a few days later, when he 'held forth in the vilest English on balloons'.[3]

Angèle returned from France without Bichette, but Georgina quickly realised that her attempt to get rid of the child was going to be a failure. Angèle was miserable without Bichette: she was sleeping badly and complained of liver pains. To make matters worse, she discovered that her husband had a girlfriend. She confronted him and he confessed all. Two days later, Angèle left England again. Georgina declared that her friend was a fool, but she was soon 'frantic' without her. She wrote to tell Angèle that she would give her 'security for life': 'It would really be too bad if you were to abandon me. Return to your little bear-cub, your little pigeon, your little cripple, who loves you with all his heart and who cannot live without his little bear-cub, his little pigeon, his little Noireaud'.[4] Georgina referred to herself as an *ourson* [male bear cub] and Angèle as an *oursonne* [female]. Angèle returned, followed a few weeks later by her sister, Marie Helluy, and Bichette. Georgina was furious. The child was 'the image of Ménier', and her behaviour had not improved. By this time Georgina had lost patience with Angèle again. 'Minette is very ill', she wrote, 'but I don't think it is much use my bothering my head about her'.

Then, at the beginning of August, Angèle told Georgina of a 'luminous idea'. All the children should be sent to Normandy, to be 'stowed' with Marie and her friend Victoria Claisse. In the meantime, Georgina, Angèle and Katie, the only one of the orphans who showed any real talent, would 'turn honest pennies by travelling about'. Georgina's initial reaction to this plan was not enthusiastic, and her doubts grew over the weeks that followed. She thought Marie Helluy 'odious'; there was 'always a row, a coaxing, roaring, threatening going on, enough to madden one'. At the end of August there was a 'fearful quarrel' with Angèle, and Georgina wrote:

> I wish to God she'd go. It would be like having a tooth out, but whatever I had to go through I could not be so miserable, so irritable and so perpetually excited, as in a state of hot water, as she keeps me in. I don't

3 GWJ, 16,28/5/1877. According to Georgina, the 'balloon' looked like 'a copper saucepan on two wheels': *Times*, 13/2/1885.

4 GW–AM, 25/6/1877. *Noireaud* means 'Blackie'.

> know what to be at; what to count on; what to expect. I feel as if I could not bear it any more without going out of my mind. Everything turns out a misery and a disappointment to me. Everything![5]

What could she do? She was desperate for a change – any change. She convinced herself that the fog and cold of a winter in London would be bad for Angèle, and that her friend needed to consult a doctor in Paris. It would also do the orphans good to spend some time improving their acquaintance with the French language. Georgina decided that they should all go to France after all.

A little over a fortnight later, Georgina and Angèle were at the quayside in Dover to wave goodbye to Marie Helluy, Bichette and five of the orphans as they set out on the first stage of their journey to the small farming village of Argueil in Normandy, where Marie lived with her friend (and lover) Victoria Claisse. Georgina and Angèle followed them three weeks later with the other five children. Georgina was not quite sure why she was going, writing, 'I never felt so sorry to go away from home, so uncertain, so sorrowful or so hopeless. The first time in my life in which I have acted or made a move without thinking I saw the end.'[6] Two spiritualist friends, Thomas and Mary Ann Lowther, had agreed to look after Tavistock House during her absence. She had at first thought of leaving Anacharsis Ménier in charge of the house, but had been warned not to do so by his wife. He was, however, given the keys to two storerooms in case Georgina asked him to send something to her.

Georgina soon began to regret leaving England. 'It pains me horribly to be so far from my home in a country of strangers, having paid out so much money and not knowing how to return', she wrote in a letter to Anacharsis Ménier. She was, she added, miserable, and she had decided that Angèle was mad. Marie told her that it would cost £150 or £200 to set up the orphanage properly and that she and Victoria would need help if they were to look after so many children. The two women were described as 'midwives and female doctors', and Angèle had told Georgina that their patrons included marquesses, countesses, baronesses, and other 'good and charitable' ladies, but there was no sign of any of these wealthy and well-connected women whilst Georgina was with Marie and Victoria. Indeed, the arrival of a new doctor in the area had deprived them of most of their former clients. Nor did they appear to have had much experience

[5] GWJ, 30/7/1877–30/8/1877.

[6] GWJ, 9/10/1877.

of caring for children. Georgina quickly came to the conclusion that they were only after her money and had no interest in her great enterprise.[7]

After a week, Georgina and Angèle set off for Paris with Katie, leaving the other children with Marie and Victoria. Quite what Georgina hoped to achieve is unclear, though she later claimed that the purpose of this visit was to consult a physician about Angèle's health. It seems to have been Angèle who suggested that she and Georgina should travel incognito, both adopting the surname of Angèle's grandmother, de Lotz. If, as Georgina claimed, they did this in order to avoid the attention of the 'Gounod clique', they were singularly unsuccessful. After a chance meeting with an acquaintance of Angèle's brother-in-law, Eugène Ménier, the news that Georgina was in Paris 'oozed out' into the French newspapers. 'Mysterious paragraphs, more or less garbled, appeared, and I felt very much annoyed', wrote Georgina:

> Then insulting letters were written by J.P. Barbier, the librettist of *Faust*, to say that all the Paris doors would be closed against an Englishwoman of my description, that I was a female Tartuffe, a pickpocket, and that I should be shown to the frontiers by the police. Besides this, Gounod and party began to go about like mad, recommencing their horrible scandals about me. The poor old man himself was got to go to a *Commissaire de Police*, and declare that I was a common London courtesan, that I should be asked to show my number, and that as I had no visible means of existence I ought to be sent to the St-Lazare prison.[8]

Georgina was certain that the hotel where they were staying was being watched, and that she herself was being followed 'to see if I plied my imputed trade'. Bravely – or, perhaps, foolishly – she decided to fight back, taking a nine-year lease of 'a nice little apartment' in the Rue du Luxembourg. She and Angèle began to buy furniture and household goods and engaged a servant. They went to the theatre and visited the cemetery at Montparnasse, where Georgina placed a large garland of *immortelles* on Gounod's mother's tomb. On the following day she sent Angèle to see Antoine Choudens, who said that he would like to meet Georgina. 'If he [Gounod] has made it up with Choudens, there is a little tiny spark of hope for me', wrote Georgina in her diary. But all her hopes were soon dashed. Somehow, Angèle managed to speak to Gounod, but he 'would not listen to a word' about Georgina, and was 'very violent and *méchant* [unpleasant]'.[9]

7 GW–Anacharsis Ménier, 14/10/1877; GWM, ii, pp. 51–4.

8 GW, *London Figaro*, 5/2/1879, p. 11.

9 GWJ, 30/10/1877, 2,17/11/1877.

On 20 November Georgina took part in a 'most beautiful' séance, at which Gounod's mother 'spoke' to her again, calling her 'my well-beloved' and telling her that she was with her all the time. At the end, Madame Gounod promised that all Georgina's prayers would be answered in exactly six weeks' time. On the following day she and Angèle attended a performance of Gounod's new opera, *Cinq-Mars*, at the Opéra-Comique. It was, Georgina thought, 'a miserable production, artistically, musically and as [to] libretto. The only pretty motif one which he composed at Tavistock House, but he has been too lazy to work it out properly, so it is insignificant.'[10]

According to Georgina, she was being 'pursued' by concert agents at this time, though this may have been out of curiosity as much as respect for her artistic talents. Nevertheless, it was arranged that she should sing Gounod's *Biondina* at the Salle Herz on 12 December. The agent who engaged her, Salazar, promised her half the net receipts and the tickets sold well. On the day before the concert, however, she was informed that the event had been cancelled by order of the *Préfecture de Police*. She blamed Gounod, whose lawyers had threatened the Salle Herz. The composer and his friends were, she was told,

> in such a state at the idea of the Parisian public getting a chance of seeing for themselves that this fearful combination of Megæra, Aspasia and Cleopatra was a soft, modest-looking, rather baby-faced Englishwoman, very nervous and plainly dressed, instead of being what she is described by the Gounod clique, a lawyer in petticoats, tall, bony, stern, about fifty years of age, with a hare lip, sticking-out enormous teeth, green spectacles, a voice like a raven and the glance of a hawk, that this must be put a stop to at any price.[11]

Georgina appealed to her old friend Lord Lyons, now British ambassador in Paris, but he refused to allow the concert to be moved to the embassy.

It was not until several months later that Georgina discovered that her enemies were not confined to the 'Gounod clique'. Many of her troubles at this time appear to have been orchestrated by the Méniers. A few weeks after leaving England, she was informed that Anacharsis Ménier was living at Tavistock House. She had left home in too much of a hurry to hand the keys over to her lodgers, but had trusted Ménier to let them in. Ménier had, however, told the Lowthers that Georgina had given him permission to occupy two rooms in the house. The Lowthers had refused to agree to this and had not moved in. They had tried to contact Georgina, but without success, as Ménier had given them a false address. He then failed to forward

[10] GWJ, 20–1/11/1877.

[11] GW, *London Figaro*, 5/2/1879, p. 11. Aspasia was a gifted Athenian courtesan.

Georgina's letters to her and ignored her repeated requests for him to send money. By the beginning of December she was accusing him of being 'a miserable adventurer, a rascal, a swindler, a braggart like Eugène, a swindler like your uncle, a miserable old crook like your mother.' She told him not to meddle in her affairs again.

Georgina also sent a threatening letter to Eugène Ménier, who wrote to Anacharsis from Paris, assuring him:

> Within a month Mrs Weldon must be so discredited and dishonoured that she will not be able to return to England. Poor women who want to fight against me, if they knew what I am preparing for them, they would not dare to speak a word against us. You know that I spare nothing, and these are vipers whose venom must be removed, and I reply to you that the operation will be carried out in a manner that she cannot fight back against. Know well that after a short campaign of 15 days, if they are not forced to leave Paris, even by the police, I will give up my name of Eugène Ménier.

Eugène was already busy spreading rumours about the orphanage, telling everyone that it should be suppressed 'from the point of view of public morals' and hinting at an unnatural relationship between Georgina and Angèle. He told his brother that the two women disgusted him and should be chased out of France, and claimed that he was doing all he could to defend the honour of the Ménier family. In his opinion, Georgina's nature was 'bad, satanic': Gounod had done well to escape her clutches and she was 'finished' in both England and France. By attacking him, Eugène, she had made 'the biggest mistake possible.'[12]

A few days after the cancellation of the concert at the Salle Herz, there occurred an event that Georgina found profoundly disturbing. On the morning of 17 December Angèle went out alone to buy food. As she left the apartment, she was approached by a man who insisted on walking to the market with her. This man offered to give Angèle money if she would agree to leave Georgina and return to England, insisting that she had to come with him immediately. Angèle refused and went back to the apartment to tell Georgina what had happened. Georgina was convinced that this was a plot to separate her from her friend and get her into Dr Blanche's lunatic asylum at Passy – from which she would never emerge. She decided to write to Lord Lyons again and to ask the *Préfet de Police* to put her under special surveillance. 'I am afraid of being assassinated or of having vitriol thrown in my face,' she wrote in her diary

12 GW–Anacharsis Ménier, 8,11/12/1877; Eugène Ménier–Anacharsis Ménier, 10/12/1877.

that evening. She made a statement to a police officer, who was clearly not convinced, though he did promise to send Gounod an official warning, telling him to keep the peace towards Georgina and to cease molesting her. There were no more such incidents after this, though the concierge at the hotel was subsequently pestered by men enquiring after Georgina.[13]

Amid all the distractions of life in Paris, Georgina had not entirely forgotten about the orphans at Argueil. Regular letters from Marie told her of the difficulty of finding anyone to help with the children. Georgina tried to find somewhere else for them to live, but nobody would take them in and she blamed the 'Gounod clique' for spreading stories about her. In spite of all that Gounod's mother had promised, her hopes had been 'raised, only to be dashed to the ground.' 'Nothing to hope for and no hope of anything. No illusion,' she wrote in her diary. She was not, however, depressed for long. A new American friend, Mr O'Sullivan, took her and Katie to see Victor Hugo, who was 'much amused by the child.' On the following day Georgina went to the Châtelet to hear *La Damnation de Faust* by Berlioz. It was, she thought, 'an awful row.' There was no theme, but the orchestration was wonderful. She even managed to persuade Angèle to take Bichette away and leave her with the Ménier family.[14]

Then disaster struck. The first signs of trouble came towards the end of January, when Georgina received a letter from Marie in Argueil, telling her that there was measles 'in the camp.' There was also an outbreak of cholerine (a mild form of cholera). Everyone had fled from the house as if the inhabitants had the plague, and there was a rumour in the countryside that the children were half-starved and fed only on oatmeal.[15] To begin with, Georgina did not understand the seriousness of the situation. On 1 February she and Katie dined with Victor Hugo, who was 'very charming and *spirituel*.' After dinner, Georgina sang to the author's guests, who included the Parisian artists Félix and Frédéric Regamey, whom she had met in London several years before. But a desperate telegram from Marie arrived two days later. 'Poor darling little Mireille,' 'the one pearl that I was able to collect among this crowd of little pieces of dung,' had died on the previous evening – a year and a day after the burial of 'poor Freddie.' Another telegram, on the following day, told her that Merthyr and Dagobert were now at death's door. Georgina decided to set off immediately, leaving Angèle and Katie in Paris.[16]

13 GW, *London Figaro*, 12/2/1879, p. 3; GWJ, 17/12/1877.
14 GWJ, 31/12/1877–6/1/1878.
15 GWJ, 25/1/1878; Marie Helluy–GW, 30/1/1878.
16 GW–Marie Helluy and Victoria Claisse, 3/2/1878; GW–AM, 6/2/1878; GWJ, 1–4/2/1878.

Georgina reached Argueil late in the evening on 4 February. Marie and Victoria were both 'broken-hearted', having hardly undressed, slept or eaten for several days. Nobody could understand how Merthyr and Dagobert could still be alive; Tommy and Johnnie were ill too, and everyone – adults and children alike – was crawling with lice. During the days that followed, Georgina did what little she could to help and busied herself with arrangements for Mireille's funeral. Because she had been baptised as a Protestant, the local officials refused to allow the child's grave to be dug in the main part of the cemetery, insisting that she should be buried among those who had been guillotined or had committed suicide. Georgina appealed to Lord Lyons, asking him to use his influence to have a part of the burial ground set aside for Protestants. She also tried frantically to find a hospital that would be willing to take Dagobert, whose infected sores made the whole place stink. The child would, Georgina thought, give everyone gangrene if he stayed in the house. On 15 February, he was taken to Rouen.

It was not long before Georgina decided that Argueil was 'the most beastly place in the world (and that includes the people)'. Marie, whom she had disliked from their first meeting in London, did not improve on closer acquaintance. 'She is a dreadful woman', Georgina wrote, 'and the more I see of her, the more odious I find her.' She called her 'the Grand Turk'. Georgina felt sorry for Victoria, who appeared to do most of the work and was constantly bullied by Marie, who rarely got up before mid-day. 'Marie talks constantly of "my" house, "my" maid, "my" this and "my" that', Georgina told Angèle. 'Victoria does not exist, and as for me, I am a dog-turd.' Georgina and Victoria moaned to each other of the two Helluy sisters' ingratitude, rudeness and lack of affection.[17] Nor, on closer inspection, were the children being very well cared for. They had, Georgina thought, being 'completely brutalized'. They were scolded and sworn at constantly, and were often too scared to move or open their mouths.

The worst was over by mid February, when Georgina decided that she needed some peace and quiet so that she could work on her book about Gounod. She took up residence at the Hôtel du Cygne in Gournay, ten miles from Argueil. Though she felt some guilt at leaving the children, Georgina was happy to be away from Marie's 'eternal roaring, grumblings and cursings'. On 26 February she thought of Gounod and noted in her diary that it was seven years to the day since she had 'made that wicked old man's acquaintance'. 'I may be a fool', she added, 'but at the bottom of my heart I'm as fond of him as ever, and I feel certain if I saw him for two

[17] GWJ, 4–18/2/1878; GW–AM, 6–19/2/1878.

minutes he would love poor Mimi over again.'[18] She made good progress with her writing and began work on an English translation of *Jean Dacier*, a play by Charles Lomon, whom she had met in Paris.

This period of calm did not last for long. The news from London had become increasingly worrying during the previous months and Georgina had asked a friend to employ a solicitor to evict Ménier. The Frenchman had refused to go, claiming that, as a married woman, Georgina did not have the right to turn him out of her husband's house. Angèle had written to her husband in December, ordering him to leave Tavistock House. He was 'a robber and a crook', and his brother was 'the most horrible man, the most miserable wretch I know'.[19] Ménier had replied that 'as Mr Weldon was trying to get his wife into a lunatic asylum it was not at all likely that he would interfere in his wife's interests'.[20] Georgina asked her mother to do what she could to persuade Harry to take the necessary steps against Ménier. This had no effect either. Then, at the end of the month, she received a letter from Louisa, begging her to 'pick up your traps, bag and baggage, and come over instantly to England'. It was clear from Louisa's letter that she herself was not going to do anything to help her daughter:

> I should think you ought before this have [*sic*] found out that your swans are all geese, your angels devils, and, if they are not so, your mismanagement of the ordinary affairs of life is so great, that it leads to the people you have to do with being antagonistic.

Louisa suggested that Georgina should contact her (and Harry's) old friend General Henry de Bathe, and told her 'If I had strength of mind or body, and wealth, I would exert every faculty to get you out of your present line, but I am powerless! I can only *grieve*, and I have much in life to grieve at.' Georgina replied that her problems were all the result of her husband's 'indolence and cowardice'. Given a little money and energy, she would be able to 'crush Gounod and his bandits' and stop them spreading lies about her. She told Louisa that she – or brother Dal – should 'prevail on Harry to get Ménier taken up without warning'. 'He is an impudent, barefaced swindler and adventurer', she added, 'he knows that I, having no title deeds to the house, can legally do nothing.' Ménier had keys to the strong-room in which Georgina had left all her jewellery, and also to her deed-box which contained valuable papers. His claim to have a written agreement with Georgina was 'all bosh'. 'The thing to manage', she begged her mother, 'is to

[18] GWJ, 19,26/2/1878.

[19] AM–Anacharsis Ménier, 18/12/1877.

[20] GW, *London Figaro*, 12/2/1879, p. 4; GW, *Reports2*, 1878–85, p. 4.

get him into prison for something like trespass and false pretences.' Louisa continued to implore Georgina to return to London immediately, telling her daughter that she had brought her troubles on herself by abusing Harry and putting her trust in Ménier.[21]

At the beginning of March, Georgina received a letter from Lise Gray, a member of her choir, telling her that 'things were going on in a most disgraceful and scandalous manner' at Tavistock House. Georgina's former maid Elizabeth Villiers, who was now working for the Gray family, had visited the house and reported that everything was filthy. Furthermore, Ménier's mistress had been living there with him and was about to give birth.[22] Equally worrying was a letter from Harry's Liverpool solicitor, William Jevons. Back in January, Georgina had written to Jevons, asking him to let Harry know that she wished to sublet Tavistock House for ten or twelve years, and to use the money thus raised to rent a house for herself and the orphans. She had received no reply. Now, however, Jevons informed her that Harry intended to sell the lease, returning to Georgina her share of the amount that had been paid for it. That night Georgina was 'too frantic to sleep.' 'It is enough to drive me wild', she added, 'This is indeed a kettle of fish! Never was such a one.' She told Angèle what had happened, begging her 'Minette, don't be ill, I beg you. I am afraid of telling you all that, but I am demoralised by the idea of losing Tavistock. My dear Tavistock! The Tavistock of my old man!' She would, she informed her mother, 'rather burn Tavistock House down, with me inside it, than lose it.' In her reply, Louisa asked her daughter not to send her any more 'mad tirades.'[23]

Whilst she waited anxiously for further news from London, Georgina began to search urgently for somewhere to stow the children, having decided that she could not leave them at Argueil any longer. On 12 March she and Angèle took a train to Gisors, fifteen miles from Gournay and approximately forty miles from Paris. There they visited the convent or hospice of the Sisters of St Thomas de Villeneuve, which stood in extensive grounds to the south of the town. Attached to the convent itself were a hospital and an orphanage and there were also apartments for 'decayed gentlewomen' and other residents. The buildings were spacious and modern, having been constructed in 1860. Georgina and Angèle saw 'a little chapel and a lovely garden' and were 'quite overjoyed' with it all. Georgina decided that it would be the ideal home for Rosie, Beryl and Pauline, and for herself too. On the following day she packed up all her belongings and took herself off

21 LFT–GW, 23/2/1878, 5/3/1878; GW–LFT, 26–28/2/1878.

22 LFT–GW, 5/3/1878; GW–AM, 8/3/1878.

23 GWJ, 8–9/3/1878; GW–AM, 8/3/1878; GW–LFT, 9/3/1878; LFT–GW, 12/3/1878.

to Gisors with Rosie. She was dismayed to be told that the girl could only be admitted to the orphanage with the permission of the administrative council, but the nuns agreed to take them both in for the time being. 'I am quite happy', Georgina wrote that evening, 'I have got a crucifix in my room and plenty of cupboards. I shall be *très bien* here.' Rosie was, however, getting on her nerves and preventing her from writing. 'She is a real brute', wrote Georgina, 'and so ungracious to the Mother Superior. If they don't accept her I shall certainly send her to a House of Correction. Kindness would be quite thrown away on her. She wants very firm, harsh discipline.'[24]

A few days after their arrival at Gisors, the bursar told Georgina that she and Rosie would have to leave. Georgina learned that the nuns had heard bad accounts from Argueil of Marie Helluy and her friend, and they supposed that Georgina was 'of the same tribe'. This suggests that the nuns had been told that they were all lesbians. Georgina was asked for references, but told them that she had none. 'I was in great trouble', she wrote, 'for never having been a servant or a governess, I did not know how to get any.' She declared that she had never done any harm, and said that she would not leave 'unless they could bring specific charges against me'. She told the bursar and nuns to write to several 'well-placed' people in London and Paris, and showed them some letters from Lord Lyons and her account books for the previous fifteen years, which she happened to have with her. Eventually the nuns relented, and Georgina and Rosie were allowed to stay for the time being.

Ignoring further letters from her mother begging her to return to London at once, Georgina stayed at Gisors for a fortnight, sewing, writing, walking in the garden and singing in the chapel. But the period of comparative quiet came to an end on 27 March, when she was 'staggered' to receive a telegram from Angèle in Paris. All the children were with her in their small apartment, having been sent from Argueil by Marie, who had taken exception to Georgina's criticisms as relayed to her by her sister. Georgina hurried back to Paris and spent the next few days searching frantically for foster parents or schools where she could leave the children. On the evening of 1 April, having finally got rid of all of them, Georgina sobbed herself to sleep, 'dead tired'.[25]

A day later, Georgina left Angèle in Paris and returned to Gisors, where she found 'awful' letters from her husband's lawyer waiting for her. She learned that Harry had already taken possession of Tavistock House and was about have everything cleared out. Jevons asked where he should send Georgina's belongings. At this point 'a voice' told her to go home at

24 GWJ, 13–14/3/1878; GW–AM, 14/3/1878.

25 GWJ, 1/4/1878; GW, *London Figaro*, 19/2/1879, pp. 3–4.

once.[26] By one o'clock the following morning she was at Calais. She crossed the Channel during the night, 'praying to Ma Mie all the time to prevent me being sick and to give me strength.'[27] Arriving at Victoria Station on Wednesday 3 April at 6.15 in the morning, Georgina went straight to 30 Danvers Street in Chelsea, where Lise Gray and Villiers were expecting her.

[26] GW–W.H. Jevons, 8 April 1878.
[27] 'Ma Mie' was Georgina's name for Gounod's mother.

15
Mad-Doctors

After resting for a day, Georgina returned to Tavistock House on the afternoon of 4 April, accompanied by Villiers and a friend, 'dear old' Professor Lloyd Birkbeck. The door was opened by James Bell, the broker's man and caretaker put into the house on Harry's behalf, and they pushed their way in. All around them were boxes full of Georgina's belongings which Ménier was about to carry off with the help of André Sauvadet, who was waiting outside in a hansom cab. Suddenly, Ménier himself emerged from the basement, where he and his Hungarian 'secretary' Alexander de Barathy were busy packing up more of Georgina's possessions. On seeing Georgina, Ménier 'turned as pale as a ghost' and rushed out of the house without a word, leaving his mistress, Olive Nicholls, behind. 'Cheer up Madam,' Bell told Georgina, 'I never saw a party run away from his debtor before.' Georgina felt some sympathy for the girl, 'the erring and deluded victim of this old scamp, this old and dirty Don Juan,' but she ordered her to leave the house. The girl went, threatening 'You will not be here long.' But Bell ('a pleasant old man') was prepared to let Georgina stay and she remained in Tavistock House, receiving visits from Harry's London lawyer, James Neal, 'a fool,' and the broker, Washington Hirschfield, 'a *fanfaron* [braggart],' both of whom were anxious to find out what was going on.

That evening Georgina wrote to Angèle to tell her what had happened:

> I have thrown Ménier out. I stopped everything. They were carrying everything away – bed linen, beds, coverlets, your velvet dress! Don't worry. I will have my revenge. I will avenge you! The house is full of *putains* [whores]. I am exhausted – dead – but too happy to have saved something. Everything is ruined: the magnificent ceiling in the music room has a hole big enough for three men to get through. It's dreadful. They have stolen everything. God knows how much has gone. The gas has been cut off. I'll have to pay 300 francs [£12]. They wanted to take my piano to pay the taxes. I haven't had time to check everything, only to undo what they were about to carry away – my dresses, things that

> you sewed, bedcovers, sheets, casseroles. It will kill you. Your brute apparently adores this girl – they are like two children.[1]

A quick search of the house had shown that Olive Nicholls had taken several parcels of children's clothes. Georgina's jewel case had been emptied and it was clear that Ménier had pawned some of her belongings. She estimated that the missing items were worth £500 or more. At least she still had Ménier's balloon, which was in the front garden – though she soon discovered that there was some doubt as to whether it actually belonged to him.

Georgina quickly realised that Neal would do nothing to help her to recover her property. 'I had never before seen this simpleton and I marvelled at him,' she wrote. Ménier had informed the lawyer that Georgina had put him into the house to manage everything in her absence and to try to sublet it. She had, Ménier claimed, treated him 'shamefully' and she owed him £178.[2] In Georgina's words:

> The simple-minded Neal had sucked in the following tales, which, he gravely informed me, were compromising if they got bruited about. I had put poison bottles about the house in various corners, which the babies found, sucked, died and were buried in the garden. I got one thousand pounds for each baby – no questions asked. Ménier had most compromising letters from me proposing all sorts of dreadful things.[3]

Ménier had hinted that there was something distasteful about the relationship between Georgina and his wife Angèle. The lawyer had been prepared to allow the Frenchman to carry off what he wanted in order, as he saw it, to shield Georgina from public exposure. Any such exposure would, he knew, inevitably affect his client as well. He had, Neal told Georgina, decided that the best approach would be to temporise. Her reaction to this was derisive: 'Temporise indeed!' she declared 'You shall see how I will temporise!! Pursue him, find him, arrest him, the lying brigand! Send for the police!'

On the following day Georgina telegraphed to Olive Nicholls's father to tell him that his daughter was dying and he should come at once. Before long both parents arrived on her doorstep. They knew nothing of what had been going on, believing that Georgina was employing Olive as her housekeeper. The next step was to track down the fugitives. Through de Barathy, who appeared to be innocent and was willing to help, they discovered that Ménier had taken a room at the Hotel Comte in Golden Square.

1 GWJ, 4/4/1878; GW–AM, 4/4/1878.
2 James Neal–William Jevons [March 1878].
3 GWL, p. 17.

That evening Mr Nicholls and Georgina went to the hotel with a policeman, whom they left at the door. Olive tried to run away when she saw Georgina, but was caught by the policeman. The room was full of boxes of Georgina's possessions, but there was no sign of Ménier. Deciding that they needed reinforcements, Georgina then went to Vine Street Police Station and returned with 'a most charming young detective', Uriah Cooke. Then they all waited: Mr and Mrs Nicholls, their 'nasty' daughter Olive, a servant ('that impudent little hussy Lizzie'), the detective and Georgina.

Some time after midnight 'the wretch himself' arrived. The dramatic – even farcical – scene that followed can be best described in Georgina's own words:

> Ménier, not knowing what had happened, put on a pleasant face as he came in without knocking, and said, 'There are a good many peoples in my room.' I came forward and said 'Detective, I give this man in charge for the theft of these things!' Ménier came and shook his fist in my face and said, 'And I give this woman in charge for murder – for the murder of leetle sheeldren.' He tried to palaver all he could, but it was in vain.[4]

Order was restored by Detective Cooke, who took them all downstairs and put them into a cab, placing one 'huge' constable inside and one on the box. Georgina felt sorry for the horse, with such a heavy load to pull. They went first to Tottenham Court Road Police Station, discovered that it was the wrong one ('of course'), and eventually ended up at the station in Hunter Street. It was not a quiet journey. As they went along Ménier shouted, 'She is von mahd vomman! She is de marderess of leetle cheeldren. She is von forgerer. She ahs forged her ahsbahn's synature. She is mahd! She know not what she say.' From time to time he threatened Georgina in French, calling her 'Ignoble femme! Miserable femme!' and telling her, 'You are indeed Gounod's Englishwoman. I'll catch you out tomorrow – you'll be ruined. I'll ruin you.' All this, too, was in French, which Georgina obligingly translated it into English for the benefit of the policemen. She suggested to Ménier that he should speak, and threaten her, in English.[5]

When they reached the police station, Ménier was searched and was found to have on him Georgina's gold watch, and duplicate keys to several rooms and drawers in her house. He also had a letter signed by Harry, which appeared to authorise him as 'a proper person in charge' at Tavistock House. He was, nevertheless, locked up for the night and the others returned to Tavistock House, where Georgina gave 'the unfortunate

4 GWJ, 5/4/1878.
5 GWL, p. 20.

Nicholls and their most unsympathetic daughter' shelter. They must have been uncomfortable, as there were only three beds in the house, all of them infested with bedbugs.

Though she had not gone to bed until three in the morning, Georgina was up early on the following day. By 10.15 she was at Bow Street Police Court where, as she wrote in her diary, she felt 'quite at home', having spent several days there during Henry Slade's trial in the autumn of 1876. The same clerk was there, and the presiding magistrate was again Frederick Flowers. Georgina was introduced to the newspaper reporter 'Papa' Grossmith, the father of her old friend George Grossmith. Ménier was brought into the dock 'looking beautifully dirty'. He claimed that Georgina had stolen his balloon, which was worth £400, and that he had taken her belongings 'as a sort of equivalent'. Georgina would have none of this, informing the court that the balloon was 'a dreadful thing' and she wanted to get rid of it. 'I soon floored him', she wrote, 'I refused to let him out on bail. He begged of me, but I replied, "I am not generous to such as you. You deserve no pity, you are a wretch!"' The case was remanded for a week and Ménier was sent to Clerkenwell Detention House.[6]

With Ménier safely out of the way, Georgina began to assess the extent of her losses. She visited de Barathy and his wife and found their rooms 'crammed' with her furniture. Tavistock House was 'a stye': 'No words can fully describe the filthy state it was in. Bugs fell from the ceiling; a dog Ménier had, had given birth to five puppies who had never been turned out of doors; and the cistern had overflowed right through the ceilings.'[7] There was a nauseating smell everywhere and the roof leaked badly. 'It will', Georgina wrote, 'take me a year of Sundays to get it right and straight'. For several days she was busy seeing 'no end of people, gas, water, locksmith, tradespeople duped by Ménier'. She was looking forward to getting her revenge: 'God willed that I should be the means of punishing one of the deepest dyed and most unblushing schemers and villains that ever lived', she wrote, adding 'The hour of my triumph has struck.' When de Barathy told her that Sauvadet wanted to bribe her to let Ménier go, her response was 'Not for a million!' She was delighted when, a few days later, she found two letters from Eugène Ménier to his brother, which were, to her, 'invaluable proofs' that they had been plotting her ruin and intended to murder both her and Angèle.[8]

6 GWJ, 6/4/1878; POB, 9 October 1878; Anacharsis Ménier–AM, 6/4/1878.
7 GWL, p. 23.
8 GWJ, 6–11/4/1878.

On 13 April they were all back at Bow Street for another court hearing. Ménier was represented by J.P. Grain, brother of the well-known entertainer Corney Grain, whilst Georgina conducted her own case for the prosecution. She produced a long list of articles, including jewellery, pictures and furniture, that Ménier had allegedly stolen whilst she was in France. She also tried to produce the two letters from Eugène, claiming that they proved that the two brothers had conspired together to destroy her character, but Flowers told her to confine herself to the accusation of theft. He asked Georgina if she had left Ménier in charge of the house and she said that she had not done so, explaining that she had expected the Lowthers to occupy it.

In his cross-examination, Grain did his best to discredit Georgina. He asked her if she was 'the charming lady' whom he had seen daily during Henry Slade's trial. When she replied 'Yes', he 'jumped at the chance of hinting' that because she had been 'deluded' into a belief in Slade, she might also have been 'deluded into a *disbelief* in his virtuous client'. Grain also insinuated that Georgina had gone to Paris with the well-known author and spiritualist Edward Maitland. Georgina had known Maitland since the early 1860s; he had called on her in Paris in January and had presented her with a copy of his latest book, *The Soul and How it Found Me*, but there is no indication that they were ever alone together.[9] She laughed at Grain's suggestion, replying that 'everybody' knew that Maitland had been in Paris with 'Mrs Dr Kingsford'. This was Anna Kingsford, the wife of a Shropshire clergyman, who was studying medicine at the University of Paris at the time. Maitland and Mrs Kingsford were, Georgina added, 'deeply and seriously engaged in the same pursuit: occultism'.[10]

Grain also referred to the 'partnership' between Georgina and Ménier's wife, and suggested that Angèle might have been her husband's accomplice. Georgina denied all this, telling the court that Angèle had warned her not to trust her husband. 'I put him [Grain] down nicely', she wrote in her diary, 'I don't think he'll like to face me.'[11] Summing up, Flowers told the court that, whatever the relationship between the various people concerned might have been, 'nothing could justify stripping the home of his employer in this way'. 'If the charge was a true one', he continued, 'it was one of the worst he had ever experienced in his life. The very fact of the man's being trusted – if he ever had been – made the crime the more infamous.' Finally, Flowers said he felt that it would be impossible for Mrs Weldon to conduct

9 GWJ, 12/1/1878.
10 GWMSM, p. 97.
11 GWJ, 13/4/1878.

her case without legal assistance, and that this illustrated the necessity of a Public Prosecutor. He remanded the case for a further week and Ménier was taken back to gaol in a Black Maria. One of the policemen, Inspector Aunger, agreed to communicate with the Treasury in the hope that they would take up the prosecution on Georgina's behalf.[12]

Georgina felt that she had acquitted herself well in court and went home 'proud and delighted, rejoiced to think the Treasury, the government, the CROWN (the British Crown!!!) was going, at last, to take up the cudgels on my behalf and see me righted.'[13] For no very obvious reason, she believed that the Ménier trial would put an end to the 'eight years of persecution, calumny and boycotting' that she had suffered at the hands of the music publishers. Her perseverance would be rewarded: everything was going to be all right at last.

On the next day, a Sunday, Georgina, Villiers and Bell set to work clearing up Tavistock House. Wearing a red dressing gown and a large dirty apron, with 'a pair of most inelegant slippers' on her feet, Georgina was at the top of a ladder dusting the music books in the library when, at about half past ten in the morning, the bell rang. Villiers opened the front door and then came to ask Georgina if she would receive 'two gentlemen named Shell and Stewart.' Thinking that the visitors must have come from the music publishers Duff and Stewart, who had recently gone bankrupt, Georgina agreed to see them. She soon realised her mistake, for she did not recognise either of the men who were shown in. One was an old man who, in Georgina's words, 'sat on a bone in the middle of his back, with his hands clasped on his stomach, the very ideal of the lean and slippered Pantaloon'; the other was about thirty, 'all blinks, winks and grins and looked like a washed Christy Minstrel.' The latter seemed to be ill at ease, clearing his throat and fidgetting, and left his companion to do most of the talking. The older man told Georgina that they were both spiritualists and said that they had read her articles on education in the *Spiritualist* newspaper. They wished to place some children in her orphanage, as the children's relations wanted them to be brought up as good spiritualists.

The reference to 'relations' settled the matter as far as Georgina was concerned. Remembering Gwen Jones and her problems with the girl's mother, she replied that she would have nothing to do with children who were encumbered with adults who might 'come and talk nonsense to them and take them away as soon as they thought them proficient enough to bring out at the Music Halls.' She could, however, recommend 'a charming

12 *Times*, 15/4/1878.

13 GWL, p. 22.

convent in France' which would take the children for £30 apiece. The men left after half an hour. Villiers and Bell watched them as they went down to the steps into the garden and noticed that they were laughing and seemed to be in particularly good spirits. 'Aren't they hugging up to each other as if they had a fine prize!', commented Bell. 'Oh bother!' replied Villiers, 'Missis has been talking Spiritualism!'[14]

That afternoon there were several more visitors, including General Sir Henry de Bathe. Georgina had known him for more than ten years and believed that he owed her a debt of gratitude. She had been kind to his much younger wife, whom he had married in 1870, having lived with her for more than thirteen years and fathered seven children by her. Georgina had visited the new Lady de Bathe shortly after her marriage, at a time when few London hostesses were prepared to associate with her.[15] Georgina had barely seen Sir Henry since her separation from Harry, though he had paid her a flying visit just over a year earlier. He tried to persuade Georgina to give up her prosecution of Ménier, telling her that the Frenchman was relying on letters from her for his defence. She was immovable, laughing at 'the idea of my letters to the horrible creature compromising me'. After ten minutes de Bathe departed 'apparently disgusted with my hopeless frivolity and want of appreciation of my danger'. He did, however, promise to return with his wife in a fortnight.[16]

In the evening Georgina received a visit from a former servant, Elizabeth (Tibby) Jordan. They were sitting chatting when the doorbell rang again. This time Bell went to the door and found two men waiting on the doorstep, claiming to be 'Messrs Shell and Stewart'. Bell, who had been absent during the previous visit of the 'spiritualists', was doubtful about the propriety of letting two strange men into the house at such a late hour. He asked them to wait and went to consult Georgina, but the men followed him in. One was an elderly gentleman, 'short and tubby', whilst the other was 'a dark, taciturn, evil-looking person'. Georgina had never seen either of them before. The men admitted that they were not 'Shell and Stewart', but claimed that they had come from them, 'so we thought it best to give the same names, as they sent us about the orphanage'. They gave the same story about wishing to settle a number of orphans and appeared to be interested in Georgina's psychic experiences.

14 GWL, pp. 23–4.

15 Henry de Bathe had inherited his father's baronetcy a few months before his marriage.

16 GWL, p. 25.

The men stayed for an hour, during which Georgina told them of the spirit voices that she had heard, of the 'splendid white light' that she had seen at the time of Gounod's flight, and of a white rabbit that had appeared at a séance. She noticed that they behaved rather oddly. At one point the older man went out of the room. He appeared to be looking for something in the passage, so Georgina sent Tibby to find out what he was up to. Whilst his companion was absent, the younger man suddenly 'became livelier'. He told Georgina that he had heard her sing at one of Gounod's concerts, and complimented her on the loveliness of her voice. He also told her that she was very beautiful and looked very young. This attempt at flattery did not endear him to Georgina, who decided that he was 'surprisingly rude and vulgar'. She could not see what any of this had to do with the orphans. The older man then returned to the room and the younger one went out for a few moments, closely watched by Tibby. 'They neither of them wanted anything in the corridor', Georgina later wrote, 'they only appeared to wait for each other, making a few observations to Elizabeth [Tibby].' The older man looked out of the window and admired the garden, asking Georgina if she spent much time there, and whether she had any particular hours for going out. He tried, unsuccessfully, to open the window, so Georgina opened it for him. She turned round and saw the man's eyes 'fixed upon me with a sort of glittering stare, or leer, which terrified me'. Now thoroughly unnerved, Georgina called to Tibby, who returned to the room followed by the younger man. He announced that it was time for him and his companion to go.

By this time, as she later wrote, Georgina had come to the conclusion that these were 'bad men seeking my ruin'. She remembered Ménier's letter to Angèle in which he had referred to Harry's desire to get her into a lunatic asylum, and decided that the Frenchman's allies were trying to do away with her so that his prosecution for theft would be dropped. She also thought of the 'kidnap attempt' in Paris and wondered if the two Méniers had conspired with Gounod. Convinced that she was in great danger, she 'got in a dreadful fright'. She and Bell managed to push 'the second batch of Messrs Shell and Stewart' (as she later referred to the two men) out of the house. She told Tibby, 'Something awful has come over me. I see black clouds floating down over me, one by one. I see all black, I feel stifled – I feel as though I were in some horrible danger! What can those men be? I am in some horrible trap.'[17] Tibby, who thought that the men were probably newspaper reporters, replied that they seemed to be 'very pleasant gentlemen'. Georgina told her to go home and then had a good look at the front

[17] GW, galley proofs of unidentified article.

door. Security had never worried her before, but she was relieved to see that there were two bolts, one at the top and one at the bottom, and a chain. She drew the bolts and fastened the chain.

Another half hour passed. Reluctant to go to bed until Villiers returned from a visit to Chelsea, Georgina stayed in the pantry with Bell, discussing the evening's events. Then a closed carriage was driven up to the door. This was unusual: the iron entrance gates leading to the front of Tavistock House had been damaged some time before by a runaway cab horse and were now usually kept closed by means of a large flagstone wedged against them. Most visitors left their carriages in Tavistock Square and walked up to the house through a smaller side gate.

Not long afterwards, someone rang the doorbell. 'I told you so,' Georgina said to Bell, 'there they are, they've come for me. Call to them from the area and tell them everybody has gone to bed.' Still unconvinced, and thinking that the 'visitor' might in fact be Villiers, Bell called out 'Who's there?' A man's voice answered, 'We want to come in. We want to see Mrs Weldon.' Cautiously, Bell opened the front door, keeping the chain up. On being told that Georgina had gone to bed, the man replied 'All the better.' He and his two female companions tried unsuccessfully to push their way in. They refused to give their names or identify themselves, but the man first ordered, and then tried to bribe, Bell to undo the chain, reminding him 'You are here for Mr Weldon.' The faithful Bell replied, 'Never mind who I am here for: you don't come in,' and slammed the door in their faces. He refused to open it again, though they continued to ring and knock for several minutes. By the time they went away Georgina was 'half dead with fright.' Convinced that the two female visitors were men dressed as women, 'and come to carry me off somewhere,' she prayed with all her strength to God to save her. Villiers, who came in shortly afterwards, and Bell both agreed that there was something seriously wrong.

After a sleepless night, Georgina was up early on Monday morning. She sent for the police inspector from Hunter Street and asked him to tell his men to look out for anyone trying to get into the house. She wrote letters to Gladstone and all the influential friends she could think of, describing the previous day's events and telling them of her fear that Ménier and Gounod were trying to get rid of her. She also sent a telegram to General de Bathe: 'COME UP AT ONCE. IT IS A MATTER OF LIFE AND DEATH.'[18] She then thought of Louisa Lowe, the secretary to the Lunacy Law Reform Association, which she had founded in 1873. Georgina had never met Mrs Lowe, but she had read in the *Spiritualist*

[18] GWL, p. 26; GW, *Doctors*, pp. 8–11; GWJ, 14/4/1878.

and *Medium and Daybreak* newspapers of her attempts draw the attention of the public to the scandalous system of private asylums.

Widespread fears that sane people were being wrongfully confined had been reinforced by newspaper reports and by best-selling 'sensation novels', such as *The Woman in White* (Wilkie Collins, 1860); *Lady Audley's Secret* (Mary Elizabeth Braddon, 1862); and *Hard Cash* (Charles Reade, 1863).[19] A Select Committee of the House of Commons had been set up at the beginning of 1877 'to inquire into the operations of Lunacy Law so far as regards security against violations of personal liberty'. Patients who were cured – or had never been insane in the first place – could find it extremely difficult to regain their liberty and Lord Shaftesbury, the head of the Lunacy Commission, had even admitted that it was in the interest of the proprietor of an asylum to keep his paying patients as long as possible.[20] Mrs Lowe, who had herself been confined in a private asylum and had given evidence to the Select Committee in 1877, had warned fellow spiritualists, especially female ones, of the dangers of being incarcerated in such institutions. Georgina decided to consult her, 'feeling certain that these mysterious visitors and visits were something to do with the vile system she had denounced'.[21] She sent a note to her old acquaintance, W.H. Harrison of the *Spiritualist*, asking for an introduction. But she did not dare to leave the house – fortunately for her, as she later discovered that cabs and people were stationed at each corner of Tavistock Square, waiting to catch her if she ventured out.

The first visitor that morning was the lawyer, James Neal, who came on the pretext of wanting to know if Georgina had heard from Harry or from William Jevons. Whilst he and Georgina were talking in the corridor, a man rang the doorbell and asked if Neal was there. Both men then went away. Then, early in the afternoon, a woman called. She told Bell, who opened the door to her, that her name was Mrs Thomson and said that she wished to see Georgina. Bell went to ask Georgina if she would receive the visitor, informing her in a whisper that he 'believed it was one of last night's females'. Georgina asked him to tell Mrs Thomson that she could not see anyone until half past six that evening – having previously arranged with the police that they should be with her by that time. The woman departed, saying that she would return later. Five minutes later the doorbell rang again. This time it was a much more welcome visitor – Louisa Lowe herself – who sent in her card. Georgina welcomed her 'joyfully' and told her what had

19 Georgina had read *The Woman in White* and *Lady Audley's Secret* in 1864.

20 Kathleen Jones, *A History of the Mental Health Services* (London, 1972), pp. 158–9. The Lunacy Commission was the government department responsible for supervising the treatment of lunatics in England and Wales.

21 GW, *Doctors*, p. 14.

happened. Mrs Lowe replied that 'in the existing state of the Lunacy Laws nothing was unlikely or impossible', and warned Georgina that she might be in 'the most horrible danger'. Their worst fears were confirmed a few minutes later when Bell came to Georgina 'ashy pale, shaking from head to foot in the greatest state of agitation' and told her 'in a hoarse whisper': 'Them three of last night have pushed their way into the hall and declare they won't leave. They want to see you.' On being informed that Georgina was out, they had replied that they would wait until she returned.[22]

Leaving the unwelcome intruders waiting in the hall, Georgina sent Louisa Lowe to fetch the police and took refuge in the library. The door had no key, so she did her best to build a barricade by piling her largest music books in front of it. Instead of going to Hunter Street, where Georgina was already well known, Louisa Lowe went to Tottenham Court Road. Nevertheless, she returned with two men. Georgina told them of her suspicions and then, with these reinforcements behind her, went into the hall and asked 'them three' what they wanted. Mrs Thomson, who seemed 'much flurried', 'mumbled something about an orphanage'. She and her companions then tried to grab Georgina, upon which Louisa Lowe shouted, 'They are assaulting you, tell the police you give them in charge!' Georgina called to the policemen, and then retreated to the library again.[23] Much later she decided that she should have pretended to agree to go with them, then 'go to dress; heat a poker red-hot, take the cayenne pepper bottle, put the pepper in a cup, throw it at them and belabour them with the poker'. It was perhaps fortunate that she did not think of this at the time.

What actually happened was that Villiers fetched two policemen from Hunter Street, who asked Mrs Thomson and her accomplices what they were doing in Georgina's house. It soon became clear that they were indeed 'madhouse keepers', and were armed with medical certificates drawn up by two doctors, Edward Rudderforth and Charles Semple, together with a lunacy order, which had apparently been signed by Harry Weldon himself. Certain that this was 'an impudent forgery', Georgina telegraphed to Harry, begging him to 'COME AT ONCE. SOME VILLAINS SENT BY THAT VILLAIN MENIER HAVE GOT INTO THE HOUSE WITH A FORGED SIGNATURE OF YOURS.' She then started writing letters to the press, to her mother and to friends in Paris to tell them of her 'extraordinary adventure'. 'I awaited with trustful calm Mr Weldon's

[22] GWL, p. 27.
[23] GW, *Doctors*, p. 16.

appearance', she later wrote, 'as well as with joyful anticipation the "happy despatch" style [with] which he would turn them all out.'[24]

With Georgina still closeted in the library, Bell, Villiers, Louisa Lowe and Lise Gray, who had arrived whilst all this was going on, confronted the intruders and examined the lunacy order. This document, which appeared to be quite legal, directed them to commit one Georgina Weldon, 'a lunatic at large', to an asylum belonging to Dr Lyttelton Stewart Forbes Winslow. There was some debate as to whether Georgina could be said to be 'at large' if she was in the library, and the 'madhouse keepers' were eventually persuaded to leave, after appealing unsuccessfully to the police to help them to secure their quarry.

After they had gone, Mrs Lowe begged Georgina to leave the house immediately, telling her that she knew from experience that being put into a lunatic asylum was 'worse than death'. Georgina would be driven mad within an hour. She 'did not know how bad husbands were'. Mrs Lowe was sure that it was all Mr Weldon's doing, and that Georgina would be 'a doomed woman' if she stayed in the house. No power on earth would be able to get her out again once she had been sent to an asylum. Reluctant to believe that Harry could be responsible for 'such a cruel, abominable act', Georgina at first refused to go. But all her companions, including Bell and the policemen, begged her to flee. Villiers knelt down and kissed her hand and stroked it, telling her 'don't be angry, I feel sure it's all Mr Weldon's doing'. She had recognised the male madhouse keeper as the man who had called that morning asking for James Neal. Believing now that Neal was in league with Ménier, Georgina finally made up her mind to go:

> So, in greatest haste, I threw my cloak over my shoulders, [put on] my bonnet [and], without waiting to put on my boots, in a pair of wonderful old slippers, ran down the Square. The policeman stopped a cab ('I am not looking at the number!' he said), I jumped into it, Mrs Lowe took me to her house and I was ... SAVED!!![25]

Georgina spent the first night after her escape from Tavistock House at Louisa Lowe's lodgings in Keppel Street. That evening she wrote in her diary:

> How wonderful are the ways of Providence: but for Mrs Lowe I should be the inmate of a lunatic asylum. Then this is what I was sent for, to help Mrs Lowe to get the Lunacy Laws altered. And with the blessing of God, who intended me for His handmaid, I will, now that the

[24] GWL, p. 27.

[25] GW, *Doctors*, pp. 17–19.

> children are safe, devote my life, as long as He chooses, to this work. How well I knew Harry was a bad, cruel wretch. How right I was to say, 'Bad as Gounod is, Harry is ten times worse.' And I have been such a good wife to him! Thank God I do not love him, and that I bear this blow, which is apparently so much worse than the loss of the old man, quite calmly. Then I was not deeply religious, as I am now.[26]

Next morning she heard that a man had rushed up to Tavistock House ten minutes after her flight, and had then 'raved and stamped up and down, shouting excitedly "Mrs Weldon is a dangerous lunatic. Where is she gone?"' Receiving no answer, he had 'rushed away distractedly.' The same man had returned at midnight with the carriage and the three madhouse keepers. He had offered a thousand pounds to anyone who would help him to capture Georgina, telling them 'We must have Mrs Weldon tonight.' The 'troop' had subsequently gone to the office of the Lunacy Law Reform Association in Berners Street, but had been forced to leave empty-handed.[27]

After one night with Louisa, Georgina decided that she would prefer a lunatic asylum to her new friend's company. 'As for remaining another day with her,' she wrote, 'I would rather have been tied up with a bag of angry fleas.' She then sought refuge with her spiritualist friends, Thomas and Mary Ann Lowther, who lived in Hammersmith. A letter from James Bell warned her to stay away from Tavistock House for the time being as 'the unpleasantness' was still 'going on' and the house was being watched day and night. 'The people' had tried to bribe him to tell them where Georgina was.[28] So she went (disguised in 'a Sister of Mercy's bonnet and vail') to 7 Porchester Terrace, the home of John Morgan Richards, a wealthy American-born druggist and dealer in patent medicines, and his wife Laura. Georgina had known the Richardses for several years; they were keen theatre-goers and Laura had supported her orphanage with gifts of children's clothes.

Georgina stayed with the Richardses for a month. She did not leave the house for the first few days, though several people came to see her and she sent and received a large number of letters. Her friends and relations were at first inclined to dismiss the attempted incarceration as a figment of her imagination, but it soon became apparent that her fears were only too well founded. Exactly when the idea of having her carried off to a lunatic asylum had entered Harry's head is unknown, but it had clearly been there for some time. Henry de Bathe's brief visit to Tavistock House early in February 1877 seems to have been prompted by Harry, though he told Georgina's mother

26 GWJ, 15/4/1878.

27 GWL, p. 28.

28 SS, 7–10/1884, p. 6; James Bell–GW, 17/4/[1878].

that it was at her daughter's own 'urgent request'. Georgina was later to claim that de Bathe, who was at the time a governor of St Luke's Hospital for the Insane in Old Street, had worked on her husband's 'weak brain' with the aim of having her locked up and exposed as an adulteress so that Harry could marry one of his fellow-conspirator's many illegitimate daughters. De Bathe reported back to Harry shortly after the visit, and his description of life at Tavistock House gave Georgina's husband the ammunition he needed for a campaign to persuade the Treherne family that her unconventional way of life should be curtailed in some way. Harry quickly wrote to Georgina's mother to tell her that de Bathe had advised him to send 'one or two first-rate doctors, like Monro or Forbes Winslow', to see his wife:

> For the impracticable projects that she unfolded to him, which she felt so sure would succeed; the filthy state of the house; and the childish mismanagement of her means, all went to convince him that for her own sake, for mine, for that of her family, and for the sake of the poor little children she is attempting to bring up, some opinion, at any rate, should be taken as to the state of her mind.

Harry also told Louisa that he was tired of his wife's 'follies' and was determined to put a stop to them. Before 'moving in the matter', Harry explained, he would like to have the agreement of Louisa and of Georgina's brother Dal.[29] But for the time being he took no further action, apart from consulting two of the doctors who had looked after Georgina's father during the last few months of his life.

Harry had bided his time during the rest of 1877, as nothing could be done whilst Georgina was in France. By the beginning of 1878, however, the idea of having his wife confined in a lunatic asylum had clearly taken root. Anacharsis Ménier knew of his intentions, as did James Neal, who informed Arthur Rawlings, 'Mrs Weldon is a mad-brained woman, as mad as can be, and I shall soon have her into a lunatic asylum. There won't be much trouble about getting Mrs Weldon into a lunatic asylum. That's a very easy matter. There's no difficulty about that.'[30] Harry had good reason to believe that Georgina's family would not intervene: Louisa had already shown him some of Georgina's letters from France and told him that she was worried about her daughter's behaviour, and Dal had frequently expressed the opinion that his sister was mad.

[29] WHW–LFT, 19/3/1877. Dr Henry Monro (1817–91) was a well-known alienist (mad-doctor). See below, p. 209, for Forbes Winslow.

[30] GWM proof, misc., p. 184.

By returning to England on 3 April, and then by her determined efforts to prosecute Ménier for stealing her property, Georgina had given her husband both the opportunity and the motive to get her out of the way. No doubt he was afraid of what might come out in the course of further court proceedings, as Ménier, who had been intercepting Georgina's post during her absence, claimed to have a number of compromising letters written by men who included Georgina's eccentric Irish admirer, Cadwalladwr Waddy. He had also been making wild accusations about Georgina's treatment of her orphans.[31] Harry may well have had suspicions about the relationship between his wife (whom he had not seen for more than two years) and one – or both – of the Méniers. He knew from past experience that opposition of any kind only made Georgina more determined and was, no doubt, alarmed by the prospect of the Treasury becoming involved. He would, at the very least, be called upon to testify in court. Who knew what else might come out when the Weldons' dirty linen was washed in public?

The events of 14 and 15 April 1878 showed every sign of desperation. Had Harry and his accomplices not acted so precipitately, their attempts to kidnap Georgina might well have been successful. In their haste, as Georgina was later to point out, they omitted to follow the correct procedures. They had also reckoned without the loyalty of Georgina's servants – including the broker's man, Bell, who was being paid by Harry himself.

It was some time before Georgina discovered the identities of her visitors on those two fateful days. The 'first batch of Shell and Stewart' were an elderly doctor, James Michell Winn, and his son-in-law (the 'washed Christy Minstrel'), Dr Forbes Winslow, the proprietor of two private lunatic asylums in Hammersmith. Winslow was a controversial alienist or psychiatrist and an enthusiastic 'ghost grabber', well known for his hostility towards spiritualists. He and his father-in-law had been sent to examine Georgina and to report on her state of mind. Clearly, an unconventional way of life and the 'mismanagement' of her household were not seen as sufficient reasons for committing her to an asylum: instead, the doctors chose to concentrate on her involvement with Spiritualism.

Spiritualism has been described as 'a haven for the repressed, the unsatisfied, and the bereaved.' To the mid-Victorian mind it was distinctly suspect.[32] It appealed particularly to women: séances, which were usually held in private houses, gave them an opportunity to meet together and discuss a variety

31 GW, *Doctors*, pp. 79–80.

32 Ronald Pearsall, *The Table-Rappers* (Stroud, Glos., 2004), p. 10.

of subjects. There was a widespread belief that women were 'spiritually superior' to men, and many mediums were female. Entering into a trance led to a loss of inhibitions, and the ability to convey messages from 'the other side' gave mediums a significant amount of power.[33] Medical men, alarmed by the popularity of Spiritualism even among educated people, caricatured its adherents as 'crazy women and feminized men engaged in superstitious, popular and fraudulent practices.' Some scientists depicted spiritualists as maniacs, and denounced the trance as a form of hysteria.[34] Forbes Winslow had been the opening speaker at a conference on 'Spiritualism in connection with Lunacy' at the Langham Hall at the end of 1876. In his pamphlet, 'Spiritualistic Madness,' published a year before his examination of Georgina, he had identified Spiritualism as the principal cause of the increase in insanity in England, particularly among 'weak-minded hysterical women.' His claim that there were in the United States 10,000 insane patients whose malady had been caused by Spiritualism had been met with widespread derision. Furthermore, Winslow and his father had both been accused of detaining people improperly in their own asylums.[35]

In the report that he wrote after his interview with Georgina on 14 April 1878, Winslow claimed that her conversation throughout the interview had been 'inconsecutive and unconnected.' Her manner and demeanour had been those of an insane person, and he was 'decidedly of opinion' that her condition was 'such as to require the immediate protection of her friends.' Dr Winn, too, was prepared to certify that Georgina was 'laboring under insane delusions of such a nature as to render it necessary for her own protection that she should be put under proper legal restraint.'[36] He and Winslow had told Harry exactly what he wanted to hear. No doubt it was Harry who sent his friend de Bathe to see Georgina that afternoon (though Harry was later to claim that he had met de Bathe 'accidentally'). After this, de Bathe signed a letter to Forbes Winslow, with a formal request that he should receive into his house as a patient one Georgina Weldon, who was 'a person of unsound mind.' Georgina would subsequently assert that de Bathe did so 'falsely and maliciously and without taking due care or making due inquiries and without reasonable or proper cause.' She also discovered that the letter signed by de Bathe had been written by Forbes Winslow himself.[37]

33 Owen, *The Darkened Room* (London, 1989), esp. pp. 27–32.

34 Judith Walkowitz, *City of Dreadful Delight* (London, 1992), pp. 172–3.

35 L. Forbes Winslow, *Spiritualistic Madness* (London, 1877), p. 32, quoted in Walkowitz, *City*, p. 174.

36 GWM proof, misc., pp. 172–3; SC, *Weldon v. Winn*, 1884.

37 SC, *Weldon v. de Bathe*, 1883.

Before an individual could be certified as a lunatic, the law directed that they should be examined separately by two suitably qualified medical practitioners, both of whom must be independent of the proprietor of the asylum in which the examinee was to be incarcerated. Hence the pantomime with 'the second batch of Shell and Stewart' on the evening of 14 April, when each man made excuses to leave the other alone with Georgina for a while. This time the visitors were Edward Rudderforth (the older of the two) and Charles Semple, two doctors who had made a profitable business out of helping to commit patients to Winslow's asylum. Once Harry had the necessary certificates, he was able to sign the lunacy order that the 'madhouse keepers' produced during their attempt to abduct Georgina on 15 April. These three were Winslow's employees, Wallace Jones and his two female assistants, Mrs Thomson (or Tomkins) and Mrs Southey. The man who had 'raved up and down' outside Tavistock House after Georgina's escape was none other than Arthur William à Beckett, Forbes Winslow's brother-in-law and an old friend of Harry Weldon. Georgina may well have been correct in her suspicion that it was à Beckett who had introduced Forbes Winslow to her husband in the first place.

16
Home Again

Anacharsis Ménier was due back in court at Bow Street on 20 April. Georgina, who did not dare to attend in person, asked a solicitor, Charles Murr, to engage counsel to tell her side of the story. She also took the precaution of having herself examined by two doctors, James Edmunds and George Wylde, both of whom certified that she was 'perfectly sane.' When the hearing opened, her barrister, John Macrae Moir, informed Frederick Flowers that the prosecutrix was unable to be present, 'steps having been taken to secure her arrest as a lunatic.' This was, Moir asserted, 'a totally illegal proceeding.' He produced the two new medical certificates, which left no room for doubt concerning Georgina's sanity, and asked for the protection of the court. Flowers replied that it was his firm belief that the case should be taken up by the Treasury 'as the lady appeared to be quite helpless in the matter.' The court was informed that a well-known solicitor, St John Wontner, had already been instructed to conduct the prosecution on behalf of the Crown, but was unavoidably absent on this occasion. It was agreed that Ménier should be remanded for a further week, though he was allowed bail. Georgina was furious.[1]

The day after the court hearing was the eighteenth anniversary of Georgina's marriage to 'that nonentity,' Harry Weldon. Feeling rather braver, she attended the City Temple church with the Richardses. She was also determined to pursue her attackers. But who were they? And what part had her family played in the proceedings? She had written to her mother immediately after her escape from the 'mad-doctors.' Louisa, who was horrified by her daughter's news, had replied immediately, telling her that she should return to her husband:

> The law binds you to Harry and whatever way he wishes you to live; with respect to your orphanage, you must do as he wishes you. It will be a thorough protection to you from these bad people you fall in [with], who fleece you.

1 *Times*, 22/4/1878.

> I never heard of anybody being seized without a medical enquiry first. I do not understand your letter in detail. I am stunned with astonishment.[2]

The letters that Georgina sent to her mother at this time have not survived, but it is clear that she accused Louisa and the rest of the family of being her husband's accomplices. She discovered that her mother had been corresponding with Harry, and had lamented her daughter's 'strange, unnatural, ungrateful and wrong behaviour' to him. Louisa had even sent Harry some of Georgina's letters, thus unwittingly giving him ammunition for his campaign against his wife.[3] In her next letter Louisa vehemently denied all her daughter's accusations, telling her that she was totally mistaken. All the family had been horrified and astonished by the attack, and Louisa herself had 'had no more to do with it than the *Pope*':

> There is no 'stabbing in the dark' or secrecy on *our* side. We have accused you of nothing, but all the world saw your eccentric ways, of taking your children about barefoot etc. etc. I *myself* have had nothing to do with making conditions now with you, tho' I think on condition of Harry giving you what he proposes, you should cease these ways that are distasteful.[4]

Unless Louisa was being utterly disingenuous, it seems that she had little idea of Harry's true part in the recent events. She tried to persuade her elder son, Dal – now the head of the family – to try to mediate between Georgina and her husband. Dal was at first reluctant to intervene, having already received an abusive letter from his sister, whom he had barely seen since her marriage. He sympathised with Harry and was not averse to the idea of finding some way of restraining Georgina – indeed, he told Louisa Lowe that he would not have helped to get his sister out of a lunatic asylum, had she been confined in one.[5] Dal felt that Georgina had already embarrassed her husband and family quite enough. In his reply to her letter to him, he told her:

> I see scarcely any chance of my being of the smallest use to you! Your whole letter to the best of my belief is one mass of delusions.
>
> The end of this affair, even if nothing worse happens to you, will be that Harry will take your allowance away, only allowing a bare maintenance, and will sell Tavistock House. This, I feel convinced, will be

2 LFT–GW, 17/4/1878.
3 GWL, p. 16.
4 LFT–GW, 24/4/1878.
5 GW–William Jevons, 4/5/1878.

> the end of your 'dreams' if you persist in your present line of thinking and acting.

Any intervention on his part was, Dal assured Georgina, 'For your sake and yours alone'. Nevertheless, he eventually agreed to do what he could, under pressure from his mother, who told him, 'Poor Harry, he is, as you say, a – fool, but I am sure he has a very kind heart and no doubt suffers dreadfully, if only from the vexation of having been the executive of such a horrible blunder.'[6]

Given that Georgina had always regarded Dal as a 'putty-brained fool', it was unlikely that she would take much notice of his advice. She did, however, agree to see him. Afterwards, Georgina thought that the meeting had gone rather well, and that she would be able to dictate her terms to Harry: 'I think I have succeeded at last in getting one of the great family of Treherne to listen to me. Harry, he [Dal] says, is in the most dreadful funk! and Dal thinks I shall get Tavistock House and my £1000 a year all safe.' She signed a draft settlement on this basis.[7] Dal told Harry what had happened and sent him a copy of the document that Georgina had signed. In return for an income of £1000 a year and free use of Tavistock House, she was to be allowed to carry on her orphanage 'as she may please, so long as the number of the children do not exceed her means'. She would retain the house and the allowance, 'so long as Mrs Weldon does not come before the public in a manner inconsistent with her birth and station'. If these conditions were broken, Harry Weldon would have the right, with the consent of his wife's family, to 'take the necessary measures to ascertain as to whether she is capable of taking care of herself'. Given the circumstances, Harry had little choice but to agree.[8]

There matters might have rested, but for Georgina's discovery of Sir Henry de Bathe's contribution to the attempt to incarcerate her. On 25 April, the day after the meeting with Dal, she went to Cloak Lane in the City to discuss the Ménier case with St John Wontner. The meeting did not start well. Wontner began by shouting at Georgina in what she thought was 'the most insulting manner'. He argued with her and contradicted her 'in the most incomprehensible fashion'. Then he let slip that Forbes Winslow had already been to see him and had shown him a certificate of lunacy, informing him that 'Mrs Weldon is a hopeless lunatic. She has been certified insane by three medical men and Sir Henry de Bathe. She does not

6 DT–GW, 23/4/1878; LFT–DT, 24/4/1878.
7 GWJ, 24/4/1878.
8 GW, proofs of unidentified article.

know what she is saying.' Winslow had asked Wontner to help him to get Georgina into his asylum, telling him 'Her family is very unhappy about her. Her relations with Ménier are gravely compromising and they wish you to persuade her to abandon the prosecution.'

Wonter was 'vexed and mortified' when he realised that this information was all new to his client. He advised Georgina to give up her pursuit of Ménier, asserting that her relations with the Frenchman were 'of a most compromising nature.' Winslow had shown him letters written by her mother and brother, which made it clear that she had made them very unhappy. Her best course, he said, was to go to Dr Winslow's asylum and give herself up. If she were as sane as she alleged, she would be able to prove herself so. All this suggested to Georgina that Wontner was colluding with Winslow, whose brother-in-law, Arthur à Beckett, was the lawyer's 'intimate personal friend.'[9] This was bad enough. But the most shattering piece of news was the revelation was that the certificate produced by Winslow had been signed by de Bathe. It is difficult to disentangle the true course of events from the mass of accusations and theories produced by Georgina over the years, but it seems clear that the original lunacy order – the one produced at Tavistock House on 15 April – had been signed by Harry Weldon alone. Such an order was not, however, valid unless it bore the signature of someone who knew the alleged lunatic well. They had to state if this was the first bout of insanity and give details of any treatment that had been administered. It was almost three years since Harry had last seen his wife, so he persuaded de Bathe to visit Georgina at Tavistock House on 14 April, after which his friend either countersigned the original order or signed a completely new one. This was dubious to say the least: though Harry apparently tried to make Georgina's family believe that de Bathe had visited her regularly, he had in fact seen her for less than half an hour over the course of three or four years.

Georgina was 'staggered' by her discovery of de Bathe's treachery. She rushed straight from Wontner's office to the de Bathes' house in Arlington Street. Sir Henry was not at home when she arrived, but his wife received Georgina kindly. It was obvious that she knew nothing about her husband's part in the recent events. Lady de Bathe blamed Harry Weldon, whom she described as a 'horrid vagabond.' Harry had, she said been telling everybody that his wife was insane for the last eighteen months 'and it was the fashion among his friends to say Mrs Weldon was quite mad.'[10] According to his wife, de Bathe had been at home all day hanging pictures on 15 April

9 GWM, vi, pp. 7–12.

10 GW–R. Venables Kyrke, 23/5/1878.

and had not received any telegrams. Georgina was beginning to believe her when de Bathe himself walked in 'as jaunty and friendly as ever'. Georgina refused to shake hands and asked him:

> 'Did you sign that Lunacy Order?' He shuffled, tried to laugh it off, said he might put it in force this minute if he chose, that it was my mother's doing, but I kept on sledgehammer fashion fixing him well 'Did you sign that Lunacy Order?' At last he began 'Well, Madarme, I don't deny I have something to do with it!' 'Did you sign that Lunacy Order?' 'Well, Madarme, yes, I ...' I waited to hear no more. I started up as if I were shot. I said 'General de Bathe, you will repent this!'

'To think I telegraphed to him, as I telegraphed to Harry, to come and save me!!!', Georgina wrote in her diary that night. 'The two last people I should have suspected!! And to think it should be them!' It was a terrible blow. But she would have her revenge, adding 'And may God give me the means, give me the allies to ruin them!'[11]

There was now little chance that Georgina would abide by the terms agreed with Dal on 24 April. She had fresh ammunition to use against her family, since de Bathe had claimed that he had 'signed me [Georgina] mad to oblige my mother'. Louisa wrote to de Bathe, begging him to disabuse her daughter of these erroneous notions and telling him that, whilst she had believed that Georgina needed 'some protection and some friend to help her', neither she (Louisa) nor any member of the Treherne family had ever contemplated the possibility of her daughter being incarcerated in a lunatic asylum. The letter that Georgina had written to her mother, accusing her of having been 'instrumental' in the attempt to carry her off, had been so shocking that Louisa had been 'almost prostrated' by the grief and sorrow that it had brought to her.[12]

Two days after Georgina's visit to de Bathe, the Ménier case came up again at Bow Street. News of the attempt to abduct Georgina had spread and the hearing aroused a considerable amount of public interest. Fearing that his client was determined to create 'a blazing scandal', St John Wontner advised her to stay at home and stop writing to the newspapers. Georgina ignored him. Although the lunacy order was still in force, she was determined to attend the hearing. She wanted to make 'a sensational name' for herself, thereby attracting the public to her concerts and bringing in money to support the orphanage. She went to the court with 'a large number of friends' and a new acquaintance, the Christian socialist, Spiritualist, poet

11 GWJ, 25/4/1878.
12 LFT–Sir Henry de Bathe, 30/4/1878.

and journalist Gerald Massey, who arrived at Bow Street 'armed with four sandwiches and a loaded pistol.'

Wontner appeared for Georgina on behalf of the Treasury. He alluded to her desire to prosecute a number of people for conspiracy to injure her character, but said that he proposed only to deal with the charge of felony against Ménier on this occasion. If there were just grounds for a further charge, this could be deal with at Ménier's trial. Edward Besley, representing Ménier, objected that the case could not continue unless the prosecutrix's husband was present, since the articles that the prisoner was alleged to have stolen belonged to Mr Weldon and not to his wife. He was right. As a married woman, Georgina had no separate personality in law: everything that she had belonged to her husband – even, as Besley reminded her, her dresses.

When Besley claimed the right to cross-examine Georgina, Wontner tried to prevent her from taking the stand again, but Frederick Flowers granted the request, albeit reluctantly. The barrister (who was, Georgina decided 'not nearly so disagreeable as Mr Grain') began by asking questions about the letters that she had written to Ménier, several of which were produced in court. He claimed that the letters showed that Georgina had authorised Ménier to act for her in her absence and had regarded him as a partner in her orphanage and other business matters. Georgina replied that her husband had never employed Ménier and she herself had never authorised the Frenchman to receive money for her or to act as her partner in any way. The court was informed that Ménier had admitted that some of the stolen property had been found in his box, but claimed that a servant had put it there without his knowledge. Doubt was cast on this when a pawnbroker's assistant produced several articles of plate from Tavistock House, including some silver spoons that had been pledged by the prisoner.

Besley's assertion that 'he should not be deterred from doing his duty because the prisoner was a foreigner' provoked the sharp rejoinder from Flowers, 'Nor shall I be prevented from doing mine because the prosecutrix is an English woman.' Wontner then asked for the case to be sent for trial, but it was eventually agreed that the hearing should be adjourned for another week. It was up to the Treasury to decide if they wished to call Harry Weldon to give evidence. Gerald Massey took Georgina home afterwards. The day's events had not gone entirely as she had hoped: St John Wontner had, she thought, been 'very nice indeed,' but she was already suspicious of him, believing him to be 'a false hound.'[13]

[13] GWJ, 27/4/1878; *Observer*, 28/4/1878, p. 3; *Times*, 29/4/1878.

On 30 April, three days after the court hearing, Georgina sent a long letter to Harry's solicitor, William Jevons. This can be best described as a declaration of war:

> How Mr Weldon can have placed himself in such an awkward position, I cannot imagine. I am very much provoked about it, for, really, I am very sorry to have to defend this absurd imputation as to my sanity. Why! I have brains of steel!!! and so he and all my putty-brained family will eventually find out. If Mr Weldon wants money, why does he not come and tell me so? I am his best friend and would gladly have had him back again and taken care of him and the money.
>
> However! it was not to be. My work in this world is evidently cut out for me. It was nothing short of a miracle which saved me from a lunatic asylum. The man who signed the Order is a man I have seen twice for ten minutes in four years. As he is rich, I hope to get heavy damages against him, for it is a most *diabolical act of revenge* for a snub to his vanity received from me many years ago. His wife knew nothing about it and told me my husband had been preparing this for years. Telling everybody I was mad! My principal reason for writing to you is to ask you for instructions from Mr Weldon about my returning to Tavistock House.
>
> I am not safe, as the Order is not cancelled till the 14th May. I am sure that imposter Dr Llewellyn Stewart Winslow [*sic*] is still on the look out for me. But he may send where he likes; there's not a policeman in London who would not protect me, and all my tradespeople and servants are *up in arms*.
>
> I ought to have that Order and Certificates placed in my hands. I want very much to return to Tavistock House. I want to get the summer clothes for the children and send them. I want to have the house done up and repaired. It has been most *shamefully* neglected and will cost about £200; and as I have got to go to this expense I *must* be guaranteed peaceful possession and my £1000 a year.
>
> The accusations which are brought against me are so utterly false and ridiculous, I cannot for one moment submit to be spoken of as Mr Weldon speaks of me as 'being given another chance' or 'if things go on properly'. I deny it most indignantly. A public enquiry is going to be made and Mr Weldon will be forced to eat his own words *publicly* if he does not do so *privately* and, if he does not prove his repentance and his sincerity by settling the whole thing as he has promised, on me. I am sure Mr Neal will tell you I have my wits very considerably about me!
>
> I am a perfect heroine at the present moment and am deluged with letters of sympathy and encouragement from perfect strangers as well as heaps of friends. I hope you will persuade Mr Weldon that he has

> [been] made the dupe or the accomplice of what might have been a very cruel act, and which, thanks be to God, is but a very foolish and reprehensible act. It injures me, perhaps irreparably.
>
> An accusation of lunacy is a stigma which, in spite of all the publicity I shall court in every way, is likely to prove detrimental to me all my life and can only be mitigated by heavy damages given against the instigator of this abominable conspiracy against me. I hope for a speedy and pleasant termination of the affair as between me and Mr Weldon, which I am sure your good sense and good heart will both prompt you to bring about.[14]

After seeing this letter, Harry wrote to Dal Treherne, telling him 'I think the time has now come for you to decide whether you can give Georgina your support any longer.' In his opinion, Georgina had broken her agreement, and he hoped that Dal would not oppose him in any steps he might be advised to take for his own protection. Dal replied that, although he considered Georgina's brain to be affected, 'I do not consider she is bad enough to warrant, for the present at any rate, such a step as putting her into a lunatic asylum.' 'The strongest and firmest means' should be tried first. Harry should send Jevons to see her, with instructions to

> explain plainly what you demand from her at the present juncture, informing her at the same time that if she does not acquiesce you will sell Tavistock House and give her an allowance sufficient only for her to be able to live decently, and that you will no longer by giving her such large means, aid and abet her in her preposterous conduct which may, in the end, bring ruin and disgrace on her, on you, and on all connected with her.

If Georgina did not consent immediately, Harry should advertise that he would not be responsible for any debts she might incur. If she still refused to behave herself, her husband should take 'any stronger measures which you may think right for her protection as well as your own.' 'Believe me,' Dal continued, 'by firmness and decision you will make her understand her position, and the money is the only point by which you can touch her, for as to her heart or good feelings are concerned [*sic*], she has neither.' Harry's response was that it was 'impossible for me to write to, and argue with, a person I firmly believe (from my own experience which has been long and bitter) *no* argument will reach.'[15] He also wrote to Sir Henry de Bathe, to whose wife and footman Georgina had sent 'a bundle of

[14] GW–William Jevons, 30/4/1878.

[15] WHW–DT, 8,12/5/1878; DT–WHW, 10/5/1878

[presumably abusive] printed papers', telling him 'I now feel wholly released from the promise I made to [Georgina's] family to hold my hand and let things [go] on as heretofore'. 'My wife is *mad*', he added, 'she is *not* the horribly wicked and loathsome creature her acts make her appear.'[16] At the same time, Georgina told one of Harry's cousins that she was convinced that '*He* must be insane to behave in this way, and he has, I am told on very good authority, a perfect fear and horror of me – quite unaccountable to *me*, for we have never had a quarrel.' It was 'the most bitter humiliation to me to find my husband not only a cur but a criminal.'[17]

Georgina was now enjoying the notoriety that her court appearances had brought. One reporter wrote, 'All musical London is aroused to partisanship, and the most harsh discordant epithets are bandied from one fanatic to another.'[18] She used the publicity to promote her newly-found determination to bring about the reform of the Lunacy Laws, telling her old friend Percy Anderson:

> God has saved me. I have grown to the knowledge that thousands of persons as sane, as good, as useful, as active as I am, are dragging weary, maddening years in these 'licensed hells', beaten by the attendants for an unsubmissive word. Kept for days in the padded room for insubordination – kept on the worst side with raving, dangerous lunatics if you attempt to escape, drugged when those devils the Commissioners in Lunacy come round; when God has saved me from all this, is it to my mother or to any one else of my family I can listen? Let them join me, heart and soul, in making an exposé which will release thousands from the cruel, unjust, *atrocious*, false imprisonment; let them repent their supercilious way of judging and treating me as if I were the imbecile of the family instead of being what I am, extraordinarily gifted by God for purposes of His own. You can only imagine that if a remarkably intelligent woman, as I am, can, *in one day*, be certified mad by four doctors, what danger hangs over us all!

In his reply, Anderson, who had already tried to intercede with Harry on Georgina's behalf, warned her that Harry might well make the payment of her allowance dependent on certain conditions, and that it would be difficult to control his right to do so. 'You may', he told her, 'have to choose between the public advocacy of lunacy reform and revenge, on the one hand, and the providing for the poor orphans on the other.' But the 'poor orphans' were no longer Georgina's main priority and she told Anderson

16 WHW–Sir Henry de Bathe, 14/5/1878.
17 GW–R. Venables Kyrke, 15/5/1878.
18 *Illustrated Police News*, 11/5/1878, p. 2.

that she had made up her mind to give them up 'and to let nothing stand between me and my mission'. She was prepared to suffer for her cause: 'I do not expect for myself any comfort or reward in this world, and I thank God I am so frugal and unluxurious I can live very cheap. Lettuce, onion, and potato salad to eat and water to drink, and kippers for a change, sufficeth me day after day.' God had undoubtedly singled her out as an instrument of His vengeance. 'Why else', she asked Anderson, 'at my age, never having thought of *Woman's Rights*, should I be given the gift of eloquence? It must be for a purpose *not my own*.'[19] Georgina was now unstoppable, informing another friend that she expected to achieve much more than Louisa Lowe: 'The world will listen to one thing only: "Sensation". If I can get indicted for libel and get a few years' imprisonment, then at [last] the Lunacy Laws will be listened to and reformed. I shall have sacrificed myself to a great cause.'[20]

Louisa Lowe was a seasoned campaigner who had used many of the same methods of presenting her case as Georgina. At first Georgina was grateful for the older woman's help, but she was not used to playing second fiddle and it was not long before she attempted to take the lead. Shortly after receiving a letter from Gladstone, promising to bring her recent experiences to the attention of the head of the Lunacy Commission, she told Louisa:

> It is a great thing, I perceive, Mr Gladstone taking it up. In time we'll do wonders, and you must not *curb my audacity*.
>
> Remember that when the storm rages fiercely the best way to save the ship is to steer full steam and full sail through the tempest. The captain may sleep if the man at the wheel has nerve.[21]

Georgina, of course, saw herself as the 'man at the wheel'. She believed that Mrs Lowe was jealous, especially when Georgina began to attract attention by addressing meetings. At the end of the first week in May she decided that there was little risk that she would now be 'nabbed' and began to go about quite freely. On 11 May she visited Tavistock House for the first time since her escape and began to make plans to clean up and renovate the building. The lunacy order finally expired on 14 May and she returned home six days later, to be told by Bell that James Neal had ordered him not to let any workmen into the house. She did not take any notice of this. 'Loaded pistols and a squirt will keep robbers, etc. off',

19 GW–PA, 11,15,23/7/1878; PA–GW, 13/7/1878.

20 GW–Lennox Browne, 17/5/1878.

21 W.E. Gladstone–GW, 27/4/1878; GW–Louisa Lowe, 2/5/1878.

she wrote in her diary. She bought 'an enormous clyster' (a device for watering plants) and a policeman's rattle.[22]

Angèle had gone into hiding in Paris with Bichette after hearing of the momentous events of 14–15 April. She returned to Tavistock House at the beginning of June. Georgina was by no means sure that she wanted Angèle there, as she was beginning to suspect that she had conspired with Anacharsis Ménier to rob and ruin her. Her doubts were reinforced when Angèle produced some letters from Eugène Ménier, accusing her of trying to get rid of Anacharsis so that she could indulge in 'revolting sexual practices' with Georgina, her 'female lover.' Though she 'almost died of laughing' when she read these letters, Georgina quickly realised that her association with Angèle could undermine her attempts to revenge herself upon the latter's husband. She informed her friend that she could only come back to Tavistock House under certain conditions. Angèle would have to give up smoking and must stop sleeping in Georgina's room. She had to stay at home if Georgina went out in the evening, and should now think of herself as a housekeeper, rather than a companion. 'I feel,' Georgina added, 'a horror for a love or an exaggerated friendship.'[23] Nevertheless, she was soon grateful for Angèle's support. Together they barricaded and bolted themselves into the house and broke all the locks, thus excluding both Bell and the broker's clerk, a Mr Hooper.

On 4 June Georgina spoke to the Lunacy Law Amendment Society at Exeter Hall. It was all 'most exciting' and she was 'much applauded.' Over the next few months the publicity given to her activities brought a succession of visitors to her door – so many, indeed, that some of the neighbours believed that she was keeping a brothel. As usual, Georgina thrived on all the attention, though she complained that she had little time for herself and was tired by all the excitement.[24] Her influential friends also seemed to be reluctant, or unable, to give her the assistance she sought. As he had promised, Gladstone had forwarded an account of her escape from the mad-doctors to Lord Shaftesbury, but the latter's reply was discouraging: the Commissioners were not 'able to found upon it any suggestion for the amendment of the Lunacy Laws.' Georgina decided that Lord Shaftesbury was 'a great humbug' and the Commissioners in Lunacy were 'a monstrous institution.'[25]

This did not prevent her from taking direct action to help women who sought her help, or from doing everything she could to publicise their plight. In the words of a contemporary, she 'practically became the

22 GW–AM, 29/5/1878.
23 Eugène Ménier–AM, 10/5/1878; GW–AM, 17/5/1878.
24 GW, *Correspondence*, p. 316; GWJ, 2–5/6/1878.
25 W.E. Gladstone–GW, 27/4/1878, 20/6/1878; GW–PA, 11/7/1878.

recognized legal adviser of women who had been wronged and ill-treated', at a time when professional female lawyers did not exist.[26] There was Mary Ann Walker, newly 'escaped' from Camberwell House asylum, where she had been sent by her husband, an officer in the Indian Army. Louisa Lowe brought Mrs Walker to Tavistock House at the end of May, and Mrs Walker asked Georgina to help to her to recover her belongings, which were still held by the asylum. Georgina took her to the Lambeth Police Court, but was informed that her companion would need to employ a solicitor to pursue her claim. Georgina replied that 'she was perfectly prepared to talk as well as any solicitor'. 'There were', she added, 'no end of ladies confined, most unjustly, in lunatic asylums, placed there by husbands who wished to get rid of them.' The magistrate, George Chance, told Georgina to consult her own solicitor, but St John Wontner refused to get involved.[27] Georgina was not too upset when Mrs Walker decided to leave Tavistock House and return to Mrs Lowe's protection.

A few weeks later, Georgina took up the cause of two Australian women, Mary Ann Platt and her widowed sister Jane Sheberras, who had spent almost six years in Camberwell House, having allegedly been sent there by 'persons' who wanted their money. Though the women had 'considerable means', they had been treated as pauper lunatics. They had both been discharged in May 1877, though Miss Platt had subsequently been sent to another asylum, from which she had eventually escaped. In August 1878 Georgina was informed that Miss Platt had been 'caught'. She went to see Frederick Flowers at Bow Street, and told him that she wished to take charge of both ladies. She asked Flowers to recommend her as 'a fit and proper person' to undertake that duty, but he refused, telling her that giving such recommendations was no part of his duty. When pressed further by Georgina on the 'general deficiency' of the Lunacy Laws, he suggested that she should take the matter up with one of the 'aspiring young members of Parliament' who might be prepared to help her. On the following day Georgina awoke, 'thinking that if there remained no other way of getting justice or the Lunacy Laws reformed, I'd go and break Sir Henry de Bathe's windows'.[28] When Miss Platt turned up at Tavistock House, Georgina took her in. The woman now appeared to be 'completely off her head'; she was very disturbed and unable to sleep, and Georgina had to get up in the night to

26 F.C. Philips, *My Varied Life* (London, 1914), pp. 265–6. Women were not able to practise law on a professional basis before the passing of the Sex Disqualification (Removal) Act of 1919.

27 *Times*, 11/6/1878; GWJ, 7–10/6/1878.

28 *Times*, 24/8/1878; GWJ, 24/8/1878.

attend to her. By the end of the first week in September, Miss Platt was 'riotous' and calling for the police'. After trying to throw herself out of a window when Georgina was out of the house, she was carried off to St Pancras workhouse by the relieving officer. Georgina wrote some years later that she herself would have allowed Miss Platt to jump, in order to draw attention to the deficiencies of the Lunacy Laws.[29]

~

All through the summer of 1878, Anacharsis Ménier remained in Newgate gaol, where he succeeded in convincing his fellow inmates that he was 'an innocent martyr'. In the meantime, his brother Eugène tried – unsuccessfully – to raise £120 in bail money, and also further funds to pay for the prisoner's defence when the case came to court again. He also told Anacharsis's solicitor, Willoughby Gunston, that people in Paris who knew Georgina and Angèle had informed him that the 'total intimacy' between them hinted at 'unnatural relations, which [are] unfortunately too common in our days'. Eugène had, he claimed, tried to keep this a secret to protect his brother, but it was now necessary to reveal it.[30]

After several further adjournments, Anacharsis Ménier's trial at the Old Bailey began on 16 September before the Recorder of London, Sir Thomas Chambers. This time, Ménier was charged with 'Stealing a mosaic necklace and other articles, the property of William Henry Weldon'. It was, in the words of Edward Grierson, 'a ludicrous trial'; Georgina thought it 'an infernal and odious comedy'. Ménier was again defended by Edward Besley. St John Wontner had withdrawn from the fray, having received a number of rude letters from Georgina during the summer, and the Treasury was represented by Douglas Straight and Frederick Mead. It was noted that, although Mr Weldon was nominally the prosecutor, 'the real prosecutrix in the case was Mrs Georgina Weldon'.[31]

Proceedings began with Georgina taking the stand and giving a long – and somewhat rambling – account of her orphanage and her dealings with the Méniers. The reporter for *The Times* described her as 'an excitable lady and an avowed believer in Spiritualism'.[32] She was indignant when Besley, cross-examining, suggested that her relationship with Ménier had been rather closer than she admitted and asked her when she had last slept with her husband. It was not until after the trial that Georgina

[29] GWJ, 7–9/9/1878; SS, 7–10/1884, pp. 5–6.

[30] GW–St John Wontner, 6/8/1878; Eugène Ménier–M. Gunston, 13/6/1878.

[31] Edward Grierson, *Storm Bird* (London, 1959), p. 174; GWM, vi, pp. 120–1; *Eastern Daily Press*, 18/9/1878, p. 4.

[32] *Times*, 18/9/1878.

realised that Besley had been hinting that it was her relationship with one (or both) of the Méniers that had driven Harry Weldon out of the house. Had she understood this at the time, Georgina could have pointed out that her husband had left Tavistock House nine months before her first meeting with Angèle, and over a year before the Frenchwoman moved into Tavistock House. Unfortunately for her, however, there were plenty of people who were prepared to believe that there must be some truth in the scandalous rumours.

Georgina then moved on to the attempt to confine her in a lunatic asylum, asking the Recorder to subpoena the doctors and force them to come to court. It was, she continued, all the result of a conspiracy. Wontner was unwilling to act on her behalf because he and Dr Winslow were friends, and Ménier was only a tool – he was acting on behalf of others who were 'more wicked than him' and had 'tried to get me away and get possession of my house'. Harry's lawyer, James Neal, had been helping Ménier to steal her property. Everyone was conspiring against her because she was a spiritualist. This was all highly entertaining for the audience, if not for the lawyers. When the trial recommenced on the following day, Georgina took her seat below the jury box, between Besley and the jury. Everyone began to laugh when Besley asked the Recorder to tell her to sit somewhere else because she was making 'insane grimaces' at him – a claim that Georgina indignantly denied. Even the Recorder 'roared with laughter and made a most merry incident of it'.

Reluctantly, Harry Weldon was called to the stand. He told the court that he had not authorised Ménier to take anything from Tavistock House; he had merely asked his solicitor to take possession of the house and 'put a proper person in charge of it'. He had ceased to live with his wife around 1875, but had never made any settlement on her. She had no property in her own right apart from her jewellery. 'I cannot explain how it is that she says I improperly tried to make her out a lunatic in order to get her money', he added, 'because she had no money.' He admitted that he had consulted 'two medical men who had charge of her father', and said that he had taken steps 'to see as to the state of her mind' after her return from France. But the idea that anyone had tried to have her taken to a lunatic asylum was 'a complete delusion on her part'.

The principal witness for the defence was Angèle's sister, Marie Helluy, who had already made a private deposition accusing Georgina of being 'very familiar' with her during her stay at Tavistock House in 1877. Georgina's campaign against Anarcharsis Ménier had, Marie claimed, been motivated by jealousy, because she wanted Angèle for herself. In her opinion, Mrs Weldon was 'afflicted with monomania'. Marie swore that Georgina had asked Ménier to pawn 'articles, silver plate and jewellery'. Georgina had, she said, discussed the management of Tavistock House with Ménier and it had been arranged that, whilst she was in France, 'Ménier, as her partner, should direct, conduct and transact all the business just as if she was here'. He was, indeed, 'very nearly like the master of the house'. Marie also claimed that Georgina had said that 'she was a ruined woman, and everything was to be sold, and had to be sold'. Georgina contradicted all of this and told the court that Marie had agreed to give evidence for Ménier only if she was paid.

Summing up for the defence, Besley said that Mrs Weldon was evidently labouring under the impression that she had been treated harshly by her husband and hoped that the prosecution would assist her in her aim of procuring an amendment of the Lunacy Laws. He maintained that she had been jealous of Ménier's mistress, Olive Nicholls, and implied that Georgina had herself been the Frenchman's mistress. Though Georgina claimed that she had been robbed of jewellery worth several hundred pounds, the only articles that could be traced to the prisoner were, he said, 'of a very trifling value':

> And the prisoner, having regard to the intimate connection that existed between him and Mrs Weldon, might very well have believed that he was justified in dealing with such articles for a temporary purpose, without the slightest idea of committing a criminal act, and that, at all events, there was a sufficient doubt in the matter to justify the jury in acquitting the prisoner.

At the end of the trial, the Recorder showed little sympathy for Georgina, telling the jury that she was 'a person of very strong opinions' and there had evidently been 'an acquaintance of great intimacy between the prisoner and herself, in consequence of which the prisoner might have felt justified in doing as he had'. If the jury believed that Ménier had 'really and honestly' acted under that impression, Sir Thomas Chambers told them, they should acquit him.[33]

The jury was out for a long time. Eventually they returned and the verdict was given. Anacharsis Ménier was found guilty, but the jury strongly recommended mercy because he was a foreigner 'and on the grounds of the intimate relationship that existed between the prosecutrix and himself'. Ménier was sentenced to six months' hard labour. Georgina's reaction was that the case had been 'disgustingly hushed up'. In her opinion Ménier deserved to serve seven years' penal servitude for his crimes. She went back to Tavistock House after the trial had ended, 'dead tired and mortified', though she was somewhat comforted by a séance that evening at which a

33 Deposition of Marie Helluy, *c.*16/8/1878; *Times*, 18/9/1878.

'guardian angel' told her to have faith in God. In a letter to Chambers, she complained that the antecedents of the prisoner had been allowed to pass in silence, whilst she had been 'dragged through the mud.' 'Perhaps I use strong language,' she added, 'but I am tempered like steel and as valiant as in the Age of Chivalry.'[34] Chambers merely sent her a brief acknowledgement.

[34] GWJ, 17/9/1878; GWM, vi, pp. 127–8: GW–Sir Thomas Chambers, 18/9/1878.

17
Rivière

At the end of 1878 Georgina was riding on the crest of a wave of support and sympathy after her escape from the mad-doctors and the Ménier trial. She was now determined to fight back with all the weapons she could muster. A brilliant self-publicist, she went on the rampage, attacking her enemies on all fronts. She did so at a time when the removal of taxes on newspapers and technological improvements had led to an explosion in the availability of news and advertising media of all kinds. Georgina made use of books, pamphlets and newspapers to publicise her views and grievances. She also appeared on concert platforms, in theatres and lecture halls and, most significantly, in the law courts. For a decade her name was rarely out of the newspapers.

Opinion on Georgina's exploits was sharply divided. To some, especially to the mainly middle-class spiritualists, she was a heroine, sacrificing her own interests to help the powerless and oppressed. An account of her career published in *The Medium and Daybreak* in 1879 can only be described as a hagiography:

> She was a brilliant star in the aristocratic firmament, and to lend her rays to any sphere less elevated was a crime too great to be condoned. But her ostracism from the self-selected few has been the gain of the many – loyal souls, who reward with generous gratitude any acts performed for their instruction or amusement. As a Musician of great natural gift, as a Composer, as a Lecturer, as an Author, as a Teacher, as a Philanthropist, as a Reformer, and as a Woman of unspotted fame, Mrs Weldon stands conspicuous before the world, as not only one woman, but a host in herself. Mrs Weldon is a presage of the better time, when those of good natural endowments, position, and education will step out from the charmed circle of exclusiveness and selfishness, and use their glorious powers for their country and the good of humanity. The evils of the world will be healed, and the sufferings of the nation alleviated ... Like all great souls, she knows not yet the grandeur of her Mission. Let her name be WELL-DONE – a name not inherited nor conferred, but deserved!

When she saw this, Georgina commented 'Lives of the Saints is nothing to mine!' and ordered 10,000 copies for her supporters.[1]

On the other hand, 'Society' as a whole – the members of the upper and upper-middle classes, including Georgina's own family – heartily disapproved of her activities. They deplored her methods, even if some of them privately agreed with her aims. The columnist 'Gadfly' wrote in the magazine *Entr'acte and Limelight*, 'Mrs Weldon is possibly a woman of very generous instincts, but she cares not to keep her light under a bushel. She knows the way to advertise herself.' As she was fortunate enough to have received 'the education and training of a lady', no excuse could be made for her 'unseemly method of getting into prominence.'[2]

Over and over again, Georgina's mother attempted to point out the error of her ways, telling her: 'Your love of publicity feeds the taste of the public who, out of vulgar curiosity, occupy themselves with an affair without a drop of sympathy.' Like 'Gadfly', Louisa believed that Georgina was behaving in a most unladylike manner: 'I do not understand your love of publicity. Most women dread seeing their names made into a topic of public conversation, whether they are right or wrong, or even if they are as innocent as the angels.' Georgina's response was predictably scathing:

> 'Most women' of whom you speak to me, who 'would recoil from this and that', in my opinion, are idiots and do not have (old as I am) either my beauty, nor my diverse talents, nor my happy, calm, and serene temperament. So why should these women seek publicity? They have nothing to show, and their mind is not of a superior kind. Find for me several dozen women of my calibre, and let them give me their opinion! If they had the same grievances as me, I believe they would do the same as me. There is no hope if one keeps quiet. It's always better to try to make a fuss.[3]

Georgina quickly developed a love–hate relationship with the press: she needed them to publicise her campaigns and her public appearances but took violent exception to unfavourable accounts of her exploits. She hated their favourite headline, 'Mrs Weldon again', believing that it 'conjured up visions of a public nuisance in divided skirts, with hooked nose, horned spectacles, and a green umbrella.'[4]

1 *Medium and Daybreak*, 17/10/1879, pp. 646–8; GWJ, 17/10/1879.
2 *Entr'acte*, 28/12/1878, p. 6; 15/11/1879, p. 11. I have not been able to identify 'Gadfly'.
3 LFT–GW, 20/11/1880, 19/7/1881; GW–LFT, 31/7/1881.
4 *Eastbourne Gazette*, 21/9/1887, p. 5.

Many people agreed, however, that Georgina had been badly treated. In October 1878 she asked Frederick Flowers for summonses against Harry, de Bathe and the four mad-doctors for 'conspiring to arrest her and drag her forcibly to a lunatic asylum', telling the magistrate that she hoped that he would 'have them all for conspiracy'. Flowers advised her to draw up a formal statement of her case and find witnesses who would back up her accusations. But when she presented her 'information' to him, he told her to consult a solicitor, as many of her allegations were too vague and it might be difficult to prove them to the satisfaction of a court. Georgina followed his advice, only to be informed that she could not take legal action against 'Winslow and the lot' because, as a married woman, she had no separate legal identity. This meant that any civil proceedings against Harry and the other men would have to be undertaken by 'a next friend of good monetary position, who might also be required to give security for costs'. A few days later, a different solicitor filed a Petition for Dissolution of Marriage with the Probate, Admiralty and Divorce division of the High Court on Georgina's behalf.[5]

The Matrimonial Causes Act of 1857 had made it easier to obtain a divorce, though it remained a complex and expensive process. The new legislation favoured the husband, who had to show that his wife had committed adultery. A wife, however, had to prove adultery, plus some aggravating offence such as incest, cruelty or desertion. Alternatively, she could sue for divorce on the grounds of cruelty alone. In Georgina's petition of 17 October 1878 she accused Harry of adultery, with a woman living in Chelsea and also with other women. At this stage, she still did not know the name of her husband's mistress. She also accused Harry of cruelty, in that he had attempted to have her forcibly removed from her home and confined in a lunatic asylum, knowing that she was quite sane at the time. Harry denied that he had committed adultery, and it soon became obvious that Georgina did not have enough evidence to prove that he was lying. He did not deny that he had been involved in the attempt to have her detained (thus contradicting the evidence that he had given on oath at the Ménier trial four months earlier), but claimed that he had genuinely believed that his wife was a person of unsound mind who needed 'care and treatment'. He had acted 'with bona fides and without malice'. Six weeks later, Georgina amended her petition, asking for a judicial separation instead of divorce. A separation was easier to obtain, as she would simply have to prove adultery or cruelty or desertion. She

5 *Times*, 14/10/1878; Morgan and Gilkes, solicitors–GW, 15/10/1878; TNA, J77/216/5905.

also wanted the court to order Harry to pay her a fixed annual allowance. Delaying tactics by Harry's lawyers meant that these proceedings were destined to run on for another two years.

In the meantime, Georgina was busy with attacks on her other enemies, and with her campaign for the reform of the Lunacy Laws. At the end of September 1878, the proprietors of St James's Hall agreed that she could hold a meeting there on 5 November. She immediately had posters and tickets printed. She would, she promised, lecture on the subject of Anacharsis Ménier's trial and on the Lunacy Laws, and it was clear that she would not be pulling any punches. She referred to the 'horrible trap' that her husband and his associates had laid for her, and accused Doctors Winslow and Winn of 'hunting in couples,' tracking down rich patients for the former's private lunatic asylum. She also claimed that Winslow had tried to bribe the police to help him to find her.[6]

In mid October one of Georgina's sympathisers and fellow Lunacy Law reform campaigners, a 'little cock sparrow' called James Salsbury, agreed that she could rent advertising space in the window of his shop at 429 Oxford Street, which housed the 'Sanitary Depot' of Messrs Nichols and Company and 'the Alpha Food Reform Restaurant and Vegetarian Dining Rooms.' Shortly afterwards, Salsbury received a letter from Forbes Winslow's solicitor threatening to prosecute him for displaying Georgina's publicity material in his shop. Georgina told the solicitors to regard her as the responsible party and address any future complaints to her. In the meantime she hired a sandwich-man to carry her posters around the streets of central London. Salsbury also stood firm: he sent £8 to Georgina as a contribution to her orphanage and started to sell photographs of her.[7]

It also occurred to Georgina that her notoriety following the Ménier trial might be a means of restarting her musical career and gaining additional publicity for her meeting at St James's Hall, so she wrote to the conductor and concert organiser, Jules Rivière, asking for permission to distribute her Lunacy Law bills 'all over' the Covent Garden Theatre, where he was conducting a series of promenade concerts. Thus began one of the most disastrous of her relationships – one that was to last for many years and cost both protagonists many hundreds of pounds. In Rivière Georgina had finally met her match.

Jules Prudence Rivère, the son of a stocking-weaver, had come London from France in 1857, speaking little English and virtually penniless. For reasons that would eventually become apparent, he was somewhat vague about his

6 GW, *Correspondence*, p. 314.
7 GWJ, 24/9/1878–5/11/1878; GWMSM, p. 151.

previous career. He claimed to be married with one child when he was naturalised as a British citizen in 1864, but was described as a bachelor when he married Amy Frances Fisher (variously described by Georgina as a dressmaker or a dancer at the Alhambra) in London in 1870. By this time he was well known as a conductor of concerts of light music, featuring military bands, 'grand operatic selections', 'pretty pieces' and ballets.[8] Many of these were promenade concerts, given in large halls that could accommodate several thousand people, where the lavish decoration would be augmented with potted plants, fountains and gaslights with coloured filters. Refreshments were available and the audience – drawn mainly from the lower middle class – was free to wander in the open area in front of the orchestra. Georgina had been to one of these concerts at Covent Garden with Nelly Craven and Freddy Warre in 1871 and had not been impressed. She had seen Rivière with his wife at a party earlier in the same year, but had not been introduced to them, as they were not 'respectable'. Madame Rivière was, she was told, 'a disreputable *danseuse de casino*, whilst her husband was a *saltimbanque en musique* [mountebank musician]. In 1873 Rivière had tried unsuccessfully to persuade Gounod to conduct some concerts for him, and had also asked to hire the music for the *Funeral March of a Marionette*: Gounod had made him pay ten guineas to use the music for a month.[9]

In 1878 Rivière hired Covent Garden from the tenants, the Swiss restaurateurs and theatre proprietors Agostino and Stefano Gatti, for five weeks with the aim of putting on a series of promenade concerts, beginning on 5 October. He was just as aware of the value of publicity as Georgina and had seen the newspaper articles about her lawsuit. So, when she asked him to display her posters and allow her to distribute some circulars, he replied that he would be happy to do so if she would sing at his concerts once a week, thinking that her name would be 'a draw'. Georgina was only too happy to accept Rivière's offer and told him that she would require no fee. Her debut, on 15 October, was (she thought) a triumph:

> All the house was surprised when I made my appearance. I had a perfect ovation. The house almost rose. I got thro' 'Le Songe' very respectably and was encored and recalled. I sang 'Welcome to Skye'. It was a success. I knelt down in a little dark corner and thanked God and my guardian angel, Victoire Gounod, who has been urging me to sing. 'Oh, that we two' encored. I gave them the 'Harlech March'.

8 Jules Prudence Rivière, *My Musical Life and Recollections* (London, 1893), p. 130.

9 POB, 1/3/1880: *Regina v. Weldon*; GWJ, 25/8/1871; GWM proof, vii, p. 111; GW, *Correspondence*, p. 202.

She felt that she was, at long last, 'regaining lost ground' in spite of the efforts of her old enemies, the music critics.[10] Rivière seemed to agree, and asked her to sing every night for the next fortnight. These further performances were, however, not an unqualified success. In the opinion of one reviewer, 'Mrs Weldon's singing will pass muster in a drawing-room, but [her] vocalisation can hardly be supposed to satisfy a public which expects a really good-class article. The reception given to this lady and her performance was of a frigid character.' Though she wrote in her diary that she was well received on most evenings, Georgina later admitted that people had 'come every night to hiss me', and her friends had 'got into rows every night'.[11]

The final night, Saturday 2 November, was Rivière's Benefit performance. Georgina and Angèle were taken to Madame Rivière's box to be introduced. Georgina did not recognise the girl, who was much younger than her husband, and concluded that she must be the conductor's second wife. Afterwards, Rivière presented her with a cheque for £10 and asked her if she would join him and his 'troupe' when they travelled to Brighton in the following week to give a series of concerts at the Dome. He promised that that he would pay all the expenses for Georgina and Angèle, and that they would have 'a room, two beds, a drawing room, a piano, all the shop'. Georgina agreed.[12]

Before the trip to Brighton, however, Georgina had to get through her meeting at St James's Hall on 5 November. In spite of all her efforts to publicise the event, the audience was much smaller than she had expected. About 200 people turned up, many of whom were disappointed to find that they were expected to pay between 1s and 5s for the privilege of hearing Georgina's lecture on the Lunacy Laws and the Ménier case. Many, no doubt, came out of curiosity, for the idea of a woman speaking from a platform was still something of a novelty at this time. Ten years earlier such an activity had been almost unheard-of: women had begun to campaign for better education, political enfranchisement, and social and legal reforms, but their energies had been channelled into committees and meetings, the writing of letters, books and pamphlets, and the presentation of petitions. This had changed in the 1870s, when members of the 'shrieking sisterhood' had begun to address public meetings.[13]

10 Rivière, *Musical Life*, p. 195; GWJ, 15/10/1878; GW, *Correspondence*, p. 4. 'Le Songe' was 'Le songe de Pauline' from Gounod's *Polyeucte*.

11 *Entr'acte*, 26/10/1878, p. 11; GW–JPR, 22/8/1879.

12 GWJ, 2/11/1878.

13 The first use of this term that I have found comes from the *Saturday Review*, and was quoted in the *Standard*, 12/3/1870, p. 5.

For Georgina, giving a lecture was a less intimidating experience than it would have been for many women, for she had been singing at private parties since childhood and at public concerts since 1870. She had spoken from the platform in the Langham Hall during her 'sociable evenings' and was already used to standing up and speaking in the law courts. At St James's Hall on 5 November 1878 she spoke to her audience for nearly two and a half hours and sang two songs. As usual, she thought that she had done well, writing afterwards in her journal: 'I turn out to be a splendid public speaker, not the least nervous and as much at home as it is possible to be. So I have the gift of eloquence and that of keeping my audience delighted and amused. I sang well.' The reporter for the *Illustrated Police News* wrote that 'Mrs Weldon has a pleasing manner, smiles profusely, and speaks in a colloquial manner and with much fluency, delivering her remarks with telling emphasis.'[14] It was quite obvious that she was not a lunatic. James Salsbury, who was in the audience, was also deeply impressed and offered to display further material relating to Lunacy Law reform in his window free of charge. He also sent Georgina a cheque for five guineas, 'trusting you may become the apostle of this movement and succeed in your mission.'[15]

On the day after Georgina's meeting she received a letter from Rivière addressed to 'Dear Prima Donna.' 'You must let the lunatics have a rest and occupy yourself about our week at Brighton,' he began. He was taking his full orchestra and chorus, and 'the principal singers from Covent Garden.' At this stage in their relationship the two were clearly on excellent terms: Rivière signed his letters 'yours devotedly,' and he even gave Georgina £10 just before they all left London on 9 November when she discovered that 'that pig Harry' had not paid her allowance for two months. The concerts were, however, a failure. The hotel bills alone came to nearly £100 and Rivière vowed that he would never give another concert in Brighton.[16]

~

Georgina also gained a new supporter at this time. James Mortimer was an American chess player and diplomat who had settled in Paris in 1860. He had subsequently taken to journalism, becoming a loyal supporter of Napoleon III. When the Emperor was deposed in 1870, Mortimer had followed him to England, where he had founded the *London Figaro*, the official newspaper of the French government-in-exile. By 1878 the twice-weekly periodical had an extensive circulation and was well known for its

14 GWJ, 5/11/1878; *Illustrated Police News*, 16/11/1878, p. 2.
15 Nichols and Co.–GW, 21/11/1878.
16 Rivière, *Musical Life*, p. 195; GWJ, 7/11/1878; GW, *Correspondence*, p. 11.

articles on politics, literature and the arts, employing a number of influential drama critics. On Saturday 26 October 1878 it included an article entitled 'Worse than the Bastille'. The article is unsigned, but must have been written by Mortimer himself:

> Is there a husband with a little money, a seared conscience, and the heart of a wolf, who is tired of his wife, and wants her out of the way, so that he may have the society of a mistress without protest or interruption? Is there a false wife, an incarnate fiend, who wants to get rid of her husband, so that she may be intimate with her paramour without the risk of a Divorce Court suit, and consequent loss of income and social *status*? Is there any one who, for devilish greed, or fraud, or revenge, wants to get rid of any person?
>
> In this realm of England it can be done, with very little trouble and without risk. The means are as sure as murder, and more cruel. The victim of fiendish lust or revenge can be put into a private lunatic asylum.

The author went on to describe how 'any two black sheep doctors' might be employed to commit a sane person to an asylum, from which they would be unable to escape. Their fate would be 'Worse than penal servitude. Worse than the Bastille. Worse than an agonising death'. Everyone, he wrote, should demand an amendment of the Lunacy Laws in order to prevent 'the most infamous and accursed iniquity of confining the sane in lunatic asylums'. Private asylums should be abolished because the proprietors had a pecuniary interest in detaining the inmates.[17]

Three days after reading this, Georgina visited the office of the *London Figaro* and met Mortimer and his sub-editor, Henry Kenward. They agreed to publish a series of letters on the subject of the Lunacy Laws. In the first one, Georgina congratulated the editor on his 'glorious article' and expressed the hope that he would take up the cause of Lunacy Law reform. In the next, published on 20 November, she described the events of 14–15 April, asking the editor to 'enlighten the public as to what really took place as regards the attempt, several times repeated, to get me into a private lunatic asylum'. 'This sort of legally carried on business', she continued, occurred every day. In spite of her efforts, 'no real public cry' had been raised against such practices.[18]

Several letters of advice and encouragement addressed to Georgina were published at the same time. One correspondent thought that she should 'adopt some means of self-protection'. Carrying a gun might be going too

[17] *London Figaro*, 26/10/1878, p. 1.
[18] GW–*London Figaro*, 29/10/1878, 20/11/1878.

far, but she could at least employ a secretary who could act as a bodyguard. Another warned her 'You may unhinge yourself and upset your own mental machinery by the work and worry all this must involve.' Georgina should 'trust this championship to masculine minds': 'Your best and most invincible safeguard is to give the lie to your enemies by your own circumspection and calmness of bearing; the least feminine lapse into excitability or hysteria would simply give them the opportunity for which, no doubt, they watch.' 'Circumspection and calmness of bearing' were, however, the last things that Georgina was interested in:

> To die as a solder falls, with his flag in his hand, is a noble death, and one which will carry the spirit to the Great Light beyond. I therefore dread nothing which may befall me. I hope for success, though I do not believe in it. I am quite ready to write what I know, if the *Figaro* wishes it, for I have neither 'private nor particular reasons' for avoiding mixing myself up in a public controversy on the subject.

The *London Figaro* did indeed want Georgina to write what she knew. In the first instalment, which appeared on 4 December with the title 'Our Lunacy Laws: The Story of Mrs Weldon, Written by Herself', she accused her husband of perjury at Anacharsis Ménier's trial, declaring that it was her intention to 'expose the whole system' and make the public 'listen and believe', even if it took the rest of her life. Over the weeks that followed, Georgina told readers of her first meeting with Harry and their life together; of the orphanage; of her unsuccessful attempts to persuade her influential friends to help her to reform the Lunacy Laws; and of the hundreds of people who had written to her asking her to publicise their grievances. If she had achieved anything, she wrote, it was 'By defying ridicule, by defying lies, by courting libel in every direction, by becoming what people call "low-bred", "vulgar", "bad taste", "thirsting for notoriety", and every accusation or reproach as "malevolent" [and] "revengeful"'. She was, she wrote, determined to bring Harry Weldon, Sir Henry de Bathe and the four mad-doctors to book.[19]

Then, on 14 February, Georgina received the 'very delightful news' that Harry and de Bathe had made a successful application to the High Court for the publishers of the *London Figaro* to be prosecuted for criminal libel. Her final article was published four days later. At the end of it was a note by Mortimer referring to the legal action and stating:

[19] *London Figaro*, 20/11/1878, p. 5; 4/12/1878, p. 11; 8/1/1879, p. 3; 15/1/1879, p. 4.

> Our sole object in publishing Mrs Weldon's story has been, and is, to permit a defenceless woman, whom we sincerely believe to have been misrepresented and ill-used, an opportunity of vindicating herself before the public. We utterly disclaim all malice in this publication, and we are actuated solely and exclusively by a sense of public duty, and the conviction that great wrongs are perpetrated under the present Lunacy Laws of England.[20]

If James Mortimer thought that this would pacify Weldon and de Bathe, he was wrong. He told Georgina that he had no money for legal expenses, but nevertheless decided to defend himself after she promised to let him have Watts's portrait of her, telling him that he could sell it if she could not raise the money by any other means. 'Naturally', she informed him, 'the more remarkable I grow, the more valuable does my picture become.' She gave Mortimer a long list of instructions for the lawyer who was to defend him, assuring him: 'You will see, the other side will not find a witness against me. I know that. Be easy. Victory is ours.' The lawsuit 'may cost a little', but she could 'earn money over and over again.' In any case, no one who knew anything about the matter thought that it would go any further.

Georgina was furious when Mortimer refused to publish any more of her articles, telling her that the case was now *sub judice*, and he would risk being committed to prison for contempt of court were he to do so. In court on 13 March he made a 'humble apology', but this was not accepted and he was forced to prepare his defence. Georgina tried to persuade him to resume the publication of her articles and letters, but he again refused. Georgina then seems to have demanded the return of her picture, claiming that Mortimer had obtained it from her under false pretences. Her letters have not survived but they were clearly abusive, as Mortimer told her that he had not replied to them 'because I have no answer to make to insults from a lady.' He also refused to give the picture back, since she had given it to him of her own free will.[21]

The case against the *London Figaro* was tried at the Guildhall on 30 June. Mortimer put up no defence and repeated his apology. His case was not helped by the fact that his sub-editor had 'disappeared' several months earlier. Georgina (who had expected to be called as a witness for the defence) did not find out about the trial until the following day, when she was 'astonished beyond measure' to find out that she had missed it. 'Of

20 *London Figaro*, 19/2/1879, p. 3.

21 James Mortimer–GW, 22,26,28/2/1879, 28/3/1879, 3/4/1879; GW–James Mortimer, 23/2/1879; GWJ, 13/3/1879.

course it went exactly as I prophesied it would!', she wrote, 'All hushed up.'[22] She was sure that everything would have turned out differently if she had been there. The jury found Mortimer guilty 'without a moment's hesitation': he was fined £100 and sent to Holloway Gaol for three months. Georgina was totally unsympathetic, claiming that the journalist had 'behaved like a whipped cur' and had 'gravely compromised' her.[23] He had thoroughly deserved all that he got and none of it was her fault. Mortimer's plight does seem to have aroused a certain amount of sympathy, though 'Gadfly' wrote that 'his short-sightedness in publishing Mrs Weldon's ravings may be said to be abnormally big.'[24] The financial results were disastrous and he was forced to sell the *London Figaro* three years later. There is no indication that Georgina contributed anything to his costs – Mortimer did not sell her portrait and it was eventually returned to her.

At the beginning of April, Georgina received a letter from Rivière informing her that he had made arrangements to give four weeks of concerts at Covent Garden in the following October. Would she, he enquired, like to organise a choir to sing at these concerts? He signed himself 'Yours devotedly, The General.' Georgina replied immediately, assuring the conductor, 'You may take it for granted that I will devote myself to being the choir's mistress.' She also told him that his previous choir of forty had not been large enough. 'You want the PEOPLE – the MASS', she asserted. She had a fine room for rehearsals, which could hold 250 people sitting down. They would be able to get up a splendid choir without paying too much if they promised to give the singers free tickets. There should be a music stall, which would sell works by Gounod of which Georgina held the copyright. She was, as usual, getting carried away and Rivière wrote back at once, urging restraint. Georgina believed that she would require from 200 to 300 singers; Rivière wanted no more than thirty or thirty-two 'good voices'. More would be too expensive, and the costs could be kept down by finding some amateurs to swell the numbers.

> One condition – *sine qua non* – is to be young, and the ladies pretty. You must be the eldest and the least pretty. The fellows who pay their shillings like to see fine girls, and I understand that. Also, the ladies' toilet (excepting yours) should be uniform. You in the midst of them – superb!

22 *Times*, 1/7/1879; GWJ, 1/7/1879.

23 GW, *Correspondence*, p. 193; GWM proof, vii, p. 99.

24 *Entr'acte*, 2/8/1879, p. 6.

Georgina's reaction to the stipulation that she should be the least pretty of the singers can only be imagined. At the age of forty-one, she was certain that she could outshine all the female members of the choir, in looks as well as voice. Rivière wanted her to sing a solo every evening, but made no definite promise concerning 'pecuniary arrangements', telling her 'we shall easily come to an understanding, as you are not of the ordinary class of artists, who ruin the directors, and rub their hands rejoicing.'[25]

Georgina was dismayed when Rivière told her that he had so far made only a verbal agreement for the hire of Covent Garden for the concerts. She urged him to draw up a written contract and get it signed as soon as possible, as her enemies would put a stop to the enterprise if they knew that she was involved. She still believed that most of her problems arose from the hostility of the composer Arthur Sullivan and the music publishers, represented by Arthur Chappell. If they could be kept out of the way, the concerts would be successful 'for I have the *public* entirely for me, and you are *popular*.' 'I don't torment myself about the pecuniary part of the business', she continued, 'and do not torment yourself. I work for glory, satisfaction, *and the sale of the music*.'

Rivière continued to insist that the choir should be a small one, telling Georgina, 'We require the quality, not the quantity: we are not the Albert Hall.' He reminded her that Gounod had been the main attraction at his own concerts because he was 'the lion of the day'. He, Rivière, was much less popular. Georgina ignored him, insisting that the key to success was 'knowing how to advertise' and suggesting that they should be billed as: 'Mrs Georgina Weldon's Concerts, Conductor M. Rivière'. They would, she added, not need 'your horrid "stars"', who would 'run away with the money'. 'People say I am a *constellation*', she continued, 'with a splendid orchestra and a splendid choir, you would, I think, save a great deal of expense.' They could expect to make a profit of £1410 a week, with the boxes in the theatre filled by the aristocracy, who would be sure to want to see her:

> I'll do my best to get accused of murder. What brings money and crowds are people accused of crime. That is what really fetches the public. If only Peace could be resuscitated and whistle 'Pop Goes the Weasel' in a comb at the Promenade Concerts every evening, you would have 10,000 – what do I say – 100,000 nightly, who would pay 2s, with pleasure and delight.

Alarm bells were sounding by now, and Rivière replied, 'I cannot follow you, you go at the devil's pace, but happily I am there to put a damper

[25] JPR–GW, 3,8/4/1879; GW–JPR, 5/4/1879.

Fig. 18. Georgina Weldon in 1879. Cabinet card by Debenham of Regent Street. Georgina is wearing the silver medal of the Parisian Société d'Encouragement au Bien.

on you.'[26] Unfortunately for Rivière, a damper was not nearly enough to discourage Georgina once she had got up a good head of steam.

Shortly after this, Georgina set off for France. The aim of this visit to was twofold: she had been asked to sing at a concert in Paris and it was high time she visited her long-neglected orphans, most of whom she had not seen for more than a year. The exceptions were Tommy and Johnnie who, to her horror, had turned up unexpectedly at Tavistock House six months

[26] GW–JPR, 25/4/1879. Charles Peace was a notorious burglar and murderer, who was hanged in 1879; JPR–GW, 2/5/1879.

earlier. They were both now aged about seven and she had no idea what to do with them. Both appear to have run wild for several months, intermittently supervised by the servants. Georgina had tried to deposit them in the local workhouse, but without success, and attempts to get Johnnie into an orphanage had also failed. In desperation, at the end of April, she had left him in Hunter Street and told the police to go and fetch him, writing afterwards in her diary: 'So now he will be properly taken care of and put into a proper school. How knocked up, disappointed, disheartened, fagged out, heart-sick I felt. What brutes people are and the rules of Society among these godly folk, how hollow and unchristian from the very foundation.'[27] It does not appear to have occurred to her that most people would have considered that dumping a young boy in the street was a somewhat unchristian act. What happened to John is unclear: there are no further references to him in the diary. Tommy remained at Tavistock House for the time being.

After crossing the Channel, Georgina met up with Angèle who had already been in France for a week. They paid a brief visit to Gisors to check on the children, and then took the train to Paris, where Georgina was delighted to see that her concert was well advertised. On 11 May, at the office of the monthly journal, the *Revue Spirite,* she sang Gounod's songs 'Ruth,' 'Le pays bien heureux' and *Biondina,* but the Prefet de Police, M. Berrillon, forbade her to make a speech. Georgina was told that Berrillon had been 'got at' by Gounod's friends Barbier and Franceschi. But she was well received and it was agreed that the concert should be repeated. She hoped that she would be able to talk to Gounod himself, even though she was told by a mutual acquaintance that the composer now believed her to be 'a kind of witch, possessed by the devil!' A few days after the first concert she caught sight of him in the Place Malesherbes, close to his house. He looked 'fat and well, but a very humpy back.' That evening she sang and made a speech at a soirée in the Café Richefeu. It was, she though, a triumph: the café was 'full! crammed' and there were 'heaps of journalists' and many acquaintances, including the Rivières, who were on their way back from a trip to Madrid. Georgina was 'as happy as possible – not a bit nervous – sang magnificently and rattled away my *causerie* [chat] with perfect verve.' 'I don't think I have done better,' she wrote on the following day, 'and went to bed perfectly happy, having begun my revenge on the Gounod, Barbier, [and] Francheschi faction. And with more hope of getting my old man back a little by my success.'[28]

[27] GWJ, 22/4/1879.

[28] GWJ, 10–17/5/1879.

Reports in the London newspapers of Georgina's expedition to Paris were, however, less favourable. 'Her manifestations of venom, always deplorable, have now become contemptible,' wrote 'Gadfly'. 'And the French people and the attacked composer laugh at their impotency.' Georgina's 'constant desire' to show to the world how badly Gounod had behaved towards her was, he thought, 'not only unnecessary, but unbecoming.' 'Gadfly' was to become even more critical of Georgina in the months that followed, especially after she sent him a letter 'full of picturesque Billingsgate.'[29] She was not, in short, behaving in a ladylike manner.

Back in London in mid May, Georgina was soon hard at work composing a circular advertising the formation of a new choir and asking for singers. 2500 copies were printed and sent out in the *Musical Standard* at the end of May, and Georgina and her helpers distributed many more by hand. The circular announced that Rivière's annual series of Grand Vocal and Orchestral Concerts at Covent Garden would begin on Saturday 11 October. M. Rivière had been fortunate enough to secure the cooperation of Mrs Georgina Weldon 'whose proficiency and excellence as a trainer of a choir has been universally acknowledged.' In order to make the Rivière choir 'as efficient as the best in London,' Mrs Weldon would hold two weekly morning classes for ladies and one evening class for men. Each member of the choir who attended regularly would be presented with 'an elegant case' containing a photograph of Georgina, and 200 complimentary tickets of admission to the Rivière concerts worth £10. Rehearsals would begin on 9 June, and anyone who was interested should apply to Mrs Weldon herself in writing.[30]

On 31 May Georgina sang in the first of a series of Saturday concerts at the Royal Aquarium in Westminster. This hall, which had cost £200,000 to build, had been opened to a great fanfare three years earlier. It was vast: no fewer than 14,000 visitors had passed through the turnstiles when Rivière gave a concert there in 1877.[31] Originally intended to combine educational facilities and exhibitions, as provided by the Crystal Palace, with cultural entertainments, the Aquarium was already failing by the time Georgina appeared there. The enormous fish tanks that gave the building its name remained empty; the acoustics were terrible; and the lofty ideals of the original prospectus were rapidly being abandoned. Tight-rope walkers, Zulus, gorillas and boxing kangaroos replaced concerts of classical music. Georgina was 'dreadfully nervous' before her first performance, but she sang Gounod's song 'Oh, happy home!' and 'got through it very well.' She

29 *Entr'acte*, 31/5/1879, p. 6; 14/6/1879, p. 6.
30 GW, *Correspondence*, p. 42.
31 Rivière, *Musical Life*, p. 192.

met several people she knew and some of the directors were 'very civil indeed', so she went home satisfied. At her second concert a week later she was 'much applauded by the orchestra and the public [and] well encored'.

The response to the choir circulars was slow to begin with and there were only four men and fifteen women at the first rehearsal. Before long, however the numbers began to grow: on 7 August about 200 turned up and Georgina reckoned that she could count on a total of 350. That there were not more was Rivière's fault: if he had not been 'so stingy about adverts' she would, she believed, have had 500. Some of the singers were old friends, former members of the Gounod choir, whilst others had sung in the Alexandra Palace choir or in Rivière's previous concerts. Teaching them was hard work: they were, Georgina thought, 'truly idiotic' and their pronunciation was 'vulgar and absurd'. At least she now had someone to help her with her paperwork in the form of a 'kind' young man called Frederick Cooper, who lived with his 'very rich' father in Gordon Square.

Between choir rehearsals, Georgina still found time to speak at public meetings. On 21 May she went to Wellington Hall in Islington where (fortified by 'a little gin') she gave the audience a short talk on 'the police of the

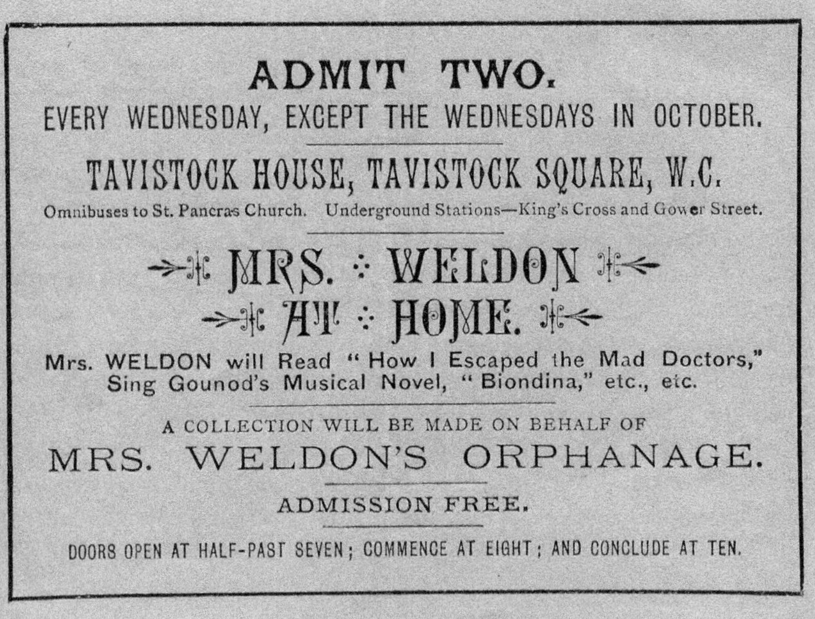

Fig. 19. Admission ticket for one of Georgina's 'At Homes' at Tavistock House, 1879.

French Republic' followed by a song.[32] A fortnight later she embarked on a series of soirées or 'At Homes' at Tavistock House itself. These took place every Wednesday evening and consisted of a mixture of talks and musical performances by Georgina and her friends and supporters, including Einar Saemundsen, 'the only Icelander in London', who had 'a tidy tenor voice' and sang 'the national airs of his country very nicely'.[33]

Georgina invited 'Gadfly' to attend one of her 'At Homes'. He declined the invitation, declaring 'I am not willing to be entertained by the pretty hostess of Tavistock House when she elects to bedaub M. Gounod with her recriminations', and adding: 'Mrs Weldon says that M. Gounod is a madman. He may have been once; but if so, pretty certain is it that he had a lucid interval when he reduced to a minimum his interest in Tavistock House.' The author of an article in the *Musical Standard*, who attended one such evening, described it as 'an entertainment of a unique kind'. The first part began with an address, given by the hostess, entitled 'How I escaped from the Mad Doctors'. This was followed by a musical programme, which included nursery rhymes composed by Georgina herself. Then Georgina performed Gounod's 'musical novel', *Biondina*: 'Possessed of a voice of wide range and great power, well under control excepting as regards a slight preponderance of the penetrating quality in the upper register, the versatile powers of the lady are eminently qualified for a work of this description.'[34] Georgina's 'At Homes' in subsequent weeks were well attended, but the takings were disappointing and rarely exceeded £4.

~

It had been arranged that Rivière should give a series of Saturday concerts at the Crystal Palace in the second half of August. The advertisements promised '150 instrumental performers; Miss Emma Thursby, Madame Antoinette Sterling and others; two military bands and efficient chorus'.[35] The 'efficient chorus' was Georgina's choir. She saw this as 'a sort of preparation' and wished that she had 500 singers. She told Rivière that he had no need for professional soloists such as Emma Thursby, the 'American Nightingale', who was on her first European concert tour, and that she, Georgina, should be the star of his concerts. She had, she claimed, 'a hundred times more celebrity than Emma Thursby'. Thursby was eight years younger than Georgina, which did not help. Nor did the fact that Rivière was prepared

32 GWJ, 21,31/5/1879, 7,13/6/1879, 8/8/1879.
33 GW–JPR, 20/6/1879.
34 *Entr'acte*, 14/6/1879, p. 6; *Musical Standard*, 5/7/1879, p. 328.
35 *Daily Telegraph*, 11/8/1879, p. 8.

to pay her £100 a week. The composer ignored Georgina, warning her 'Do not pose yourself as a star or else cite me the concerts where you have made your fortune. Be calm and all will go right.' A degree of exasperation was beginning to creep into his letters. He told her to stop advertising 'or you will have 5000 [choristers] one of these days, and then you would have to get a Weldon Hall built in Regent's Park.'

On 14 August Rivière came to a rehearsal for the first time, having hitherto left it to Georgina to audition potential choristers.[36] He was, Georgina wrote, 'agreeably surprised,' in spite of the fact that the choir was 'in reality very higgledy piggledy.' A day later they all went to Store Street Hall for the final rehearsal. It was not entirely satisfactory and Georgina wished that she had had more time to practise. On the following day Georgina and Angèle, with three boxes full of music and one containing Georgina's dress, set off for Sydenham. The concert began at 7.30. In addition to Georgina and a choir of more than 260 singers, the performers included a 'scratch band.' There were two soloists apart from Georgina and Emma Thursby: the popular American contralto Antoinette Sterling and the soprano Giulia Welmi. As usual, Georgina believed that she was the real star of the show: though she was an amateur and the others were all professionals, she had been 'twenty times more applauded than anyone else.' The critic from the *Morning Post* commented, however, that 'the special merit' of Mrs Georgina Weldon's performance 'may be difficult to chronicle.'[37]

Two days after the performance, Rivière called at Tavistock House. He seemed depressed and told Georgina that the evening had lost him more than £100. The whole thing had been 'a *fiasco*.' 'Every one seems so delighted at the concert,' he added, 'especially those who have not paid their admission.' Georgina suggested that she should conduct at the next Crystal Palace concert by herself. This would, she argued, be 'a great attraction.' She could see that the directors of the Crystal Palace were against her, but Rivière should tell them 'to go and be hanged!' The conductor ignored her. The next concert was 'a second disaster.' The third, on Saturday 30 August, was much more satisfactory from Georgina's point of view: she had 'great success' in Gounod's 'Ruth' and was 'encored doubly.' At the end, she was presented with three bouquets. She was – in her own eyes, at least, 'the success of the evening.' Rivière did not agree.[38]

36 GW–JPR, 26/7/1879; JPR–GW, 10/6/1879, 28/7/1879, 5,7,12/8/1879.

37 GWJ, 14,16/8/1879; *Morning Post*, 18/8/1879, p. 6.

38 GWJ, 18,30/8/1879; JPR–GW, 17,25/8/1879; GW–JPR, 20/8/1879.

18
Covent Garden

Trouble had been brewing for several months. In spite of Rivière's confident assertion that he and Georgina would 'easily come to an understanding' where pecuniary matters were concerned, there were continual wrangles over money. Though she had not been promised any fees, Georgina expected Rivière to refund the money she paid out (without consulting him) for printing music, advertising and other expenses. When he grumbled, she told him to be quiet.[1] They continued to disagree on the size and composition of the choir. Rivière had left the auditioning of the singers to Georgina, but later claimed that she had never refused to let anyone join, and that they all 'sang like parrots'.[2] Georgina still insisted that she could sing better than any professional 'star' and told Rivière that members of her choir, such as Einar Saemundsen, were perfectly capable of singing solos. The Icelander could sing songs in his native language, and would be an attraction, as 'people would expect him to come on to the platform in skins, in a sleigh, and with Esquimaux dogs!' Rivière was not enthusiastic.

They also argued about the music stall, the concert programmes, the number of free tickets to be given to members of the choir, and the dresses for the female singers. Georgina was sure that extensive advertising was still needed, and took every opportunity to send out information on Spiritualism and the Lunacy Laws with the choir circulars. Rivière told her to stop, informing her that he was not prepared to advertise her 'private affairs' during his concerts. Ignoring him, she ordered 50,000 envelopes with advertisements relating to the Lunacy Laws printed inside them and sent 25,000 of them to Rivière. He refused to use them. Georgina's relentless attention-seeking was making him increasingly unhappy and he was beginning to feel that the notoriety that had attracted him to her in the first

1 GW–JPR, 20/7/1879. Much of the information on Georgina's dealings with Rivière is taken from her printed (unpublished) Rivière volumes.

2 POB, 23/3/1885: *Regina v. Weldon*; *Times*, 28/3/1885.

place had become a liability. One day in August she informed him, 'The newspapers are full of me. I have been to three police courts today, and have blown up two magistrates as they deserve' He replied:

> I do not know if your friends approve your line of conduct, and whether they encourage you to run after this police court celebrity, but all I can tell you is, it does you the greatest harm in the artistic world. The directors of the Crystal Palace, the artistes, the world in general, love you for your talents, but they blame strongly what they call your eccentricities. All these articles in the public newspapers cannot do good to our common cause, I mean the concerts at Covent Garden, and I am the first to suffer by it.[3]

This letter was like a red rag to a bull. Georgina responded with a torrent of abuse. Rivière was, she wrote, 'an IMBECILE':

> All these charming creatures to whom you listen, and who worry you, are dusters and dirty dusters! Listen to your own ears! Who is the pet? Who gets the triumph? Who got all the applause last Saturday? Me!! So hold your tongue. I am only too much in the right, my General. I know what I am about, and that is just what enrages 'my dear friends'! I laugh at them!

In another letter she told him 'I shall not change my ways *in the slightest degree*, you may take your oath on that, and I shall beat them all in the end bravely and loyally at the point of my sword.'[4] Rivière replied 'You may call me an *Imbecile*, and call me all the names you please – it is absolutely indifferent to me.' Georgina's 'triumph' at the last concert was, moreover, one of the problems: 'The Directors [of the Crystal Palace] find that the applause prodigally bestowed on you by your choir is of bad taste, and fear that it may cause a counter-demonstration on the part of the public.' 'I begin to think,' he added, 'we shall not agree at all easily; our way of looking at things is not at all the same.' Of course, Georgina had no intention of taking any notice of the conductor's warnings. She decided that Rivière was jealous of her because she was so popular.

The battle of wills continued. By the beginning of September, Rivière had had enough. He gave Georgina the name of his lawyers, informing her: 'I decline to have you as my partner, or adviser, in the management of my concerts, our ideas being quite different. You can therefore dismiss

3 GW–JPR, 20/6/1879, 19/8/1879; JPR–GW, 17/6/1879, 2,14,20,25/8/1879.
4 GW–JPR, 20/8/1879.

your choir, or reduce it to my number. I will not give in one inch.'[5] He then relented slightly and proposed that they should go to arbitration, but Georgina ignored him. She continued with the rehearsals and started selling dresses to the ladies of the choir. She informed Rivière that she would accept 200 tickets for each of 120 choristers, but insisted that he would have to pay all expenses. He replied that this could mean that 1000 might expect to be admitted free to any individual concert, which could ruin him. When Georgina complained that he showed no sign of appreciating her own singing, he told her

> I never show any enthusiasm to anybody; I am not in the habit of shaking hands with the singers after they have done, or to pat them on the shoulder, and, in my opinion, the performers ought to leave the public to applaud the soloists. Perhaps you would like me to dance a jig after each of your songs.

They continued to argue about the number of free tickets, until, on 12 September, Rivière issued an ultimatum. If Georgina would not sign 'a proper agreement,' he would do without her choir altogether.

That evening, Georgina read Rivière's latest letter to the choir. They received it 'with hisses,' but decided to accept the conductor's terms. Georgina then wrote to Rivière, laying down her own terms, which were refused two days later.[6] Four days after this, Rivière's friends handed what Georgina later described as 'an underhand circular full of unscrupulous lies' to the members of the choir as they left Tavistock House after their evening rehearsal. In it Rivière recited the problems that had arisen as a result of Georgina's determination to have a choir much larger than he required. 'Nothing,' he claimed, 'could induce Mrs Weldon to stop advertising or to reduce the choir to reasonable proportions.' He invited all members of the choir to meet him on the following evening at his 'place of business,' 28 Leicester Square.

Three of the male choristers then went to see Rivière and asked him, instead, to attend a rehearsal a few days later. Georgina saw these men as traitors and later claimed that they had been 'paid to come into the choir to make mischief.' By this time she was sulking. She told Frederick Cooper to inform Rivière's lawyers, Dod and Longstaffe, that 'she declined to receive any money whatever' from M. Rivière for herself, but he should give Cooper £300 to cover expenses, including the salaries for the lead singers she had engaged. She would not sing solos at any of the concerts, but would expect to receive the profits from a Benefit Concert planned for 5 November. The

5 JPR–GW, 21/8/1879, 2–3/9/1879; GW–JPR, 22/8/1879.
6 JPR–GW, 10,12/9/1879; GW–JPR, 13/9/1879.

lawyers replied on their client's behalf, informing her that the conductor objected to paying for the choir before the concerts began, but would put £300 on deposit in the joint names of himself and Cooper, to be drawn on to cover the choir's expenses at the rate of £60 a week.[7]

Fearing that the choir was turning against her, and still determined to get her own way, Georgina now sent Angèle to Paris to dig up as much dirt on Rivière as she could find. She remembered a conversation that she had had with the conductor at the beginning of the year, when he had hinted that there were events in his early life that he would rather keep hidden. She already knew that the 'Madame Rivière' whom she had met in 1871 was not the woman with whom the Frenchman was now living. When challenged about this, Rivière had replied enigmatically that he had been married 'once and a half' and had asked Georgina not to disturb 'a sleeping cat'. Several mutual acquaintances had, moreover, hinted at a murky past. Georgina wanted as much ammunition as she could gather for the battles that were to come.

On 23 September the conductor and his partner Samuel Hayes duly turned up at a choir rehearsal at Store Street Hall. Georgina spent some time reading Rivière's circular out to the choir, challenging its contents paragraph by paragraph. When she reached the words 'Nothing could induce Mrs Weldon to stop advertising', the choir burst out laughing. Georgina then openly accused Rivière of cheating her and falsifying the accounts of the previous year's concerts at Covent Garden, claiming that he had 'swindled her into the whole thing'. At this, Hayes brandished his umbrella and shrieked 'Swindled! Swindled!' upon which Georgina 'calmly' replied 'I repeat the word *swindled*'. Rivière exclaimed 'I did not come here to be cross-examined', put on his hat, and stormed out with Hayes and a number of sympathisers.[8]

Rivière then made another attempt to sack Georgina, on the grounds that they had never entered into a formal contract and the terms that she had tried to impose on him were impossible.[9] When the members of the choir were informed of this at a rehearsal that evening, the men ('extraordinary fools', according to Georgina) begged her not to disappoint them. They had been working for five months; they had promised tickets to all their friends; and they 'did not like to be made fools of'. Georgina burst into tears and appealed to them to authorise her to break off all relations with Rivière.

7 JPR–Mrs Weldon's Choir, 19/9/1879; W.H.F. Cooper–Dod and Longstaffe, 21/9/1879; Dod and Longstaffe–W.H.F. Cooper, 22/9/1879

8 GWJ, 23/9/1879.

9 Dod and Longstaffe–GW, 24/9/1879.

But the choristers were adamant, telling her 'Others had had dealings with Rivière for years, and people would only say I was mad to be so sticklish.' She eventually gave way and agreed to talk to the conductor again.

A truce was negotiated, but this did not last long. Angèle returned from France with information about a certain Jules Prudence Rivière, a *fumiste* or seller of stoves, who had been sentenced to ten years' penal servitude as a fraudulent bankrupt. Georgina wrote immediately to Rivière to tell him what she had found out. This provoked a letter from Dod and Longstaffe to Cooper, informing him that Rivière would decline to sign any agreement with Georgina unless she gave a satisfactory explanation for her 'remarkable and most ill-advised letter.' Rivière also wrote an open letter to the choir, which was read out at the next rehearsal. In it, the conductor informed them that he had, with 'deep regret' been compelled to break off negotiations with Mrs Weldon as to the Covent Garden concerts. In view of the time and trouble the singers had devoted to numerous rehearsals he would, however, give them 500 free admissions every night for their friends and would honour the personal season tickets that had already been distributed.[10] Rivière's letter provoked 'a commotion' at the rehearsal, but it does seem to have produced the desired effect. Under pressure from Angèle and the choir, Georgina went to Dod and Longstaffe's offices on the following day and a contract was signed. Frederick Cooper signed for Georgina, it having been realised rather late in the day that, as a married woman and being 'under coverture,' she was not legally able to enter into a contract. She did, however, countersign the document, confirming it and undertaking 'that the same shall be performed in all respects.

In the contract of 3 October 1879, Georgina promised that she and her choir would sing at Rivière's Promenade Concerts at Covent Garden 'in a proper and efficient manner' under the conductor's direction. The size of the choir on each evening should be limited, and Rivière would be entitled to select the music to be sung and approve the soloists. Mrs Weldon would train the choir and sing one solo apart from them each evening, in addition to solos during the choir's pieces. Further clauses related to the clothes to be worn by the choir; the organisation of the music stall; and the allocation of free tickets. Rivière would, as previously agreed, deposit £300 in the London and Westminster Bank, out of which £60 a week would be paid to Frederick Cooper to defray expenses. Once the concerts were over, Rivière would pay half the clear net profits to Georgina, and the concert on 5 November would be solely for her benefit after the deduction of £150 to

[10] GW–JPR, 29/9/1879; Dod and Longstaffe–W.H.F. Cooper, 30/9/1879; JPR–Mrs Weldon's Choir, 1/10/1879.

cover 'regular expenses'. Finally it was agreed that Rivière and his employees, and Georgina and the choir, should treat each other 'with proper respect': neither of them should speak disrespectfully of the other, or 'make any imputation upon the other calculated to bring him or her into odium or contempt'. Georgina was also persuaded to copy and sign a letter drawn up by one of the lawyers and addressed to the choir, in which she promised to 'make things square between the choir and Mr Rivière'. She withdrew the imputations she had cast on Rivière and apologised for using 'any language calculated to wound and annoy him' This letter was read to the choir at a rehearsal later that evening. Somewhat surprisingly, Georgina thought that she had beaten Rivière, who came to Tavistock House that night, looking 'like a sheep led to the slaughter'. She later denied that she had made any kind of apology and claimed that she had been forced to sign this 'swindling document' as a result of an 'artfully contrived and most infernal plot'.

Georgina and the choir only had time for two rehearsals at Covent Garden itself before the performances began on 6 October. After this, they were contracted to perform on five nights a week for five weeks. At first all seemed to go fairly smoothly, though 'Gadfly' was not impressed:

> Mrs Georgina Weldon loves notoriety, and will have it if it is to be had by a little more than moderate straining after. To watch her at Covent Garden, where she and her choir are singing just now, is quite a 'sight'. She adjusts her pince-nez, cracks a joke with the trombone, smiles amiably at the ophicleide, and giving a friendly nod to the side-drums, clambers up the inclined orchestra until she reaches the bosom of her faithful chorus. There she will deliver in most demonstrative fashion the instructions which she wishes faithfully carried out in some piece in which her choir will soon take part, and during which time she will be far away in front singing the solo part.
>
> She seems to dress in an eminently original style, and with an evident disregard of popular prejudices. Previous to trotting out her voice she will be very liberal in her nods and smiles to the various members of the orchestra, and when she begins to sing the visitor is not positively enthralled; you may then understand that her appearance as a public vocalist is due in a great measure to the insatiable thirst for notoriety which seems to be apparent in every action of this pretty lady's life. I don't mean to say that Mrs Weldon is not a fairly good singer in a drawing-room, but I have yet to be convinced that she sings effectively in Covent Garden Theatre.[11]

[11] *Entr'acte*, 18/10/1879, p. 11. An ophicleide is a type of keyed wind instrument.

After a week, Georgina was suffering from 'acute bronchitis, sore throat and inflammation' and could 'neither speak nor breathe'. She went to rehearsals almost every day, but was unable to take part for ten days. Without her, the choir's singing was 'perfectly shocking'.[12] Before long, Georgina and Rivière were barely on speaking terms, and communicating mainly via Frederick Cooper. There were continuing disagreements about the programmes and Georgina complained about the lack of rehearsal time and the fact that her name was not advertised as prominently as that of Emma Thursby. There were also problems with the choir's tickets, and accusations of rudeness. As Rivière had predicted, the size and composition of the choir fluctuated wildly from one evening to another: on 9 October 160 turned up and they were so tightly packed on the stage that some fainted or were obliged to leave 'on account of the pressure and heat'. It is also clear from a letter written by one of the female singers that Cooper found it difficult to keep control of the choir when Georgina was away:

> I must complain of a number of the choir who, during your absence, and in spite of all Mr Cooper could do, laugh, talk, and flirt with the tenors; also the second sopranos (some of them) come into the front row, and the first go at the back where they can talk and laugh with the men.[13]

Rivière had threatened to dismiss them again if their behaviour did not improve.

Then on 20 October, when Georgina was absent, the choir 'came to smash' during the popular song 'Come back to Erin'. Rivière was furious and called out 'For shame!' This so unnerved the choir that they were unable to continue. Rivière then accused them of going wrong on purpose and told them that they need not come on the following evening. But there was another concert three days later, and Georgina was finally well enough to sing again. She was well received, and sang 'Annie Laurie' as an encore. Afterwards, she wrote, 'I went to bed very happy, thinking my popularity would soon cause a reform in the Lunacy Laws.[14] Rivière was, however, less pleased. Anxious to avoid extending the concerts, which already lasted from 8 to 11.30 p.m., he had decreed that encores should be avoided if possible. If the audience insisted, and if he gave permission, the last verse or movement of the previous piece might be repeated. Under no circumstances should a different piece be performed. Georgina argued that this rule did not apply to her, because she had accompanied herself on the piano in her rendition of 'Annie Laurie', and the orchestra had not been involved.

12 *Daily News*, 6/3/1880, p. 2.

13 GW–JPR, 10/10/1879; Louise Thompson–GW, 21/10/1879.

14 GWJ, 21–23/10/1879.

Rivière was later to claim that Georgina had defiantly 'snapped' her fingers in his face as she walked onto the platform. On the day after the concert he forbade her to sing any more solos. 'I shall go to law with him', she vowed, and wrote a letter to the conductor's secretary, William Selby, in which she expressed the opinion that 'Mr Rivière had much better have stuck to his old profession of stove-selling than taking upon himself that of giving himself the airs of a conductor and managing superior artists'. She would, she added, continue to give encores if she chose and would take Rivière to court if he tried to stop her singing.[15]

The following evening, Saturday 25 October, was Balaclava Night, an important date in the concert calendar when several patriotic pieces of music were to be played. With ten military bands engaged, there would be no room on the stage at Covent Garden for the choir. Rivière had suggested that twenty-four of the best female singers should sit in two of the boxes, from where they would sing 'See the conquering hero comes' in unison at the end of the 'British Army Quadrille'. The theatre was 'crammed' with drunken medical students when the doors were closed at 8.15. Most of the audience were brandishing copies of an effusive article about Georgina that had just been published in *The Medium and Daybreak*. Georgina had ordered 10,000 offprints and she and her friends had already spent several days making them up and distributing them. A copy was handed to each member of the audience as they entered the theatre.

The events of that evening were to be the subject of so many hours of discussion and pages of print that it is difficult to work out exactly what happened, but some things are clear. The choir were to sing only in the second half of the evening, so they and Georgina entered their double box during the interval. When they saw Georgina, the audience began to call out 'Bravo! Mrs Weldon' and there was 'a lot of cheering and counter-demonstrations from other people'. Samuel Hayes came storming into the box, 'with his hat on the back of his head, in a jovial state', and shouted: 'What the devil are you kicking up a row here for? The choir shall be dismissed for this on Monday!' The crowd shouted 'Knock his hat off, pitch him over the front'. Hayes (who later claimed that he had merely said: 'This is a temple of art and not a place of demonstration') left the box and the noise continued. Hayes then returned, 'said something rude' and told Georgina to leave the box, but she ignored him. When he returned for the third time, very obviously drunk, someone in the pit called out, 'Take your hat off before the ladies'. Georgina then told him, 'very severely', 'If I were to say a word to these people they would drag you out of the place'. It was twenty minutes before the audience

15 GWJ, 24/10/1879; GW–William Selby, 24/10/1879.

calmed down and the concert began again. But – it was later claimed – at ten o'clock, whilst Rivière was conducting the 'British Army Quadrille,' Georgina began 'demonstrating – bowing and acknowledging the plaudits.' Rivière later accused her of 'flourishing about' deliberately, in order to annoy him, and encouraging the audience to 'hoot and shout and misbehave themselves.' But the choir sang 'See the conquering hero,' as arranged, and Georgina then left the theatre. She was later told that the crowd had kept up the applause for twenty minutes after her departure.[16]

During the weekend that followed, Georgina and Angèle concocted a circular for distribution to Georgina's supporters:

> Mrs Georgina Weldon was much gratified at the kind sympathy shown her by the people at Covent Garden on Saturday October 25, and begs to inform them that she is not allowed to sing by M. Rivière because he is jealous and afraid of her popularity. In behaving thus, M. Rivière breaks his contract, and Mrs Weldon clearly has her remedy in a court of law. But in the meanwhile, this act of impertinent tyranny on his part, non-explained, might be misconstrued, and do her a real injury. She therefore in self-defence (without any observation as to what and who M. Rivière was in his own country 22 years ago) desires to say to the public that, health permitting, she will be at Covent Garden every evening; and that should the public wish her to do so, she will sing as is her right. She has no idea of being unfairly treated because certain parties have thought it worthwhile to make her out a lunatic, and appeals to the people for justice.

This circular, printed on yellow paper, was handed to members of the audience as they entered the theatre on the following Monday. The choir was there, and so was Georgina, though she seated herself in a box rather than on the stage. Again, accounts of what happened that evening vary. According to Georgina she sat quietly behind a curtain, whilst Rivière claimed that she tried to conduct the choir from her box behind his back, and threw some of the yellow circulars down to the promenaders, who began to move about and call out 'Georgina' and 'Bravo Mrs Weldon!' Rivière also said that Georgina should have been on the stage with the choir when they sang a selection from Wagner's *Rienzi* and that the choristers had, as a result, 'made a disgrace of the whole affair, singing out of time and out of tune.'

After the concert, Georgina sent Selby a list of requirements for her Benefit on 5 November. She would, she told him, conduct, and would not require Mr Rivière's services. A reply came back immediately from Rivière

16 *Standard*, 17/11/1884, p. 3; POB, 23/3/1885: *Regina v. Weldon*.

himself: he would not allow her or the choir to sing again at his concerts. He gave as his reasons the 'inefficiency' of the choir and Georgina's failure to sit with them on the previous evening, as was her duty. It was clear that the 'yellow circular' had been the final straw. A further letter, from Selby, informed her that her Benefit would not take place, as she had 'forfeited all claim on Mr Rivière by breach of contract'. Georgina responded by threatening to take Rivière to court.[17] At a rehearsal at Store Street Hall the members of the choir presented her with 'a most beautiful gold watch set in a thick gold bracelet' with the inscription, 'To Mrs Georgina Weldon by the members of her choir, as a slight token of their admiration of her great musical genius, November 5th 1879'. It had evidently been ordered and engraved before Rivière announced the cancellation of the Benefit Concert.

Georgina went to Covent Garden again after the rehearsal with Angèle and two other friends, having reserved a box in the name of one of the girls in the choir. There are several versions of what happened there. According to the newspaper and court reports, Georgina ascended the grand staircase and handed her voucher to the box-keeper, who asked 'Are you Mrs Weldon?' She replied that she was. The box-keeper told her that he had been given orders not to admit her. When she asked who had given the orders, he replied 'the management' then added 'Mr Rivière'. At this point Samuel Hayes came out of the refreshment rooms and declared that he would take responsibility for the refusal to admit Georgina and her companions. They were joined by the Gattis' secretary, James Sidney, who accused Georgina of being 'a filthy woman who wrote filthy publications like that filthy 'Town Talk'.[18] Georgina retaliated by pushing his hat off and asked to be given into custody. Sidney, who later claimed that she had struck him a violent blow in the eye with the back of her hand, 'dimming his sight for a time', replied that he would have her arrested. At some stage in the 'general altercation', Angèle bit, or tried to bite, Sidney. Georgina, who was told that she was being excluded from the theatre because she had distributed handbills there, was 'conducted' down the stairs by Sidney, who asked a policeman, Inspector Cruse, to take Georgina's name and address, saying, 'She has assaulted me and I want her out of the theatre'. Cruse replied that he already knew who she was. Georgina insisted that she should be locked up, but the inspector wisely refused to do as she asked.[19]

17 GW–William Selby, 28/10/1879; JPR–GW, 28 October 1879; William Selby–GW, 29/10/1879; GW–JPR, [29/10/1879].

18 'Town Talk' was a regular column in the satirical newspaper, *Fun*.

19 *Times*, 7/11/1879.

On the next day Georgina sent for a doctor to look at Angèle's arm, which was badly bruised. She then hurried to Bow Street, where the elderly magistrate Sir James Ingham was sitting. He was, she wrote, 'very nasty and hypocritical', but he granted her a summons for assault against Samuel Hayes. Later in the same day James Sidney was granted a summons for assault against Georgina, after claiming that she had struck him in the eye with her hand, cutting it with a diamond ring. That evening Georgina went to Covent Garden again and found that the police were 'three deep' to prevent her going in. 'What a tremendous woman I must be', she wrote with some satisfaction. On the next day, Georgina and Angèle both took out summonses for assault against Sidney. A further unsuccessful attempt to enter Covent Garden provoked a characteristic outburst in her diary:

> One would say such things cannot take place in England! Hout-tout! When a man tries to get his wife who is not a sneak into a lunatic asylum, 'Throw her to the dogs', that's the cry. What business has she to object, or to try to reform matters statesmen let slide! Thank God women have had no hand in our laws.

At Bow Street on 1 November, Frederick Flowers granted Georgina subpoenas against the two Gattis, Ernest Gye (the Gattis' manager), and several others. Later, at Covent Garden, she was refused entry yet again.[20] She also made an unsuccessful attempt to have a Receiver in Chancery appointed by the High Court to attend Covent Garden and take all the receipts on 5 November, the date of her now-cancelled Benefit Concert. On that evening, Georgina and her friends walked up and down outside the theatre, distributing copies of *The Medium and Daybreak*, together with envelopes containing tickets of admission to her 'At Homes' at Tavistock House. Georgina also handed tickets for the evening's concert to every passer-by. The police eventually stopped her, due to the disturbances caused when the ticket-holders were refused admission to the theatre.

They all ended up in court on Thursday 6 November. In the morning, Georgina had a visit from Alexander Bodson, a Belgian musician, who told her 'heaps about that devil Rivière'. 'We have', she wrote, 'proof of his being a bigamist, perjurer and fraudulent bankrupt.' Later that day, 'a crowd of choir and friends' accompanied her to Bow Street where, to her dismay, Sir James Ingham was sitting again. The court was 'full of Gatti and Co.'s friends', and Georgina's were 'studiously kept out'. She had decided to represent herself, certain that she could do better than any professional lawyer.

[20] GWJ, 30–1/10/1879, 1/11/1879; *Morning Post*, 31/10/1879, p. 7; 1/11/1879, p. 7.

Georgina's summons was heard first. Her main witness was Angèle, who 'was great fun and brought all out about Rivière like a torrent' and ended by inviting the court to prosecute her for libel. She produced a medical certificate describing the bruises, which had, she claimed, been caused by Sidney's violence in ejecting her from the theatre.

Georgina continued to examine her witnesses until half past five, when Ingham decided that he had heard enough. He dismissed Georgina's summons against Hayes, who claimed that he had 'merely moved his hand'. The summons against Sidney was also dismissed on the grounds that he had the right to turn her out of the theatre. Georgina, on the other hand, had assaulted him. Angèle was more successful: it was agreed that she had been 'rather roughly handled' by Sidney. Georgina and Sidney were both bound over in their own recognisances of £50 to keep the peace for three months, and Georgina concluded that they had all somehow 'come off square'. This, her first appearance in court as prosecutrix, reinforced her belief that she did not need to employ a lawyer. That evening she went to Covent Garden once again and was dragged downstairs by three policemen, after which she 'commenced to address the ladies and gentleman coming out' and had to be removed from the front of the theatre by force.[21]

'Gadfly', who occasionally showed a grudging admiration for Georgina in spite of himself, thought that she had let herself down badly:

> I have spoken of Mrs Weldon often; I have been watching her career for some time past; and painfully deluded, as I have always thought her, I cannot but think she makes herself responsible for acts which, but a few years ago, she would have recoiled from. The Mrs Weldon of ten years back would hardly have admitted that she hit off a gentleman's hat from his head. That she does it now is a proof that the desirable gentleness of a woman no longer finds an abiding place in Mrs Weldon.
>
> At one time I was under the impression that she was somewhat of an ill-used woman; but now I see her quarrelling with everybody who declines to permit her to practise her fads and advertise herself in her own approved manner, I am compelled to believe her a woman of vulgar ostentatiousness, and, for the sake of any self-respect she may have, I would advise her to do her best to crucify that abnormal craving for notoriety, which has done so much to bring her into ridicule.

[21] GWJ, 6–7/11/1879; *Morning Post*, 6/11/1879, p. 6; 7/11/1879, p. 3; *Times*, 5–7/11/1879.

Georgina was, however, a useful source of journalistic copy: a few months later 'Gadfly's colleague wrote in the 'Merry-go-Round' column that he was 'disposed to regard her as a kind of pick-up to a slack season.' When everything was 'as dull as ditchwater,' he added, 'I sigh for my Weldon.'[22] She was to provide newspaper readers with plenty of entertainment in the years that followed.

22 *Entr'acte*, 15/11/1879, p. 11; 24/1/1880, p. 4.

19
Disaster

Georgina's 'At Homes' at Tavistock House had continued throughout September 1879. The room was almost always full, due to the publicity generated by her appearances at the Aquarium and in the police courts. The programmes were the usual mixture of readings and lectures (mainly by the hostess) and musical items. The takings, however, remained low. Georgina claimed that she was raising money to support her orphanage, but members of the audience may well have wondered what had happened to the orphans themselves. Most of them were still in France and Georgina quickly disposed of the only one left in London, 'that little wretch' Tommy, who was 'planted' at a place where he would be 'trained on board ship'. Georgina was only too pleased to see him go.[1]

As Rivière had deprived her of her Benefit Concert, Georgina decided to hold one of her own. On 5 November, the day of the cancelled concert at Covent Garden, she booked St James's Hall for St Cecilia's Day, 22 November. She sent a circular to the members of the choir, informing them

> As you all know, I work for my orphanage and the reform of an iniquitous system which has broken my life and, well-nigh, my heart. I have no desire and no pleasure in public singing myself, and I have the sense to know that I am too old to dream of making a career. The choir is a great pleasure to me, and I entertain a sincere feeling of affectionate regard towards many of its members. I am, however, advised there are several backbiting, slanderous tongues among them. I am in a most extraordinarily difficult position, the target for lies, and, till now, the victim of injustice in its most cruel and cowardly form. I have to contend against public and private pique; against hundreds of thousand pounds sterling a year, which are able to buy up the very courts where justice is supposed to be meted out to the subjects of this realm, and the newspapers which are supposed to give fair play.[2]

1 GWJ, 13/9/1879.

2 GW, *Correspondence*, pp. 164, 168.

Apart from one or two 'turncoats', the choir remained loyal. Georgina received numerous letters of support and most of the singers still came to rehearsals.

Even she had to admit that the concert on 22 November was not a total success. The audience numbered fewer than 500 and the hall, which could hold 2000, seemed empty. In the absence of Rivière, Georgina was accompanist, conductor and soloist. The evening began with a performance of Gounod's *Gallia*, with Georgina as the soloist and James Hallé at the organ. His playing was, Georgina thought, 'too beautiful.' Other performers included Einar Saemundsen ('drunk'), who sang two Scandinavian songs, and the soprano Elène Webster, who sang songs by Gounod. 'Lady Glinka,' 'The Circassian violinist,' and her brother Media, a cornettist, played solos. Georgina had persuaded Julius Benedict to take part; he accompanied her as she sang his song 'The maiden's dream' and then conducted the orchestra as they played his overture 'Die Minnesinger.' According to Georgina, everything (apart from Saemundsen's songs) 'went splendidly and was vociferously applauded.' Nevertheless, the concert was a disaster from the financial point of view: Georgina estimated that she had lost at least £125.[3] The music critic of *The World* reckoned that the takings could not have covered as much as a quarter of the evening's expenses, though he complimented Georgina herself, writing 'Mrs Weldon is a lady of extraordinary attainments, an organisation of rare gifts, and although she led an orchestra for the first time in her life, she led with a determination, a calm, and a degree of intelligence which more than one of our would-be conductors cannot boast of.'[4] Miscellaneous concerts such as Georgina's were, however, going out of fashion at this time. Instead of novelty and quantity, the more sophisticated music-lovers now looked for balance and high quality.[5] Georgina's concerts must have been hard work for her audiences, for they often lasted for several hours and the quality of the performers was variable.

Matters went from bad to worse when, at the end of November, Georgina embarked on a concert tour promoted by a new acquaintance, Donald Shaw. Although Georgina was subsequently to describe him as a 'penniless adventurer,' Shaw was an educated man who had previously been a captain in the 86th Regiment of Foot. He seemed to know nothing about music, but Georgina, Angèle and Frederick Cooper nevertheless set off for Manchester with him and a group of Spanish students. Shaw

3 GWJ, 22/11/1879; GW, *Correspondence*, pp. 165–7.

4 *World*, 26/11/1879.

5 Asa Briggs and Janet Lovegrove, *Victorian Music: A Social and Cultural History* (Brighton, Sussex, 2018), p. 203.

SUPPLEMENT TO THE ILLUSTRATED SPORTING AND DRAMATIC NEWS, December 6, 1879.—281

HUMOURS OF THE PAST MONTH.

Fig. 20. 'Chamber of Horrors', cartoon from *The Illustrated Sporting and Dramatic News*, December 1879. 'A Novelty: Mrs Weldon conducts herself'.

subsequently published a description of their trip, which differed considerably from Georgina's own account:

> [Mrs Weldon] made it a *sine qua non,* and refused to budge an inch unless I agreed to permit her to be accompanied by a huge Frenchwoman whom she called her companion [Angèle], and a sickly youth whom she designated her secretary. I was not only to cart this worthy couple about first-class, but to pay for their board and lodgings. As the French person was as voracious as a cormorant, and as the secretary was apparently suffering from some complaint that impelled him to eat inordinately three or four times a day, and as provincial hotels are proverbially expensive when the ordinary routine is in the least deviated from, and as nothing but the best and most *recherché* menu was considered good enough for the worthy trio, my bill and my feelings after a three days' experience may be easier imagined than described.[6]

In Manchester the audiences were 'wretched,' never numbering more than seven or eight. The final straw came when they moved on to Newcastle, where it was freezing cold and there was deep snow everywhere. Georgina was due to give a concert that evening, but when they all got to the hall they found that it was completely empty. Eventually one 'solitary, unhappy man' appeared, but it turned out that he was the music critic of the local newspaper who had been given a free ticket. The concert was cancelled and the rest of the tour abandoned. It had lasted less than a fortnight and Shaw estimated that he had lost £440. Georgina later claimed that the failure had been entirely Shaw's fault, as he had failed to advertise her properly.

In the meantime, the legal manoeuvres continued. Rivière commenced a civil action claiming damages for breach of contract against Frederick Cooper, as Georgina's agent. The unfortunate young man received the writ on 1 November, accepting it in the mistaken belief that it was a cheque for £60. Two days later, Cooper had a writ served on Rivière, alleging breach of contract. Georgina, who was busy compiling a dossier of Rivière's iniquities, also made a number of allegations against him in letters to friends and acquaintances. Rivière was, Georgina informed them, 'one of the biggest scoundrels unhung,' an escaped felon, who had been condemned to ten years' forced labour for either forgery or fraudulent bankruptcy. He had also falsified his marriage certificate and committed bigamy. His first wife, who was still alive, had come to England three years ago and had been given £1000 to go away quietly. 'I am very hard up now owing to Rivière's

6 Donald Shaw ['D.S.'], *Eighteen Months' Imprisonment* (London, 1882–4), quoted in SC, *Weldon v. George Routledge and Sons*, 1885.

swindling,' Georgina told one correspondent, 'though I expect, if he does not run away, to get a good sum out of him, besides heavy damages.' Rivière 'must be done for in time': he would never dare to stay in England once the truth about him came out.[7]

On 7 December the tenor Monari Rocca, came to see Georgina, 'almost crying,' and confessed that he had told Rivière about the letter she had sent him. Later that day, Georgina was informed that Rivière was planning to summons her for libel and telling everyone that she would be sent to prison.[8] The summons was delivered to Tavistock House two days later. It quickly became apparent that the recipients of several other letters had shown them to Rivière. Georgina and Angèle duly presented themselves at Clerkenwell Police Court, where they found Rivière and his allies, including two of the defectors from the choir, waiting for them. The conductor was represented by Montagu Williams; Georgina, who was defending herself, was allowed to sit at the solicitors' table. Several of her 'false, malicious and defamatory' libels were read out and Rivière was examined, together with two of this witnesses. When Georgina told the court that she could prove that everything she had written was true, the magistrate cautioned her and asked her to confine her answer to the authorship of the letters. Georgina replied that she did not wish to deny them and only wanted to say that they had not been maliciously written. The magistrate was not convinced. He committed her for trial at the Central Criminal Court, informing her that she would go to gaol if she could not find two sureties in £250 each for her own appearance, in addition to a recognisance of her own for the sum of £500. None of her friends could come up with the money immediately and Georgina was packed off to Newgate in a cab.

Newgate Gaol was a gloomy granite building used to hold prisoners awaiting trial at the Central Criminal Court (Old Bailey) next door. Despite its notorious reputation, Georgina rather enjoyed her night there:

> It was very comfortable, and so warm, in the cell, no. 5. Matron, sub-matron and laundry matron very kind. I had a lovely hot bath and went to bed at 8 o'clock. [On the following morning] Got up at 7.30. Ate gruel, very good, for breakfast. Two doctors came to see me. I was weighed – 10 stone 11 pounds; height 5 foot 5½ inches. Had a long talk with the chaplain, who I floored.

She met the governor, who reminded her of her father. On the following day she was bailed out by her brother Dal and Freddy Warre and allowed to

7 POB, 1/3/1880: *Regina v. Weldon.*

8 GWJ, 7/12/1879.

return home to await her trial, which was adjourned until the next sessions. During the weeks that followed she took part in a series of concerts at the Aquarium, in which she led the orchestra as well as conducting the choir and singing. Not everyone was impressed by these performances. One reviewer commented 'To say that Mrs Weldon shows a genius for conducting would be a flagrant absurdity' – though he conceded that she had, at least, been conversant with the score. Georgina's estimate of the size of the audience at these concerts was more than double that admitted to by the Aquarium staff and she was convinced that they were cheating her. Before long, the conductor, Charles Dubois, was claiming that each concert had lost £80. It was no wonder that he appeared to be 'worn out and irritated'.[9]

By now Georgina was again in desperate need of money. She asked her mother to lend her £500, telling her that the bailiffs had already been to the house three times. 'I have had enough to make a thousand million women mad, but thank God I remain calm and in good health, and I couldn't care less about going to prison, except for Madame Ménier's sake.' She would, she told Louisa, be able to repay her after she came out of gaol: she was so popular with the public that she would get lots of musical engagements. Louisa turned her down, claiming unconvincingly that she had no money.

At the end of the year Georgina's usual optimism seems to have deserted her. She wrote in her diary:

> What a life of turmoil and struggle this book represents and perhaps the next will contain far sadder and more heart-rending tales of tyranny, cruelty and injustice. Perhaps I shall get a year's imprisonment for calling a thief a thief. Judge and jury are sure to prefer Barabbas to Jesus. Now ruin is heaped upon ruin [and I have] no-one to protect me. Everyone combining to ruin me and the poor children if possible.[10]

Determined to find further evidence to support her allegations against Rivière, she sent Angèle back to Paris to obtain additional documentation. When Angèle returned, she brought her husband's two nieces, Jeanne and Bichette with her. They were followed by the children's father, Henri Duprat, the 'filthy communard' who had accused Anacharsis Ménier of stealing the children several years earlier. Duprat moved into Tavistock House and made himself useful cooking and helping Georgina to paste scraps into her books.

9 *Entr'acte*, 20/12/1879, p. 4; GWJ, 20,27/12/1879.
10 GW–LFT, 19/12/1879; GWJ, 31/12/1879.

On 12 January 1880 Georgina went to the Old Bailey to hear the formal indictment for libel. She pleaded 'Not Guilty' and put in a justification 'extending to five yards in length', repeating her allegations about Rivière's past misdeeds and giving six reasons why she should not be prosecuted. This did not have the desired effect, and the trial *Regina v. Weldon* finally started in the New Court at the Old Bailey on 4 March, before Sir Thomas Chambers, the judge who had presided over Anacharsis Ménier's trial in 1878. Georgina was permitted to sit close to her counsel, rather than in the dock. She was represented by Samuel Danks Waddy, QC, MP 'a psalm-singing Wesley preacher' (who was, he said, not related in any way to her erstwhile admirer Cadwalladwr Waddy) and a Mr Moseley.[11] Rivière's lawyers were Mr Lawrence, QC, and Montagu Williams. Lawrence opened the case for the prosecution, reciting Georgina's alleged libels. He said that the defendant would not only have to prove that the libels were true, 'in every detail and every particular', but also that their publication was for the public interest. The recipients of the letters were called to give evidence for the prosecution. Rivière was then examined and cross-examined: he gave his version of his dealings with Georgina and denied swindling her.

In his speech for the defence, Waddy told the jury that Rivière's employees had a right to know about him, as did the 100 or 200 young women in Georgina's choir. Georgina had said nothing that was not 'substantially' true – indeed, Rivière had admitted this. His client had certainly used some 'severe' expressions, but these did not amount to libel. The question of whether Rivière had swindled Georgina was the subject of action at common law and should be fought out in its proper place. 'At considerable length', Waddy contrasted Rivière's conduct with that of the defendant who, he said, 'had given herself up to works of benevolence, and retired from that society she had so long adorned'. He called several of Georgina's friends as witnesses. After Waddy had finished, the Recorder commented that Rivière had not committed any offence against English law and said that he did not see how it was possible to show justification or public benefit.

The trial ended on the following day. In summing up, Chambers (whom Georgina described as 'antagonistic') said that there was no doubt that Mrs Weldon was responsible for 'odious libels and serious imputations'. She claimed that she had published them for the public benefit, but she had made agreements with Rivière for the concerts at the Crystal Palace and Covent Garden after finding out about his past. M. Rivière had carried on his profession as a musical publisher and conductor in England for many years without reproach, and Georgina was the only person who had ever

11 GWJ, 31/12/1880.

made any complaints against him. Chambers did not see how it was for the public benefit that the transactions of Rivière's early life should be exposed. The jury retired for half an hour and returned with a verdict of 'guilty'. Waddy asked for sentence to be postponed since civil actions between Rivière and Georgina were pending. Chambers agreed, on condition Georgina could again find sureties as before. In the meantime, she was bound over to keep the peace.

A number of Georgina's friends were in court for the verdict and they all crowded round and kissed her. All were 'quite indignant' with the outcome of the case.[12] Others were less sympathetic: the reporter for the *London Daily News* wrote that Georgina had, through her counsel, subjected Rivière to 'a cross-examination extending over his whole life, much of which was both scandalous and irrelevant, and a good deal of which would have been stopped by a strong Judge'. Georgina had 'completely failed', and there was no reason to be dissatisfied with the verdict of the jury. 'Gadfly' commented that Georgina had clearly believed that the fact that she was a woman would shield her from the consequences of her acts, but 'this has proved a mistaken and cowardly assumption'.[13]

Georgina spent the next few weeks assembling her papers for the civil actions for damages and plotting further attacks on her enemies. On one day alone she sent off forty-seven letters to potential witnesses. By the beginning of May she was busy coaching Frederick Cooper and her witnesses for their forthcoming court appearances.[14] Proceedings started on 5 May at the Westminster Sessions House in Broad Sanctuary, before Baron Pollock. Rivière was represented by Mr Lawrence and Mr Finlay; Cooper represented himself 'for and on behalf of' Georgina. Rivière accused Cooper of breaking the agreement of 3 October 1879 and asked for £1000 in damages and the remainder of the sum of £300 that he had deposited in the bank to cover the costs of the Covent Garden concerts. In his counter-claim, Cooper demanded damages of £5000; the residue of the £300 (now said to be £180); a declaration that Georgina was entitled to receive the profits of her Benefit Concert on 5 November; and Georgina's share of the takings from the concerts at Covent Garden.

The trial ended three days later. Rivière had won, and he was awarded £50 damages and costs. The judge decreed that he was also entitled to the £180 that was still in the bank. Georgina blamed Cooper. 'He is very obstinate', she wrote, 'and it is like dragging fifty tons up hill trying to get him

12 *Times*, 4–6/3/1880; GWJ, 3–5/3/1880; POB, 1/3/1880: *Regina v. Weldon*.

13 *Daily News*, 6/3/1880, p. 6; *Entr'acte*, 13/3/1880, p. 11.

14 GWJ, 2–3/5/1880.

to ask as I desire.'[15] In the days that followed she attempted to take out summonses for perjury against Rivière's witnesses ('arch fiends'), though her solicitor tried to discourage her. She felt thoroughly sorry for herself: 'I was weak and sensitive and cried a good deal today. The newspaper reports are as disagreeable as possible, of course. It is so heart-sickening to see such lies and injustice pursue me everywhere. Real persecution!' She felt 'quite broken hearted, 'at bay, like a poor hunted deer'. It was 'very hard when one sees too well that the sun of one's youth has set for ever'.

Having been given notice to appear at the Old Bailey for sentencing on 24 May, Georgina busied herself making arrangements for her papers to be removed from Tavistock House to a place of safety 'in case of sudden invasion'. 'One never knows what a cowardly hound like my husband would do, should I get shut up by that villainous old Recorder, Sir Thomas Chambers', she wrote.[16] She was helped by two new friends, the widow and son of Edward Kenealy, the Irish barrister and founder of the Magna Charta Association who had defended the Tichborne Claimant, Arthur Orton, 'with violent partisanship' in 1873 and 1874.[17] Kenealy had subsequently been struck off. He had attended one of Georgina's 'At Homes' at Tavistock House in June 1879 and she had subsequently become an ardent Tichbornite, though she had previously considered that Orton was 'a beast' whose sentence (to fourteen years of penal servitude with hard labour, for perjury) was too lenient. By the spring of 1880 the Claimant's son, who called himself Roger Tichborne, was living with the Kenealys in Tavistock Square. Georgina saw him as a victim like herself, commenting, 'My case and his are parallel cases of English justice.'[18]

Henri Duprat accompanied Georgina when she went to the Old Bailey on 24 May – her forty-third birthday. Angèle stayed behind to guard Tavistock House, promising that she would be killed before she would let 'the enemy' steal Georgina's papers. The Recorder told Georgina he saw no provocation at all for the 'serious libels' she had uttered against Rivère. She had attempted to destroy the conductor's character 'by raking up old stories and giving them a different aspect to that which they properly bore'. It was no use fining her, he told Georgina, 'because you have already wasted large sums in this profitless and vindictive undertaking'. She could not be put upon her own recognisances because she was a married woman. The

15 *Times*, 7/5/1880; GWJ, 6/5/1880.

16 GWJ, 11–15,23/5/1880.

17 Orton claimed to be Roger Tichborne, heir to a baronetcy, who was presumed to have died in a shipwreck in 1854 when he was 25. He was tried and found guilty of perjury in 1874.

18 GWJ, 1/3/1874, 4/6/1879, 23/5/1880.

only course open to him was to send her to prison for four months from the date of her conviction. She was handed over to a female warder and taken from the court to Newgate.[19]

Angèle rushed straight to the prison when she heard what had happened, but was not permitted to see her friend. She returned to Tavistock House 'in a state of suffering, both moral and physical.' Later that day, James Neal, Harry Weldon's solicitor, presented himself at the front door with the aim of taking possession of the house. Angèle refused to let him in. Neal and his associates then besieged the house for four hours until, faced with no fewer than eight men threatening to break down the door, Angèle had to give up. They then 'rummaged about' in the whole house for three hours and Neal put seals on the door of the strongroom and on the drawer where some of Georgina's jewellery was kept. He told Angèle, 'Mrs Weldon is no better than she ought to be, and it is high time she should be put a stop to.'[20] He reacted with fury when Angèle refused to give him Georgina's jewel box and papers, telling him that she had put them all in a safe place. Neal offered her money, but she still refused. Eventually the men retreated, leaving behind three guards, one of whom was so drunk that he could not stand up. At some time during the night Angèle and Henri Duprat smuggled the remaining papers out of the house and took them to Mrs Kenealy. Afterwards, Angèle retired to bed 'with death in [her] heart.'

After a sleepless night, Angèle rose at five on the following morning, her only comfort being the fact that all Georgina's papers had been saved. Neal was supposed to come at ten with instructions from Harry Weldon, but failed to turn up. In the meantime the maid, Harriet, went on strike, telling Angèle that she could not stay in the kitchen: 'These men are unbearable. Since the morning one of them has been to look for beer five times. He has urinated along the walls, in the kitchen, in a bowl; the other behaves in an indecent manner with the girls.' Angèle went to the police station to complain, but was told there was nothing that could be done as the men were there by Mr Weldon's orders. She then sent a telegram to Neal, who showed up at 3, together with Harry Weldon. Harry gave Angèle twenty-four hours' notice to quit. She and a friend, Lucie Michou, packed until 2.30 the following morning, when they finally went to bed, hungry and exhausted. Neal's men were still in the house on the following morning, and their behaviour had not improved, as Angèle told Georgina:

[19] *Daily Telegraph*, 25/5/1880, p. 5.

[20] GWM proof, misc., p. 184.

> They have rummaged everywhere, they have installed themselves in [your] room, lit the gas, installed themselves on your sofa, smoked, taken books etc. My God, my poor friend, if you suffer in prison, my suffering is not less. I have to see all this and say nothing. Oh! It is too cruel. Charlotte [one of the maids] found them in the music room: they play the piano, dance, sing, smoke, make an infernal row.[21]

She left the house at 9 o'clock to look for lodgings, eventually finding two furnished rooms just round the corner at 45 Burton Crescent. On returning to Tavistock House, she was refused entry and had to wait for Neal, who let her in so that she could collect her belongings. Much had to be left behind when Angèle and the two Duprat children were finally turned out of the house at 10.30 p.m. She spent that night in her new lodgings, in a bed full of bugs, crying and unable to sleep.

Georgina did not find out what had happened for several days. She had been called to the matron's room, where the governor of the gaol, Sidney Smith, informed her that she was to be sent to Tothill Fields Prison, reputedly a less intimidating institution than Newgate. But Georgina protested: she liked the matron, Mrs Belsham, and her assistants, who were 'nice, kind women' and had no desire to leave Newgate. Left alone in Mrs Belsham's room whilst the matron took the governor back to the gate, Georgina spotted a newspaper, and was horrified to read the 'fatal news' of the invasion and ransacking of Tavistock House. When the matron returned, she asked 'through blinding tears' if what she had read was true. 'My agony of mind was indescribable', she wrote later, 'I had not till then felt any anxiety. I never felt anxious about the house, as it never struck me he [Harry] could do such a barbarous thing as to touch the house unless there was some pretext for doing so'. She immediately sent a petition to the Home Secretary, Sir William Vernon Harcourt, telling him: 'I feel strongly I have been made a kind of outlaw, that I have no protection from the laws, that a most violent prejudice exists against me, which taints all I say or do not say, which distorts all I do or do not do.'[22] The petition was ignored. After this, there was nothing that she could do other than sit out her sentence.

Since the date of her conviction was reckoned as 1 March, Georgina was only in Newgate for just over five weeks. She was not uncomfortable: indeed she later looked back on her time in the prison with a degree of nostalgia:

> If I had not had these dreadful troubles about the turning out of Minette, fear of losing my papers and then the house, I may safely say

21 GWJ, 25–26/5/1880.

22 GW, *Correspondence*, pp. 234–6.

> I never was more happy than I was at Newgate. All was regular and quiet. I had plenty of work to do: I mended linen, all the ordinary's wardrobe, nine and a half pairs of stockings for the prison. I practised my singing. What bothered me most was not being allowed my own warm underclothing, so I could not keep warm. And as for the shoes, of course I could not get them on my feet, so in time I got my own way pretty well about clothes, though the governor was sillily fussy, and my wearing mitts I had knitted myself were [*sic*] an awful worry. I had to bother more than was necessary for a pen'orth of glycerine for my nose, to get my toothbrush, my injection (the doctor wanted to dose me with pills). No brush, only a horse comb. I managed to get a tin of water night and morning for my washing.
>
> I did not mind the smallness of my cell, nor my bed being so hard after a bit, and I used to sit and work in the infirmary. I love being quite alone, so that was quite a treat, and lovely thoughts came to me. No feeling of care, of any kind of responsibility. I owed no-one anything, no kindness, no help. I was helpless, and all I cared for was to be as cheerful as possible, so as not to distress the kind matrons, or please the governor, the chaplain, or old Mappison the chief warder by seeming to care or be down-hearted. I used to sing as loud as I could in chapel, and pleased them all.[23]

Georgina was permitted to write and receive letters, and Angèle sent food. She was not forced to walk in the exercise yard with her 'companions in crime' the vast majority of whom were men. She felt heartily sorry for some of them. There was 'poor little Emma Pleasance', who was awaiting her trial for murdering two of her children; and Frank Amor, a violinist who had been sent to prison for setting fire to his bed when he was 'cranky from drink and the loss of a child'.

Angèle was not allowed to see Georgina, but her lawyer, Pain, came regularly. Other visitors included 'a psalm-singing old maid', Miss Martin, who introduced herself to prisoners armed with a Bible. Miss Martin endeared herself to Georgina by smuggling sewing materials into the prison so that she could mend the chaplain's surplice. She did not think much of the chaplain himself, however, and found his sermons 'too utterly stupid'. At night she dreamt of the old cottage at Beaumaris and the pug Dan Tucker. She even began to think more fondly of her father:

> How punished in the spirit poor Papa must be to see his daughter treated so. He was an honest, well-meaning man, so let me hope I am the means of his purgatory and that he may not long be earth-bound!

23 GWJ, 31/12/1880. The ordinary was the chaplain of Newgate.

> This treatment of me must be the punishment to his pride – for it certainly can't be for *my* sins, as I have such a happy spirit, good temper, and so few wants that no-one is so well able as I am to bear my trials.

She was totally unrepentant, comparing herself with the Tichborne Claimant and believing that her sentence was a farce. She, 'an honest, brave, respectable English lady', had been 'imprisoned as a common felon for saying a French thief was what he is!' She began to plot her revenge on her husband. Her application for a judicial separation had still not been granted and she was afraid that Harry might try to divorce her. Georgina decided to strike first by initiating a suit against him for the restitution of conjugal rights. Unless he agreed to live with her again, a decree for restitution would, she hoped, force Harry to make an out-of-court settlement on her. His only alternative would be to agree to a judicial separation with generous financial provision. If he refused, he could be sent to gaol. Georgina was certain that her husband could find no defence, 'except a pack of the most infamous lies, one more ridiculous than the other'. He was, in short, a 'filthy blackguard'. She became even more determined when, shortly before her release from Newgate, she received the news that Harry was planning to cut her annual income down from £1000 to £500.[24]

In the meantime Angèle and Pain were busy rallying support for Georgina. Sixty-five members of the choir met together and agreed that they would carry on with rehearsals whilst Georgina was away, each one paying 6d to meet the costs. On Wednesday 9 June a public meeting was called at St Andrew's Hall 'to consider the great injustice that had been done to Mrs Weldon in sentencing her to a term of imprisonment for simply stating what she believed to be the truth'.[25] The chairman, Captain William Morrison, vice-president of the Magna Charta Association, addressed the audience, as did several other people, including Mrs Kenealy's son, Maurice. Though originally formed to support the Tichborne Claimant, the Magna Charta Association had become 'a radical people's movement' by this time; its members also campaigned for civil liberties and law reform, and against the Contagious Diseases Acts and compulsory vaccination for smallpox.[26] It was unanimously agreed at the meeting that a petition should be presented to the Home Secretary. In this document, the petitioners pointed out that Georgina was, as far as they knew, the only woman who had been imprisoned for libel 'in modern times', and claimed

24 GWJ, 31/12/1880.

25 GWJ, 10/6/1880; *Times*, 10/6/1880.

26 Rohan McWilliam, *The Tichborne Claimant: A Victorian Sensation* (London and New York, 2007), pp. 113–28, 145–69.

that the judge's summing up and remarks on passing sentence had been 'prejudiced and untrue.' Georgina should be released or made a first-class demeanant. 'As women in this country are not enfranchised, and have no power or voice in making or framing the Laws of Libel, some consideration ought to be shown to them when, through ignorance, they break the said laws.'[27] Those who knew Georgina might well have reflected that she had broken the law through recklessness, rather than ignorance.

A deputation including Angèle, the two children, Lucie Michou and several members of the choir, took the memorial to the House of Commons on 11 June. The Speaker refused to see them, but graciously agreed to give the document to the Home Secretary. The reply came back a week later: the Home Secretary regretted that, having carefully considered all the circumstances of the case, he did not feel justified in advising any interference.[28] A letter from Georgina's mother to the Home Secretary was similarly unsuccessful. But her supporters did not give up, and it was agreed that another meeting should be held on 13 July, by which time Georgina would be out of gaol. Her old friend Thomas Lowther, now the editor of a campaigning magazine called the *People's Cross*, promised to publish her story.

Georgina emerged from Newgate early on the last day of June, having lost half a stone during her sentence. The road was lined with vehicles, including hansom cabs and one or two private carriages. Most of the vehicles were occupied by women, some wearing thick veils, who peered out through the windows. Other supporters stood in the street clutching fruit and bunches of flowers. When Angèle arrived with the two children, Pain insisted that she should sit and wait in a carriage with him, rather than outside on the pavement – otherwise, he told her, the governor would not let Georgina come out. When Georgina appeared there was 'a shrill cry of delight and welcome,' and the crowd called out 'Three cheers for Mrs Weldon!' According to one bystander, she was dressed, 'with her usual carelessness of effect,' in 'a dingy waterproof cloak and a somewhat battered hat.' But she was not allowed to speak: Pain pushed her into the carriage and she was driven off to Burton Crescent, bowing and waving from the window 'amid the cheers of the crowd.'[29]

Later that day, Georgina went to see her mother and told her that she wished to live with Harry again. Louisa Treherne's letter to her son-in-law informing him of this startling fact received an instant response from his lawyer: Mr Weldon had no intention of returning to his wife, but had kindly

27 GW, *Correspondence*, pp. 179–80.
28 A.F.O. Liddell–W. Chapman, 18/6/1880.
29 *Derby Daily Telegraph*, 9/7/1880, p. 2.

taken apartments for her at 51 Welbeck Street. Georgina's reaction to this was predictable. Neal was informed that:

Fig. 21. Georgina Weldon in her stage prison costume, 1880.

> I am not Mr Weldon's mistress, I am his wife. I have committed no fault in my marriage relations, and I will not be banished to apartments. Where my husband's home is, there is my home. If he does not find me a home according to my right, I will accept none that is inferior, and no conditions which are insulting and dishonorable to me. It is my right to dwell under my husband's own roof. I love a quiet life, and nothing would please me better than to live happily with my husband in quiet retirement.

Georgina asked if Mr Weldon was expecting her at the College of Arms, where he now had 'the best rooms' following his promotion to Windsor Herald earlier in the year; or at 9 Albert Mansions, his private lodgings. The reply to this was unequivocal: she would not be received at either address.[30] She stayed at 45 Burton Crescent.

During the weeks after her release from Newgate, Georgina occupied herself by writing notes for her article for the *People's Cross*; looking for evidence that she could use in her campaign against Harry; and preparing for the meeting on 13 July, which was to be held at the Great Central Hall in Bishopsgate. One of her detractors commented:

> I don't know how her prison experiences can possibly interest a respectable and miscellaneous audience, but Mrs Weldon is endowed with an abnormal amount of vanity, and she believes that anything she may do or suffer must necessarily be of some moment to a generous public. She has experienced that kind of treatment which ladies are not usually subjected to, simply because she has chosen to behave herself as ladies generally do *not* behave.[31]

[30] GWJ, 16/4/1880; *The People's Cross* [August 1880], p. 7.

[31] *Entr'acte*, 17/7/1880, p. 4.

Nevertheless, the room was 'crowded to excess' and hundreds had to be sent away. It was, Georgina, thought, 'a most glorious evening'. She told the audience, 'She knew it was not considered respectable for a woman to appear in public, but she was speaking in the cause of liberty and justice, and did not care a button what was thought of her.'[32] The meeting is described in a special issue of the *People's Cross*, which was issued a few weeks later with a portrait of Georgina in her prison dress on the cover:

> Even the hideous prison garb – which by a perverted ingenuity is contrived with a view to degrade woman, and strip her as far as possible of her personal beauty – cannot hide the exquisite tenderness that flashes in those eyes, or the general beneficence that sits enthroned on those comely features.
>
> It is through much suffering, as well by the force of personal character, that Mrs Weldon has become a popular favourite; and that she is popular is abundantly clear from the numbers that crowd to the meetings she has held in different parts of London since her release from Newgate. Men of the world, and woman of fashion, crowd up to see the heroine of so many adventures, whose bravery survives all her afflictions. They long to look on the plucky little woman, who baulked the 'mad-doctors', and braved the officials in their own castle.
>
> On the first occasion after her release, and much to the amusement of the crowd, Mrs Weldon appeared in a facsimile of her prison dress – gown, jacket, cap, apron and all. Nor did she forget to hold in her hand the huge cotton pocket-handkerchief, the pattern of which is a brown ground with huge white spots sprinkled all over, and the size, enough for a small table-cloth.
>
> No announcement of this dress in character had been made, and when Mrs Weldon put in appearance the hideous garb, the wild, but sympathetic enthusiasm of the house, knew no bounds, and expressed itself in vociferous cheers.
>
> How Mrs Weldon found her way to Newgate, we need not here repeat; the public knows already. But the public does not know how she bore herself under the infliction. Even her persecutors, if they knew, must now think it was a pity to imprison so high-spirited a woman, who disdained to make her punishment real by the reproaches of remorse. In her innermost soul she persuaded herself she was no sinner, and thus found it easy to raise herself, in her own consciousness, to the dignity of martyrdom. Newgate has no terrors for such proud spirits.[33]

32 GWJ, 13/7/1880; *Reynolds's Newspaper*, 18/7/1880, p. 5.

33 *People's Cross* [August 1880], p. 9.

As usual, the takings at the meeting were disappointing and barely covered the expenses.

By the time Georgina came out of Newgate, Tavistock House had been cleared, and all the remaining contents had been taken to James Shoolbred and Co.'s furniture depository in Tottenham Court Road. Georgina told her mother 'I have only one dress to put on, no sponges, no combs, no brushes, no books, no Bible. Nothing at all.' She and Angèle had been obliged to buy mattresses, pillows and blankets and were both '*miserable*.' They could not gain access to their belongings until 6 August. Once there, Georgina finally broke down as she surveyed the wreckage of her former life: 'Oh, it was heart-rending to go over our furniture etc. Everything topsy-turvy, everything spoilt, injured, higgledy piddledy [*sic*], everywhere and anywhere. Everything packed up with dust. It breaks my heart altogether. I wish I could hate everything and everybody.'[34] They were not allowed to take anything away without Harry's permission – but Harry had gone to ground. His absence was, no doubt, prolonged by the receipt of a 'very reasonable' letter from Georgina at the beginning of August, followed by 'an ultimatum' a few days later. A week after this, her new lawyer, Thomas Disney Leaver, filed a petition for the restitution of conjugal rights in the Divorce Division of the High Court.[35] Then, on Friday 13 August, Georgina and Angèle set off for Clerkenwell Police Court, where Georgina asked the magistrate, Thomas Barstow, for a summons against 'Mr William Henry Weldon (Windsor Herald), College of Arms' for detaining her property. She also asked for Barstow's assistance in publicising the disappearance of her husband:

> who, she said, was a fine, tall man, forty-three years of age, with fine teeth, and a very smooth and fine complexion, had been missing for more than six weeks, and although she had been doing all she could to find him, her efforts had been of no avail. He left her in 1875, without any quarrel or disagreement. She should very much like to see her husband, also to get her property.[36]

That afternoon Georgina received a note giving her and Angèle permission to collect their possessions. The two women spent the next fortnight at Shoolbred's, sorting and repacking. On 25 August Leaver served Harry's lawyer with a copy of the petition for the restitution of conjugal rights.[37] A few days later Georgina sent eleven parcels of papers and other belongings

34 GW–LFT, 27/7/1880, 4/8/1880; GWJ, 6/8/1880.
35 GWJ, 31/7/1880, 9/8/1880; GW–LFT, 4/8/1880; TNA, J 77/247/7063.
36 *People's Cross*, [August 1880], p. 10.
37 GWJ, 25/8/1880.

off to Gisors and on 1 September she, Angèle and the two Duprat children set off for France. It was time Georgina got to know her orphans again, but her decision to leave the country may also have been prompted by financial problems. The Rivière affair had cost her more than a thousand pounds in choir expenses, advertising and legal fees – she owned the lawyer Pain alone £200 – and she had not paid the £50 damages or the costs awarded to Rivière in May.[38]

[38] GWM proof, misc., p. 210.

20
Conjugal Rights

Georgina and her companions reached Gisors on the afternoon of 2 September 1880. Four of the orphans were still in the nuns' orphanage there: Pauline ('improved'), Beryl ('blind in one eye'), Sapho/Katie ('very pretty and nice and clever'), and Baucis ('grown immensely').[1] Rosie, the eldest girl, had died of typhoid fever earlier in the year, whilst the two boys, Dagobert and Merthyr, had been boarded out in the town. None of them could speak a word of English.

Once again, Georgina's spirits were refreshed by the calm, quiet atmosphere of the convent. It was 'a port of refuge, of peace, of comfort' – and not expensive. She and Angèle were given 'splendid' lodgings in the hospice: a salon with two bedrooms, with 'heaps of cupboards' for their belongings. 'I would like to spend the rest of my life here', Georgina told her mother, 'but it is my duty to live with my husband.'[2] She was not best pleased when Angèle insisted that the two Duprat children could not possibly be put into the orphanage, but must stay with them. James Salsbury sent newspapers from London, and Georgina wrote and received letters almost every day. In November she learned that 'Mrs Weldon's Choir' had been dissolved and merged into the 'Dilettante Choir'. The impending lawsuit against Harry was never far from her mind: she bombarded Thomas Disney Leaver with instructions and busied herself collecting and copying letters that might be useful. Towards the end of the month, she was 'horrified and disgusted beyond measure' to receive a letter from brother Dal telling her that Harry was accusing her of adultery, having found an 'incriminating' letter addressed to Sir Henry Thompson amongst some papers that had been picked up at Tavistock House. This letter, which was fourteen years old, appears to have been Georgina's reply to a declaration of love from Sir Henry, which Harry had forbidden her to send. She believed that it had been destroyed at the

1 The child originally named Sapho was now called Baucis, whilst Katie had been renamed Sapho.

2 GW–LFT, 4,9/9/1880.

time. Georgina, who now realised that she had been naive and unwise in allowing Sir Henry to get so close to her, told Dal that it was all Harry's fault, as he had encouraged her to lead the older man on. Dal, in return, asked her why she was bringing the action for the restitution of conjugal rights, telling her that she had, 'a strange idea of happiness' if she wished to live with a man whom she had described as 'mad, bad, evil, coarse, a rascal … and other tender epithets.' If she merely wished to annoy and dishonour her husband more than she had already done, Dal continued, it was hardly rational of her to require that he should receive her under his roof. She was 'like an enraged bull which buts a brick wall and breaks its head.'

Georgina replied with the usual torrent of abuse, informing her brother that Harry had been 'invaded by a morbid fear of her' and that he was a sex-maniac. Nevertheless, the worse he was, the more it was her duty to live with him.[3] She was furious with her family for interfering in her affairs. They were all 'immeasurably inferior to me in spirit, in principles, in character and talents.' 'Oh!' she raged, 'the existence of my family is indeed a malediction to me! They are like Banquo's ghost. Never useful and always deleterious.' She did, however, concede that 'they don't mean harm.'

An old legal friend, W.F. Low, was asked to act as an intermediary. After some consultation, he informed Georgina that Harry had agreed to increase her allowance to £600 a year and give her a lump sum of £250 (her share of the proceeds from the sale of the lease of Tavistock House) if she would withdraw the suit for restitution and sign a deed of separation. At the same time, all papers on both sides should be given up and destroyed. If Georgina refused and the lawsuit went against her, her allowance would cease and she would have no claim on Harry's estate if he were to predecease her. Georgina's reply was immediate and unequivocal: she required 'public reparation for years of calumny and insult'; the restoration of her home; and a settlement of £1000 a year. She would, moreover, not 'for £5000 a year' consent to the destruction of a single letter. A married woman's home was under her husband's roof, she told Low. Harry had taken away her house and must now receive her in his own home.[4]

At the end of 1880 Georgina reflected on the events of 'another very peculiar year.' She was, she wrote, 'perfectly happy and materially comfortable' at the Hospice, but felt that she had been 'beaten by foul play and a persecution of 14 years nearly.' 'I am,' she continued 'what my sister Florence used to call me, "a poor old scape-goat".' She was certain, nevertheless, that she had been 'endowed and chosen by Providence for a certain purpose.'

3 GWJ, 21/11/1880; GW–DT, 21,30/11/1880; DT–GW, 27/11/1880.

4 GW–LFT, 30/10/1880; GWJ, 21,25/11/1880; GWMSM, p. 153.

That purpose was, she now felt, the publication of her life and papers. Anyone who knew Georgina a little might, however, have laughed when they read her claim: 'I duly feel the unimportance of individual self and the absurdity of fancying that brilliant triumph can ever attend the efforts of anyone so unworldly, so unselfish, so *pot-au-feu*, as I am.'[5]

The conjugal rights business dragged on during the first months of 1881, with Harry and James Neal doing their best to ensure that it would never come to court. In January Neal filed an Answer to Georgina's petition, in which it was claimed that she had committed adultery 'on divers occasions' and 'at divers places,' including Great Ormond Street, Tavistock House and the Princes Gate Hotel in South Kensington. Harry and Georgina had separated by mutual consent in August 1874. She had not suggested that they should live together again before instituting the suit against him, the sole purpose of which was to force him to make her an allowance 'larger than is reasonable.'[6]

Georgina dismissed the accusation of adultery as 'the cynical joke of an imbecilic maniac' and told Leaver that the statement was 'even *more* wonderful than I expected.' 'I wonder,' she added, 'Mr Weldon has not begun since the year 1801 to accuse me of adultery.' Every single assertion in the statement should be denied 'emphatically and entirely.' If her husband persisted, he should be summonsed 'to mention the names of the men I have committed adultery with, on what dates and in which rooms of the houses he mentions.' She assured the lawyer that 'every particular is entirely false.' She also informed him that she neither she nor Harry had ever suggested a separation, and continued:

> I refuse to be separated. He always said I could 'live with the Devil,' being such a good, amiable creature. Mr Weldon is of a very desponding, hypochondriacal temperament. I believe he is insane or has a diseased brain, and he certainly wants me to take care of him and what remains of his property.

'I daresay,' she added, 'he never expected the "worm could turn".' Harry was trying to get rid of her 'for the sole reason that I was not as good a bedfellow as some bad women are, and that was my *only* defect.' She had tried to get her husband back 'in every possible way' and did not see why they could not live together in spite of all that had happened. There was, she asserted,

5 A pot-au-feu is a stew of meat and vegetables. Does Georgina mean 'ordinary, homely?' GWJ, 31/12/1880.

6 TNA, J77/247/7063. 44 Great Ormond Street was Freddy Warre's house; the Princes Gate Hotel was the hotel belonging to Alfred Nodskou where Georgina stayed on her way back to Tavistock House in July 1875.

'nothing to prevent a husband and wife who are not on speaking terms from living under the same roof'. She had never had any quarrel with her husband and did not see any reason why they should not get on 'just as contentedly as before', once had had got over his 'evidently insane dislike' of her.

In Harry's next Answer, which was filed on 14 March, he alleged that his wife had committed adultery with Sir Henry Thompson, the singer George Werrenrath and Cadwalladwr Waddy, but he was still vague about the precise dates. Georgina replied that she had not seen Thompson for sixteen years, whilst Werrenrath was 'a vulgar baker's boy, with skin the colour of pastry, a bloated Teuton, hideous, never in my good graces in any form'. She had not seen him for four years. Waddy was 'an insane person with whom she had never had the slightest acquaintance'. Harry knew as well as she did that 'he might as well accuse the Virgin Mary of adultery as accuse me'. She would, she told Leaver, resist any attempt to have the case heard *in camera*: if this were to be done it would be with the sole aim of 'screening' Harry and Sir Henry. When she won – as, of course, she would do – Harry would 'safely sneak off' and no one would know why. 'I'll stir Heaven and Earth before this shall happen', she declared.[7]

~

At the end of March, Georgina and Angèle travelled to Paris for the first performance of Gounod's new opera, *Le Tribut de Zamora*, in Paris. After the failure of *Polyeucte* three years earlier, the composer was hoping that this new work would revive his reputation as an operatic composer. The evening was a critical success, but Georgina was not impressed. In her opinion, Gounod was 'not very well received', and the first two acts of the opera were very dull. It was 'a degrading, revolting libretto'. She thought that Gounod himself looked bad-tempered and weary. His appearance was dishevelled, and she longed to 'wash his hair and make him a beautiful *crinière* [mane]'. One wonders at his reaction if he received the '*immortelle* garlands' that Georgina had bought for him earlier that day, especially if he remembered the similar garland that had caused so much trouble at the time of the final performance of *Gallia* at the Opéra-Comique ten years earlier. Georgina fervently hoped that he would be cross.[8] In spite of her disapproval of *Zamora*, she and Angèle went to two further performances in the days that followed. She bought the music and decided that there was 'a great deal to be done with it', though it had been ruined by the bad performance. Two days after their return to Gisors, Angèle set off for England

7 GW–LFT, 18/3/1881; GW–T.D. Leaver, 27/1/1881, 6/2/1881.

8 GWJ, 1/4/1881.

with Baucis, whose mother had asked for her. Angèle also spent some time looking for somewhere for them all to live, settling on 33 Loughborough Road in the middle-class suburb of Brixton. In mid-May she took four of the orphans back to London.

~

In the meantime, Georgina had received the news that, as she had anticipated, Harry and his lawyers were trying to have the case for restitution heard *in camera*, claiming that their aim was to avoid a public scandal. If the case were to be heard in public, they argued, everyone would soon know that Georgina was 'given over to a vice of which one cannot speak – although not a matrimonial offence recognised by the law.' Georgina's reaction was one of utter contempt. She informed her mother that she would 'move heaven and earth to put a stop to that little game' and spent the next few weeks locked in her room in the hospice, sorting and copying letters.[9]

In mid June, however, Georgina was forced to return to England. She had fallen out with Leaver and needed to meet her new lawyer, John Rae. The house in Brixton was, she thought, 'very handy and comfortable,' but Angèle was discontented, mainly because she had been ordered her to keep a low profile. With the conjugal rights business pending, Georgina did not wish her husband to know that Angèle and the children were back in London. Nor did she want his lawyers to enquire too closely into her own living arrangements or her relationship with the Frenchwoman. Now, Georgina found that Angèle looked 'very changed and thin' and was 'very dull and does nothing but cry.' The children were ill too. Georgina was not sympathetic, though she did engage a girl, Eva Morand, to help 'as governess and to work.'[10] Three months later, she brought the rest of the children from Gisors to Brixton, having come to the reluctant conclusion that she would have to stay in England for the time being so that she could concentrate on her campaign against Harry.

At the end of November, Georgina received the exciting news that Harry had spent the summer on a houseboat at Mapledurham with a 'magnificently dressed woman' who had a son aged thirteen 'the very image of Mr Weldon.'[11] 'Now we see the reason why he abandoned me at Müllberg in the winter of 1869–70,' she told her mother, adding sadly, 'It makes me *furibond* [furious], especially because he knows how happy I would have been to have a baby to care for. I told him that no matter what bastard he

[9] GW–LFT, 28/5/1881.
[10] GWJ, 2,17,23/6/1881.
[11] GWJ, 30/11/1881.

might have, I would be happy to look after it.'[12] Attempts to find out more about this woman and her child over the next few months were, however, unsuccessful. Equally fruitless were Georgina's attempts to get Harry to court. Neal was proving to be a master of prevarication, as one obstacle after another was put in her way. In December she sang at the Aquarium, where the audiences were poor but she earned the grand sum of £44. At the same time she was busy correcting the proofs of her Gounod book, which, thanks to 'Alpha' Salsbury's help, was almost ready for publication. She was also trying to work out how she could dispose of Beryl, having decided that the girl was 'a lump of vice'.[13] In January Angèle left Beryl at the orphanage attached to the convent of *Virgo Fidelis* [the Faithful Virgin] in Norwood. Georgina was not sorry to see her go, though Beryl had been with her for six years. She was much more worried about her pet canary, which was suffering from 'the pip'.

Georgina informed John Rae that she was not prepared to countenance any kind of compromise with her husband: '[I will] never, never, never [accept a settlement]. I will have it pushed to the bitterest end. I have been too deeply injured. Beggared or not, I do not care.' Rae therefore filed Georgina's reply to Harry's accusations of adultery at the beginning of February 1882. Of course she denied everything – adding that, if she *had* committed adultery as alleged, her husband had 'connived thereat'; had been 'guilty of conduct conducing thereto'; and had 'condoned the same'. In Harry's Rejoinder, which was filed a week later, he, in turn, swore that all his wife's allegations were untrue. This was, Georgina thought, 'cheek!'[14] No date had yet been set for the court hearing, but she busied herself inspecting the letters that Harry proposed to produce as evidence and compiling a list of possible witnesses. Several of these were served with subpoenas, including 'old Rawlings' and his son Alfred, and Georgina's former pupil, Nita Gaëtano (now Mrs Lynedoch Moncrieff). Georgina was delighted to hear from Angèle that Nita was now 'tremendously stout, has an immense moustache, coarse skin, and looks a thoroughly disappointed, discontented woman'. Georgina also familiarised herself with the procedure of the Divorce Court at Westminster, attending on no fewer than seven days in May. She took an instant dislike to Frederick Inderwick, the barrister (and specialist in matrimonial cases) who was to represent Harry.[15]

12 GW–LFT, 1/12/1881. Harry was not the child's father.

13 GWJ, 27/12/1881.

14 TNA, J77/247/7063; GWJ, 3/3/1882.

15 GWJ, 16–26/5/1882, 7/7/1882.

Despite the best efforts of Harry Weldon and his lawyers, proceedings in 'the great case *Weldon v. Weldon*' finally began on 13 July 1882 in the Probate, Divorce and Admiralty Division of the High Court at Westminster before the president, Mr Justice Hannen, and a special jury. Harry and his lawyers had continued their efforts to stop the case coming to court up to the last moment: on 12 July Georgina had received a letter from Harry which confirmed her belief that he was anxious to avoid the publicity that would follow a court appearance:

> We have now been living entirely apart for seven years. Surely it is possible we can come to some agreement to continue to do so. There is room in the world for us both without being compelled to inflict daily on each other feelings and views and acts which are wholly antagonistic. Life is so short, why endeavour to add to what remains of it to us certain misery? I am quite willing to settle as far as I can a reasonable allowance on you, when you will be able to pursue your objects in life unfettered by me, which you could never do it we lived together.

Georgina's reaction when she read this was one of contempt. Harry was, she thought, 'a pitiful cur'.[16] She had no intention of living with him, but she wanted to frighten him into settling a decent income on her.

Harry had already withdrawn his defence, so the court proceedings should have been a formality, but Georgina was determined to vindicate herself in open court, convinced that, if she did not do so, everyone would believe that she had been Gounod's mistress. In fact, Harry had never accused her of adultery with Gounod – having presumably been advised by his lawyers that to do so would invite the response that he must have colluded in any such relationship, as they were all living under the same roof at the time. Nor, in spite of their previous threats, had the lawyers made any reference to Georgina's relationship with Angèle.

Georgina's great opportunity came when she entered the witness box and her counsel, Arthur Bayford, asked her if she had committed adultery, expecting a brief and formal denial, in which nobody would be named. He – and the rest of the court – got much more than they expected. 'Certainly not', she replied, 'It is an infamous lie and Mr Weldon knows it', adding, when it became clear that Bayford was not going to ask any more questions, 'Neither with Sir Henry Thompson, Cadwalladwr Waddy, and Werrenrath.' The judge stopped her at this point, telling her 'I should not have allowed you in the box if I had thought you would have said anything.' Georgina promptly retorted, 'I knew you would not. It is a scandal and a disgrace the

[16] WHW–GW, 12/7/1882; GWJ, 13/7/1882.

way every case I bring into Court gets hushed up'. She did, however, obey the judge's order to leave the box. Hannen directed the jury to find that Mrs Weldon was not guilty. They did so at once and he pronounced a decree for the restitution of conjugal rights, with costs. Georgina had, as she wrote in her diary 'come off victorious at all points' in spite of the best efforts of her own counsel to thwart her. The lawyers were all a 'disgusting set of blackguards, liars and scoundrels'.[17]

Savouring her triumph, Georgina wrote to Harry, the 'pitiful cur', that evening. 'My darling old Poompsey Keat', she began:

> You are a silly old *feelo*, and trying to tell lies and beat your wise and purky little Tooss must have filled Jevons', Neal's and Rae's pockets, and you would have done better to have given in at once.
>
> You are quite mistaken if you think I am pebble-eyed or peach-jammy. *I* have no object in life. At 45 years of age a woman may rest upon her oars. I have done my *best*, but my '*best*' being unlike people's '*bad*', I have been too bothered to continue in the same and think I may just as well become as worldly, well-dressed etc. as your fortune can allow me to be.

She signed herself 'Your ever faithful and loving Tatkin and wife'. She followed this missive two days later with an extraordinary letter, four thousand words long, in which she expressed all her bitterness and resentment:

> I find that as long as a man is in a tidy position, is supposed to have money, gives dinner parties, yacht lunches and musical entertainments, he has no lack of admirers and supporters, and that, although had you been convicted of having cheated of 5s worth at cards, you would be cut by all respectable (?) Society, you may *and have* cheated your wife of her money, of her reputation, of her home, of her liberty; you may *and have* stood by (if not contrived) to get your wife imprisoned for calling a French adventurer what he was – a convicted felon, a bigamist and a perjurer, and who had swindled her out of at least £2000, and *you* are upheld by respectable Society and *my* friends go to your dinners and shake you by the hand.

Harry was, she continued, 'a diseased, morbid, morose creature', whose 'only home luxury was unbridled sensuality' and whose 'hands were up every woman's petticoats'. Nevertheless, she wrote, she could see no reason for believing that they would be miserable if they were to live together again:

17 GWJ, 13/7/1882; *Times*, 14/7/1882. The report in *The Times* omits all the names of men with whom Georgina was alleged to have committed adultery.

> You were never interesting or a companion to me, but all our correspondence proves that we were (at all events, *I* was) extremely attached to each other. I shall now expect less than ever any intellectual amusement with you. I look younger and prettier than your vulgar mistresses, and look fifteen years your junior, so I am quite handsome enough for you, and I hope I should have a wholesome moral effect upon you, for you cannot be in your senses to have behaved as you have, and I still hope to get you to repent your sins.

'In India,' she added, 'women are forbidden by English law to make *suttees* of their bodies, but here, unless they prostitute their *bodies*, prejudice forces clever women to make suttees of their minds.' Now that he was Windsor Herald, Harry had a very good income, with 'a nice apartment, rent free, at the College of Arms' – all thanks to the influence of *her* friend, Sir William Alexander. Had she been a man, it would have been Georgina who was a herald, and not Harry, and it was not fair that he should keep her out of the College. She was quite willing to live there and save the rent at 9 Albert Mansions. She intended to come to him without delay. She did not want him to give her an allowance, though 'You will like me to spend money on dress and ornaments, and I can work you a fine tabard and keep some plants.' This would make her perfectly happy, and she would also like his 'nice house-boat.' 'How can you suppose that I can wish to live anywhere but under your roof?,' she asked him, 'there, at least, I am safe. If anything happened to me there, the suspicion would fall on you and you would risk being hanged. You would not like that.' Warming to her subject, she continued:

> Remark, if you have not before, how like your skull and chin are to Lefroy's. Your voice, Lamson's soft and pleasant voice. It is not your fault, my poor old man, if you have these instincts. The most elementary rules of phrenology will teach you this and will teach you I have the most perfect-shaped head. I can no more help being good than you can help being bad. You have a diseased, ill-balanced brain, and I have always been happy and merry because the proportions of my brain are perfect.

Percy Mapleton Lefroy and Dr George Lamson were both notorious murderers. Harry should 'bow to the inevitable,' repent his 'evil, sly, underhand ways,' and 'live for ever happily with his ever-loving and pretty wife.'

A week after she wrote this, Georgina discovered that Harry had leased his apartment in Albert Mansions to a friend. His reply to her communication, when it came, was infuriatingly brief; he merely referred her back to his previous letter. Harry himself was once again to prove remarkably elusive, and he had many people on his side. 'Gadfly' wrote: '[Mr Weldon] has endured a wonderful lot of annoyances and humiliations at the hands of his wife, and he shall have my sympathies.' Mrs Weldon appeared to be unable to 'maintain anything like a ladylike repose for two consecutive minutes,' and her fondness for asserting herself had become 'a mania.'[18] It was to be more than a year before Harry could be served with the restitution order.

~

The orphanage was now largely defunct – Georgina had already got rid of all the boys, and only two little girls, Katie/Sapho and Pauline, were left. By mid July, the French and English editions of her Gounod book were, at long last, finished. She sent out several review copies and was gratified by a 'pretty good' notice in *Vanity Fair*. This was 'not complimentary,' but she hoped that it would make people buy the book. She set to work composing a 'Preface' to the book, in which she accused the composer of being in league with her enemies. She also referred to Harry's 'desertion' of her and gave an account of her suit for the restitution of conjugal rights. She ended with the words, 'I have done my best, in the public interest, to expose several public abuses; I hope I shall not be considered deserting my colours if I now retire into private life.' There were many people in the next few years who were to wish that she had done so.[19]

In July Georgina discovered that the long-delayed first performance of Gounod's oratorio *The Redemption* was in the programme for the Birmingham Music Festival. She was already familiar with the work, for the composer had been working on it during his stay at Tavistock House. She was determined to hear it, especially when she discovered that Gounod, her beloved 'old man' was coming to conduct it, having been offered £4000 by the festival committee. She wrote off immediately for tickets and a room at the Queen's Hotel, where the composer and his party were to stay. Her excitement grew when she heard, on 14 August, that Gounod and his son Jean had arrived in Birmingham. On the same day, however, she received a letter informing her that the Queen's Hotel was 'all full' and she would have to stay somewhere else. A friend brought her the score of *The Redemption* and she scanned it eagerly. It did not, she thought 'promise well in pianoforte score' and some of the English words were 'wretched.'[20]

[18] GW–WHW, 13,15/7/1882; WHW–GW, 23/7/1882; *Entr'acte*, 22/7/1882, pp. 11–12.

[19] GW, 'Preface,' pp. ii, xii–xv.

[20] GWJ, 21,24/8/1882.

On 26 August Georgina set off by train for Birmingham armed with bundles of her 'Preface', leaving Angèle in London with the children. She found a room at the Grand Hotel and then went to the Town Hall. Standing outside, she could hear that a rehearsal of *The Redemption* was in progress. 'I felt like a deserving angel kept out of Paradise', she wrote sadly. 'It is very hard, but though I could have had several cries, I was too proud to show anything.' It was, however, all good publicity for her book. She consoled herself by buying two 'hideous' new photographs of Gounod. 'He has grown so fat and blowsy, and looks so hard and wicked. My dear beautiful old man, who is so cruel to me.' She hired a piano and bought all the music for the festival, including both *The Redemption* and *Graziella*, a new work by Julius Benedict.[21] On 29 August she took the opportunity to distribute her 'Preface' at two of the concerts. Several copies found their way into the hands of the musicians and members of the festival committee. As a result, an emergency meeting was held, at which the committee members, believing 'that there was a great probability of an unseemly scene occurring in the Town Hall' if Georgina were to attend Gounod's concert, took the unanimous decision that she should be excluded and that a strict watch should be kept at the entrances to the Hall.

The first performance of *The Redemption* took place on the following day. Georgina dressed in her best clothes and set off for the Town Hall in good time with the score under her arm. On the way there, she stopped to look at a 'new and good' photograph of Gounod in a shop window and met an old friend, the composer Alberto Randegger. As they stood chatting, a note was thrust into Georgina's hand. It was from Robert Impey, the secretary to the festival committee, who informed her that she would not be allowed inside the Town Hall for any performances conducted by Gounod. 'Of course', she wrote, 'I pushed my way to the Hall'. There she was met by one of the stewards, J.W. Farmer, and two policemen, who refused to let her in. At that point, 'a technical assault was committed'. Accounts of these events differ, but Farmer appears to have put one or both hands on Georgina's shoulder and pushed her away from the entrance.

After this, Georgina gave up her attempt to get into the Hall. This, it turned out, was a wise decision since, as she was later informed, the festival committee hoped that she would 'make a row, in a rage', so that they could have her locked up without the option of a fine. Instead, she went to the Police Court to ask for a summons for assault, which was refused. The stipendiary magistrate, Thomas Kynnersley, advised Georgina to consult a solicitor and told her that she should seek her remedy in a civil court. She

[21] GWJ, 26/8/1882.

reminded him that, as a married woman, she could not do so without her husband's permission – permission that her husband (even if she could find him) would be sure to deny her. Unable to find a solicitor that day, she tried to get her own back by giving an interview to a reporter from the *Birmingham Mail.* The performance that she missed was 'a frantic success': 400 singers and an orchestra of 140 thrilled an audience of several thousand. It would be remembered as one of the greatest triumphs in the history of the Birmingham Music Festival.[22]

Georgina tried again to take out a summons on the following day. The court was full and the events of the previous day were in all the local and London newspapers. Some were more accurate than others: one even claimed that she had gone to the Town Hall with a pistol in her pocket. An article in the *Birmingham Daily Gazette* was, Georgina thought, libellous. On the other hand, she was delighted by the publicity. 'The newspapers are full of me', she told Angèle with glee, 'articles without end: in the trains, the trams, the buses – the lawyers, everyone is talking about me. It's Providence.'[23] She hoped that Gounod would read the newspapers and remember her – even if it was for the wrong reasons: 'What consolation to think he *cannot* forget me. He must hear, he must see my name. So I am something in his life – dear old man, who I have loved so, and who I do love so much.'

The magistrate still refused to grant Georgina a summons, but she found a solicitor who agreed to help her to bring an action against the festival committee for all her expenses and tickets, and another one against the *Birmingham Daily Gazette* for libel. She took particular exception to their suggestion that she was 'A lady whose name has been brought prominently before the public in connection with certain notorious litigation proceedings' and that her 'presence at a musical celebration is not usually regarded as conducive to entire harmony'.[24] For the time being, however, there was nothing she could do. She was informed that the musicians were 'altogether on my side', but was unable to get into the second performance of *The Redemption* and returned to London a day later.

The 'Birmingham affair' also reached the French newspapers, including *Le Figaro*, which published an article by its London correspondent, Thomas Johnson, on 3 September. It was not complimentary. 'Dame Weldon', it was claimed, 'never loses a chance of making as much fuss as she can about her very unattractive personality.' Nobody who knew Georgina could have

22 GWJ, 30–31/8/1882; *Birmingham Daily Post*, 9/9/1882, p. 5; James Harding, *Gounod* (London, 1973), p. 207.

23 GW–AM, 2/9/1882.

24 GWJ, 31/8/1882; *Birmingham Daily Gazette*, 31/8/1882.

been surprised at her reaction to this. On Friday 8 September she asked 'my dear Mr Flowers' at Bow Street for a summons for libel against Johnson. Flowers commented that the article was 'very vulgar', but looked 'much like the ordinary writing of people with strong views'. He did, however, grant the summons.[25] He was no doubt dismayed when Georgina returned again on the following day, this time to ask for a summons against Percy Betts ('Cherubino') of the *London Figaro*, who had told his readers that her publications were 'indecent and scandalous'. This time Flowers advised her to 'treat the *Figaro* in the same way they seem disposed to treat you' – in other words, to ignore them. Georgina had no option but to give way.[26] The case against Johnson was dismissed a week later, on the grounds that Georgina could not prove the publication of the libel and had produced no evidence that Johnson had written the article. Afterwards, Georgina wrote in her diary 'I shall try again and get him [Johnson] well thrashed by a navvy, if possible. There's no redress!'[27]

A few days after this, Georgina and Villiers set off for Birmingham again. They were to stay there, apart from a few short excursions by Georgina, for four months. The main aims of this visit were to publicise Georgina's grievances against the Birmingham Festival Committee and to pursue her claim for damages. For several weeks she waged a tireless campaign by means of newspaper advertisements, handbills, posters and lectures. The subject of her talk at the Masonic Hall on 5 October was advertised as 'English Laws and Customs', but she spent most of the time telling the audience about the recent music festival and complaining about the press coverage of her exploits. She had, she said, 'suffered as much as it was possible to suffer from the press', who had been paid by her enemies to ruin her. After speaking for more than two hours, she sang several songs, accompanying herself on the piano.[28] Further lectures in Birmingham attracted large audiences: a meeting at Middleton Hall on 22 October was 'packed' and 150 people had to stand. This time Georgina gave them 'Mad Doctors and Sir Henry de Bathe'. One of her supporters 'spoke up and passed a resolution condemning the action of the Birmingham Festival Committee'.[29] Less successful was a tour of the Midlands, which took Georgina and Villiers firstly to Dudley, where the Public Hall was 'very empty' and Georgina's share of the takings was less than £4. The

25 *Birmingham Daily Post*, 9/9/1882, p. 5; *Times*, 9/9/1882; GWJ, 8/9/1882; SC, *Weldon v. T. Johnson*, 1883.

26 *Reynolds's Newspaper*, 10/9/1882, p. 4; *Times*, 11/9/1882.

27 GWJ, 15/9/1882.

28 *South Wales Daily News*, 7/10/1882, p. 4.

29 GWJ, 23/10/1882.

Fig. 22. 'Georgina Victrix (Mrs. Weldon gets her cheque.)'. Cartoon of Georgina and John Jaffray by E.C. Mountford, from *The Dart*, January 1883.

newspaper report of this event is nevertheless of interest, as it describes the impression that Georgina made on someone who had never encountered her before:

> Mrs Weldon is tall and handsome, with a pleasing and intellectual countenance, at the same time indicative of that determination which has characterised her during the past few years. She gave abundant evidence last night that she is also a lady of refinement, and possessed of no mean vocal and musical talent.

The reporter was particularly impressed by the 'versatility as well as the ability of Mrs Weldon's vocal powers,' though he thought that she would secure a better 'house' next time if she 'excised the history from her entertainment, and confined herself entirely to singing songs.'[30] Although most of her audiences during the rest of the tour were enthusiastic, the takings were miserable. Georgina found the whole affair very discouraging, writing 'What hard struggling for a few pounds, when I ought to get hundreds!'[31] In Worcester and Great Malvern the receipts did not even cover the travelling expenses, and the remaining meetings in Birmingham were no more successful.

~

Georgina should have had her day in court on 19 December, when her action against John Jaffray, chairman of the Birmingham Musical Festival Committee, was to be heard at the Birmingham County Court. She claimed £50 damages for breach of contract and the money expended in her vain attempt to attend Gounod's concert. But when the day came she was ill with influenza and unable to get out of bed. Her solicitor, Frank Adcock (who had already tried to give up the case, probably because Georgina seemed to be reluctant to pay his bills), agreed to accept £30 on her behalf and the case was withdrawn. Georgina was disgusted, commenting 'it is shameful, and I feel now as if fate were too much against me.' She felt too ill to travel for several weeks, but finally returned home to Brixton at the end of January. She was, however, cheered by a 'capital' cartoon in the *Dart*, showing Jaffray giving her a cheque for £30. She wrote in her journal, 'I hope it will make people believe I really won the day,' and sent Villiers out to buy six dozen copies of the magazine.[32]

30 *Dudley and District News*, 28/10/1882, p. 8.

31 GWJ, 27/10/1882.

32 GWJ, 19/12/1882, 30/1/1883; *Times*, 21/12/1882; *The Dart*, 5 January 1883.

21
Revenge

In September 1882 Georgina bought copies of two Acts of Parliament. One was the Newspaper Libel Act of 1882, which was relevant to her ongoing battles in the wake of the 'Birmingham Affair'. The other was the Married Women's Property Act, also of 1882. At first she found the latter 'very puzzling', but after discussing it with one of her new acquaintances in Birmingham it gradually began to dawn on her that changes in the law might enable her to take revenge on her enemies. On 2 January 1883 she wrote in her new diary, 'Hail 1883! Married Women's Property Act comes into force, so I suppose my reputation is now become my own property, and that I shall be able to sue for damages to any extent if libelled or insulted from henceforth.' At last she had the opportunity to 'clear off old scores'. 'I am no longer an outlaw', she told her mother.[1] Inside the front cover of the book she wrote the motto, '*Nemo me impune lacessit*' [nobody wounds me with impunity]. It was a declaration of war.

The Married Women's Property Act, which came into force on 1 January 1883, gave a wife the right, for the first time, to enter into contracts and sue or be sued with respect to her separate property. Before this date, everything belonged to her husband and she had no legal identity apart from him, and no property under her own control. If, like Georgina, she was separated from her husband and had little or no contact with him, she was utterly powerless. Now, however, she could attack her persecutors, whether Harry liked it or not.

Whilst she was deciding on a plan of action, Georgina continued to attend meetings of the Magna Chartists, Salvation Army and other campaigning groups. At the beginning of March she went to Bow Street to ask Frederick Flowers for a summons for libel against Dr Forbes Winslow, as a result of the publication of a series of letters to the *British Medical Journal* in 1878 and 1879. In these, Winslow had attempted to justify his attempt to have Georgina forcibly incarcerated in his lunatic asylum and

1 GWJ, 2/1/1883; GW–LFT, 1/1/1883.

had defended the whole system of private lunatic asylums.[2] As Flowers seemed disinclined to help her on this occasion, she returned home, 'tired, nervous and excited, thinking over the impossibility of getting a fair hearing'. Perhaps, she thought, she should 'go to Winslow and throw an ounce of cayenne pepper in his face and sprinkle vitriol all over his room, carpet, papers etc.' Then he would have her arrested, and she would be able to stand up in court and tell everybody what he had done to her.[3] Georgina was disappointed on the days that followed to find that no newspaper reported her application. If all the editors were determined to ignore her, she decided, she would publish her own monthly newspaper, which would be called *Social Salvation*. Maurice Kenealy, who had published several of her articles and letters in his Magna Chartist paper, the *Englishman*, during the previous year, agreed to let her make use of his office, at 11 Fleur-de-Lis Court.

The first issue of *Social Salvation* was ready by the end of April. There would be twenty issues altogether, published between May 1883 and the end of 1884, each one consisting of four pages. In theory there were several editors, but it was soon noted that virtually everything was written by Georgina herself, who sometimes adopted the pseudonym 'Stormy Petrel'. At the beginning of the first issue she set out her manifesto. The 'editors' had, she wrote, only one object, 'The Public Benefit':

> We advocate Social Reform and Salvation in every branch. We advocate Food Reform. We object to Compulsory Vaccination [and] Vivisection. We advocate the Repeal of the Contagious Diseases Act, Marriage with a Deceased Wife's Sister, the Affirmation Bill, Amendment of the Marriage Laws, and the suppression of the following passage in the Marriage Service, as it now stands and has stood for centuries; a crying satire on the legal status of woman; a legal lie on the lips of a civilised nation:
> WITH MY BODY I THEE WORSHIP, AND WITH ALL MY WORLDY GOODS I THEE ENDOW.[4]

In the event, few of these subjects were ever covered and most of the articles consisted of accounts of Georgina's life and recitals of her own grievances. Some, however, were more wide-ranging. In March 1884 Georgina expressed her own radical views on the place of women in society:

[2] See, for example, *British Medical Journal*, 25/1/1879, pp. 128–9.

[3] GWJ, 3/3/1883.

[4] SS, 5/1883, p. 1.

> Parliament, Board Schools, all Educational establishments, should inculcate into the female mind the absolute necessity of depending upon their own selves for their livelihood. Primogeniture must be abolished, sons and daughters must equally share the parental fortune. Women must insist on being paid as well as men. Let them no longer look upon themselves as the head servant to keep the man's home nice and comfortable.

She encouraged any woman who was prevented from earning her own money 'in consequence of the inconvenience of child-bearing' to 'grab away' all she could of her husband's money in case he deserted her later on. She should, in short, 'make hay while the sun shines'.[5] There were also the inevitable attacks on the Earl of Shaftesbury, the mad-doctors, music publishers, theatrical agents, the legal profession and the newspapers.

Sales were slow, and Georgina reduced the price from a penny to a halfpenny after a friend told her that the first three numbers of any new publication had to be given away in order to create a demand. Another informed her, 'You can't get a paper to go until you create a demand by advertising and spending £1000 at least.' *Social Salvation* kept her busy, but she found time to attend meetings about the assisted emigration of paupers, and Land Reform. She also spent several hours sitting for a new acquaintance, the French artist Théobald Chartran, who wanted to paint a full-length portrait for the following year's Paris Salon. Georgina hoped that Gounod would see it.[6]

In mid June Maurice Kenealy offered to sell Georgina the *Englishman* for £150, telling her that it brought in £20 a week and that he longed to go to America. He was almost certainly overstating the profits: in an editorial published in 1882 he had appealed to the paper's readers for money to keep the newspaper going, telling them that the circulation was so low that it was hardly worth publishing it.[7] At first Georgina was enthusiastic, but she eventually gave up the idea and concentrated on *Social Salvation*.

She soon had a new ally who, she hoped, would help her to attain her ultimate aim of attacking her enemies through the law courts. This was Alexander Chaffers, a sixty-year-old solicitor, who had gained notoriety ten years earlier by attempting to blackmail the wife of Sir Travers Twiss, Queen Victoria's Advocate-General. At his trial at Southwark Police Court in 1872, Chaffers had insisted on cross-examining Lady Twiss, and had

5 SS, 3/1884, p. 3.

6 GWJ, 6–7/6/1883.

7 Rohan McWilliam, *The Tichborne Claimant* (London and New York, 2007), p. 182.

Fig. 23. Portrait of Georgina Weldon by Théobald Chartran, 1883.

been so aggressive and unpleasant that she had refused to appear again on the following day and had left England for the Continent. This sensational development – widely reported at the time – had led to the collapse of the prosecution. Sir Travers Twiss had resigned all his offices a few days later. The magistrate at Southwark had told Chaffers that he would be 'an object of contempt to all honest and well-thinking men' for the rest of his life.[8] After this, Chaffers had disappeared into obscurity. In 1879 he had entered St Pancras workhouse as a pauper, and he had long since failed to renew the annual certificate that permitted him to practise as a solicitor.

8 PMG, 14/3/1872, p. 2.

In 1882 Chaffers discovered that Lady Twiss had returned to London and applied for a summons against her for 'wilful and corrupt perjury' in the evidence that she had given in court in 1872. When the application was refused, Chaffers tried to summons Sir Travers Twiss, also for perjury, again without success. Georgina, who invariably supported anyone who claimed to have been treated badly by the English legal system, wrote a letter to the *Englishman* about Chaffers after reading about these applications.[9] Chaffers wrote to her at the end of June 1883, and on 2 July he presented himself in Fleur-de-Lis Court, where she was working on the third issue of *Social Salvation*. Georgina quickly realised that Chaffers could be useful to her: he shared her sense of grievance and thirst for litigation, and he had a legal training. The 'poor old fellow' was also hard up and would be grateful for anything she might give him to keep him out of the workhouse. He would be much cheaper than a practising solicitor. It was soon arranged that she would pay him 10s a week.[10]

Georgina now had an assistant. She soon had an office of her own too. From the end of July she rented 9 Red Lion Court, off Fleet Street and only a few hundred yards from 'those new dens of infamy', the recently-opened Royal Courts of Justice in the Strand.[11] But she was still meeting with failure on all fronts at this time. Frederick Flowers refused her second request for a summons against Winslow because he 'could not see the slightest grounds for her allegations of libel.' If she was dissatisfied with his decision, Flowers told her, she could apply to a superior court. An attempt to persuade Maurice Kenealy to publish an article on 'Mrs Weldon and Dr Winslow' in the *Englishman* was similarly unsuccessful. Georgina decided that the man was 'a toad.'[12]

Undaunted, Georgina and Chaffers were ready to launch their great legal campaign by the end of August. Georgina found a young solicitors' clerk called Lever ('an old Tichbornite'), who was prepared to serve writs for her. On 1 September he served the first one, claiming £5000 for trespass and slander, on Harry's solicitor, James Neal, who was said to be 'stunned.' Service on the mad-doctors Forbes Winslow and Edward Rudderforth soon followed. Both were also 'stunned', and claimed that they had 'acted according to instructions.' By 6 September Lever had also served Edward Lloyd, the publisher of the *Daily Chronicle*; Jules Rivière; Sir Henry de

9 *Times*, 28/4/1882, 1,22/5/1882, 5/6/1882; GWJ, 6/8/1882; GWM proof, vii, pp. 78–81; *Lloyd's Weekly Newspaper*, 23/5/1886, p. 2. See also Michael Taggart, 'Alexander Chaffers and the Genesis of the Vexatious Actions Act 1896', *Cambridge Law Journal*, 63(3), 2004, pp. 656–84.

10 GWJ, 5,10/7/1883.

11 GWJ, 28/12/1882.

12 *Times*, 13/8/1883; GWJ, 31/8/1883.

Bathe; and Thomas Johnson of *Le Figaro*. His greatest coup was to catch the elusive Harry Weldon at the Garrick Club, a feat that he only achieved because Harry mistook him for Georgina's former solicitor, Thomas Disney Leaver, thus reinforcing Georgina's suspicion that the latter had been in league with her husband. Lever served Harry with a writ claiming damages for slander, together with the order for the restitution of conjugal rights that he had managed to avoid for more than a year. That evening Lever was elected a member of the Westminster Branch of the Magna Charta Association. Before long, he had served Frank Adcock and Dr Semple too. The former (whom Georgina had asked for £31 15s, due in Birmingham) offered, in an 'impudent' letter, to settle for £25. Georgina sent him 'a stunner' in response. 'Now I must look out the other ruffians,' she wrote in her diary.[13] On 21 September she issued a further five writs, mostly for libels in Birmingham. In the meantime she continued to publicise her grievances in every way she could. On 13 September printed handbills advertising the *Englishman* and *Social Salvation* on one side, and Georgina's legal actions on the other, were distributed over the town of Hastings from a hot air balloon by one of her 'champions,' Joseph Simmons. Georgina also attended Magna Chartist meetings almost every Sunday, most often at Peckham Rye or Clerkenwell. At one meeting, Hull, the chairman at Clerkenwell, was so drunk that he was forced to leave the chair and Georgina was elected in his stead.[14]

At the beginning of October, 'a poor thin miserable creature, smelling fearfully strong of beer, stale onions and tobacco, with a suspicion of kipper or bloater' came into the office in Red Lion Court. This was 'Captain' Henry Harcourt, who, like Chaffers, had a somewhat chequered past and a profound sense of grievance, which led him to spend much of his time 'raving at open-air meetings against Miscarriages of Justice, Judges, and the Law in general.' Harcourt brought with him an account of his experiences entitled 'Prison Horrors' and was hoping that Georgina would help him to publish it. A heavy drinker, he had served two prison sentences as a result (he claimed) of mistaken identity. Georgina gave him a sovereign because he looked 'so wretched and ill.' Before long, she had taken him on as a 'messenger.'[15]

There was still no word from Harry, so Georgina sent him a note, dictated by Chaffers. This time Harry replied, telling her that 'our living together again could only entail certain misery on both of us.' He was, he continued, still quite willing to settle a proper allowance on his wife. It was obvious

13 GWJ, 1–8/9/1883.

14 SS, 10/1883, p. 1; GWJ, 23/9/1883.

15 GWM proof, vii, pp. 60–9; GWJ, 3/10/1883.

that he had no intention of complying with the order for restitution. Three days after receiving this letter, Georgina appeared again before Mr Justice Hannen to ask for a writ of attachment against her husband. If this were to be granted, Harry could be sent to prison. Harry was again represented by 'Mr Inaudible Inderwick', who said that his client was anxious to obey the order of the court 'as far as possible', and was willing to make 'an ample settlement' on his wife. Hannen gave Harry a week to comply with the order. Six days later, Harry wrote to Georgina, telling her he had taken a furnished house in Acton for her and had engaged two servants. He would pay the rent so long as the house was occupied and would continue her allowance of £500 a year. If she wanted to live somewhere else, he would be 'quite willing to make what arrangements I can to meet your wishes'.[16] He also filed an affidavit to the same effect with the court.

Nobody who knew Georgina could have been surprised when she refused to accept this offer – which was, in her opinion, absurd and 'the acme of impudence'. But on the following day, Hannen decided that he needed further time to decide whether her husband had complied with the order for restitution.[17] In an article in *Social Salvation*, Georgina railed against a law which compelled a woman to say, 'I want to go to bed with my husband', 'and thereby exposes her to all sorts of obscene jokes, lustful allusions, lascivious innuendos, disgusting letters, and indecent pamphlets'. 'Men made the law [for the restitution of conjugal rights], and this law has generally unblushingly served the *man's* purpose, for what hesitation need he show when asking to go to bed with his wife?' The law should be changed. 'Mrs Weldon, we believe', she told her readers, 'is destined to effect a reform in the lunacy, libel and other laws, as well as the marriage laws'.[18] She filed her own affidavit, claiming that Harry had deserted her and had then conspired with several others to entrap her and incarcerate her 'as a lunatic or person of unsound mind'; he had taken Tavistock House away from her and reduced her allowance from £1000 to £500 a year; he kept several mistresses, and had, moreover, 'suitable' apartments at the College of Arms, where he held the appointment of Windsor Herald solely through Georgina's influence.[19]

On 27 November Hannen granted Georgina's request for the attachment of her husband. He did so extremely reluctantly, telling the court that he did not approve of a law that gave him no discretion. The order for restitution meant that Harry was obliged to live under the same roof as

16 WHW–GW, 3,12/11/1883; GWJ, 6/11/1883; *Times*, 7/11/1883.
17 GWJ, 13/11/1883; *Times*, 14/11/1883.
18 SS, 12/1883, p. 2.
19 TNA, J77/247/7063.

Georgina unless he had 'lawful cause' for not doing so: providing her with a separate residence was not enough. The judge also decreed that Harry would have to pay Georgina's costs. Harry was, however, given a further fortnight in which to comply with the previous court order and was also given leave to appeal.[20]

Serving writs was one thing; getting Georgina's opponents into court was quite another. They all played for time. The delays continued during the early weeks of 1884. In January Georgina sent in an amended Statement of Claim, in which she accused Harry of slandering her in conversations with a number of different people (including her mother and brother) between 1876 and 1881. He had allegedly told Josiah Foster (a builder employed by Georgina) in 1879 that his wife was 'the best, the purest, the chastest woman alive, but hopelessly insane since nine years in consequence of a quarrel with her family'. Dal Treherne had been informed that his sister was an adulteress; whilst Louisa Treherne had learned that her daughter was 'a hopeless lunatic'. Harry had also libelled her by signing a medical certificate in order to commit her to a lunatic asylum. Georgina demanded damages of £10,000.[21] The case finally came to court on 28 February, when Georgina appeared in person before the Lord Chief Justice, Lord Coleridge, and Mr Justice Watkin Williams in the Queen's Bench Division of the High Court. She brought with her several 'voluminous' bundles of documents, and thought that she got 'a very good innings' against Harry's 'giggling' barrister, Wood Hill. Lord Coleridge was 'charming' but it did not take him long to dismiss the case on the grounds that the Married Women's Property Act did not give her the right to sue her husband in this instance. Georgina was highly indignant. 'So', she informed the court, a husband could libel his wife or 'do anything he likes'. It was, she added, 'a very good thing that we were not told this before we got married, or else the men would be very badly off'. The response, according to the newspaper report, was 'great laughter'. Laughter also greeted Georgina's parting shot, 'I don't see that the Married Women's Property Act is of much good.'[22]

In the meantime, Harcourt was busy delivering subpoenas to everyone who might be connected, however remotely, with Georgina's forthcoming action against Forbes Winslow. Many were bemused; most were 'very unwilling'. One old friend, Lennox Browne, returned the subpoena and the shilling that accompanied it. 'What a sneak and toady he is!', Georgina commented, 'worse than I thought – a real humbug!' Brother Apsley, whom

[20] GWJ, 27/11/1883; *Times*, 28/11/1883.

[21] SC, *Weldon v. Weldon*, 1884.

[22] *Exeter Flying Post*, 5/3/1884, p. 3

Georgina had hardly seen since her marriage, was 'very rude'; the Duke of Bedford's agent, John Bourne, was 'mad'; and Forbes Winslow himself was 'all in a shake.' Two of the recipients even attacked the unfortunate Harcourt. Harcourt had both of them summonsed for assault. At Bow Street he told Frederick Flowers, 'I have served 60 or 80 summonses and have been called all sorts of names.' He was, he added, 'a servant who has three little children to keep; two of them are cripples, and have no mother.' Flowers was not sympathetic.[23]

'The great case of *Weldon v. Winslow*' came before Mr Baron Huddleston and a Special Jury in the Court of Queen's Bench on 13 March 1884. By this time Georgina had engaged another assistant, a young shorthand writer of Dutch-Jewish origin called Barnett (or Bernard) De Bear. She did not trust the newspapers and wanted to make sure that she had her own reports of all the court proceedings. De Bear, 'a pretty boy with lovely eyes,' who was eventually to become the principal of Pitman's Commercial School, was paid the princely sum of 30s a week.[24]

Confident that she could present her case better than any lawyer, Georgina chose to act as her own prosecutor. She was not the first female plaintiff in person: Rosanna Fray, who had given up employing lawyers around 1860, was described on her death in 1888 as 'one of the most trying and persistent and obstinate of female litigants in person.'[25] Miss Fray was, however, a spinster. Georgina may have been the first married woman to represent herself in this way; she was certainly the best known and the most successful before the First World War. Over the five years that followed *Weldon v. Winslow*, her appearances in the High Court came increasingly to resemble theatrical performances, with herself as the leading lady; the jury and lawyers as members of the cast (the judge and opposing counsel were usually the villains); the court officials as stage-hands; and the general public as the enthralled audience. She even adopted a quasi-judicial costume, consisting of a black silk dress, with black cape and hood.[26] When Georgina was on the stage, there was barely a spare seat in the house.

Many of Georgina's friends (and foes) were in court on the first day of *Weldon v. Winslow*. They included St John Wontner, the de Bathes, Frederick Flowers, Freddy Warre, sister Zizi (Emily) 'looking old and ugly,' 'the Doctors,' and Angèle with Eva Morand and her sister Eugénie. Georgina was suing Dr Forbes Winslow for libel, assault and false imprisonment,

23 GWJ, 12–28/2/1884, 6–7/3/1884; *Times*, 18/2/1884, 7/3/1884.

24 GWJ, 10/1/1906.

25 *Morpeth Herald*, 2/6/1888, p. 2. See below, pp. 338–40, for Rosanna Fray.

26 See below, p. 315, Fig. 24.

for which she claimed damages of £10,000. Although she was suffering from the effects of a sleepless night and the onset of a heavy period, she impressed the reporter for *The Times*, who recorded that she opened her case by addressing the court 'with great fluency for more than three hours.' After this, Forbes Winslow's Statement of Defence was read. He claimed that Georgina had never been in possession of Tavistock House and denied that he had libelled her. His letters to the *British Medical Journal* had, he claimed, been 'privileged and without malice.' The alleged trespasses had been committed under the written authority of Sir Henry de Bathe, together with two medical certificates, written by Drs Rudderforth and Semple.

Georgina then gave the court a detailed account of her life since October 1877. She had still not finished her opening speech when the court rose at 4 p.m. She tried to continue on the following morning, but the judge's patience was soon exhausted. He told Georgina to take her Statement of Claim in her hand and prove her case. After she had described the events of 14 April 1878 at some length, she entered the witness box to be cross-examined by the eminent defence counsel, Edward Clarke, QC. Clarke's main aim was to show that Georgina had, for several years, been trying to publicise her grievances by provoking Winslow and her other enemies in every way she could. Obligingly, Georgina agreed that this was exactly what she had been attempting to do, in the belief that 'the only way was to libel everybody all round, so that they might be forced to attack me.' She told the court that she was not ashamed of anything she had done. Her assertion that 'If a man comes and tries to carry you off to a lunatic asylum, he deserves anything that he gets' was greeted with laughter.[27]

After this, Georgina began to examine her witnesses. She called James Edmunds, one of the doctors who had seen her at her own request, who stated that he had examined her for three hours and had found that she was thoroughly sane, 'although she had peculiar ideas on the education of young children and the simplification of ladies' dress.' Under cross-examination by Clarke, however, Dr Edmunds became less helpful. He agreed that delusions as to hearing supernatural voices were indications of an unsound mind, but said that he should not consider them a ground for 'certificating' a person. Where such delusions were found, he continued, 'He should ask the patient if he or she obeyed such voices. If the patient told him he did, he should consider it a mark of craziness.'[28]

27 *Times*, 15/3/1884.
28 *Daily Chronicle*, 15/3/1885, quoted in Edward Grierson, *Storm Bird* (London, 1959), pp. 208–9.

Georgina then re-examined Edmunds:

GEORGINA:	John Wesley was a medium and heard voices. Should you say he was crazy?
DR EDMUNDS:	No.
GEORGINA:	St Paul, when he went down to persecute the Christians, heard a voice saying 'Why persecutest thou me.' Now, should you consider that St Paul was a crazy person?
(Loud laughter).	
DR EDMUNDS:	I am afraid I should have to say he was in a little crazy condition.
GEORGINA:	Do you think Balaam was out of his mind when he heard his ass speak?
DR EDMUNDS:	I think he must have been a little crazy.
(Laughter).	
GEORGINA:	Then there was Joan of Arc. Was she crazy?
DR EDMUNDS:	A little, I think.
GEORGINA:	I am a Spiritualist, and do not believe in Mad Doctors, but I do believe in spirits, which are much less harmful.
(Laughter).[29]	

Georgina commented in her diary that the doctor had been 'very priggish' and had almost ruined the case, but she had 'completely saved the position.'

Next into the witness box was a police inspector, William de Maid, who testified that Forbes Winslow had come to him late in the evening of 14 April 1878 and asked for his help in removing Georgina to his lunatic asylum. Winslow had described his quarry as 'a lunatic wandering at large.' The policeman had refused, on the grounds that, since Georgina was at the time barricaded in her own house, she could not be said to be 'at large.' After this, Georgina called Forbes Winslow himself – a move that Edward Grierson described as 'a tactical error.'[30]

The years had not been kind to Dr Lyttelton Stewart Forbes Winslow, who was now forty years old. According to Georgina, he had been 'a slim,

[29] *Standard*, 15/3/1884, p. 2.

[30] GWJ, 14/3/1884; *Times*, 15/3/1884; Grierson, *Storm Bird*, p. 210.

skipjack clerk of a man, with lots of hair on his head' when she first met him. Now he was bald and had 'decidedly aged.'[31] His defence of his actions in attempting to have her carried off to his lunatic asylum, Brandenburgh House in Hammersmith, had won him few friends in the press. The medical Establishment viewed him as a publicity seeker and he was fast becoming an outcast. After his death in 1913 the obituarist for the *Lancet* wrote dismissively that Winslow had been 'well known in lay circles as an alienist who had written semi-popular books.'[32]

The combative doctor began by defending his actions in April 1878. He had, he said, written all the answers in the Lunacy Order 'at the dictation of Mr Weldon,' who had asked him if he knew of an asylum. Winslow had offered to take Mrs Weldon into his own institution and Mr Weldon had told him to 'take the necessary steps.' Two 'independent medical gentlemen' were required to certify as to the state of Mrs Weldon's mind, and Winslow had communicated with Drs Rudderforth and Semple at Mr Weldon's request. Winslow added that Mr Weldon had been subpoenaed as a witness on his behalf, though it soon became clear that the lawyers did not actually intend to put Harry into the witness box. The court broke up shortly after this and Georgina found 'a perfect mob' waiting for her outside. She had to get into a cab to escape them. She went back to Red Lion Court and ordered Harcourt to subpoena Harry to appear as a witness for her. He did so at two o'clock in the following morning, at 9 Albert Mansions. Harcourt said that Harry had appeared to be 'boosey.' 'Never saw him boosey myself,' commented Georgina, 'He'll go to the bad altogether. A cur!'[33]

The next day was a Saturday, so the court sat only until 1 p.m. The morning was taken up with Georgina's examination of Winslow, who stated that Harry Weldon had paid him thirty guineas, out of which he had paid the fees to Rudderforth and Semple. Once the report that Winslow had sent to Harry after his visit to Georgina on 14 April 1878 had been read to the court, she pressed the doctor for further details of his dealings with her husband. Winslow said that he had had no reason to suppose that Harry would have given him false information about her behaviour, adding 'I do not suppose that he told me of all your peculiarities.' Georgina then continued:

GEORGINA:	But he told you a great deal too much. (Laughter.) Did I not tell you that if I was

31 *Pall Mall Gazette*, 20/3/1884, p. 11.

32 *Lancet*, 14/6/1913, quoted in Molly Whittington-Egan, *Doctor Forbes Winslow* (Great Malvern, 2000), p. 267.

33 *Times*, 15/3/1884; GWJ, 15/3/1884.

	threatened with a great danger, I had been distinctly warned.
WINSLOW:	You did.
GEORGINA:	Do you call that a delusion?
WINSLOW:	Yes.
GEORGINA:	But yet I was distinctly warned when I refused to open the door to your madhouse keeper. (Great laughter).

At this point the judge intervened, telling Georgina that she was trying to cross-examine her own witness, and doing it in such a way to cast ridicule on him. The witness had a right to be protected from this. The questioning continued. Winslow admitted that he would have received ten guineas a week for keeping Georgina but insisted that he had been right in attempting to have her removed to an asylum. Georgina then said that she had sent Winslow tickets for her lecture at St James's Hall on 5 November 1878 and asked him why he had not come. Baron Huddleston remarked that she could hardly have expected Winslow to go and meet her there 'in the presence of an audience made up entirely of those who sympathized with her'. The court then adjourned for the weekend.[34]

On the following Monday so many people wanted to see Georgina in action that many of them were unable to gain admission. Her interrogation of Forbes Winslow began again. At one point the doctor claimed to be a specialist in lunacy:

GEORGINA:	Brought up to it?
WINSLOW:	Yes
GEORGINA:	I suppose it is a kind of a breed? (Laughter).
HUDDLESTON:	You must not take advantage of your position to ridicule the witness.
GEORGINA:	But, my Lord, children do inherit the aptitudes of their parents. (Laughter.) (To Winslow): Your father was a mad-doctor?
WINSLOW:	Yes.
(The judge repeated his ruling.)	
GEORGINA:	May I ask him some questions on his own book?

[34] *Standard*, 17/3/1884, p. 3; *Times*, 17/3/1884.

HUDDLESTON: No, it would not be evidence.

GEORGINA: You have no idea, my lord, how careful he says in his book that mad-doctors should be.

HUDDLESTON: I have no doubt they ought to be.

GEORGINA: But he does not follow his own advice, my lord. (Laughter.) The defendant says in his book that our lunacy laws are so perfect. I want to know whether he thinks so now?

HUDDLESTON: I can't allow that. The question is not before the court.[35]

After Winslow, it was his father-in-law's turn to go into the witness box. Next came Sir Henry de Bathe, who told Georgina that she had said things that had led him to the conclusion that she was of unsound mind. He 'had some experience of insanity', being a governor and treasurer of St Luke's Hospital for the Insane. After him, Dr Rudderforth described his visit to Tavistock House on 14 April and claimed that Georgina had told him that her rabbit 'had a devil'. She had spoken of a vision in which she had seen an essay written by Christ, which it would have taken three months to read. Gounod had formed a wish to injure her throat so as to spoil her voice. She had also said that her dog had an angel in it. By this time the judge had had enough, and the case was adjourned until the following morning. Georgina was cheered as she left the court. The crowd then followed her, cheering all the way, to Red Lion Court.[36]

Tuesday 18 March was the last day of the trial. Georgina began by calling Dr Semple, who backed up his colleague and told the court that Georgina had 'talked incessantly on all sorts of subjects'. Further witnesses included Elizabeth Villiers and Frederick Flowers. The latter had, he said, seen Georgina 'very frequently', but he had 'not noticed anything at all' to lead him to the conclusion that she was out of her mind. Indeed, her manner at Bow Street had been 'as cool and intelligent as it has been today'. Harry was called, looking 'horrid, vulgar, etc.'. He told the court that he had heard that Georgina did not keep Tavistock House clean; that she was 'negligent in her person'; and that she had a white rabbit which was allowed to run about on the dining room table during meals. He had discussed the matter with Georgina's family. When Dr Winslow asked him if there was any insanity

35 *Standard*, 18/3/1884, p. 3; *Daily Chronicle*, 17/3/1884, quoted in Grierson, *Storm Bird*, p. 211.

36 *Times*, 18/3/1884; GWJ, 17/3/1884.

in the Treherne family, Harry had told him that Georgina's father had been 'taken care of' during the latter part of his life. Harry considered that Winslow had 'woefully mismanaged' the whole business. He had agreed to pay the doctor 'about £400 a year' to look after his wife.

After Georgina had run out of witnesses, Edward Clarke submitted that there was no case to go to the jury as Dr Winslow had complied with the law. Where Georgina's accusation of libel was concerned, she had totally failed to prove that Winslow had been guilty of malice towards her. After a further speech from Georgina, which was greeted with 'great applause', the judge began to sum up. It was clear that the case had caused him some disquiet, and that he was not without sympathy for Georgina:

> It is somewhat startling – it is positively shocking, that if a pauper, or as Mrs Weldon puts it, a crossing-sweeper, should sign an order and another crossing-sweeper should make a statement, and that then two medical men who had never had a day's practice in their lives and would for a small sum of money grant their certificates, a person may be lodged in a private lunatic asylum, and that this order and the statement and these certificates are a perfect answer to any action.[37]

Huddleston added that he had no doubt that all the parties in the case had acted conscientiously, though the proceedings had been 'strangely precipitate'. He was, nevertheless, bound to hold that there was no case to go to the jury, as the requirements of the Lunacy Acts had been complied with. He regretted that the plaintiff could have no redress for the 'serious inconveniences to which she had been put', but he had no option other than to non-suit her. According to Georgina, this decision was greeted with 'dead silence'. Even the jury looked 'much disappointed'.

Though the costs of the hearing were awarded against Georgina, she felt that she had won 'a grand moral victory'. On the first page of the next issue of *Social Salvation*, Georgina described herself as 'A torpedo boat among men-of-war'. 'Till the Winslow case came into Court', she wrote, 'I was a "public nuisance"; now I am considered a *public benefactress*.'[38] She was sure that she would get her costs quite easily by singing at music halls. There were 'thousands' waiting for her outside the court and she was again cheered all the way back to her office.[39] On the following day she served notice of motion for a new trial. As an article on 'Ladies at Law' in the *Pall Mall Gazette* had put it a few years earlier, 'Once [a woman] has

37 *Morning Post*, 19/3/1884, p. 3.
38 SS, 4–5/1884, pp. 1, 5.
39 *Times*, 19/3/1884; GWJ, 17/3/1884.

dabbled in law she is like a tiger that has tasted blood. She cannot stop.' The tone of this article is tongue-in-cheek, but it nevertheless reflects growing disquiet at the ever-increasing number of female litigants. They were an unwelcome distraction to the juries and to the members of the all-male legal profession: 'A law court ought to be a sort of male harem: female witnesses should be compelled to wear impenetrable veils and unbecoming dresses: and the most frightful and cross-grained old laundresses should be trained to guard its portals, and sew up in a crinoline any daring female intruder.' In 1896 an elderly judge, Lord Justice Lindley, told the students of St Thomas's Hospital, 'He sometimes saw ladies judicially, but seldom with pleasure, and if the Liturgy were ever altered in his lifetime he would suggest the addition of the words "From female litigants, in person, good Lord deliver us."'[40]

[40] PMG, 7/2/1865, p. 7; *Cornishman*, 8/10/1896, p. 3. There is no indication that Lindley had ever come face-to-face with Georgina Weldon, though he must have known about her activities.

22
The New Portia

Details of Georgina's exploits were now filling the columns of the national and regional newspapers. On 19 March 1884, the day after the Winslow trial ended, she received a visit from a Mr Morley from the *Pall Mall Gazette*.[1] The interview, which was published on the following day, gives a vivid picture of Georgina and her office in Red Lion Court:

> I knocked at the door, and it was opened by Mr Chaffers. I presented my card, and in a minute found myself seated at Mrs Weldon's desk. There could be no doubt, from the appearance of the room, that it was devoted to business, and to a business in which much paper was required. Mrs Weldon was buried in papers – on the desk before her were scattered documents, manuscripts, letters, books, newspapers; the pigeon-holes were stuffed full of them; a table behind groaned under their weight. Two loaves found a precarious resting-place in another mass, packed up out of reach. In fact, Mrs Weldon is a woman of affairs. And a very clever woman. 'Then you are not disheartened, Mrs Weldon?' 'Disheartened! Good gracious, no, indeed. I have just made a motion to set aside the nonsuit, and asked for a new trial on the ground of misdirection – and all the rest of it. Then I have an action against Sir Henry de Bathe, and an action against – but there – there is no end to them.' This indomitable woman stood up at her desk, and, with her arms extended, pointed proudly, with a look of especial elation, to a shelf under the window where lay, neatly docketed, a number of legal documents. 'There are my seventeen cases. My children, they are all going on. They *shall* all go on. Through this court, through that one. Superior, inferior. Before my lord this judge, and my lord that judge. There are no intricacies, no subtleties that shall be too much for me. I will *never* let them rest. I will *never* cease from troubling them until I have swept every cobweb away.'

[1] This was probably the journalist Charles Roberts Morley (1853–1916).

She showed Morley the cover of the January issue of *Social Salvation*, which had been created for her by a young engraver, George Sanford:

> Look at the symbolical title page. Here I am, standing on the dark Rock of Intrigue. I carry with me reformed marriage law, reformed libel law, musical reform. In my left hand I grasp the Lunacy Laws, in my right I hold up triumphantly the mirror of truth. And the sun, to represent social salvation, is rising in the background.[2]

Keeping track of seventeen cases was a full-time job. Three days after the interview, Georgina and Harcourt were sitting in the office, 'in peaceful security', when de Bear rushed in and told them that her case against Edward Lloyd of the *Daily Chronicle* was on in the Court of Queen's Bench before Baron Huddleston. Georgina was horrified, having 'prepared nothing', but she and Angèle hurried off to the Law Courts.

Georgina had accused Lloyd of libelling her in a leading article on the Rivière trial published in March 1880 and was asking for damages of £5000. She took particular exception to his claims that she had fallen out with Rivière and had sung from a private box at Covent Garden. As usual, her opening speech went on for a long time. She began by informing the court that she intended to defend herself in person, as employing counsel and a solicitor would, she believed, 'be an act of absolute insanity'. It was owing entirely to the professional lawyers that she had lost her case against Rivière in the Central Criminal Court: 'Nobody understood anything about it'. All of this was greeted with much hilarity, as was Georgina's description of herself. Nobody had more common sense than she had, she claimed, but 'it was alleged she was eccentric because she wore short hair, low-heeled boots, and did not resort to crinoline and dress improvers, and dressed quietly in black'. Nor was it true that she had fallen out with Rivière – indeed, 'I never had a dispute with anybody in all my life'.[3]

One can almost hear the judge sighing as he said, 'I see you have a very large brief'. He was quite right: she proceeded to give a detailed account of herself and her grievances against Rivière and those who were associated with him. 'Although this action might appear trivial', she added, 'what she wanted to prove by it was that the whole Press of this country was against her because she was a respectable lady'. Lord Huddleston was extremely patient, but even he remarked at one point that 'some matters which might appear to her to be of great importance had really no bearing on the case'. 'A court of justice', he added, 'is not a place in which persons are to be

2 PMG, 20/3/1884, p. 11.
3 GW, *Reports2*, p. 175.

permitted to ventilate any particular idiosyncrasy they may have, or any particular feeling of their own.' Furthermore, he told her, 'I am not going to allow the case to be prolonged by your reading every possible document that can be brought into it.' When Georgina replied huffily 'Of course, I am not a lawyer', he continued:

> Mrs Weldon, I cannot help it. I have, on former occasions, as I have on this, given you every possible latitude and every possible advantage, but your case must be conducted in a court of justice according to law. There are certain rules of evidence and certain rules of practice which have been laid down, and which cannot be deviated from simply because you don't happen to be acquainted with the particular points.

Georgina's cross-examination by Lloyd's counsel, Charles Hopwood, QC, is a vivid example both of her quick wit, and of her ability to drive professional lawyers to distraction:

HOPWOOD: May I ask you, within three or four, how many dozen actions you have on at this moment?

GEORGINA: I think I have 17. (Laughter).

HOPWOOD: Only 17?

GEORGINA: You see it is about 12 years since I have been able to bring them.

HOPWOOD: You have an office for this purpose?

GEORGINA: I have.

HOPWOOD: Who are your legal advisers?

GEORGINA: Mrs Weldon, I should say. (Laughter).

HOPWOOD: Have you a clerk who is out on ticket-of-leave?

GEORGINA: No, I think not.

HOPWOOD: You think not?

GEORGINA: I am certain of it.

HOPWOOD: Who is Mr Harcourt?

GEORGINA: He is a man who 20 years ago was sentenced to 12 years penal servitude, but according to the learned Recorder he is a very estimable man. (Laughter).

HOPWOOD: He is your clerk?

GEORGINA:	Yes, he is the most devoted creature in the world. He has been out eight years.
HOPWOOD:	Who is your other adviser?
GEORGINA:	Mrs Weldon. (Laughter).
HOPWOOD:	You furnish all the law?
GEORGINA:	Yes.
HOPWOOD:	And not the eloquence only?
GEORGINA:	No. (Laughter).

The hearing lasted for three days, and might have lasted longer if most of Georgina's witnesses (apart from Angèle) had not failed to appear. Lloyd's defence was that the whole affair had been 'fairly and impartially reported', and the leading article related to a matter of public interest. His counsel told the jury that Georgina was 'a cruel and malevolent woman': 'She objected to being called eccentric at a time when she was pursuing a course which must stamp her with eccentricity. She was possessed by an insane love of notoriety, and was plainly a woman who was clamorous of public admiration.' He asked the jury to give a verdict that would 'bring her back to that sense of decorum of which she had, as he trusted it might prove, only temporarily lost sight'. After deliberating for 'a very short time', the jury found for Edward Lloyd and awarded him his costs.[4] Georgina's own reaction was predictable: 'After much blarney, lies etc. on the part of Huddleston, the set of proverbial asses, a British jury, found for the defendant!!!'

Georgina had now had costs awarded against her twice in less than a week and she owed 'heaps of money' to James Salsbury. She was therefore delighted when Edwin Villiers, the manager of the London Pavilion Music Hall, engaged her for a month and agreed to pay her thirty guineas a week.[5] Georgina had visited a music hall for the first time in the previous year. This was the Trocadero in Leicester Square, which was much more respectable than she had expected: 'I thought it would be awfully fast, and I never was at anything more quiet and slow'.[6] Music halls, which had originally catered mainly for the working class, were moving upmarket at this time, and the Trocadero (formerly the Argyle Rooms) had recently been 'completely metamorphosed into a charming concert hall'. There were comfortable seats in the hall itself, and the public could also make use of 'handsome

4 *Daily Chronicle*, 22–24/3/1884; *Times*, 22–25/3/1884; SC, *Weldon v. Lloyd*, 1883.

5 GWJ, 24–28/3/1884.

6 GWJ, 11/5/1883.

saloons and retiring rooms'.[7] The London Pavilion was smaller, and had originated as an entertainment room attached to the Black Horse Inn in Tichbourne Street. It had been opened in 1859, when it had been described as a 'magnificent establishment, fitted up most luxuriously and elegantly'.[8]

Georgina performed at the London Pavilion for the first time on 7 April. That evening, she dressed herself 'very simply, in my black silk Jersey and merino petticoat', and made her bow 'at 10.30 precisely'. The audience was 'most enthusiastic' and cheered her for five minutes without stopping. After Villiers had made a speech introducing her, she sang Gounod's 'Ruth', followed by 'Jeanie with the light brown hair' and 'Men of Harlech'. She was back again on the following evening, 'less nervous, quite cheeky in fact'. Again, she was given a 'grand' reception, and was recalled twice. Villiers told her that she was 'an unprecedented attraction', and offered to pay her £50 so long as she 'belonged' to him and did not sing anywhere else. A notice published after her death tells a somewhat different story. Georgina's voice was said to have lost much of its freshness by this time, 'and her engagement was due more to her notoriety than her charm as a vocalist'.[9]

Georgina had good reason to be feeling 'cheeky' on 8 April. She had spent most of the day in the Court of Queen's Bench, this time before Mr Justice Watkin Williams and Mr Justice Manisty, asking for a new trial in her action against Forbes Winslow. Like Baron Huddleston three weeks earlier, the judges clearly felt a considerable degree of disquiet at the way the whole affair had been managed. They noted that a question had already been asked in Parliament about the power of summarily confining persons for supposed lunacy. To Georgina's 'intense delight', they agreed that she was entitled to a new trial. Giving his judgment 'at considerable length', Manisty said that the circumstances of the case were 'most peculiar':

> The case is one of the most important that has come into court for many years. It involves consequences such as have not, perhaps, been considered as they ought to be considered at the trial, or during the arguments in this court. It is a case involving the liberty of the person under the most extraordinary circumstances.

There was, he continued, an important difference between a person who was 'merely of unsound mind' and one who was in such a state that they had to be consigned to an asylum. Georgina had 'perhaps entertained some strange notions or delusions', but she had done nothing to annoy anyone

7 *Era*, 30/9/1882, p. 24.
8 *Era*, 23/10/1859, p. 8.
9 GWJ, 7–15/4/1884; *Era*, 14/1/1914, p. 29.

and had been 'in no sense dangerous to anyone'. The fact was that Forbes Winslow was the registered proprietor of an asylum; having advised Mr Weldon that his wife should be sent to an asylum, and having been asked which asylum she should go to, he had suggested his own. He should have refused to take any part in 'the proceedings' and told Mr Weldon to get someone else to act in the matter. It had also been 'most improper' of Winslow to select the medical men who were to examine Mrs Weldon. Winslow had stated that it was 'imperative' that Mrs Weldon should be secured, but she did not appear to have done a single act to render it necessary to shut her up. He had libelled her, and there was evidence that he had done so maliciously. This was not a case of a medical man merely giving an honest opinion, since Winslow was the registered proprietor of the asylum to which the lady was to be sent. It was for a jury to decide whether the doctor had acted honestly or with some indirect motive (that is, maliciously). Watkin Williams agreed with his colleague and delivered judgment to the same effect.[10] 'Thank God', was Georgina's reaction, 'All is for the best'. That night she went to bed late, exhausted but happy.[11] Many people congratulated her and for a few days she had to have a police escort as she went about her business to keep the crowds at bay.

The press reaction to Georgina's victory was favourable, and she was even mentioned in a leader in *The Times* calling for the urgent reform of the Lunacy Laws. Such was her fame that Leslie Ward ('Spy') began work on a caricature, which was published in *Vanity Fair* on 3 May. Cartoons had been published in the magazine every week since the beginning of 1869: Georgina was only the thirteenth woman to be depicted, and the third without a title (the other two were the actress Sarah Bernhardt and a nun). When Georgina saw Ward's portrait of her, which showed her dressed in her special court outfit, she commented that it was 'not very like, but it is pretty, young and innocent'.[12] The anonymous memoir accompanying the cartoon described her as 'a very energetic lady, entirely unshackled by conventional ideas'. By her remarkable success as an advocate in the courts of law she had endowed the recently-opened 'Palace of Justice' with 'a new Portia'. The writer praised her 'indomitable courage, a marvellous energy, and an incredible activity and industry', and wondered how any unprejudiced person could be brought to believe that she was a lunatic.[13]

10 *Times*, 2–3,9/4/1884.

11 GWJ, 8/4/1884.

12 GWJ, 12/4/1884.

13 Portia was the heroine of Shakespeare's *Merchant of Venice*, who disguised herself as a lawyer in one scene. *Vanity Fair* published over 2000 such prints between 1869 and 1914: only 20 were of women. The women were usually more

After her death, an obituarist recalled the impression that Georgina had made on those who saw her in her heyday:

> Mrs Weldon exemplified the aptitude which many women have for law, and also the advantage which they may easily have as advocates. She was a remarkably pretty woman, with a beautiful voice and no small histrionic gifts. When she came into court in the professional costume which she adopted, a black satin hood drawn together round her face – the face of a roguish schoolgirl, with a peach-like complexion, dimpled cheeks, and a pair of irresistible eyes, all set off by a heap of short-cropped curly grey hair – she was a suitor to deprive any jury of their wits, disarm counsel for the other side, and mollify any judge who had ever been a young man. Add to this that she knew all her advantages as a lady litigant, and used them, and it is not difficult to understand her success.[14]

Fig. 24. Cartoon of Georgina Weldon by Leslie Ward ('Spy') from *Vanity Fair*, May 1884.

In 1884 the new 'Portia of the Law Courts' wrote 'I am sure I have never flirted a quarter so much in all my life as I do now! The Law Courts really are a perfect field for flirting.' She found her celebrity 'amusing and, I may say, advantageous', though it was all rather tiring. The atmosphere of the vast Gothic Revival building in the Strand was oppressive, and it and its surroundings were 'not what ladies are prepared for or brought up to, nor what they ought to be subjected to.' The solicitors and their clerks all smoked and drank too much, and the fumes, combined with the stench of unwashed feet, were 'enough to knock you down.' It was all, if the truth be told, 'enough to deter the stoutest heart from prosecuting a lawsuit, or even *wishing* for justice.'[15]

---

sympathetically portrayed than the men: Eleanor Doughty, 'I spy with my little eye', *Country Life*, 22 January 2020, pp. 54–5.

14 *Liverpool Echo*, 21/1/1914, p. 6.

15 SS, 7–10/1884, p 7; *Times*, 9/4/1884; GWJ, 9/4/1884; SS, 11/1884, p. 3.

Sometimes Georgina rested on a sofa in her office in Red Lion Court, out of sight of visitors, whilst Harcourt, Chaffers and de Bear worked away at her legal papers. One day she was amused to hear Walter Rawlings telling Harcourt that she had never taught him or his brothers anything. They had all, he said, been pupils of Gounod (something that Georgina vehemently denied). Walter believed that he should be earning £500 a year.[16] Nevertheless, Georgina began to employ him on and off to run errands and sell *Social Salvation*. Before long she was renting a bedroom above the office, sleeping there during the week and only returning to Brixton at weekends to have a hot bath and play cribbage with Angèle, who was laid up for much of the summer, having broken both ankles alighting drunkenly from a cab one evening after accompanying Georgina to the London Pavilion.

~

Georgina continued to perform at the London Pavilion on five or six nights a week until the end of October, changing her clothes and making herself up 'in artistic fashion' with fard (white face paint) and rouge to go there late in the evening, after spending the whole day in her office, in court, or arguing with judges in their chambers. For a fortnight in late April and early May she also defied Edwin Villiers and appeared at the South London Music Hall in Lambeth, earning an additional £30 a week and often singing at both music halls in the same evening.

To begin with, Georgina liked the London Pavilion. The audiences were well behaved, and so quiet that Villiers complained that he lost money because they sat still and listened to her, instead of getting up and buying the refreshments from which he expected to make his profits. But, as the weeks went on, they became increasingly restless. Georgina decided that she preferred the South London and that the Pavilion was 'a hole' in comparison. One night there was a 'beastly row', so she looked 'as cross as possible' and vowed to sing 'Bolero' no more 'as they yowl over it on the high notes'. On the following evening there was 'the same stupid lot' and she made her opinion of them quite clear: 'I look at them like this "I don't like you, but I am paid to sing, so I do so, not because I like it"'. Things did not improve, and the audiences on the days that followed were 'beastly' and 'villainous'. On 10 May two 'well dressed men' came to 'fistycuffs' while Georgina was singing 'Men of Harlech' and the whole house rose to its feet. Georgina played the march several times over, then, finding that this had no effect, played 'God save the Queen' and order was restored.[17]

16 GWJ, 27/2/1884.

17 GWJ, 2,6–10/5/1884, p. 4.

Fig. 25. Georgina Weldon in costume as 'Sergeant Buzfuz', 1884.

It was Edwin Villiers who suggested that Georgina should add to her repertoire by writing and performing a skit based on Serjeant Buzfuz's address to the jury in the trial scene of *Bardell* v. *Pickwick* from Charles Dickens's *Pickwick Papers.* She thought this an excellent idea, so bought a QC's gown and wig and had herself photographed in this costume. The first few performances were quite successful, but one at the London Pavilion in September was a disaster. She was loudly hissed, 'whereupon she ceased, and told the audience that if that kind of thing were repeated she should retire from the stage. She was as good as her word, for, hissing once again being audible, she walked off the stage'. 'Merry-go-Round' commented that 'It is not often that Mrs Weldon is to be found in this retiring mood.'[18] It was to be some time before she dared to inflict 'Buzfuz' on an audience again. In the autumn of 1884 Georgina told her mother that she had earned so much money that she could afford to stop singing for several months. The novelty of appearing on the music hall stage had evidently worn off. That she had been forced to do so in the first place was, as usual, her family's fault. It was due to their 'injurious and mysterious attacks' that she had been forced to 'descend into a squalid cave, stinking of tobacco and drink, with a frightful audience of swine and muck.'[19]

Reducing her theatrical engagements gave Georgina more time to concentrate on the lawsuits that were still making their slow way through the tortuous legal process – a process eloquently described by Edward Grierson, who had experienced it at first hand:

[18] *Entr'acte*, 20/9/1884, p. 4.

[19] GW–LFT, 4/11/1884.

> Seventeen High Court actions have on the face of them a substantial sound. But the reality was a great deal more impressive and more burdensome than anyone who is not a practitioner at the courts can conceive. For actions are not just a matter of getting up in front of a judge and jury and being eloquent. There are Statements of Claim to be drawn; Defences to be studied, Replies and even Replications to be made. Interrogatories may be administered. There has to be 'Discovery of Documents', at which the parties disclose and exchange the correspondence to be used at the trial. There may be motions to strike out causes of action and offending paragraphs in the pleadings, and these may be pursued through a Master, a Judge, a Divisional Court, up to the Court of Appeal.

It was, in Grierson's opinion, 'a marvel that she did not really go insane and enter one of Dr Winslow's establishments.' On the contrary, she thrived on the pressure of keeping so many balls in the air at the same time. Grierson also commented that, in spite of the time she spent studying law books, Georgina was 'never learned in the law.'[20] She showed a nonchalant disregard for the usual procedure, hoping to charm the male judges and get her own way through the force of her personality. Sometimes it worked; sometimes it did not.

Egged on by Chaffers, Georgina even decided to sue Gounod. 'At last I've got him, the old scoundrel', she wrote triumphantly:

> Oh! You have utterly ruined me: husband, home, reputation, honour, dreams, ideals, health; you devastated me; you made me despair; you broke my heart, my hopes, my faith; you prevented me from building my school, from bringing up my children. But God will avenge me, at last the hour of retribution will come!

The writ was issued and the action officially commenced on 12 May. Now, Georgina thought, 'it will not be left to Posterity to know upon the side of which was Faith, Devotion, etc.!!! The old devil!'[21]

On 26 May Georgina was back in the Court of Queen's Bench for the second round of her battle against Thomas Johnson of *Le Figaro*, whom she had tried unsuccessfully to sue for libel two years earlier. As usual, the court was packed – the spectators including, bizarrely, Forbes Winslow 'drawn like a moth to the flame.' This time the judge, Lord Coleridge, was more sympathetic, though he eventually began to grow weary as Georgina insisted, as usual, on reading out every letter and article that had even the

20 Edward Grierson, *Storm Bird* (London, 1959), p. 226.

21 GWJ, 17/4/1884, 12/5/1884.

remotest connection with the case. Her principal witness was Harcourt, who told the court that Johnson had admitted to him that he was the author of the allegedly libellous article. Though Willie Mathews, Johnson's counsel, tried to discredit Harcourt, Lord Coleridge was having none of it. In his summing up he told the jury that no one had the right to hold another up to odium or disrespect unless there was a legal justification. The press had a right of comment on matters of public interest, but it had no right to interfere with private character. The jury took only ten minutes to consider their verdict. Georgina had won and they awarded her damages of £500. Though she had claimed £4000, she was delighted. It would, she thought, 'make others tremble'. Her supporters applauded, and she gave 'an oration' outside the court.[22]

Georgina's next action in the Court of Queen's Bench, on 2 and 3 July, was less successful. This was her attempt to sue Harry's solicitor, James Neal, for slander and trespass. Neal pleaded the Statute of Limitations as a defence, but the judge, Mr Justice A.L. Smith, ruled that this was inadmissible following the passing of the Married Women's Property Act. He soon tired of Georgina, however, and told her that she was wasting the time of the court. 'My lord', replied Georgina, 'I have heard counsel wasting the time of the court more than I do. I have had my time wasted for seven years.' This was greeted with 'a laugh'. Eventually the judge asked Georgina how much longer she expected to be. Her reply, 'My lord, I never can tell', produced more laughter. The judge's summing up was not favourable. Georgina had failed to prove that Neal's words had caused her any 'temporal damage'. She had admitted that her servants had let Neal into the house, so he was not guilty of trespass. He therefore gave judgment for Neal, with costs. This provoked a furious outburst from Georgina, which was widely reported in the press on the following day. She said that she would certainly ask for a new trial and a stay of execution.[23]

Less than a week later, she was back again, this time before Mr Justice Hawkins. Now the defendant was Charles Semple, one of the doctors who had bluffed their way into Tavistock House and discussed Spiritualism with Georgina before certifying her as a lunatic on 14 April 1878. Semple was represented by Edward Clarke, QC, whom Georgina had already encountered at Forbes Winslow's trial, and by C.H. Anderson. Once again, Georgina represented herself. She was suing Semple for unlawful entry into Tavistock House and for having written of her 'falsely and maliciously' in a medical certificate. She also accused him of collusion with her husband

22 GWJ, 26/5/1884; *Times*, 27/5/1884.

23 *Reynolds's Newspaper*, 6/7/1884, p. 8; *Times*, 3–4/7/1884.

and Forbes Winslow and others, and claimed that Semple 'had not personally examined her as required by the Lunacy Act, 1853, but improperly and fraudulently, for the purpose of gain, filled up the lunacy certificate'. She asked for damages of £5000. Semple denied collusion and the imputation of fraud and said that he had 'duly' examined Georgina. He also denied that Tavistock House had belonged to her. It was, he said, her husband's property. He had not entered the house wrongfully, but by leave of Harry Weldon. He had not given the certificate falsely or maliciously, and had in any case given it under circumstances that rendered the occasion privileged.

Georgina then began to call her witnesses. When Clarke objected that much of their evidence was irrelevant, the judge replied, in words he may well have regretted later on, 'I would rather take too much evidence than too little'. He had not encountered Georgina before. Georgina called Charles Spencer Perceval, Secretary to the Lunacy Commission, who informed the court that there had been 440 orders for admission into Forbes Winslow's two asylums in Hammersmith between 1866 and 1884. He was unable to say how many of them had been signed by Semple. When Georgina observed that this was 'unsatisfactory' the judge said that 'he was sure Mr Perceval only desired to give as accurate information as possible'. Georgina's reply was greeted with laughter, 'My lord, I have not as much confidence in the Lunacy Commissioners as your lordship appears to have'. Not to be outdone, Hawkins said 'He had not at present had any personal experience of them. (Much laughter.) He did not know what might happen to him in the future (renewed laughter), but at present he certainly had none. (Laughter.)'[24] Georgina asked if it was the usual practice for the proprietor of a lunatic asylum himself to fill in the forms of orders for admission into his institution. Perceval replied that he did not know. Further questioning produced the information that the Commissioners 'could not interfere, except as to persons actually under confinement for lunacy, and not in such cases as hers'. At this point the judge interrupted and asked whether the keeper of a lunatic asylum was obliged to register a lunacy order that was given to him, or give notice of it to the Commissioners. The answer was 'No, not until the patient is admitted under it'. 'Then', commented Hawkins, 'If a person was captured and kept for some days before being lodged in an asylum, there would be no information of it to the Commissioners'. Again, the answer was 'No'. When asked if the Commissioners would visit the asylum after a person had been admitted, Perceval replied that they went six times a year unless there were 'special circumstances'. Georgina asked if there had not been 'special circumstances' in her case, and Perceval informed the court

[24] *Times*, 11/7/1884.

that he had 'no experience in those matters'. 'Then', said Georgina, 'I think we must have one of the Lunacy Commissioners, my lord.' This produced laughter, but the judge agreed that a Commissioner could be called.

The hapless Perceval was then allowed to leave the witness box and was replaced by Dr James Edmunds, who had given evidence during the Winslow case a few months earlier. Under cross-examination, Edmunds expanded his previous statement concerning the hearing of 'spirit voices': 'Asked whether hearing fancied voices was not a proof of insanity, he said it occurred in persons of unsound mind, but it was not necessarily a proof of unsound mind. All persons, he added, were, in a sense, of unsound mind.' This produced 'much laughter'. Further hilarity followed the next exchange:

HAWKINS: That is the very question I was going to ask. (Great laughter.)

EDMUNDS: All persons, except your lordship, are in a sense, or to some extent, unsound in mind. (Much laughter.) There is, however, a distinction between harmless unsoundness and dangerous unsoundness.

Edmunds added that in his opinion only those who were likely to be dangerous to themselves or to others should be detained as lunatics. On re-examination by Georgina, he said that he had always thought that St Paul 'either had a sunstroke or an epileptic fit'. John Wesley, too, had been 'insane for a time, in seasons of exultation, such as earnest religious men sometimes experience'. 'But', asked Georgina 'Do you think on that account he was fit to be certified and sent to Dr Forbes Winslow's asylum?' 'Certainly not', replied Edmunds. Georgina's next witness was Dr George Wylde, the other doctor who had pronounced her sane in April 1878. He said that in his opinion she was 'a very clever and humorous woman, with a little excitability, such as was very often observable in interesting women'. Under cross-examination, Wylde admitted that he was a spiritualist. But, he added, '400,000,000 of our fellow men, Hindoos and Buddhists' also believed that they could see spirits. He believed that they were deluded, but not insane. As for Mrs Weldon, he thought she was eccentric, but not mad.

By the third day, Friday 11 July, Georgina's action against Charles Semple was exciting 'great interest' and the court was crowded. The Poet Laureate, Alfred, Lord Tennyson, even came in and stayed for a short time. The spectators were not disappointed. The day's proceedings began with Georgina's examination of James Neal. This time Harry's solicitor had a much less easy ride. He was in the witness box for two hours, during which Georgina did her best to show that he had acted in collusion with Semple. She thought afterwards that she had 'roasted him nicely'. Neal said that he had known nothing of the first attempt to incarcerate Georgina until the following day, when he had gone to see her, but he was distinctly evasive when questioned about the reason for his visit, claiming that he did not remember much about it. With growing impatience the judge intervened, asking 'Do you really mean that your memory is a blank about it all?' 'It is', replied Neal. He continued to stonewall, though he did eventually admit that he had ordered the caretaker to admit Dr Winslow's people to the house when they returned.

Georgina then tried another tack. She said that Neal had seen her regularly in the days leading up to 14 April and asked if he did not think her husband was mad to want to put her into a lunatic asylum. 'I did not form an opinion upon the question', was the unhelpful reply. But Neal subsequently admitted that he had stated 'to some person, and perhaps to Mr Weldon' that he did not believe that she was insane. 'And yet', said Georgina, 'you took steps to have me shut up in an asylum!' Georgina also called Washington Hirschfield, whom Neal had employed to make an inventory of the contents of Tavistock House before removing Ménier. Hirschfield said that he had not thought that Mrs Weldon was insane; indeed he had been 'paralyzed' when he heard that she was to be removed to an asylum. He swore that he had received a card from Neal on 15 April warning him 'not to interfere', and said that Neal had subsequently asked him to go with him to Tavistock House. Semple's counsel objected that this was 'very irrelevant'.

After examining two more witnesses, Georgina called Dr Forbes Winslow. Winslow had other matters on his mind at this time, for he was engaged in a battle with his brother-in-law Arthur William à Beckett for control of the family's asylums. Georgina, who had had plenty of time to hone her skills in questioning witnesses since the trial four months earlier, began by asking Winslow when he had first become acquainted with her husband. The doctor replied that the first contact had been on 13 April 1878, when Mr Weldon had come to his house in Cavendish Square and told him that 'his wife had taken a number of children to the Continent, and had left them uncared for, in consequence, as she said, of a voice from Heaven; and that there were letters written by her mother to the effect that she was anxious as to her daughter's condition'. Some of these letters were produced, as were a number of letters from Georgina to her mother, which, she said, contradicted Harry's claims. Why, she asked, had Winslow believed what Harry told him?

GEORGINA: Did you know he had not seen me for years?

WINSLOW: Yes, he said you had driven him out of his house.

GEORGINA: Oh, indeed. How?

WINSLOW: He said you picked up a lot of children in the streets and they upset water over his head, and it ran through, and he was driven from room to room until he was fairly driven out of the house.

GEORGINA: And did it never occur to you that he was out of his mind in talking such stuff? (Great laughter.)

WINSLOW: Certainly not.

GEORGINA: Well, you thought it your painful duty to shut me up in your asylum?

(Semple's counsel objected).

GEORGINA: Oh, then it was a pleasant duty, was it? (Great laughter.)

Georgina proceeded to read the report that Winslow had given to Harry after visiting her on 14 April 1878. She then asked him 'sarcastically', 'I suppose I seemed so pleased to see you, that you constituted yourself at once my friend?' 'No', was the reply:

GEORGINA: It was very sad, was it not, to find a poor woman in such a condition?

(Winslow did not answer.)

GEORGINA: Were you sad? Did you go away sad? (Much laughter.)

WINSLOW: It is not my temperament to be sad.

HAWKINS: Especially when you have a patient for an asylum. (Laughter.)

GEORGINA: And you laughed heartily as you departed, as my witnesses have stated.

(Winslow laughed.)

GEORGINA: You laughed as you went away?

WINSLOW: I took no note of it. I am not aware of it. It is possible.

And so it continued until the trial was adjourned.

Georgina's first witness on the following day was none other than the Earl of Shaftesbury. Now aged eighty-three, the great philanthropist and reformer had been a member of the Lunacy Commission since 1828, and chairman since 1845. 'The old villain,' as Georgina called him, had refused to help her in the summer of 1878 and she was not inclined to give him an easy time. When Shaftesbury stated that licensed madhouses were 'conducted upon the principle of profit,' Semple's counsel objected. The judge intervened: 'It is obvious, is it not? It is not to be supposed that anybody will keep a lunatic asylum except for profit.' He would, he continued, 'like to know this, whether it was the practice of keepers of asylums to send out their own agents and servants to arrest persons as lunatics.' Shaftesbury replied that it was 'a moot point, on which opinions of keepers of asylums themselves differed.' 'Surely,' asked Hawkins with growing incredulity, 'it cannot be contended that a doctor has a right to arrest me – on an order for my reception into his lunatic asylum – just as though he were a policeman arresting me for some offence?'

Georgina continued to question Lord Shaftesbury, eliciting the information that 'The doctors who gave the certificates ought to be quite independent of the proprietor of the lunatic asylum.' Once the Earl had left the witness-box, Forbes Winslow was recalled. Georgina produced a long letter that she had sent to her mother on 26 February 1878, giving 'an account of her tribulations and trials.' After reading the letter to the court 'with much emotion,' and 'almost breaking down,' she asked Winslow 'Now, having read that letter, do you mean to say it gave you an impression of my being insane?' At this point a juror fainted and had to be removed from the court – it is not clear if this was due to the length of the letter or the nature of its contents. He eventually returned, still looking very ill, and the judge decided to adjourn the trial until the following Tuesday.

The court was 'crammed' on the fifth day of the trial. Georgina continued her interrogation of Forbes Winslow, assisted by the judge who made it quite clear that he did not like what he was hearing:

HAWKINS: Pray, is it usual for your servants to go and take possession of the alleged lunatic?

WINSLOW: It is always done by all proprietors of asylums.

HAWKINS: Then it is time it was altered, and it is not so laid down in the law books.

Winslow claimed that his mother, not he, had been the proprietor of the asylum, but eventually agreed, under further questioning by the judge, that he had been 'the manager, and responsible as if you were the actual proprietor.' He admitted that neither he nor any other medical man had asked

Georgina's own doctor about her, nor had they consulted anyone else who knew her well – though he had stated in his own book that 'inquiries ought to be made, especially as to whether supposed "delusions" are not based upon facts'.[25] This was, Winslow claimed 'a peculiar case' because Georgina's husband had not seen her for three years. 'Surely', commented the judge, 'that was the very reason why you should have inquired of somebody else.' Hawkins asked Winslow if he had purposely abstained from making enquiries, and the doctor replied that 'it did not occur to me'.

When Georgina asked for the lists of people admitted to the Winslow family's asylums in the hope of showing that many of them had been signed in by Semple, Winslow objected that they were privileged communications. Having been overruled by the judge, he produced some bundles of certificates and began to shuffle through them. Georgina observed that he had had ample notice to produce them. Grudgingly, Winslow at last found the certificates Georgina wanted. 'And here they are', he said, 'I am not bound to sort them for you.' After this, Winslow was examined by the counsel for the defence. He told the court that he had been acquainted with Semple for twenty years and knew him to be 'a competent person to make examinations for lunatic asylums'. Semple had given certificates for Winslow's asylums, and none of the Commissioners had ever objected to these certificates. In Winslow's opinion, Semple was justified in giving his certificate concerning Georgina.

After further discussion, Wallace Jones was called as a witness. He said that he was secretary to Dr Forbes Winslow and sometimes received his patients. 'And sometimes you seize them, don't you?' added Georgina. Several people laughed. On the following day Jones gave his account of the events of 14 and 15 April, but there was much that he claimed to have forgotten. He did, he said, remember one of the nurses asking Mrs Weldon to go with them. When his quarry seemed to be reluctant to co-operate, he had told the women to 'take her'. He had left the house because Mrs Lowe had pushed him out. Jones informed the court that he had been in Winslow's service for eighteen years. He refused to say how much he was paid, or whether he received any commission on captures.

Later in the same day, Georgina called her mother as a witness. Louisa Treherne said that she had never heard of Dr Semple, and that he had not come to ask her any questions about her daughter being put into a lunatic asylum. Nobody in the family, she said, had thought that Georgina was mad 'in the slightest degree'. She had not played any part in the attempt to have her daughter locked up. 'No one was more horrified than yourself?' asked Georgina.

[25] Presumably Lyttelton S. Winslow, *Manual of Lunacy* (London, 1874).

Edward Clarke tried to object to 'this kind of question,' but Georgina answered sweetly, 'My mother thinks it is a very natural question for a daughter to put to her mother.' She went on to ask if her mother had written to the papers. Clarke tried to object again, but Louisa ignored him and said 'Yes.' Then, 'amid much merriment,' Georgina exclaimed, 'She has answered "Yes". I have no more questions to ask of her. Mamma dear, you may now go.'

Finally, Georgina herself entered the witness-box. She told the court of her marriage to Harry Weldon and of their life together at Tavistock House. When Clarke protested that this was not evidence, she replied that she was trying to show her right to the house. When Clarke objected again, the judge said that he could not prevent the plaintiff giving evidence to show that she was sufficiently in possession to enable her to bring an action for trespass. Georgina then moved on to her separation from Harry, her time in France with the orphans, and her problems with Anacharsis Ménier. After this, she told the court of the dramatic events of 14 and 15 April 1878 and her interviews with Semple and Rudderforth. They had, she said, got everything wrong. She was still in the witness box when the proceedings were adjourned once again. On the seventh day of the trial, Friday 18 July, Georgina described her escape from the mad-doctors and told the court that she had gone to Hammersmith, quite close to Dr Winslow's asylums. Hawkins, who evidently had a sense of humour, asked 'You did not call?' 'No, my lord,' replied Georgina, 'I did not return his call.' Having finished her evidence, she was cross-examined by Anderson. She told him that she had not, as far as she could recollect, seen Dr Semple before 14 April 1878, adding 'He had no ill will to me; quite the contrary. I think he liked me when he saw me very much indeed.' The audience began to laugh. Anderson asked 'Did he do more than his duty?' and Georgina replied (to more laughter), 'Oh, I think it was rather a pleasure than otherwise. He would have liked to take me to the seaside, I dare say.' Doctors Rudderforth and Semple had examined her together for three-quarters of an hour; Semple had been with her alone for five minutes at the most, and he had done most of the talking: 'He spoke flatteringly, and told me I looked very young, and I told him he was very impudent.' She had spent three or four minutes alone with Rudderforth.

After James Bell had been examined and confirmed Georgina's story, she informed the judge that she had finished presenting her case. At this point Edward Clarke stood up and submitted that there was no case to go to the jury. The plaintiff had not been in possession of Tavistock House when these events took place, so there had been no trespass – and the doctors had, in any case, entered the house with the permission of Georgina's husband. There was, Clarke also said, no evidence that Semple had not examined Georgina separately, as was required. The judge disagreed on both counts. Clarke continued to argue, but Hawkins was adamant: he had no intention of stopping the proceedings.

After a further adjournment, Anderson began to present the case for the defence on Wednesday 23 July. He called Charles Semple first. Semple, who was now thirty-nine, said that he was a member of the Royal College of Physicians and had been in practice for about fifteen years. He had had 'a good deal of experience in unsoundness of mind in public asylums and had studied the subject for twenty years'. He had 'for many years been in the habit of examining persons to see if they were insane' and had 'frequently been consulted on the subject'. He gave his account of the events of 14 April 1878 to the court, claiming that he had spent a quarter of an hour alone with Georgina, during which time she had 'talked incessantly'. He had 'conscientiously believed' her to be insane, and he had made a separate examination as required by the Lunacy Act. Cross-examined by Georgina, he said that he had known Dr Forbes Winslow for twenty years and dined with him nine or ten times a year. When she asked if he had studied at Winslow's asylum, he replied that he had been 'a good deal there', but had not studied lunacy there. He was 'not at Dr Winslow's asylum for study, but rather for pleasure'.

HAWKINS: Pleasure at a lunatic asylum?

GEORGINA: To give the lunatics pleasure. (Laughter.) You went rather oftener to Dr Winslow's asylum than to any other?

SEMPLE: Perhaps I did, but not for study. I was not paid for going.

Semple said that he had certified in forty-three cases for Winslow's asylum between 1874 and 1884. He could not remember any other case in which the alleged lunatic had not been received into an asylum and had never been sued before. He admitted that his father had been sued in similar circumstances and had been ordered to pay damages.[26]

The next witness was Semple's companion on 14 April 1878, Dr Edward Rudderforth. Aged about seventy and a member of the Royal College of Surgeons, Rudderforth said that he had 'some knowledge of lunacy', though he was not a specialist. He had been alone with Georgina for twenty or thirty minutes and had written his certificate by himself, without colluding with Dr Semple in any way. At this point the trial was adjourned again. By this time the members of the jury were becoming restless. One of them

[26] The case, *Hall v. Semple*, was reported in *The Times* in 12/1862.

protested against the length of the proceedings: 'We are,' he said, 'working men, whose time is of value to us and the loss of time in coming here day after day is very great.' The judge heartily agreed.

On Friday 25 July, the ninth day, Georgina cross-examined Dr Rudderforth. After her examination of Semple, he cannot have expected an easy time. He had, he said, been paid five guineas for his visit to Tavistock House and had received it the same evening from Dr Winslow. The fee was larger than usual because it was a night visit:

GEORGINA:	What, you put it down as a night visit to a raging lunatic, did you? (A laugh.)
RUDDERFORTH:	I was paid five guineas for certifying you to be a lunatic.
GEORGINA:	And you took it quietly, as a piece of luck? (Laughter.)
RUDDERFORTH:	No, I took it for services rendered, and the services rendered were well worth the money. (Laughter.) There is a great responsibility about it.
HAWKINS:	A very great responsibility indeed.
GEORGINA:	I dare say if you had known what would follow you would not have given the certificate for £500.
RUDDERFORTH:	No, indeed, I would not. (Much laughter, in which Mrs Weldon heartily joined.)
GEORGINA:	Was I the first poor woman who resisted capture?
RUDDERFORTH:	I do not know.

Then, at last, came the final speeches. Edward Clarke told the court that Dr Semple had believed that the plaintiff 'ought be subjected to care and treatment,' and had made out his certificate accordingly. He would gain nothing by Mrs Weldon being sent to Dr Winslow's asylum; he had only performed his duty and there was nothing to justify a verdict against him. Georgina then addressed the jury. It was, she said, not her fault that the trial had lasted so long, as she had been obliged to call 'hostile witnesses, from whom it was difficult to extract anything.' These people, who all knew her to be sane, had all been acting in collusion to have her locked up. 'Could anything be conceived more horrible than to seize her at night and carry her off to a lunatic asylum, no doubt gagged and in a strait-waistcoat, and probably before long mad or dead through terror and excitement?' She believed that the lunacy certificates had been dictated to Semple and Rudderforth by Dr Winslow. There was, she said 'an admirable Manual of Lunacy' by Winslow, 'really quite pathetic and philanthropic as to the painful duty of getting hold of well-paying patients', but none of the symptoms he mentioned applied to herself. She was pleased to have come before a jury, and hoped that they would give a verdict in accordance with common sense and justice 'and read a lesson to those who thus abused the Lunacy Laws and perpetrated abuses connived at by the Commissioners of Lunacy'. By this time it was four o'clock and the judge deferred his summing up until after the weekend.

On Monday 28 July Mr Justice Hawkins spoke for nearly four hours without a break. In the words of Edward Grierson, his summing-up was 'admirable and brilliant – the work of a liberal minded man who had suddenly been made aware of dangerous abuses of the law'.[27] The case was, Hawkins said, 'of great importance, not only to the parties, but to the public'. The jury had to decide, without prejudice or sympathy, whether Mrs Weldon had established her case against Dr Semple, and, if so, to decide what damages should be awarded. Where lunacy orders were concerned, 'the state of the law was such as to fill him with alarm when he contemplated it'. Any friend or relation who chose to think a person insane might sign an order to remove him to an asylum. Before the order was put in force, certificates should be drawn up by two medical men, but no oath was required and there was no requirement that their qualifications should be described. He hoped that the law would be altered: it was not for him to say in what way, but he was of the belief that the law, in the state in which it was, 'must be calculated to fill everybody who contemplated it with terror and alarm'. The jury must not, however, allow this to affect their minds at all against Dr Semple, who was not responsible for the fraud and cruelty of others, though he was liable for his own acts and his own conduct.

The judge went on to tell the jury about the laws relating to lunacy orders and the requirement that the person who signed the order must have seen the alleged lunatic within the last month. But Sir Henry de Bathe had not seen Mrs Weldon since 1877, and her husband had not seen her since 1874. It seemed 'almost incredible' that two English gentlemen who had not seen a woman for a year, or for three years, should have given an order to confine her as a lunatic 'in a country where liberty was boasted of, and not even a criminal could be incarcerated without the order of a magistrate, or someone in authority'. Could it, he asked, be lawful for the keeper of an asylum, who

27 Grierson, *Storm Bird*, p. 221.

was prohibited from certifying a lunatic himself, to nominate those who certified? Dr Semple was not responsible for any misconduct that might have occurred before he was called in; he was only responsible for his own conduct. He was bound to exercise 'reasonable care' in the examination of Mrs Weldon. If he did not do so, and his negligence was 'gross and culpable', then he would be responsible and would be liable to pay damages. The jury had to decide whether Rudderforth and Semple really had examined Mrs Weldon separately, and whether they had signed the certificates recklessly.

Finally, Hawkins asked the jury no fewer than seventeen questions. Twelve related to the main issue: was Mrs Weldon really of unsound mind at the time in question? Did the jury believe her version of the events of the day in question, or did they believe the doctors? The remaining five related to the alleged trespass: was Mrs Weldon in possession of Tavistock House, and had the doctors entered the house without her permission? The case was, the judge added, 'of serious importance to the liberty of the subject'. He now left it in the hands of the jury. The jury was out was out for an hour and twenty minutes. When they returned to the court they gave their verdict: every one of the judge's questions was answered in Georgina's favour. They awarded her damages of £1000, plus £20 for the trespass. It was a spectacular victory, and there was 'an immense crowd' waiting outside the Law Courts to greet and cheer Georgina. That evening she performed at the London Pavilion as usual, and received a 'pretty fan bouquet'.

The Semple trial was the subject of a leader in *The Times* on the following day. 'Mrs Weldon has been signally victorious in one of her many battles', it began. The writer, who noted the 'preposterous length' to which the inquiry had run, commented that the judge had 'virtually invited' the jury to find for her. He named Drs Forbes Winslow, Semple and Rudderforth, and thought that they had all given 'an unsatisfactory account of their share in the transaction'. 'It would', he added 'be scandalous if each case of suspected lunacy were sifted with no more intelligence than was displayed with regard to Mrs Weldon.' The judge's comments on the part played by Harry Weldon and Sir Henry de Bathe were also noted. But the real importance of the case was 'that it secures the triumph of the agitation against the lunacy laws in their present shape'. Their reform was 'henceforth only a matter of time'.[28]

For Georgina, however, the outcome of the Semple trial was more immediate. It left the way open for actions against the remaining mad-doctors and Sir Henry de Bathe.

[28] The main sources for the Semple trial are *Times*, 10–29/7/1884; GWJ, 9–28/7/1884.

23
Swings and Roundabouts

Throughout the summer and autumn of 1884 Georgina and her assistants continued to work away in the cramped, stuffy office in Red Lion Court. Harcourt, Chaffers, de Bear and Walter Rawlings were joined by another clerk, 'little' William Holmes, who claimed to have spent five years in penal servitude. He had 'lovely' handwriting and was 'such a contrast to Old Misery' (Harcourt). Harcourt and Chaffers were both prickly and quick to take offence. They were jealous of each other and of their companions, and there were frequent quarrels. But was plenty of work to do, as a number of her fellow lady-litigants looked to Georgina for help and advice. As she told her mother, 'I am a kind of female Don Quixote. All the unfortunates knock on my door.'[1]

The first of these 'unfortunates' was Louisa Trevelyan, the wife of Colonel Harington Trevelyan, a veteran of the Charge of the Light Brigade. The two had married in 1858 and had several children, but by the end of 1883, when Georgina first encountered Mrs Trevelyan, she was 'a poor crushed woman,' separated from her husband and penniless. She moved into 33 Loughborough Road and Georgina helped her to retrieve her clothes from the pawnbrokers. Colonel Trevelyan was supposed to pay his wife £300 a year, but she had received nothing for two years. Georgina was determined to force him to pay up.[2] Before long, however, Mrs Trevelyan began to stay out all night. One evening she returned late, obviously drunk, made 'a great row' and smashed a window. Georgina had to send for the police, who took her away. When she was arrested for stealing a jacket and brought before the magistrate at Marylebone Police Court, Georgina refused to bail her out. Mrs Trevelyan was 'an extremely nice person,' she wrote, but directly she went out 'she disgraced, not only her family but her sex.'[3] A few weeks later Mrs Trevelyan was in the workhouse, but she continued to appear at the Law Courts from time to time.[4]

1 GW–LFT, 4/11/1884.
2 GWJ, 7/1/1884; SS, 3/1884, p. 2, 2/1884, p. 2.
3 GWJ, 27–8/2/1884; *Times*, 8/3/1884.
4 GWJ, 3/4/1884.

Another protégée was Mary Ann Trower, who was already 'well-known in the Chancery Courts as a litigant in person'.[5] She was the second wife of Frederick Trower, a colonial broker, who had died in 1876, less than a year after their wedding. Most of Mr Trower's property had been settled on the children of his first marriage and his widow had inherited nothing but debts. She had been sent to gaol in 1879 after refusing to cooperate with her late husband's creditors, and had subsequently launched a number of unsuccessful legal actions in an attempt to obtain what she believed to be her rightful inheritance. Georgina met her for the first time in June 1884 and heard her 'marvellous history', which, inevitably, included the claim that she was entitled to 'a good deal of money'. She accompanied Mrs Trower on her visits to the Law Courts and tried to assist her at her numerous court hearings. She also sent Harcourt to distrain on the tenants of a house in Kensal Town that Mrs Trower claimed to own, in spite of a court order forbidding any such action. He succeeded in carrying off a deal table and eight chairs.[6] As a result, they all – Harcourt, Mrs Trower and Georgina – ended up in the Court of Chancery on 31 October, accused of disobeying the court order. The court was 'crowded to extinction' with Georgina's supporters and other onlookers, who included 'divers lady litigants, conspicuous amongst whom were Miss Fray and Mrs Trevelyan'. Georgina noted in her diary two days before this that she had seen Mrs Trevelyan at the Law Courts 'in workhouse garb', guarded by Miss Fray 'like an old crow'. Georgina disliked Rosanna Fray, whom she had known for several years.[7]

The counsel for the prosecution commented that 'Mrs Weldon appeared not only to take the law into her hands, but other people's law into her hands'. It was clear that Georgina had acted on her own initiative, without telling Mrs Trower what she intended to do. She agreed to return the furniture, but refused to pay the costs of the action, telling the judge 'If I were sent to prison, the public would pay the costs and get me out'. On being told that she could be gaoled for contempt, and that her supporters would not be able to have her released, she again refused to pay the costs and dared the judge to send her to Holloway. He duly made the order, committing both Georgina and Harcourt to prison. But, as she recorded in her diary, 'as no-one took us there [to prison] we went home and heard no more of it, except the newspapers, the bills etc. all flaring away "Mrs Weldon sent to prison!"' 'Everyone', she added, 'will know about Mrs Trower's case

5 *Times*, 1/11/1884.
6 GWJ, 11/6/1884, 21/10/1884.
7 *Daily News*, 1/11/1884, p. 7.

now.'[8] Nevertheless, she and Harcourt returned on 4 November to purge their contempt. They apologised and promised the judge that they would not interfere with the property again and would pay the costs. It was not long before Georgina gave up on Mrs Trower too, having decided that the woman was 'a little suspicious cross-grained toad.'[9]

The spectators at the Chancery Court hearing on 31 October had included Forbes Winslow. A month later he and Georgina met again in the Court of Queen's Bench for the second round of *Weldon v. Winslow*, this time before Mr Justice Denman. The trial, which covered much of the same ground as the first one, was another marathon, lasting five days in all. On this occasion, Winslow represented himself, as he could no longer afford to pay a barrister. As Edward Grierson put it: '[This enabled] the public to see these two remarkable characters face to face, matching irrelevance with irrelevance, till poor Mr Justice Denman was in despair over the pair of them.'[10]

It soon became clear that Winslow was no match for Georgina, who enjoyed cross-examining him so much that the judge had to reprimand her. She asked him why he and his father-in-law, Dr Winn had apparently left Tavistock Square 'laughing' on 14 April 1878. Was it not, she asked, 'a sad thing to have to deal with persons out of their mind?' The judge rebuked her for creating an impression that she herself looked upon it as 'to a certain degree a matter of levity.' Georgina went on to examine Winn, forcing him to admit that the Commissioners in Lunacy had complained of his conduct in 1875. It emerged that he had certified that the death of a patient who had died at the asylum belonging to Forbes Winslow's father was the result of natural causes, but the body had later been exhumed and an examination had produced evidence of poison. The Commissioners had subsequently written to Dr Winslow to tell him that Dr Winn's conduct in the matter had been 'gravely culpable.' Winn's only explanation was that 'Such cases often occur in asylums.'

Towards the end of the fourth day, Winslow summed up his case. He asserted that there was 'every reason for his believing that [Mrs Weldon] suffered from a monomania of voices.' Some people might say that she was eccentric, rather than insane 'But such a view would not be correct. Eccentricity is innate, it is born in the subject.' The judge begged to disagree and rebuked Winslow for delivering a lecture to the jury. Winslow continued: 'Only those who had to deal with the victims of mental disease know how slight the demarcation was between a harmless and a dangerous lunatic.'

8 GWJ, 31/10/1884.

9 *Morning Post*, 1/11/1884, p. 3; *Daily News*, 5/11/1884, p. 2; *Times*, 1,5,13/11/1884; GWJ, 10/4/1885.

10 Edward Grierson, *Storm Bird* (London, 1959), p. 224.

He had, he said 'been examined as a witness in nearly every lunacy case of importance during recent years, yet his character and reputation had never been called in question.' According to the *Times* court reporter, the learned judge had 'repeatedly' to correct Winslow during his speech. It would, Denman said, 'soon become necessary for the courts to make a rule to prevent suitors appearing in person.' It was 'intolerable that the patience of juries should be tried and public time wasted with evidence and topics which were quite irrelevant.'

In his own summing-up, the judge told the jury that they had to decide if Winslow had been acting *bona fide* under a sense of duty. Did he have an 'unworthy' motive, such as a desire to further Georgina's husband's wishes, or to gain a patient for his mother's asylum? He felt bound to say that 'even if she were to be thought eccentric in her method of pursuing them, the objects of Mrs Weldon seemed to be of a benevolent character.' The jury also had to decide if Forbes Winslow had acted as he did 'through mere error' or through malice. They jury was out for two and a half hours and found for Georgina on two out of three points, awarding her damages of £500, plus her costs. It was a significant victory, but Georgina, who had asked for £10,000, was not pleased. The members of the jury were, in her opinion, 'utter fools' and 'idiotic imbeciles.' Two days later she issued yet another writ against Winslow.[11]

Winslow was probably fair game, but it is difficult to see anything other than sheer spite and vindictiveness as the motivation for some of Georgina's other legal proceedings at this time. One victim was James Sidney, who had accused her of giving him a black eye when he attempted to throw her out of Covent Garden in October 1879. Georgina tried – quite without justification, it seems – to have him prosecuted for bigamy in the autumn of 1884. She failed. Her greatest fury was, however, reserved for Jules Rivière, the conductor who had had her imprisoned for libel in 1880. She was determined to get him back into court, convinced that she had only lost the previous action because her counsel had not presented her case properly. Encouraged by her successes against Semple, Thomas Johnson of *Le Figaro*, and Winslow, she thought she could do better.

In her statement of claim, delivered to Rivière's lawyers in November 1883, Georgina claimed £10,000 for breach of contract and assault. The lawyers fought tooth and nail to prevent the case coming to court, but in August 1884 the Master of the Rolls, William Baliol Brett, decided that there was a case to answer where the alleged assault was concerned,

[11] GWJ, 29/11/1884; *Times*, 26–9/11/1884, 1/12/1884.

though Georgina could not sue on her other claims.[12] The second Rivière trial opened in the Court of Queen's Bench on Saturday 15 November 1884. It was to last for seven days, spread out over a period of just under a month and would have lasted for much longer if the judge, Mr Justice Wills, had not quickly taken control. He had been a judge for only four months and had not encountered Georgina before. Clearly horrified when he saw the length of her statement of claim, he held the 'volume' up to the jury, and exclaimed 'It is hardly necessary to read all that. It is a pure waste of time; nobody ever does it.' Ignoring him, Georgina began to recount the whole history of her relationship with Rivière. After a while Rivière's counsel, Henry Matthews, QC, interrupted, and pointed out that there was only 'one short and very small issue to try, namely whether Mr Rivière assaulted Mrs Weldon.' The exchange that followed was to be the first of many:

WILLS:	[To Georgina] What you have to do now is to open to the jury and tell them shortly the case you are going to make about the assault.
GEORGINA:	I am sorry to say I cannot do it shortly.
WILLS:	Then at length; either shortly or at length, open to the jury the case you are going to make about the assault.[13]

It quickly became a battle of wills, with the judge doing his best to keep Georgina to the point, and she becoming increasingly grumpy and uncooperative. Before long she was referring to the judge in her diary as 'the little red louse.'

Having been forced to curtail her opening speech, Georgina put Rivière himself in the witness-box and proceeded to examine him. She kept him there for over three hours and – in her own opinion – 'bowled him out over and over again.' He was, she wrote, 'a lying old thief.' As the day wore on, the judge announced, 'in a most lamentable, dejected tone,' 'I don't think parties in waiting will be wanted today, and they had better not come till further notice.'[14] Rivière was still in the box when the court was adjourned. Further adjournments followed as the two sides argued over the precise nature of Rivière's agreement with Covent Garden and the question of whether he did, or did not, have the right to exclude Georgina from the

12 GW, *Reports2*, pp. 149–51; *Standard*, 4/8/1884, p. 3.

13 GW, *Reports3*, p. 4.

14 GWJ, 15/11/1884; GW, *Reports3*, p. 19.

theatre. Georgina bickered with the judge continually, scolding him and treating him with gross disrespect. At one point she told him

> THE JURY, my lord, UNDERSTAND PLAIN ENGLISH LIKE I DO; I can read the case, and your lordship can read the case. If your lordship says 'I WON'T LET YOU PUT THE FACTS BEFORE THE JURY', HOW CAN I PUT THE FACTS? I am not at all wishing to be disrespectful to his lordship. I look upon the jury as the People.[15]

The capital letters are Georgina's own. Witness after witness told the court in minute detail what had happened at Covent Garden in the autumn of 1879 until everyone – apart from Georgina – was exhausted.

It was not until 11 December that Henry Matthews was able to address the jury on Rivière's behalf. 'He regretted with Mr Rivière', he began, 'that a cause of action so trumpery should have occupied their time so long':

> Without saying anything disparaging of Mrs Weldon, for she appeared to possess many qualities which ought to make her the ornament of her own sex and the delight of his, she appeared to pursue anyone who had the misfortune to come in conflict with her with a pertinacity of vengeance. She somehow delighted to drag her wrongs before the public, both as a wife and as a woman, for it was idle to ignore her many other quarrels and law-suits.

She had 'chosen to hang her grievances against the Lunacy Laws on the peg of M. Rivière's Promenade Concerts' and 'could not be described as anything else but a source of discord whenever she showed herself'. She 'seemed to him to have lunatics and the Lunacy Laws on the brain'. The management of Covent Garden had been quite right to anticipate a row and to prevent her from entering her box.

On Friday 12 December, the last day of the trial, Mr Justice Wills summed up. He began by telling the jury that the case had 'occupied an enormous time, quite disproportionate to anything that was to be gained by it, chiefly owing to both parties having elected that as material which, in his judgment, was not material at all'. His main criticism was reserved for Georgina. He 'hoped the jury would not listen to the appeal that had been repeatedly made to them, with every form of personal disrespect to himself, to disregard the law just because Mrs Weldon did not like it'.[16] The jury had to consider whether M. Rivière had been a lessee of Covent Garden in 1879.

[15] GW, *Reports3*, p. 56.

[16] *Times*, 11–13/12/1884; GW, *Reports3*, p. 115.

Fig. 26. 'The Wolf and the Fox': *Weldon v. Rivière*, 12 December 1884, by Leon Michou. Georgina Weldon's victory 'after seven days hard fighting'.

Had more violence than was necessary been used in order to remove Mrs Weldon? Could Mrs Weldon's account of the events of 29 October 1879 be relied on, in view of the fact that she had declared that she 'would ruin M. Rivière, no matter how long it might take or what it might cost'?

The jury was out for half an hour. When they returned they gave their verdict 'Messrs Rivière and Hayes were not sub-lessees of the theatre, and no unnecessary violence had been used.' According to the *Times* reporter, this announcement 'created some surprise in Court.' The judge informed the jury that, as they had found that the defendant had no right in the theatre, it was a case for substantial damages. They retired again, this time for an hour and a half. Eventually, at 4 p.m. they returned and announced that 'there was no chance of their agreeing'. It was later rumoured that nine of the jurymen had wanted Georgina to be awarded £1000; the other three insisted on one farthing.[17] The judge warned the jury that he would have to discharge them, but they still said that their difference was 'hopeless'. In the end it was Georgina who – to everyone's astonishment – agreed to compromise. She told the judge that 'the matter of damages was quite immaterial to her'. She would take a verdict without damages, and would be content with £50 for costs. The judge hastily agreed. Georgina was, once again, 'greatly cheered' as she left the court. Later she wrote in her diary 'Wills must be "mad". It is grand. I think this verdict will scare a good many people'. A few days later almost all the 'comic papers' had portraits of her in wig and gown.[18]

~

In her persecution of Rivière and Sidney, Georgina had made reckless allegations for which she had no certain proof. But woe betide anyone who dared to criticise her. They would be pursued with what Henry Matthews had described as 'a pertinacity of vengeance'. Thus Henry Pottinger Stephens, the editor of the *Topical Times*, was served with a writ in November for daring to suggest that Georgina's prosecution of Sidney had been unjustified. 'Men may come and men may go', the article began, 'but Mrs Weldon goes on for ever.' 'Mrs Weldon was annoyed', Stephens continued, 'and when she is annoyed it is good to get out of her way.' Georgina claimed £1000 damages, but – unusually – this dispute seems to have been settled amicably and out of court.[19]

Another recipient of a writ at this time was Georgina's fellow 'lady litigant', Rosanna Fray. Miss Fray had entered the service of the Countess of Zetland as head lady's maid in 1854, but had been dismissed without a character after eight weeks after falling out with the housekeeper, who had accused her of making 'improper overtures' to the groom of the chambers, and of being addicted to strong drink. Miss Fray had then sued the housekeeper for slander, and the Earl of Zetland for wrongful dismissal. The Court of Queen's Bench had awarded her £100 for the slander, and the Earl had paid £300 to settle the case out of court.[20] Miss Fray had received only £50 of this money; the rest had been retained by her lawyer to settle his fees. She

17 GW–*The Englishman*, 27 December 1884.
18 GWJ, 12/12/1884; *Times*, 17–18/11/1884, 9–13/12/1884; GW, *Reports3*.
19 *Topical Times*, 25/10/1884; SC, *GW and Henry Pottinger Stephens*, 1884.
20 *Lloyd's Weekly Newspaper*, 12/8/1860, p. 6; *Morning Post*, 3/7/1855, p. 6.

had then sued the lawyer for negligence. Further suits had followed; in 1859 Miss Fray owed her lawyers £169 and was imprisoned for debt. She had continued to frequent the law courts for the next twenty-five years, usually representing herself as she had lost faith in the legal profession and was 'wholly without means.' Some people believed that she was the model for Charles Dickens's Miss Flite, but *Bleak House* was first published in 1852–3, more than two years before Miss Fray's first appearance in court, so this is clearly incorrect.[21]

It was noted in 1885 that Rosanna Fray had first 'set up as a female lawyer' nearly thirty years earlier, and that she was still at it '"coaching" all her sex who have a grievance – legal or matrimonial.' 'Mrs Weldon' was said to be 'a baby in law suits' compared to Miss Fray.[22] They had met for the first time in October 1878. At first Georgina had thought that Miss Fray was 'a great woman,' but it was not long before the two women fell out: early in the following year Georgina referred to her new acquaintance as 'the dirty old baggage.'[23] In early December 1884 Georgina discovered that Miss Fray had been telling malicious stories about her. She had accused Georgina and Angèle of being 'filthy women, unspeakable beasts' who 'bring poor children up for immoral purposes and send them to France.' Mrs Weldon was a thief who had swindled her out of £30 and Tavistock House had been 'no better than a brothel': 'There's not a more immoral woman in London than Mrs Weldon. She is a perfect beast with the men and so is that horrid Frenchwoman.' After hearing the verdict in *Weldon v. Rivière* in December, Miss Fray had accused Georgina of bribing the jury. She had also written to Forbes Winslow, telling him, 'When I knew Mrs Weldon in 1878 and '79 she was suffering from a disordered mind, and at times of a very dangerous character.'[24] Georgina decided that she had to 'put a stop to' Miss Fray, and a writ, accusing the older woman of slander and libel and claiming damages of £100, was issued on 1 January 1885. This led to a state of open warfare between the two 'fair litigants.' Everyone in the Law Courts was said to be talking about the case and 'longing for the encounter between the two ladies.'[25] They were to be disappointed. The matter was still unsettled at the time of Rosanna Fray's death in 1888 when, under the headline 'Death of a well-known female litigant,' a reporter commented, 'Unlike many of the female litigants who plead their own cause, Miss Fray was a very well-behaved woman.'

[21] See, for example, *Thame Gazette*, 4/5/1869, p. 5.

[22] *Northampton Daily Chronicle*, 1/9/1885; *Morpeth Herald*, 2/6/1888, p. 2.

[23] GWJ, 21/11/1878, 4/1/1879.

[24] R.D. Fray–L.S. Forbes Winslow, 2/12/1884.

[25] SC, *Weldon v. Fray*, 1885; *Nottingham Evening Post*, 19/1/1885, p. 2.

Another finished his article with the words, 'The Fray is ended.' Georgina merely wrote in her journal, 'Good riddance to bad rubbish.'[26]

Then there was 'Captain' Donald Shaw, who had organised Georgina's disastrous tour of the provinces at the end of 1879. In 1882–4 Shaw had published a book entitled *Eighteen Months' Imprisonment*, which included a chapter entitled 'Georgina.' This was, she claimed, 'A wholly false, malicious, untrue libel.' She fired off a letter to the publishers, George Routledge and Sons, threatening to sue Shaw. 'He,' she noted, 'has money.' On 1 January 1885, writs against Routledge and the booksellers W.H. Smith were issued for 'false and malicious libels,' for which Georgina claimed damages of £10,000. A further writ, this time against Mudie's Select Library was issued a few days later. It is clear from Georgina's diary that she was hoping for 'real money.' 'So,' she wrote, 'after all I may end by making money thro' that scamp.'[27] Not for the first time, she was to be sadly disappointed: Mudie's and Routledge apologised and paid £26 5s and £25 respectively; W.H. Smith paid £75 to prevent a 'lengthy legal argument,' but without admitting that they were liable.[28]

~

At the end of 1884 Georgina reflected on 'a wonderful year, which must infinitely displease the musical trade and press, whose efforts since fourteen years have been strained to prevent my becoming celebrated.' The 'degraded villains' had 'striven to crush' her in every way, but, 'in spite of judges, QCs, and all the fry of legal sharks,' she had 'conquered all along the line.' Though costs had been awarded against her several times, she had so far not paid a penny. She did, however, admit that her own legal expenses had been 'very heavy.'[29]

She began the New Year with a fresh onslaught on Harry Weldon, having so far utterly failed to have the attachment order of 27 November 1883 enforced. In theory, Harry could have been sent to prison, but in 1884 the Matrimonial Causes Act had been rushed through Parliament, abolishing the use of attachment in cases such as Georgina's.[30] Lawyers soon began to refer to it as the 'Weldon Relief Act,' though there was some doubt as to whether its effect was retrospective. In the Divorce Court on 27 January 1885 Georgina argued that the Act did not apply to her case and asked for the order to be issued immediately. Mr Justice Hannen told her that the

26 *Morpeth Herald*, 2/6/1888, p. 2; *Dundee Evening Telegraph*, 16/5/1888, p. 2; GWJ, 12/5/1888.

27 GWJ, 20,30/12/1884, 10/1/1885; SC, *GW v. W.H. Smith*, 1885.

28 *Times*, 17/3/1886.

29 GWJ, 31/12/1884.

30 The Act was sponsored by Mr Justice Hannen.

court had the power to fix the allowance that her husband should make to her. 'Will that do for you?' he asked. Georgina's reply was uncompromising, 'No, my Lord. I should like to know where he is. I should like to get at him.' Hannen's judgment, given a week later, was not in Georgina's favour. The court had, he said, no discretion to enforce the writ of attachment; nor did it have the power to have Harry taken into custody in order to compel him to pay the costs of the case. Georgina decided that Hannen was 'a scoundrel' and vowed to take the case to the Court of Appeal.[31]

Georgina also attacked her husband on a second front at this time. The second *Weldon v. Weldon* trial began in the Court of Chancery on 4 February before the vice-chancellor, Sir James Bacon, who celebrated his eighty-seventh birthday during the trial. It soon became clear that he was as deaf as a post. Some of his deafness may have been selective: a means of taking control of Georgina's tirades. This time she was suing Harry for failing to allow her to make a career as a singer, as he had promised before their marriage. She also claimed that he had agreed to give her full control of his money as well as her own and had promised to settle £800 a year on her. She wanted, she said, to live in his apartments at the College of Arms. She also wanted the £1000 a year that he had agreed to give her after they separated. He had never entered into a formal deed of separation as he had promised, and had deprived her of her home. She wanted an account of all the money Harry had received and spent between 1860 and 1884, and a list of all the articles taken out of Tavistock House by Anacharsis Ménier in 1878. She claimed £20,000 for breach of contract.

The trial lasted for six days. By the second day Georgina was 'nearly killed' with shouting at the judge. She was determined that the court should hear almost a hundred letters that had passed between her and Harry, though she had to ask an officer of the court to read some of them for her. Bacon soon interrupted, telling Georgina that 'He could not have the time of the Court wasted by the reading of letters which had nothing whatever to do with the question before the Court.' Georgina ploughed on regardless. On the last day she made her final speech, finishing with the threat 'I will yet show to the world that I am brave and true and pure, and that my husband is a sneaking cur! There!' After this, the judge summed up 'without,' Georgina wrote, 'having heard a word of the evidence.' In fact, it is clear that he had heard only too well. He told the court that the case was 'as clear in point of law as could be imagined.' He had 'listened for some days to what was called evidence, but which was wholly disconnected from the case upon the record.' There was 'not a particle of evidence' that the plaintiff had been interfered with in

31 GWJ, 27/1/1885, 3/2/1885; *Times*, 28/1/1885, 4/2/1885.

making use of her vocal talent as a profession. Nor was there any evidence that she was to have control of her own and her husband's money: she had no money of her own 'and it would be preposterous if the Court of Chancery were to allow a wife to have the control of her husband's moneys.' Georgina had not proved the existence of agreements that Harry should settle £800 or £1000 a year on her: a husband was 'at liberty to make such payments to his wife as he thought fit and to curtail them if necessary.' Mr Weldon had always been the owner of Tavistock House and had never assigned it to his wife, and no deed of separation had ever been signed. Georgina's case had 'wholly failed.' Bacon directed judgment to be entered for the defendant and dismissed the action with costs.[32]

Of more lasting significance was Georgina's appearance at the Old Bailey at the end of the following month. Not content with her unexpected victory over Rivière in December, she had continued to harry the conductor, determined to confront him in court yet again. It is impossible to disagree with Edward Grierson, who commented, 'Whatever the rights of [Georgina's] original grievance, her actions against Rivière had become little better than persecutions. She was obsessed with hatred of him. And Rivière returned that hatred.'[33] It was not long before Rivière rose to Georgina's bait. On 13 February 1885 he had her served with a summons for libel. An article by Georgina entitled 'Evil Influence of the Stage', published in *Social Salvation* in June 1883, had included the usual outpouring of abuse against the conductor, and the libels had been repeated in subsequent issues.[34] Georgina's defence was that she had published *Social Salvation* 'without any reason for doing so other than the desire to improve the laws and customs of this country.' The alleged libels were not libels at all, as they were 'neither malicious or [*sic*] scandalous or defamatory.' She wished to be prosecuted so that she could attract the nation's attention to 'the danger and infamy of the Libel and Slander Laws.'[35] Georgina's wish for a further day – or days – in court would soon be granted.

The second trial of *Regina v. Weldon* opened at the Old Bailey on 25 March 1885. The court was 'crammed' with spectators, anticipating several days of knockabout entertainment. They were not to be disappointed. Presenting the case for the prosecution, Montagu Williams said that Rivière had felt compelled to institute proceedings against Georgina because she had made his life a misery. He would prove the publication of the libels, and

32 GWJ, 4–12/2/1885; *Times*, 5–13/2/1885.
33 Grierson, *Storm Bird*, p. 236.
34 GW, *Reports4*, p. 21; GW, *Correspondence*, pp. 236–7; SS, 6/1883, p. 3.
35 GW, *Reports4*, pp. 24–5.

it would then be up to her to prove that they were true and had been published for the public good. In her reply, Georgina began by telling the court that she proposed to describe exactly what had happened when she was tried for libelling Rivière in 1880.[36] The judge immediately told her that they were not sitting as a Court of Appeal and he could not retry the previous case. They all struggled on, with Georgina determined to tell the court all about 'the sea of intrigue which has encircled me for 15 years,' and the judge, Sir William Charley, trying desperately – and not always successfully – to keep her to the point:

GEORGINA: Because I was jolly and good tempered, and gave the sunshine of my life to those who have so little, it is only for that I am persecuted. I was a lady, I went to the best parties, into the very highest society. Because I shut myself up, and because I tried to get justice –

CHARLEY: M. Rivière had nothing to do with that.

GEORGINA: My lord, it is to do with it! You let them go on with their lies without stopping them, and you dare to sit there and see and listen to the agony I am in, and then tell me it is nothing to do with it. How dare you do it? How dare you do it, sir? It is enough to drive me out of my mind to hear you talk like that and constantly interrupting me. I say it is a scandal the way that Judges deal with persons who plead their own causes. My word has never been doubted. I have been in the witness-box over and over again. Men tried to hint that I was a woman of no character, but once again, there was the light of truth, the light of heaven shining on me. These men who sell their tongues, who sell their brains, who sell their pens to tell lies to try and put me down, they know they daren't ask me a question.[37]

After this, Georgina called Rivière himself. She kept him in the box for nearly three days, examining him minutely on his life history and the details of his relationship with her. A torrent of mockery and scorn was poured over the composer's head, as she belittled his talents and questioned his morals. She was enjoying herself. She also took great pleasure in needling Montagu Williams, who was, she believed, a close friend of her husband. At one point

[36] GW, *Reports4*, p. 45.
[37] GW, *Reports4*, p. 51.

she told him: 'Do try and comprehend what the judge has said.' His reply showed the depth of his irritation: 'Mrs Weldon, you teach children, you teach men, and you may teach judges, but don't try to teach me.' She told him not to make his client say 'such silly things'; later she ordered him to 'hold your tongue.' The jury, she added, didn't 'care twopence' for all his 'jargon.'

And so it continued. 'Merry-go-Round' was certain that Georgina would not have got away with her attempts to bully and insult witnesses, counsel and judge if she had not been a woman.[38] As usual, she insisted on reading out every document that could possibly have any connection with the case. Towards the end of the second day she told the judge that she had got as far as 25 May 1879. Charley replied, 'I am very sorry to hear it', and the jury 'gave a kind of groan.' After this, the spectators were entertained by an exchange between the judge and Harcourt, whom Montagu Williams accused of 'keeping up a running commentary in the hearing of the jury.' 'Merry-go-Round' wrote: 'Mrs Weldon's power of abuse can be safely said to be above the average, but she pales before Harcourt, who certainly would not disgrace Billingsgate.' On the following day Harcourt had to be removed from the courtroom by the police after accusing the prosecutors of 'telegraphing' to Rivière, who was still in the witness-box. He was still there at 7 o'clock that evening, when the court finally rose, much to the relief of the judge and jurors, who had already begged Georgina several times to stop reading all her letters and to 'just pick out the pertinent points.'

By Saturday 28 March, the fourth day of the trial, everyone – apart from Georgina – had had enough. Just after ten o'clock the judge told her that she had been wasting the time of the court and gave her notice that he would call upon Montagu Williams to cross-examine Rivière in three hours' time.[39] Needless to say, Georgina was still examining Rivière at one o'clock. Indeed, she was questioning him at four o'clock, when the court was adjourned until the following Monday. Unfortunately for her, her obvious delight in torturing the conductor had alienated many observers. As 'Merry-go-Round' commented: 'A great deal of latitude – perhaps too much – was allowed her, but with the liberal amount of rope allowed her she contrived to strangle herself.'[40]

The reason for Georgina's ultimate downfall, however, was her inability to prove that Rivière was a bigamist. Montagu Williams's final address to the jury was damning. The whole cause of the quarrel between Georgina and Rivière, he said, was 'malice in its very worst degree.' Not one of Georgina's

[38] *Entr'acte*, 4/4/1885, p. 4.
[39] GW, *Reports4*, p. 124.
[40] *Entr'acte*, 4/4/1885.

charges against his client had been proved: they all arose from her 'egregious vanity and an insatiable thirst for notoriety'. She had told Rivière that she was a great musical star who would make his fortune; instead, she had 'utterly failed'. Others, she claimed, had succeeded in the musical profession because they were immoral, not because of their talents. She thought that she was different: 'I am married; I am the most talented artist that ever lived; and because I am the most moral, I cannot succeed.' She had made Rivière's life 'a hell upon earth'. Having been imprisoned once for libelling him, she had 'repeated, and enlarged upon, and repeated' the libels in her 'pretty rag', *Social Salvation*. Finally, Williams asked the jury by their verdict, 'instead of endorsing this title of *Social Salvation*' to 'throw it from you as if it were a leprous thing, and to characterise it as a Social Plague-spot'.

Sir William Charley's language was more temperate, though he did ask the jury to 'recollect how she [Georgina] sprang upon me, almost like a tigress, on the first day, when I stopped her going into the Lunacy Laws'. (Georgina claimed that this was a lie.) He ended by telling them 'It is difficult for me to see how you can avoid coming to the conclusion that she has not successfully shown that [Rivière] was a bigamist'. The jury agreed: they were out for just twenty minutes. Their verdict was 'guilty', though they 'strongly recommended' the defendant 'to the mercy of the court'. The judge sentenced Georgina to imprisonment without hard labour for six months. She also had to enter into recognisances for £100 for her good behaviour for two years. Costs were awarded against her.

Georgina tells us what happened next:

> Mrs Weldon was forthwith taken off to Millbank; undressed; dressed in prison clothes, no underclothing, and kept in a cell for five days and five nights at a temperature between 51 degrees and 56 degrees Fahrenheight, then removed to Holloway Gaol, where she remained till the 21st September 1885.[41]

[41] GW, *Reports4*, pp. 191, 201; *Times*, 26–31/3/1885.

24
Holloway

On Monday 30 March 1885 Georgina was taken straight from the Old Bailey to Millbank Prison, a fortress-like building on the left bank of the Thames, close to Vauxhall Bridge. It was cold, damp and run-down and would be closed in 1890 and then demolished. Angèle visited Georgina on the following day and found her 'dying of cold, she had no *pantalon* [underpants], she was crying and she told me she would die.' There were many who believed that she had got what she deserved. She had, above all, behaved in an unladylike manner:

> Mrs Weldon says 'I'm a lady.' She certainly possesses much talent, and she has enjoyed a good education; but I am not by any means sure that her recent achievements have been those which would be voluntarily attempted by a person who before everything is a lady. When a woman is a lady, the fact does not require anything in the shape of advertisement; it is felt and understood.[1]

Angèle and Harcourt did their best to whip up support, contacting Georgina's friends and all the newspapers they could think of. Harcourt lobbied the members of the jury, nine of whom signed a petition to Sir William Harcourt, the Home Secretary, asking him to remit or alleviate the sentence. One supporter, Pauline Cranstoun, went to Sir William Charley with the request that Georgina should be treated as if she were a 'first class misdemeanant.' This would entitle her to privileges that were usually denied to prisoners who had been convicted of criminal offences. Pauline was successful and Georgina was moved to Holloway after a week.

Holloway had been opened in 1852 as the City of London's House of Correction. Modelled on Warwick Castle, it had pseudo-medieval battlements and turrets and was surrounded by an eighteen-foot-high brick wall. The building could hold up to 400 prisoners, mostly men but with a small number of women as well. As a first class demeanant, Georgina had

[1] *Entr'acte*, 11/4/1885, p. 12.

her own room away from the common prisoners and was not obliged to work. She could buy her own food and wine from outside and wear her own clothes. She could also entertain visitors and write and receive letters without supervision. First-class prisoners were, in short, 'the aristocrats of the gaol.' Their punishment was 'separation from the rest of the world … with no serious discomfort or lasting disgrace.'[2]

To Georgina, Holloway was 'a beautiful place' after the 'awful suffering and privation' that she had been through at 'that vile den,' Millbank, where they had 'actually brought me a bundle of oakum to pick.'[3] At Holloway she had 'such a nice room, warm, bright.' The matron, Miss Maria Jackman, was 'very nice' and lent her a pen and a comb. Georgina and Miss Jackman walked in the 'so-called garden, a very dilapidated affair,' and Georgina went to see the governor, Lieutenant Colonel Everard Stepney Milman, 'a dear old soul, who appears to be bursting with fat, inside and out.'

Some visitors were more welcome than others. Georgina made friends with the prison doctor, Gordon, who was 'very amusing and chatty,' but she took a particular dislike to the locum chaplain, a man called Stubbs. She had 'a quiet row' with him 'as I won't listen to canting stereotyped rubbish about the Word of God.' One of her first visitors was her former adversary Forbes Winslow – now a supporter, in spite of the fact that she had done her best to ruin him. He promised to do what he could to get her out of prison and sent her oil and vinegar. Winslow was as good as his word, appealing to the Home Secretary for a writ of *habeas corpus*. This was refused. John Corbett, MP, asked a question about Georgina in the House of Commons, but it received 'the usual stereotyped answer,' which was greeted with laughter. Another blow came when she was summoned to the governor's office to be presented with a bill of costs (for £170) from Rivière's solicitor, who was none other than her old enemy St John Wontner. This was, she thought, 'quite wrong.' In a letter to two of the jurymen she claimed that she had been found guilty as a result of a conspiracy. Nevertheless, as she informed another juryman, she was determined to continue with her campaigns. He should not grieve about the verdict, as

> I shall probably get a Court of Criminal Appeal and a reform of the libel laws through it, just as by hammering away for seven years I have got the Lunacy Laws amended and the nation's attention thoroughly alive to the dangers we all ran.

2 George Sims, quoted in Caitlin Davies, *Bad Girls* (London, 2018), p. 26. Much of the general information on Holloway is taken from this book.

3 PMG, 23/9/1885, p. 12.

> It is the destiny of reformers to be made martyrs of, and crucified by their countrymen. Barabbas was preferred to Jesus. It will always be so. It is the law of 'Society'.[4]

On the whole, however, she was quite content, writing in her diary, 'I am much happier here than at the office, tormented all day by one thing or another. Here is peace and quietness, and I am able to learn and improve my mind.' Friends brought gifts of plants and food and she soon had a new project. The playwright George Lander brought the first two acts of his play *An Heroic Woman* and she agreed to help him to write a new version, which would include elements of her own life story. She was so excited after his visit that she had to retire to bed with 'a vile headache'. After this, Lander came regularly and they worked on the play together. Georgina soon began to suspect that he was a drunkard, and decided that she did not think much of his dialogue. She could do much better. She worked away at her legal papers too, as she was still hoping to prosecute Rivière for perjury and conspiracy. Her attempt to obtain compensation from Gounod was also moving towards a conclusion.

Georgina's High Court action against the composer in the previous year had not been defended and she had been awarded £1500 for her work as his amanuensis, with £140 for his board and lodging at Tavistock House. The action had been sent to the Middlesex Sheriff's Court for the assessment of the damages claimed by Georgina after the publication in France of a number of 'malicious and defamatory' articles which, she believed, been 'paid for and caused to be published' by Gounod himself. Thus it was that Georgina left Holloway on 7 May, on a writ of *habeas corpus ad testificandum*, and was driven to the court in a carriage, accompanied by the governor and attended by her 'lady-in-waiting', Miss Jackman, with a footman on the box in full uniform. Examined by her counsel, Bowen Rowlands, QC, she denied that there had ever been any 'improper intimacy' between herself and Gounod. She told the composer's counsel, the Hon. Alfred Lyttelton, that 'she ascribed all her domestic unhappiness and troubles to the libellous articles and slanderous statements emanating from M. Gounod, in which there was a not a particle of truth'.[5]

The 'most sympathetic' jury was out for only fifteen minutes. Their verdict was unanimous: they awarded Georgina £10,000 in damages in addition to the £1640 already granted, and her costs.[6] She was overjoyed,

4 GWJ, 6–13/4/1885; GW, *Correspondence*, pp. 261–3.

5 GWJ, 10/4/1885–7/5/1885; *Times*, 8/5/1885.

6 This was thought to be the largest amount given for libel up to that date: F.C. Philips, *My Varied Life* (London, 1914), p. 258.

and the verdict was greeted with 'loud applause' by the crowded court. Outside, she was cheered by 'a large gathering of people', as she was driven away in a cab accompanied by the prison officials. Georgina immediately sent a telegram to her old friend Pierre Gailhard at the Opéra to tell him the 'glorious news'. 'Oh the excitement in Paris and the rage of the old man!' she wrote in her diary that evening. 'I shall be able to get judgment against him in Paris and bother him for the remainder of his life!' On the following day she made a new will, leaving all the money to Angèle, who would be 'quite rich!' Georgina hoped, however, to live to be 'a jolly old lady, 90 years old'.

For the next few weeks the newspapers and magazines were full of articles about Georgina and Gounod. She was delighted, and certain that she would now be able to vanquish all her foes, as she was now 'more celebrated than any actress, vocalist or author'. She was, she believed, now 'spoken of in a breath with Mrs [Elizabeth] Fry and Florence Nightingale' – and they had not had 'one hundredth part of what I have had to contend with'.[7] All this publicity was a great embarrassment for the Home Office, who sent an official to Holloway with a special order for Georgina's release. She refused it 'most obstinately', telling the governor that she would not go unless her sentence was annulled. This was a step too far, and Georgina stayed in the prison. Letters to the newspapers on a variety of subjects kept her in the public eye, however, as the *Glasgow Evening News* reported on 8 August: 'The redoubtable Mrs Weldon, we observe, is not done. She is still in Holloway Jail in body, but in spirit she is outside, free as air, concerned in everything that pertains to the welfare of her country and of her fellow men and women.'[8] She wrote 'desperate' letters about a cockatoo, which had been caught by the chain on its leg on the top of the church steeple opposite her window, and was rewarded by being elected to the Balloon Society. She also received the 'Order of Merit from *Ally Sloper*'. The latter, which puzzled her, took its name from a popular comic strip character.

Georgina kept pot plants in her room and began to make a garden in the prison grounds. Forbes Winslow came regularly, as did Charles Semple, the mad-doctor who had been ordered to pay her damages of £1000 a year earlier. Winslow promised Georgina that he could get 'a mild lunatic' who could live with her and Angèle – a useful source of income, no doubt. In the meantime, the Magna Chartists were making preparations for her release. On 7 August they held a 'grand meeting' at the Crown Tavern at which a committee was formed, with Forbes Winslow as president and Semple as vice-president; the arctic explorer William Parker Snow as Hon. Secretary;

7 GWJ, 7–8/5/1885, 5/6/1885.

8 GWJ, 21/6/1885; *Glasgow Evening News*, 8/8/1885.

and Pauline Cranstoun as treasurer. A third mad-doctor, Edward Rudderforth, was a committee member. Harcourt attended another meeting a fortnight later and 'misconducted himself', so he was turned out. 'I suppose he is mad with rage', Georgina wrote, 'What a real brute he is.'[9]

On 20 August Georgina was 'greatly excited' by the news that Gounod was coming to the Birmingham Music Festival to conduct his new oratorio, *Mors et Vita*. She was torn between her hopes that he would 'grow good and friendly again' and the desire for revenge – and for her £11,640. A few days later the papers the papers reported that the composer had not turned up after all. 'So I have the laugh on my side', Georgina wrote. 'What a good thing not to die of a broken heart! Ha! Ha!' A friend sent her a copy of the *Owl* with a cartoon showing Gounod in France and Georgina in England warning him off. Her triumph was, she thought, 'complete' – though she was still no nearer to getting her money, and she failed in an attempt to have a receiver appointed to collect for her benefit all money due to Gounod from the directors of the Birmingham Music Festival.[10] In a letter to one of the newspapers she claimed that the original idea for *Mors et Vita* was hers. She had, once again, been 'frustrated out of the fruits of all my labours, of all my talent, of all my genius.'[11]

As the day of Georgina's release drew near, there was speculation in the columns of the newspapers as to what she would do next. Everyone agreed that the law courts had been very dull without her. The 'Mrs Weldon Release Committee' made plans for a 'Public Reception and Testimonial' for 22 September, the day she was due to leave Holloway. On the previous day, however, the news came that the Home Office, anticipating trouble, had ordered her immediate release. The governor, who had been ordered to tell no one of the change of plans, gave her his photograph as a parting memento. Georgina and the matron were carried off with all Georgina's luggage to 58 Gower Street, a rented house in Bloomsbury to which Angèle, the orphans and sundry servants had moved from Brixton in June.

The government's attempts to prevent a demonstration of support for Georgina were in vain. On the next day she dressed herself carefully in her best clothes. A friend sent an open barouche (which Georgina described, disparagingly, as 'rather dog-in-front') and four horses, with coachman and groom, and she was driven to Holloway. Outside the closed gates of the gaol, she found a crowd of several thousand people, who had stopped all the traffic. They received her with loud cheers: 'Her friends hurried to greet

9 GWJ, 4–7/8/1885, 21/8/1885.
10 GWJ, 26–8/8/1885.
11 *Nottingham Journal*, 31/8/1885.

her. A tremendous rush of people anxious to get a glimpse of her pushed forward, and swept a mounted policeman, horse and all, along with them. Except that a boy was knocked down and bruised by the horse's feet, no accident occurred.'

Led by the Nottingham Magna Charta Band, they all set off, some carrying banners on which were written slogans such as 'All Honour and Long Life to Georgina Weldon', 'The Brave Exponent of Injustice', 'The Champion of the People's Right' and 'The Heroine of Lunacy Law Reform'. The procession followed a pre-arranged route, along the Thames embankment and up Northumberland Avenue, with cheering spectators at the windows along the way: 'Mothers lifted their offspring shoulder high; fathers shoved and elbowed; costers stood up in their carts; cabbies joked from their boxes; the drivers on their 'buses; invalids were wheeled in their bath-chairs, and all craned their necks to catch a glimpse of Mrs Weldon.'[12] In Piccadilly the horses were taken out of the shafts, and the carriage was 'lugged' to the Reformers' Tree in Hyde Park where Georgina spoke to the crowd. She called for the creation of a Court of Criminal Appeal, 'remarking that it was a disgrace to England that it was the only country boasting of civilisation that had no institution of the kind for the protection of the people'. A resolution to this effect was proposed 'and enthusiastically carried by heaps of people, some say 17,000'. That evening, after a brief rest at 58 Gower Street, Georgina attended a meeting of her Magna Chartist supporters, chaired by Forbes Winslow.[13]

The newspapers were only too pleased to welcome Georgina back. The *Pall Mall Gazette* printed two verses of a 'poem of many stanzas' that she had sent them. One of these begins 'For six long months, through cunning deep as hell, I've been the inmate of a prison cell.' Georgina goes on to describe herself as 'A second Joan of Arc'. Her release was even reported in the *Greenock Telegraph*:

> What with dull trade, duller politics, and the dullest of world's weather which is awaiting us in the immediate future, it was feared that the winter we are now entering upon would be an intolerably flat one; but no. Mrs Weldon, the 'universal genius – the advocate, actress, songstress and orator,' as a London paper styles her – is out of prison, and she will keep the British public merry. Fighting, funny, quaint, enduring, and irrepressible Mrs Weldon! A sort of female Ishmael![14]

12 PMG, 23/9/1885, p. 12.

13 GWJ, 22/9/1885; *Times*, 23/9/1885.

14 PMG, 22/9/1885, p. 3; *Greenock Telegraph*, 23/9/1885, p. 2.

Two days after emerging from Holloway, Georgina went to the Law Courts, where everyone was 'so delighted' to see her. They were to see plenty more of her over the months that followed, as she tried to get new hearings for her multitudinous actions and appeals. She was not short of public support: on 24 September she and Angèle walked from the Old Bailey to the Mansion House, cheered as they went along, with two policemen in front and four behind. For several days there was 'a commotion' wherever she went. This had its disadvantages, as she soon discovered: when she and Angèle went to Peckham Rye in Winslow's carriage they were mobbed by a crowd that Georgina estimated at ten or twenty thousand. The carriage was almost overturned; the horse had to be taken out of the shafts and the police restored order with some difficulty. The theme of the meeting was Georgina's new campaign for a Court of Criminal Appeal. But in spite of the size of the crowd, the collection taken at the meeting produced only £2 4s 4½d. Georgina's interest in the Court of Criminal Appeal seems to have faded after this. Such a court was eventually established in 1907 in the face of opposition from the Home Office and many members of the legal profession.

At the same time Georgina was busy with rehearsals for George Lander's melodrama, which she had completely rewritten, and in which she was to star as the heroine, Hester Stanhope. The play, which was now named *Not Alone*, presented a highly-coloured version of her own dealings with the mad-doctors. Hester Stanhope, was 'an anti-vaccinator, an anti-vivisectionist, a teetotaller, and a vegetarian'. Her husband, Raymond (the villain of the piece), had grown tired of her because she was 'an awful bore':

> She somehow manages to provoke everybody. Her mother never could get her to care about dress or Society. She sang most beautifully, but she was so shy and awkward, her talents were of very little use to her. She had beautiful shoulders and arms; you could not get her to wear a low-necked dress. She had lovely golden brown hair; she cut it off. She was most ridiculously frugal; she would insist on wearing a large kitchen apron.

Hester was a philanthropist, who devoted herself 'morning, noon and night' to teaching (in her husband's words) 'a parcel of dirty gutter children she insists on bringing up as her own'. Raymond, a thinly-disguised version of Harry Weldon, was 'always of a very indolent turn of mind, owing to a torpid liver'. 'I do not think he ever really enjoyed anything, poor fellow', Hester informed one of the mad-doctors, 'I often wished I could have parted with some of my good spirits and energy to him'.[15]

[15] George Lander, *Not Alone* (London, 1886), pp. 10, 19.

The first performance of *Not Alone* was scheduled for 12 October at the Grand Theatre in Birmingham. In addition to Georgina, the company was made up of a mixture of professionals and amateurs, including Lise Gray, who was to be Georgina's understudy, Eva Morand and Sapho. The rehearsals began on 1 October at the Grand Theatre, Islington. All did not go smoothly: Georgina soon fell out with Lander, who objected to her being named as joint author of the play; the theatre was cold; and no one had 'the least idea what the drama is about.'[16] Nevertheless, after rehearsing for just ten days, they all set off for Birmingham, taking with them a hedgehog called Peter, which had a part in the play. Georgina was delighted to find that she was 'splendidly billed.' She thought that the first performance went 'wonderfully' and the newspaper reports on the following day were 'civil.' Perhaps she did not see the review in *The Era*: the critic wrote that 'It would be idle to say that there is not a feeling of relief felt when the piece is over,' though he did commend Georgina's 'many touches of real histrionic ability.' When Eva told her that the theatre manager Charles Wilmot, who came on the third day to see how they were getting on, seemed 'jealous and vexed,' Georgina commented 'I have proved such a success [that he] feels I am quite independent of him.' That evening she was, in her own words, 'quite cheeky' – especially after drinking some gin and lemonade.[17] But in spite of 'capital' performances and 'splendid' houses, the theatre was never full and the takings for the week were disappointing. The hedgehog, which was blind in one eye, died shortly after the last performance, but was soon replaced.

The play ran for six nights in Birmingham, after which Georgina returned to Gower Street on the day before the first London performance, at the Grand Theatre in Islington on Monday 19 October. The critic from *The Era* found the play amusing, but not necessarily for the right reasons, writing, 'It soon became evident that serious consideration of a piece abounding in so much unintentional humour was difficult, if not impossible.' Great hilarity had been occasioned 'by the obvious difficulty of Mrs Weldon, with her no longer sylph-like form, escaping through the high window of the madhouse.' Her costume in the first three acts, 'being of a funereal cast, somewhat accented the liberal style of her figural conformation.' The critic did praise Georgina's 'thoroughly efficient' performance, and thought that she played the heroine's part 'with perfect self-command and *aplomb*.' Over all, there was 'some good work' in *Not Alone*, but the dialogue was often 'fearfully tedious'; some of the lines were absurd; and there was 'a crudeness about the construction of the piece which is, we fear, ineradicable.' *Entr'act*

16 GWJ, 3–4/10/1885.

17 GWJ, 12/10/1885; *Era*, 17/10/1885, p. 14.

and Limelight was less polite: the play was 'rubbish,' and nobody would have gone to see it if the leading actress had not been so notorious. Mrs Weldon should not have been allowed to 'ventilate her grievances and offensively caricature her alleged persecutors on the stage.'[18] The theatre was full on the evenings that followed, but – having received only £22 for her share of the takings in Birmingham – Georgina quickly became convinced that she was being 'robbed.' To make matters worse, she sprained her ankle. That evening she limped through the performance and was 'greatly applauded throughout.' Her benefit performance on the penultimate evening, was 'a complete failure,' and only £46 was taken. She was glad it was all over, though she needed money badly.[19]

~

By this time, the new legal term had begun. At the opening of the Law Courts on 26 October Georgina was 'warmly welcomed by everybody,' and she and Angèle settled down to watch the procession of judges. They included the 'darling' Master of the Rolls, Lord Esher: 'I was applauding him, he caught sight of me, gave such a sweet smile and shook his head at me, as if to say "Oh, you naughty little girl!" I was *so* delighted and I did blush so!' She would have been less delighted if she had heard Lord Esher's comments on her legal career a few months earlier:

> I wish I could say something to prevent this unfortunate person from bringing such a multitude of actions. In respect of some matters she appears to have been harshly used, but she is continually bringing actions without taking any reputable advice, and assuming to conduct them herself without knowing even the rudiments of law, thereby wasting the time of the courts.[20]

Georgina was back in court on 19 November, before Lord Chief Justice Coleridge, for the first day of her long-awaited action against Sir Henry de Bathe for his part in the mad-doctors' affair. Georgina was suing de Bathe for trespass in 'wrongfully entering' Tavistock House on 2 February 1877 in collusion with Harry Weldon and others.' He had also libelled her by telling her husband that the condition of her mind should be enquired into. On 14 April 1878, he had 'falsely and maliciously' signed a request for Forbes Winslow to receive her into his asylum as a person of unsound mind. Furthermore, he had caused her to be 'assaulted and imprisoned'

18 *Era*, 24/10/1885, p. 14; *Entr'acte*, 24/10/1885, p. 4.
19 GWJ, 7/11/1885.
20 GWJ, 26/10/1885; *Times*, 7/5/1885.

on 14 and 15 April, 'in consequence of which, and through his behaviour having caused an irreparable breach between her and her husband', he had deprived her of an income of £300 a year. As a result, Georgina had been 'shunned and avoided by her former friends and the society in which she previously moved, and prejudiced irretrievably in the eyes of the public'. She claimed damages of £10,000. De Bathe's defence was that his entry into Tavistock House in 1877 had not been wrongful, as it was in the possession of Georgina's husband, not Georgina herself. The words he had spoken to Harry Weldon were not actionable and he had not slandered Georgina. The letter to Forbes Winslow had been signed in good faith, without malice, in the belief that his claims were true. Furthermore, Georgina's mother had written to Harry expressing grave doubts as to her daughter's state of mind.

On the first two days Georgina called several witnesses, including her mother and her brother Apsley. They all testified to her sanity and claimed that they had known nothing about the attempt to have her locked up. For the defence, Charles Russell, QC, said that the question was not whether Georgina had been of unsound mind in April 1878, but whether Sir Henry de Bathe 'might reasonably have believed that she was so'. De Bathe had, Russell continued, acted honestly and with none of the bad motives attributed to him, 'but on the contrary believing he had the sanction of her nearest relations'.

On the third day de Bathe himself was examined. He did not make a good impression, becoming confused when asked about his two visits to Georgina in 1877 and 1878. He claimed that he had been 'actuated by no motive but kindness and affection'. Georgina cross-examined him for several hours. She believed afterwards that he had 'damned his own case completely': she had shown him up as a ruffian and had 'turned him inside out'. It soon became apparent that Lord Coleridge was not happy with de Bathe's evidence. When de Bathe referred to Georgina's state of mind 'derived from the strange ideas, the vision, the voices etc', the judge interrupted:

LORD COLERIDGE: But do you think that every one who has ideas different from other people is to be shut up as a lunatic?

DE BATHE: No, certainly not; but if a man had acted as I did – honestly without malice – then he is justified.

LORD COLERIDGE: The mere absence of malice is not enough; there must be reasonable care. You must know, as a man of the world, that many sane people have supposed they had visions?

DE BATHE: Yes, but there were the voices.

Georgina accused de Bathe of failing to make any enquiries before signing the order for her to be carried off to the asylum. His reply, 'I had nothing to do with it,' was too much for the judge, who interrupted again:

Lord Coleridge:	Yes you had, for you signed the order. You were the person who did it; without your signature it could not have been done. It was you who set the proceedings in motion, and if Mrs Weldon had in fact been taken and incarcerated; if a jury should have found that she was not insane, you would certainly have been liable.

De Bathe denied that he had suggested that Georgina should be taken to a lunatic asylum. He had only 'desired that she should be put under care.' The judge's response was damning:

> Lord Coleridge pointed out that the order was for her reception into an asylum; and the asylum of the medical man who filled it up. Without that order she could not have been taken there. 'What a state we should be in if any one could be put into a lunatic asylum on the authority of a friend.'

'I think,' wrote Georgina that evening, 'the Chief is now on my side and rather disgusted with de Bathe.'

The next day was Sunday, but Georgina was back at the Courts before midday on Monday. The building was 'besieged' and both of Georgina's brothers accompanied her. She continued her cross-examination of de Bathe, the 'lying, impudent thief.' Again, Coleridge helped her:

Lord Coleridge:	You knew that one of the reports on which you gave the order was Dr Winslow's own?
De Bathe:	Yes I did.
Lord Coleridge:	Did you know that you were authorizing the imprisonment of Mrs Weldon in the establishment kept by Dr Winslow, on a report drawn up by himself?
De Bathe:	No, that did not enter into my mind.
Lord Coleridge:	It did not! Why, the order you signed is addressed to Dr Winslow?
De Bathe:	Yes it is.

LORD COLERIDGE:	And it authorizes him to receive her into his house.
DE BATHE:	Yes it does.

In the judge's summing-up he stated that there was no evidence as to the alleged trespass or assault. But there remained a very serious question, which demanded the jury's most serious attention. Had de Bathe 'maliciously and unlawfully' asserted that Georgina was of unsound mind? Had he made reasonable enquiries and taken reasonable care to arrive at a just belief?

> He had signed an order for the reception and detention of Mrs Weldon in a lunatic asylum; and if she was not a lunatic a greater or more cruel wrong could hardly be done by one person to another. He was, therefore, doing an act in which he was bound by the most sacred obligation to take the utmost care.

De Bathe would, the judge told the jury, be liable to pay damages if he had signed an order describing Mrs Weldon as insane 'improperly and without due enquiry'. Georgina thought Lord Coleridge had spoken 'infamously, all in de Bathe's favor' and was afraid that she would only get a farthing's damages, but to her astonishment the jury returned with a verdict for her after only half an hour's discussion. They awarded her £1000. Outside the Courts a 'great crowd' was waiting to cheer her. Less than a week later she received de Bathe's cheque, which, as she later discovered, was actually paid by Harry Weldon, who had managed to avoid being called as a witness during the trial.

On 25 November Georgina was back before Lord Coleridge, pursuing yet another action against Rivière. After a lengthy argument on technical points, both sides were persuaded to settle, and all civil and criminal proceedings were thus stopped. 'So there's very little left now', wrote Georgina that evening

> I can now turn my attention to the stage, singing etc. I am very glad, having my talents at my back, to leave litigation. I hope I shall be able to do more by lecturing and acting than I have managed to do in the Courts of Justice. My opinion of Judges and Magistrates remains of the very worst. I am convinced that 'Law' and 'Justice' is a mere market for a certain set of men.[21]

[21] *Times*, 20–4/11/1885; GWJ, 21–5/11/1885.

On the following day, however, Henry Harcourt appeared at Bow Street Police Court, charged with attempting to 'corrupt and influence' the jury during Georgina's action against Rivière in November and December of the previous year. This trial lasted, on and off, for three weeks. The chief prosecution witness was Georgina's former clerk, William Holmes, who now had a grudge against her. Georgina had taken his wife and children into her house earlier in the year, but had eventually got the police to turn them out, as Mrs Holmes was 'constantly drunk and smoked a short black pipe.' Angèle had then dismissed Holmes himself whilst Georgina was in Holloway. Holmes had also made a number of serious allegations concerning the household at 33 Loughborough Road. Angèle and Eva Morand had, he said, performed an abortion on the orphan Pauline; the dog 'carried French letters upstairs,' and 'suet was melted down to be used for unnatural machines.' Georgina 'bribed all the juries and tricked all the panels, and Harcourt gave them all money.' Georgina also discovered that Holmes had informed the Society for the Protection of Women and Children at 85 Strand that she and Angèle kept children for immoral purposes, and 'sold' them. He had told them the stories of the abortion, and the dog. 'In fact,' commented Georgina, he had 'conveyed the idea that we were vile, abominable women.' The society had refused to have anything to do with the case on the grounds that it was due to come into court anyway. Georgina tried, unsuccessfully, to have Holmes summonsed for slander.

On 17 December St John Wontner informed the court that his client, M. Rivière, wished to abide by his agreement with Georgina that they should drop all litigation against each other. 'If the witnesses were cross-examined,' he added, 'matters might be introduced that would lead to an undesirable issue.' With a sigh of relief, Sir James Ingham dismissed the summons against Harcourt 'without comment.' Georgina was 'disgusted' and vowed to 'do something to show up Wontner and Co.'[22]

~

Performances of *Not Alone* in London in December 1885 and January 1886 were poorly attended and the takings failed to cover expenses. Undaunted, Georgina and her company set off on the last day of February for a tour of the provinces which was to last for seven months. They started in Liverpool, where they were met by 'a large crowd hurraing as the train entered the station, and such a fighting and struggling.' They performed *Not Alone* at Carl Rosa's Royal Court Theatre (a 'nice, snug, comfortable theatre') for

[22] *Times*, 18/12/1885; GWJ, 17/12/1885.

the first time on the following evening. It was freezing cold, wet and windy, and the snow ankle deep. Georgina found that none of the cast knew their lines properly and decided that they were 'a bunch of idiots'. The audience was not enthusiastic and there was the occasional 'ripple of seemingly inexplicable laughter'. Unruffled, Georgina 'serenely' performed her part 'with the greatest good nature'. One critic thought that she exhibited 'much intention and aptitude' and could become 'an artist of wide range and ample force' if her mind were less occupied elsewhere.[23] The takings were, however, still disappointing, and they remained so for the rest of the tour, which took them to Scotland, Wales, and a number of towns in central and south-west England. They stayed in most towns for a week, usually moving on Sunday, and sleeping in hotels or lodgings, many of which were cold and inadequately furnished. Georgina soon began to wish that she could return home. The life of a touring actor was, she told Angèle, 'the most tiresome, the most odious that one can imagine'. It was made even worse by the fact that they were not earning anything. It was 'enough to kill you'.[24] She was also critical of her fellow actors, especially the men. One was 'idiotic', another 'vulgar and offensive'. A third was 'simply vile'. One of the stage managers told her that they were all 'well known fossils'. 'They are worse than that', she commented, 'No museum would care to have any part of them'.[25] One of the 'fossils', Gervan Clifford, who played the anti-hero Raymond Stanhope, dropped dead suddenly in Paisley and was replaced by his understudy, Charles Sennett, whom Georgina loathed. Sennett was 'atrocious, an abortion, a toad on two crooked legs.' If they could not get rid of him, she told Angèle, there would soon be two more dead, 'as I shall assassinate him and then be hung'.[26]

In a few places, however, the tour resembled a triumphal progress. In Manchester Georgina was greeted at the station by 'a demonstrative public welcome', with a band in uniform and a carriage drawn by four grey horses. Thousands of people cheered her as she was driven to the Grand Hotel, and listened to her as she spoke from a window. That evening she lectured to a large audience at the Prince's Theatre on her experiences in the law courts. The reporter for the *Manchester Times* wrote that her 'manner was unconstrained and natural, and her clear voice was heard in all parts of the theatre'. She sang well, though the lecture itself was 'of somewhat invertebrate construction'. But he did not think much of *Not Alone*, which he

23 GW–AM, 1/3/1886; *Stage*, 5/3/1886, p. 10.
24 GW–AM, 26/3/1886.
25 GWJ, 20,26/3/1886.
26 GW–AM, 20–2/5/1886.

thought weak.[27] In Cardiff, the theatre critic of the *South Wales Daily News* wrote Georgina a letter in which he gave an honest appraisal of the play and Georgina's own acting:

> I am sorry to see that you do not find your provincial tour the success you expected. The friends who advised you to tour could not have known much about provincial taste, nor the inconveniences so disagreeble to a cultured lady, which are attendant upon the horrid dressing rooms usually found in provincial theatres (e.g. Swansea) and the dismal lodgings one has to put up with. The weakness in *Not Alone* is the piece, *not* Mrs Weldon. Without you, it would not pay expenses in any town.
>
> On the stage you studiously avoid acting, you imagine yourself in your own drawing room, you are a lady, and you think that behaving in a ladylike manner, without trick of voice or gesture, you will please the public. I grant that theoretically you are right, but the British public, that is the pit and gallerys [*sic*] who are the *paying* public, love to see things a bit idealised, and as they pay, they must be considered.
>
> As you have no doubt discovered, there is much in the theatrical art that is hideous sham, seen behind the footlights. Nothing is more feigned, and yet nothing is more absolutely essential to success than the complete obliteration of the individual in the presentation of a part.[28]

The idea of self-obliteration was, of course, entirely alien to Georgina.

Other critics were more complimentary. The reporter for the *Western Mail* wrote that Georgina had 'an excellent presence, a most pleasing face, and a highly cultivated voice'. Her acting was 'marked throughout by conscious power and dignity, and shows, moreover, considerable mastery of pathos and passion'. During a lengthy interview for the same newspaper, which was published in Cardiff, Georgina clearly felt the need to emphasise her Welsh roots: though she admitted that she herself had not been born in Wales, she claimed that her parents, uncles and aunts had all been born in the Principality. In fact they had all been born in London. She also claimed that she had been able to speak Welsh 'very fluently' a few years ago 'but feared that she was losing her command of the language'. There is no indication that she had ever known more than a few words, though she had learned some Welsh songs.[29]

27 GWJ, 23–9/5/1886; *Manchester Times*, 29/5/1886, p. 7.

28 J.J. Bisgood–GW, 16/9/1886.

29 *Western Mail*, 14/9/1886, p. 3.

As she travelled, Georgina collected a growing menagerie. In addition to the hedgehog Peter II (which refused to unroll itself) she acquired three marmosets and a white rat. Her decision to take the marmosets on stage with her was not entirely successful, as at least two critics mistook them for rats. In Birmingham she bought 'two little hedgehogs (one dying, blind etc.)' from 'a wretched little stinking Genoese'.[30] One of the new hedgehogs promptly died, and Peter tried to kill the other. It was not long before that one died too. In Plymouth she added a canary to her collection, and by the end of the tour she had a kitten as well.

In July Georgina bought a tricycle from the Humber bicycle company. This was soon in all the newspapers, and she was interviewed by a reporter from the *Cyclist* magazine. In Coventry she rode the tricycle three times round the racecourse. She was, she thought, 'getting on nicely' and the exercise was good for her, though she was stiff and lame at first. She attracted a good deal of attention when cycling to the theatres and back to her lodgings. She often fell off and hurt herself. One evening in Swansea she appeared on stage covered in arnica and bandages, and had to be carried on and off again.[31] She was later elected to the Swansea Cycling Club and the Cyclists' Touring Club.

The tour ended in Coventry on 25 September. On the last night they took only £10: it was a 'vile house and noisy'. This was, Georgina wrote: 'A sorry ending to a sorry beginning and an unlucky tour, which they are all very sorry was over. I am very glad. I wanted to gauge the British public in all ways and see if I can depend on anything ever so small.'[32] But she was not going home at once: instead she embarked on a four-week lecture tour, which took her to Birmingham and then Nuneaton, where the receipts were meagre due to the rival attraction of Wombwell's Menagerie. And so it continued, at Market Harborough, Lichfield, Burton-on-Trent (where they encountered Wombwell's Menagerie again) and Nantwich. From there Georgina travelled via Crewe to Anglesey to visit her old servants Robert and Mary Hughes in Holyhead. From the train she looked out for 'all the old spots', Conway Castle, Bangor, and the red light at Penmon lighthouse. She thought she saw the lamp opposite 'my dear little old cottage' at Tros-yr-afon

> and the tears came in my eyes to think how all there seemed the same … all human beings so changed, and I a sorrow-stricken weary woman nearly 50, so different to the bright lovely young creature who lived so

30 GWJ, 9/8/1886.

31 *Western Mail*, 15/9/1886, p. 2; GWJ, 9–11/9/1886.

32 GWJ, 26/9/1886.

> many years so poor and so contented, believing she had saved from ruin and redeemed for life the miserable sneaking cur she had the generous folly to marry.[33]

Robert and Mary were at the station in Holyhead to meet her and she spent two happy days talking of old times before setting off on her travels again. The audiences were almost uniformly 'wretched'. Georgina finally arrived back at 58 Gower Street in the early hours of 23 October.

[33] GWJ, 2/10/1886.

25
Gower Street

Georgina's tour of the provinces had been, as she herself admitted, 'a complete failure'. As usual, she believed that this was the fault of the journalists and critics who had libelled and boycotted her, and the theatre managers who had failed to advertise her properly.[1] The next three years were to see a series of increasingly desperate attempts to keep herself in the public eye and to air her many grievances. The costs of her unsuccessful legal battles mounted up and she desperately needed to supplement her income of little more than £600 a year.

At first Georgina's confidence in her popularity in London seemed to be well founded. On 8 November (1886) she 'went off gaily on my tricycle and got quite safe to the Law Courts'. She spent the day there until, according to *The Times*:

> About 4 o'clock considerable commotion was caused outside the main entrance of the Royal Courts of Justice by the appearance of Mrs Georgina Weldon on a tricycle, on which was painted in large letters 'Mrs Weldon's Crystal Tricycle'. It appears that on the conclusion of her business at the Courts Mrs Weldon was on her way to a rehearsal at Sanger's Amphitheatre, where she is to appear on Thursday next as Sargent Buzfuz in the sketch of '*Bardell* v. *Pickwick*'. So large a crowd, however, had been attracted by the appearance of the tricycle in the Strand bearing her name that her progress thereon was entirely stopped, and she was obliged to abandon her vehicle to the care of a friendly cabman and take refuge within the Courts again.[2]

For the next eighteen months or so she found it easy to get engagements in London music halls. In December she appeared for five nights at Deacon's in Clerkenwell, 'a beastly *bouge* [dump]'. The audiences there were disappointing. She was more successful in Peckham early in the following

1 SC, *Weldon v. Weldon*, 1888.

2 *Times*, 9/11/1886.

Fig. 27. Georgina Weldon and 'that devilish cat' Angèle Ménier in fancy dress, 1887. Cabinet card by Elliott and Fry of Baker Street.

year. The house was 'packed, immensely enthusiastic'. She sang Gounod's 'Oh! dille tu!' and her own composition, 'Song of the sparrow', with 'Annie Laurie' as an encore. On the same evening she went on to Shoreditch and sang 'I can't get my conjugal rights', a comic song which had been written specially for her.[3] A total of twenty-one engagements in March brought in nearly £100 and she was optimistic that she would be able to earn a decent living from her public appearances.[4]

3 She had bought it from Charles Dubois a year earlier.

4 GWJ, 19/3/1887.

For many years, Georgina had been on the periphery of the London theatrical world. Now, for a short while, she moved closer to its centre. Most significantly, she renewed her friendship with 'Nelly Watts', now the famous actress Ellen Terry. Ellen sent Georgina 'a nice affectionate little note' towards the end of 1886 and then gave her tickets for a box at the Lyceum Theatre early in the following year. Georgina and Angèle went to a performance of W.G. Wills' highly successful adaptation of Goethe's *Faust* on 14 January. The *mise en scène* was 'most splendid' and Ellen was 'so pretty and nice as Margaret'. Georgina had never admired the acting of Henry Irving, who played the part of Mephistopheles. She found him 'incomprehensible', but had to admit that 'as it is a grotesque part it is a good, or rather bearable, part for him'.[5] She and Angèle also attended Ellen's benefit performance at the Lyceum on 13 June. The play was *Much Ado about Nothing*: Ellen was 'quite charming' as Beatrice, and Irving 'tho' with his usual tricks' was 'very quaint and funny as Benedick'. Afterwards, they went onto the stage, where refreshments were provided and everybody was 'very cordial'. They talked to Laura Richards, whom Georgina introduced to Irving, and saw Ellen's sister Kate Lewis 'looking well, with three hideous daughters'. Ten days later they enjoyed *Much Ado about Nothing* again, from the 'best box', which Irving had given them. This time, Georgina was less impressed by his performance: 'Strange, Irving, who is so thoughtful and clever, should be such a bad actor – bad walk, bad movements, bad voice!!! Marvellous! Nellie exquisite. She came and had a little chat and said she was quite jealous because I had got the boxes from Irving and not from her!'

A few weeks later, Georgina and Angèle joined about fifty others on a trip to Hampton Court. It was a 'most delightful' day and they enjoyed themselves 'frantically'. Georgina's new friends were a Bohemian crowd, of whom the rest of her family would certainly have disapproved. 'I don't believe they are a bit worse than people in the highest Society', Georgina wrote' 'but there's less disguise about it and consequently [less] humbug.' Before long, however, she began to find it difficult to keep up with them. On 12 August she sang 'Annie Laurie' at the Cambridge Music Hall, at a benefit for the popular star Jenny Hill, and then attended a supper party which went on to 'an ungodly hour'. She did not get to bed until four o'clock the following morning. 'How strong people must be to be able to rake', she wrote in her diary that evening. On the next day there was another trip to Hampton Court. 'It was a lovely day', she commented, 'but I got very tired, thanks to yesterday morning. In fact, one must have an ox's constitution to go on as these people do, and how they drink!'[6]

[5] GWJ, 14/1/1887.

[6] GWJ, 13/6/1887–14/8/1887.

Georgina had been elected to the Balloon Society during her stay in Holloway, and she and Angèle occasionally attended meetings in London. In May 1887 she actually went up in a balloon for the first – and only – time, with her old friend, the 'aeronaut' Joseph Simmons. It was Whit Monday and she had been engaged to sing to the crowds gathered in the Montpellier Gardens in Cheltenham. The day did not start well: it was icy cold and she was 'nearly frozen to death' at the rehearsal. But everything went off 'very well indeed'. By her reckoning there were more than 8,000 people there during the day, and 12,000 in the evening. Newspaper reports described Georgina as the 'chief attraction' of the event. Wearing a dress of red Suarah silk under a handsome mantle of crimson plush, with a cream-coloured bonnet, she 'gave the effect of juvenility and old-fashionedness combined'. Many ladies declared that it was worth paying an extra sixpence to get a better view. Georgina sang four of her favourite songs and then made a captive ascent, during which she first sat in the car and then stood up to give her audience a better view. With the balloon still in the air, the basket was towed around the gardens so that everyone could see her. She stayed that evening to watch the fireworks, and eventually retired to bed, too tired to sleep well, but 'delighted with the success'.[7] A year later, Simmons was killed when his balloon crashed.[8]

In February 1887 Georgina met the soap manufacturer Thomas Barratt, a partner in the firm A. and F. Pears. Barratt, 'the father of modern advertising', had pioneered the use of celebrity endorsements to advertise Pears' Soap. Georgina was delighted when he offered to take her to be photographed 'and stick me in all the busses like Mrs Langtry and [Miss May] Fortescue'. This was, she thought 'My last chance'. If only Pears' Soap advertised her properly, she would get plenty of engagements. She composed a testimonial, 'MRS GEORGINA WELDON WRITES, 24 May 1887, "I am 50 to-day, but thanks to Pears' Soap my COMPLEXION is only 17". By mid November the advertisement was in all the omnibuses. 'It looks very nice, I think', wrote Georgina, but 'few people think it good enough.' Although she believed that it did her 'a deal of good' her diaries suggest that requests for her to sing and lecture came in less and less frequently from the middle of 1888.[9]

~

7 GWJ, 30/5/1887; *Cheltenham Examiner*, 1/6/1887, p. 8.

8 GWJ, 28/8/1888.

9 T.F.G. Coates, 'Mr Thomas J. Barratt, "The father of modern advertising"', *Modern Business*, September 1908, pp. 107–15; GWJ, 31/3/1887, 26/11/1887, 16/4/1888.

Fig. 28. Georgina Weldon in an advertisement for Pears' Soap, 1887.

During this time Georgina also continued to act as an unofficial legal adviser, especially to victims of the mad-doctors. The campaign to reform the Lunacy Laws had been vigorously pursued during the 1880s by Georgina, the Lunacy Law Reform Association, and other societies such as the Magna Chartists. A number of bills had been introduced into parliament, but none had been passed. Georgina had watched their progress with interest, claiming (somewhat prematurely) in 1880 that the inclusion of the Lunacy Laws in the Queen's Speech was 'a great triumph for me.' In 1886 she studied the new Lunacy Law Amendment bill carefully, and wrote to the newspapers objecting to a clause prohibiting civil or criminal action against a mad-doctor for locking up a lunatic, so long as he had acted 'in good faith and with reasonable care.' She was not at all happy with the bill that was to become the 1890 Lunacy Act, commenting that 'the principal thing they have contrived is extra protection for the Doctors.'[10] The 1890 Act did, nevertheless, oblige those petitioning for lunacy orders to justify their request before a magistrate. The new rules also expressly prohibited any kind of relationship between the petitioners and the doctors; between the doctors themselves; and between any of these and the manager of the institution where the alleged lunatic was to be confined.

The alleged lunatics who sought Georgina's advice at this time included Louisa Tanfani, who had been confined in lunatic asylums in the early 1860s. She had married an Italian, Achille Tanfani, in 1869 and the two had settled in Rome. In 1878 Louisa's trustee, her elder sister Adelaide, had informed Signor Tanfani that his wife was a lunatic, and had taken Louisa to London by force. Louisa had then been held in Forbes Winslow's asylum in Hammersmith for four months, until the Commissioners in Lunacy ordered her release. In 1886, after contacting Georgina, Louisa sued Winslow for damages, but lost. She then tried to sue Frederick Spurgin, one of the doctors who had certified her, for culpable negligence. The judge ruled that there was no case to answer, because too much time had passed between her release from the asylum and the commencement of her action against Spurgin. Egged on by Georgina, Louisa tried to appeal, but had to give up because of the expense. Georgina was disgusted, describing Louisa as 'an idiot' and commenting unsympathetically 'I should say she would end her days in a lunatic asylum, and serve her right!'[11]

Another former inmate of an asylum was Arthur Irwin, a retired surveyor of taxes who had married a barmaid, Nora Collins, in 1883. Irwin had lost money after the marriage by gambling on the Stock Exchange. When, early

[10] GWJ, 6/2/1880, 14/4/1889; PMG, 18/2/1887, p. 11.

[11] Louisa Tanfani–GW, 8/2/[1885]; *Times*, 9–10/11/1886, 1/12/1886; GWJ, 16/2/1887.

in 1887, he had been found unconscious after taking a sleeping draught, it was suspected that he had tried to commit suicide. He had been taken, first to a hospital, and then to a lunatic asylum where he had stayed for six months, eventually being discharged into the care of his wife. Shortly after his return home, he had discovered a number of letters that indicated that his wife had been having an affair with a married solicitor, John Granville Layard. As the affair had clearly been going on for several months, Irwin began to suspect that his wife and Layard had colluded to have him removed from the scene. He was subsequently to claim that, far from trying to kill himself, he had been deliberately poisoned by his wife.

Georgina met Arthur Irwin for the first time at the end of October 1887. Believing that he had been hard done by, she tried to help him. She hired a van and, with Irwin, Harcourt and four other men, made 'a splendid raid' on the Irwins' house in Hammersmith, carrying off some of the furniture and several letters from Layard to Nora Irwin, 'clearly proving adultery on many occasions.' Two days later, with Georgina's help, Irwin filed a petition for divorce from his 'little impudent brazen-faced hussy of a barmaid.' He moved into 58 Gower Street, but proved to be a difficult guest, arguing constantly with Harcourt and being 'greedy, mean and ungrateful.' Georgina quickly decided that he was intolerable.[12] When the case reached the Divorce Court on 11 July 1888, Layard's counsel announced that his client would not deny adultery, but denied any involvement in Irwin's confinement in a lunatic asylum. Nora Irwin accused her husband of cruelty and refused to state whether she had committed adultery. Her counsel, however, did not dispute the accusation. The jury awarded Arthur Irwin damages of £750 and the judge pronounced a decree *nisi*.[13]

On the following day, a highly coloured account of the court proceedings appeared in the *Pall Mall Gazette*. Georgina was 'heartily congratulated' on her 'brilliant success.' When the police had refused to do anything to help Arthur Irwin, Mrs Weldon had taken the case in hand: she

> rescued the injured husband, ran to earth the guilty wife, burst open by crowbars and sledge-hammers her place of retreat, unearthed the man who sold the drug [allegedly used to poison Irwin], maintained the husband until his case could be heard, and finally, yesterday, had the rare satisfaction of compelling the Court to admit that the case had been proved up to the hilt.[14]

[12] GWJ, 28/11/1887, 6–7/12/1887, 5/2/1888.

[13] *Times*, 12/7/1888; GWJ, 11/7/1888.

[14] PMG, 12/7/1888, p. 4.

In the following year Layard and 'the hussy, whore and poisoness' Nora Irwin sued the *Pall Mall Gazette* for alleging that they had 'conspired together to shut up a sane man in a lunatic asylum and take his money'. The jury awarded damages of £1000 to Nora Irwin and £500 to Layard. They also won £300 each in a similar action against another magazine, *Modern Society*.[15] As for Arthur Irwin, Georgina threw 'the old beast' and his furniture out of her house a week after the Divorce Court hearing in 1888.

~

Amongst the most regular (and most surprising) visitors to 58 Gower Street at this time were the two mad-doctors, Forbes Winslow and Charles Semple, both of whom were now down on their luck, at least partly as a result of Georgina's legal actions against them. Winslow had other problems as well: from 1881 to 1885 he had been involved in a number of actions in the Court of Chancery, as a result of which he had been forced to retire from the position of manager of his family's lunatic asylums without receiving any kind of compensation. By the end of 1885 he was bankrupt. Georgina, who thought that he was 'law mad', felt sorry for him, and tried to help him.[16] With little work to occupy him, Winslow took to writing comic songs. Georgina would sing two of these songs, 'Three old girls at law' and 'Am I not the lawyers' friend?' during her music hall performances. The words have unfortunately not survived. Winslow was useful as a companion at the Law Courts and on the occasional theatre visit, but Georgina never had a very high opinion of him, describing him as 'a shuffling booby'. In the second half of 1888 he had a new interest: the hunt for the Whitechapel murderer, 'Jack the Ripper'. As a well-known alienist, he believed that he was qualified to assist in the search for 'some kind of frightful madman', but the police treated him as 'an ordinary member of the public, a crankish amateur sleuth'.[17]

Like Winslow, Charles Semple looked to Georgina for help and support. One of his daughters, born in May 1886, was named Georgina Angèle and he asked Georgina to be godmother.[18] If Winslow was 'law mad', Semple was 'music mad', coming to Georgina for singing lessons and even performing with her on several occasions. Semple may have hoped to supplement his income from his dwindling medical practice, as he was 'absolutely penniless' by this time, and was declared bankrupt in February 1887. His main

15 GWJ, 4/4/1889; *Times*, 5/4/1889.

16 GWJ, 25/1/1886.

17 GWJ, 17/3/1888; Molly Whittington-Egan, *Doctor Forbes Winslow* (Great Malvern, 2000), pp. 170–1.

18 GWJ, 14/5/1886.

creditor was Georgina herself – he still owed her the £1020 in damages for libel and trespass that she had been awarded as a result of her sensational legal action against him in July 1884.[19]

Semple's wife died in March 1887. Two days later he came to dinner at 58 Gower Street. Georgina was rather shocked when the grieving widower sang and played the piano, while his wife was 'lying unburied, blood gushing out of her nose, ears, mouth etc.!' Nevertheless, she suggested that Semple and his four young daughters should move in with her and Angèle. They all arrived at the beginning of April, with all their furniture and other belongings, and Semple's 'sole remaining lunatic', Fanny Blenkin. Georgina soon began to have second thoughts: Miss Blenkin gave no trouble, but the children were 'insufferable' and Semple drank.[20] He was also lazy and reluctant to practise his piano playing or singing, so that he sang 'like a pig' and accompanied her 'vilely'. Of course, it all ended in tears. The children left in August without saying goodbye to anyone, after which Semple made several unsuccessful attempts to retrieve Miss Blenkin, a comparatively wealthy woman. Miss Blenkin stayed with Georgina until mid September, when she was taken to Burgess Hill. As for Semple himself, Georgina decided that he was 'an evil, mean, low, dishonest, lazy cur', one of the 'heartless beasts' who took in lunatics for money and looked on them as 'so much cattle'.[21]

At the beginning of 1888 Georgina issued a writ against W.H. Smith and Son, asking for £10,000 for 'false and malicious libels' because they had sold a weekly journal called *Men and Women* and a book entitled *Great Musical Composers* at their bookstall at Euston Station.[22] Both publications included accounts of Georgina's relationship with Gounod. Moreover, she claimed, Smith's had since 1871 'sold, published and circulated' a great quantity of 'absolutely false, wilful, malicious and injurious notices and articles', which held her up to 'public ridicule, contempt, hatred and derision'.[23] To her astonishment, the counsel for the booksellers admitted in court that some parts of *Great Musical Composers* were libellous, and said that his clients 'deeply regretted that they should, however innocently, have been made the means of diffusing a book containing these passages'. 'I hope this triumph will be the means of grabbing £8,000', Georgina wrote in her diary. As usual, she was to be disappointed, though she did eventually

19 *Times*, 6/4/1887.
20 GWJ, 27/3/1887–9/4/1887.
21 GWJ, 26/8/1887.
22 The book was written by George T. Ferris.
23 SC, *Weldon v. W.H. Smith and Son*, 1888.

receive £500 and her costs.[24] In the meantime, however, she was still very hard up, writing in mid May, 'We are getting very low in funds. What ever shall we do if we cannot soon get in something from the libels I know not. Utter smash and ruin.'[25]

At the end of May, Georgina went before 'that fiend' Lord Coleridge again. The plaintiff in this case was nominally Angèle Ménier, while the defendants were Georgina and her husband. It is, however, clear that the pleadings had all been drawn up by Georgina, and that the purpose of the action was to get money out of Harry. Angèle claimed damages for the breach of an agreement she had entered into with Georgina in 1877, and compensation for the loss of her goods when Tavistock House had been cleared in 1880. Unusually, they managed to get Harry Weldon into court, where he 'put a bold front on the matter, and [made] an appearance looking bloated, stiff and beastly.' He stated that he knew nothing about the agreement of 1877 and had never given his wife any authority to enter into a contract on his behalf or to act as his agent. After three days, the judge summed up 'in complete sympathy with the kind, noble and generous Weldon' and 'of course, the asinine jury gave an immediate verdict for him.' Harry had won, and Georgina had to pay him his costs which came to £210 13s 1d. She sent him a cheque for £150, which was returned, and eventually, very reluctantly, she sent the whole sum in cash. The payment to Harry absorbed a large chunk of the £500 from W.H. Smith and Georgina was soon short of money again. She wrote to Lord Wimborne, the elder brother of her former admirer Merthyr Guest, offering to sell him Watts's portrait of her. A sale was agreed in the autumn and Lord Wimborne sent her £500. 'Now we are safe for one year', Georgina wrote on 18 October. She soon needed the money, for another attempt to get damages (£10,000) from James Neal ended in failure and she was ordered to pay her opponent's costs.[26]

On Monday 12 November, three years after they had agreed to abandon all actions against each other, Georgina and Jules Rivière met in court for what was to be the final round of their epic struggle. The judge on this occasion was 'that vile old devil' Mr Baron Huddleston. This time Georgina was demanding damages from Rivière, Henry Harcourt and William Holmes for 'an alleged conspiracy to defame her character and ruin her position in the musical profession.' She opened her case by referring back to the prosecution of Harcourt for bribing her juries in November and December 1885. This was, she claimed, a sham, the result of a conspiracy to defame her. Harcourt admitted under cross-examination that he had

[24] *Times*, 13/4/1888; GWJ, 12/4/1888.
[25] GWJ, 12/5/1888; SC, *Weldon v. Weldon*, 1888.
[26] Lord Wimborne–GW, 18/10/1888; GWJ, 18,26,29/10/1888; *Times*, 27,30/10/1888.

conspired with the other defendants, but said that he had done it 'for a good purpose and in order to save his benefactress', and that he was not ashamed of it. The jury did not believe a word of this, and Georgina's case was not helped by the fact that her witnesses kept contradicting each other. The jury found for the defendants and Lord Huddleston gave judgment with costs to Rivière, Holmes and Mrs Holmes, and without costs to Harcourt 'because I consider that he was only made a defendant by Mrs Weldon in order to assist her in this disgraceful case.' The judge then went on to say that 'in all his experience he had never before tried so scandalous and disgraceful a case in all its particulars.' He had a public duty to perform, he said, 'and would be wanting in courage and firmness if he shrank from that duty.' He agreed with the jury that Harcourt and his witnesses were lying, and suggested that the witnesses had been 'induced to come here and support this incredible story by some indirect means.' Finally, the judge gave his opinion that the Treasury should charge Georgina, Harcourt and their witnesses with perjury or conspiracy, or both. It was, he added, his duty to take care that the public were protected from what, in his judgment, was 'a most scandalous conspiracy.' Georgina asked Huddleston to stay execution as she intended to appeal, but he immediately refused. Georgina, who had expected to be nonsuited, was stunned, whilst Angèle was 'fearfully excited.'[27]

Two of the witnesses called at 58 Gower Street a few days later. They promised to help Georgina to 'hold meetings, raise defence funds and get old Huddleston turned off the Bench if possible.' Georgina thought that it was 'really almost a joke, when one considers that the Royal Courts of Justice is quilted with perjury, that I should be accused!' On the following day her 'contemptible old mother' sent her maid to Gower Street to beg Georgina to escape to Holland. Georgina was as defiant as usual: 'Ha! Ha! Me run away!! I sent her a piece of my mind.' She was disappointed to find that the affair was not reported in the newspapers. Before long she was informed that Rivière was claiming £167 for costs, whilst William Holmes wanted £88.

In mid November Georgina became convinced that her creditors were paying men to watch the house. She hardly dared to go out, and gave orders to her servants to let no one in unless they knew who they were. At the end of the year she wrote despairingly in her diary: 'I have failed in everything and been put to frightful expense. I owe no end of money to Mayo [her printer] – see no hopes of any settlement, can get no engagement, only keep pretty well by dint of constant care. What shall I do?'[28] The only good news was that the Treasury had declined to take any action against her for

[27] GWJ, 9,12–15/11/1888; *Times*, 16/11/1888.

[28] GWJ, 17–18/11/1888, 1,29/12/1888.

perjury or conspiracy. She returned to her attempts to win damages for libel. These were largely unsuccessful, though she did manage to get £100 in cash out of the printers of *Men and Women*.[29]

~

Georgina's office in Red Lion Court had been given up during her stay in Holloway in 1885. After her return from her theatrical tour in the following year, therefore, she spent much more time at 58 Gower Street with Angèle and the children, and an ever-changing assortment of servants and hangers-on. This led to renewed tension and disputes between Georgina and Angèle, who had previously taken on most of the responsibility for managing the household with little interference from Georgina. By now, she had largely lost interest in her two remaining orphans, Pauline and Sapho, who were aged about seventeen and twelve respectively. Both girls left Gower Street in the following year. According to Georgina, Angèle had been plotting to get rid of them for several months because they 'knew too much about her'. Many years later, Georgina discovered that Sapho and Pauline had both been terrified of Angèle. They 'trembled in all their limbs, enough to make them feel ill, just to hear her at a distance. She frightened them horribly, threatening them with all kinds of horrible things that I would do to them'.[30]

Sapho, who had always been Georgina's favourite, would reappear later on. But at this time Georgina showed much more interest in her menagerie, which continued to grow in spite of some unfortunate losses. After all the marmosets had died, she consoled herself by breeding canaries, though both adults and babies showed an alarming tendency to expire suddenly. She also acquired two pugs, Binnie and Judge, both of which proved to be more durable.[31] For a while she had a newt and some fish, none of which survived very long. A grey parrot called Polly flew away after a few months and was never seen again. Then, early in 1889, Georgina acquired two monkeys: a small female that she named Tittileelee and a male called Dagobert. She spent much of her time in the garden of 58 Gower Street, enlisting the assistance of her shorthand clerk George Faithfull, a washerwoman's son. Faithfull did not know much about plants, but he was obliging and useful for digging holes and trimming trees and shrubs. There was also a new friend, Thomas Titley, a chemist who had been sentenced

29 GWJ, 16–17,20/2/1889, 6/3/1889; *Times*, 18,21/2/1889.

30 GWM, ii, pp. 176–7, GWM, v, p. 3.

31 Her two old pugs, Dan Tucker and Jarba, had both been put to sleep in 1875 and buried in the garden at Tavistock House.

to eighteen months' hard labour in 1880 for 'having unlawfully supplied certain noxious drugs for the purpose of procuring abortion.' He knew about dogs and monkeys, and was helpful when Georgina's animals fell ill.

Harcourt, too, proved to be surprisingly useful. He 'loved' gardening and helped Georgina to sow seeds and tidy up. She also employed him to spy on Harry and his mistress, and 'nearly died of laughter' when Harcourt turned up in disguise:

> I went into the hall and beheld a tall, thin, scraggy man, close shaven with a very black waxed moustache, black hair, green goggles, a fishing rod in his hand and a fish basket on his side. Very well dressed – a fishing cap on his head – I began by asking this gentleman what he wanted, whereupon he burst into loud laughter and I recognised … Harcourt!!!

He was, she wrote, 'an admirable detective' – 'his patience was marvellous. He was scrupulously honest. His enquiries were very cheap. Where a professional detective would have cost £10, he spent £1.'[32] Harcourt's loyalty led Georgina to overlook his belligerence and weakness for strong drink.

~

This period of comparative peace did not last long. Angèle had now become 'a female nightmare, a monster'; there were tantrums and rows and she appeared to be 'demented.' She left for France in July, taking Lydia, the youngest of the Morand sisters, with her. The excuse for this visit was a desire to visit the *Exposition Universelle*, the World Fair on the Champ de Mars, the entrance to which was the newly-built Eiffel Tower. Angèle did not ask Georgina to go with her. The inhabitants of 58 Gower Street were all glad to see her go. They had been longing to tell Georgina to throw her out, but had believed that she was entirely in her friend's power. Now they began to talk, and Georgina listened. She was 'astounded,' especially when their stories were confirmed by her former servant, Elizabeth Villiers. Angèle had, they all told her, frequently boasted of her power over Georgina, claiming that she had papers and letters that could have her friend 'shut up for life.' 'I've got her! I've got her in my hands,' Angèle had gloated. It was she who was mistress of the house, and Georgina could not turn her out even if she wanted to. 'They pitied me,' Georgina wrote, 'for being in the power of such an old bat.' They all told her that they would leave if Angèle ever came back again.[33]

[32] GWJ, 9/2/1888; proof of GWM, vii, pp. 59–69.

[33] GWM, ii, pp. 40, 181, 186, 201; GWM, v, pp. 1–5

A search of Angèle's room produced 'hundreds' of letters, including some of Georgina's that she had believed to be lost. Georgina was now convinced that the Frenchwoman was both 'mad and bad', and had been 'a scheming villain from the commencement'.[34] She composed a 'great letter', fifty-two pages long, which she sent to France by registered post at a cost of 2s 8d. In it she poured out all the bitterness and resentment that had built up during the thirteen years of her relationship with Angèle. She no longer wished, she wrote, to keep with her 'a person who, whilst saying that they are my friend, denigrates and calumniates me in the most odious fashion, and who makes herself hated by everyone who approaches her'.[35]

It is clear from this letter than Angèle had told someone – we do not know whom – that Georgina had 'debauched' Eva Morand. Georgina indignantly denied this (as did Eva herself), telling Angèle 'I don't know why you invented something so horrid about me. You who know that, although I don't like men much, I would rather have to do with a hundred men than with one woman.' Georgina had, she wrote, only allowed her friend to sleep in her room 'because you were nervous and didn't like sleeping alone'. Angèle had told Eugénie Morand 'horrors' about Georgina and Freddy Warre, though there can be little doubt that the latter was homosexual. Georgina had also learned about Angèle's affair with Henry Marsh Clifford, 'a vulgar actor' and a member of the original cast of *Not Alone*. Eva had been persuaded to act as a lookout, warning the couple of Georgina's approach by coughing or ringing a bell.

Angèle had complained that Georgina had not paid her. But, Georgina claimed, she had been amply compensated in other ways:

> Why should I pay a person who smokes, who dresses like you do, who covers her hands with jewels, and has such a risqué way of speaking? Then, I never need a companion, or to pay her. If you had not got your hooks into me I would probably have found a woman who would join in the expenses. I could always have had Lise Gray or one of her sisters with me. Moreover, having you always with me, mimicking my clothes (especially when circumstances forced me to look a little smart) alienated me from the world. I did my best to convince you of that, but in vain.

Finally, Georgina told Angèle that she never wanted to see her again, but would give her £400 if she returned the jewellery, papers and other

[34] GWJ, 10–11/8/1889.
[35] GW–AM, started 24/7/1889, sent 3/9/1889.

belongings that she had taken.[36] She had Angèle's own possessions packed up and taken to the docks.

Four days after sending the 'great letter', Georgina received an 'impudent' reply. Two weeks later 'the old devil' herself turned up at the house with a man and demanded admittance. Faithfull refused to let them in, but it was obvious that this would not be the end of the matter. Georgina's problem was that the lease of 58 Gower Street, which had been signed whilst she was in Holloway, was in Angèle's name. On the day after Angèle's return, Georgina received a 'most outrageous' solicitor's letter, ordering her and everyone else to leave the house. Harcourt threatened to shoot Angèle and told Georgina that she was 'worse than ever he thought she was'. But all advised her to go, and to store the belongings that she could not take with her with friends. Defeated, and still convinced that the house was being watched, she agreed to leave, though it 'quite broke' her heart.[37] It took them all five days to pack, but by 22 September the house was virtually empty. At 8.15 that evening Georgina left Charing Cross, with Eugénie Morand, a maid called Annie Kleinheinz, two pugs, two monkeys and an unspecified number of birds. Lise Gray and all the (now homeless) inhabitants of 58 Gower Street were there to wave goodbye to them.

[36] GWM, ii, pp. 167–86, 202.

[37] GWJ, 17,21/9/1889.

26
Gisors

Georgina and her companions arrived at the Hotel de Flandres in Calais on 23 September 1889 at one o'clock in the morning. Letters from home informed her that Angèle had been seen sitting on a doorstep in Gower Street. 'Oh! What will she do when she hears how she has been sold, and me *flown*!' Georgina gloated. After a week in Calais they all moved on to an apartment in Boulogne, where Georgina walked on the sands with the dogs and remembered Crow, with whom she had been there thirty-four years earlier. On 21 October they reached their final destination, the hospice at Gisors where the nuns gave them 'a kind welcome'.[1] There had been no time to make long-term plans and it is not clear how long Georgina intended to stay. The hospice was a refuge, where she could recover from the trauma of the disintegration of her relationship with Angèle and the collapse of her dreams and ambitions. It was to be her home for the next six years and an occasional retreat for a further eight.

Regular reports came from London. Lise Gray wrote that she had met Angèle, who vowed that she would 'spare no pains' to ruin Georgina, threatening to take her to court to recover money that she was allegedly owed. Nothing ever came of this; Georgina never heard from Angèle again. Titley, Faithfull and the others had been busy packing up Georgina's belongings, and twenty-eight boxes and cases duly arrived at the hospice. Georgina busied herself unpacking them and settling in. As a paying boarder, she occupied a comfortable suite of five rooms opening off a corridor at the top of the building.

~

The Hospice of St Thomas de Villeneuve stood in a large garden bounded on one side by the River Epte, a tributary of the Seine.[2] There was also a farmyard, and the nuns kept cows and chickens. It was not long before Georgina persuaded the mother superior to let her have a piece of land of

1 GWJ, 26–28/9/1889, 21/10/1889.
2 The building was bombed by the Luftwaffe during the Second World War.

Fig. 29. Gisors in 1911. The Hospice, where Georgina Weldon lived, is in the top left-hand corner.

her own; she eventually took over half the garden. She concentrated most of her efforts on growing fruit and vegetables, but there were flowers as well. Keeping the garden going was 'perfect slavery'.[3] There were continual battles with birds, caterpillars, snails and slugs, and the climate was unfavourable: frost and snow killed her plants during the freezing winters, whilst incessant watering was needed during the hot, dry summers. She took to wearing the uniform of the *pensionnaires*, which was so much more practical for physical work than her more ladylike clothes. It consisted of a dress of thick blue material with a cape and pockets in front. In the summer she wore a white cap; in the winter a cap of thick fur which came down over her ears.

Georgina's presence was something of a mixed blessing for the board of governors. It was certainly impossible to ignore her. Shortly after her arrival she began to complain about the terrible stench from the cesspit, which had not been emptied since the construction of the hospice thirty years earlier. She made them clean it out. The chimneys smoked, but the bursar refused to have them swept, telling her that they were all 'used to it'. There were ongoing arguments about the rooms that she occupied and the rent she paid for them. The cooking was poor and the wine even worse, so Georgina bought supplies of her own and a stove, so that she and her maids

3 Philip Treherne, *A Plaintiff in Person* (London, 1923), p. 126; GWJ, 8/9/1893.

Fig. 30. The entrance to the large greenhouse built by Georgina Weldon in the garden at the Hospice, Gisors, 1893. Left to right: Chevalier (gardener), Michèle le Borgne (maid), Georgina Weldon, Lucie Michou (friend), Charlotte Hue (maid) with Judge, Père Graffin (gardener), Marguerite Graffin (maid), with a basket of tortoises.

could prepare some of their own food. The bursar and mother superior worried that the weight of her belongings would cause the building to collapse – twenty-three more boxes followed the original twenty-eight, and she also bought numerous pieces of furniture. The bursar ('a beast') tried to veto all her projects. All these minor irritations led her to conclude that France was 'a mean, dirty, beastly, pretentious country.' However, she paid for the construction of two greenhouses, a henhouse, and a new laundry and drying ground for the hospice, and supplied them with fruit, vegetables and flowers, and honey from her own hives. She was delighted when her name was included in the list of benefactors inscribed on a marble slab.[4]

Word soon got round that there was a wealthy Englishwoman living in the hospice, and a number of hopeful supplicants turned up at her door. Georgina sent most of them away empty-handed: she was not, as they believed, the 'head fool' of the town; and she was no longer interested in children 'or charities, or benevolence of any description, if I can help it.'

4 GWJ, 21/2/1890, 17/6/1892.

When two women came to collect money for the seminarians she only gave them fifty centimes. 'I don't care for *séminaristes*', she wrote. 'I think the Government ought not to allow anyone but young fellows with at least £20 a year to take to the Church.' Those who tried to take advantage of Georgina often got more than they bargained for: when some friends from England came to stay, she hired a horse and trap so that she could show them the countryside. Both horse and vehicle proved to be 'of archaeological appearance'; the horse was 'a poor old veteran fit for the knackers' and she took pity on it and returned home after a drive of two or three miles. The owner, M. Barat, demanded 15 francs; when Georgina refused to pay more than 6 francs and 50 centimes, Barat took her to court. When the judge discovered that he usually charged 10 francs for a day's hire, but had asked Georgina for 15 francs for a drive lasting two hours, the case collapsed. Costs of 73 francs were awarded against Barat.[5]

She was content on the whole. She got on well with most of the other inhabitants of the hospice, though there were complaints about the barking of the dogs and the unruly behaviour of the monkeys, which had an unfortunate habit of climbing into other people's rooms through open windows and stealing or destroying their belongings. But they did not last long: Tittilee's sudden death after six months was 'a terrible blow', after which she sent the other monkey, Dagobert, to Thomas Titley in London. She never kept monkeys again.

Georgina made friends with several of the nuns, including the mother superior ('*Notre Mère*'), who brought her eggs, and Soeur Louisa, who helped her in the garden. The nuns tried to persuade her that Spiritualism was '*diablerie*' [devilry] and never gave up hope of converting her to Roman Catholicism. She promised that she would do so 'when the hens will have teeth.' In 1894 she told a reporter from *The New York World* that she had no religion but that the sisters 'do good.'[6] She also acquired a retinue of helpers after Eugénie and Annie had returned to London. Some were more successful than others: a middle-aged Breton maid was 'a treasure all round', whilst an odd-job man and gardener had 'no more head than a pin.' One gardener was found guilty of attempting to ravish a local girl and sentenced to three years in prison.

More successful was the pensioner Louis Graffin (Père Graffin), who moved into two of Georgina's rooms with his wife in September 1892. Aged seventy-six, he had been a professional gardener for forty-three years.

5 GWJ, 11/7/1890, 7/11/1892, 5/4/1890–9/5/1890; Treherne, *Plaintiff*, pp. 128–31. There were 25 francs to the pound at this time.

6 GWJ, 25/9/1891, 11/2/1892; *The New York World*, 21/1/1894.

Despite his advanced years, he seemed to be 'healthy and robust', though his wife, two years older, looked delicate.[7] Mère Graffin died at the beginning of the following year, and Georgina helped to lay her out. After this, she took Père Graffin under her wing: he worked in the garden and they played cards together in the evenings. But she soon began to complain about him: Père Graffin was obsessed with growing geraniums and threw all Georgina's plants out of the greenhouse to make room for them. He also demonstrated an alarming fondness for the brandy bottle. By the end of the year he had gone into a decline. He died in February 1894, just over a year after his wife.

In October 1892 Georgina took on a new maid, the Graffins' married granddaughter Charlotte Hue. Charlotte, who was about thirty years old, was 'very quick and handy in her work' and soon made herself indispensable. Inevitably – as always happened with Georgina and her employees – this honeymoon period did not last. After a few months Georgina began to complain about Charlotte's untidiness and her 'constant *cachotteries* [mysteries], dodges, lies and *potins* [gossiping]'. She did not get on with the other servants, so there were regular rows and sulks. The woman was, Georgina decided, 'a kind of Madame Ménier No. 2'.[8]

~

In the meantime, Georgina had found a new interest, one that was to occupy her thoughts for more than a decade, bringing her into a new social circle and reviving her long-standing interest in Spiritualism. This was the fate of Louis-Charles, the ten-year-old son of Louis XVI and Marie-Antoinette who, it was generally believed, had died in the Temple prison in Paris in 1795 after two years of solitary confinement. Rumours that the uncrowned king, Louis XVII, had in fact survived and that the dead boy had been a substitute had begun to circulate almost immediately. Over the years that followed, more than a hundred young 'dauphins' had attempted to claim their inheritance.[9]

As a child, Georgina had 'sobbed with all my heart over the tales of the ill-usage the Dauphin was subjected to'.[10] At Schloss Hard in 1852–3 she had hidden herself away in the library to read Anna Lindsay's books about the French Revolution, and had become convinced that the young boy had somehow been spirited out of the Temple. Like many of her family and friends, she believed the claims of one of the more plausible 'false dauphins',

[7] GWJ, 11/9/1892.

[8] GWJ, 21/10/1892, 16/8/1893.

[9] Deborah Cadbury, *The Lost King of France* (London, 2002), pp. ix–xii.

[10] GW, *Louis XVII*, p. 9.

a Prussian clockmaker named Karl Wilhelm Naundorff, who had died in 1845 leaving a number of 'princes and princesses' to pursue his claims. Attempts to institute legal proceedings had been thrown out in 1851 and 1872, but the Naundorffists had refused to give up. They were still pursuing their claims vigorously in Paris in the 1890s.

Georgina, who felt that she had always been 'ill-used', sympathised with 'Louis XVII', believing that her own life had been 'almost as storm-tossed' as his. She decided that destiny had chosen her to be his champion: she would be 'one of the means of scenting out the trail and exposing the villainy of a monstrous historical fraud'.[11] From the beginning of 1890 onwards she spent every spare moment studying the subject. In November of that year she met the well-known Spiritualist Lady Caithness (also known as the Duchesse de Pomar). Lady Caithness, a wealthy widow who lived in a luxurious house in the Avenue de Wagram in Paris, believed that Mary Queen of Scots was her guardian angel. She dressed like her heroine, with whom she was known to converse through the medium of table-rapping and the planchette. Georgina, who had already read Lady Caithness's book, *A Midnight Visit to Holyrood*, thought her 'charming and loveable'. The two women hit it off immediately, for Lady Caithness and her son, the Duc de Medina Pomar, were both supporters of Naundorff and his family. Georgina was invited take part in a series of séances with the mediums Madame and Mademoiselle Rodière, with whom she was already acquainted. At the first, Gounod's mother 'appeared immediately' and 'went to fetch Louis XVII', who 'answered a great many questions' One evening Georgina went out for a walk with a friend and passed Gounod's mansion, 20 Place Malesherbes. Georgina longed for the composer to look out of his window and see her, but there was no sign of him.

Georgina also met the Comte de Duranti, the author of a book about 'Louis XVII', at his house on the Boulevard Haussmann. The count introduced her to 'Prince Louis de Bourbon', one of Naundorff's grandsons, an officer in the Dutch army. Georgina thought that he was 'an ugly little fellow', who looked like Louis XIV. She invited him and Duranti to visit her and Lady Caithness in the Avenue de Wagram on the following day. They were present at 'a splendid séance' at which Gounod's mother appeared again and, to Georgina's delight, addressed her as 'Ma chère Georgina'. After a most satisfactory stay in Paris she went home, writing in her diary a few days later:

11 GW, 'Spiritualism'.

> Since I have been at Gisors, the only ray of happiness, interest or pleasure has been my visit to Paris and my renewed serious intercourse with the spirits. Their apparent lies and advice had seemed so wrong, but now I see that what I have gone through is education. I have been educated up, so as to understand *la Question de Louis XVII* as no one else can![12]

She returned to her studies 'with renewed ardour'. At a séance with the Rodières at the beginning of 1891, she received further 'messages' from Victoire Gounod and 'Charles Louis' (Naundorff). The latter warned her of the difficulty of the fight against 'the enemies of the throne' and she went away feeling 'quite melancholy'.[13] On 14 July she railed against the 'crackers, popguns, fireworks, bands in all directions in commemoration of the hideous Revolution of 1789'. 'Scratch the Gaul', she continued, 'and you find the tiger monkey. They are not even pure-bred savages!' In the following year she wrote 'All music is dead in me. All my energy has gone into flowers and Louis XVII'. She visited the Comte de Duranti again and found 'the poor little Prince Louis' there. The young man said that he had left the army 'on the advice of Marie Stuart'. But he was no longer in favour with Lady Caithness, having borrowed 1500 francs from her. Georgina gave him 'a good jawing', though she felt sorry for him, writing: 'Anyone can see he has the stuff of commandment in him. Blood of 66 Kings. Poor fellow. I wish I had millions. They would all go on the cause.'[14] Her generosity was soon to be severely tested.

Less than a fortnight later, 'Prince Louis' turned up in Gisors. He told Georgina that he needed money so that he could bribe someone to steal some papers from the 'Secret Archive' in Berlin. These papers had allegedly been confiscated from Naundorff by the Prussian chief of police. They would, the 'prince' claimed, prove beyond doubt that his grandfather really was Louis XVII and his family would be able to claim 'millions'. He only needed Georgina's money for five days, It seemed 'too good to be true', but Georgina lent him 650 francs. After a few days Louis was back again, with a story about a bundle of papers labelled 'Naundorff, Louis XVII'. It was, he said 'very expedient to get them at once'. This time she gave him 520 francs in gold and a cheque for £60.[15] Before long, however, she began to wish she had not been so 'precipitate'. 'Everything with me', she wrote, 'always turns out a desperate trouble and rumpus'. By the end of the month, when 'His Royal Highness'

12 GWJ, 21–30/11/1890.

13 GWJ, 3/1/1891.

14 GWJ, 14,21/7/1892, 18/8/1892.

15 GWJ, 30/8/1892, 5/9/1892.

had neither been to see her nor written, she had decided that he was 'a real Bourbon' and that they were 'all cads'. She informed the police that Louis was 'a real natural born thief and liar' and refused to see him when he came to the hospice again. The police referred her to the public prosecutor and before long the newspapers reported that she was taking legal action against the 'prince'. She hoped that Gounod had heard of the 'riot'.

In Paris a few weeks later, Georgina met the Baron de Gaugler, the author of a recent book about Louis XVII and another avowed supporter of the claims of the Naundorff family. What he told her about them was, however, not encouraging: they were all 'poor, penniless individuals' who laboured under the delusion that 'a grand upset of everything' would soon restore them to their rightful position in society. At a séance with the Rodières that evening, 'Charles Louis' told Georgina that she was 'the instrument intended to make the truth known because I did not care about the world, or what people said, or about popularity, that I espoused an unpopular cause from wholly honest motives'.[16] Shortly after this Georgina was introduced to 'Prince Louis's aunt, the 'poor unfortunate' Christine Schoenlau, widow of Naundorff's son Charles Edmond, 'Duc d'Anjou', who was staying with the Durantis. 'A highly colored, raw-boned, plain woman, very silent and with all the appearance of a common servant', Christine had arrived unexpectedly in Paris 'without shoes to her feet or a penny in her pocket'. Georgina rashly offered to have the woman at Gisors and it was agreed that she should go there, incognita, and stay in lodgings. Christine spoke no English, and little French, but Georgina was able to communicate with her in 'double Dutch, German and French'. She was clearly no friend of 'Prince Louis', and informed Georgina that 'His Royal Highness' had deserted from the army after being caught with a boy aged fifteen and arrested. Georgina was disgusted, asking herself 'Can it be right or proper I should take any steps to rehabilitate that creature?' The 'Queen Regent, Christine de Bourbon' duly arrived in Gisors on 19 December. She soon began to drive everyone mad and Georgina decided that she was a lunatic. After two months in Gisors, to Georgina's 'inexpressible relief and delight', the 'Queen Regent' was packed off back to Paris and thence to her own family in Brussels.[17]

In spite of all these distractions, Georgina had not entirely given up her interest in music. Her friends in Gisors included the Josset family: old Monsieur and Madame, and their son Alfred, a composer who taught music at a school for poor and disabled boys run by the order of St-Jean de Dieu

[16] GWJ, 10–12/9/1892, 4,26/11/1892; Baron de Gaugler, *L'enfant du Temple* (Paris, 1891).

[17] GWJ, 8–9/12/1892, 21/2/1893.

at 223 rue Lecourbe in Paris. Many of the pupils were blind, but some were taught to sing and play musical instruments. One such was Jules Rousseau, a blind boy from Gisors, who had been appointed organist at the parish church of St-Gervais and St-Protais in 1891, when he was only sixteen.[18] Georgina liked Jules, a talented musician who also wrote songs. She was persuaded to sing one of his compositions, 'Avril', at a concert at the school in May 1893, but only agreed on condition her name was not advertised, as she was terrified that Angèle Ménier would turn up. The Jossets had met 'the fishfag' (as Georgina now called her), who had returned to France in 1891 and was now living in the Parisian suburb of Levallois-Perret, teaching English and music. The hall at 223 rue Lecourbe held about 1500 people, and there were 120 performers. With the help of 'a stiff glass of wine', Georgina overcame her nerves and got through the song 'to the great pleasure of the audience'. She was even asked for an encore.[19]

In October 1893 Georgina received the news that she had been dreading for years: Gounod was dead. She comforted herself with the knowledge that he had been unconscious for some time before his death, 'so he no more said Goodbye to them than he has said Goodbye to me'. She had never entirely given up hope of a reconciliation, though she had not spoken to him for nearly twenty years. She had last seen him in 1887, when he had conducted the five-hundredth performance of *Faust* at the Paris Opéra.[20] Now she scanned the newspapers for references to herself and her relationship with the composer, firing off letters to any who dared to say anything uncomplimentary. When one of her letters was published in the *Petit Journal*, she was 'quite delighted to think of the discomfiture of the Gounod crew'. She sent copies to everyone she could think of, including the composer's son, Jean. On hearing that Gounod was to be buried in the family vault of his in-laws at Auteuil on the western fringe of Paris, she wrote again to the *Petit Journal*, demanding that he should rest with other famous Frenchmen in the Panthéon. Gounod himself had wanted to be interred at Montparnasse with his parents and she had promised him that she would be buried there too. Three days later, on 27 October, Gounod was laid to rest at Auteuil. Georgina sent 500 francs to the president of the town council of Paris, the head of a fund to pay for a monument: when her name appeared on a list of contributors three weeks later she noted with satisfaction, 'How annoyed the clique must be'.

18 He was organist there until 1940.

19 GWJ, 18/5/1893.

20 GWJ, 4/11/1887.

Fig. 31. Georgina Weldon at Gisors in her Hospice outfit with Judge, October 1893. The newspaper reports Gounod's death.

One of Georgina's first thoughts on hearing of Gounod's death had been that she should go to Paris and have 'a séance all to myself'. She longed to communicate with her 'old man' and was sure that he would now return to her. Ten days after the funeral she set off, finding lodgings in the Rue Hamelin. At a séance with the Rodières, Gounod's mother made her presence known at once. She told Georgina that Charles could not come yet, but she would bring him to her at Lady Caithness's house.[21] During the days that followed Georgina visited several mediums, astrologers and fortune-tellers in Paris, none of whom told her anything useful. Back at the hospice, she experimented with her maid Charlotte and Charlotte's sister

[21] GWJ, 17–24/10/1893, 9–10,22/11/1893.

Marguerite, who had recently come to work for her as well, but nothing happened. Georgina noted with regret that the two young Frenchwomen much preferred the card game *Nain Jaune* to séances.[22]

Georgina had to wait six months for Gounod to communicate with her. This time the 'medium' was Amélie, the widow of the French sculptor Jean-Baptiste Carpeaux. Amélie had visited Tavistock House regularly in 1873 when her husband was sculpting a bust of Gounod, but Georgina had then had no contact with her until June 1892, when she wrote out of the blue. Georgina, who had described Amélie in 1874 as 'the filthiest slut that ever was heard of', was surprised to find that the Frenchwoman now looked 'tidy, clean and pleasant' – and ten years younger than she had done in London. She was, moreover, 'a very *savante* Spiritualist'.[23] Georgina decided that she liked her very much. Amélie sent plants to Georgina at Gisors and Georgina visited Amélie at her home in Auteuil. A particular attraction of Auteuil was that it was where Gounod was buried. In May 1894 they held a séance at which Gounod and his mother appeared. The composer seemed to be affectionate and pleased to be with her. Georgina went to bed that night, tired but happy, believing that 'The old man loves me.'[24]

Having decided that she herself was no medium, Georgina needed one in Gisors who could summon up Gounod for her. She did not have long to wait. On 10 June she had a 'highly satisfactory' séance with Edgard Josset, a visiting pharmacist from Rouen who was 'full about Spiritualism', together with Jules Rousseau and Charlotte. The first words rapped out were 'J'aime Mimi'. This had to be Gounod, who seemed to want to 'quarrel and discuss'. He also promised that he would dictate music to Georgina. It is clear from Georgina's journal that the 'medium' was Charlotte, for the rapping noises were heard only when she was at the table. 'This', wrote Georgina, 'is unexpected bliss!' After this there were séances every day – sometimes several times a day. Gounod 'communicated' by rapping as they recited the alphabet, a slow process. Attempts to persuade him to use a written alphabet failed: he could apparently hear and feel, but not see. On some occasions he was cooperative, even chatty; on others he was grumpy and would say nothing at all. From time to time his mother came too, but Gounod appeared to be jealous of her and reluctant to let her speak. He told Georgina he was happy 'because my love has taken hold of him, that I have always loved him, but *he* has been unfaithful and not loved me'. The

22 This card game was called 'Pope Joan' in England.

23 GW–Dr Edward Chepmell, 15/5/1874; GWJ, 14/11/1893.

24 GWJ, 20/5/1894.

composer cried, and seemed to be repentant. Georgina was delighted to hear that he never went near his wife.[25]

After this, Georgina refused to take any decision, important or unimportant, without consulting Gounod. The advantages of this for Charlotte are obvious: Georgina had long complained that her maid was rude, dirty, untidy, a liar and a thief; now she was entirely dependent on her. Charlotte could manipulate her mistress as she wished. But why was Georgina, an intelligent woman in many ways, so gullible? The truth must that she was so desperate to renew her relationship with her 'old man' that she would believe anything that brought her what she wanted. She did wonder if Charlotte's 'deep duplicity' was bringing 'false spirits', but she did not suspect that the so-called spirits did not exist at all.[26]

It was not long before Gounod began to communicate through Jules as well, writing (terrible) poetry:

> Ton image vibre en mon coeur
> Comme une corde en une lyre.
> Et pour moi ton divin sourire
> Est l'accord le plus enchanteur.[27]

Georgina was delighted:

> Fancy what joy, after 20 long years, to find my faithfulness unto Death so well rewarded. Heavens only knows what he may not inspire us with. Poetry and composition. Bless the dear old man. Here is the proof that 'love is stronger than Death'. There is no Death! Nothing can be lost to Love.[28]

Sometime later she wrote 'Beatrice had her Dante, Laura had her Petrarca, and Tasso had a lady he lauded in verse, but they were only living men, while *my* poet laureate is a living spirit!'[29] Gounod even seemed to be interested in the fate of the Dauphin. He promised to carry out some research and tell Georgina what had happened to the boy. She was convinced that 'Spirits, in time, can certainly learn and teach us', and was dismayed when he failed to come up with anything interesting.[30]

25 GWJ, 10,23/6/1894.
26 GWJ, 31/8/1894.
27 'Your image vibrates in my heart like a string on a lyre. And for me your divine smile is the most enchanting harmony.'
28 GWJ, 30/6/1894.
29 GWJ, 29/6/1894, 7/2/1895.
30 GWJ, 1/8/1894.

Gounod-Charlotte-Jules quickly became a tyrant – and a capricious one at that. On one occasion Georgina cancelled a visit to Paris because he did not want her to go. He often told her to go to bed early. He sulked when she reprimanded him for claiming that he had suffered as much as she. If he had suffered, she informed him, it was 'entirely his own doing'. He had, moreover, promised to dictate verses and music, but had failed to do so. But she admitted that she was 'in perpetual fear' that he would leave her. After one particularly unsatisfactory evening session she wrote, 'all he generally says is useless repetitions and platitudes'. He also appeared to be reluctant to allow his mother to talk to Georgina, and rapped 'No' loudly when Georgina said that she would like to communicate with her own father.[31]

There were other problems too. Since Jules was blind, Georgina often asked Charlotte to guide him. Before long rumours about the two were circulating in Gisors, whipped up by Jules's aunt, who appears to have written a number of anonymous letters, including a love letter in Braille, allegedly sent by Charlotte to Jules. There may have been something in these stories: during one séance Georgina caught her maid 'fondling' the boy. Everyone believed, moreover, that Charlotte was trying to get rid of her sickly husband, Paulin Hue. She was even accused of poisoning him. Georgina sought Gounod's advice, but he unfortunately suggested that Charlotte's young son, Adrien, should be taken to Paris, so that his father could not claim him in the case of a separation. The result of this was that Charlotte was accused of kidnapping the boy. Some believed that Georgina was helping Charlotte to divorce her husband so that she could marry Jules. The good people of Gisors were also suspicious of Georgina's relationship with Charlotte, and they and the nuns, as devout Catholics, did not at all approve of Georgina's obsession with Spiritualism. The church authorities threatened to dismiss Jules from his post as organist.[32]

In mid October the Countess of Caithness sent Georgina two invitations that she had been given by Gounod's widow to a mass to be held in Paris on the first anniversary of the composer's death. Georgina was very excited. She and Charlotte consulted Gounod and he came at once, 'loud and strong'. Yes, she was to go to Paris and must take a 'lyre of flowers' to the cemetery after the mass. Charlotte made 'a most lovely lyre of blue-beard [*Caryopteris*], ageratums, small white asters and foliage grass and white dahlias'. On 16 October, just as Georgina was getting ready for the bus to the station, a telegram came from brother Apsley: their mother had died early that morning. But this did not deter Georgina: she was off to Paris

31 GWJ, 13/8/1894, 25/1/1895, 5/2/1895.

32 GWJ, 27/8/1894, 6/12/1894, 9/1/1895.

by the 12.20 train, taking the lyre with her. She then took a cab to Auteuil, where there was time for a quick séance with Madame Carpeaux (Gounod told her that he did not like his tomb) before returning to the centre of Paris. On the following day she attended the 'lovely' requiem mass at the Madeleine, which was 'crammed full'. She saw Verdi entering the church, but missed seeing Gounod's family as she was sitting in a side aisle. She vowed that she would get a better seat next time.[33]

With the rumours about Charlotte and Jules flying around Gisors, Georgina began to think that it might be a good idea to move to Auteuil. Jules was 'in a dreadful way' and Charlotte was 'all but quite mad, poor thing'. When she saw that her husband had put a notice in the local paper informing readers that he would not take responsibility for her debts, Charlotte rushed out of the room screaming, then went into a fit, with 'blood and froth oozing from her mouth'. Georgina, who was feeling poorly at the time, began yelling too, and they had to send for the doctor. That evening they were all too upset to hold a séance.[34] Charlotte was in hysterics for several days and her state of mind was not improved by the discovery that her husband had sold all her furniture.

By the end of March 1894 Georgina had made up her mind. She would rent Madame Carpeaux's house at Auteuil and take Charlotte – and perhaps also Jules – with her. But first she needed to go to England, for a major family row was brewing over her mother's will. Georgina had no faith in the lawyers; Apsley was well-meaning, but lazy and weak – and she did not trust Dal or Emily an inch. She told the managers of the hospice that she would keep two rooms and give up the rest of the apartment, and spoke to a carrier about transporting some of her belongings to Auteuil.[35] The next few weeks were spent 'packing up and packing away'. Finally, on 28 April, Georgina and Charlotte left Gisors for Dieppe by train, leaving Marguerite at the hospice with the two surviving members of Georgina's menagerie, the pug, Judge, and a cat, Minou.

33 GWJ, 14–17/10/1894.

34 GWJ, 6,9/12/1894.

35 GWJ, 27/3/1895.

27
The Trehernes

Had she married with her parents' consent, a dowry of £7000 should have been paid on Georgina's marriage in 1860. But she and Harry had not received a penny: her father had disinherited her and had left her nothing in his will when he died in 1867. Her mother had given Georgina £100 a year thereafter, and had been horrified when, in 1884, Georgina had threatened to take steps to dispute the will on the grounds that her father had been insane when the document was drawn up and signed, just over two years before his death. Louisa had persuaded her not to do so, promising to ensure that Georgina was provided for in her own will. But her power to do so was severely compromised by the fact that in 1863 she and her husband, with their eldest son Dal and their trustees, had entered into an agreement under which Dal would receive £50,222 18s after his mother's death, for his own use 'absolutely and beneficially'. In fact, it appears, a large portion of this money had been advanced to Dal long before his mother died. Georgina later claimed that her brother had squandered about £70,000 'in riotous living, gambling, mad extravagance and bad investments'.[1]

A letter sent by Dal Treherne to his sister Emily in 1893 suggests that Emily and her husband Ashley George (Bill) Williams had received only £2000 when they married in 1871, and that £5000, the remainder of her dowry, was still owing. When Emily and Bill threatened to take Dal to court, he replied: 'I cannot believe that a brother or sister of mine would lend themselves to a step which might prove my ruin!! I have 3 children and £20,000 (less £2,000 still remaining of unpaid debts) to leave them as their fortunes!!!' Clearly, there was one rule for Dal, and a different one for the rest of the family.

It is also clear that Dal and Emily had been advised that the agreement of 1863 was illegal and had no force in law. They were both terrified that Georgina would find out and take action against them.[2] In an attempt to remedy the situation, they and their younger brother, Apsley, had a 'deed

1 GWMSM, p. 115.
2 DT–Emily Williams, 17/5/1893; Emily Williams–DT, 22/5/1893.

of family arrangement' drawn up in 1893. The next step was to persuade Georgina to sign it. In June she was 'Astonished beyond measure at receiving an aggravating manifesto from the Head of the family!!!' Dal proposed binding himself to pay her £160 a year on their mother's death. She was highly suspicious, writing 'Something must be up!' And why should she not receive 'two hundred and a sum'?[3] Ten days later Apsley informed her that Dal had agreed to give her £200 a year. He brought the deed to her in Gisors at the beginning of August and she signed it immediately, an action that she would come to regret. But at the time she believed that it would 'prevent Dal playing further ducks and drakes'. Dal himself turned up on the following day. Georgina, who had not seen him for eight years, thought he looked 'very old, short of wind, very ugly and loud'. He was, in her opinion, a '*Fanfarone buffone*! [a braggart and a buffoon]'. He had got what he wanted and only stayed for a few hours.[4]

In July 1894 Georgina received a disturbing letter from Dal. The Welsh copper-works in which much of the family's money was invested was in trouble and neither her mother nor her brothers could expect any income from it that year.[5] By this time Louisa, who had given up her house in London in 1881, was living in Hampshire with Bill and Emily. In October Emily asked Georgina and Apsley to make some contribution towards keeping their mother. Both found this 'incredible'. Georgina wrote: 'I have been robbed and injured in every way by them for 34 years. Bill and Zizi [Emily] have profited by thousands a year Mama has had since 1867!!! and even before, of which I got but a pittance.'

~

Nine days after this, Georgina received a telegram from Apsley, informing her that Louisa had died that morning. She wondered if Emily had poisoned the old lady because she had run out of money. A few days later she was 'fearfully excited and disgusted' when she received a copy of her mother's will from the family solicitor, Augustus Drake. The document had been signed less than a month before Louisa's death and the executors were Emily and her brother-in-law George Curzon, who had remained close to the Trehernes since his first wife's death in 1868. Instead of the £2000 that she had expected, Georgina was to receive just £50. Apsley was to have £3000; Dal was forgiven a debt of £3000; George Curzon was given £100 – and everything else was to go to Emily. Georgina had good reason to be

[3] GWJ, 22/6/1893.
[4] GWJ, 2–3/8/1893.
[5] GWJ, 23/7/1894.

suspicious: according to Apsley's son, Philip Treherne, Louisa had been 'incapable of managing her own affairs' for a year before she died, so she may well have been *non compos mentis* when the will was signed. Georgina wrote immediately to the Home Secretary to insist on a post mortem.[6] She was still not convinced when Apsley sent her a copy of a doctor's letter, stating that their mother had died of heart failure. Given that Louisa was eighty-three, it seems likely that this was correct.

Georgina was determined to oppose probate of the will. At first Apsley and Dal seemed inclined to follow her lead, but both quickly backed out. Her family were, Georgina decided, 'all sneaks'. Her fury was increased when Dal told her that he wanted to delay payment of the £200 due under the agreement they had all signed in 1893 and asked her to lend him £3000. She spent much of her time reading old family letters, 'which make my blood boil as well as grieve'.[7] Augustus Drake, who travelled to Gisors from Lewes in Sussex to see Georgina, did his best to persuade her that she had no chance of upsetting her mother's will, but he did hold out some hope of disputing that of her father. In his opinion, he said, the deed of 1863 and subsequent deeds appointing the capital to Dal were irregular and 'tainted with fraud'. These were words that he would subsequently wish he had not spoken. Drake thought that Georgina was entitled to a quarter of the estate, but was 'much disappointed' to discover that she had been 'foolish enough' to sign the 'deed of family arrangement' in 1893. He was, he said, 'dreadfully afraid' that the deed had 'cut the ground from underneath' her feet.[8]

Georgina and Charlotte left Gisors on 28 April 1895 and headed for Lewes, where they settled themselves into lodgings at 57 High Street, not far from Augustus Drake's office. The lawyer, who tried to persuade Georgina to sign a paper stating that she would abide by the provisions of her mother's will, must have been rather surprised when she told him that she had to talk to Gounod first. That evening 'Gounod' told her that she should consult Apsley before signing. He also warned her not to discuss Spiritualism with people she did not know well. No doubt Charlotte was worried that there would be another attempt to have her mistress certified insane. In the meantime, having heard from France that her separation from Paulin Hue was now official, Charlotte lost no time in picking up a new admirer, Joe Hardwick, whose parents kept a draper's shop in the town.

6 GWJ, 7,16,21/10/1894; Philip Treherne, *A Plaintiff in Person* (London, 1923), p. 170.

7 GWJ, 1/2/1894.

8 GWJ, 7/3/1895, 6/4/1895.

Gounod apparently approved of this, but Georgina was not at all happy. She did not want her maid to go 'flaunting herself all day and evening' with the young man.

Apart from her desire to contest her mother's will, Georgina had further reasons for wishing to spend some time in England. Her departure from 58 Gower Street in September 1889 had been so precipitate that she had left many of her belongings behind. These included clothes, furniture, books, pictures and silver plate, some of which had gone into store, whilst other items had been distributed among friends and employees, including the Morands, Lise Gray, Thomas Titley and George Faithfull, who had got married a few weeks earlier. For several years Georgina had been trying to persuade Faithfull to let her have a list of the things that he had taken, but he had been curiously reluctant to so. Believing that Georgina would never return to London, he had informed one of her friends that he intended to 'stick to everything' and that she had given it all to him.

Immediately after her arrival in Lewes, Georgina asked the indefatigable Harcourt ('Old Misery') to find out where Faithfull and his wife were living. He soon located them in Shepherd's Bush. A fortnight later, Georgina set off for London 'with good heart' and met up with Harcourt, who was 'looking more hideous and stinking worse than ever'. Together with Lavinia Newham, a friend who lived nearby, they set off with a van, having told the local police what they proposed to do. At the Faithfulls' house, 43 Netherwood Road, they somehow got in and carried off Georgina's barometer, rosewood console, sewing machine, knife cleaner and a piece of stair carpet. Faithfull's wife, Polly, called the police and accused Harcourt of burglary. He was taken to the police station in Addison Road, with Georgina and Mrs Newham following in a hansom cab. After arguing for three-quarters of an hour, they were all allowed to go free.[9]

Six weeks later, Georgina and her friends met the Faithfulls at the Brompton County Court. Georgina claimed £50 for the 'unlawful detention' of two Japanese vases, which had been a wedding present. Unlike Georgina, who represented herself as usual, George Faithfull had employed a barrister, who argued that the articles concerned had been given to his client before Georgina left for France in 1889. Faithfull counter-claimed for £50 12s 6d, for trespass and damage to the door at his house. The judge, blaming Georgina for her haste in 'divesting herself of her property to prevent Madame Ménier getting it', found for Faithfull. In addition to his costs, Faithfull was awarded £30 for trespass and annoyance; and £5 for the

9 GWJ, 20/2/1891, 20–2/5/1895.

goods that Georgina and her companions had removed.[10] Georgina, who felt 'weary, heartsick and worn out', decided that the judge was 'a beast'. She was even more depressed when Faithfull's bill of costs arrived: it came to £33. When the court charges were added to this she was informed that she owed nearly £60. She said that she would rather go to prison than give him a halfpenny. The judgment was reversed in the following year and Georgina was awarded £516. She never got her money, though she continued to pursue Faithfull through the courts until he was declared bankrupt two years later.[11]

Georgina had moved to London at the beginning of June so that she was closer to the Law Courts. In addition to her vendetta against Faithfull, she was pursuing claims against music sellers, publishers and printers, in a largely unsuccessful attempt to recover royalties owed for the sale of sheet music of which she owned the copyright. These proceedings were so convoluted that they are now almost impossible to follow – even Georgina herself often lost track of what was happening. At the same time, her attempts to prove that she was entitled to a larger share of her mother's estate seemed to be making little progress. The clerks and attendants at the Law Courts were pleased to see her again, but the lawyers were much less welcoming. One of the court reporters told Georgina that he could not understand 'why the judges and some barristers hated me so, as everybody else was so fond of me'. One reason, no doubt, was that the courts were besieged by amateur litigants at this time. These litigants in person were described a few years later as 'the terror of the Bar, and (with some fortunate exceptions) the aversion of the Bench'. One of the most pestilential was Georgina's former assistant, Alexander Chaffers, whom she met wandering around the Law Courts in December. He had been thrown out of the British Museum, and haunted the courts because he had nowhere else to go. His 'litigation mania' had led Chaffers to file no fewer than forty-eight proceedings against leading personages since the beginning of the decade. Costs were almost invariably awarded against him, but he never paid a penny.[12] The activities of Chaffers and others like him (including Georgina herself) led to the passing in 1896 of the Vexatious Actions Act, which gave the courts the power to restrain a litigant's ability to initiate or continue civil or criminal proceedings. Several of these amateur litigants were female: on

10 GWJ, 5,10/7/1895, *Lloyds Weekly Newspaper*, 7/7/1895, p. 9, 14/7/1895, p. 12.

11 GWJ, 12–17/7/1895, 16/6/1896, 10/8/1896; *Times*, 11/8/1896.

12 GWJ, 11/8/1895, 11/12/1895, 15/1/1896; Michael Taggart, 'Alexander Chaffers', *Cambridge Law Journal*, 63(3), 2004, pp. 656–84.

one occasion Georgina found the ladies' waiting room at the Law Courts 'full of noisy, hysterical, giggling women.'[13]

A particularly notorious tormentor of the judges was Mary Cathcart, whom Georgina had first encountered at the beginning of 1889. She had thought at the time that the woman was 'cracked, cracked as ever she can be!'[14] Unlike Georgina, Mary was an heiress with money of her own. In July 1887, when she was over forty, she had married a distant cousin, James Taylor Cathcart of Pitcairlie, of whom her mother did not approve. Cathcart was only twenty-nine and his income was about £300 a year, whilst the annual revenue from Mary's estates was approximately £4000.[15] The marriage had not been a success. Mary had left her husband after two months, claiming that he had committed adultery with a maidservant, and had refused to return to him. James Cathcart's subsequent threat to treat his wife 'like Mrs Weldon' illustrates the lasting impact of the attempt to incarcerate Georgina in a lunatic asylum ten years earlier. When Georgina met her, Mrs Cathcart was preparing to file a petition for divorce on the grounds of adultery and cruelty. This was subsequently changed to a request for a decree of judicial separation, which was refused. Two years later, she visited the Law Courts to ask for a protection order against her husband, who was trying to have her certified as a lunatic so that he could administer her property. She was unceremoniously dragged from the building to a carriage waiting just outside and taken to Dr William Wood's lunatic asylum, the Priory at Roehampton, where she was certified as 'a proper subject for restraint.'

Later in the same year, after a sixteen-day hearing before James Bulwer, QC, a Master in Lunacy, a special jury found that Mrs Cathcart was capable of managing her own affairs. The Master ordered that she should be released from the asylum at once. From this time onwards she had pursued her lawyers and agents, and anyone else who might conceivably have conspired against her, through the law courts. Like Georgina, Mrs Cathcart mistrusted lawyers and preferred to represent herself in court. Unfortunately, she knew much less about the law than Georgina. Some years later she was described as 'a lady who wanted to litigate to the crack of doom.' 'Such a person,' the Recorder, Sir Charles Hall, observed at the Central Criminal Court, 'would be perfect prey for harpies and low-scheming attornies.'[16] In 1895, Mrs Cathcart was still 'rampaging about' the Law Courts', having made herself thoroughly unpopular with all the staff by her

13 GWJ, 5/3/1896.
14 GWJ, 1/2/1889.
15 *Birmingham Daily Post*, 6/3/1891, p. 5; 7/3/1891, p. 5.
16 *Daily News*, 2/11/1898, p. 7.

rudeness and unruly behaviour. But she liked Georgina and the two women became friends. Georgina did her best to help Mrs Cathcart, but believed that she was her own worst enemy. It was no use talking sense to her: she was 'as mad as a March hare' and would probably end up in Holloway.[17]

~

These months in London in 1895 gave Georgina plenty of opportunities to renew old friendships. On Sundays she usually visited the hospitable Grays, who treated her as a member of their own lively and chaotic family. Lise Gray's niece Marjory Pegram (who would eventually inherit Georgina's papers) remembered that she 'never looked anything but ravishingly beautiful, though she wore a grey wig. She was always the centre of attention: 'When she talked, which she did with great clarity and wit, her whole face sparkled with animation and intelligence. She made the simplest incident sound important.' Georgina also saw much more of her own family than she had done for many years, and attended the second wedding of her brother Apsley, at Holy Trinity, Chelsea, in June. She liked Apsley's bride, Edith Winn, and thought that the groom (now aged nearly fifty-three, and twenty-four years older than Edith) looked 'wonderfully young.'[18] But she was not pleased when, a year later, her new sister-in-law gave birth to a baby boy, Edmund. Georgina also met, for the first time, Agnes, Countess Waldstein, who had married her brother Dal in 1883. Agnes, of whom Dal's rabidly anti-Catholic father would most certainly have disapproved, was a Hungarian noblewoman, widow of a Bohemian count, by whom she had one son, Georg (Gino). Georgina was prepared to dislike Agnes, but found to her surprise that she liked her 'immensely.' Agnes tried hard to be friendly and seemed to be 'most sympathetic.' She also seemed to take good care of Dal.[19] But Georgina had no contact at all with her sister Emily, the 'Black Wolf,' whom she had not seen for ten years.

At the end of August 1895 Georgina and Charlotte moved into 272 Kings Road, Chelsea, not far from the Grays. The accommodation was far from ideal: the landlady, Agnes Lambley, had done all the mending, carpentry work and painting herself, 'in a most amateur fashion,' and the doors and windows did not close properly. Things were going badly: Georgina wrote that she felt as if her brain was 'so confused, so pent up in difficulties – like a poor mouse in a trap with several openings.' Gounod was no help –

[17] GWJ, 30/7/1895, 11/1/1896, 26/3/1896, 8,16/4/1896. Mary Cathcart was in Chiswick House lunatic asylum in 1911.

[18] Edward Grierson, *Storm Bird* (London, 1959), pp. 474–5; GWJ, 20/6/1895.

[19] GWJ, 26/10/1895, 13/11/1895.

recently they had been able to get nothing but 'banalities and nonsense' out of him. The séances became rather more interesting and productive after Louis Castella arrived on the scene. Born in France, he was a language teacher, though Georgina describes his command of his native language as 'so dreadful it is absolutely painful'. He certainly had a number of somewhat dubious connections, for he was recommended to Georgina as an interpreter by Louise Michel, the notorious French revolutionary and anarchist, who had fled to London in 1890, fearing that her enemies would have her confined in a lunatic asylum. Georgina had heard Michel speaking in 1883, and had thought her 'a most interesting, intellectual idealist with indomitable energy'. Before long, Castella moved into 272 Kings Road, and into Charlotte's bed – ejecting the faithful Joe Hardwick, who had travelled to London to visit her almost every Sunday since she and Georgina had left Lewes. Georgina did not like Castella much, thinking him 'full of flare and words and wind', but she put up with him because he claimed to be a medium. Quite soon, 'Gounod' started writing poetry again – indeed, he became quite prolific, spewing out interminable verses on subjects such as the iniquity of judges, the injustice of court proceedings, and the lunatic ravings of Georgina's father. By the end of 1899 he had written a total of 5380 lines. Georgina was particularly impressed by a 49-line poem in Latin. 'What a marvellous thing it is', she wrote, 'and yet it explains so much'. The 'precious old man' was 'happiness without end'.

In May 1896 Georgina, Charlotte and Castella left 272 Kings Road, having fallen out with Mrs Lambley whom Georgina described as a *trumeau* (literally 'shin of beef') and 'an awful old sow'. On 8 May there was a 'rumpus royal'. Mrs Lambley and her daughter 'screamed like 2000 peacocks' and Castella 'raved like a bull'. Mrs Lambley accused Charlotte of turning the house into a brothel, claiming that she had seen Castella and Joe in the younger woman's bed. Georgina told Mrs Lambley that she was out of her mind. They were all given notice to quit and told to get out of the house within a week. They moved next door, to 274 Kings Road, with Mrs Lambley 'snorting with rage and fury'. A further move, in March of the following year, took them to 7 Bramerton Street in Chelsea, which even had 'a bathroom and two WCs'. The landlord, a 'nice old man' called Mr Wüstermann, played the flute and claimed to be an old admirer. Inevitably, however, they were soon disappointed. The house was filthy dirty and the street was noisy. The chimneys smoked, the kitchen range did not work, and the water-heater soon broke down.[20] Having decided that 'Old Wüstermann' was a fraud, Georgina escaped to Gisors for a month, returning from Dieppe to Newhaven on the *Tamise* at the beginning

20 GWJ, 27/8/1895–11/10/1895, 8/2/1896–12/8/1896.

of May. It was a rough crossing and she was very seasick. As she lay groaning in a deckchair, the ship lurched and the chair was overturned, throwing her onto her head and breaking a bone in her thumb. The stewardess, 'a kind of French female hog' was unsympathetic. Georgina vowed that she would sue the shipping company.[21]

~

The first round of the battle over Louisa Treherne's will began at the end of October 1897, this time in the Court of Chancery rather than Georgina's usual stamping-ground, the Court of Queen's Bench. The defendants were her mother's executors, sister Emily and George Curzon. Georgina claimed that the deeds under which her parents' marriage settlement had been set aside, and she herself disinherited, had been fraudulent, and that she had only agreed not to contest her father's will because her mother had promised to provide for her in her own will – a promise that had not been kept. In their statement of defence, the executors had pointed out that Georgina had signed the 'deed of family arrangement' in 1893 and that Dal had been paying her £200 a year, as agreed, since their mother's death.

Georgina's two brothers had, very wisely, decided to be out of the country when the case was heard. She and Castella arrived at the Law Courts on the morning of 1 November to find Emily, 'looking bricky and black and rich in black velvet', waiting with 'that little red-nosed cad' George Curzon. Georgina ignored them and spoke instead to Harcourt, who had come to enjoy the entertainment. Proceedings began in earnest on the afternoon of 3 November, before the 'charming, gentlemanlike' Mr Justice Byrne. Philip Treherne and his fiancée Beatrice (Beata) Hammersley hid in the gallery, to watch and 'glare down on the ruffians'. By 5 November Georgina thought she was winning: 'I was indeed on the Throne of Perk, and had £5000 worth of annoyance today out of the lot'. Her opponents were 'caricatures of mental agony'. Five days later, Byrne reserved his judgment. Georgina was still optimistic, writing 'even if some legal hitch baulks me, I have had £25,000 worth of annoyance'. But a few days afterwards, to her 'utter surprise' Byrne gave judgment against her on the basis that she had made an agreement with her mother, which had been carried out. Georgina told the judge that he had understood nothing of the case. She would go to the Court of Appeal and, if necessary, to the House of Lords. As they all left the court, she informed Emily and her husband that 'it will all be the worse for you in the end'.[22] Two days later she set down her notice of appeal. In July she had also issued a writ for conspiracy against Emily and her husband,

21 GWJ, 5/5/1897.
22 GWJ, 1–15/11/1897.

together with George Curzon, brother Apsley and the lawyer Augustus Drake, claiming £10,000 damages from each, together with her share of the family jewels 'etcetera'.

Early in the following year *Weldon v. Williams* was dismissed with costs by the Court of Appeal. The costs of both actions came to £433: after her legacy of £50 from her mother had been deducted, Georgina still owed £383, but she was confident that she would be awarded this much – and more – when her conspiracy action came to court. At Philip and Beata Treherne's wedding on 20 July she reduced her sister-in-law Edith to tears by telling her that she intended to carry on with her campaign. Georgina was implacable, though Apsley was seriously ill – too ill to come to the wedding. Her brother was, she thought, 'a perfidious devil'. But she was to be disappointed. At the end of the year she was informed by a Master in Chancery that her family's 'infamies' were not actionable. In the meantime, Emily and her lawyers issued a writ of sequestration in an attempt to force Dal to pay Georgina's £200 a year to them.[23]

[23] GWJ, 2/2/1898, 20/7/1898, 28/10/1898, 7–9/12/1898.

28
A New Century

For the next six years Georgina divided her time between England and France. She spent several months each summer at Gisors, but also rented an apartment in Paris, at 2 Rue de Narbonne. By the mid 1890s her interest in the supposed descendants of Louis XVII had waned. Instead, in 1898 she took up the cause of Alfred Dreyfus, a young French artillery officer of Alsatian-Jewish descent who had been accused of communicating French military secrets to the German Embassy in Paris. In 1894 he had been tried and found guilty of treason and sentenced to deportation for life to Devil's Island, a disease-ridden penal colony off the coast of French Guiana. A widespread belief that Dreyfus had been framed had led to a campaign to persuade the government to reopen the case. This culminated in the publication on 13 January 1898, on the front page of the Parisian newspaper *L'Aurore* (the Dawn) of an open letter, 'J'accuse', by Émile Zola. The eminent author hoped to provoke the authorities into prosecuting him for libel so that new evidence exonerating Dreyfus could be made public. The 'Dreyfus Affair', as it became known, developed into a full-blown political scandal that was to divide French society for the next eight years, with the anticlerical, pro-republican Dreyfusards lined up against the pro-Army, predominantly Catholic, and anti-Semitic anti-Dreyfusards.

The Dreyfus affair included all the ingredients that most attracted Georgina – involving, as it appeared to do, persecution by the establishment and a miscarriage of justice. It will be remembered that she had previously been a passionate supporter of two imposters, the Tichborne claimant and Naundorff. This time, for once, she was on the side of reason. She had long admired Zola and was immediately drawn into the Dreyfusard camp. It was, she wrote in her diary, all 'a ridiculous mare's nest, [an] anti-Semitic crusade'. She was, however, critical of Zola's letter: 'It is not strong and he puts on white gloves instead of using his fists, and speaks far too civilly of Justice etc. He can't hold a candle to me. The beginning is especially weak.' She began to write letters to the French and British newspapers. When Zola was sentenced to a year in gaol, she sent him a postcard. The French were, in her opinion, 'the most abject fools. They have been given the chance of protesting, and they have missed their chance!'[1] She had to be careful what she said to her friends in Paris, for many were anti-Dreyfusards, including Pierre Gailhard and Amélie Carpeaux. So were all the nuns at Gisors, whose suspicion of anyone who did not share their religious beliefs extended to Protestants as well as Jews. They informed Georgina that they often said *Ave Marias* for her conversion. She was, however, a hopeless case, vowing that she would never give money to any Roman Catholic charity 'and help to atrophy the brains of the French rising generation.'[2]

Before long, Gounod/Castella had composed a 268-line poem about the Dreyfus Affair, entitled 'Le Complot de l'État Major' (the Conspiracy of the General Staff). Georgina wrote a preface and had a thousand copies printed.[3] She sent them out to all her friends and acquaintances in France and England. She even sent one to her old admirer, 'Crow'. Whether he ever read it is unknown, but some people certainly did: at the end of January 1899 'Le Complot' was the subject of a short article in the *Los Angeles Herald* under the headline 'Georgina Weldon, France's Prophetess of Evil':

> Georgina Weldon is the latest Parisian sensation. She is the high priestess of the Dreyfusards, and she has startled Paris with a pamphlet in which she predicts the downfall of the nation. It is written in verse of no mean order. Its author is now immured in a convent of the provinces, but there are Dreyfusards who desire to carry her through the streets of Paris in a chariot.[4]

The article was accompanied by a drawing of a young nun, who bore no resemblance whatsoever to Georgina herself.

~

At the end of May 1899, Georgina received a mysterious note from Angèle Ménier's brother, Émile Helluy. He did not say what he wanted, but she concluded that Angèle must have died. A further, much longer, letter from Émile confirmed this. Émile had fallen out with the rest of his family, and also with Angèle's brother-in-law Eugène Ménier, and they were all quarrelling over the £700 or so that Angèle had left. It soon became clear that Émile was hoping that Georgina would help to pay his legal fees. She decided that he was 'an ASS', but worth cultivating in the hope that he would help her to

1 GWJ, 25,29/1/1898, 24/2/1898.
2 GWJ, 9/5/1898, 13/11/1899.
3 GWJ, 24/12/1898.
4 *Los Angeles Herald*, 25/1/1899.

recover the documents and personal belongings that Angèle had stolen from her. She paid him 1000 francs and he sent her some papers. At the same time, a search in one of the store-rooms at the hospice produced a wooden box labelled 'Ménier', full of documents relating to Anacharsis Ménier's trial in 1878, many of which Georgina had never seen before. It was 'too wonderful.' She was so excited that she had to take a dose of potassium bromide to calm her down. Hoping for further revelations, she gave Émile more money, paying out at about 9000 francs altogether. After a while, she decided that he was 'a born *escroc* [crook] and fool', who was merely using her money to pay off his own debts.[5] She refused to give him any more.

Subsequent attempts to recover the money from the Helluy family were unsuccessful – indeed, their lawyer claimed in 1905 that Georgina owed them 3000 francs. They never received a centime of this. Somehow, however, most of Angèle's estate ended up in the hands of Eugène Ménier. The only compensation for Georgina was the thought that Angèle herself would not have been at all happy about this: 'It is laughable', she wrote, 'Fancy the torturing rage of the fishfag's spirit!'[6] She spent the next few months copying out all the newly-discovered papers. Everything that she read brought back her feelings of resentment at the way she had been treated by her family. She also began to understand the significance of an 'enigmatical' letter that she had received from Oscar Wilde in the middle of the previous year. Philip Treherne had met the (by now) infamous author in Paris, and Georgina had then written to Wilde, telling him that she would like to meet him, as she understood that he was repentant and had given up his 'unnatural and insane penchants'. Wilde had replied immediately, warning her not to judge the lives other people by 'an alien standard', and adding:

> Those very expressions, *unnatural and insane* were often used of you in reference to your conduct as a wife, with duties of affection, and a woman with duties of rational conduct. You know that they were unjustly so used. I know it too. But there were many who had a different estimate. They make the harsh error of judging another person's life without understanding it. Do not you – of all people – commit the same error.[7]

Georgina began to fear that the reputation of the 'Queen of the Law Courts' would 'descend to posterity like that of a female Oscar Wilde'. She was now determined to publish her memoirs as soon as possible. As 'the most intelligent and intellectual person in the world, devoted to a cause that is good,

5 GWJ, 3/5/1899, 12,30/12/1900.
6 GWJ, 10/6/1905.
7 Oscar Wilde–GW, 31/5/1898.

useful, and worthy of every kind of praise', it was her duty to tell the public about the 'extraordinary persecution' that she had been subjected to. Otherwise, thanks to her husband and family, she would be remembered as 'a mad, unhinged, nymphomaniac who did not know how to behave, giving men black eyes, setting fire to the theatre, bawling and having to be taken away by the police'. 'No, that will not happen!' she vowed. 'I will write the truth!' It would, she thought, be 'a deal too much for one volume'. She set to work on the first one at the end of January 1901 and produced sixteen pages within two days. It was hard work, but she was enjoying herself. 'I do hope', she wrote, I shall get some of my money back from Weldon and show up Our Judges!!!' Someone sent a copy of the first proofs to Eugène Ménier, who immediately threatened to sue the printer, Darantière of Dijon, for defamation and blackmail, claiming that the work was 'libellous to the first degree'.[8]

The memoirs were to be published in French to save money, so much of Georgina's time was spent translating letters to and from her mother and 'other family twaddle'. At the same time she was busy correcting the proofs of another book of poems by 'the spirit of Gounod', to be entitled *Après Vingt Ans* [After Twenty Years].[9] She devoted all her spare time to writing and proof-reading; within a little over a year she had paid the printers £680 and received the first six printed volumes of *Mémoires de Georgina Weldon: Justice (?) Anglaise*. A few months later, convinced that she would finally be vindicated, she took delivery of thirty-two parcels of books to be distributed among the judges at the Royal Courts of Justice. She also sent a set to Forbes Winslow, with whom she had fallen out again, but he refused to read them.[10] Georgina does not say how many copies of the books were printed altogether, but it is clear that her estimate of the likely sales was wildly over-optimistic. Eighteen months later she was informed that the binders in Paris still had 12,000 volumes of her memoirs in their warehouse, and that she would have to pay them £6 a year if she wanted to leave the books there any longer. She was forced to admit that they had already become a 'white elephant'.[11]

~

Of all the orphans whom Georgina had taken into her house and subsequently discarded, the only one whose loss she ever appears to have regretted was Sapho/Katie, who had always been her favourite. She heard

8 GWM, i, pp. 71–4; GWM, v, pp. 174–7, 225–7; GWJ, 31/12/1899, 25/1/1901–1/2/1901.

9 The book was published in 1902.

10 GWJ, 13/3/1901, 25/3/1902, 11/7/1902, 14/9/1903.

11 GWJ, 6,25/3/1904.

nothing from or of the girl for ten years until, in August 1898, she learned that Sapho had contacted Forbes Winslow. Now aged twenty-four, she was working in a dress-shop, was engaged to be married, and 'wants to know who she is, poor little thing.' A few days later Georgina, who was at Gisors, received a letter from Sapho herself, which made her cry. She would, she wrote, 'be glad to see the poor little thing again.' Two days after her return to London in mid October, Sapho visited Georgina at 7 Bramerton Street. The girl looked 'very nice, tidy, well dressed' and had a 'nice voice.' She told Georgina all about the iniquities of 'that filthy fishfag [Angèle Ménier],' who had 'debauched the very children.'[12]

Georgina soon decided that she would like to take Sapho into her own household, writing 'I know it is only right and proper she should return home, and she is a nice little thing, and loves her Grannie.' But Charlotte and Castella quickly scuppered this plan. 'Gounod' declared that he would hold no more séances if Sapho moved into 7 Bramerton Street. He had, Georgina believed, 'always hated the children.' 'I despise him for it,' she added 'and myself for compromising with him.' He was 'an old devil.' But she was terrified that Gounod would refuse to communicate with her, so she obeyed – up to a point. Secretly, she continued to see and correspond with Sapho for several years, giving her money and clothes. The two met for the last time in Paris in 1904, when Georgina finally decided that her former protégée was 'a most deceitful, underhand puss' who could not be trusted. Gounod had been right about her all along.[13]

Georgina was much less pleased to hear from Beryl, who had been dumped in an orphanage in London at the beginning of 1882. Now aged about thirty and working as a chambermaid in Paris, Beryl called at 2 Rue de Narbonne in June 1900 and spoke to the concierge. She told him that Madame Ménier had beaten and ill-treated her and the other orphans, but that she was very fond of Georgina. Georgina, who had never liked the girl much, suspected that Angèle's sister, Marie Helluy, had sent her to spy out the land. She told the concierge to send Beryl away if she came back.

A third orphan reappeared a few years later. This was 'Baucis,' born in London in 1875. She was illegitimate, but her mother, Mary Ann Winchester, had subsequently married and had taken Baucis (now called Alice) to live with her and her new husband. It turned out that Mary Ann was the sister of Sapho's mother-in-law. Mary Ann visited Georgina in Brighton in May 1903 and lost no time in informing her that Sapho was 'no good' and drank 'a good deal.' Three days later, Baucis/Alice herself turned up

12 GWJ, 25/8/1898, 2,27/9/1898, 17/10/1898.

13 GWJ, 18–21/10/1898, 8/7/1904.

and told Georgina that she had been 'hankering' for her ever since she left. Georgina decided that the girl could be useful: she kept her with her for a few days and then took her to Gisors. But Alice (now, confusingly, renamed Madeleine) appeared to be delicate and was not as cooperative as Georgina had hoped. She was, moreover, inclined to sulk, and was 'dreadfully vulgar, awkward, gawky, her voice and accent excruciating'.[14]

~

In the autumn of 1901 Georgina was delighted to receive a visit from a long-lost relative. This was Hugh Treherne ('Bubi'), the son of Uncle George and his second wife, Juliana Geier. Georgina had not seen Hugh since 1876, when he was eleven years old. Two years after this, the care of the now-orphaned boy had been committed to his half-sister Nandine Butler and his late mother's sister, Katinka Geier. Nandine had already received a settlement on her marriage, so George had left almost everything that he possessed to Hugh, subject to a generous annuity of £500 for life to Katinka. Hugh's fortune was to be held in trust for him until he was twenty-five. Unfortunately, as it turned out, one of his trustees was George's nephew Dal Treherne. The other was another nephew, the lawyer George Gilbert Treherne.[15]

Hugh had been sent to Eton in 1880 and had subsequently studied electrical engineering in London, though there is no evidence that he ever had a job of any kind. When he came of age at the end of 1889, he found that much of his father's money had disappeared. He was later to claim that this was the result of mismanagement by his trustees. No doubt he had heard about Georgina's quarrels with Dal and hoped that she might be able to help him to take legal action against the trustees. Hugh wrote to Georgina for the first time at the end of 1900 and she sent him some of her books. When he turned up at Gisors on a bicycle a year later, he told her how he had been 'fleeced' by 'the Honorable Colonel West Kent Light Infantry Militia' (Dal) and 'the Brigand' (George). His father's income had been £4000 or £5000 a year, and Hugh should have inherited £34,000 in money and investments, but there was only about £14,000 left.[16] Georgina felt sorry for him. He had, she thought, been 'the general milch cow of the family'. The 'poor boy' had been 'persistently snubbed and trampled upon' and appeared to be 'frightened of everybody and everything'. She was afraid that he had brain damage, having nearly killed himself at the age of

[14] GWJ, 11/5/1903, 9/7/1903.

[15] Son of Georgina's uncle, Rees Goring Thomas. He had changed his surname from Thomas to Treherne in 1856.

[16] GWJ, 14–15,29/10/1901, 24/3/1910.

twenty-three by running up a hill in the sun: 'It affected his heart, affected his memory; he can't work, read – he can't apply himself to any regular work. What a misfortune!' When Georgina offered to do what she could to help Hugh, he accepted, in spite of a postcard from Dal warning him 'not to use GW as his lawyer'.[17]

~

In May 1900 Georgina had received a letter from the widow of her friend Thomas Titley, who had been managing her financial affairs whilst she was in France. Titley had just died, having been in poor health for some time. Georgina immediately began to worry about retrieving her sheet music and orchestral scores from his widow – and also the money that must be due to her. She thought there should be at least £280, but it was difficult to be sure as Titley had always been reluctant to let her have detailed accounts. It was not long before Mrs Titley claimed that she owed Georgina nothing: on the contrary, Georgina owed her £200. Georgina was sure that Titley must have been in league with Faithfull and decided to take his widow and executors to court. This impending action brought her, somewhat reluctantly, to England in the summer of 1902. She went into lodgings at 40 Russell Square, Brighton, having told Charlotte and Castella to leave the house in London a year earlier. Not before time, Georgina had decided that the two were, 'regular swindlers, no more, no less', after discovering that they had been keeping the rent money that she sent them for themselves and not paying it to the landlord.[18] She had only put up with them for so long because of Castella's apparent ability to communicate with Gounod, but the composer's messages had now become few and far between. Even his poetry had begun to dry up and he was showing a disconcerting tendency to repeat himself. Georgina never admitted – to herself or anyone else – that she had been duped, though she did think it strange that the composer was prepared to communicate through 'such rascals'.

Ten days after her arrival in Brighton, Georgina's lawyer, James Rossiter informed her that Thomas Titley's executors wished to settle out of court for £250. She agreed, albeit reluctantly, feeling that she had 'no strength to fight'. She decided to stay on in Brighton, a town that she had known all her life, where she still had a few friends. It was not too far from Newhaven and she could get up to London easily by train. By this time she was suffering from neuralgia and rheumatism, and she hoped that the Turkish Baths in Brighton would help to relieve her aches and pains. Her legal career had not yet come to an end, though her recent actions had been largely

[17] GW–Agnes Waldstein, 3/4/1902; GWJ, 31/10/1901, 2/11/1901, 9/12/1901.
[18] GWJ, 6/1/1901, 31/12/1901.

unsuccessful. In November 1898 she had attempted to sue the London, Brighton, and South Coast Railway Company for damage to her property, and the injury to her right thumb, sustained during the stormy Channel crossing in the May of the previous year. She had, she claimed 'escaped death by a miracle' and wanted £300. The case was rapidly dismissed, as Georgina could produce no evidence that the company had been negligent. She had, she thought, been as badly treated as Dreyfus, declaring 'His are a flea-bite to my experiences!'[19]

~

Georgina was still in Brighton in February 1903 when she read in the *Daily Telegraph* that her old friend 'Crow' had died at his palace in Bemfica near Lisbon. She had thought of him every year on his birthday and on the anniversary of their final meeting in 1855. Now she was desperately upset, though she believed that he had let her down:

> My dearly beloved Crow. Oh my love, and my love who loved me so! How queer it seems to me he should have left me without one word during all these years of trouble. Had he been in trouble, how I would have flown to his side to help or to console him!

She hoped that Gounod would 'receive him kindly in his sphere' for her sake.[20] She decided that she would like to visit Crow's grave, though it was so far away and she was, as usual, short of money. Then, in Paris in September, Georgina dined with her friend Otto Friedrichs, a collector of Naundorff memorabilia, and met a Portuguese lady who had known Crow. This was Alice Colaço, whose husband was a professor at the conservatory of music in Lisbon. Alice told Georgina that Crow's wife, the Marquesa da Fronteira, was still alive, aged eighty-one, 'almost blind, very decrepit.' Crow had always been a good husband to her, but it was well known that he did not care for her. He had suffered from diabetes and his legs had become very 'crookly,' but he had been 'the nicest, dearest, funniest man they ever knew.'[21]

Ten days later, the Colaços visited Georgina at her apartment in the Rue de Narbonne. They told Georgina that Crow had eaten and drunk too much, and that he had become 'a miserable wreck.' Georgina wondered why he had not asked her to go and nurse him. Now she wanted more than ever to go to Portugal. 'Why should not I spend the whole winter there instead of Brighton? Give those crawly lawyers etc more time to digest

19 GWJ, 2/11/1898; *Times*, 3/11/1898.
20 GWJ, 14/2/1903.
21 GWJ, 15/9/1903.

and read, mark, learn my books.'[22] She hoped that a few months in a warmer climate would be beneficial to her health, though such a long journey was a formidable undertaking for a woman of sixty-six whose ailments included rheumatism, neuralgia, piles, fistula, skin rashes and digestive problems. She made up her mind to go, and invited a new friend, Grace Ashford, to accompany her. Georgina had first met Grace a year or so earlier when she had been governess to James Rossiter's daughters. The young woman seemed to be keen to go to Portugal but was unable to leave at once, so it was agreed that Georgina would travel alone and Grace would follow her later.

Shortly after midday on 10 November, Georgina set off from the Gare d'Orsay in Paris on the thirty-six-hour journey to Lisbon, taking 70 kilos of luggage with her. Although she had reserved a *wagon-lit*, she was forced to spend a sleepless night on a mattress in the corridor: climbing up to the top bunk would be bad enough, but climbing down during the night to visit the lavatory would be impossible. The train reached Lisbon two days later and Georgina found an apartment in the small resort town of Estoril, a few miles along the coast. The apartment was clean, with an indoor WC and plenty of room, but the doors and windows did not fit and the draughts were terrible. The Sirocco was blowing and the weather was cold, wet and stormy. A few days after her arrival, Georgina's new landlady, Madame Raff, took her to Bemfica, just outside Lisbon, where they looked at Crow's home, the Palácio Fronteira, from a distance. Finding that Bemfica was 'an ugly neighbourhood', she felt 'sorry and disillusioned'.[23]

After Grace arrived on 14 December, Georgina got down to work indexing her journals. The weather improved and the two women walked on the beach and sat in the garden of a nearby *quinta*. They made friends with a retired doctor, Daniel Gelásio Dalgado, who had come to stay in Estoril for his health.[24] In mid February they were joined by the lawyer James Rossiter, who had travelled all the way from England to see Georgina. He stayed for nearly a fortnight, having apparently come mainly for a holiday, though he brought some legal papers with him as well. He also brought the first four volumes of a series entitled 'Bell's Miniature Series of Musicians'. An account of Gounod's life included a 'libellous and scurrilous titbit' about Georgina, 'composed of lies artfully piled one upon the other'.[25] Georgina studied it carefully and began to plan her next legal fight.

22 GWJ, 24/9/1903.
23 GWJ, 19/11/1903.
24 GWJ, 25,30/1/1904.
25 GWJ, 17/2/1904.

Together, Georgina, Grace, James Rossiter and Dr Dalgado paid a visit to Bemfica. With the help of an introduction from a friend of Dr Dalgado, they persuaded the porter to let them into the Palácio Fronteira. As they entered the entrance hall, they were met by Crow's widow, the old Marquesa da Fronteira. She was much better-looking than Georgina (who had always referred to her as 'The Scarecrow') expected: '[She] is quite as tall as I am, thin, holds herself very well and is, decidedly, a good looking old lady, although she was considered very plain.' For once, even Georgina was lost for words:

> She was very nice, shook hands with the Doctor and me, and said how sorry she was she had an appointment in Lisbon, else would so like to have taken us round herself. How sorry *she* was *he* was no longer there to take us round himself. I do not suppose she knew or understood who I was. I was really more glad to see *her* than anything else. I would so like to have kissed her. As it was, I cried nearly all the time I was there. The piano had not been opened since his death. The butler opened it for me and I played a few chords. I was too stupefied to remember anything. I thought it so wonderful that after nearly 50 years his piano should be opened for me, and that I should be the first, after he had last touched it, to strike the notes!

The piano was, however, 'an dreadful old tin kettle'. They were shown all over the house and gardens, where Georgina sat in an arbour and hoped that Crow had thought of her there. She picked a few flowers that she could press and take home. Back in Estoril, she wrote that she was glad that Crow 'really had a very nice ladylike wife', adding 'What does it matter? Beauty!' But she still believed that Crow would have been happier with her: he would have lived much longer and they would both have been artists 'and even richer than the Marqueza'.[26]

~

Shortly after Georgina's return to France in mid-May, she received a letter from Otto Friedrichs, who was 'frantic' for her to go to Delft for the inauguration of a new tomb for 'Louis XVII'. After his death in 1845, Naundorff's body had been buried in the old cemetery there; this was now to be closed, and the remains were to be moved to a new cemetery. Otto had been asked to put on an exhibition of some of his Naundorff-related items. Georgina was fond of 'poor dear Otto', though she had been very rude about his book, which had been published a few months earlier, describing it as 'awful rot'.[27]

26 GWJ, 23–25/2/1904, 29/4/1905.
27 GWJ, 13/3/1904.

She decided that she would like to go to Delft, and asked Grace Ashford to accompany her. They arrived early in the afternoon of 16 June. Otto visited them that evening, together with 'Prince Henri', one of Naundorff's grandsons and the younger brother of the 'Prince Louis' who had obtained money from Georgina under false pretences in 1892. Georgina was not impressed: Henri was 'a little man like his mother; therefore very ugly and common-looking'. Nevertheless, he had 'that curious commanding tone … When he decides something, you feel he must be obeyed'. He made a long speech to Georgina about the emotion that he felt on meeting her, and the regret he felt about his brother's bad behaviour towards her. '[He] talks about the *respect de son nom* as if the Bourbons were not a race of scoundrels of the deepest dye.'

Georgina was not much more impressed by the other members of the 'Bourbon' family. Several had refused to come to the re-interment because of quarrels over precedence, and most of them were not speaking to each other. They were, Georgina thought, just like the Trehernes. On 18 June she rode in the second carriage in the procession to the New Cemetery, with 'Prince Henri' in full uniform, 'Princesse Henri', and Otto, who was now 'distracted'. She was pleased to see her wreath of 'roses of France' on the hearse, though dismayed to discover that the inscription on it read '*à Grand père* [to Grandfather]'. Naundorff's only surviving child, his daughter 'Princess' Marie-Thérèse, made a 'wonderful' speech. Georgina thought that she was very imposing, and the image of her father. The 'princess' also looked 'wonderfully like' Georgina's own mother. It was a moving scene: 'She did cry so. It was a historical incident which made me blubber to see her throw herself on the coffin and sob her heart out, overwhelmed with the sorrows of 110 years or more. Injustice of the most revolting description.' Georgina was disappointed to note that dignitaries appeared to be rather thin on the ground, though the president of a local historical society did say a few words.[28]

~

Just before leaving for Portugal, Georgina had asked her former landlady to look for a flat in Brighton for her. Now, on her return from her foreign travels, the hunt began in earnest: James Rossiter, Hugh Treherne and Grace Ashford all did their best to find somewhere suitable. Georgina might have preferred London, but Lise Gray advised her that the rents there were 'quite terrible'. A flat like 2 Rue de Narbonne would have cost £150 a year, which was much more than she could afford.[29] It was James Rossiter

[28] GWJ, 16–18/6/1904.

[29] GWJ, 7–8/8/1904.

who suggested Sillwood House in Sillwood Street, a Regency house where the top floor was to let. By mid October Georgina heard that the landlady had agreed to rent it to her, in spite of some reservations due to her reputation for litigiousness. Grace Ashford, who was to live with her, began to organise the necessary redecoration and building work, and Georgina started to pack. She said goodbye to all the nuns and left the hospice on 16 November. She took 112 kilos of luggage with her, having already sent 243 kilos (a third of a ton) to Brighton. She never returned to Gisors.

29
Sillwood House

Georgina arrived at Sillwood House late in the evening on 16 November 1904. This was to be her base for the remaining years of her life, though she spent most of her time in London until 1912 when illness finally prevented her from travelling. The original intention seems to have been for her to rent a flat, but it was not long before she took over the whole house. Whilst she was away, Grace Ashford and her younger sister Annie acted as caretakers and housekeepers. Occasional lodgers helped to subsidise the household expenses.

Georgina travelled to Paris for the last time in mid May 1905, returning to Brighton two months later to prepare for a new round of legal actions. One evening she and Annie Ashford went to the theatre to see Ellen Terry in *Alice-Sit-by-the-Fire,* a comedy written especially for the actress by J.M. Barrie. Georgina was critical of her old friend, whom she had not seen for nearly twenty years: 'Ellen charming, fascinating, but as she [has] grown so stout, and being so tall, she is ponderous, and the way her figure is strapped up is a marvel. It does not look natural. I would not do it. She blacks up her eyes too much.' On the following day the two women spent two hours together and 'jabbered our heads off'.[1]

~

In the second week of October, Georgina sent nine cases and baskets and an armchair to the Salisbury Hotel, just off Fleet Street, where she had rented a room. It was only ten minutes' walk from the Royal Courts of Justice, and very convenient. When the Courts reopened, she vowed that she would not go near 'the beastly place' – but she was there almost every day.[2] She was soon involved in a convoluted series of claims against everyone who had had anything to do with the biography of Gounod published in the previous year. She also renewed her attacks on the booksellers and librarians, W.H.

1 GWJ, 21–22/9/1905.
2 GWJ, 24/10/1905.

Smith. They had all, she claimed, contributed to holding her up to 'hatred, ridicule and contempt,' and had forced her once again 'into that litigation which has occasioned her to be contemptuously treated in Courts of Justice and elsewhere, and unjustly twitted and bantered and spoken of and "at" as though she were a low designing courtezan, a common scold, without either talent, birth, education or reputation.'

Georgina claimed sums varying from £2000 to £10,000, and asked for an injunction to prevent the sale of further copies of the book. She also demanded that all remaining copies should be called in and destroyed. At the same time she alleged that Novello's and several other music publishers had 'sold, circulated and pirated' several songs by Gounod, but had not paid the royalties due to her. Writs and Statement of Claim flew around the Royal Courts of Justice, to the amusement of the attendants and the dismay of the judges who had the unenviable task of wading through the mass of paperwork. Even Georgina was beginning to despair. She feared that she would 'die in harness': she now tired easily and often felt unwell. Indeed, she was 'a miserable machine, worn out in spite of joyful temperament by incessant grief, trouble, annoyance, pin-pricks and moral thumps.'[3] The Law Courts made her feel ill, and she was sure that she was being poisoned by 'the moral atmosphere of iniquity' there.[4] She took up smoking, which was recommended as a cure for asthma. It seemed to help a little. She was short of money, too, as the costs of her legal actions were invariably awarded against her. Her difficulties were increased by the sudden death of her friend and solicitor, James Rossiter, on his way home from a visit to her in December 1906. The news made Georgina feel 'so wan, forlorn, hopeless.' Her mood did not improve when she discovered that Rossiter's affairs had been chaotic: money that she had given him for safekeeping had not been kept in a separate account; there was 'a tremendous bill of costs' against her; and Rossiter had owed money to 'hosts of people.'[5]

~

Georgina gave up the lease of her Paris apartment in 1906, and her rooms in the hospice at Gisors in the following year, an acknowledgement that her health and stamina were beginning to fail. But hard luck stories could still rouse her to action. There was Henry Hess, the German-born editor of a pro-British South African scandal sheet called *The Critic*, which had been suppressed by the Boer leader and President of the Republic, Paul Kruger,

3 GWJ, 1/8/1905, 31/12/1905.

4 GWJ, 1/6/1907.

5 GWJ, 9/12/1906, 16/1/1907, 2/12/1907.

in 1897. Hess visited Georgina in March 1906, claiming that he had been 'crushed by law suits' and had no money. He wanted a job. 'I felt so sorry,' wrote Georgina. 'This is the fate of crusaders. To go to the wall while the wicked flourish.' She 'made him' take a sovereign, which she could ill afford.[6]

Then there was Mary Rathbone Wilmot, the Anglo-Indian daughter of a colonel in the Bombay Infantry, who was living in Kentish Town with her 'husband', George Wilmot, a gentleman's collar cutter, and a two-year-old son, in 1881. Mary's father had died in 1885: she was his only child, but appears to have been illegitimate under English law. Claiming that she had been 'swindled' out of her rightful inheritance, she had made regular appearances in the Court of Chancery, where most of her pleadings had been struck out as being frivolous or vexatious. Georgina thought her 'a very amusing, interesting little character'. She was particularly impressed with her new friend's 'passage at arms' with the Chancery Master, Binns Smith, in the Lord Chancellor's Court' in 1906:

> The Judge wanted to force her to sign a document and threatened her with Holloway Gaol and threw a deed at her, whereupon she, like a little tiger, seized three inkstands, pens, papers, everything she could lay hands on, and threw them at the Judge, who had to run away streaming with ink. Pens sticking in his wig ... A wonderful scene. The Court doors were locked.[7]

Like Hess, Mary Wilmot was now poverty stricken, having sold her home and her jewellery to fund her legal battles. Georgina tried to help 'the poor little starving creature' and gave her food. But she could not 'make head nor tail of her history' and found that her papers were in a state of 'wild confusion'. Before long she had decided that Mary, though unlucky, was 'very foolish'. Georgina began to find her demands exhausting and refused to lend her any more money.

~

Georgina's political sympathies had always been anti-establishment. She read the left-of-centre *Daily Chronicle* and described herself in 1883 as 'a red-hot Radical'.[8] She had felt a sneaking admiration for the anarchists who were active in Paris during the 1890s. At the end of May 1906 she read of the attempted assassination of Alfonso XIII, King of Spain and his bride,

6 GWJ, 12–13/3/1906.
7 GWJ, 20/3/1906.
8 SS, 7/1883, p. 2.

Victoria Eugenia. She thought that the anarchists' tactics were wrong: their real targets should be the legal profession:

> Why do they not commence by blowing up all law courts, judges, and lawyers of every grade? The people are so short-sighted, they do not realise where the root of all mischief lies. Lawyers, trained and steeped in lies, are the real corrupters of the brains and morals of the nations.[9]

In the following year she wrote, 'The higher classes really are loathsome. Who would not be a Socialist!' On the other hand, she believed that her female servants should know their place. Too much education was undesirable for the lower classes:

> I prefer servants who cannot read and write, because they have a good memory, and are attentive, and remember how to cook a dish when one has once described how it is to be done, or shown them how to do it. I prefer servants, in fact, who are what they are, who have to clean, sew, mend and cook, and are happy to accomplish the task they are allotted to do ... The servant, therefore, who does not read or write, enjoys her work, and is not in a hurry to get her work done, so that she may read the last novel.[10]

Fully occupied with her own personal grievances as she was, Georgina had previously shown only a limited interest in the wider campaign for women's rights. Back in 1882 she had heard Josephine Butler speak at a meeting calling for the repeal of the Contagious Diseases Acts, which allowed the police to arrest women suspected of being prostitutes and have them forcibly examined to find out if they had a sexually transmitted disease. Georgina had commented: 'Those brutal men! Why is not every male who is not a fine or healthy specimen of humanity castrated before he is 7 years old? That would prevent the beasts throwing themselves like bulls and boars on all the women. Poor things. I wonder women can endure men.'[11] Georgina had admired Annie Besant, whose campaigns included the promotion of birth control, and had met Anna Kingsford, one of the first English women to obtain a degree in medicine. She also knew the suffragists Jessie Craigen and Helen Taylor. She had been asked to join them in the 1880s, but had refused because they 'never seemed to me to come to the help of any ill-treated woman.' She seems to have borne a grudge against these women, together with a number of other prominent female philanthropists and reformers,

9 GWJ, 31/5/1906.

10 GWJ, 2/12/1907; GW, *Musical Reform*, p. 73.

11 GWJ, 8/11/1882.

because they had failed to reply when she had written to them to ask for help. She had, moreover, been 'insulted and misrepresented' in a newspaper edited by the prominent activist Emily Faithfull.[12]

In 1908 Georgina wrote disparagingly of 'the old-fashioned *ladylike* crawlers who have been feebly agitating for the past fifty years without anyone seeming to realise that they existed.' In the early years of the twentieth century, as the campaign for women's suffrage began to gain momentum, she changed her mind. She mentioned the suffragettes in her diary for the first time in October 1906. Two years later she wore a 'Votes for Women' badge, and praised the prominent campaigners Charlotte Despard, Emmeline Pethick-Lawrence and the Pankhursts in one of her pamphlets, writing that their methods appealed to her and had answered her former objections.[13] In February 1908 Emmeline Pankhurst led a deputation to the House of Commons. She and her companions were arrested and sentenced to six weeks in gaol for obstruction. On hearing of her release, Georgina told Lise Gray:

> I am so glad the Suffragettes are getting on. Surely they will succeed in getting Prison Reform. Curious no one complains of their underclothing being taken off. Surely they all wear combinations? I see they were treated worse than I was, but I *liked* solitary confinement. I learnt such a lot by heart.[14]

A few months later Georgina received a letter from Mabel Tuke, 'the Secretary of the National Women's something or another union.' This was the Women's Social and Political Union, which had been set up by Emmeline Pankhurst in Manchester in 1903, but had moved its base to London three years later. It was their strategy of 'aggressive picketing, noisy interruptions and causing maximum public nuisance' that so attracted Georgina.[15] Miss Tuke wrote of processions and meetings. 'Fancy *me* marching in a procession!!!', commented Georgina. She did not join the non-militant National Union of Women's Suffrage Societies in their procession from the Embankment to the Royal Albert Hall on 13 June, though she did go to the meeting afterwards. The streets were so crowded that it took her two hours to get to

12 SS, 2/1884, p. 2. The women listed by Georgina were Florence Nightingale, Jessie Craigen, Frances Cobbe, Angela Burdett-Coutts, Florence Fenwick Miller, Rose Crawshay, Helen Taylor, Elisabeth Surr, Emily Faithfull and Louisa Sims. The newspaper to which Georgina refers was presumably the monthly *Victoria Magazine*.

13 GW, 'Sanctity of Marriage and Conflict of Sex.'

14 GW–Lise Gray, 22/3/1908.

15 F.C. Philips, *My Varied Life* (London, 1914), p. 179.

the Albert Hall. She heard Millicent Fawcett, Lady Henry Somerset and Dr Anna Shaw speak, but merely commented that they had 'very good voices'. She was, however, disappointed at not being asked to sit on the platform, complaining of the 'sneakishness and jealousy of the women, not asking me'. She was, she believed, 'a real pioneer. No amateur'.[16] Later that year she joined the suffragists outside Holloway Gaol as they serenaded Emmeline and Christabel Pankhurst, who had been serving a three-month sentence for incitement to disorder. 'Quantities' of men were joining the campaign now, as well as the women.[17] Three years later, on 21 November 1911, there was a 'tremendous suffragette row' and 223 women were arrested. 'They are brave!', Georgina wrote approvingly in her diary, though she still believed that women 'would make no better use of the Vote than men do'. The imprisonment of Mrs Pankhurst and Fred and Emmeline Pethick-Lawrence for nine months in May 1912, following a major window-smashing session, was 'a diabolical tyranny and injustice'. After reading Mrs Pankhurst's 'great' defence speech she wrote, 'We are not worthy to tie their shoes'.[18]

In May 1907 Georgina left the Salisbury Hotel and moved in with an old friend, Elizabeth Buchanan, a wood engraver and artist who had a flat at 75 Lamb's Conduit Street. The flat was dirty and untidy and Georgina soon found that her friend irritated her: 'She is too drivellingly coster [common] and commonplace. Thinks she is witty'. Georgina continued to complain about Elizabeth, but she lodged with her friend during her visits to London for the next five years. Relations with the two Ashford girls could be difficult too. They were 'perfect girls in their way, but bone disagreeable'. They looked after Sillwood House well and kept it clean, but their precise status was uncertain and they were becoming increasingly 'pert and uncooperative'. Georgina decided that they had 'a great deal too much liberty'. They 'jeered and sneered' at everything she suggested, and were 'uppish, domineering and dictatorial'.[19] She became 'rather anxious as to their tyranny' feeling that she would be 'regularly rough ridden over and bullied' if she were to become 'decrepid'. The sisters were jealous of Elizabeth Buchanan and openly hostile towards her. Georgina eventually told them that only one should stay at Sillwood House when she was there. She could cope with one at a time, but not both.

16 GWJ, 2,13/6/1908.
17 GWJ, 14/11/1908.
18 GWJ, 21/11/1911, 3/3/1912, 23,27/5/1912.
19 GWJ, 17/5/1907, 16–17,31/8/1907, 8/9/1907, 31/12/1907.

At a low moment in September 1907 Georgina wrote: 'The sun indeed has gone down on my beautiful past. All hopes have faded away and are dead, except of reincarnation and succeeding in getting my ideal, yet so simple, school together.' In London, she wandered sadly around the site of Tavistock House, which had been demolished in 1901. There was no sign of the mulberry tree or the ivy-covered wall at the bottom of the garden that she remembered so well.[20] But she had not given up yet. At the beginning of 1908 she borrowed a braille typewriter and taught herself to use it so that she could write to Jules Rousseau in Gisors. Plans to write a history of Louis XVII in braille never came to anything, but she did write and publish a short book (her last) entitled *Louis XVII or The Arab Jew*, which was to be sold for the benefit of the National Lending Library for the Blind. Like most of Georgina's books, it is virtually unreadable, jumping from Jules Rousseau to Dreyfus, via Louis XVII and Georgina herself.

In July of the following year Georgina was informed that her brother Dal had died. She expressed no sorrow, merely noting in her journal that she had received 'a splendid mourning card from Agnes regarding the death of the Honourable in the most pompous terms.' The card was followed by 'a long and gushing letter' from her sister-in-law, who had been 'quite taken in by the *fanfarone buffone*.'[21] It took some time for the consequences of his death to sink in. Dal had been paying her £200 a year since 1894, but this money was not secured in any way. Nor had Hugh Treherne's claim against Dal and his other trustee, George Treherne, been settled. Hugh had not spoken to Georgina for three years: after learning that he 'pretended' to be in love with Grace Ashford, she had forbidden him to visit Sillwood House when she was not there and he had taken umbrage. They now began to correspond again and she met him in London in June 1909. She also met Agnes, who appeared to be prepared to settle and had offered Hugh £650 a year. Agnes told Georgina that Hugh had always been considered to be 'of weak mind and nerves' (she had allegedly referred to him in the past as 'the village idiot'), and that the mad-doctor George Fielding Blandford had been consulted about him in 1880 when he was sixteen. There had been talk of having him declared to be of unsound mind. Agnes believed, moreover, that Hugh could not be expected to have any noble sentiments or the feelings of a gentleman 'on

[20] GWJ, 2,8/9/1907, 2/10/1907. The site is now occupied by the headquarters of the British Medical Association.

[21] GWJ, 29–31/7/1908.

account of his plebian Jewish mother.'[22] Georgina agreed that Hugh was 'no doubt very queer and very unreliable', but she thought that he was 'more respectable and careful than either Dal or George.'[23]

All attempts at a compromise soon broke down; 'exciting' letters were sent and received, and matters became even more complicated as Hugh's half-sister, Nandine Butler, entered the picture. Even the lawyers admitted that it was 'a shocking case, a nightmare.'[24] Once again, Hugh turned to Georgina for help. Georgina decided that her sister-in-law was 'as false as they make them' and began to refer to her as 'the noble widow', 'St Agnes' and 'the Saintly Snake'. Agnes accused Georgina of stirring up trouble and forbade Hugh to communicate with her. Georgina, meanwhile, began to fear that her own annuity would be stopped. She was not best pleased when she discovered that her nephew Philip Treherne had advised Agnes that 'the only way to cope with Aunt Georgina is to be vague and mysterious'. The Trehernes were, she thought, 'an awful crew of sharpers'. Dal, Apsley and Emily were all thieves, and Agnes and Bill (Emily's husband) were even worse. Bill had probably poisoned his mother-in-law, and they were all 'capable of anything.'[25] Before long, Hugh was on the edge of a nervous breakdown, his moods veering between depression and levity. Georgina put him to work researching the history of his family and their property in the British Museum and at Somerset House. A visit to Dal's bank convinced her that her brother and George Treherne had done their best to cheat both her and Hugh.[26] She asked the Law Society how she could get 'the rogue' George Treherne struck off the roll of solicitors and was furious when they declined to take up the case.

In May 1910 Georgina appeared before Mr Justice Joyce in the Chancery Division of the High Court for the first hearing of her own case, *Weldon v. Treherne*. After taking her seat in the well of the court with 'a mass of legal documents' in front of her, she told the judge that she wanted the annuity to which she was entitled and informed him that she was 'destitute for life' because she had been tricked. For once, the judge ('an old dear') was on Georgina's side. When Temple Gurdon, the barrister representing Agnes, claimed that there was only £40 left for distribution, Joyce pointed out that Gurdon had retained £2000, and told him, 'if I can decide it against you I will'. 'If I were in Mrs Weldon's position', the judge added, 'I should be annoyed'. The case was adjourned so that Gurdon could consult with

22 GWJ, 8/2/1910.
23 GWJ, 22/6/1909, 14/7/1909, 31/12/1909.
24 GWJ, 14/4/1910.
25 GWJ, 12/6/1909, 8/10/1909, 30/4/1910.
26 GWJ, 13,18–19/4/1910.

his client, but they were all back in court a fortnight later on 24 May, Georgina's seventy-third birthday.

The reporter from the *Cardiff Times* was impressed by Georgina. She was, he wrote, 'Now an old lady, dressed in black, with snow-white hair and cap', but she had in years gone by done 'notable work'. Gurdon said that 'Countess Waldstein Treherne' had taken upon herself the duty of paying £200 a year to Mrs Weldon, but the payments had been suspended after the latter had instituted legal proceedings. Georgina had written letters which had spoken in a derogatory manner of Colonel Treherne (Dal) and members of the family [and] 'had caused her much pain and grief'. Agnes had offered to enter into a bond to guarantee that she would pay the money, but Georgina said this was not good enough. Her sister-in-law might die 'any day'. She was 'a very flighty kind of person' and might marry again. She should buy an annuity for Georgina.[27]

Back in court again on 11 June, the judge unwisely offered to read all Georgina's papers, and asked what day would suit her for a further hearing. She said any day would suit her, as she was 'devoted to this case'. 'I am' she informed the court, 'old and weary, and it was very cruel to keep me working like this.' 'If he reads that lot', she wrote in her diary, 'he will be well edified, and I hope he will give me all I want.' Two days later, however, Mr Justice Joyce appeared to have 'read nothing and understood nothing'. He said 'No' to everything, but told Georgina she would get her annuity all right if she would only keep quiet. He would not give her the order she wanted. She was slightly pacified when he 'absolutely refused' to award costs against her. Typically, she decided to go to the Court of Appeal.[28] Finding that she was unlikely to be successful she wrote:

> I feel brought to bay. Hunted down by these abominable laws, made for the protection and propagation of fraud. I feel as if I could do nothing but cry – helpless. It is hard to be cheated with impudent impunity. I wish cursing did any good. I'd curse Harpagon [brother Apsley] day and night.[29]

On 21 July Georgina returned to the Royal Courts of Justice to see the heralds at Temple Bar to proclaim the coronation of George V. She saw the performance 'splendidly'. Harry Weldon, now Norroy King of Arms, was in the last carriage and she got a good look at him. She was relieved to see that he looked 'very well and healthy'. Having failed to force him to make any kind

27 GWJ, 24/5/1910; *Cardiff Times*, 14/5/1910, p. 9, 28/5/1910, p. 12.

28 GWJ, 10–13/6/1910; *Cardiff Times*, 18/6/1910, p. 5.

29 GWJ, 8/7/1910.

of settlement on her, she needed him to stay alive. A year later she was highly amused to see a photograph of her husband in the *Daily Mirror*. He had been fined 10s with 2s costs for failing to take out a licence to use armorial bearings – a somewhat embarrassing experience for one of the king's heralds.[30]

By this time it was obvious that neither Georgina's nor Hugh's claim against Agnes would be settled separately: there had to be some kind of general arrangement. Georgina, however, did not trust Hugh not to betray her, describing him as a 'weathercock, bully, skunk, and coward and miser.' He was, in short, a typical Treherne. She was afraid that he would give in to Agnes, who kept sending him 'torrents of verbosity' in German. Agnes had stopped communicating directly with Georgina, having decided that it was impossible to reason with her. But she came to London in June 1911 and it seemed as if she and George Treherne had 'caved in completely' and were prepared to give Hugh everything he wanted. Georgina wrote in her diary: 'Let us be truly thankful. The strife is o'er!' In court on 16 June she stood up before Mr Justice Joyce and announced, 'My Lord, I am Mrs Weldon, plaintiff in person, and I agree with the terms.' The judge said he was 'very glad.' He smiled, and everyone else laughed when Georgina added, 'It is all my doing, my Lord.'[31] She gave all her friends at the Royal Courts of Justice the good news.

Georgina's delight was premature: it soon transpired that Agnes, who had not understood the terms of the agreement, had announced that she would neither give in nor sign anything. They were back to square one. Georgina told Hugh that there should be no further talk of compromise: they should go to court. She would not, she vowed, give up her own action against Agnes for less than £2000. Hugh, laid up in Switzerland with an attack of rheumatoid arthritis, seemed to back her up: he told her at the beginning of 1912 to 'Withdraw nothing. Sign nothing. See them d[amne]d.' Georgina began to suspect, however, that the illness was 'a mere blind' and that Hugh was simply too scared to return to England to face her. She got her lawyer to write to him, and to inform him that the case would be tried without him if he refused to return.[32]

At the same time, Georgina was trying to fight yet another legal battle, this time against the Times Book Club, which had distributed a biography of Gounod containing 'false, malicious and libellous' allegations against her.[33] The case was finally heard before Mr Justice Ridley in the Court of King's Bench at the end of June 1911, a few days after the agreement with

30 GWJ, 21/7/1910, 14/10/1911.

31 GWJ, 19/12/1910, 3/1/1911, 15–16/6/1911.

32 GWJ, 19/1/1912, 15/5/1912.

33 The book was P.L. Hillemacher, *Charles Gounod* (Paris, 1906).

Agnes had collapsed. Georgina took an instant dislike to Ridley, whom she described as 'a little beast'. He had, she wrote afterwards, been 'as hostile as possible from the start'.[34] She was not on her best form: she had not prepared her case thoroughly and became easily flustered when the judge snubbed and interrupted her.

The defendants were represented by the brilliant – and extremely expensive – barrister and MP, F.E. Smith, KC. He informed the court that his case rested on a denial that his clients had shown 'the slightest neglect of any kind from first to last' and implied that Georgina had brought the case for financial reasons. The exchange that followed often degenerated into a comedy routine:

SMITH: I am asking you. You wanted money.

GEORGINA: Of course I want money, and so do you – more than anybody else.

SMITH: But I am not giving evidence, and you are.

RIDLEY: I do not think you ought to be rude to Counsel, Mrs Weldon.

GEORGINA: I am not rude, I am answering the question.

RIDLEY: You made the observation. He made no rude observation to you. I must ask you to behave in the witness box.

GEORGINA: I know how to behave.

RIDLEY: I do not think you do. You are presuming on your old campaigns.

SMITH: I am sorry to be disagreeable to you.

RIDLEY: You must behave like any other witness.

GEORGINA: Yes – like a fool.

In his speech for the defence, Smith told the jury that a library could not be expected to read every book that they stocked and that the book had been withdrawn as soon as his clients had been informed that Mrs Weldon objected to it. These proceedings, he continued, represented 'one of the most peremptory, unreasonable and unfounded complaints against a library that has ever been brought'.[35] The plaintiff should be suing the author

[34] GWJ, 23/6/1911.

[35] *Times Book Company*, p. 97.

of the book, not the distributors. The jury agreed with him and Georgina lost her case. As usual, she threatened to take it to the Court of Appeal. Afterwards, she complained of F.E. Smith's 'langourous [*sic*] attitudes, his unfair cross-examination, and the lying way he represented the case to the jury'. His name was added to the list of 'beasts' who had been responsible for her downfall. Georgina's appeal was dismissed with costs five months later. She was disappointed to find that the newspaper reports on the following day were 'very meagre'. This was to be her last appearance in court; she visited the Royal Courts of Justice for the last time on 1 July 1912. By this time the Times Book Club was pursuing her for their costs, which came to £400. It seems unlikely that they were ever paid.

In 1911 yet another biography of Gounod was published. Georgina liked this one: the French authors, Jacques-Gabriel Prod'homme and Arthur Dandelot, did not say anything too objectionable about her, but they did point out some of the composer's faults. Georgina's reaction to it expressed some of the bitter feelings of betrayal that had built up since Gounod's abandonment of her in 1874:

> I felt a supreme disgust in seeing his hypocritical, Jesuitical, exaggerated character piercing through every line. Prod'homme only speaks of his excess of gesticulation once, but how it did annoy me. He hints at his 'nauseous garrulity' (as Wagner called it), but no notion of his real character, tergiversations, prevarications, cowardice and treachery or absurdities are hinted at. Although Prod'homme records no bad action, neither does he record a single good one. Admiral Tartuffe, splendid dissembler! As Gambart most truly said, 'Man of Sand'.

Gounod's music had gone out of fashion too. 'Old man gone, and I fast going', she wrote on 21 July 1912, the forty-fourth anniversary of her sister Flo's death, and the forty-first of the 'happy day' she had sung *Gallia* at the Albert Hall.[36]

The year 1911 also saw a reconciliation of sorts with Georgina's brother Apsley, who came to see her from time to time. They compared notes on the villainy of their brother Dal. But there was to be no such rapprochement with sister Emily, who seems to have cut herself off from all her siblings after their mother's death. Georgina was informed that Dal had tried to 'make friends' with his younger sister, but she had refused, on the grounds that if she spoke to him, none of her husband's family would ever speak to

[36] The book was J.G. Prod'homme, *Gounod* (Geneva, 1911); GWJ, 10–11/10/1911, 21/7/1912.

her again.[37] Georgina never saw Emily again after their brief meeting in the Royal Courts of Justice in 1897.

In spite of her reservations about them, Georgina kept the two Ashford girls at Sillwood House until 1911. She was, however, distinctly unsympathetic when, in April 1911, Annie informed her that Grace was consumptive and had been advised to go away for change of air or to a sanatorium. She asked Georgina for £100. Georgina refused, telling Annie that her sister's illness was all her own fault. She would never recover and there was no point in 'wasting money on a poor girl who becomes a burden to herself and everybody else.' Hoping that this might be an opportunity to get rid of both girls, Georgina gave them an ultimatum, which brought Grace herself to London, 'not looking very ill.' The gloves were now off. Grace told Georgina that she had hated being at Gisors and that Brighton had not been much better. Georgina was unjust and inhuman and she soon tired of people. Grace stormed off in a furious temper.[38] On Georgina's next visit to Brighton she found Sillwood House empty, with nothing in the larder but a mouldy loaf of bread, some rotten carrots, and onions and potatoes that had begun to sprout. She offered Ellen Gunn, Hugh Treherne's former housekeeper, a job. Georgina did see the Ashford girls occasionally after this, but they never lived with her again.

Georgina's own health continued to deteriorate. Most of her teeth had gone, and digestive problems and neuralgia were added to her other troubles. But she was not ready to give up yet, writing, 'So many small and silly things amuse me: sweeping my room, dusting, *ma vaisselle* [washing up], and keeping everything clean, tidy, in order. Life cannot be dull, especially when one has £100 a year.'[39] She was still reading the newspapers every day, following closely the activities of the suffragettes (smashing windows all over central London); the effects of the first national coal strike; Scott and Amundsen's race to the South Pole; and the sinking of the *Titanic* (with her friend W.T. Stead on board), all in the first few months of 1912. In May she read in the *Daily Chronicle* of the trial of Katie Malecka, the British-born daughter of an Englishwoman and a Russian-born political refugee. Miss Malecka, who had gone to Russian Poland as a governess in 1909, had been arrested in Warsaw two years later, accused of consorting with Polish Socialists and promoting secession from the Russian Empire. In the spring of 1912 she had been found guilty of conspiring against the Russian government and sentenced to four years' penal servitude. It was

[37] GWJ, 22/11/1903.
[38] GWJ, 19/4/1911, 8/5/1911.
[39] GWJ, 28/11/1911. In fact she still had at least £500 a year.

rumoured that she would be sent to Siberia.[40] This news threw Georgina, who had never liked the sound of the Tsar and believed that Russia must be 'a hell on earth', into 'a fearful state of excitement and indignation'. She hurried down to the Royal Courts of Justice and asked all her friends among the clerks and attendants if they would sign a petition calling for Miss Malecka to be released. She soon had more than a thousand signatures, and was confident that she would have two thousand before long. On 10 June, however, came the news that Miss Malecka had been pardoned by Nicholas II on condition she left Russian territory immediately and never came back. She returned to England four days later.

On 25 July Georgina went to 44 Bedford Square, the home of the literary hostess Lady Ottoline Morrell and her husband Philip, to hear Katie Malecka read 'an admirable lecture'. The young woman was 'Small, thin, very plain, wears spectacles. Very quiet and unpretentious'. Georgina was thanked for her efforts. She told them she was disappointed that she had not been able to get more signatures. Some people had told her that Miss Malecka must have 'done something dreadful' to be given such a long sentence. This, Georgina thought, showed their 'shocking ignorance of Russian history'.[41]

Just over a week after Miss Malecka's lecture, Georgina left London for Brighton for the last time. Ellen Gunn had been looking after the house and everything was clean and tidy, but Georgina soon decided that her housekeeper was 'an obstinate, ignorant, self-opinionated fool'. She was, however, soon glad of Mrs Gunn's help, as a painfully swollen leg, followed by sciatica, made it difficult to walk. 'I have been moving about too much', she decided:

> Old age, decidedly, has its disadvantages, although it is much pleasanter, morally, to be aged than youthful, with all the horrid males sniffing after you with all their pains and their aches, moral and, as it turns out, physical. Pains a young girl knows nothing about. Absolutely worthless l.o.v.e. Not one of my numberless swains having, not only not come to my help, but, rather, helped to kick me down.[42]

Suffering from terrible pain and unable to sleep, Georgina spent most of the time in bed. 'It is not worth living like this', she wrote. 'It does seem hard that blackguard Dal should have died suddenly, a painless death, and I to suffer so awfully.' She asked the doctor, Harold Baines, for morphine.

40 *Spectator*, 18/5/1912, p. 6; GWJ, 11/5/1912.
41 GWJ, 25/7/1912.
42 GWJ, 7/8/1912, 7/9/1912.

He refused and gave her aspirin instead.[43] It did not work, and she turned to her favourite homeopathic remedies, which were equally ineffective. Finally, the doctor relented and gave her morphine, which reduced the pain but made her sleepy.

~

On 1 November the great family inheritance dispute, *Treherne v. Treherne and Comrades*, was settled at long last. Mr Justice Joyce, who gave judgment in the Court of Chancery, was reported to have been concerned about Georgina. On the following day one of the lawyers came down from London with papers for her to sign. Two days after this she wrote in her diary 'Quiet all day. Pain very slicing. The Doctor called.' At this point the entries cease for six months. Georgina was, however, *compos mentis* enough to make the final version of her will on 21 November. It was witnessed by Dr Baines and Ellen Gunn.

The next entry in Georgina's diary, dated 11 May 1913, shows signs of having been written under the influence of morphine or delirium:

> Journal ceased suddenly through illness. Finally rendered incapable for ever by the manoeuvres of the firm of George Gilbert Treherne Treherne, 7 Bloomsbury Square, and a Brighton Doctor who got me tortured and mutilated by the Secret Society 'L'Etoile Polaire' – a hellish institution. Too ill to write more. G.W.[44]

She seems to have rallied after this. On 16 May she had herself photographed in bed – Mrs Gunn thought this 'rather a funny idea' – and she was corresponding with Philip and Beata Treherne, and with Lise Gray, in June and July. By the end of August she was 'sitting up and doing crazy work'.[45]

Regular entries in the diaries begin again on 1 September. The writing is firm, almost as it was before Georgina's illness. The first entry is in French because, Georgina explains, she does not want Mrs Gunn to read it. The later entries are mostly in English. Georgina writes that she has been close to death for several months, and bed-ridden for a year, suffering 'the martyrdom of neuritis, constipation, wind, dropsy, loss of the left leg, the right leg very bad. My arms hurt, so do my elbows, and my right side'. She also had bedsores.[46] She had a succession of nurses, including

43 GWJ, 22/9/1912.
44 GWJ, 4/11/1912, 11/5/1913. 'L'Etoile Polaire' may be a reference to the Masons.
45 Elizabeth Buchanan–GW, 25/8/1913. 'Crazy work' is a form of patchwork.
46 GWJ, 1/9/1913.

Lise Gray, who came as often as she could. In spite of all her troubles, however, Georgina was able to send a donation of a guinea to the National Lending Library for the Blind.

On 26 September Georgina heard that her brother Apsley had died on the previous day. He was seventy-one and had been suffering from pneumonia. She wrote to his widow

> Oh! it *is* a shock, and poor dear was *so* jolly last time he came down. He never expected to die yet, and I never thought I should follow him to the grave. I don't think I *can* last. I am in pain and misery everywhere. Over 12 months of it. I long to die.[47]

She felt sorry for Edith, who was left with three children aged seventeen, thirteen and six, and very little money. There were fears that the oldest, Edmund, would have to leave Eton, but his housemaster took pity on him and agreed to keep him for £30 instead of £260. Georgina sent her nephew £5. Her writing is clear until 3 November, when it begins to deteriorate. On 10 November she wrote 'Bad night – nothing good. I am all in a muddle'. After this the pain overcame her and she wrote no more.[48] She died at Sillwood House on 11 January 1914, aged seventy-six. The death was certified by Dr Baines, who gave the cause as 'decay of nature'. The informant was Ellen Gunn.

~

Georgina had decided that she wanted to be buried in the family vault on the west side of the main entrance to St Dunstan's church in Mayfield. This could be seen as somewhat perverse, given that the only other occupants of the brick-lined vault were her much-reviled father and her younger siblings Cordelia and Gilbert, who had both died young. She may have reflected that her father, who had shunned her for the last seven years of his life, would have hated to have her so close to him in death. On 15 January, a bright, cold day, her coffin was taken from Brighton to Mayfield station by train, and then to the church in a glass hearse, which was followed by several carriages carrying the mourners. The chief mourners were Philip and Beata Treherne, Edith Treherne, Lise Gray and her brother Alfred, and two of Georgina's maids. The list of floral tributes includes one from Baucis/Alice/Madeleine, the only one of Georgina's orphans who remained

47 GW–Edith Treherne, 1/10/1913.

48 The entry for 10 November is now the last one in the final diary. The next page seems, however to have been cut out: Edward Grierson's notes suggest that entries continued sporadically until 29 November.

in contact with her until the end. There were also wreaths from Grace and Annie (Ashford) and 'Bubi' (Hugh Treherne). The reporter from the *Kent and Sussex Courier* noted that Georgina and her two sisters had sung 'very prominently in the Parish Church Choir, about 57 years ago'.[49]

Georgina left everything that she had to Lise Gray, the only person who had never let her down. 'Put not your faith in anyone but the Grays,' she had written in 1896. The net value of her personal estate was £2541, which suggests that she probably had received the £2000 due under the settlement with Hugh Treherne and Agnes Waldstein in 1912.[50]

~

By the time of Georgina's death Grace Ashford had become Mrs Hugh Treherne. Hugh and Grace had married on 5 June 1913 at Grantchester near Cambridge, where Grace's parents lived. They married without Georgina's blessing – she had tried to keep them apart in the past, and had told Hugh not to write to her again. She seems to have abused the newly-married couple in letters to other people, accusing them of trying to 'clapperclaw' her money. No doubt she was motivated in part by jealousy, but it seems likely that she, and the rest of the family also believed that Hugh had married beneath him. Grace Treherne died in a nursing home in Cambridge in 1916 aged 41; her widower died in 1931. No member of the Treherne family was mentioned in his will.

Philip Treherne died in 1922 aged 50. His book about Georgina Weldon, *A Plaintiff in Person*, was published in the following year. Philip's widow, Beatrice (Beata) Treherne died in 1953. They had no children.

Of Georgina's siblings, only her younger sister Emily Williams outlived her. Emily died in 1916 aged 77. Four of Emily's children survived to adulthood; the last died in 1960, but there are no descendants alive today. There are, however, descendants of Georgina's two brothers in Britain, Italy, the Netherlands, Australia and America.

Harry Weldon married his long-term mistress, Annie Lowe, on 26 February 1914, just over six weeks after Georgina's death. He was knighted in 1919 and died a few months later, on 25 August, aged 82. Annie died in 1931, leaving one son by her first husband, Stanley Lowe, but no children by Harry Weldon.

49 *Kent and Sussex Courier*, 16/1/1914, p. 10.

50 GWJ, 2/2/1896. The value of the personal estate was subsequently resworn at £622, perhaps because some creditors had come forward.

30
Angel or Devil?

Georgina would no doubt have been pleased by the number of publications that took notice of her death, though she would not have been happy with everything that was written. Back in 1902 she had complained about the fact that her name did not appear in *Who's Who*, either in her own right or under her husband's name.[1] She had even written her own entry:

> Weldon, Georgina. Vocalist, composer, musical conductor, educationalist; trained Gounod's Choir, Mrs Weldon's Choir; founded Mrs Weldon's Orphanage. Celebrated through her successful agitation of Copyright Laws, Married Women's Property, Lunacy Laws and Litigation in person; also for Criminal Court of Appeal. Gained her suit for RCR (1882), against Forbes Winslow, MD, Sir Henry de Bathe, Gounod, Rivière and many others, being awarded heavy damages during 1884–86. Contributed many letters and articles on Spiritualism, Musical Reform, Education etc. Recreation: Requires none.

To which she added:

> I have no hesitation in saying that my work has been more useful, more brave, more loyal, more arduous, more painful and more ungrateful than any woman's work recorded in *Who's Who*. Why, therefore, honor me by singling me out for boycottage? I bravely, laboriously, successfully – as a torpedo among men of war – steered my way alone and blew all calumnies and insinuations to blazes. I believe myself to be the bravest woman in the world.

The obituary in the *Daily Telegraph* paid more attention to Georgina's friendship with Gounod, which 'has been described as romantic' but 'turned to woeful discord', and to her fame as a litigant: 'A handsome woman, proud of her abilities and strong of will, she rather courted than

[1] GWJ, 16/9/1902

avoided law suits'.[2] The notice in the *Daily Mirror* was headed 'A Famous Woman Litigant who Liked the Way Fish was Cooked', and told how the 'aged litigant' had described her time in Holloway Gaol as the happiest days of her life because 'the way they cooked fish there was a dream'. She was, the journalist added, 'the most celebrated woman litigant in the history of the British Law Courts'.[3] One of the longest articles appeared in *Truth*. The author had clearly had first-hand experience of Georgina's way of operating in the Law Courts:

> For two or three years she was a terror to His Majesty's judges, a source of considerable income to the Bar, of amusement to the public, and of copy to the reporters. She had been grievously injured, but in the end she 'got her own back' with interest from all who had wronged her, and it was impossible to help admiring the pluck, pertinacity, and cleverness with which she did it. She was quite unscrupulous. If a judge was against her, she would endeavour to make him put himself in the wrong, provoking him by the most impudent remarks, delivered with an air of angelic simplicity.[4]

Ten years after Georgina's death, the journalist and MP T.P. O'Connor wrote about her at some length after the publication of Philip Treherne's book, *A Plaintiff in Person*. O'Connor had never spoken to her, but he had encountered her often at the Law Courts in the 1880s, and he thought that 'she remained and remains something of an enigma'. He commented on her beauty and the fact that 'One of the curiosities of her face – perhaps also of her character – was that it retained almost to the end an expression of baby-like innocence'. He remembered watching Georgina as she sang in a concert:

> Here was about as flagrant a contradiction of appearance and of character as even the mysterious problem of feminine character ever presented. And yet – and yet – as I gazed on the face, I thought I saw some signs of the terrible things in her which had scandalized, amused, and bewildered the world for years. For I could not help remarking, in spite of the babyishness of the expression, another and quite as conspicuous an expression – the expression of intense egotism and self-consciousness. While the baby lips were uttering notes of exquisite harmony – she really was a wonderful singer – there was this haunting impression of self-consciousness, of vanity,

2 *Daily Telegraph*, 13/1/1914.

3 *Daily Mirror*, 14/1/1914.

4 *Truth*, January 1914, quoted in *Liverpool Echo*, 21/1/1914, p. 6.

> of that gigantic self-esteem – which became in this woman of unconquerable purpose a voracious appetite for the melodrama – with herself as the heroine.

At the end of the second of his two articles O'Connor wrote 'Such then, was the woman. I have done my utmost to lay the materials before my readers with impartiality; I must leave them to answer the question – was she angel or devil, or a little bit of both?'[5] Almost a hundred years later, the jury is still out. T.P. O'Connor describes Philip Treherne's biography of his aunt (1923) as 'pious'; Edward Grierson (1959) wrote of her 'gay and pugnacious spirit' and believed that 'It was her fate to attempt too much, with ambitions that always outran her talents by that margin that makes the difference in our specialist world.'[6] More recently, Brian Thompson, who clearly took an instant dislike to Georgina, treated her as a figure of fun, 'one of the great undiscovered eccentrics of the nineteenth century'.[7]

Georgina's sister-in-law Agnes Waldstein told her in 1902 that she was born 'half a century too soon'.[8] A hundred and fifty years might be more appropriate: one can see Georgina thriving in the celebrity culture of the twenty-first century and she would no doubt have embraced modern social media with enthusiasm. She was supremely egotistical, and would today be described as a control freak. Despite frequent protestations as to her shyness and desire to live a quiet, solitary life, she loved to be the centre of attention. Susannah Gocher, Lise Gray's younger sister, wrote of Georgina, 'She dominated in every gathering – she had probably done so all her life.' Susannah admired her, but 'happened to prefer our more normal life to the atmosphere of heroine worship'.[9]

Georgina brought many of her troubles on herself, often because her ambitions and expectations were entirely unrealistic. 'Give her her head', wrote one commentator', 'and she bolts, kicks over the traces, and never knows when to stop'. There was some truth in the contemporary comment, 'She is not quite mad, and yet she is not quite sane'.[10] She threw herself at a man of whom her family disapproved and then, once married, found that she could not live with him. She blamed her husband for her failure to realise her dream of a stellar singing career: she clearly had a beautiful voice, but she was unwilling to take lessons or direction from anyone else,

5 *T.P.'s and Cassells Weekly*, 5/1/1924, pp. 391–2; 12/1/1924, pp. 419–20.
6 Edward Grierson, *Storm Bird* (London, 1959), p. 282.
7 Brian Thompson, *A Corner of Paradise* (London, 2014), p. 146.
8 Agnes Waldstein–GW, 23/4/1902.
9 Susannah Gocher, recollections of Georgina Weldon.
10 *Entr'acte*, 16/9/1882, pp. 12–13; *Birmingham Daily Post*, 9/7/1880, p. 7.

and was too insistent on her status as a lady to make a life for herself in the concert hall or on the stage. She smothered Gounod and bossed him around until he ran away; she established an orphanage, although she did not really like children; and she rampaged around the Law Courts firing off writs to anyone who dared to cross her, insulting the judges and running up costs that she had no intention of paying. She was a terrible judge of character: there were no half measures, and everyone was either a 'dear' or a 'beast'. She made it possible for several people – most notably Angèle Ménier and her husband, and Charlotte Hue – to take advantage of her, refusing to listen to friends who tried to point out their faults. And nothing was ever Georgina's fault: during her long life she accumulated a long list of people, from Arthur Sullivan to F.E. Smith, whom she blamed for her downfall. She was almost paranoid in her certainty that everyone had conspired against her and, certain that she was so much cleverer than everyone else, had a fatal tendency to underestimate her enemies, most disastrously Harry Weldon (who almost had her carried off to a lunatic asylum), and Jules Rivière, who had her sent to gaol – twice. Her lack of self-knowledge can be stunning: in 1884 she asked the readers of *The Englishman*:

> What has carried me through these many years of struggle? What has preserved my temper; my good nature; my happy, joyous temperament? What? Nothing but my unclouded conscience, my inner consciousness of always being in the right, and my family motto: 'For God and for my country'. These have carried me through years of unequal struggle; through circumstances of untold grief.

In 1902 Agnes Waldstein begged Georgina to 'try and see things *for once* with the eye of an impartial stranger to all the people acting in the sad Drama of your life'.[11] Her plea fell on deaf ears.

Georgina could be cruel, spiteful and vindictive, and she displayed a single-minded determination to pursue her own interests, no matter what the cost to other people might be. The barrister F.C. Philips, who knew her, wrote: 'Her attitude was that of the old knight-errant who did not trouble himself very much about the abstract principles of law or justice, but rode out to discover individual cases of oppression and to decide them on his own authority and to redress them according to his own judgment.'[12]

And yet – she was extraordinarily energetic, utterly fearless, and determined to do what she believed to be right. She could be kind and generous, and she spent much of her time attempting to help people whom she

[11] GW–*The Englishman*, 27/12/1884; Agnes Waldstein–GW, 23/4/1902.

[12] F.C. Philips, *My Varied Life* (London, 1914), pp. 265–6.

believed to have been wronged in some way. Like other pioneering women, Georgina was forced to fight against 'the tyranny of niceness' at a time when expectations of female behaviour were bound by rigid conventions.[13] Women were expected to shun notoriety, and Georgina was castigated because she had '[lost] sight of that decorous sort of conduct which we expect, not only from a lady, but from every scrupulous woman.'[14] Her conviction that she was always in the right led her to transgress the boundaries that circumscribed the behaviour of most of her female contemporaries. Her campaigns – most prominently the publicity that she gave to the need for the reform of the Lunacy Laws – led to changes that were of benefit to other people as well as herself. In the words of a modern feminist historian, 'She never gave in to the conspiratorial desire to keep her quiet. Thus, her private wrongs became public wrongs.'[15]

In Edward Grierson's opinion it is as a lawyer that Georgina chiefly deserves to be remembered. She was 'not the first, but certainly the most effective woman advocate before the coming of the professional.' Opponents who underestimated her did so at their peril: 'She behaved like a woman, but she thought and expressed herself as a man, and would and could make herself extremely disagreeable if she chose to do so.'[16] A journalist who sat through the Semple trial in 1884 thought that Georgina had 'proved the thorough soundness and clearness of her mind by arguing difficult points of law in a manner which has won her the highest compliments from the judges.' Her name would, he believed, 'be handed down in the law reports together with those of the greatest lawyers now practising.'[17]

Angel or Devil? It is probably true, as T.P. O'Connor suggested, that Georgina was 'a little bit of both.'

13 Helen Lewis, *Difficult Women* (London, 2020), p. 309.

14 *Entr'acte*, 9/9/1882, p. 12;

15 Kristin Kalsem, *In Contempt* (Ohio State University, 2012), p. 137.

16 F.C. Philips, quoted in Philip Treherne, *A Plaintiff in Person* (London, 1923), pp. 93–4.

17 Grierson, *Storm Bird*, pp. 226–8; *Life*, 8/1884, p. 163.

Bibliography

Primary (unpublished) materials

Private collections

Treherne family

Journals of Georgina Weldon (GWJ) 1852–4, 1860–1913; 'index' to journals (includes some entries from missing journals, 1854–60); manuscript memoirs of Georgina Weldon (GWMSM) *c.*1903; printed proofs of unpublished volumes of Georgina's Weldon's memoirs; letters to and from Georgina Weldon, Harry Weldon, Dal Treherne, Louisa Treherne, Charles Gounod, James Neal, and Eugène, Anacharsis and Angèle Ménier; manuscript book by Georgina Weldon beginning 'today is the 7th January 1870' (GWT); scrap-books compiled by Georgina Weldon; statements of claim (SC) and other printed material relating to Georgina Weldon's court cases; programmes and other printed material relating to Georgina Weldon's concerts

Unpublished printed volumes compiled by Georgina Weldon

Correspondence used in *Rivière v. Cooper* and other cases [1880–1885] (1885) [*Correspondence*]

Newspaper and Shorthand Reports, Notes and Pleadings of Trial and Proceedings, 1878–1885, ii (1885) [*Reports*2]

Newspaper and Shorthand Reports, Notes and Pleadings of Trial and Proceedings, 1878–1885, iii (1885) [*Reports*3]

Shorthand and Newspaper Reports: Regina v. Weldon, iv (1885) [*Reports* 4]

Weldon v. *The Times Book Company, Ltd.*, 26 June 1911, shorthand notes [*Times Book Company*]

Lindholm collection, letters 1857, 1863, 1872

Borthwick Institute, York

Probate Court of York, Thomas Weldon, Handsworth, 1847

British Library

Holland House, Add. MS 51352

East Sussex Record Office, Brighton

XA38/2 (microfilm)

The National Archives

Prerogative Court of Canterbury (PCC) wills, PROB11/1841/133, PROB11/1880/459; J77/216/5905, J77/247/7063

Proceedings of the Old Bailey (searched via www.oldbaileyonline.org): t18780916–747; t18800301–272; t18850323–438

Watts Gallery, Compton, Surrey

Transcript of letter, G.W. Watts to Georgina Weldon, 28 October 1857

Published works by Georgina Weldon [GW]

'An Appeal for Mrs Weldon's Orphanage' (1876) ['Appeal']

Après Vingt Ans et autres poésies (with 'Ch. Gounod (*esprit*)', Paris and London, 1902)

'Death-Blow to Spiritualism, Is It?' (1882) ['Death-Blow']

'French and British Law and Justice: England As It is: Is the Law an Honourable Profession?' (1906) [GWL]

The Ghastly Consequences of living in Charles Dickens' House (London, 1882), [*Consequences*]

The History of my Orphanage or, the Outpourings of an Alleged Lunatic (1878) [*History*]

'Hints for Pronunciation in Singing, with Proposals for a Self-Supporting Academy' (1872) ['Hints']

How I escaped the Mad Doctors (London, 1879) [*Doctors*]

'Louis XVII of France, Founder of Modern Spiritualism', *Borderland*, 4, 1895 ['Spiritualism']

Louis XVII, or The Arab Jew (London, 1908) [*Louis XVII*]

Mémoires Weldon, Justice (?) Anglaise, d'où résulta un procès en France (Affaire Ménier-Helluy) (Gisors (Eure) and London, 1902) [GWM]

Musical Reform (Music and Art Association, London, 1875)
My Orphanage and Gounod in England (2 parts, first published in French, 1882, English translation by 'N.N.', 1882) [GWO]
'Our Lunacy Laws: The Story of Mrs Weldon, written by Herself', *The London Figaro*, 8/1/1879, 15/1/1879, 29/1/1879, 12/2/1879, 19/2/1879 [*London Figaro*]
'Preface' to *My Orphanage and Gounod in England* (London, 1882) ['Preface']
'The Quarrel of the Royal Albert Hall Company with M. Ch. Gounod (Windsor, 1873) ['Quarrel']
'Sanctity of Marriage and Conflict of Sex' (1908)

Secondary materials

Anon., *Wonderful London* (London, 1878)
Bessborough, Earl of (ed.), *Lady Charlotte Schreiber: Extracts from her Journal, 1853–1891* (London, 1952)
Briggs, Asa, and Lovegrove, Janet, *Victorian Music: A Social and Cultural History* (Brighton, Sussex, 2018)
Bruley, Yves, *Charles Gounod* (Paris, 2015)
Cadbury, Deborah, *The Lost King of France: The Tragic Story of Marie-Antoinette's Favourite Son* (London, 2002)
Campbell, Katie, *Paradise of Exiles: The Anglo-American Gardens of Florence* (London, 2009)
Coates, T.F.G., 'Mr Thomas J. Barratt, "The father of modern advertising"', *Modern Business*, September 1908
Condé, Gérard, *Charles Gounod* (Paris, 2009)
Corbeau-Parsons, Caroline, 'Crossing the Channel', in Caroline Corbeau-Parsons (ed.), *Impressionists in London: French Artists in Exile 1870–1904* (London, 2017)
Davies, Caitlin, *Bad Girls: A History of Rebels and Renegades* (London, 2018)
Doughty, Eleanor, 'I spy with my little eye', *Country Life*, 22 January 2020.
Duranti, Comte de, *Recherches sur Louis XVII* (Paris, 1885)
Ferris, George T., *Great Musical Composers: German, French and Italian* (London, 1887)
Gaugler, Baron de, *L'enfant du Temple: étude historique* (Paris, 1891)
Gould, Veronica Franklin, *G.F. Watts: The Last Great Victorian* (New Haven and London, 2004)

Grierson, Edward, *Storm Bird: The Strange Life of Georgina Weldon* (London, 1959)

Guest, Revel, and John, Angela V., *Lady Charlotte: A Biography of the Nineteenth Century* (London, 1989)

Harcourt, H., 'Prison Horrors' (London, 1883)

Harding, James, *Gounod* (London, 1973)

Harrison, W.H., *Rifts in the Veil* (London, 1878)

Hawkesley, Lucinda, *Katey: The Life and Loves of Dickens's Artist Daughter* (London, 2006)

Hillemacher, P.L., *Charles Gounod* (Paris, 1906)

Jones, Kathleen, *A History of the Mental Health Services* (London, 1972)

Kalsem, Kristin, *In Contempt: Nineteenth-Century Women, Law and Literature* (Ohio State University, 2012)

Lander, George, and Weldon, Georgina, *Not Alone* (London, 1886)

Lewis, Helen, *Difficult Women: A History of Feminism in 11 Fights* (London, 2020)

McWilliam, Rohan, *The Tichborne Claimant: A Victorian Sensation* (London and New York, 2007)

Malecka, Katie, *Saved from Siberia: The True Story of My Treatment at the Hands of the Russian Police* (London, 1913)

Neville-Sington, Pamela, *Fanny Trollope: The Life and Adventures of a Clever Woman* (London, 1997)

Owen, Alex, *The Darkened Room: Women, Power and Spiritualism in Late Nineteenth Century England* (London, 1989)

Pearsall, Ronald, *The Table-Rappers: The Victorians and the Occult* (Stroud, Glos., 2004)

Philips, F.C., *My Varied Life* (London, 1914)

Porter, Roy, Nicholson, Helen, and Bennett, Bridgett (eds), *Women, Madness and Spiritualism* (London, 2003)

Prod'homme, J.G., and Dandelot, A., *Gounod: sa vie et ses oeuvres* (Geneva, 1911)

Rivière, Jules Prudence, *My Musical Life and Recollections* (London, 1893)

Shaw, Donald ['D.S.'], *Eighteen Months' Imprisonment* (London, 1882–4)

Taggart, Michael, 'Alexander Chaffers and the Genesis of the Vexatious Actions Act 1896', *Cambridge Law Journal*, 63(3), 2004

Terry, Ellen, *The Story of My Life* (London, 1908)

Thompson, Brian, *A Corner of Paradise* (London, 2014)

——, *A Monkey among Crocodiles: The Disastrous Life of Mrs Georgina Weldon* (London, 2000)

Tomalin, Claire, *The Invisible Woman: The Story of Nelly Ternan and Charles Dickens* (London, 1991)

Treherne, Philip, *A Plaintiff in Person: Life of Mrs Weldon* (London, 1923)
Trollope, Thomas Adolphus, *What I Remember*, ii (London, 1887)
Urich, John, 'Gounod's Life and Works in England', translation of article in the *Frankfurter Zeitung* (1876)
Walkowitz, Judith, *City of Dreadful Delight: Narratives of Sexual Danger in Late-Victorian London* (London, 1992)
White, Jerry, *London in the Nineteenth Century* (London, 2007)
Whittington-Egan, Molly, *Doctor Forbes Winslow: Defender of the Insane* (Great Malvern, 2000)
Wilson, John Marius, *Imperial Gazetteer of England and Wales* (London, 1870–2)
Winslow, Lyttelton S., *Manual of Lunacy: A Handbook relating to the Legal Care and Treatment of the Insane* (London, 1874)
Winslow, L. Forbes, *Spiritualistic Madness* (London, 1877)
Wise, Sarah, *Inconvenient People: Lunacy, Liberty and the Mad-Doctors in Victorian England* (paperback edn, London, 2013)

Unpublished thesis

Nicholson, Helen, 'Spirited Performances: A Critical Study of the Life of Georgina Weldon (1837–1914)', University of Manchester Ph.D. thesis, 2000

Online resources

ancestry.co.uk
books.google.co.uk
British Library newspapers (gale.com)
findmypast.co.uk (British newspaper collection)
freebmd.org.uk
oldbaileyonline.org
oxforddnb.com
times digital archive (gale.com)

Index

Page numbers in bold type refer to illustrations and their captions